Vinuraj V S

Sams **Teach Yourself**

SharePoint® 2010 Development

in **24 Hours**

SAMS 800 East 96th Street, Indianapolis, Indiana 46240 USA

Sams Teach Yourself SharePoint® 2010 Development in 24 Hours
Copyright © 2012 by Pearson Education, Inc.

All rights reserved. No part of this book shall be reproduced, stored in a retrieval system, or transmitted by any means, electronic, mechanical, photocopying, recording, or otherwise, without written permission from the publisher. No patent liability is assumed with respect to the use of the information contained herein. Although every precaution has been taken in the preparation of this book, the publisher and author assume no responsibility for errors or omissions. Nor is any liability assumed for damages resulting from the use of the information contained herein.

ISBN-13: 978-0-672-33579-2
ISBN-10: 0-672-33579-4

The Library of Congress Cataloging-in-Publication Data is on file.

Printed in the United States of America

First Printing March 2012

Trademarks

All terms mentioned in this book that are known to be trademarks or service marks have been appropriately capitalized. Sams Publishing cannot attest to the accuracy of this information. Use of a term in this book should not be regarded as affecting the validity of any trademark or service mark.

Warning and Disclaimer

Every effort has been made to make this book as complete and as accurate as possible, but no warranty or fitness is implied. The information provided is on an "as is" basis. The authors and the publisher shall have neither liability nor responsibility to any person or entity with respect to any loss or damages arising from the information contained in this book.

Bulk Sales

Sams Publishing offers excellent discounts on this book when ordered in quantity for bulk purchases or special sales. For more information, please contact

 U.S. Corporate and Government Sales
 1-800-382-3419
 corpsales@pearsontechgroup.com

For sales outside of the U.S., please contact

 International Sales
 international@pearson.com

Editor-in-Chief
Greg Wiegand

Executive Editor
Neil Rowe

Development Editor
Mark Renfrow

Managing Editor
Kristy Hart

Project Editor
Betsy Harris

Copy Editor
Geneil Breeze

Indexer
Tim Wright

Proofreader
Leslie Joseph

Technical Editor
J. Boyd Nolan

Publishing Coordinator
Cindy Teeters

Book Designer
Gary Adair

Compositor
Nonie Ratcliff

Contents at a Glance

Introduction xv

Part 1: Understanding the Basics

HOUR 1 Introducing SharePoint 2010 1
2 Understanding the SharePoint 2010 Architecture 25
3 Starting Development with SharePoint 2010 41
4 Walking Through the Available Site and List Templates
in SharePoint 2010 65

Part 2: Developing in SharePoint 2010

HOUR 5 Working with Web Parts and Web Pages 91
6 Working with More SharePoint 2010 User Interface
Components 125
7 Understanding SharePoint 2010 Server Side
Development 151
8 Understanding Client Object Model in SharePoint 2010 183
9 Creating Silverlight User Interfaces for SharePoint 2010
Solutions 197

Part 3: Managing Content in SharePoint 2010

HOUR 10 Managing Data in SharePoint 2010 213
11 Understanding Advanced Data Management Concepts
in SharePoint 2010 231
12 Enterprise Content Management—Understanding Document
Management 255
13 Enterprise Content Management—Understanding Records
and Web Content Management 277
14 Understanding Business Connectivity Services 299
15 Understanding SharePoint 2010 Workflows 317

Part 4: Administering and Configuring SharePoint 2010

HOUR 16 Understanding SharePoint 2010 Central Administration 337
    17 Securing SharePoint 2010 361
    18 Introducing SharePoint Search 377
    19 Working with SharePoint Designer 2010 397

Part 5: Advanced SharePoint 2010

HOUR 20 Understanding Service Applications 413
    21 Understanding the Architecture of Sandboxed Solutions 427
    22 Introducing Business Intelligence with SharePoint 2010—
Working with Visio and Excel Services 447
    23 Introducing Business Intelligence with SharePoint 2010—
Working with PerformancePoint Services 469
    24 Understanding InfoPath Form Services 487

    Index 507

Table of Contents

Introduction   xv

Part 1: Understanding the Basics

HOUR 1: Introducing SharePoint 2010   1

    Why SharePoint?   2
    History of SharePoint   6
    Features of SharePoint 2010   7
    Installing SharePoint   10
    Walking Through Visual Studio 2010 and SharePoint Designer 2010   17
    Summary   23
    Q&A   24

HOUR 2: Understanding the SharePoint 2010 Architecture   25

    Understanding ASP.NET Versus SharePoint   25
    Understanding the 14 Hive and SharePoint Virtual Directories   29
    Understanding SharePoint and SQL   32
    Introducing the SharePoint Hierarchy   35
    Understanding Timer Jobs   36
    Introducing Service Applications   38
    Summary   39
    Q&A   39

HOUR 3: Starting Development with SharePoint 2010   41

    Understanding SharePoint Solutions as Deployment Units   44
    Introducing SharePoint Features   56
    Debugging SharePoint Solutions   60
    Summary   63
    Q&A   64

HOUR 4: Walking Through the Available Site and List Templates in SharePoint 2010   65

    Understanding and Working with Out of the Box Lists and Libraries   65
    Understanding and Working with Out of the Box Site Templates   77

Sams Teach Yourself SharePoint 2010 Development in 24 Hours

| Summary | 89 |
| Q&A | 89 |

Part 2: Developing in SharePoint 2010

HOUR 5: Working with Web Parts and Web Pages — 91

Overview of SharePoint Controls	91
Developing Delegate Controls	100
Programming with Web Parts	102
SharePoint 2010 Safeguard Against XSS	120
Web Part Pages and Wiki Pages	121
Summary	123
Q&A	123

HOUR 6: Working with More SharePoint 2010 User Interface Components — 125

Writing Custom Actions	125
Programming Ribbons	127
Understanding Master Pages	135
Understanding Applications Pages	142
Understanding SharePoint 2010 Navigation	145
Summary	148
Q&A	148

HOUR 7: Understanding SharePoint 2010 Server Side Development — 151

Jump Start Programming with the Object Model	152
Exploring the Object Model	153
Understanding the Object Model in Relation to Server and Site Architecture	154
Troubleshooting and Monitoring Performance with the Developer Dashboard	168
Creating a Custom Timer Job	172
Modifying the web.config with SPWebConfigModifications	176
Understanding the Event Receivers	178
Summary	181
Q&A	181

HOUR 8: Understanding Client Object Model in SharePoint 2010 — 183

| Understanding Client Object Model Fundamentals | 184 |
| Exploring Context in Client Object Model | 186 |

Contents

Exploring the JavaScript Client Object Model	192
Summary	195
Q&A	195

HOUR 9: Creating Silverlight User Interfaces for SharePoint 2010 Solutions   197

Introducing Silverlight	197
Understanding Silverlight Architecture	198
Creating the Hello World Silverlight Application	200
Hosting the Silverlight Application in SharePoint 2010	205
Consuming Silverlight Data in SharePoint 2010	207
Summary	212
Q&A	212

Part 3: Managing Content in SharePoint 2010

HOUR 10: Managing Data in SharePoint 2010   213

Programming SharePoint Lists and Libraries	213
Understanding Site Columns	215
Understanding Content Types	221
Creating Custom List Definitions	228
Summary	229
Q&A	230

HOUR 11: Understanding Advanced Data Management Concepts in SharePoint 2010   231

Creating Custom Field Types	231
Understanding Lists and List Item Event Receivers	237
Performing List Data Querying and Manipulation	245
Summary	253
Q&A	254

HOUR 12: Enterprise Content Management—Understanding Document Management   255

Understanding Enterprise Content Management	256
Managing Documents Using Document IDs	257
Managing Document Sets	259
Understanding Managed Metadata	262
Synchronizing Content Types with the Content Type Publishing Hubs	271
Summary	275
Q&A	275

Sams Teach Yourself SharePoint 2010 Development in 24 Hours

HOUR 13: Enterprise Content Management—Understanding Records
and Web Content Management **277**

    Understanding Records Management in SharePoint 277
    Exploring the New Web Content Management Features 290
    Summary 297
    Q&A 297

HOUR 14: Understanding Business Connectivity Services **299**

    Creating External Content Types and External Lists
    Through SharePoint Designer 2010 299
    Creating External Content Types and External Lists
    Through Visual Studio 307
    Summary 315
    Q&A 316

HOUR 15: Understanding SharePoint 2010 Workflows **317**

    Understanding Out of the Box SharePoint Workflows 317
    Working with Workflows in SharePoint Designer 323
    Working with Workflows in Visual Studio 327
    Summary 334
    Q&A 334

Part 4: Administering and Configuring SharePoint 2010

HOUR 16: Understanding SharePoint 2010 Central Administration **337**

    Starting with SharePoint 2010 Central Administration 337
    Understanding Application Management 338
    Understanding System Settings in SharePoint Central Administration 342
    Understanding Monitoring in SharePoint Central Administration 344
    Understanding Backup and Restore in SharePoint
    Central Administration 347
    Understanding Security in SharePoint Central Administration 352
    Understanding Upgrade and Migration in SharePoint
    Central Administration 354
    Understanding General Application Settings in SharePoint Central
    Administration 355
    Configuring with PowerShell 358
    Summary 359
    Q&A 359

Contents

HOUR 17: Securing SharePoint 2010 — 361
- Understanding Claims Based Authentication — 361
- Configuring Claims Based Authentication for SharePoint 2010 — 362
- Understanding Authorization in SharePoint 2010 — 369
- Using the SharePoint Security Object Model — 372
- Summary — 375
- Q&A — 376

HOUR 18: Introducing SharePoint Search — 377
- Understanding Search Options for SharePoint 2010 — 377
- Understanding the SharePoint 2010 Search Components — 378
- Configuring SharePoint 2010 Search — 379
- Understanding the Search Center Site — 388
- Writing Custom Search Queries Using the Query Object Model — 392
- Summary — 395
- Q&A — 395

HOUR 19: Working with SharePoint Designer 2010 — 397
- Understanding the SharePoint Designer 2010 Interface — 397
- Uses of SharePoint Designer 2010 — 399
- Summary — 411
- Q&A — 412

Part 5: Advanced SharePoint 2010

HOUR 20: Understanding Service Applications — 413
- Understanding the Service Applications Architecture — 413
- Understanding the Existing Service Applications in SharePoint 2010 — 415
- Summary — 425
- Q&A — 425

HOUR 21: Understanding the Architecture of Sandboxed Solutions — 427
- Understanding Sandboxed Solutions — 428
- A Look Under the Hood — 429
- Administering Sandboxed Solutions — 430
- A Brief Look at Sandboxed Solution Restrictions — 437
- Developing a Full Trust Proxy — 438
- Developing Sandboxed Solution Validators — 441

Summary	445
Q&A	445

HOUR 22: Introducing Business Intelligence with SharePoint 2010— Working with Visio and Excel Services   447

Exploring the Business Intelligence Center Site Template	447
Exploring Business Intelligence Web Parts	448
Consuming Visio Diagrams with Visio Services	457
Exploring Excel Services	462
Summary	466
Q&A	467

HOUR 23: Introducing Business Intelligence with SharePoint 2010— Working with PerformancePoint Services   469

Introducing PerformancePoint Services	469
Configuring PerformancePoint Services	470
Downloading and Setting Up Adventure Works Sample Databases	472
Exploring the PerformancePoint Services Dashboard Designer	474
Creating Your First Dashboard	476
Summary	484
Q&A	484

HOUR 24: Understanding InfoPath Form Services   487

Introducing InfoPath 2010	487
Modifying List Forms in InfoPath	488
Creating InfoPath Form Templates	493
Summary	506
Q&A	506

Index	507

About the Authors

Sohail Sayed is a software consultant who has worked exclusively with SharePoint for the past three years. **Manpreet Singh** is a software consultant with extensive expertise developing business intelligence solutions with Microsoft SharePoint. **Vinuraj V S** has extensive expertise in developing enterprise solutions with SharePoint, ASP.NET, Silverlight, WCF, WF, and related technologies. The authors have worked on multiple SharePoint implementations, including one of the world's largest BPOS SharePoint implementations and multiple SharePoint on-premises web content management implementations. In addition, they have worked on Business Intelligence and custom .NET applications.

Dedication

Sohail:
To my parents, Amina and Hasanali, and my sister, Furhat. In addition, to my teachers from whom I have learned so much in life, especially Sandeep Gavand and Pranjali Verma. And to my very special friend Vivek Sharma.
Finally to a lot of friends who played their part in motivating me and supporting me; I am blessed to have them as friends.

Manpreet:
To my parents and my wife.

And to my grandfather, Captain Jagat Singh, who couldn't be here to see this day.

Vinuraj:
To my parents, K V Panicker and Santha Kumari, and my siblings, Manuraj and Anuraj, for supporting me through every walk of life.

And to my friend Jabir.

Acknowledgments

This book would not have been possible without contributions from some special people whom we would like to thank from the deepest corners of our heart. First and foremost we would like to thank our friend and colleague Sachin Joshi, who inspired us to proceed with this endeavor and guided us whenever we felt without direction. Thank you, Sachin; we are truly indebted to you.

We also would like to thank the entire Pearson team, especially Betsy Harris, Geneil Breeze, Mark Renfrow, and J. Boyd Nolan. We would also like to thank Neil and Loretta for taking our proposal from a dream into a reality. Thanks to everyone; you all rock!!

Sohail
Manpreet
Vinu

We Want to Hear from You!

As the reader of this book, *you* are our most important critic and commentator. We value your opinion and want to know what we're doing right, what we could do better, what areas you'd like to see us publish in, and any other words of wisdom you're willing to pass our way.

You can email or write me directly to let me know what you did or didn't like about this book—as well as what we can do to make our books stronger.

Please note that I cannot help you with technical problems related to the topic of this book, and that due to the high volume of mail I receive, I might not be able to reply to every message.

When you write, please be sure to include this book's title and author as well as your name and phone number or email address. I will carefully review your comments and share them with the author and editors who worked on the book.

E-mail: feedback@samspublishing.com

Mail: Greg Wiegand
Editor-in-Chief
Sams Publishing
800 East 96th Street
Indianapolis, IN 46240 USA

Reader Services

Visit our website and register this book at informit.com/register for convenient access to any updates, downloads, or errata that might be available for this book.

Introduction

How This Book Is Organized

The chapters of this book are divided into five parts:

Part 1, "Understanding the Basics," explores the basics of SharePoint 2010.

Part 2, "Developing in SharePoint 2010," explores the various aspects of customizing SharePoint and writing custom code in SharePoint 2010.

Part 3, "Managing Content in SharePoint 2010," explores the capabilities of managing content in SharePoint 2010.

Part 4, "Administering and Configuring SharePoint 2010," explores administering SharePoint 2010.

Part 5, "Advanced SharePoint 2010," explores advanced concepts such as Service Applications, Business Intelligence, and InfoPath Services in SharePoint 2010.

How to Use This Book

Code lines, commands, statements, classes, and any other code-related terms appear in a monospace typeface. Occasionally, when a line of code is too long to fit on a printed line in the book, a code-continuation arrow (➥) is used to signal the continuation.

Each chapter begins with a list of topics and an overview and ends with a summary and Q&A session. Within the chapters, you'll find the following elements that provide additional information:

By the Way notes give extra information on the current topic.

Did You Know? tips offer advice or describe an additional way of accomplishing something.

Watch Out! cautions signal you to be careful of potential problems and give you information on how to avoid or fix them.

HOUR 1

Introducing SharePoint 2010

What You'll Learn in This Hour:

- ▶ Why SharePoint?
- ▶ History of SharePoint
- ▶ Features of SharePoint 2010
- ▶ Installing SharePoint
- ▶ Walking through Visual Studio 2010 and SharePoint Designer 2010

> **By the Way**
>
> Due to the complexity of the topics discussed, some figures in this book are very detailed and are intended only to provide a high-level view of concepts. Those figures are representational and not intended to be read in detail.

SharePoint has become one of Microsoft's most popular products, and its popularity continues to grow. It is a strategic technology that enables collaboration among people in a way that traditional web applications could never achieve. With each new version SharePoint becomes more powerful in terms of features and ease of use. However, SharePoint is a big product, and some of its features themselves are huge. It takes time for a person to master even individual features, and may be impossible for a single person to know everything about SharePoint. The best way to learn is to read a good book like this one and to practice. The best way to master SharePoint is of course working on a live implementation (though it will take many implementations before you get a chance to work on the majority of the features of SharePoint). Considering the vastness of SharePoint it also is impossible to cover everything in a single book. This book is structured so that you get a good, detailed understanding of most of the features of SharePoint. For the few topics not covered in detail, the book provides a good starting point consisting of a high level overview of the topic and pointers to other sources. This book assumes that you don't know anything about SharePoint. Therefore, features that existed in SharePoint 2007 are described along with features that are new in SharePoint 2010.

Why SharePoint?

All successful technologies help a person to do something better, faster, and for less money. The same is true of Microsoft SharePoint Foundation Server 2010. Most people would define SharePoint as a great collaboration platform. While that is true, another equally justified way of defining SharePoint is a platform to manage information that will greatly improve your life and may some day save you or your organization's skin as well. SharePoint helps you manage information like no other application. From simply acting as a repository for data to performing intelligent operations on data SharePoint does just about everything involved in managing data. Intelligent operations or processing includes classifying data through metadata and tagging to make it easier to find, routing data to different locations based on rules, archiving data, freezing the state of data, auditing all operations performed on data, disposing of data based on rules, processing data through complex workflows, and much more. A scenario will help you understand all this.

XYZ Biz is a company that handles the details related to awarding government contracts. For example when a government agency decides to build a new highway, it outsources all the work related to inviting quotes for contracts, evaluating the quotes, and awarding the contracts. Though XYZ Biz makes good money it has to tread carefully through this whole process or it will land in a legal soup. A couple of times companies that didn't get the contract complained of foul play and corruption against XYZ Biz. Fortunately XYZ Biz has a strong implementation of SharePoint Server 2010 that helps it keep all legal documents and evidence handy. It also ensures that the processes related to sending out tenders, evaluating tenders, and awarding contracts are automated.

- The requests for quotes are announced on a SharePoint site hosted on the Internet. Normally an employee of XYZ Biz writes out the invitation. Once he checks in the page a workflow sends the page to a manager for approval. The manager modifies the page and approves it. The workflow sends the page to the Legal department of XYZ Biz for a second level of approval. The Legal guys verify the document and then approve it, which results in the page getting published and becoming viewable by all on the Internet.

- Companies upload their quotes on the SharePoint site. While uploading they are prompted to fill in a host of metadata without which the documents cannot be checked in. Once uploaded a workflow is initiated and a mail gets sent to the appropriate person in XYZ Biz. This document then goes through multiple levels of approvals and is finally processed as per the workflow.

- The documents are moved to various locations based on the metadata so it becomes easy to classify them. These also get tagged for easy searching.

- Also the documents, once submitted, get frozen—that is, no changes can be made to them—and they become records that can be used as evidence in case of any lawsuits.

- After a specific time the records get archived. They can still be retrieved whenever required.

- The documents are easily retrievable even if they are routed and stored at different locations. This is thanks to the document id feature of SharePoint, which ensures that the documents can be retrieved through the same URL regardless of their locations.

The preceding scenario gives a simplistic outline of what can be achieved using a few features of SharePoint. Keep in mind that SharePoint has many more features, and much more is possible that was not covered here, as you will see as you read further in this book.

Saying that SharePoint greatly simplifies collaboration among large teams is a huge understatement. SharePoint simplifies collaboration like never before and does a lot more. Here is another scenario to help you better understand the problems that SharePoint solves.

XYZ Manufacturing is a company that deals with manufacturing. A large part of its business process involves writing documents such as purchase quotes, purchase orders, purchase invoices, sales quotes, sales orders, sales invoices, and so on. These documents are usually written in a Word document with a specified template. These documents are complex, and it takes a few days and contributions from multiple team members to complete them. In addition once completed the documents are emailed to multiple departments for approval. Either the documents are approved or comments are sent back for changes to be made. Once the whole process is completed the documents are emailed to the customer. After the customer approves the changes the documents are considered final. Any new changes in the future need to be done on a new copy of the document so that the original agreed upon document is always available to review. In addition due to legal reasons some documents need to be preserved for a span of at least one year. Sometimes employees have to search for documents from a vast store of thousands of documents.

Business is good, and XYZ Manufacturing has grown from 15 employees to 500 employees in the last five years. To increase efficiency, teams of 15 to 20 people have been formed who work together on the complex documents. With the increase in the number of employees the company faces new problems in ensuring seamless collaboration among employees. Some of the recent incidents highlight the problems:

- A few weeks ago an employee working on a sales order overwrote the updates done by another employee who was also working on the same document.
- In another incident an employee sent an incomplete document for approval.
- Two weeks ago an employee sent a sales order to the customer. All hell broke out when it was realized that the document was not approved.
- Another employee sent the wrong copy of the document to the customer. The poor employee got confused in the many emails in which the documents were sent to and fro as an attachment.
- A few days ago XYZ Manufacturing found that some documents were permanently deleted that should have been retained for legal reasons.
- XYZ Manufacturing realized that most employees are doing rework as it has become impossible to search for the right document from the thousands of historical documents.
- Multiple meetings have been happening for one of the sales orders, and the information is dispersed in email. Because information is dispersed in individual mail boxes, it has become extremely difficult to track information, which has greatly reduced productivity in meetings.
- Reporting critical statistics has become impossible.

The scenario might be a bit exaggerated, but these are the kinds of issues faced when the size of a company grows and you do not have a good way to manage the processes. Faced with these new problems XYZ Manufacturing decided to implement Microsoft SharePoint Server 2010. The following explains how SharePoint helped to solve each of the preceding problems:

- The first advantage that XYZ Manufacturing got, which was an important factor, was a short duration and the ease with which the SharePoint implementation was done in the company. Also the company didn't have to do many administrative duties such as re-creating users, and they were able to use the Active Directory user and groups thanks to the brilliant integration of SharePoint with the Active Directory.
- The implementation team also quickly identified the different kinds of teams that were going to use the SharePoint application. A team site was created for

each team (more on this later). Administrative privileges were provided on the team site to some users in each of the teams who were identified to be the System Administrator for the team site.

- ▶ Training was imparted to the users. Thanks to the consistency that SharePoint provided in various features across the application the learning curve was small and efficient.
- ▶ Now the employee can prepare a document as a draft in a central location and prevent the document from being available to other users unless the document is complete. When the user wants to make the document available to other users she checks in the document.
- ▶ The check in/check out feature of SharePoint also prevents accidental overwriting of the document by another user.
- ▶ Once the document was complete it can easily be sent for approval using a workflow. Thanks to the workflow it is now ensured that the document never goes directly to the client. Also the comments are now recorded in one location rather than being dispersed in emails.
- ▶ The fact that the document is in a central place in SharePoint and not in multiple emails avoids the confusion of identifying the latest and complete version of the document.
- ▶ The versioning feature also helps track the history of the document without needing to store multiple copies of the document. It also is easy to store and track comments and other metadata information for each of the versions.
- ▶ Documents accidentally deleted are now easily retrievable thanks to SharePoint's Recycle Bin.
- ▶ Using various features of SharePoint, such as Record Retention and Information Management Policies, documents can now be stored for the specified period automatically. This helps overcome the issue of document storage for legal reasons.
- ▶ The powerful SharePoint search functionality makes searching for historical data easy.
- ▶ Using Meeting Workspaces the team can now track all information from multiple meetings at one place.
- ▶ Using the powerful Business Intelligence features of SharePoint the team can now track various critical statistics and adjust accordingly.

Don't worry if you cannot fully understand everything mentioned here, especially if you are new to SharePoint. All these features will be covered in detail throughout the book. For people who have worked on Microsoft Office SharePoint 2007, most of the features should look familiar. The important point is that the preceding scenario represents the possibilities using just the out of the box features of SharePoint. You just need to configure a few things here and there; zero code writing is required. And of course SharePoint provides a rich mechanism to implement customizations through code that can greatly expand the SharePoint's capability. Further applications of SharePoint become clearer as you progress in this book.

History of SharePoint

A quick look at the history of SharePoint clearly indicates how SharePoint has evolved to become one of the fastest growing products for Microsoft. SharePoint first came on the scene in 2001 in the form of two products: SharePoint Team Services and SharePoint Portal Server 2001. Both these products were just a start and had limited functionality compared to what SharePoint today provides. However the products quickly became popular. Customers liked the WYSIWYG HTML editing of SharePoint Team Services and the web part declarative and reusable editing of SharePoint Portal but wanted to use both models on the same site.

Then came the next release of SharePoint in 2003. SharePoint Team Services evolved into a more scalable and flexible platform and SharePoint Portal Services was built on top of it. Some features of SharePoint 2003 are listed here:

- Real-time presence and communication
- Standard site templates
- People and groups lists
- Calendar
- Surveys
- Document collaboration
- Issue tracking
- My Sites

The next release of SharePoint happened in 2007 in the form of Windows SharePoint Services 3.0 and Microsoft Office Server 2007 and took the product to a new level. Content management was the biggest area of improvement in this version. Microsoft had a separate product for content management before this release, but with this release the content management features were integrated into SharePoint itself. With the addition of new features such as workflows, document and records management, Excel Services, and InfoPath Form Services better integration with Microsoft Office and integration with Information Rights Management were added. In addition search functionality was highly enhanced in the 2007 release.

SharePoint 2010 is the latest and current version of SharePoint. Like the 2007 release this version of SharePoint comes in two parts. The first is SharePoint Foundation 2010, which is the platform for SharePoint Server 2010. You can consider SharePoint Foundation 2010 the equivalent of Windows SharePoint Services 3.0 and SharePoint Server 2010 as the equivalent of Microsoft Office SharePoint Server 2007 though both provide many more features than their predecessors.

Features of SharePoint 2010

SharePoint 2010 comes up with a lot of innovative features. These can be mainly classified into six different areas, as listed in the following sections.

Understanding Sites in SharePoint 2010

You can consider SharePoint 2010 Sites as a single platform for all your business websites—intranet, extranet, and Internet sites. SharePoint enables you to create a variety of sites and also simplifies the management of these sites. From a team site for colleagues, to an extranet site for partners, to an Internet site for customers, people can share and publish information using one familiar system. Many features help to build the SharePoint 2010 Sites experience. Some of these worth mentioning are the out of the box web parts, the SharePoint ribbon, multilingual user interface, mobile connectivity, support for Office web apps, cross browser support, and a host of out of the box site templates.

Understanding Communities in SharePoint 2010

As mentioned earlier SharePoint 2010 is a great tool for collaboration. It helps people work together in ways that are most effective for them by providing great collaboration tools that anyone can use to share ideas, find people and expertise, and locate business information. Even better, SharePoint 2010 lets you manage these tools from a single, powerful platform. It enables your people to become more creative and productive through a variety of features such as blogs, wikis, integration with Microsoft Exchange Server and Office Communications Server, Colleague

Suggestions and Colleague Network features, tagging features, My Profile, memberships, and much more.

Understanding Content in SharePoint 2010

SharePoint 2010 Content further enhances the content management features of SharePoint 2007 and makes Enterprise Content Management (ECM) easy for everyone. It consists of the following features:

- Content Organizer
- Document Sets
- Managed metadata service
- Metadata-driven navigation
- Multistage disposition
- Rich media management
- Shared content types
- Unique document IDs
- Word automation services

Understanding Search in SharePoint 2010

SharePoint 2010 provides a rich user experience in terms of search. It provides intranet search, people search, and a platform to build search-driven applications—all on a single, cost-effective infrastructure. But what's so unique about SharePoint 2010 search is its combination of relevance, refinement, and people. This new approach to search provides an experience that is highly personalized, efficient, and effective. The search features vary from simple site search to enterprise scale search. Search is discussed further in future hours.

Understanding Insights in SharePoint 2010

SharePoint 2010 provides highly advanced business intelligence features that let everyone access the business information they need to make good decisions. It includes the following features:

- Business Intelligence Center
- Calculated KPIs
- Chart web parts

- Dashboards
- Data Connection Library
- Decomposition tree
- Excel Services
- Excel Services and Power Pivot for SharePoint
- PerformancePoint Services
- Visio Services

The use of well-known applications and interfaces makes people comfortable from the start, and they know how to get the data they need. For example, anyone can use Excel Services to publish Microsoft Excel workbooks in SharePoint 2010. From there, an entire team can access and analyze the same data and rest assured that everyone has the right information.

Understanding Composites in SharePoint 2010

SharePoint 2010 Composites helps to build custom solutions on SharePoint that automate processes and connect disparate information. From simple sites to complex applications, you can rapidly respond to specific business needs with custom solutions. The following list, which you can consider as building blocks for custom solutions, helps you appreciate this capability of SharePoint:

- Browser-based customizations
- Business Connectivity Services
- Business Data Connectivity Service
- Client Object Model (OM)
- Developer Dashboard
- Event receivers
- External data column
- External lists
- Language Integrated Query (LINQ) for SharePoint
- REST and ATOM data feeds
- Ribbon and dialog framework
- Sandboxed solutions

- SharePoint Designer
- SharePoint Service Architecture
- SharePoint timer jobs
- Silverlight web part
- Solution packages
- Visual Studio 2010 SharePoint developer tools
- Windows 7 support
- Workflow
- Workflow models
- Business Connectivity Services profile page
- Workflow templates
- Access Services
- Business Data Integration with the Office Client
- Business data web parts
- InfoPath Forms Services

Installing SharePoint

Even though the experience of installing SharePoint 2010 varies depending on the physical topology of the SharePoint farm that you intend to build, it is a fairly easy process. This section covers installing SharePoint on a Windows 2008 Server environment on a single machine. In addition the section also looks at the additional steps needed to install SharePoint 2010 on Windows 7. (Yes, you read it right. You can install SharePoint on Windows 7, but it should be only for learning or development purposes.)

Understanding Prerequisites and Hardware Configuration for SharePoint 2010

The first thing you need to set up before installing SharePoint 2010 is the hardware configuration and the prerequisites. The hardware requirements for installing SharePoint on a single server are listed in Table 1.1.

TABLE 1.1 Hardware Configurations

Component	Minimum Requirement
Processor	64-bit, four cores.
RAM	4GB for developer or evaluation use. 8GB for production use in a single server or multiple server farm.
Hard disk	80GB for system drive. For production use, you need additional free disk space for day-to-day operations. Maintain twice as much free space as you have RAM for production environments. For more information, see Capacity management and sizing for SharePoint Server 2010 in TechNet (http://technet.microsoft.com/en-us/library/cc261700.aspx).

The following must be installed as prerequisites before installing SharePoint Server 2010. These are installed automatically through the prerequisites preparation tool that comes with the SharePoint Server 2010 installation.

- Web Server (IIS) role
- Application Server role
- Microsoft .NET Framework version 3.5 SP1
- Microsoft Sync Framework Runtime v1.0 (x64)
- Microsoft Filter Pack 2.0
- Microsoft Chart Controls for the Microsoft .NET Framework 3.5
- Windows PowerShell 2.0
- SQL Server 2008 Native Client
- Microsoft SQL Server 2008 Analysis Services ADOMD.NET
- ADO.NET Data Services Update for .NET Framework 3.5 SP1
- A hotfix for the .NET Framework 3.5 SP1 that provides a method to support token authentication without transport security or message encryption in WCF
- Windows Identity Foundation (WIF)

You find more details on the minimum hardware configurations for the various topologies and the prerequisites at http://technet.microsoft.com/en-us/library/cc262485.aspx.

Understanding SharePoint SKUs in SharePoint 2010

SharePoint 2010 mainly comes in three editions. You can find details of the features supported by them at http://SharePoint.microsoft.com/en-us/buy/Pages/Editions-Comparison.aspx. SharePoint Foundation 2010 is the base for the other editions, which build upon that edition. The SKUs are as follows:

▶ SharePoint Foundation 2010

▶ SharePoint Server 2010 Standard Version

▶ SharePoint Server 2010 Enterprise Edition

Try It Yourself

Install SharePoint on a Single Windows Server 2008 R2 Machine

This section lists the steps required to install SharePoint on a single Windows Server 2008 R2 machine. This could also be a virtualized environment, and the steps remain the same. If you intend to install SharePoint 2010 on Windows 7, please refer to http://msdn.microsoft.com/en-us/library/ee554869.aspx.

Before we start installing SharePoint 2010 ensure that the environment meets the prerequisites and hardware configuration as specified in the earlier section.

To start installing SharePoint 2010, follow these steps:

1. If not already done you need to set up the Active Directory.

2. Install Visual Studio 2010. This is a required step if you plan to use this as a development environment.

3. Next install the office client. You can install either the 64-bit or 32-bit office client. Installing 64-bit office client provides very little advantage over the 32-bit, and what you go with shouldn't matter much. However, if you are planning to install SharePoint Designer 2007 to use for SharePoint 2007 sites, then you need to go with the 32-bit office client.

4. Install the SharePoint Designer 2010 64-bit or 32-bit based on the version of office client you installed in Step 3.

5. Install Microsoft SQL Server. This needs to be 64-bit version and should be Microsoft SQL Server 2005 SP3 or better. I prefer going with Microsoft SQL Server 2008 R2 or you will need to install additional cumulative updates. For more

details, refer to the link provided in the section "Understanding Prerequisites and Hardware Configuration for SharePoint 2010" earlier in the hour.

   a. You need to set the firewall to allow incoming connections to the SQL Server. In addition download and install the Microsoft certificate revocation list from http://crl.microsoft.com/pki/crl/products/MicrosoftRootAuthority.crl. Ignore any warning related to installing SQL Server on the domain controller.

   b. Run the setup and install the database engine, analysis services, and reporting services.

   c. Choose to start the SQL Server agent, database engine, analysis services and reporting services.

   d. Enable mixed mode authentication and add the appropriate user as the SQL Server administrator. (In my case it is the current user administrator.)

   e. Similarly, in analysis services configuration and reporting services configuration add the appropriate user as the administrator.

   f. Proceed to the next steps in the wizard and finish the installation.

6. Run the SharePoint 2010 installation. You need to first install the prerequisites. Ensure that all are installed successfully. If any fail verify the logs and take the appropriate steps.

7. Next install SharePoint 2010 Server. Once the installation is finished run the SharePoint Products and Technologies Configuration Wizard. You are prompted at the end of the installation. Make sure the check box is selected and click OK.

8. In the Configuration Wizard, do the following:

   a. Choose to create a new server farm.

   b. Specify a service account. I usually create an AD account with the name "SharePointfarm." Ensure that the AD account is added to the SQL Server instance and has the DBCreator and DBSecurity roles. Add the account splearn\SharePointwebapp as the config account and specify splearn as your SQL Server database.

By the Way

You could use the domain administrator account as a service account. But it is recommended to use a different account for this purpose. In fact it is recommended to use a different account for each service in a production environment.

HOUR 1: Introducing SharePoint 2010

    c. Specify port 9999 as your Central Administration website port number.

    d. Wait for the Configuration Wizard to finish.

9. Once completed, open the Central Administration by going to Start Menu, All Programs, Microsoft SharePoint 2010 Products, SharePoint 2010 Central Administration. You can also browse it by typing **http://** <<*machine name* >>: <<*port no* >>. **For example: http://localhost:9999** (In my case the port number will be 9999 as specified in the Configuration Wizard in the previous step.) You now have the SharePoint 2010 configured on your machine.

Try It Yourself

Create Your First SharePoint Web Application

If not already created, you need to create you first web application and site collection for use in future hours. To create your first web application, follow these steps:

1. Browse to the SharePoint 2010 Central Administration by going to Start, All Programs, Microsoft SharePoint 2010 Products, SharePoint 2010 Central Administration.

2. In the Central Administration screen, go to Application Management and then select Manage Web Application.

3. Click the New button in the ribbon under the Web Applications tab.

4. Select the following configuration:

    - Authentication: Classic Mode Authentication
    - Port: 80
    - Host Header: Blank
    - Path: Leave default
    - Authentication Provider: NTLM
    - Allow Anonymous: No
    - Use Secure Socket Layer (SSL): No

5. Select Create New Application Pool as shown in Figure 1.1 and make the account configurable. Select an appropriate account from the drop-down list under the Configurable radio button. If the drop-down list is disabled, you need to register a new managed account by clicking on the link Register New

Managed Account. Enter the appropriate username and password. You can use the administrator account, but on production it is advisable to have a dedicated account for this. Click OK.

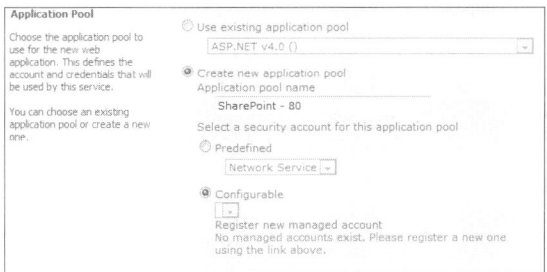

FIGURE 1.1
Create or select an application pool for a new web application.

6. Leave the rest of the settings as default and click OK.

7. The web application takes some time to create. When completed you see the screen shown in Figure 1.2 with the link to create a site collection.

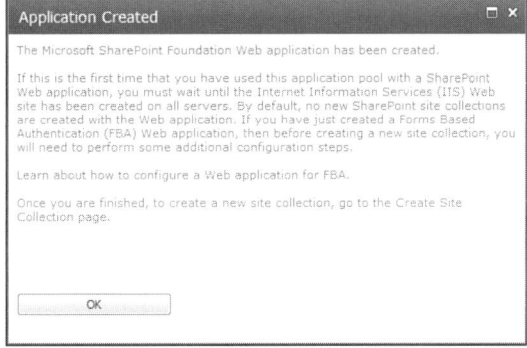

FIGURE 1.2
Application Created dialog with link to create a new site collection

8. Click the Create Site Collection page.

9. Enter a title and select the Team Site template. Enter the primary site collection administrator and click OK.

10. The site collection is created and you can now access it through the URL http://localhost. In my case, this is http://splearn. This URL will be referenced in subsequent hours.

HOUR 1: Introducing SharePoint 2010

11. You also need to activate the publishing features for your team site as it is required in future hours. To activate the publishing feature, follow these steps:

    a. Browse the site and go to Site Actions, Site Settings.

    b. Under the Site Collection Administration section click Site Collection Features. Activate the SharePoint Server Publishing Infrastructure feature.

    c. Go back to Site Actions, Site Settings.

    d. Under the Site Actions section, click Site Features and activate the SharePoint Server Publishing feature.

You are all set now. Don't worry too much if you don't understand all the steps. They are discussed in detail in subsequent hours.

By the Way

You use the site just created in all the subsequent hours.

By the Way

The SharePoint 2010 Central Administration provides a vast set of configuration options. These options are discussed in Hour 16, "Understanding SharePoint 2010 Central Administration."

Introducing Virtualization

Virtualization is a technology that is becoming more popular day by day. In simple terms virtualization enables you to build virtual machines that run within your host operating system. This offers many advantages:

- Virtualization keeps your host environment clean and light. All the installations are done in your virtual machine. The host environment just needs to have the basic prerequisites for running the virtual machines.

- You can create snapshots, which are like restore points that record an important stage of the virtual machine. For example, suppose you just installed SharePoint 2010 and you take a snapshot of the virtual machine. You can easily revert back to this stage by restoring the snapshot if something goes wrong. This is especially helpful in automated deployment testing on SharePoint where you need to daily run deployment scripts. Another advantage is reverting back to a previous build in production when you realize the new build has major issues.

- You can create multiple copies of the VM and distribute it to other team members by just copying the virtual hard disks. This saves a lot of time when you are doing SharePoint development as a team and want every team member to have an environment consistent with yours.
- You can run multiple environments within the same machine.

The main disadvantage of virtualization is that it requires a powerful host operating system and power hardware as well. Virtualization looks to be the way to go in the case of SharePoint 2010, provided you have a powerful hosting environment.

SharePoint on Cloud is becoming popular. Microsoft provides online hosting of SharePoint 2010 through Microsoft SharePoint Online, and virtualization is a technology used extensively here.

Walking Through Visual Studio 2010 and SharePoint Designer 2010

This last section of this hour walks you through Visual Studio 2010 support for SharePoint 2010 and SharePoint Designer 2010. SharePoint does provide lots of features out of the box. But in certain scenarios, out of the box features will not be sufficient to address all your needs. This is where the customization of SharePoint comes into the picture. Visual Studio 2010 enables you to do custom development in SharePoint 2010.

Introducing Visual Studio 2010 Support for SharePoint 2010

Developers have often complained that there are no good development tools for SharePoint 2007 in Visual Studio. In fact there was no out of the box support for creating SharePoint 2007 projects in Visual Studio. You needed to install Visual Studio Extensions for SharePoint separately to be able to develop for SharePoint in Visual

Studio. This has drastically changed with the release of SharePoint 2010 and Visual Studio 2010. Installing SharePoint 2010 installs a host of project templates for SharePoint in Visual Studio. The various templates available are shown in the Figure 1.3.

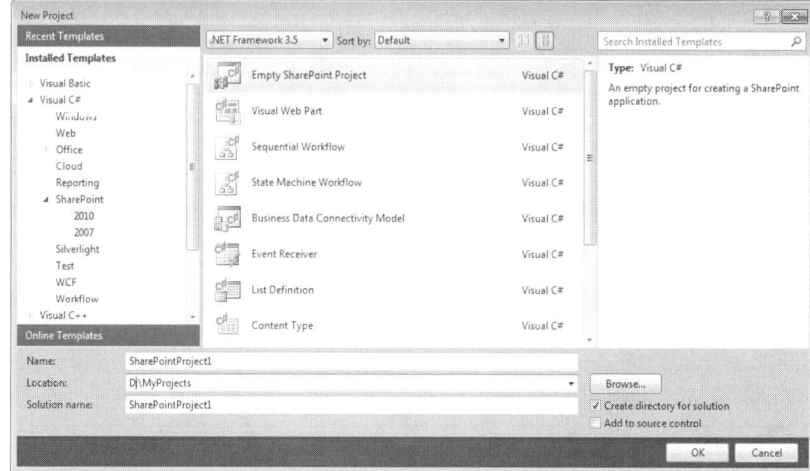

FIGURE 1.3
Visual Studio project templates for new SharePoint project

▶ **Empty SharePoint Project**—This project type creates an empty SharePoint project where you can add one or more items later on.

▶ **Visual Web Part**—Web parts and SharePoint are inseparable. You can create web parts in two ways. One way is to build the web part completely in code as in the case of a custom control. The other way is to build a web part by adding a User Control to it. The advantage of this is that you can use the drag and drop features of the Visual Studio to build the user interface. The Visual Web Part template type helps you to create a web part using a user control. You create both a Visual web part and a simple web part in Hour 5, "Working with Web Parts and Web Pages."

▶ **Sequential Workflow**—Workflows are an important feature of SharePoint. Sequential workflows are a type of workflow where control goes in sequence based on some branching logic and requires minimum human interaction. These workflows can be considered similar to flowcharts. This type of template helps you to create sequential workflows.

▶ **State Machine Workflow**—In state machine workflows control flows through multiple states based on some conditions. This control flow is too complex to be represented by the branching logic of sequential workflows because the control flow can transition from any state to any other state based on various conditions. This can result in a large number of branches too complex to be handled in a sequential workflow. In state machine workflows states are defined, and the transition from one state to another is defined in each individual state. State machine workflows are best defined for processes involving many human interactions. Examples of both workflows are presented in Hour 15, "Understanding SharePoint 2010 Workflows."

▶ **Business Data Connectivity Model**—This project type helps you to connect SharePoint with external data and represent that data in SharePoint.

▶ **Event Receiver**—You can hook to various events in SharePoint using event receivers. These events can be like creation/modification or deletion of a new list, list item, or site. This project type helps you to create event receivers, which you learn more about in Hour 11, "Understanding Advanced Data Management Concepts in SharePoint 2010."

▶ **List Definition**—In SharePoint, data is represented in lists and libraries. The List Definition template helps you to create custom lists or libraries.

▶ **Content Type**—Content types are an important concept in SharePoint, and they represent the schema of data in SharePoint lists and libraries. Content types can be considered a collection of columns (where a column is the most atomic unit representing data, similar to columns in SQL). But content types are much more and can include information such as workflows, information management policies, publishing information, and much more. You learn more about content types in Hour 10, "Managing Data in SharePoint 2010," and Hour 11.

▶ **Module**—Modules help you deploy files to SharePoint lists and libraries. You will use modules extensively when doing SharePoint development.

▶ **Site Definition**—This type of template can help you to create a customized site template.

▶ **Import Reusable Workflow**—This project type helps you to import a reusable, declarative workflow created in SharePoint Designer 2010 into Visual Studio.

▶ **Import SharePoint Solution Package**—Import SharePoint Solution Package projects let you import an existing SharePoint site, exported to a .wsp file, into Visual Studio. Once imported into Visual Studio, you can customize the individual components of the template and redeploy them.

In addition to the preceding templates you can find the SharePoint 2007 Sequential Workflow template and SharePoint 2007 State Machine Workflow template.

HOUR 1: Introducing SharePoint 2010

Go ahead and create a new Empty SharePoint Project. Name it SharePointProjectTest. You see the screen shown in Figure 1.4.

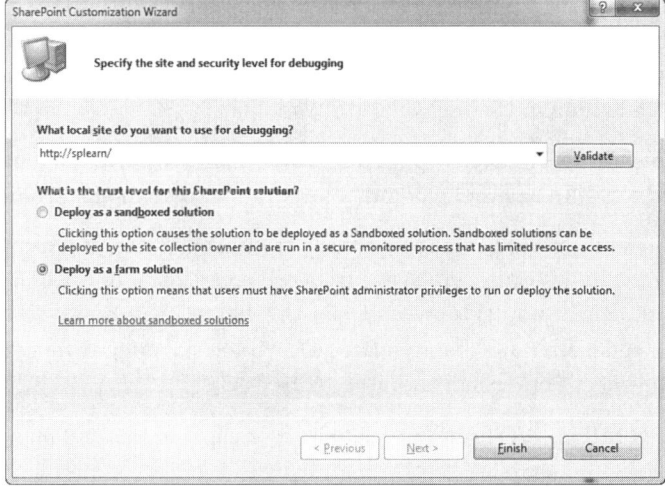

FIGURE 1.4
Configure the project as a sandboxed solution or a farm solution.

You are prompted to deploy the solution as a sandboxed solution or as a farm solution. Sandboxed solutions are discussed in subsequent hours. For now select Deploy as a Farm Solution. Enter the URL of the SharePoint site where you want to deploy the solution. This is also the URL that will be used for debugging. Click Finish. An empty SharePoint project is created. In the Solution Explorer right-click the project. You see the screen shown in Figure 1.5.

You can see the following additional items compared to a normal class library project created in C#.

▶ **Deploy**—Deploys the solution to the URL specified in the previous screen, which is http://splearn.

▶ **Package**—Packages the solution and creates a WSP. WSP stands for Windows SharePoint Solution Packages and represents a unit of deployment in SharePoint.

▶ **Retract**—Retracts an already deployed solution package.

Click Properties in the right-click menu. In the corresponding window click SharePoint in the left section. You see the screen shown in Figure 1.6.

Walking Through Visual Studio 2010 and SharePoint Designer 2010 21

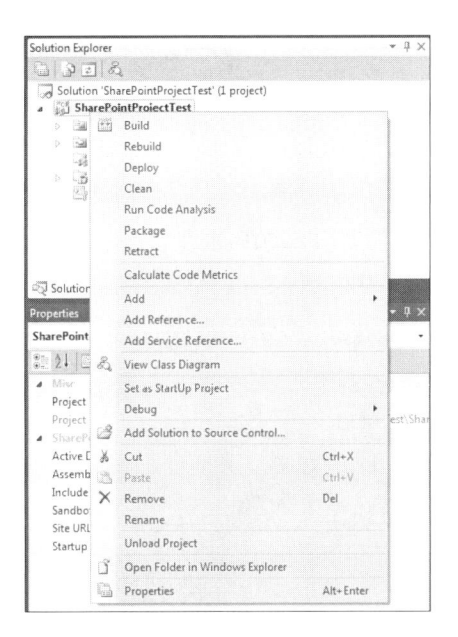

FIGURE 1.5
Build, Deploy, and Package options

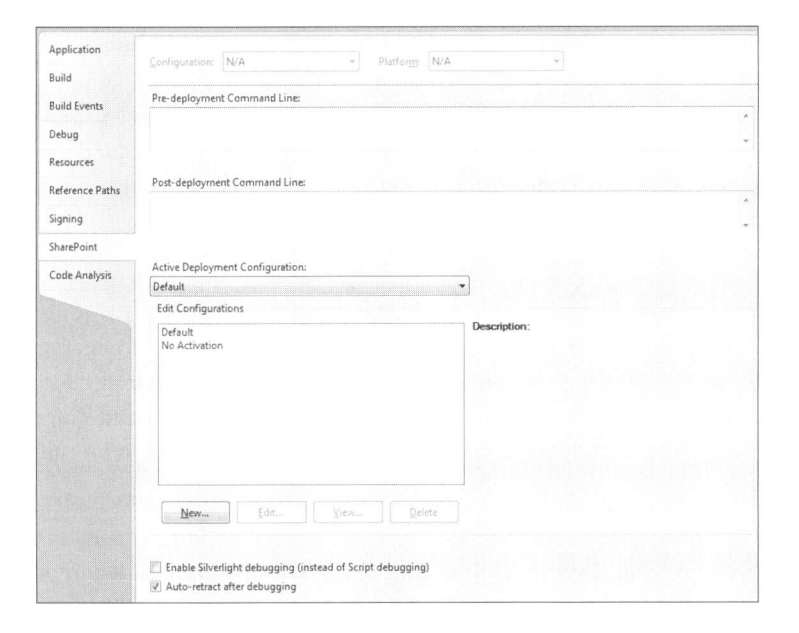

FIGURE 1.6
Select the Active Deployment Configuration.

This represents the various types of configurations for deploying a SharePoint solution. You can see the Active Deployment Configuration as Default. Select Default and click View. This is shown in Figure 1.7.

FIGURE 1.7
Deployment steps for the Default deployment configuration

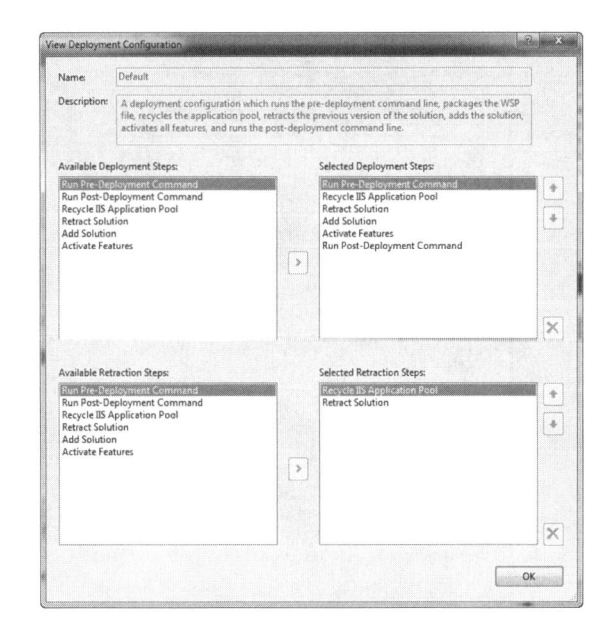

Figure 1.7 shows various steps involved in deployment when the active configuration is Default. There is also a No Activation configuration, which does not activate the features. Don't worry if you are new to SharePoint and don't understand the terms; they are discussed later in the book. You won't write any code or deploy anything for now. This is just intended as an overview of Visual Studio integration with SharePoint.

Introducing SharePoint Designer 2010

SharePoint Designer or SPD as it is known is a tool that enables you to perform more advanced tasks than the configurations done through the user interface but that don't require custom code. The full description of tasks that can be done through the SPD is outside the scope of this book, but just be aware a lot can be done through SPD.

If you followed the steps in the previous section you should have SharePoint Designer 2010 installed on your machine. Go to the Start Menu, All Programs, Microsoft SharePoint Designer 2010. Click Open Site and enter the URL of your SharePoint site. You see the screen shown in Figure 1.8.

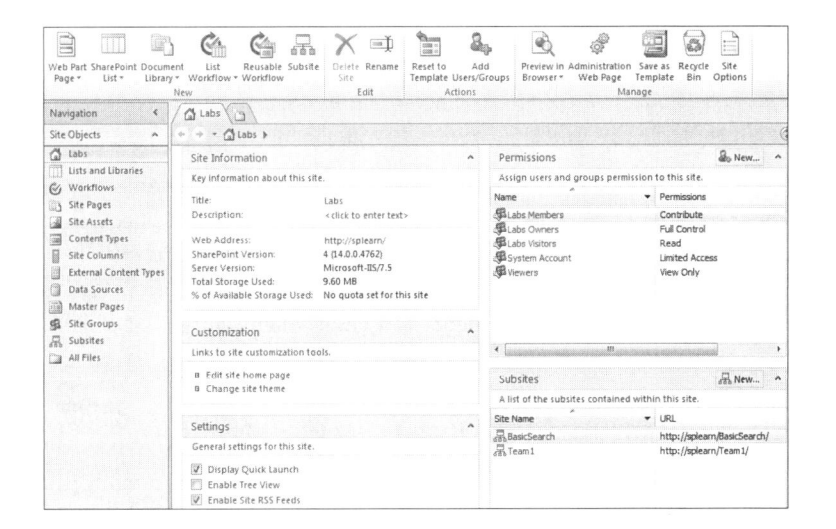

FIGURE 1.8
SharePoint Designer 2010

If you are familiar with SPD 2007 you will immediately notice the differences in SPD 2010. The notable differences are the ribbon, a navigation pane focusing on SharePoint artifacts, a breadcrumb with helpful navigation, and the concept of gallery pages, settings pages, and editors. The SharePoint navigation pane on the left is the place from where you can access the various artifacts of your SharePoint site and modify them. The ribbons present a host of commands and are context based—that is, the commands on the ribbon change based on what you are editing. You use the SPD several times in subsequent hours. For now you can just play around by visiting the various sections in the left navigation pane.

Summary

This hour was a starting point for understanding SharePoint 2010. You saw a brief description of what problems SharePoint can solve and took a high level look at SharePoint's features. You also saw the step-by-step details for installing SharePoint on a standalone Windows 2008 Server machine and the additional steps necessary to install SharePoint on Windows 7. And you took a brief look at SharePoint 2010 support in Visual Studio 2010 and the SharePoint Designer 2010.

You probably have questions about SharePoint's architecture and what installing SharePoint does to your machine. These questions and more are answered in the next hour.

Q&A

Q. Can I use SharePoint 2010 in place of creating custom ASP.NET applications?

A. SharePoint 2010 is a product built using the ASP.NET Framework. It is not intended to replace ASP.NET. While SharePoint provides many features out of the box, SharePoint 2010 is good for specific scenarios such as document management, collaboration, and so on. You still need to build custom ASP.NET applications for other requirements, especially when high transactional data operations are involved.

Q. Why does SharePoint 2010 not support 32-bit platforms?

A. 64-bit platforms provide a considerable improvement in performance compared to 32-bit platforms. SharePoint 2010 takes advantage of the 64-bit platform to achieve higher performance compared to SharePoint 2007. Therefore, it does not support 32-bit platforms.

Q. Can I install SharePoint Designer 2010 on a 32-bit platform or can it be installed only on 64-bit platforms?

A. Yes, you can install SharePoint Designer 2010 on 32-bit platforms also. The prerequisite is that the version of Office must also be 32 bit.

Q. Can we use SharePoint 2010 Designer to connect to SharePoint 2007 sites?

A. No, you cannot connect to SharePoint 2007 sites using SharePoint Designer 2010. For that you need to use SharePoint Designer 2007.

HOUR 2

Understanding the SharePoint 2010 Architecture

What You'll Learn in This Hour:

- Understanding ASP.NET versus SharePoint
- Understanding the 14 Hive and SharePoint virtual directories
- Understanding SharePoint and SQL
- Introducing the SharePoint hierarchy
- Understanding Timer jobs
- Introducing service applications

> **By the Way**
>
> Due to the complexity of the topics discussed, some figures in this book are very detailed and are intended only to provide a high-level view of concepts. Those figures are representational and not intended to be read in detail.

This hour explains the architecture of SharePoint 2010 and how it integrates with Internet Information Services (IIS) and ASP.NET. You learn exactly what happens behind the scenes when you install SharePoint and how SharePoint uses the wonderful extensibility of ASP.NET to build new components over ASP.NET.

Understanding ASP.NET Versus SharePoint

If you followed the instructions in Hour 1, "Introducing SharePoint 2010," you should have SharePoint 2010 installed on your machine. If you take a quick peek into the IIS you see at least two new websites—a website for SharePoint Central Administration and another one for SharePoint Web Services. Open the SharePoint Central Administration by going to Start Menu, All Programs, Microsoft SharePoint 2010 Products, SharePoint 2010 Central Administration. You see a URL like http:// <<machine name>>:<<port no.>> /Default.aspx. Now select SharePoint Central Administration v4 and open the Content View on the right. You do not find any Default.aspx page. So from where exactly is the default.aspx page being fetched? What changes does installing SharePoint Server 2010 make to your environment? To understand all that and more let us first go through a few concepts of ASP.NET.

ASP.NET is the Microsoft Framework that integrates with IIS to help you build highly advanced and robust web applications. A good understanding of how ASP.NET builds on IIS goes a long way toward helping you understand the SharePoint architecture.

You can think of ASP.NET as a request processing engine. It builds on the extensible architecture of the Internet Information Server (IIS). The ASP.NET Framework is implemented as an ISAPI extension named aspnet_isapi.dll. Whenever a user requests an ASP.NET page or a client application makes a call to an ASP.NET Web Service, IIS picks up the request. At the lowest level ASP.NET interfaces with IIS through an ISAPI extension. This request usually is routed to a page with a .aspx extension, but this varies depending on the implementation of the HTTP handler set up to handle the specified extension. In IIS .aspx is mapped through an Application Extension (aka as a script map) that is mapped to the ASP.NET ISAPI DLL—aspnet_isapi.dll. Every request that fires ASP.NET must go through an extension that is registered and points at aspnet_isapi.dll.

IIS starts a worker process if it does not already exist and routes the request to this worker process. This worker process handles the processing of the aspx page. The IIS just acts as a routing mechanism for the requests and response. The worker process corresponds to the Application Pool of the website for which the request was made and runs under the context of the identity defined in the Application Pool configuration. The worker process then routes the request to an appropriate HTTP handler based on the configuration defined in the web.config of the virtual directory or machine.config. Usually this request is processed by the PageHandlerFactory class, which is the default implementation of HTTP handler for aspx pages. Also on the way the request gets processed by various HTTP modules as specified in the configuration. The HTTP handler processes the request and returns the response, which might again be processed on the way by HTTP modules based on the defined configuration. This architecture based on the processing by HTTP handlers has many advantages. It frees the IIS from performing processing directly. In addition there is the concept of a VirtualPathProvider, which abstracts the details of where the files are stored from the ASP.NET runtime. By default in ASP.NET this fetches the file from the file system.

The preceding discussion represents a brief overview of the low level architecture of ASP.NET. ASP.NET is, however, a rich framework that makes web development easy due to multiple reasons, some of which are listed here:

- **A rich and vast class library**—ASP.NET boasts a rich set of classes that save a lot of effort. Creating an aspx page requires you to simply inherit from the Sytem.Web.UI.Page class. A rich set of controls, such as GridView, ListView, TreeView, and many more, help in building complex user interfaces. Also the programming model behind this is powerful, providing you hooks in the form of events at almost every place in the life cycle of the page.

- **User controls and custom controls**—In addition to the previous points, ASP.NET provides you the ability to easily create your own reusable controls in the form of custom controls and user controls. The difference between both is that in the case of user controls you get a nice interface in the Integrated Development Environment (IDE) that is the Visual Studio to drag and drop other controls, while in the case of custom controls you need to build the user interface in the code.

- **Master pages**—Master pages is a powerful concept introduced in ASP.NET 2.0. Master pages enable you to easily achieve a consistent user interface across the application. You define within the master page the elements that are common across all the pages in the application. You also define content placeholders, which are basically sections that the individual pages overwrite to define their individual user interface, within the master page. As you will see SharePoint implements the concept of master pages extensively.

- **Extensible architecture**—The ASP.NET architecture is extensible, and almost all components can be overridden and replaced by custom components. In later sections you see how SharePoint builds over it.

There is a lot more to ASP.NET, and you will find many good books on it. Let us now see how SharePoint relates to ASP.NET. In a way you can consider SharePoint to be a web application built over ASP.NET. SharePoint transforms an ASP.NET website in IIS into something called a SharePoint web application by adding IIS metabase entries and a lot of web.config entries specific to SharePoint. Using the SPVirtualPathProvider SharePoint fetches the web files from the SQL server. The following lists the changes that installing SharePoint makes to your environment.

- Deploys DLLs related to the SharePoint framework to GAC.
- Creates a special folder called SharePoint root or the 14 Hive at C:\Program Files\Common Files\Microsoft Shared\Web Server Extensions\14. This is an important folder and contains important files for SharePoint to work.

HOUR 2: Understanding the SharePoint 2010 Architecture

- Creates and configures a few IIS websites with their configuration updated to turn them into SharePoint web applications. You see the websites for SharePoint Central Administration and SharePoint Web Services. The SharePoint Central Administration site is located at C:\inetpub\wwwroot\wss\VirtualDirectories in the folder that in most cases has the same name as the port number you specified during installation. The SharePoint Web Services website is located at C:\Program Files\Common Files\Microsoft Shared\Web Server Extensions\14\Web Services\Root.

- Creates the web.config files that contain the additional entries for SharePoint as follows:

    - A custom section group called SharePoint is added. This section contains many other entries, the most notable of which is the `SafeControls` section. You need to add entries for the web parts in this section or you will not be able to run the web part. The following lists the structure of the SharePoint section:

        ```
        <SharePoint>
        <SafeMode />
        <WebPartLimits />
        <WebPartCache />
        <WebPartControls />
        <SafeControls />
        <PeoplePickerWildcards />
        <MergedActions />
        <BlobCache />
        <RuntimeFilter />
        </SharePoint>
        ```

    - The next section is the `Microsoft.SharePoint.Client` section, which is newly introduced in SharePoint 2010 and is present for the client object model.

    - Next you can see the `System.Web` section. This section contains entries for custom trust levels called WSS_medium and WSS_minimal. These code access security policies make your SharePoint installation more secure. In addition you see standard ASP.NET concepts such as sitemap providers and WebParts. You also find that the httpModules element is empty.

    - The `System.WebServer` element is a new section with IIS 7. In this element you see the various httpModules configured. This is because SharePoint 2010 works in the integrated pipeline mode. SharePoint removes a number of out of the box HTTP modules. Some of these are the anonymous identification, file authorization, ASP.NET profiles, webDav module, and ASP.NET session module. This is something you need to keep in mind when developing for SharePoint as many of these things applicable in ASP.NET are not applicable in SharePoint.

▶ Next is the `System.ServiceModel` section, which enables ASP.NET compatibility for WCF services. You see more about this in upcoming hours.

▶ Next you have a huge runtime section that specifies many assemblyBinding elements. These elements redirect calls of older versions of SharePoint DLLs to newer versions of DLLs transparently without the calling programs ever knowing about it. Thus if you had a DLL compiled to target SharePoint version 12 (SharePoint 2007), that would automatically be routed to SharePoint 14 (SharePoint 2010).

Understanding the 14 Hive and SharePoint Virtual Directories

As mentioned in the previous section a special folder is created at C:\Program Files\Common Files\Microsoft Shared\Web Server Extensions\14. This is called the SharePoint root or the 14 Hive. The 14 Hive is an important folder, and it contains important files for SharePoint. Some important subfolders in the 14 Hive are shown in Table 2.1.

TABLE 2.1 SharePoint Virtual Directories

Folder Name	Use
ADMISAPI	Contains the soap services for Central Administration. If this directory is altered, remote site creation and other methods exposed in the service will not function correctly.
BIN	Contains the important .exe files, such as the OWSTimer, which is the SharePoint timer service, the stsadm.exe, psconfig.exe, and other important utilities.
CONFIG	Contains files used to extend IIS websites with SharePoint Server. If this directory or its contents are altered, web application provisioning will not function correctly.
DATA	The root location where local data is stored, including search indexes.
ISAPI	Contains the files for various web services for SharePoint. The various DLLs of SharePoint can also be found here. These DLLs are also installed in the GAC.

TABLE 2.1 Continued

Folder Name	Use
LOGS	Contains setup and ULS logs. These logs are helpful in debugging errors in your farm.
USERCODE	Contains files used to support your sandboxed solutions. You learn more about sandboxed solutions in Hour 21, "Understanding the Architecture of Sandboxed Solutions."
WEBCLIENTS	Contains files related to the new Client Object Model.
WEBSERVICES	Contains new .wcf or .svc related files.
TEMPLATE	An important folder in the 14 Hive; you will refer to it regularly during development time. This folder is the location for many files that you will deploy as part of your custom code. Following are the important subdirectories in the TEMPLATE folder.
CONTROLTEMPLATES	The location where you will deploy your user controls. In addition you will find many user controls already existing in this folder that are being used by SharePoint.
FEATURES	An important folder that contains the files for SharePoint features. SharePoint features are a great way to add functionality to your SharePoint application and can be toggled on and off based on the activation or the deactivation of the corresponding SharePoint feature. You learn more about SharePoint features in Hour 3, "Starting Development with SharePoint 2010."
GLOBAL	Contains some master pages and list definitions.
IMAGES	Contains various image files used by SharePoint. This is also the location to deploy your images that are to be used by multiple site collections within multiple web applications.
LAYOUTS	Another important directory in SharePoint. This folder contains the application pages mostly used in administration tasks. In SharePoint terms an application page is a physical ".aspx" page that resides on the file system. SharePoint also contains site pages that are pages stored in the SharePoint content database in SQL Server.
SITETEMPLATES	You can create multiple types of sites in SharePoint. These sites are based on a site template. A site template defines various characteristics of a site that will be created using this site template. These characteristics may include the lists and libraries within site, web parts, SharePoint features activated, look and feel, and so on. The site template definitions are stored within the SITETEMPLATES folder.

Understanding the 14 Hive and SharePoint Virtual Directories

TABLE 2.1 Continued

Folder Name	Use
THEMES	Contains the various files for SharePoint themes.
XML	Contains .xml files used for various purposes. One of those is information about custom field controls.

Now that you have looked at the physical structure of the 14 Hive, open the IIS Manager (inetmgr.exe) and expand the SharePoint Central Administration website so that the various virtual directories can be visible as shown in the image in Figure 2.1.

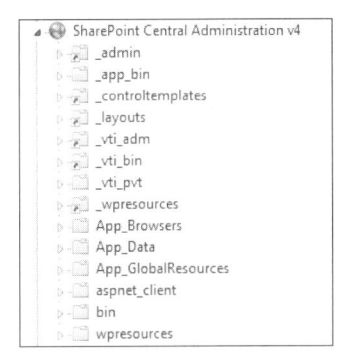

FIGURE 2.1 SharePoint website virtual directories

Most of these virtual directories point to the folders in the 14 Hive and are present in all the SharePoint websites. Table 2.2 lists the virtual directories.

TABLE 2.2 SharePoint Virtual Directories

Virtual Directory	Physical Directory location
_controltemplates	Points to the <14 Hive>\TEMPLATE\CONTROLTEMPLATES folder. As indicated earlier, this is the folder where the user controls are deployed in SharePoint. This virtual directory is present in all the SharePoint websites.
_layouts	Points to the <14 Hive>\TEMPLATE\LAYOUTS folder. This is present for all SharePoint websites.
_vti_bin	Points toward the <14 Hive>\ISAPI folder and hosts the various web services of SharePoint. This is also present for all the SharePoint websites.

In addition to the preceding directories list _wpresources points to C:\Program Files\Common Files\Microsoft Shared\Web Server Extensions\wpresources. This contains a web.config file that is used in web part resources for the Global Assembly Cache (GAC) and is present for all the SharePoint websites. Additional virtual directories are specific to the Central Administration website.

Understanding SharePoint and SQL

Installing SharePoint results in the creation of a number of databases in the SQL Server, as follows:

▶ **Configuration database (SharePoint 2010 Foundation)**—An important database generally called SharePoint_Config. This database stores and manages data associated to all the SharePoint databases in the farm, IIS websites, trusted solutions, WSP packages, site templates, and web application and farm settings. This database is generally small in size.

> **By the Way**
>
> The configuration database should reside on the same SQL server instance as the Central Administration database because they have a strong dependency on each other.

▶ **Central administration content database (SharePoint 2010 Foundation)**—The content database from for the Central Administration website. The name of the database will be in the form SharePoint_AdminContent_GUID.

> **By the Way**
>
> Only one instance of the Central Administration content database and configuration database will be created per farm.

▶ **Content database (SharePoint 2010 Foundation)**—Stores all the content stored in SharePoint websites, including list configuration and data; files/documents from SharePoint libraries, including the ones stored in the web part galleries, master page galleries, and so on; web part properties; audit logs; sandboxed solutions; and so on. It also stores data for Office web applications (Excel, Access, OneNote, InfoPath, and so on). These databases start with WSS_Content.

▶ **Usage database (SharePoint 2010 Foundation)**—Supports the new Usage and Health Data Collection Service Application service.

Understanding SharePoint and SQL 33

- **Business data connectivity (SharePoint 2010 Foundation)**—Supports BCS services. It stores the external content types and associated metadata. These databases follow the naming convention of Bdc_Service_DB_GUID.

> **Watch Out!**
> The business data connectivity database stores only the external content types and associated metadata and not the actual data from the external systems.

- **Application registry database (SharePoint 2010 Foundation)**—Stores data required to support backward compatibility for Business Data Connectivity (BDC) from SharePoint 2007. This database is used only during the upgrade process and can actually be deleted after the upgrade is complete. This database follows the naming convention of Application_Registry_Service_DB_GUID.

- **Subscription settings database (SharePoint 2010 Foundation)**—Supports the Subscription Settings Service. This database is used to support the new partitioning feature for SharePoint 2010.

- **Search administration database (SharePoint 2010 Standard)**—Used by the SharePoint 2010 Search service. It stores the configuration information associated to search and Access Control List (ACL), which is used for securing content that is indexed.

- **Crawl database (SharePoint 2010 Standard)**—Also used by the SharePoint 2010 Search service. This database stores the state of the crawled data and the crawl history.

> **Watch Out!**
> The crawl database can grow to be very large based on the amount of content that you are indexing.

- **Property database (SharePoint 2010 Standard)**—Another database used to support SharePoint 2010 Search service. This database stores information associated to crawled data (that is, properties, history, and crawl queries).

- **Web analytics staging database (SharePoint 2010 Standard)**—Stores temporary usage data collected from the usage database. The data comes to this database in an unaggregated format and the Web Analytics Service takes this data, processes it, aggregates it, and then sends it to the web analytics reporting database. This database is cleaned out every 24 hours but is then refilled with new data that has been collected.

- **Web analytics reporting database (SharePoint 2010 Standard)**—A new database for SharePoint 2010 used to support the Web Analytics Service. This database stores all the aggregated analytics data collected across the SharePoint 2010 farm. This is the database the usage reports run against, and there is only one of these databases per farm. This database can grow to become very large relative to the amount of data stored in the entire farm. This database only has analytics data; it does not have any actual data from the content databases. By default, data is stored in here for up to 25 months.

- **State database (SharePoint 2010 Standard)**—The state service is used to support storing temporary data across HTTP requests. This database is utilized by InfoPath Form Services, Visio Services, Exchange, Chart Web Part, and so on. The space required for this database is driven by the services that use this database. Multiple state databases can be added through PowerShell commands.

- **Profile database (SharePoint 2010 Standard)**—Used by the User Profile service to store profile data. This database will not become very big and the size is based on the amount of data stored about each user. The database needs to support heavy read operations to get user data that is accessed commonly (user permissions are not stored here; they are in the content database).

- **Synchronization database (SharePoint 2010 Standard)**—Another database used by the User Profile service. Its purpose is to store the configuration of the service that brings user profile data into SharePoint. It is also used to stage data being synchronized from directory services like Active Directory. The size of this database is relative to the number of users and groups being synchronized. This database needs to support both heavy reading and writing when the synchronization service is running.

- **Social tagging database (SharePoint 2010 Standard)**—Used by the User Profile service for storing social tags and notes created by users for content in SharePoint.

- **Managed Metadata Service database (SharePoint 2010 Standard)**—Database used by the new Managed Metadata Service.

- **Secure store database (SharePoint 2010 Standard)**—Used by the secure store service of SharePoint 2010. This is the new SharePoint 2010 service to support Single Sign-On. It stores user credentials and passwords.

- **Word automation services database (SharePoint 2010 Enterprise)**—This database is used by the Word Automation service.

▶ **PerformancePoint database (SharePoint 2010 Enterprise)**—Used to support PerformancePoint. It stores temporary objects and settings needed to support dashboards.

▶ **FAST Search administration database (SharePoint 2010 FAST)**—Stores information for FAST Search. FAST Search is a new search technology for SharePoint 2010. This is in addition to the existing SharePoint Search technologies.

Introducing the SharePoint Hierarchy

SharePoint sites are a part of the hierarchy that is important to understand. At the top of this hierarchy is the SharePoint farm. A SharePoint farm represents everything in a SharePoint installation—the servers that include your web front-end servers (these are the ones that serve the web pages), index server, database servers, and all other servers that may provide different types of services. The SharePoint farm includes the IIS websites, including the Central Administration, Windows services, web services, and everything else related to a SharePoint installation.

One level down from the SharePoint farm are the SharePoint web applications. The SharePoint web applications are ASP.NET web applications with configurations that turn them into SharePoint web applications. The Central Administration is one of the important web applications.

Next comes the site collection. A SharePoint application can have one or more content databases. Content databases store site collections. Site collections as the name suggests are a collection of SharePoint sites that come last in the SharePoint hierarchy. Also every web application can have multiple site collections but only one root site collection. Site collections also define a boundary of many things. For example, you give user permissions within a site collection, and it won't impact other site collections.

SharePoint sites are at the bottom of the hierarchy, and every site collection must have at least one site that is the top level site for the site collection. A site collection can have only one top level site, but you can have multiple levels of subsites and multiple subsites at the same level.

If all this sounds too confusing, don't worry; in Hour 4, "Walking Through the Available Site and List Templates in SharePoint 2010," you learn how to create web applications, site collections, and different types of sites. Within a short time of working on SharePoint you will have this hierarchy memorized.

Understanding Timer Jobs

Timer jobs are a great feature of SharePoint. Timer jobs run in the background in a specific Windows service for SharePoint Server and perform various tasks for SharePoint. These include infrastructure tasks for the Timer service, such as clearing the timer job history and recycling the Timer service, and tasks for web applications, such as sending email alerts. The SharePoint 2010 Timer service (SPTimerv4) runs timer jobs. In SharePoint 2010 management of timer jobs is easier than in previous versions. Also SharePoint 2010 adds 21 new timer jobs in addition to the 39 timer jobs present in SharePoint 2007. You can see the list of timer jobs by going to the Central Administration, Monitoring, Review Job Definitions (under the Timer Jobs section), as shown in Figure 2.2.

FIGURE 2.2
Timer job definitions

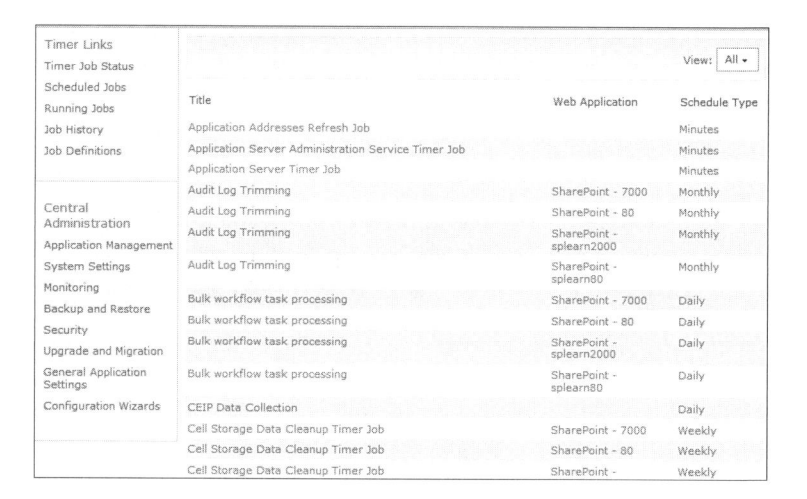

Title	Web Application	Schedule Type
Application Addresses Refresh Job		Minutes
Application Server Administration Service Timer Job		Minutes
Application Server Timer Job		Minutes
Audit Log Trimming	SharePoint - 7000	Monthly
Audit Log Trimming	SharePoint - 80	Monthly
Audit Log Trimming	SharePoint - splearn2000	Monthly
Audit Log Trimming	SharePoint - splearn80	Monthly
Bulk workflow task processing	SharePoint - 7000	Daily
Bulk workflow task processing	SharePoint - 80	Daily
Bulk workflow task processing	SharePoint - splearn2000	Daily
Bulk workflow task processing	SharePoint - splearn80	Daily
CEIP Data Collection		Daily
Cell Storage Data Cleanup Timer Job	SharePoint - 7000	Weekly
Cell Storage Data Cleanup Timer Job	SharePoint - 80	Weekly
Cell Storage Data Cleanup Timer Job	SharePoint -	Weekly

You can see three columns. Title shows the name of the timer job. The second column is Web Application and represents the web application for which the timer job runs. The third column, Schedule Type, shows the type of schedule under which the timer job runs. For some timer jobs this shows as disabled, which means the timer job is disabled and will not run. Click any of the timer jobs and you see the screen shown in Figure 2.3.

This screen provides configuration options for the timer job. You can update the schedule for the timer job or disable the timer job from this screen. You can also make the timer job run explicitly by clicking on the Run Now button.

In addition you can see the status of various running timer jobs at Central Administration, Monitoring, Check Job Status (under the Timer Jobs section), as shown in Figure 2.4.

Understanding Timer Jobs   37

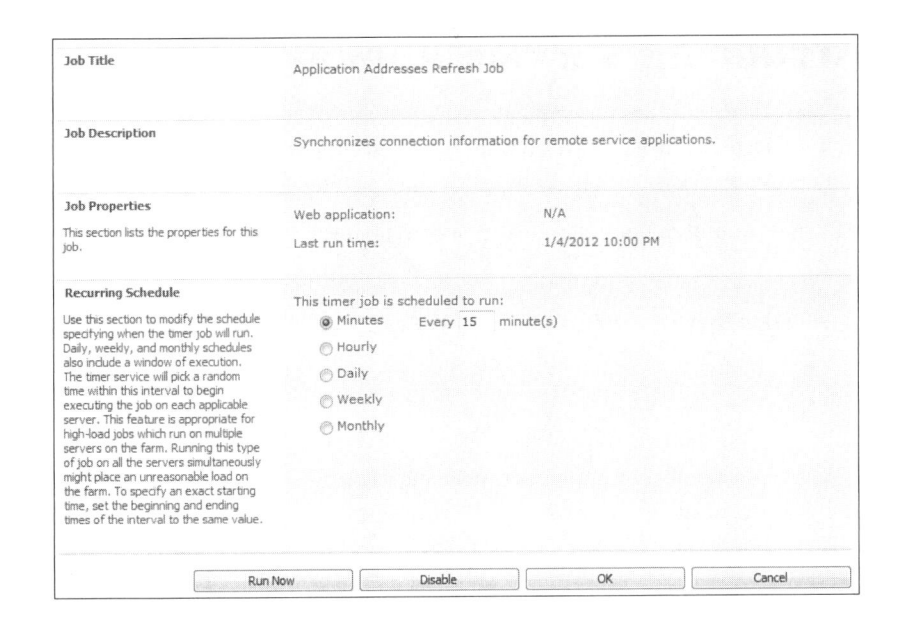

FIGURE 2.3
Timer job schedule

FIGURE 2.4
Timer job status

You can also create custom timer jobs. You learn how to create one in Hour 7, "Understanding SharePoint 2010 Server Side Development."

Introducing Service Applications

SharePoint 2007 had the concept of shared service provider or SSP, which was a single web application in which you configure various important services for SharePoint such as user profiles and search. SSPs suffered with a few limitations:

- You could not appoint administrators on a per-service-level.
- The services of an SSP could not be shared across farms, and the SSP was a concept available only in SharePoint server.
- One web application could be managed by only a single shared service provider at a given time.

This has seen a significant improvement in SharePoint 2010 in the form of the managed services concept. Each service is an individually manageable entity. This has the following advantages:

- You can now appoint administrators on a per-service basis.
- These users are then given access to Central Administration. However, they can manage only the designated service.
- Rather than providing all the services to a given site you can now assign specific services to a site. The administrator can pick and choose which services are made available to which websites.
- Farms can share services. This opens up immense scalability options and also a great deal of flexibility in the overall architecture considering things such as security, availability, and so on.
- One other point to consider is that not every service is shareable. You can also alter your custom services and, depending on the nature of the service, if it makes sense to share it you have the ability to share it.

To access the service applications browse to Central Administration, Application Management, Manage Service Applications under the Service Applications section. You see the list of service applications as shown in Figure 2.5.

> **By the Way**
> We have the whole Hour 20, "Understanding Service Applications," dedicated to the Manage Services concept.

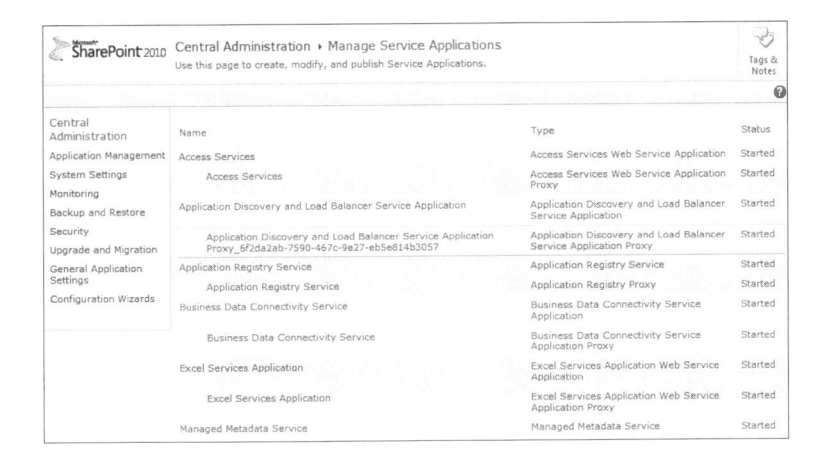

FIGURE 2.5
Service applications

Summary

This hour looked at the architecture of SharePoint 2010 and the changes installing SharePoint 2010 makes to your environment. The integration of SharePoint 2010 with ASP.NET and the configuration changes required for SharePoint were discussed, as well as the 14 Hive folder structure and the various important virtual directories. This hour explored database configurations and the SharePoint hierarchy; timer jobs and service applications also were discussed.

Hopefully you have a good understanding of the SharePoint architecture. By now you have done enough exploring of theoretical concepts and are probably ready to do some practical tasks. That's what you do in the next two hours. In Hour 3 you jump into coding, and in Hour 4 you take a quick tour of SharePoint 2010 and then learn a lot of practical lessons.

Q&A

Q. *How does SharePoint retrieve ASP.NET pages from the content databases?*

A. ASP.NET 2.0 introduced a new pluggable component type known as a virtual path provider. The idea behind a virtual path provider is that it abstracts the details of where page files are stored away from the ASP.NET runtime. SharePoint retrieves ASP.NET pages from the content databases using this concept through the SPVirtualPathProvider class.

Q. *Can we have a SharePoint Farm for just a service application?*

A. Yes. You can now have an entire farm that can scale out, whose job is only to provide services to other farms.

HOUR 3

Starting Development with SharePoint 2010

What You'll Learn in This Hour:

- ▶ Understanding SharePoint solutions as deployment units
- ▶ Introducing SharePoint features
- ▶ Debugging SharePoint solutions

> **By the Way**
> Due to the complexity of the topics discussed, some figures in this book are very detailed and are intended only to provide a high-level view of concepts. Those figures are representational and not intended to be read in detail.

Hour 1, "Introducing SharePoint 2010," gave you an overview of SharePoint 2010, and Hour 2, "Understanding the SharePoint 2010 Architecture," looked at SharePoint's architecture. If you are the typical developer, by now you are probably anxious to write some code. In this hour you begin by writing code in SharePoint 2010 in the form of a console application. After that you learn about SharePoint features and solutions, and then write your first SharePoint feature. Finally you learn about debugging techniques in SharePoint and how they differ from a normal ASP.NET application.

▼ **Try It Yourself**

Write a Simple Console Application

You write your first SharePoint 2010 code in the form of a console application.

> **By the Way**
> Although this is not a project type that you will use frequently, console applications are really useful when playing around with the SharePoint object model for learning purposes or to test some code quickly.

▼

HOUR 3: Starting Development with SharePoint 2010

Writing a console app is simple:

1. Open Visual Studio 2010 and create a new Visual C# project of type Console Application as shown in Figure 3.1.

FIGURE 3.1
New Project screen

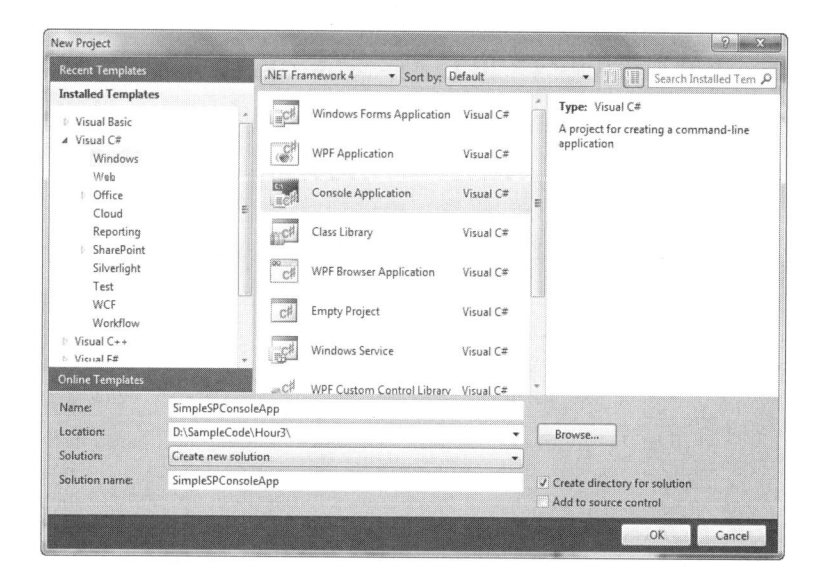

2. Add a reference to the Microsoft.SharePoint.dll from the .NET tab. If you cannot find it there you will find it in the <14 hive>\ISAPI folder.

3. Add the following using statement:

   ```
   using Microsoft.SharePoint;
   ```

4. Add the following code inside the Main method:

> **By the Way**
>
> You may need to replace http://splearn with the appropriate URL if the URL of your SharePoint site is different.

```
using (SPSite site = new SPSite("http://splearn"))
    {
        using (SPWeb web = site.OpenWeb())
        {
            Console.WriteLine(web.Title);
            Console.ReadKey();
        }
    }
```

Starting Development with SharePoint 2010

Watch Out!

Notice the using statements while creating the SPSite and SPWeb objects. It is important that you dispose these objects in any SharePoint application, or they will cause a memory leak and drastically impact the performance of your SharePoint application.

5. If you try to run the program by pressing F5 or clicking on the Start Debugging button, the program throws an exception indicating the web application was not found.

6. This is because by default the platform for your project is x86 and your SharePoint application needs to run under a x64 platform. To change this go to your project properties and under the Build section change the platform to x64 or AnyCPU. In addition ensure that the Target Framework is set to .Net Framework 3.5 in the Application tab of the project properties.

7. Run the program again by pressing F5 or clicking the Start Debugging button. You should see the title of your site.

You just wrote your first code and used two important objects of the SharePoint Object model that you will find yourself using almost everywhere. The SPSite represents a SharePoint site collection. The SPWeb represents a site within the site collection. In this case we are accessing the top level site by making a call to the OpenWeb() function of the SPSite. We could have also accessed the top level site by accessing the RootWeb property of the SPSite. However, it was important for you to see the OpenWeb() method and overload that you will be using to access the subsites method as well. Hour 7, "Understanding SharePoint 2010 Server Side Development," discusses most objects of the SharePoint object model in detail. However, it is helpful to get acquainted with a few of the objects that you will use frequently. You might have observed that SPSite and SPWeb represent the site collection and the site in the SharePoint hierarchy that we looked at in Hour 2. Following are the other objects in the SharePoint hierarchy:

▶ **SPFarm**—This class represents a SharePoint farm and is a part of the Microsoft.SharePoint.Administration namespace. You can access the local farm instance through the SPFarm.Local object.

▶ **SPWebApplication**—This class represents a SharePoint web application and is also a part of the Microsoft.SharePoint.Administration namespace. You can access the WebApplication instance of a site through the WebApplication property of the SPSite class instance.

▶ **SPContext**—This is an important class that represents the context of the request in SharePoint. You can access various important objects of SharePoint like the SPSite and SPWeb instances for the current request through this object. To get access to this object you call SPContext.Current.

> **Watch Out!**
>
> You should never dispose objects from SPContext or it will have unpredictable effects on your SharePoint applications.

> **Watch Out!**
>
> The SPContext.Current will be always null in a console application.

You will see as you proceed further in this book that SharePoint provides a rich object model, and you learn about many objects in detail.

Understanding SharePoint Solutions as Deployment Units

Although console applications are a great way to play around with the SharePoint API, you will not be using them to deploy new functionality to SharePoint. The recommended way to deploy functionality is through SharePoint solutions, which are cab files with a .wsp extension, which stands for Windows SharePoint Solution Packages. The most important file in the WSP file is the manifest.xml. This file contains information about the other files in the solution. In SharePoint 2010 you can create two types of solutions: farm solutions and sandboxed solutions.

Understanding Farm Solutions

A farm solution is a SharePoint solution that is deployed to the Solution Store in Central Administration of your SharePoint farm. People who have worked with SharePoint 2007 will find this familiar.

Try It Yourself

Write a Farm Solution

You now write your first SharePoint web part. Basically it is a simple "Hello World" web part that contains a user control. For those who are new, web parts are like

Understanding SharePoint Solutions as Deployment Units | 45

widgets that can be added dynamically to a page and can be personalized. To write the web part, follow these steps:

1. Open Visual Studio and create a new Empty SharePoint Project named HelloWorldFarm as shown in Figure 3.2.

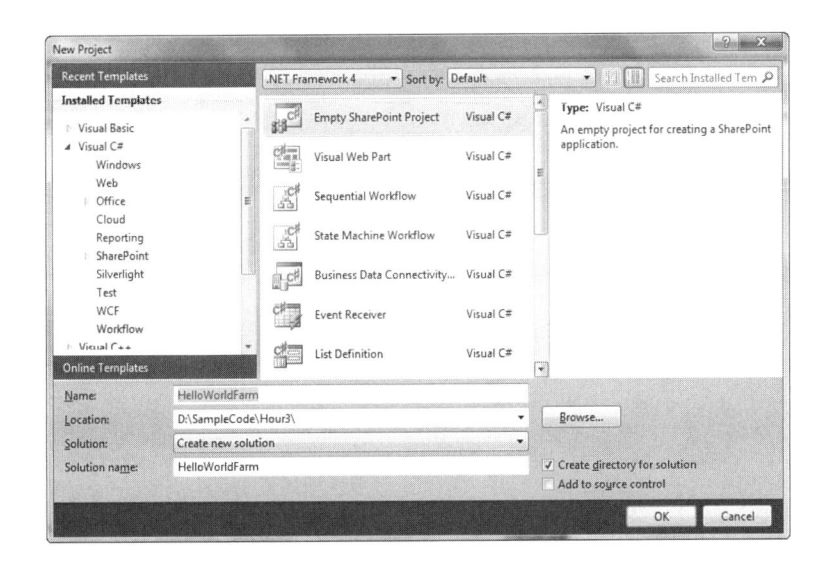

FIGURE 3.2
New Project screen

2. Select Deploy as a Farm Solution as the trust level for the solution, as shown in Figure 3.3, and click Finish.

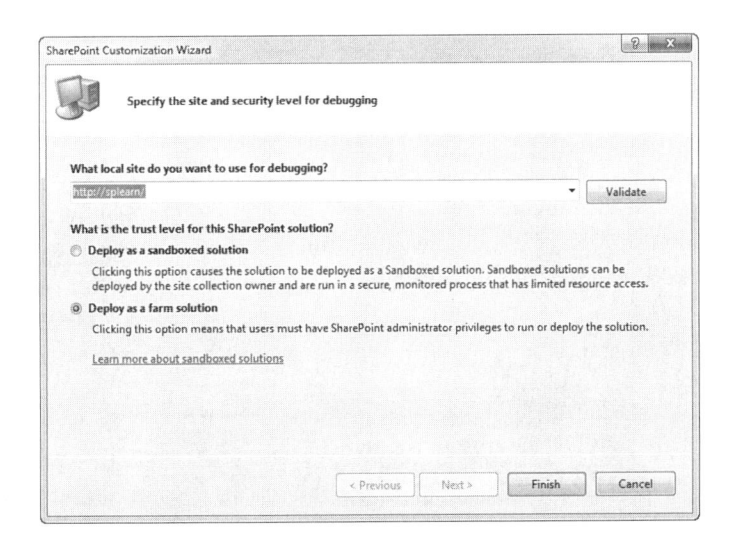

FIGURE 3.3
Creating a farm solution

HOUR 3: Starting Development with SharePoint 2010

3. Right-click the project and select Add, New Item.

4. Select Visual Web Part, name it HelloWorldVWP, and click Add, as shown in Figure 3.4. A visual web part is simply a web part with a user control that makes it easier to build the user interface of your web part by enabling you to drag and drop controls on the user control.

FIGURE 3.4
Add New Item screen

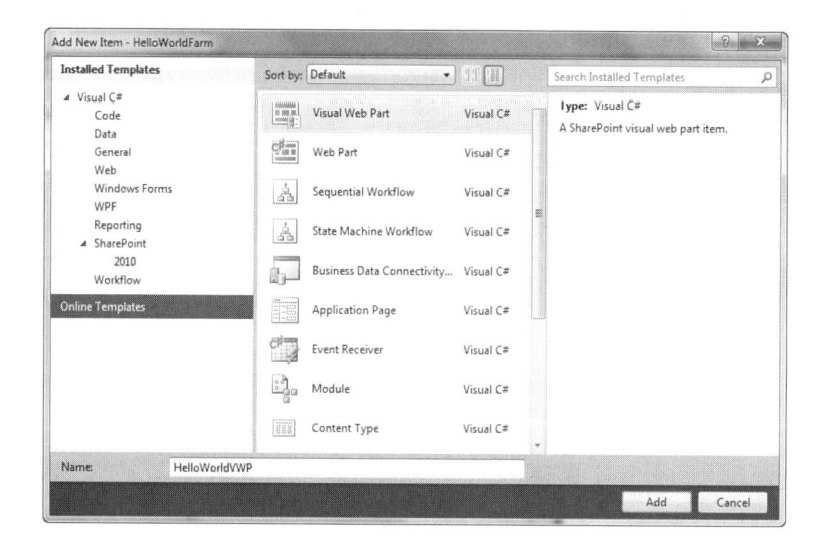

5. A new web part is added to your project. The project structure should look similar to Figure 3.5.

FIGURE 3.5
Project structure for HelloWorldFarm project

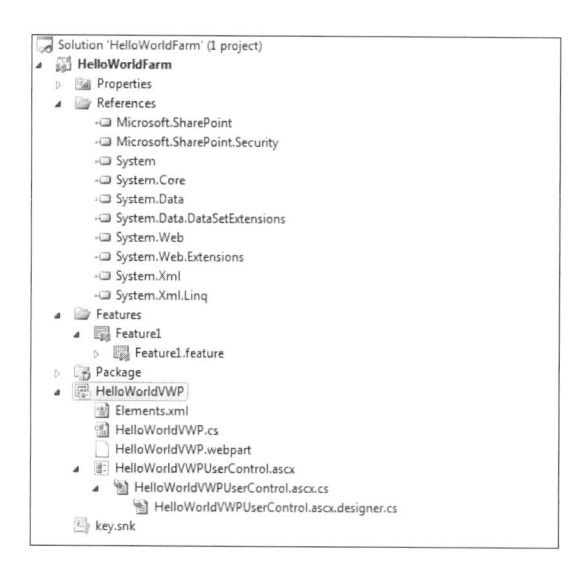

Understanding SharePoint Solutions as Deployment Units 47

Hour 5, "Working with Web Parts and Web Pages," discusses in detail most of these files. You can see in your solution something called Feature1 under Features. You learn more about features in the "Introducing SharePoint Features" section later in this hour. For now just understand that features enable you to toggle a functionality On or Off in SharePoint and that most functionality is deployed in SharePoint as SharePoint features.

6. Double-click Feature1. You see the feature designer as shown in Figure 3.6. Change the title to HelloWorldVWP.

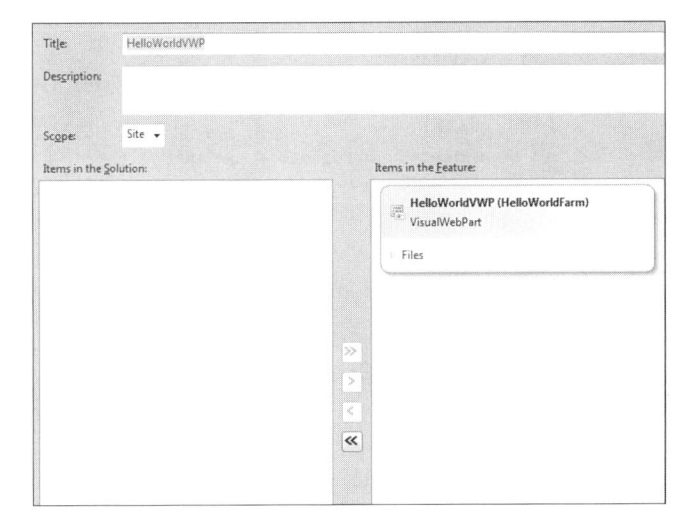

FIGURE 3.6
Visual Studio 2010 feature designer

7. Select Feature1 in the Solution Explorer and rename it to HelloWorldVWP.

8. Open HelloWorldVWPUserControl.ascx and add the following at the end:
   ```
   <asp:Label runat="server" ID="lblHelloWorld"
   Text="Hello World - My First Visual Webpart" />
   ```

9. Now build the solution.

10. Once the build has succeeded deploy the solution by right-clicking on the project and then clicking Deploy. If you look at the output window you can see a lot of information on what is happening during deployment. Remember in Hour 1 we looked at the deployment configurations in the Visual Studio. You will find that the output in the output window corresponds to the steps of the default deployment configuration.

```
Active Deployment Configuration: Default
Run Pre-Deployment Command:
  Skipping deployment step because a pre-deployment command is not
specified.
Recycle IIS Application Pool:
  Skipping application pool recycle
because no matching package on the server was found.
Retract Solution:
  Skipping package retraction because no matching package on the server was
found.
Add Solution:
  Adding solution 'HelloWorldFarm.wsp'...
  Deploying solution 'HelloWorldFarm.wsp'...
Activate Features:
  Activating feature 'HellowWorldVWP' ...
Run Post-Deployment Command:
  Skipping deployment step because a post-deployment command is not
specified.
========== Build: 1 succeeded or up-to-date, 0 failed, 0 skipped ==========
========== Deploy: 1 succeeded, 0 failed, 0 skipped ==========
```

You have now built and deployed your first SharePoint solution. In the preceding output you can see that your HelloWorldVWP feature was activated while deploying. This means that the web part is now available for adding to the pages in the site.

In the preceding scenario we deployed the solution directly through Visual Studio. But we could have just as easily packaged the solution by right-clicking on the project and clicking on Package. We could then deploy the solution using the following stsadm commands.

```
Stsadm -o addsolution -filename HelloWorldFarm.wsp
Stsadm -o deploysolution -name HelloWorldFarm.wsp
➥-url http://splearn –allowgacdeployment
```

By the Way

Stsadm is a command line tool that you will be coming across frequently. This tool is present in the <14 Hive>\Bin folder. You need to include this folder in the `Path` environment variable to be able to use this command as indicated here.

1. Go to Start, All Programs, Control Panel, System.
2. On the Advanced tab, click the Environment Variables button.
3. Select the variable path and click the Edit button.
4. Add the following to the end of the Variable value field: Change the drive if SharePoint is not installed in c: drive.

    ```
    ;C:\Program Files\Common Files\Microsoft Shared\Web Server
    ➥ Extensions\14\BIN
    ```

5. Click OK.

Understanding SharePoint Solutions as Deployment Units 49

> **By the Way**
>
> The preceding deployment could have been done through PowerShell commands in place of the `stsadm` commands. Even though the `stsadm` commands still work in SharePoint 2010 it is recommended to use PowerShell in SharePoint 2010. PowerShell is discussed in more detail in Hour 16, "Understanding SharePoint 2010 Central Administration."

You can see the contents of the .wsp file generated when you packaged the solution. To view the contents of the .wsp, perform the following steps:

1. Go to the Bin\Debug folder of your project. Rename HelloWorldFarm.wsp to HelloWorldFarm.wsp.cab.

2. Open the .cab file and you should see the contents of the solution, as shown in Figure 3.7.

3. Select the Details view and notice the path column.

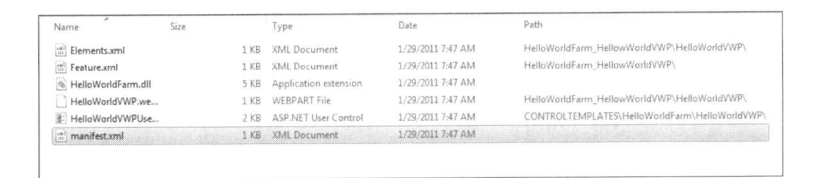

FIGURE 3.7
Contents of the WSP file

4. Open the manifest.xml file. You can see it contains all the information about the contents of the solution, as shown in Figure 3.8.

```xml
<?xml version="1.0" encoding="utf-8" ?>
<Solution xmlns="http://schemas.microsoft.com/sharepoint/" SolutionId="3bf583ab-e8e3-4075-b6cf-
    4c33e40c5867" SharePointProductVersion="14.0">
    <Assemblies>
        <Assembly Location="HelloWorldFarm.dll" DeploymentTarget="GlobalAssemblyCache">
            <SafeControls>
                <SafeControl Assembly="HelloWorldFarm, Version=1.0.0.0, Culture=neutral,
                    PublicKeyToken=eca0b390ee89e03e" Namespace="HelloWorldFarm.HelloWorldVWP"
                    TypeName="*" />
            </SafeControls>
        </Assembly>
    </Assemblies>
    <TemplateFiles>
        <TemplateFile
            Location="CONTROLTEMPLATES\HelloWorldFarm\HelloWorldVWP\HelloWorldVWPUserControl.ascx" />
    </TemplateFiles>
    <FeatureManifests>
        <FeatureManifest Location="HelloWorldFarm_HellowWorldVWP\Feature.xml" />
    </FeatureManifests>
</Solution>
```

FIGURE 3.8
Sample manifest.xml

5. You can also find the SafeControl tag for the web.config file, which is required to allow the web part to run on your site.

HOUR 3: Starting Development with SharePoint 2010

6. Now browse to the <14 Hive>\Template\Features folder and you should see a directory named HelloWorldFarm_HelloWorldVWP. Notice that this maps to the path column in the WSP file. Also go to the <14 Hive>\Template\CONTROLTEMPLATES folder. You can see your HelloWorldFarm folder in there. Notice again that this maps to the path column in your WSP file.

Browse to your SharePoint 2010 Central Administration site. Navigate to System Setting and under Farm Management click Manage Farm Solutions. You should see your solution along with other solutions, as shown in Figure 3.9.

FIGURE 3.9
Solution Store in the SharePoint 2010 Central Administration

Name	Status	Deployed To
applicationtemplatecore.wsp	Deployed	Globally deployed.
helloworldfarm.wsp	Deployed	http://splearn

Finally you can see your web part in action. Follow these steps:

1. Browse to your SharePoint site (in my case it is http://splearn).
2. Select the Page tab on the ribbon and click Edit. Two new tabs—FormatText and Insert—appear.
3. Go to the Insert tab and click web part. The list of web parts appears below the tab.
4. Select Custom under Categories on the left side. You see your HelloWorldVWP web part, as shown in Figure 3.10.

FIGURE 3.10
Insert web part screen

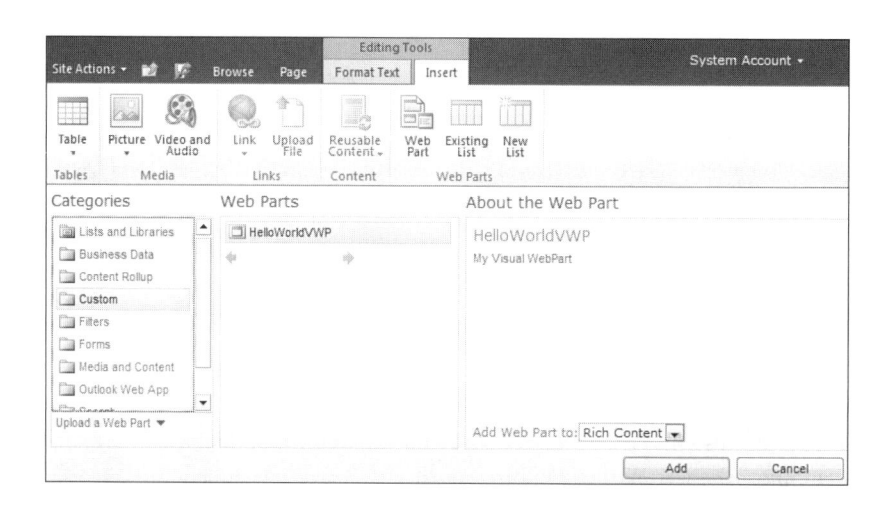

5. Click Add and the web part is added at the top, as displayed in Figure 3.11.

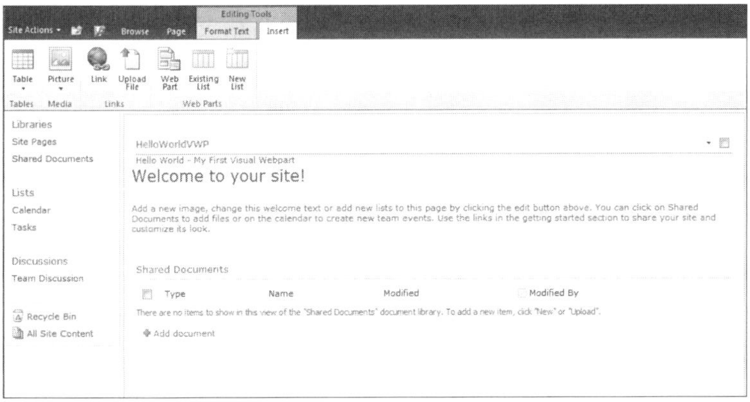

FIGURE 3.11
HelloWorldVWP web part added to top zone

One of the most important factors that differentiate a farm solution from a sandboxed solution is that the farm solution is always deployed to your Central Administration Solution Store. Farm solutions can run any type of code without any restrictions. This can be at times counterproductive as there is an increased chance that some code can bring your entire farm down.

Understanding Sandboxed Solutions

Sandboxed solutions are newly introduced in SharePoint 2010. Sandboxed solutions are not deployed to your Central Administration Solution Store like farm solutions. They are deployed to the solutions gallery of your site collection. Also they run with a lot of restrictions compared to farm solutions. In addition sandboxed solutions do not run under the worker process like farm solutions but in a special process known as the Sandboxed Code Service. You can see this service by browsing to SharePoint 2010 Central Administration, System Settings, Manage Services on Server. There you can find the Microsoft SharePoint Foundation Sandboxed Code Service as shown in Figure 3.12. Make sure that this is started.

FIGURE 3.12
The Manage Service On Server screen in SharePoint 2010 Central Administration

Service	Status	Action
Application Registry Service	Started	Stop
Business Data Connectivity Service	Started	Stop
Central Administration	Started	Stop
Claims to Windows Token Service	Started	Stop
Document Conversions Launcher Service	Started	Stop
Document Conversions Load Balancer Service	Started	Stop
Lotus Notes Connector	Stopped	Start
Managed Metadata Web Service	Started	Stop
Microsoft SharePoint Foundation Incoming E-Mail	Started	Stop
Microsoft SharePoint Foundation Sandboxed Code Service	Started	Stop
Microsoft SharePoint Foundation Subscription Settings Service	Started	Stop
Microsoft SharePoint Foundation Web Application	Started	Stop
Microsoft SharePoint Foundation Workflow Timer Service	Started	Stop
Search Query and Site Settings Service	Started	Stop
Secure Store Service	Started	Stop
SharePoint Foundation Search	Started	Stop
SharePoint Server Search	Started	Stop
User Profile Service	Started	Stop
User Profile Synchronization Service	Starting	
Web Analytics Data Processing Service	Started	Stop
Web Analytics Web Service	Started	Stop
Word Automation Services	Started	Stop

Try It Yourself

Write a Sandboxed Solution

You learn about sandboxed solutions in detail in Hour 21, "Understanding the Architecture of Sandboxed Solutions," but here you create a simple web part as a sandboxed solution. To create a new web part for a sandboxed solution, follow these steps:

1. Create a new Empty SharePoint Project and name it HelloWorldSandBoxed.

2. Select Deploy as a Sandboxed Solution for the trust level and click Finish.

3. Right-click the project and select Add, New Item.

4. Select the Web Part template, name it HelloWorldWP, and click Add. Note that you cannot select the Visual Web Part template as it requires you to deploy the user control to the CONTROLTEMPLATES folder and one of the restrictions of sandboxed solutions is that they cannot deploy files to the file system.

5. Select the project and look at the properties window shown in Figure 3.13. You can see the Sandboxed Solution property set to True, which indicates this is a sandboxed solution.

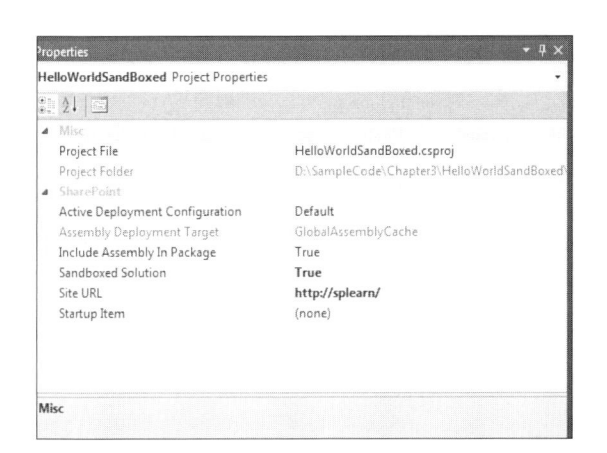

Understanding SharePoint Solutions as Deployment Units 53

FIGURE 3.13
Properties window

6. Open the HelloWorldWP.cs and add the following to the CreateChildControls method:

```
Label lbl = new Label()
{ Text = "Hello World - My first sandboxed solution in SharePoint 2010" };
this.Controls.Add(lbl);
```

7. Rename the feature title and feature node to HelloWorldWP.

8. Right-click the project and click Deploy Solution. You should see the following in the output window of your Visual Studio. You can see that the application pool was not restarted as sandboxed solutions do not run in the worker process.

```
Active Deployment Configuration: Default
Run Pre-Deployment Command:
  Skipping deployment step because a pre-deployment command is not
specified.
Recycle IIS Application Pool:
  Skipping application pool recycle
because a sandboxed solution is being deployed.
Retract Solution:
  Skipping package retraction because no matching
package on the server was found.
Add Solution:
  Adding solution 'HelloWorldSandBoxed.wsp'...
  Deploying solution 'HelloWorldSandBoxed.wsp'...
Activate Features:
  Activating feature 'HelloWorldWP' ...
Run Post-Deployment Command:
  Skipping deployment step because a post-deployment command is not
specified.
========== Build: 1 succeeded or up-to-date, 0 failed, 0 skipped ==========
========== Deploy: 1 succeeded, 0 failed, 0 skipped ==========
```

HOUR 3: Starting Development with SharePoint 2010

9. Now go to the Solutions gallery of your SharePoint site by going to Site Actions, Site Settings, Solutions under Galleries. In Figure 3.20 you can see that the status is activated. This is as per our deployment configuration in Visual Studio.

FIGURE 3.14
Site Collection Solution Gallery

10. Now go ahead and add the web part to your site (see Figure 3.15).

FIGURE 3.15
HelloWorldWP web part

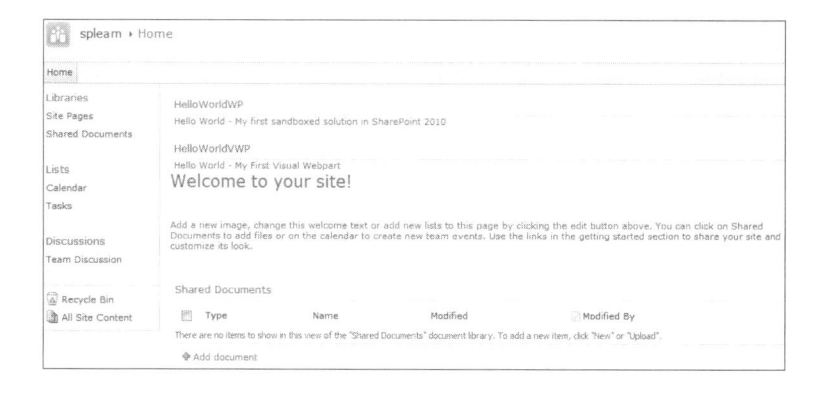

Though we created and deployed simple web parts without much functionality, the steps to create and deploy web parts will be applicable to most of the other things including more complex web parts and other project types in SharePoint. However you need to know when you should create sandboxed solutions and when you should create farm solutions. Sandboxed solutions are the recommended way to go in SharePoint 2010 as they can be monitored more easily and due to restrictions imposed on them cannot cause issues that rogue code in a farm solution might. Sandboxed solutions are an important topic, and Hour 21 is devoted to them. You should go with a farm solution only if you cannot achieve the functionality through a sandboxed solution due to the restrictions imposed on them. Even then various workarounds are available for overcoming the sandboxed solutions' restrictions as you see later.

Understanding Sandboxed Solutions Restrictions

It is important to know the restrictions imposed on sandboxed solutions if you are to be able to work with them. Following are the SharePoint project items that will not work with a sandboxed solution:

- Visual web parts
- Application pages
- Custom action group
- HideCustomAction element
- Content type binding
- Web application-scoped features
- Farm-scoped features
- Workflows with code

Don't worry if you do not understand all the items listed here. You will come across all these items in subsequent hours. In addition to the previous items, you can access only the following from the SharePoint object model in a sandboxed solution:

- All of Microsoft.SharePoint, except
    - SPSite constructor
    - SPSecurity
    - SPWorkItem and SPWorkItemCollection
    - SPAlertCollection.Add
    - SPAlertTemplateCollection.Add
    - SPUserSolution and SPUserSolutionCollection
    - SPTransformUtilities
    - Microsoft.SharePoint.Navigation
- Microsoft.SharePoint.Utilities, except
    - SPUtility.SendEmail
    - SPUtility.GetNTFullNameandEmailFromLogin
- Microsoft.SharePoint.Workflow
- Microsoft.SharePoint.WebPartPages, except
    - SPWebPartManager
    - SPWebPartConnection
    - WebPartZone

▶ WebPartPage

▶ ToolPane

▶ ToolPart

In addition to the preceding restrictions the administrator can apply further restrictions to the API. The `Microsoft.SharePoint.Administration.SPWebService` class provides a collection in the form of the API block list that enables an administrator to specify additional types in the API to block.

Introducing SharePoint Features

As indicated earlier features in SharePoint enable you to toggle functionality On or Off. All features created using farm solutions are deployed to a corresponding folder in the <14 Hive>\Template\FEATURES directory. You find a feature.xml file within this directory. Features created using sandboxed solutions get deployed to the database.

You already created a couple of features in this hour in a farm solution and in a sandboxed solution. To see these features activated, go to Site Actions, Site Settings, Site Collection Features under the Site Collection Administration section (see Figure 3.16).

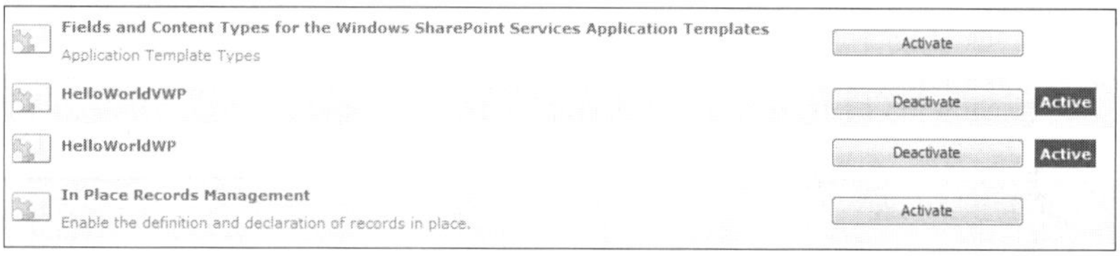

FIGURE 3.16
Site Collection features

Let's see more details of the feature.xml file. If not already open, open the HelloWorldFarm project created earlier. Double-click the HelloWorldVWP feature under Features. A designer opens up, as shown in Figure 3.17.

Here you can change the Title, Description, and Scope of the feature. In addition you have the option to remove or add files to your feature. A feature can be scoped to Web, Site, WebApplication or Farm. A Web scoped feature is available only within the site and can be activated by going to Site Actions, Site Settings, Manage Site Features under the Site Actions section. A Site scoped feature is available within the site collection and can be activated by going to Site Actions, Site Settings, Manage Site Collection Features under the Site Collection Administration section. A WebApplication scoped feature usually provides functionality at the web application

Introducing SharePoint Features | 57

level. An example is a feature that does modifications to the web.config file. You can activate the WebApplication feature by selecting SharePoint 2010 Central Administration, Application Management, Manage Web Applications. Select a web application and click Manage Features in the ribbon. You will see a pop-up, as shown in Figure 3.18.

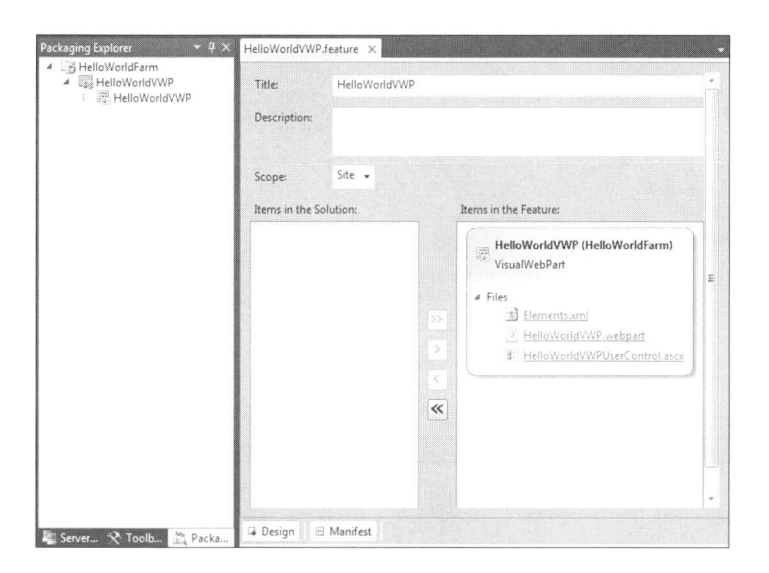

FIGURE 3.17
Visual Studio 2010 Feature Designer

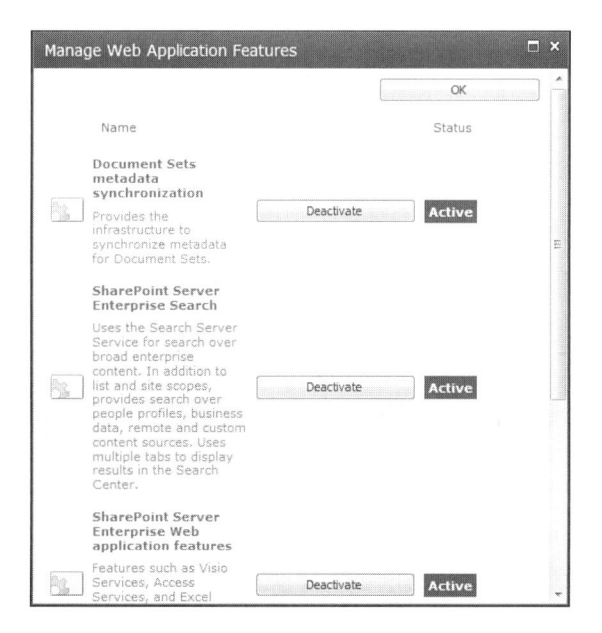

FIGURE 3.18
Web Application features

HOUR 3: Starting Development with SharePoint 2010

Finally, Farm scoped features are activated once in the entire farm. These can again be activated from SharePoint 2010 Central Administration, System Settings, Manage Farm Features. This is shown in Figure 3.19.

FIGURE 3.19
Farm features

> **By the Way**
>
> You cannot create Farm and WebApplication scoped features using a sandboxed solution.

Coming back to the feature designer in the Visual Studio, click Manifest at the bottom of the designer. Here you can see the XML for the feature, as shown in Figure 3.20.

FIGURE 3.20
Feature Manifest

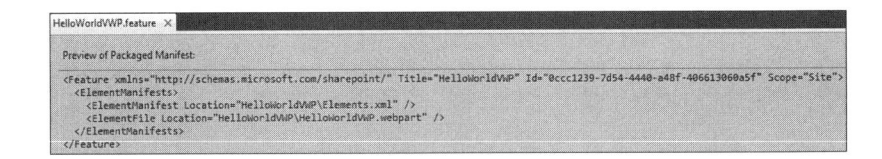

The `id` attribute specifies the feature id that uniquely identifies the feature. In addition the `ElementManifest` attribute specifies the list of files in the feature. Many other elements can be within your feature XML. You find the list of all elements at http://msdn.microsoft.com/en-us/library/ms475601.aspx.

You can see that feature.xml is read-only in this view. You can edit this by expanding the Edit Options at the bottom (see Figure 3.21). Any changes that you make to it will actually happen to HelloWorldVWP.Template.xml, which you can see if you expand the HelloWorldVWP.feature in the Solution Explorer.

FIGURE 3.21
Feature Manifest editor

It is also important to understand the concept of feature receivers. A feature receiver is a class that inherits from the `SPFeatureReceiver` base class and handles various events of a feature. To add a feature receiver class, right-click the HelloWorldWP feature and click Add Event Receiver, as shown in Figure 3.22.

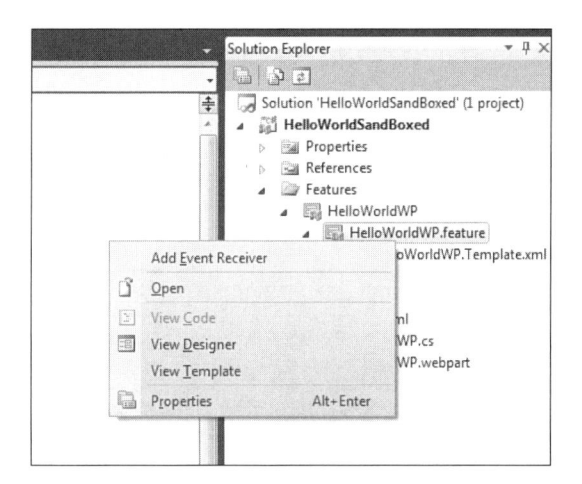

FIGURE 3.22
Adding an event receiver

A new feature receiver is added. Double-click the HelloWorldWP feature and click the manifest to see the feature XML. You can see the following two attributes added to the feature element:

▶ ReceiverAssembly="HelloWorldSandBoxed, Version=1.0.0.0,
  Culture=neutral, PublicKeyToken=96e1896643f851d0

▶ ReceiverClass="$SharePoint.Type.abe8d3c9-a062-4a4a-9b4e-
  d3ec5525d231.FullName$"

This is how the feature receiver class gets associated with the feature. The `Receiver` class attribute is resolved to the correct name of the class during deployment.

Open the HelloWorldWP.EventReceiver.cs file and you can see various methods that will be commented by default. You can uncomment and use these based on your requirements. Table 3.1 lists descriptions of these functions.

TABLE 3.1 Events of a SharePoint Feature

Function Name	Description
FeatureActivated	Called when the feature is activated. Use this when you want to perform some action through code on feature activation.
FeatureDeactivating	Called when you deactivate a feature. You usually write code in this to undo the changes that were done in the FeatureActivated event.
FeatureInstalled	Called when the feature is installed.
FeatureUninstalling	Called when a feature is uninstalled.
FeatureUpgrading	Newly introduced in SharePoint 2010. This is called when the version of the feature is upgraded.

By the Way

The `FeatureUpgrading` event is associated with a feature through a different XML element compared to the other events.

You work with features in upcoming hours.

Debugging SharePoint Solutions

Debugging code is as important as writing the code itself. There are few differences in debugging SharePoint code as compared to traditional ASP.NET applications. In ASP.NET you can just set the breakpoint in the code. Press F5 and you can debug the code line by line. It is not as simple in SharePoint because you already have a web application up and running to which you are deploying your customizations. Following are the various techniques to debug code in SharePoint.

Disabling Custom Errors

Custom errors are the way to hide the yellow error screen and show more user friendly messages. Unfortunately they don't help much in understanding the root cause of issues, and we normally turn these off during the development phase. In SharePoint you normally see a screen showing unexpected error or limited error detail. To see it for yourself go to the farm solution project created earlier in this hour and add `throw new Exception();` in the `CreateChildControls` method. Build and redeploy the solution and refresh the page where the web part is hosted. You see the custom error screen shown in Figure 3.23.

FIGURE 3.23
Custom error screen

To disable custom errors, open the web.config file for you web application. You can usually find it at C:\Inetpub\wwwroot\wss\VirtualDirectories in a folder that corresponds to the port number of your web application. Search for the `customErrors` tag and set the `mode` attribute to `Off` or `RemoteOnly`. Then find the `SafeMode` tag and set the `CallStack` and `AllowPageLevelTrace` attributes to `true`. Refresh the page and you see more detailed error information as shown in Figure 3.24.

FIGURE 3.24
The error screen when custom errors are turned off

Introducing Developer Dashboard

SharePoint 2010 comes with a developer dashboard that you will find useful in debugging especially in a production environment. The developer dashboard provides a lot of information such as the stack trace of the current execution and also the SQL queries currently executing. To enable the developer dashboard execute the following command:

```
stsadm -o setproperty -pn developer-dashboard -pv OnDemand
```

The other options for this are `On` and `Off` in place of `OnDemand`. After executing this command, refresh your site and you can see a new icon on the top left after the username. Click it and you can see the developer dashboard at the bottom of the same page, as shown in Figure 3.25. Note that you need to remove the `throw new Exception();` statement that we added in the previous section and redeploy the solution, or else the page will continue to show the error screen.

FIGURE 3.25
Developer dashboard

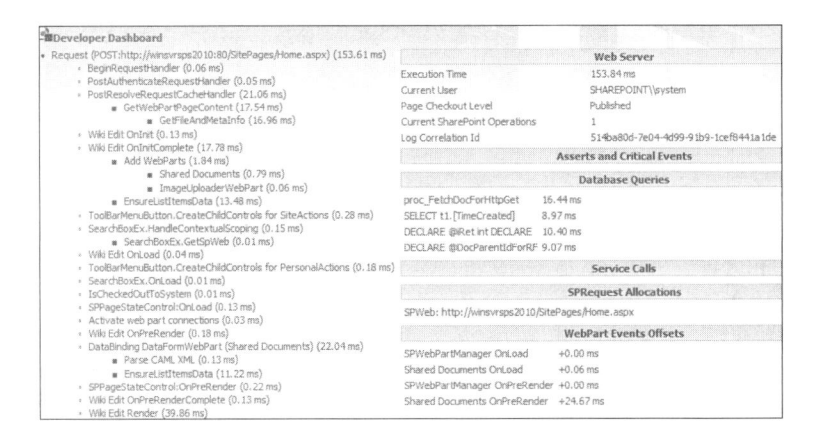

Debugging in Visual Studio

In traditional ASP.NET applications debugging can be started from within the Visual Studio. In SharePoint 2010 you need to attach to the worker process for debugging. Open the HelloWorldFarm project created earlier. Browse to the site where you deployed the web part. Open the HelloWorldVWP.cs file and add a breakpoint at the `CreateChildControls` method. Now go to the Debug menu and select Attach to Process. Make sure that Show Processes from All Users and Show Processes in All Sessions are selected. You may see multiple w3p.exe in the list. Attach to the appropriate process. If you are unsure which is the right w3p process you can simply attach to all the w3p processes as shown in Figure 3.26.

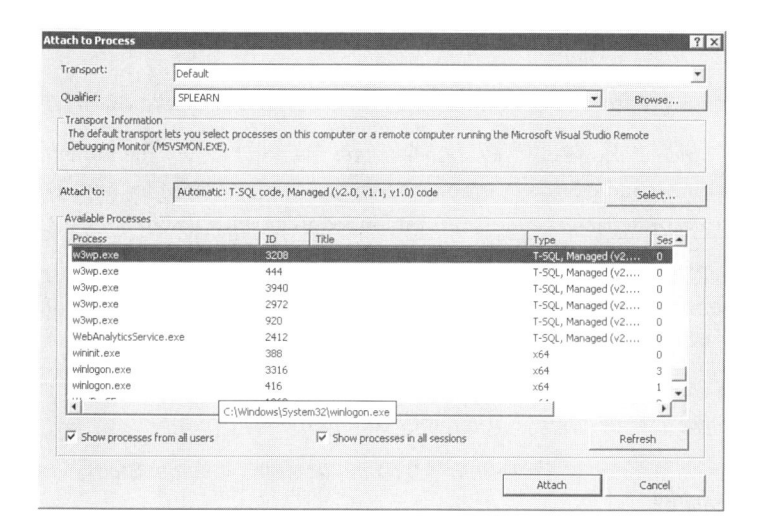

FIGURE 3.26
Attach to Process in Visual Studio 2010

> **Did You Know?**
> Sometimes the breakpoints do not load even after attaching the debugger. To solve this problem click the Select button in the Attach to Process screen and select only the Managed (v2.0,v1.1,v1.0) option.

Refresh the page and you can step into the code.

Debugging a sandboxed solution in Visual Studio is similar but requires you to attach to the SPUCWorkerProcess.exe.

Summary

This hour gave you a good head start into developing solutions and features for SharePoint 2010. You created your first web parts as both a farm solution and as a sandboxed solution. You learned that sandboxed solutions are the recommended way to develop code in SharePoint 2010 and also learned about the restrictions imposed on sandboxed solutions. In addition you looked at features.

Debugging in SharePoint 2010 is another important topic as you continue in your journey to learn SharePoint and later when developing real world solutions in SharePoint. Hopefully by now you have a good idea how to write and deploy solutions for SharePoint in Visual Studio 2010.

Q&A

Q. *Can we create SharePoint packages without Visual Studio 2010?*

A. Yes. Since a SharePoint package is a .cab file you can use the makecab command to build a SharePoint package manually. You need to have a valid manifest file. However, it is recommended to go with Visual Studio 2010 as the manual process can get complex.

Q. *If sandboxed solutions have so many restrictions, how can we achieve functionality through them when we need to call the restricted API?*

A. You can build sandboxed proxies and call them in sandboxed solutions to achieve functionality that requires calling the restricted APIs.

Q. *How do we debug SharePoint 2010 applications if Visual Studio is not installed?*

A. Multiple options are available. If you are finished logging in your code, the logs at <14 Hive>\Logs will be of great help. You can also use tools such as DebugView to check for any exceptions occurring in the code. Finally you can try remote debugging if you have the required privileges.

HOUR 4

Walking Through the Available Site and List Templates in SharePoint 2010

What You'll Learn in This Hour:

▶ Understanding and working with out of the box lists and libraries
▶ Understanding and working with out of the box site templates

> **By the Way**
>
> Due to the complexity of the topics discussed, some figures in this book are very detailed and are intended only to provide a high-level view of concepts. Those figures are representational and not intended to be read in detail.

One of the keys to becoming a successful developer is understanding where things are in your SharePoint application. It is important to understand the various site templates you can use to create sites and the different types of lists and libraries within SharePoint. Understanding these out of the box features is important so that you don't re-create elements that already exist.

Understanding and Working with Out of the Box Lists and Libraries

Everything in SharePoint is stored in lists. Libraries are lists that can store documents, videos, audio, and other types of files. In this discussion the term "list" refers to both lists and libraries. You can consider lists and libraries to be the basic data structure for storing data in SharePoint. Data in SharePoint lists is stored in the form of rows and columns. The column of a list can be a site column that is a column created at the site level that can be reused across multiple lists. Or the column can be a list column specific to the list and cannot be reused at other places.

Columns are usually associated to the lists through content types, which you can consider a collection of columns with a lot of other things added to them such as workflows, event receivers, and so on. A list can contain multiple content types.

A list can also contain versioning settings, workflows, event receivers, views and more. Views in SharePoint lists enable you to see data from different perspectives. You can have a view that shows items created by you or assigned to you. Another view might show data sorted according to importance. You can also have views that display data in graphical format.

As you go further into your SharePoint journey you realize the importance of understanding the lists and libraries. Although Hour 10, "Managing Data in SharePoint 2010," discusses custom lists and libraries in depth, this hour looks at some of the out of the box list and library templates.

Custom Lists

This is the most basic list template in SharePoint. A custom list contains a single column called Title. This list template must be used when you want to create a list customized according to your requirements. You can create a new custom list by going to Site Actions, View All Site Content. On this page click Create and a pop-up appears. Click List in the left menu to just see the available list templates. You can see the option to create a new custom list as well as many other types of lists as shown in Figure 4.1.

> **By the Way**
>
> The type of lists available for creation varies based on the site template of the parent site.

Click More Options to see more configuration options for creating the list as shown in Figure 4.2.

Announcements

The Announcement list as the name suggests is used for storing and displaying announcements. The Announcement list contains a Title, Body, and an Expires date time field.

Understanding and Working with Out of the Box Lists and Libraries 67

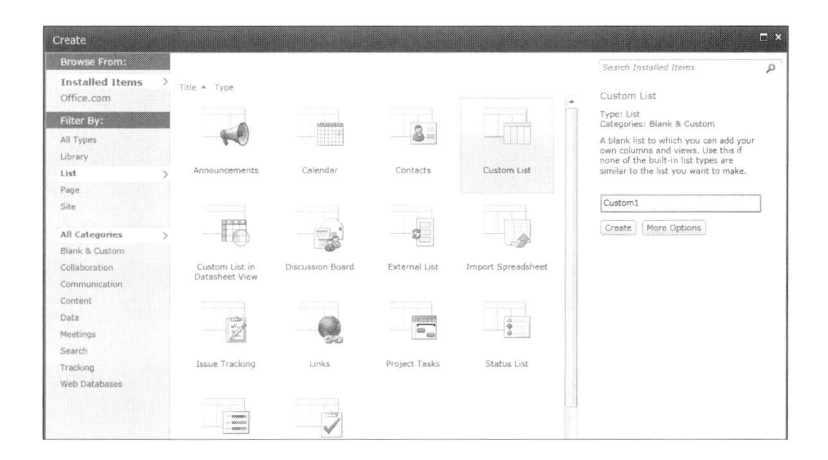

FIGURE 4.1
Creating a custom list

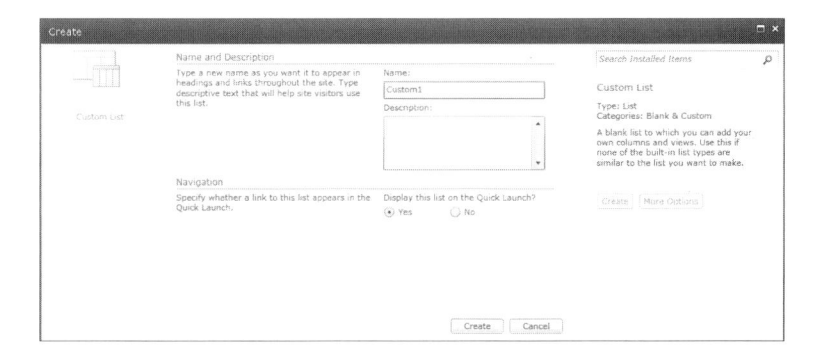

FIGURE 4.2
Configuration options for creating a custom list

Document Library

A document library is a list based on documents. You can upload documents to a document library and add metadata for the document. You can create a new document library by going to Site Actions, View All Site Content. On this page click Create and a pop-up appears. Click the Library link in the left menu to just see the available library templates. You can see the option to create a new document library as well as many other types of libraries. This is shown in Figure 4.3.

Click More Options to see more configuration options for the library. Here you can configure the versioning settings and the document template for the document library as shown in Figure 4.4.

HOUR 4: Walking Through the Available Site and List Templates in SharePoint 2010

FIGURE 4.3
Creating a document library

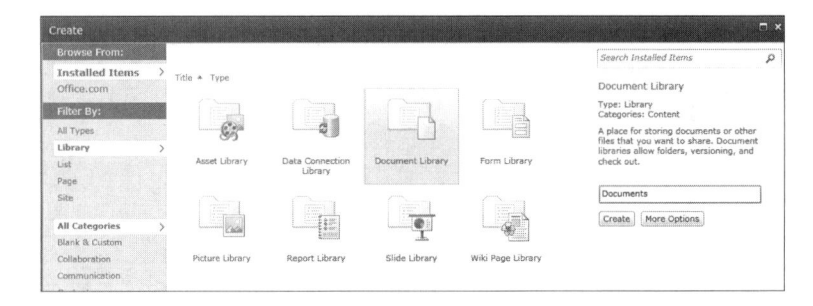

FIGURE 4.4
Configuration options for creating a document library

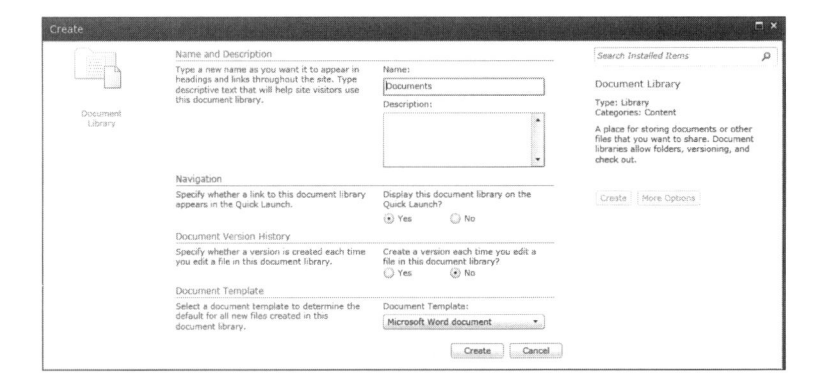

Calendar List

The Calendar list is used to create and track events and meeting information. It can show the scheduled meeting and event information in various views. You can create a single event or a recurring event. Figure 4.5 shows the New Item screen for the Calendar list.

You can also create a recurring event. In addition you can associate the event with a meeting workspace, which enables you to store additional information such as agenda and documents for the meeting.

Understanding and Working with Out of the Box Lists and Libraries

FIGURE 4.5
Creating a new event in a Calendar list

Try It Yourself

Create a Recurring Event in the Calendar List

Follow these steps to create a new recurring event and associate it with a meeting workspace:

1. If not already created, create a Calendar list.

2. Create a new event and check the Make This a Repeating Event box and the Use a Meeting Workspace to Organize Attendees, Agendas, Documents, Minutes, and Other Details for This Event box (see Figure 4.6). Click Save.

3. You are prompted to create a new meeting workspace as shown in Figure 4.7. Enter the desired title and URL for the meeting workspace and click OK.

4. You are now prompted to select a template for the meeting workspace as shown in Figure 4.8. You learn more about these templates later in this hour. For now select the Basic Meeting Workspace template and click OK.

FIGURE 4.6
Creating a recurring event

FIGURE 4.7
Creating a new meeting workspace for a calendar event

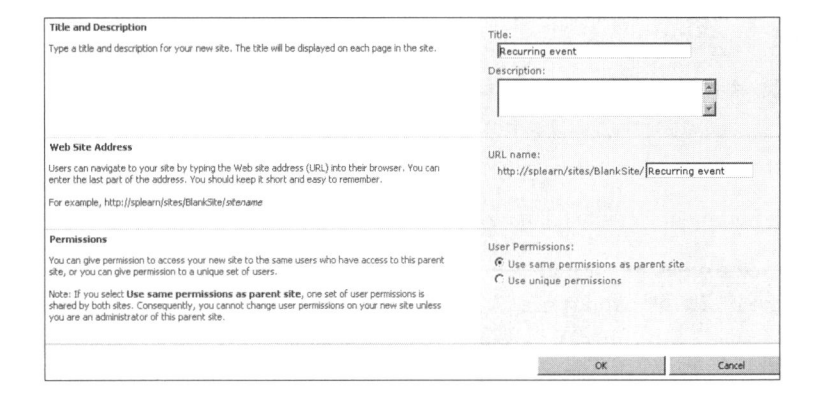

FIGURE 4.8
Selecting the Basic Meeting Workspace template

Understanding and Working with Out of the Box Lists and Libraries

5. You see the home page for the meeting workspace and a navigation pane on the left showing various dates, as shown in Figure 4.9.

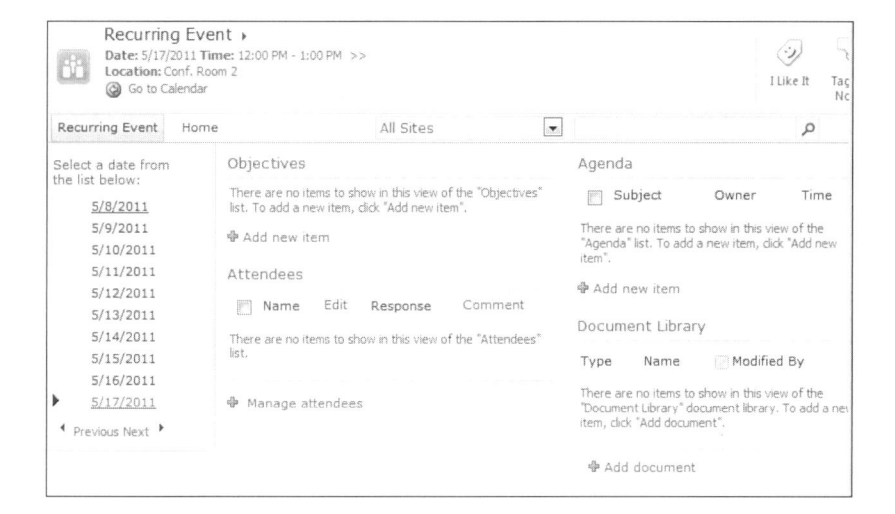

FIGURE 4.9 Meeting workspace linked to a calendar event

6. Add a new item to the Objectives list. Then navigate to another date. The item cannot be seen when you navigate to another date. Navigate back to the previous date, and you can see the item you created. This is a useful feature of the meeting workspace that allows you to associate list data with specific instances of the meeting.

In addition to the preceding steps you can also sync the calendar information to Outlook. To do this, go to the Calendar tab in the ribbon and click the Connect to Outlook button. You can now see a new calendar in Outlook.

Discussion Board

The Discussion Board list allows creating newsgroup style discussions. The discussion board makes it easy to manage discussion threads. In addition you have content approval enabled for all the posts.

Tasks

The Tasks list allows you to manage tasks. You can create new tasks, specify the dependency on other tasks, and track the completion of the tasks. Figure 4.10 shows the New Item screen for the Tasks list.

HOUR 4: Walking Through the Available Site and List Templates in SharePoint 2010

FIGURE 4.10
Creating a new Tasks list

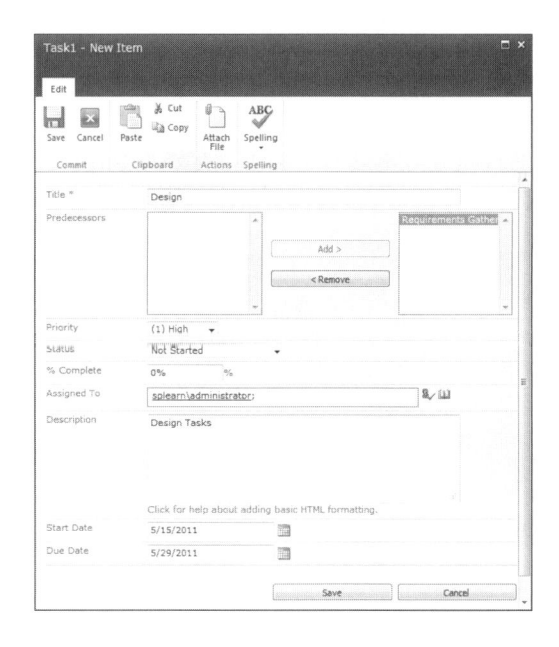

You can create a Gantt View to see the tasks in an intuitive Graphical format. To Create a Gantt View go to the Tasks list. In the List tab of the ribbon click Create View, as shown in Figure 4.11.

FIGURE 4.11
The List tab in the ribbon

Click the Gantt View (see Figure 4.12).

FIGURE 4.12
Creating a Gantt View

Understanding and Working with Out of the Box Lists and Libraries

Give an appropriate name to the view, as shown in Figure 4.13.

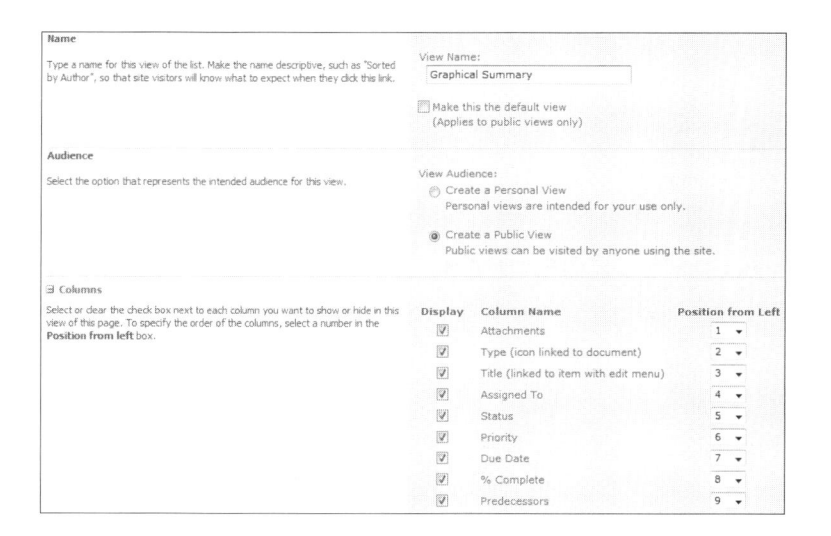

FIGURE 4.13 Options for creating a new view

Select Gantt Columns as shown in Figure 4.14 and click OK.

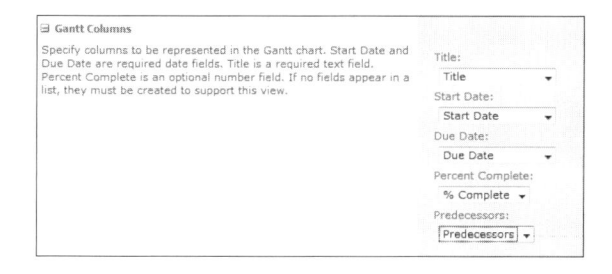

FIGURE 4.14 Selection of columns for the Gantt View

You can now see the Gantt View for the tasks as shown in Figure 4.15.

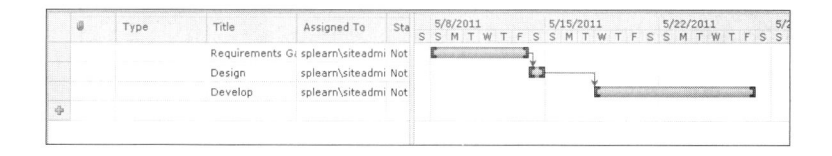

FIGURE 4.15 Gantt View for the Tasks list

In addition to tracking personal tasks, the Tasks list is also used by workflows to track workflow tasks, which you see in subsequent hours.

HOUR 4: Walking Through the Available Site and List Templates in SharePoint 2010

Contacts List

The Contacts list allows you to store contact information. This information can be synced with Outlook. Figure 4.16 shows the New Item form for the Contacts list.

FIGURE 4.16
Creating a new item for a Contacts list

Survey List

The Survey list allows you to quickly and easily create surveys. Create a new survey named Survey1, as shown in Figure 4.17.

FIGURE 4.17
Creating a new survey

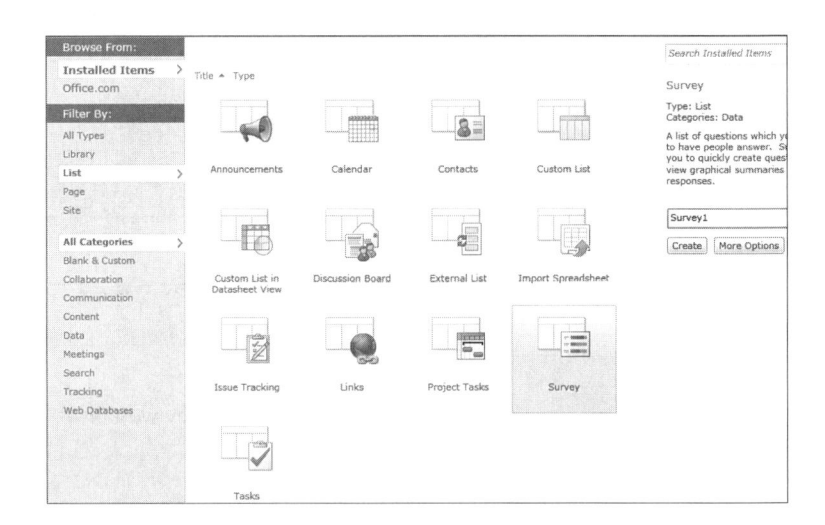

Understanding and Working with Out of the Box Lists and Libraries

After clicking on the Create button you are presented with a screen to create the survey questions. Here you can specify the question text, type of question, branching logic, and so on. Enter a few questions as shown in Figure 4.18.

FIGURE 4.18
Creating a new question for a Survey list

After you have set up the survey click Finish. You are presented with a screen that allows you to respond to the survey. This is shown in Figure 4.19.

FIGURE 4.19
Survey overview

Respond to the survey. You can see the Number of Responses field changes to 1 after you respond. In addition you can see the individual response by clicking on Show

All Responses. You can also see a graphic summary of the responses by clicking on Show a Graphical Summary of Responses as shown in Figure 4.20.

FIGURE 4.20
Graphical summary for a Survey list

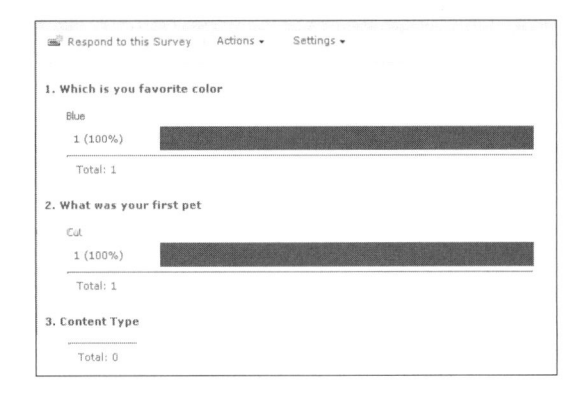

Lists in Meeting Workspaces

The meeting workspaces contain a few special lists available only within the Meeting Workspace templates. These include the Attendees list, Objectives list, Agenda list, and Decisions list. By default the lists in the meeting workspaces link data to a meeting instance. For example, if a meeting workspace is linked with multiple events or a recurring event, any data you create will be associated to the currently selected event date. Navigating to different dates shows different data based on the association. You can also make the list a series item, that is, the data will be shared across the meeting instances. To do this go to the list settings; from the List tab in the ribbon, go to Advanced Settings.

Select Yes for Share List Items Across All Meetings (Series Items), as shown in Figure 4.21.

Watch Out!

Once a list has been changed to a series item it cannot be changed back.

In addition to the list templates discussed previously, the Asset library is used to store digital assets such as video and audio files and the Picture library stores image files. Now is a good time for you to play around with the out of the box lists and libraries.

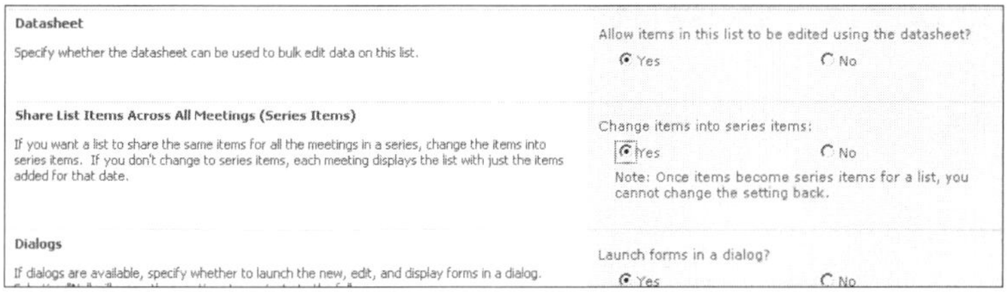
Datasheet
Specify whether the datasheet can be used to bulk edit data on this list.
Allow items in this list to be edited using the datasheet?
Yes No
Share List Items Across All Meetings (Series Items)
If you want a list to share the same items for all the meetings in a series, change the items into series items. If you don't change to series items, each meeting displays the list with just the items added for that date.
Change items into series items:
Yes No
Note: Once items become series items for a list, you cannot change the setting back.
Dialogs
If dialogs are available, specify whether to launch the new, edit, and display forms in a dialog.
Launch forms in a dialog?
Yes No

FIGURE 4.21 Converting a list to a Series Items list

Understanding and Working with Out of the Box Site Templates

You can create a variety of types of sites in SharePoint 2010 by selecting the various templates that come out of the box with SharePoint 2010. You might have already seen the various templates available when creating a site collection earlier. These templates are mainly classified under four categories: Collaboration, Meetings, Enterprise, and Publishing. This section looks at some commonly used site templates.

Team Site

The Team Site template is one of the most used templates in SharePoint. As the name suggests the site enables effective collaboration for a team. Like in a SharePoint 2007 team site, the SharePoint 2010 team site contains a Shared Documents library, Calendar list, Announcement list, Links list, Tasks list, and Team Discussion discussion board. In addition SharePoint 2010 offers new lists and libraries such as the Site Assets library for storing media files and the Site Pages library to store site pages. Figure 4.22 shows the home page of a team site.

In team sites everything is a wiki. You can edit the pages like a wiki page. Just click Edit and start typing or insert web parts on the page. This is shown in Figure 4.23.

Blank Site

The Blank Site template is the simplest template. It does not contain any lists or libraries except for the Style Library. You may use this template when you want to create your content on a totally blank site.

HOUR 4: Walking Through the Available Site and List Templates in SharePoint 2010

FIGURE 4.22
Team site home page

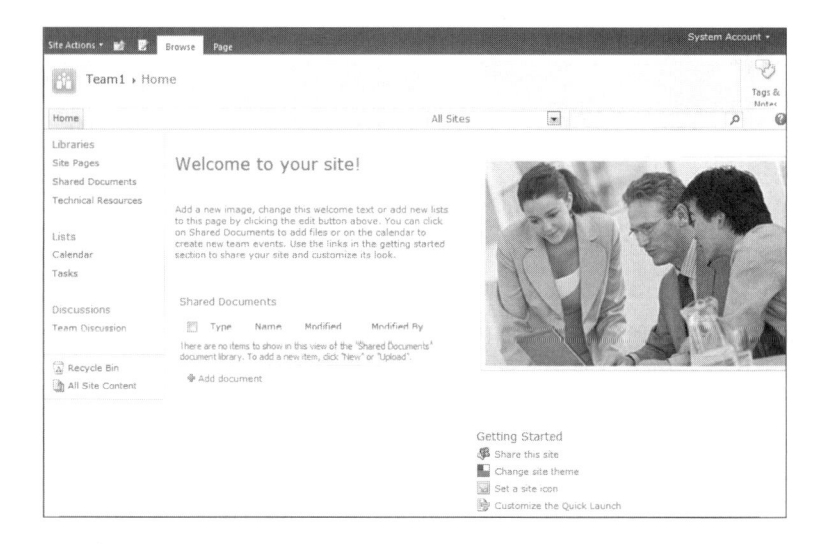

FIGURE 4.23
Team site home page in Edit mode

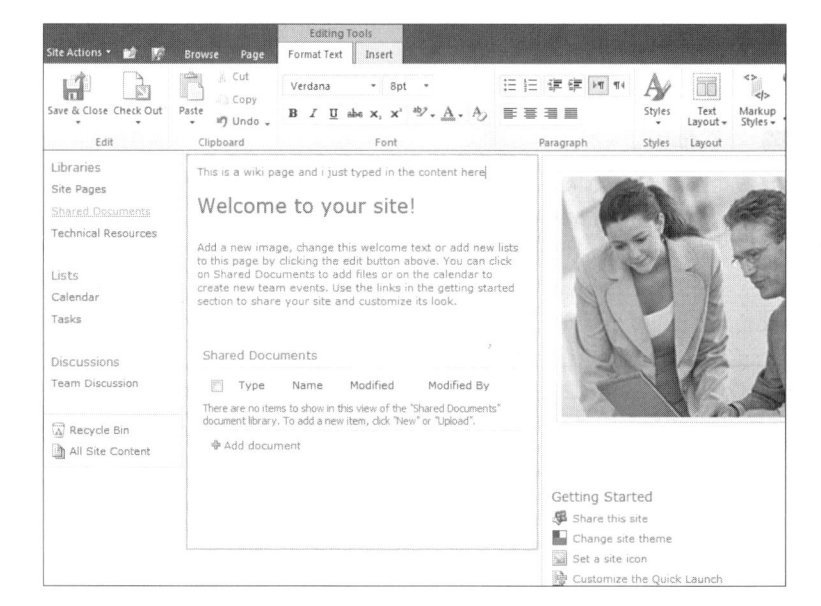

Document Workspace

A document workspace is a place for multiple members of your team to work together on a document. The document workspace provides a document library for storing the primary document and supporting files. It also contains a Tasks list for creating and tracking tasks, and a Links list for storing resources related to the document. In addition there are the Calendar and Announcements lists. Figure 4.24 shows the Document Workspace home page.

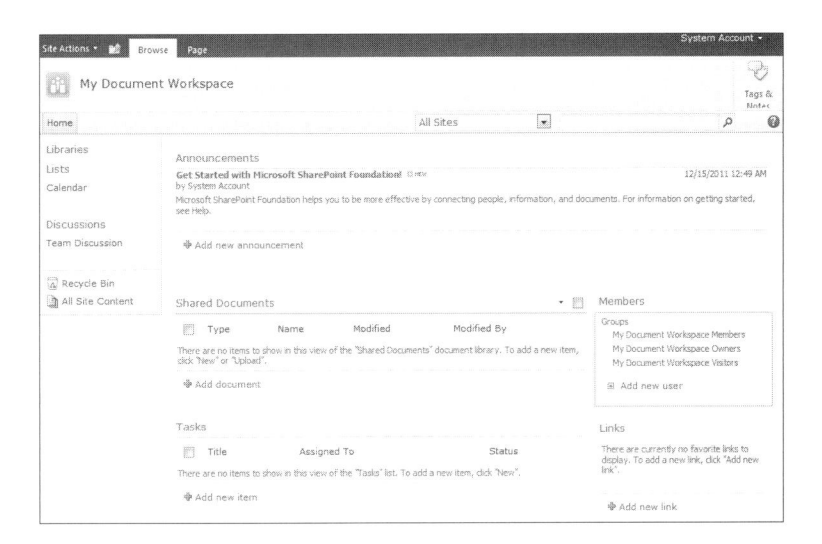

FIGURE 4.24 Document Workspace home page

Blog

Blogs are sites where users can write posts and other users can comment on them. They are part of the social networking features provided by SharePoint 2010.

The blog site contains the Posts lists to store posts, Categories list to store categories for blogs, and Comments list and Photos library. Figure 4.25 shows the home page of a blog site.

To create a new post, click Create a Post under Blogs Tools on the right. You can assign multiple categories to the post. To create new categories click Add New Category on the left navigation of the blog home page. Figure 4.26 shows the screen to create a new blog post.

Once you save the post you need to approve it for the post to be visible to everyone. Go to the Manage Posts link on the right under Blog Tools in the home page. Select the post you want to approve and click Approve/Reject from the ribbon (see Figure 4.27). Once the post is approved you can see it on the home page and also add comments to it.

Group Work Site

The Group Work Site template is a new template in SharePoint 2010. Figure 4.28 shows the home page of the Group Work Site template.

HOUR 4: Walking Through the Available Site and List Templates in SharePoint 2010

FIGURE 4.25
Blog site home page

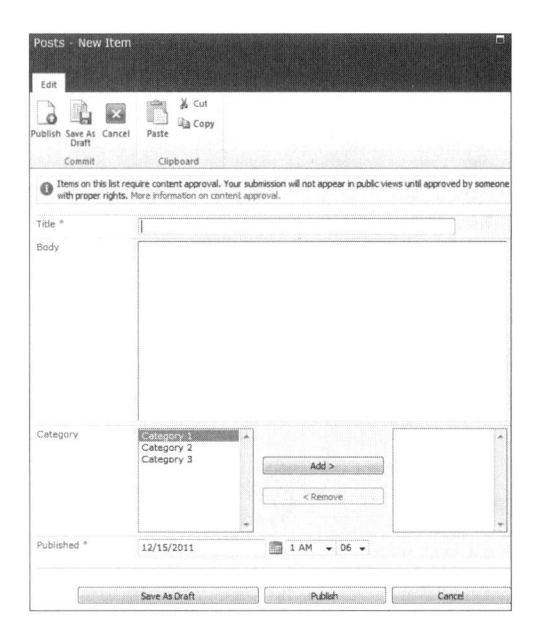

FIGURE 4.26
Creating a new blog post

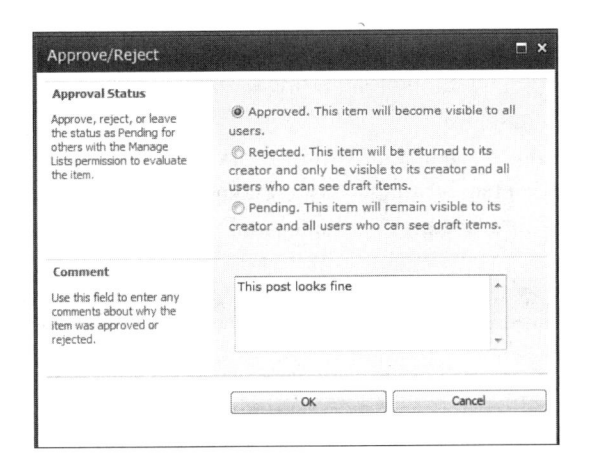

FIGURE 4.27
Approving a new blog post

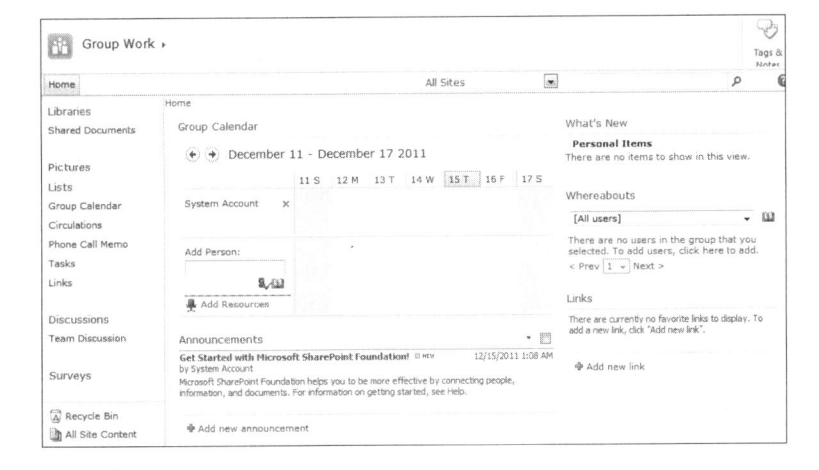

FIGURE 4.28
The Group Work Site template

Like the Team Site template the Group Work Site template is also for enabling effective collaboration within a team, and like the Team Site template the Group Work Site template contains the Announcement list, discussion board, Tasks list, Links list, and Shared Documents library. In addition, the Group Work Site template contains the following lists:

▶ **Circulations list**—Allows circulating information among various team members and request and track confirmations

▶ **Phone Call Memo list**—Can be used to store follow-up information related to phone calls

▶ **Whereabouts list**—Enables you to store information about the locations of the team members

HOUR 4: Walking Through the Available Site and List Templates in SharePoint 2010

▶ **Resources list**—Can be used to store the information on various resources such as meeting rooms, projectors, and so on

In addition to the preceding lists, the Group Work Site replaces the Calendar list of the Team Site with a more advanced Group Calendar list. The Group Calendar list enables you to see the schedule of multiple team members as shown in Figure 4.29.

FIGURE 4.29
Group Work Calendar

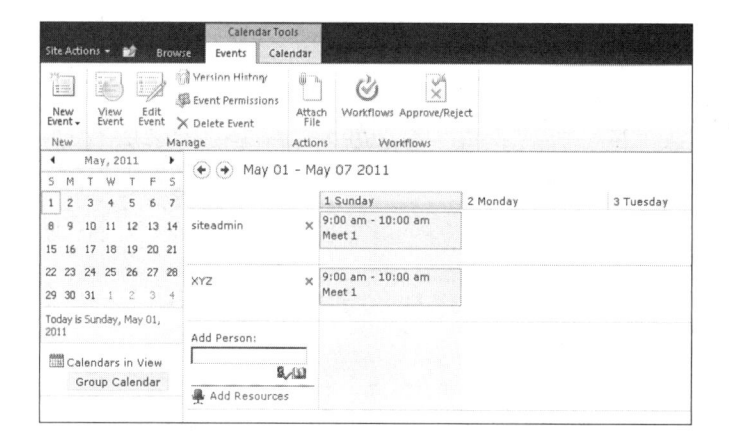

In addition the Group Calendar list enables you to specify resources created in the Resources list and also allows checking for conflicts in booking the resources as shown in Figure 4.30.

Meeting Workspace Templates

Meeting workspaces enable you to track information related to meetings. They usually work in conjunction with a calendar. Go to a Calendar list in a team site and create a new calendar item in it. Select the Workspace check box and click Save (see Figure 4.31).

You are taken to a new screen that provides the option to create a new meeting workspace or to select an existing one. Click OK to proceed further (see Figure 4.32).

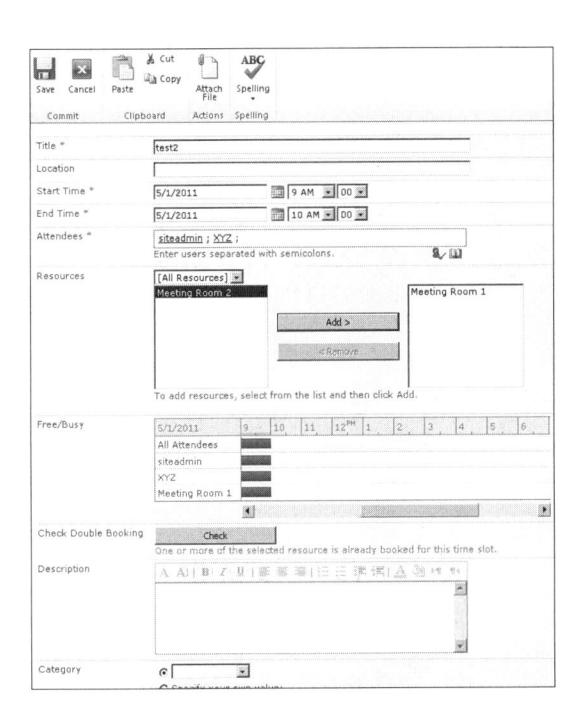

Understanding and Working with Out of the Box Site Templates

FIGURE 4.30
Creating a new item in a Group Calendar list

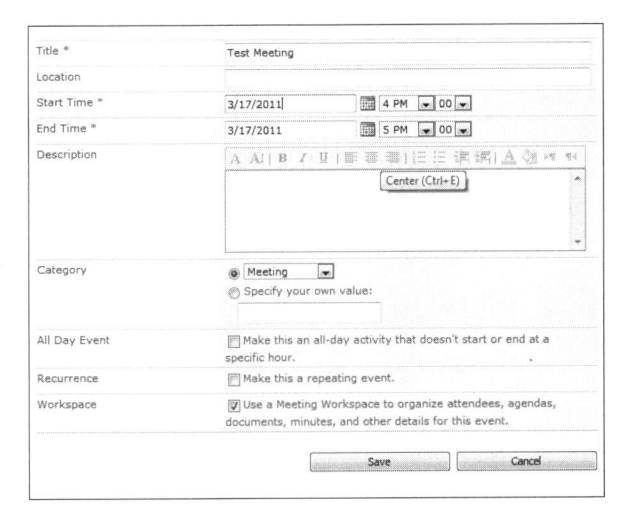

FIGURE 4.31
Creating a new event in Group Calendar

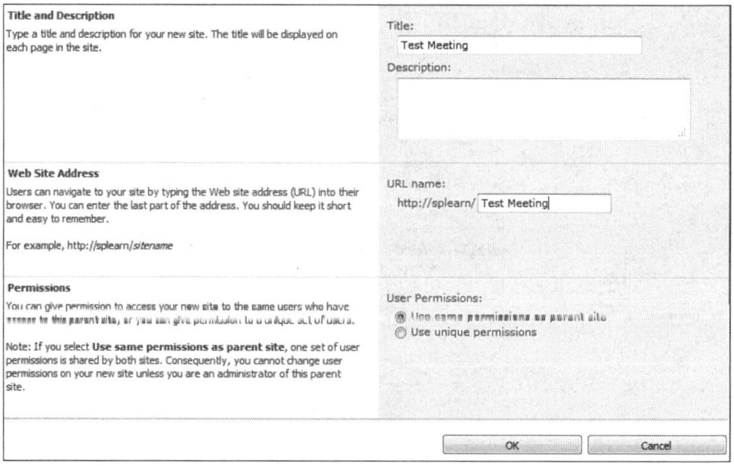

HOUR 4: Walking Through the Available Site and List Templates in SharePoint 2010

FIGURE 4.32
Creating a new meeting workspace

You now get the option to select a meeting workspace template. Select Basic Meeting Workspace and click OK. A new site of type Basic Meeting Workspace is created and linked to your event in the calendar. Add one more event and this time instead of creating a new meeting workspace select the one you just created and click OK (see Figure 4.33).

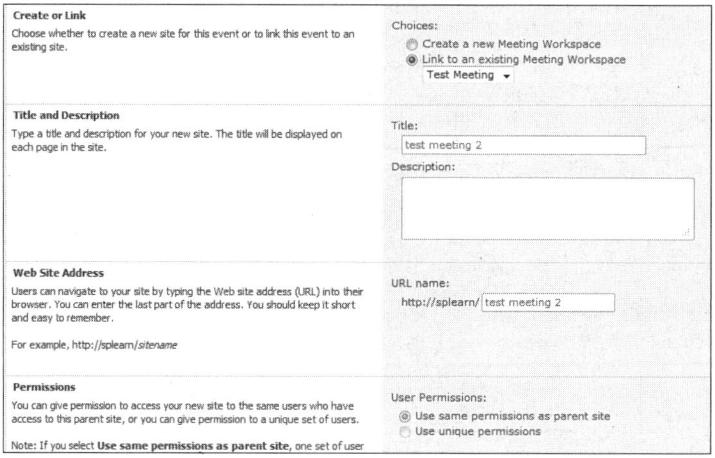

FIGURE 4.33
Linking to an existing meeting workspace

You should now see in the left a navigation mechanism to browse to show the different meeting dates. You can create the following different types of meeting workspaces.

Basic Meeting Workspace

The Basic Meeting Workspace contains the Objectives, Attendees, and Agenda lists. These lists form the basics required for managing the meetings.

Blank Meeting Workspace

The Blank Meeting Workspace template creates a blank site template that can be used as a meeting workspace. The Blank Meeting Workspace contains only the Attendees list by default.

Decision Meeting Workspace

The Decision Meeting Workspace template provides features for tracking decisions made during the meetings. It contains the Agenda list, Attendees list, Decisions list, Objectives list, and Tasks list. In addition it contains a document library named Document Library.

Social Meeting Workspace

The Social Meeting Workspace template allows tracking of social occasions. It contains the Attendees list, Things to Bring list, Directions list, a discussion board, and a Picture library. The Things To Bring list tracks information about items that each attendee needs to bring to the meetings. The Directions list enables you to track any custom text. In addition the Picture library enables you to share pictures, and the Discussion Board enables you to plan the social occasions making this template a Social Meeting Workspace.

Multipage Meeting Workspace

The Multipage Meeting Workspace template as the name suggests enables you to create multiple pages in the meeting workspace. It contains the Agenda list, Attendees list, and the Objectives list.

Document Center

The Document Center template is for effectively managing documents. Figure 4.34 shows the home page of a Document Center.

The Document Center template contains a document library named Documents. Three web parts on the home page display data from this library in different views (Newest Documents, Highest Rated Documents, and Modified By Me). In addition the Documents Center has many features related to document management enabled by default such as the Document Id feature, Document Sets feature, major

HOUR 4: Walking Through the Available Site and List Templates in SharePoint 2010

and minor versioning, and required checkout. You learn more about these features in Hour 12, "Enterprise Content Management—Understanding Document Management."

FIGURE 4.34
Document Center

Records Center

The Records Center site template enables effective record management. As you learn in Hour 12 records management involves maintaining the records of an enterprise from creation to disposal. Figure 4.35 shows the home page of a Records Center.

FIGURE 4.35
Records Center

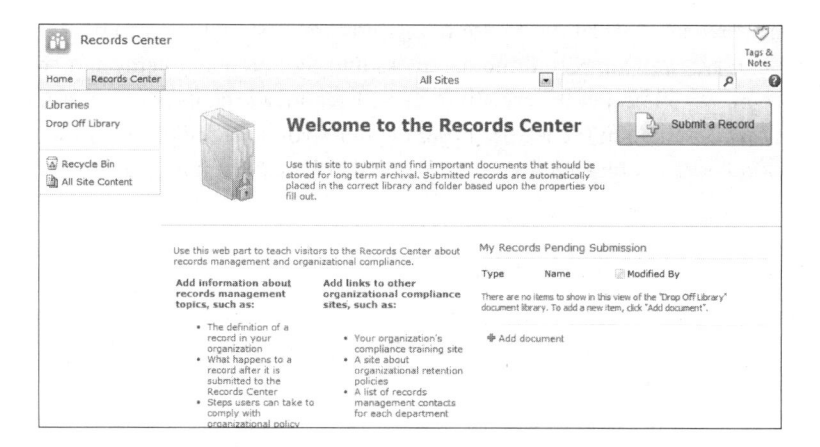

The Records Center contains the following two special libraries:

- ▶ **Drop Off Library**—This library routes the documents uploaded to it to different libraries based on rules that can be configured.

- ▶ **Records Library**—Documents uploaded to this library get automatically declared as Records and the item is frozen.

In addition the Records Center has by default features required for Records Management enabled. You learn about these features in Hour 12 and Hour 13, "Enterprise Content Management—Understanding Records and Web Content Management."

My Site Host

The My Site Host template allows you to create a site that will be used for hosting My Sites. My Sites are personalized sites that can be created for each user and allow users to share personal information with others much like Facebook or Orkut. Figure 4.36 shows the home page of a My Site.

FIGURE 4.36
My Site

Publishing Portal

The Publishing Portal template is typically used to create sites that are Internet facing. This template has the SharePoint Publishing features enabled on it by default. It contains the Pages library, which allows you to create new site pages. The Pages library has Content Approval enabled by default, which ensures that any page created goes through the cycle of approval before it can be published and viewable by end users of the site. The Publishing Portal site includes a home page, a sample press releases subsite, a Search Center, and a login page. Figure 4.37 shows the home page of a site created using the Publishing Portal template.

> **Did You Know?**
> The Publishing Portal site can be easily customized to achieve specific branding and you will find a different look and feel of the Publishing Portal sites in production.

FIGURE 4.37
Publishing Portal

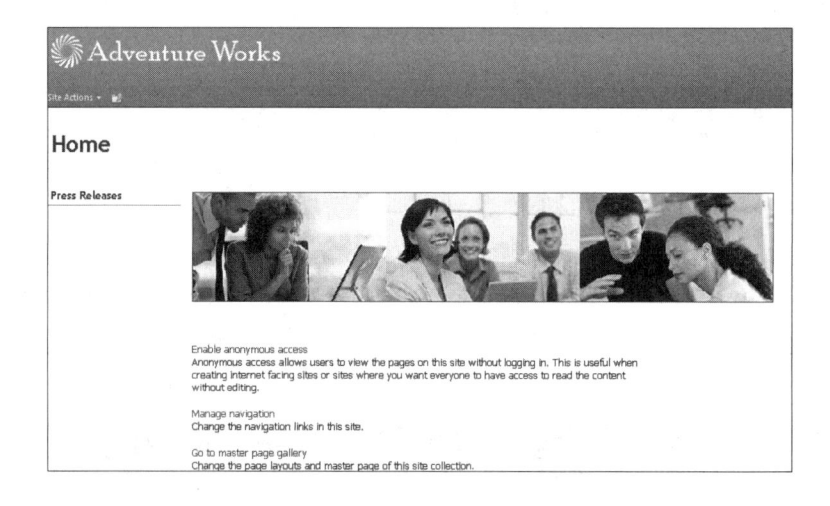

Enterprise Wiki

The Enterprise Wiki template is used to create a wiki site. Figure 4.38 shows the Enterprise Wiki home page.

FIGURE 4.38
Enterprise Wiki home page

The Enterprise Wiki contains new features compared to SharePoint 2007 such as Ratings and Categories.

In addition SharePoint 2010 contains many other templates that you can explore on your own.

Summary

This hour walked you through most of the out of the box features of SharePoint. The site templates and list templates are an important feature in SharePoint, and you need to have a good understanding of them. It's a good idea to spend some time playing around and exploring these. In the next hour you look at another important topic—web parts.

Q&A

Q. Can we create a site from a blank site template and then upgrade to other templates?

A. You can have functionality available in other site templates in a site created through the Blank Site template by activating the required features. However you cannot have the functionality of the Meeting Site template in a Blank Site template.

Q. Can different types of list types be nested? For example, can a picture list be hosted as a folder in a document list?

A. No, you cannot nest different types of list. However, you can create your own list definitions by inheriting from the existing ones and modify the behavior as required.

HOUR 5

Working with Web Parts and Web Pages

What You'll Learn in This Hour:

- Overview of SharePoint controls
- Developing delegate controls
- Programming with web parts
- SharePoint 2010 safeguard against XSS
- Web part pages and wiki pages

> **By the Way**
>
> Due to the complexity of the topics discussed, some figures in this book are very detailed and are intended only to provide a high-level view of concepts. Those figures are representational and not intended to be read in detail.

SharePoint development is often thought of as synonymous with web part development. This is because web parts are the most commonly developed SharePoint control. However you will develop many other types of controls as a SharePoint developer. This hour explores various types of controls that you can develop to extend SharePoint. First user controls and custom controls are discussed, followed by a quick look at delegate controls. And finally the discussion focuses on web parts, editor parts, visual web parts, and web pages.

Overview of SharePoint Controls

Controls are nothing but reusable user interface components that execute when a SharePoint page is requested and render the generated markup to the web browser. SharePoint controls can be classified broadly under the following two categories:

- User controls
- Custom controls or web controls

HOUR 5: Working with Web Parts and Web Pages

The major difference between a user control and a custom control is that user controls are much easier to develop due to a high level of visual design support available for these controls. The user interface elements are coded separately using the template markup code and stored in .ascx file. Visual designers such as Visual Studio facilitate the development process by allowing you to drag and drop the standard web controls (such as text boxes, labels, and so on) onto the designer surface. Thus the development process for user controls is similar to that of developing ASP.NET pages, the only difference being the template markup file has .ascx extension in place of .aspx and user controls inherit from the `System.Web.UI.UserControl` class instead of `System.Web.UI.Page` class.

Web controls on the other hand contain only the assembly code. The user interface elements are also emitted using the assembly code, contained in a .cs (for C# development) or .vb (for Visual Basic development) file. Due to the absence of separate template markup code for user interface elements, no design time support is available for custom controls.

To better appreciate the features and functionalities provided by user and custom controls this hour looks at the steps involved in creating user and custom controls.

Developing User Controls

As discussed earlier, user controls are developed similarly to ASP.NET page development. In fact they can also be thought of as ASP.NET pages having a .ascx extension. Like the ASP.NET web forms, user controls also have two separate files associated with them, one containing the markup code and the other containing the assembly code.

Did You Know?
> You can also merge the markup code and the assembly code to write inline code blocks in the markup file. However, this is generally not considered a good practice, as it reduces code readability.

All the out of the box SharePoint user controls are stored in the TEMPLATE\CONTROLTEMPLATES folder under the SharePoint root (or the 14 hive). Any user control you develop should also go into this directory.

By the Way
> Since the markup code file for a user control (that is, an ASCX file) must be placed under the TEMPLATE\CONTROLTEMPLATES folder, user controls can be deployed only as farm solutions.

Overview of SharePoint Controls 93

Try It Yourself
Create a User Control

Let's develop a user control to upload pictures to a picture library created in a top level SharePoint site. Refer to the UserAndCustomControl project in the accompanying code samples for this hour for complete code listings for this example.

1. Create an *Empty* SharePoint Project in Visual Studio 2010, name it as UserAndCustomControl and configure it to be deployed as a farm solution.

2. Next add a new User Control item to the project, name it as ImageUploaderUserControl, and open it in designer mode.

3. Drag and drop the required control elements from the toolbox onto the designer surface, a File Upload control, a Button control, and a label in this case.

4. Rename the button and the label text so that your user control looks something similar to Figure 5.1.

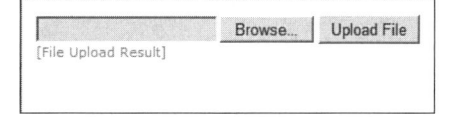

FIGURE 5.1
Image Uploader user control

5. Once the user interface elements of the control are ready, double-click the Upload File button and add the following code to the button's Click event:

```
protected void ButtonUpload_Click(object sender, EventArgs e)
{
    try
    {
        // Get root web reference
        SPWeb rootWeb = SPContext.Current.Site.RootWeb;

        // Get reference to MyPictureLibrary
        SPPictureLibrary myPictureLibrary =
rootWeb.GetList("MyPictureLibrary") as SPPictureLibrary;

        // Get the FileBytes from the File Upload Control
        byte[] fileBytes = this.FileUpload1.FileBytes;

        // Prepare destination Url and upload the file
        string fileName =
Path.GetFileName(this.FileUpload1.PostedFile.FileName);
        SPFile file =
        myPictureLibrary.RootFolder.Files.Add(
                                        fileName,
                                        fileBytes,
                                        true);
```

```
            file.Update();
            this.LabelUploadResult.Text = "Upload Successful!";
        }
        catch (Exception ex)
        {
            this.LabelUploadResult.Text = "Upload Failed:" + ex.Message;
        }
    }
```

The preceding code gets a reference to the top level site in the current site collection and uploads the picture file selected by the user using the File Upload control to a picture library called MyPictureLibrary in the top-level site. The result of the file upload operation, whether success or failure, is displayed using the `UploadResult` label. Ensure that you have the picture library MyPictureLibrary already created. Later in the hour in the discussion related to web parts, you learn how the end user can configure the library name using the web browser itself.

6. To test this user control, add a new Application Page, called ControlDemo.aspx, to the project and add the following `Register` tag in the page to register the control:

```
<%@ Register TagPrefix="uc" TagName="FileUploader"
Src="~/_controltemplates/ImageUploaderUserControl/
➥ImageUploaderUserControl.ascx" %>
```

7. Once the control is registered on the page, you can use the following markup code to add the user control anywhere inside the page:

```
<uc:FileUploader ID="PictureUploader" runat="server" />
```

8. Build and deploy the solution using Visual Studio and browse to http://<<YouServerName>>/_layouts/ControlDemo/ControlDemo.aspx to see the control in action.

9. Select a file using the Browse button and then click the Upload button, to upload the file to MyPictureLibrary of the top level site.

10. Examine the MyPictureLibrary of the top level site in the current site collection to verify that your image file was uploaded successfully.

This example demonstrates how easy it can be to develop a user control, making use of Visual Studio's design time support for developing user interface components.

Developing Custom Controls

As discussed earlier, custom controls contain only the assembly code, and the user interface elements are also emitted using the assembly code. Due to the absence of

Overview of SharePoint Controls 95

separate template mark-up code for user interface elements, no design time support is available for custom controls.

Try It Yourself
Create a Custom Control

In this section we develop a custom control to display pictures uploaded using the `ImageUploaderUserControl` user control we developed earlier.

1. To create a custom control, insert an Empty Element item in the UserAndCustomControl project that we developed in the preceding section. Name this empty element item ImageViewerCustomControl.

2. Add a new class file and call it ImageViewerCustomControl.cs, under the ImageViewerCustomControl element. Your project should now have a user control named `ImageUploaderUserControl`, a custom control named `ImageViewerCustomControl`, and an application page to test these controls, as shown in Figure 5.2.

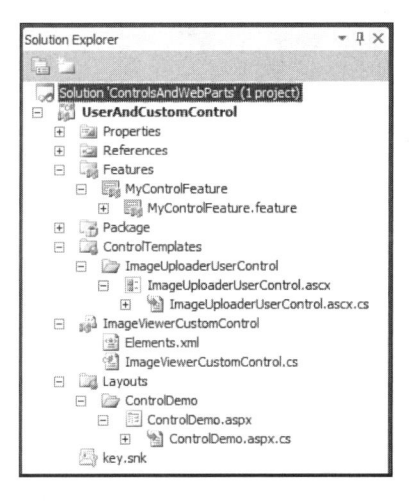

FIGURE 5.2
Developing an Image Viewer custom control

3. As a first step, modify the definition of the `ImageViewerCustomControl` class and change it to inherit from the `System.Web.UI.Control` class. All the custom controls that you create should inherit from this class. In fact the user controls also derive ultimately from the `System.Web.UI.Control` class (the `UserControl` class inherits from the `TemplateControl` class, which ultimately extends the `System.Web.UI.Control` control class).

HOUR 5: Working with Web Parts and Web Pages

The `System.Web.UI.Control` class provides a number of methods that you can override to develop your user controls. Out of these the most commonly overridden method is the `CreateChildControls` method, which, as the name suggests, is used to insert the custom control's child controls into its controls collection.

4. Override the `CreateChildControls` method to loop through the picture library and add as many ASP.NET image controls to the custom control's control collection to render the images in the picture library. Also add the ASP.NET Panel to the controls collection of the custom control to serve as a container for these image controls. One image control is added for every picture in the picture library, as illustrated in the following code snippet:

```
protected override void CreateChildControls()
{
    try
    {
        // Get root web reference
        SPWeb rootWeb = SPContext.Current.Site.RootWeb;

        // Get reference to MyPictureLibrary
        SPPictureLibrary myPictureLibrary =
        rootWeb.GetList("MyPictureLibrary")
        as SPPictureLibrary;

        // Add a Panel to controls collection
        Panel panel = new Panel();
        panel.Width = 353;
        panel.BorderColor = System.Drawing.Color.Gray;
        panel.BorderStyle = BorderStyle.Solid;
        panel.BorderWidth = 1;
        this.Controls.Add(panel);

        foreach (SPListItem item in myPictureLibrary.Items)
        {
            // Create a new image control and set its
            // image url to point to the Picture
            Image image=new Image();
            image.ImageUrl =Path.Combine(rootWeb.Url,item.Url);

            // Add image control to the Panel's Controls Collection
            panel.Controls.Add(image);
        }
    }
    catch (Exception ex)
    {
        // Display any exceptions
        this.Controls.Add(new LiteralControl(ex.Message));
    }
}
```

5. Add the following `Register` tag in the application page (ControlDemo.aspx) to register the control on the page:

   ```
   <%@ Register TagPrefix="cc"
   Assembly="$SharePoint.Project.AssemblyFullName$"
   Namespace="UserAndCustomControl.CustomControl" %>
   ```

6. Once registered, add the following markup code (below the user control's section) on the page to insert the custom control in the page:

   ```
   <cc:ImageViewerCustomControl ID="ImageViewer" runat="server" />
   ```

7. Build and deploy the solution using Visual Studio and navigate to the ControlsDemo.aspx application page, which should now look something like Figure 5.3.

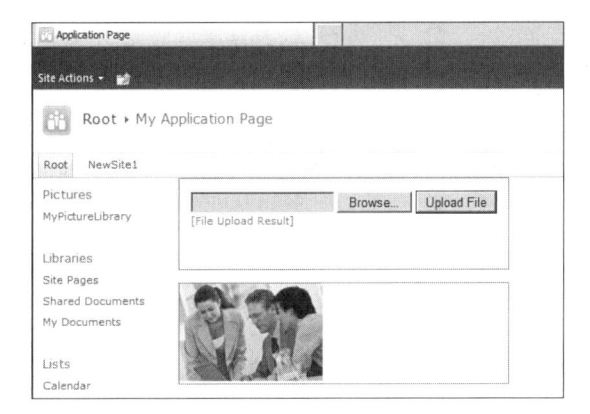

FIGURE 5.3 Image Viewer Custom Control in Action

8. Test the control by uploading an image ("Hello World" in our case) using the Image Uploader user control, and verify that the same image gets displayed in the Image Viewer custom control as well. As you upload more images, additional Image controls are added to the Image Viewer custom control to render all those images on the page.

In the preceding example, notice that we did not write any template markup code to design the control's user interface. The user interface elements were also created through the assembly code by overriding the `CreateChildControls` method. Also, there was no design time support when it came to developing the control's user interface.

> **Did You Know?**
>
> As a rule of thumb, you should develop user controls when the user interface is more or less static, or you need the controls to render a large number of child controls, as in the case of data entry forms containing many form fields. Custom controls are preferable in situations where you want to create dynamic user interfaces and need a lot of control-on-control rendering.

Understanding the Concept of Safe Mode Processing

In the preceding two scenarios, you tested the user and the custom control by adding them to an application page. The process for deploying these controls on master pages and site pages is also similar. You can customize the master page or a site page, add the required registration tag, and then use the control in the page. However, one important additional step is required for using the custom controls on the customized SharePoint master and site pages.

Before discussing this additional step, let's first have a look at the concept of safe mode processing. By default, the SharePoint security model blocks execution of inline code blocks and unapproved controls in the content served from the content databases. This important security measure prevents users from inserting faulty/malicious code blocks in customized pages and also prevents them from deploying unapproved controls and web parts.

Since the customized pages are served from the content database against the file system, safe mode processing enforces restrictions on the controls that can be added to these pages. The allowed set of controls are called *safe controls*. Therefore to use the earlier developed custom control on the site pages, you must register it as a safe control in your site's web.config.

If you open your web applications web.config and look for the `SafeControls` tag, you find entries similar to Figure 5.4.

FIGURE 5.4
Safe control entries in web.config

```
<SharePoint>
    <SafeMode MaxControls="200" CallStack="true" DirectFileDependencies="10" TotalFileDependencies="50" AllowP
        <PageParserPaths>
        </PageParserPaths>
    </SafeMode>
    <WebPartLimits MaxZoneParts="50" PropertySize="1048576" />
    <WebPartCache Storage="CacheObject" />
    <WebPartControls DatasheetControlGuid="65BCBEE4-7728-41a0-97BE-14E1CAE36AAE" />
    <SafeControls>
        <SafeControl Assembly="System.Web, Version=1.0.5000.0, Culture=neutral, PublicKeyToken=b03f5f7f11d50a3a"
        <SafeControl Assembly="System.Web, Version=1.0.5000.0, Culture=neutral, PublicKeyToken=b03f5f7f11d50a3a"
```

Overview of SharePoint Controls

To register your custom control as a safe control you can directly edit the web.config shown in Figure 5.4 and add an entry similar to the following:

```
<SafeControl
    Assembly="[Fully Qualified Assembly Name]"
    Namespace="ImageUploaderUserControlProject.ImageViewerCustomControl"
    TypeName="*" />
```

Or, as always, you can let Visual Studio do all the work for you. Right-click the `ImageViewerCustomControl` element in your project and select Safe Mode Entries from the properties window. Click the Add button, as illustrated in Figure 5.5. Deploy the solution and examine the web.config again. You will find that Visual Studio added the required safe control entry into the web.config and now you are free to use the control on the customized site and master pages.

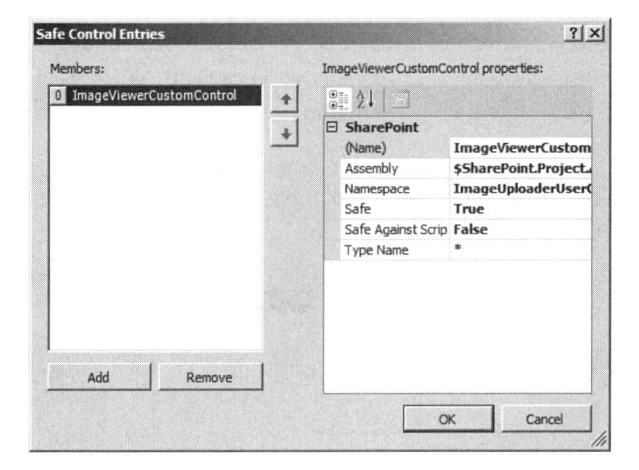

FIGURE 5.5
Registering a control as Safe using Visual Studio

In case you are wondering why we don't need to do this for the user controls, examine the web.config again and look for the following safe control entry:

```
<SafeControl Src="~/_controltemplates/*"
IncludeSubFolders="True" Safe="True"
AllowRemoteDesigner="True"
SafeAgainstScript="True" />
```

As discussed earlier, the user controls are deployed to the CONTROLTEMPLATES folder under the SharePoint root (or 14 hive). Hence all the user controls are already registered as safe controls and there is no need to explicitly add a safe control entry for them.

HOUR 5: Working with Web Parts and Web Pages

> **By the Way**
>
> The concept of safe mode processing is not applicable to the application pages. This is because application pages are served from the file system and not from the content database. Therefore, you can use custom controls on application pages without the need of registering them as safe controls.

Developing Delegate Controls

Delegate controls provide a superior way of control replacement or substitution based on ControlID and a Sequence number. By using delegate controls, you can replace existing controls on a page with your own controls without customizing or modifying the page markup code. The delegate controls are enclosed in `SharePoint:DelegateControl` tag. If you examine the contents of the v4.master page (out of the box SharePoint 2010 master page) and search for this tag, you would notice that controls such as Top Navigation's Data Source, Search box, and so on are delegate controls, which means that you can easily replace them with your own custom controls.

For example, let's replace the links on the top navigation panel based on a custom site map provider, by using delegate controls, as shown in Figure 5.6.

FIGURE 5.6
Using delegate controls to replace SiteMapProvider for top navigation

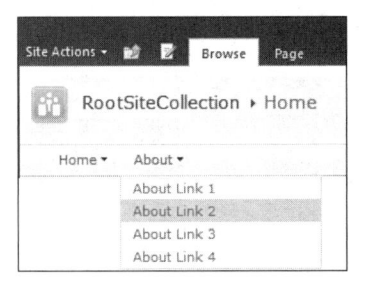

The v4.master page contains the following definition for the top navigation panel:

```
<SharePoint:DelegateControl runat="server"
ControlId="TopNavigationDataSource" Id="topNavigationDelegate">
    <Template_Controls>
        <asp:SiteMapDataSource
          ShowStartingNode="False"
          SiteMapProvider="SPNavigationProvider"
          id="topSiteMap"
          runat="server"
          StartingNodeUrl="sid:1002" />
    </Template_Controls>
</SharePoint:DelegateControl>
```

Developing Delegate Controls   101

As you can see, the contents of the top navigation panel are based on a SiteMapDataSource and SPNavigationProvider. Also, make note of the delegate control's ID (that is, TopNavigationDataSource) and data source's ID (that is, topSiteMap). You will need these to replace the out of the box data source of the top navigation with your custom data source. Let's create a custom site map provider and replace that with the out of the box navigation provider. To do that, create an Empty SharePoint project in Visual Studio and add a custom.sitemap file containing your navigation links, as shown here:

```xml
<?xml version="1.0" encoding="utf-8" ?>
<siteMap xmlns="http://schemas.microsoft.com/AspNet/SiteMap-File-1.0" >
  <siteMapNode roles ="*">
    <siteMapNode title="Home" roles ="*">
      <siteMapNode url="dummy1" title="Home Link 1" roles ="*"/>
      <siteMapNode url="dummy2" title="Home Link 2"  roles ="*" />
      <siteMapNode url="dummy3" title="Home Link 3"  roles ="*">
      </siteMapNode>
    </siteMapNode>
    <siteMapNode title="About" roles ="*">
      <siteMapNode url="dummy4" title="About Link 1" roles ="*"/>
      <siteMapNode url="dummy5" title="About Link 2"  roles ="*" />
      <siteMapNode url="dummy6" title="About Link 3"  roles ="*" />
      <siteMapNode url="dummy7" title="About Link 4"  roles ="*" />
    </siteMapNode>
  </siteMapNode>
</siteMap>
```

You want this file to be deployed to the TEMPLATE/LAYOUTS folder under the SharePoint root, so make sure that you add this file under the SharePoint mapped Layouts folder in the project.

Next add an Empty Element into the project and insert the following contents into the Elements.xml file:

```xml
<?xml version="1.0" encoding="utf-8"?>
<Elements xmlns="http://schemas.microsoft.com/sharepoint/">
  <Control
     Id="TopNavigationDataSource"
     Sequence="1"
     ControlClass="System.Web.UI.WebControls.SiteMapDataSource"
     ControlAssembly="System.Web,
     version=2.0.3600.0, Culture=neutral,
     PublicKeyToken=b03f5f7f11d50a3a">
    <Property Name="ID">topSiteMap</Property>
    <Property Name="SiteMapProvider">CustomSiteMapProvider</Property>
    <Property Name="ShowStartingNode">true</Property>
  </Control>
</Elements>
```

In the preceding XML fragment, the Id attribute specifies the control ID of the out of the box top navigation's data source (we made note of this earlier). The sequence

HOUR 5: Working with Web Parts and Web Pages

value of 1 ensures that the navigation provider overrides the out of the box navigation provider. (A lower value implies higher precedence.) The `ControlClass` and `ControlAssembly` attribute indicate that the control being defined is of type `SiteMapDataSource`, which is defined in the System.Web assembly. The last three `Property` elements define our custom site map provider and indicate that the starting node should be visible.

Add the following entry into your web application's web.config to register the Custom Sitemap Provider:

```
<add name="CustomSiteMapProvider"
siteMapFile="_layouts/DelegateControlDemo/custom.sitemap"
 type="Microsoft.SharePoint.Navigation.SPXmlContentMapProvider,
Microsoft.SharePoint, Version=14.0.0.0, Culture=neutral,
PublicKeyToken=71e9bce111e9429c" />
```

Watch Out!

> Manual modifications to the web.config should generally be avoided, as these may get deleted with the installation of Service Packs. SharePoint provides a way to edit the web.config programmatically as well using the `SPWebConfigModifications` class. Modifications done using this class are persisted in the configuration database. This is discussed more in Hour 7, "Understanding SharePoint 2010 Server Side Development," while exploring SharePoint server side development.

Validate the correctness of the `SiteMapFile` attribute, which should point to the custom.sitemap file, containing the navigation links.

Further, rename the Feature element in the project to `DelegateControlDemoFeature` so that you can easily identify the feature later on when examining the feature list.

Deploy the solution, and as always, Visual Studio by default activates the associated feature, which is `DelegateControlDemoFeature`. Verify that after the successful feature activation (which happens as a part of deployment), the links in the top navigation appear as specified in your custom.sitemap file. If you deactivate the feature `DelegateControlDemoFeature` the sitemap data source should automatically default to the out of the box one.

Programming with Web Parts

The user and custom controls developed earlier had two limitations:

▶ They worked only for MyPictureLibrary, and there was no way an end user could configure the name of the picture library.

▶ Further, the end user could not add or remove these controls on just any page using the web browser.

Web parts offer a solution to these limitations, in an elegant and standardized way.

Web parts are specialized custom controls designed to support user customization. Web parts enable business users to manipulate content, appearance, and behavior of site pages using the web browser. Web parts are rendered inside Chrome, in the web part zones, on the web part pages. Chrome is responsible for providing a standardized user experience when dealing with web parts.

Web parts are managed by the Web Part Manager. Web Part Manager is responsible for serializing and deserializing web parts to the content databases, managing web part functionality as well as the web part events. The `SPWebPartManager` class provides implementation of Web Part Manager in the SharePoint world.

> **Did You Know?**
>
> The concept of web parts was first introduced in WSS 2.0 and later on adopted in ASP.NET. The legacy `WebPart` class is still bundled with SharePoint 2010 and is present in the `Microsoft.SharePoint.WebPartPages.WebPart` namespace.

Web part definitions are stored in SharePoint in the form of XML-based template files. The template file contains information required by the Web Part Manager to create an instance of the web part. The document library where these files are stored is called the Web Part Gallery. Every site collection has exactly one Web Part Gallery, existing at the top level site.

The Image Viewer Web Part

To further understand how web parts solve the issues discussed in the beginning of this section, let's convert the Image Viewer custom control to an Image Viewer web part, which extends the `WebPart` class present in the `System.Net.Web.UI.WebControls.WebParts` namespace.

Try It Yourself

Develop a Web Part

1. Fire up Visual Studio and create a new Empty SharePoint Project by name ImageViewerWebPart.

2. Configure the project to be deployed as a *sandboxed solution*.

3. Add a new Web Part item into the project and call it ImageViewerWebPart.

4. At this point you notice that Visual Studio has already created a class called `ImageViewerWebPart` for you and overridden the `CreateChildControls` method. As was the case with the custom controls, you override this method most of the time when developing web parts. Copy the same source code that you had written while developing the `ImageViewerCustomControl` and paste it inside this function.

5. Rename the feature associated with the project to ImageViewerWebPartFeature.

6. Build and deploy the solution, using Visual Studio, and at this point you are ready to use the web part in your site pages.

7. To test the web part, deploy it on one of your site pages. Edit a site page and select the Insert Web Part option. The web part appears under the Custom web parts folder in the Web Part Gallery. Once added to a site page, your web part should now look similar to Figure 5.7.

FIGURE 5.7
The Image Viewer web part

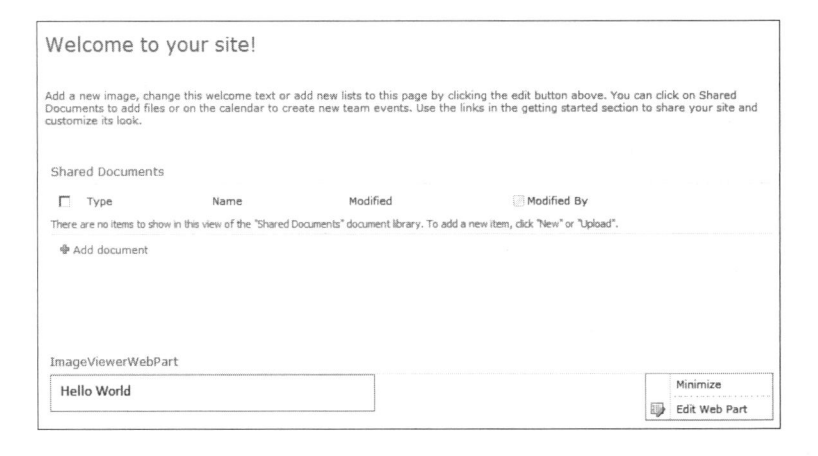

The web part resembles the custom control developed earlier; however, now it is rendered inside Chrome, which provides additional things such as a border and a toolbar with a menu. In addition to these visual elements, you can now add or remove the web part using the browser on any of the site pages. The important point to note here is that you get all these additional goodies for free, by just inheriting from the `WebPart` class instead of the `Control` class earlier.

> **Did You Know?**
>
> As you dirty your hands with web part development, it is possible that you create a web part that causes your entire page to crash because of a missing null check or an unhandled exception, for example. In such scenarios you can navigate to the Web Part Maintenance page and remove the defective web part from the page. You can navigate to the Web Part Maintenance page by adding Contents=1 to the web part page URL.
>
> For example, to view the Web Part Maintenance page for the http://<< yourservername >>/SitePages/Home.aspx page, you can use the following URL: http://<< yourservername >>/SitePages/Home.aspx?Contents=1

Moving from a custom control to web part has already solved our second issue (listed in the beginning of this section), that is, the end users can add or remove the web parts to a site page using a web browser. To solve the other issue—allowing users to easily configure the name of the picture library—let's look at the idea of customization and personalization.

Customization and Personalization

There are two ways you can modify properties of a web part. *Customization* (or the shared view modification) refers to a change by a privileged user that is visible to and affects all users. *Personalization* (or the user view modification) on the other hand affects only the user doing the change and does not affect the view of other users.

Let's create a new property, `PictureLibraryName`, and let end users configure this using the web browser. Decorate this property with the following three attributes:

- Personalizable(PersonalizationScope.Shared)
- WebBrowsable
- Category("Configuration")

The `WebBrowsable` attribute ensures that the property is visible in the Web Part editor and the `Category` specifies the group name under which the property appears in the Web Part editor.

Build and deploy the solution using Visual Studio and navigate to the site page where you added your web part earlier. Notice that the web part prompts you with a message to configure the picture library, as shown in Figure 5.8.

HOUR 5: Working with Web Parts and Web Pages

FIGURE 5.8
Prompt to configure the picture library

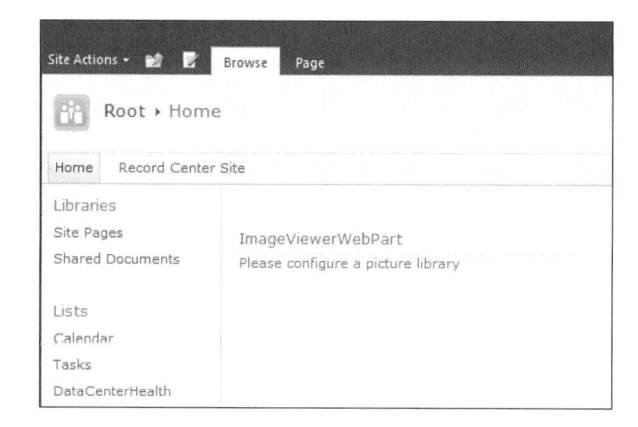

Use the Edit Web Part option provided by the menu in the web part Chrome, to edit the web part. The Web Part editor should now display your property under the Configuration category as shown in Figure 5.9.

FIGURE 5.9
Configuring the picture library in the Web Part editor

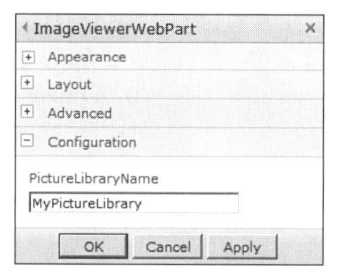

Enter the name of a picture library, created at the top-level site and click OK to save your changes. The web part should now display the images in the configured picture library. Notice that even if you close and open the web browser and navigate to the same page, your changes are persisted. The Web Part Manager is now responsible for repopulating your configuration (that is, the picture library name) every time you reload the page.

Configuring Web Parts with Editor Parts

Although things worked well with the web part so far, there is still one thing missing in the web part configuration. While configuring the picture library name, the user is free to enter anything in the text box as we are not doing any sort of validations against the picture library name. Additionally, rather than having validation logic in place, it would be even better if you can show a drop-down list of values to the users so that there is very little chance of making a mistake. The editor parts help us to achieve exactly the same effect.

Editor parts are specialized web controls meant for designing property editing interfaces. Let's examine the process of developing an editor part to edit our Picture Library Name property in a more elegant and user friendly way.

All your editor parts should inherit from the System.Web.UI.WebControls. WebParts.EditorPart class. The System.Web.UI.WebControls.WebParts class provides you with an option to override the CreateEditorParts method, which you can override and return an EditorPartCollection containing your list of editor parts (with each editor part inheriting from the EditorPart class) along with the EditorPartCollection returned by the base class, as shown in the following code:

```
public override EditorPartCollection CreateEditorParts()
{
    // Get the base editor part collection
    EditorPartCollection baseCollection = base.CreateEditorParts();

    // Create new ImageViewerEditorPart object
    ImageUploaderEditorPart imageViewerEditorPart = new
ImageUploaderEditorPart();
    imageViewerEditorPart.ID = "ImageViewerEditorPart";

    // Create new ImageViewerEditorPart list, multiple custom editor parts
    // can be added to the list
    List<EditorPart> editorPartList = new List<EditorPart>();
    editorPartList.Add(imageViewerEditorPart);

    // Return new EditorPartCollection passing on the
    // references to base collection and
    // our newly created editor part list
    return new EditorPartCollection(baseCollection, editorPartList);
}
```

In this code, ImageViewerEditorPart is the custom editor part created by inheriting from the EditorPart class.

To create an editor part, at the minimum, you should override the following methods of the EditorPart base class:

- CreateChildControls
- OnPreRender
- SyncChanges
- ApplyChanges

HOUR 5: Working with Web Parts and Web Pages

The following discusses the implementation of each of these methods, to create the `ImageViewerEditorPart`:

- **CreateChildControls**—In this method we create two child controls, a literal control to show the caption Select a Picture Library and a drop-down list to display available picture libraries in the top-level site and add these controls to the controls collection of the editor part.

- **OnPreRender**—The OnPreRender method contains the core functionality of the editor part. Here we check whether the count of items in the drop-down list is zero. If it is, then we populate it with the list of picture libraries. If the list is already populated, we call the SyncChanges method to synchronize the selected value in the drop-down list with the picture library name value returned web part.

- **SyncChanges**—Sets the selected value in the picture library drop-down list.

- **ApplyChanges**—Applies the user selection to the web part.

Refer to the code samples for this hour for implementation details.

> **By the Way**
>
> Note that if you carefully examine the editor part you see two configuration sections for the picture library name setting, as shown in Figure 5.10. This is because, although we added an editor part to allow users to configure the value via the drop-down list, we still did not remove the `WebBrowsable` attribute from the `PictureLibraryName` property.

FIGURE 5.10
Two configuration sections to configure the picture library name

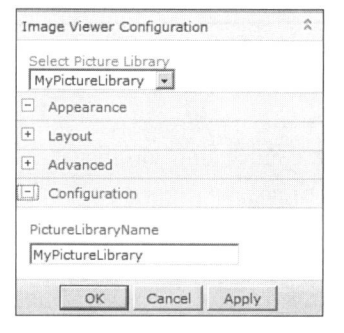

Since now you are controlling the modifications to the property via your editor part, there is no need to make the property `WebBrowsable`; therefore, we can safely remove this attribute now. As soon as you do so and redeploy the solution, the configuration section containing the text box to specify the picture library name will no longer appear in the web part editor.

Programming with Visual Web Parts

Visual web parts, as the name suggests, aim to ease the process of designing the user interface for the web parts, by leveraging Visual Studio's design time support for user interface creation. To achieve this effect, visual web parts combine the functionalities offered by user controls with the web parts. A visual web part contains a user control and an associated code behind the file, and a class inheriting from the web part class (which acts as a wrapper for the user control), in addition to other files created in a standard web part project element. Visual Studio 2010 provides a project template as well to create visual web parts. This project can only be deployed as a farm solution, since the associated user control template file must be deployed to the CONTROLTEMPLATES folder under the SharePoint root (or the 14 hive). Visual web parts are useful in scenarios where you have a user interface with many child controls. Controlling the layout and rendering of child controls can be challenging in such scenarios, thus increasing the need for design time support to create the visual elements of the control.

Try It Yourself
Create a Visual Web Part

To better understand visual web parts, try converting your ImageUploaderUserControl to a visual web part by following these steps:

1. Fire up Visual Studio and create a new Visual Web Part project named ImageUploaderVisualWebPart.

2. Delete the VisualWebPart1 item that Visual Studio adds to your project by default.

3. Add a new Visual Web Part item to the project and call it ImageUploaderVisualWebPart. At this point you should have a project structure similar to Figure 5.11.

4. Examine the contents of the ImageUploaderVisualWebPart class generated by Visual Studio. The ImageUploaderVisualWebPart class inherits from the System.Web.UI.WebControls.WebParts class, loads the underlying user control from the CONTROLTEMPLATES folder, and adds the same to the web part's control collection. Thus in effect it is acting only as a wrapper for the underlying user control. When you use the Visual Web Part control template, Visual Studio automatically generates the following code to perform these tasks:

HOUR 5: Working with Web Parts and Web Pages

```
[ToolboxItemAttribute(false)]
public class ImageUploaderVisualWebPart : WebPart
{
    // Visual Studio might automatically update this
➥path when you change the Visual Web Part project item.
    private const string _ascxPath =
    @"~/_CONTROLTEMPLATES/ImageUploaderVisualWebPart/
➥ImageUploaderVisualWebPart/ImageUploaderVisualWebPartUserControl.ascx";
    private ImageUploaderVisualWebPartUserControl userControl;

    protected override void CreateChildControls()
    {
        Control control = Page.LoadControl(_ascxPath);
        Controls.Add(control);
    }
}
```

FIGURE 5.11
Developing a visual web part

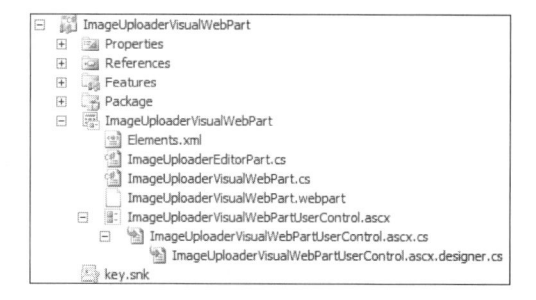

5. Now modify the ImageUploaderUserControl.ascx and ImageUploaderUserControl.cs files and copy the code from the ImageUploaderUserControl developed earlier.

6. Further, also create an editor part to enable the user to select the picture library from the drop-down list into which the image file will be uploaded. Let's call this editor part ImageUploaderEditorPart and copy the exact same code from the ImageViewerEditorPart.

7. Create a public property called PictureLibraryName both inside the ImageUploaderVisualWebPart class and ImageUploaderUserControl class. When the user configures the PictureLibraryName property from the editor part, we pass down the value to the underlying user control, from the wrapper web part. To achieve this, instead of casting the user control to the Control class object, cast it to an object of the ImageUploaderUserControl class. Your code should now look something similar to the following:

```
public class ImageUploaderVisualWebPart : WebPart
{
    // Visual Studio might automatically update this path
➥when you change the Visual Web Part project item.
```

Programming with Web Parts

```
    private const string _ascxPath = @"~/_CONTROLTEMPLATES/
➥ImageUploaderVisualWebPart/ImageUploaderVisualWebPart/
➥ImageUploaderVisualWebPartUserControl.ascx";
    private ImageUploaderVisualWebPartUserControl userControl;

    [Personalizable(PersonalizationScope.Shared),
Category("Configuration")]
    public string PictureLibraryName
    {
        get;
        set;
    }

    protected override void CreateChildControls()
    {
        userControl = Page.LoadControl(_ascxPath) as
        ImageUploaderVisualWebPartUserControl;
        userControl.PictureLibraryName = this.PictureLibraryName;
        Controls.Add(userControl);
    }

    public override EditorPartCollection CreateEditorParts()
    {
        // Get the base editor part collection
        EditorPartCollection baseCollection = base.CreateEditorParts();

        // Create new ImageViewerEditorPart object
        ImageUploaderEditorPart imageViewerEditorPart
        = new ImageUploaderEditorPart();
        imageViewerEditorPart.ID = "ImageViewerEditorPart";

        // Create new ImageViewerEditorPart list, multiple custom editor
➥parts
        // can be added to the list
        List<EditorPart> editorPartList = new List<EditorPart>();
        editorPartList.Add(imageViewerEditorPart);

        // Return new EditorPartCollection passing on
➥the references to base collection and
        // our newly created editor part list
        return new EditorPartCollection(baseCollection, editorPartList);
    }
}
```

8. That's it; the ImageUploaderVisualWebPart is ready and should now function similarly to the user control developed earlier.

9. Build and deploy the solution using Visual Studio and add the web part to a site page.

Thus you see that by using a wrapper web part and an underlying user control, you can get the benefits of design time support, which otherwise is not available while developing web parts.

Did You Know?

> Did you know that traditionally SharePoint developers have used the user control technique to build web parts? The user interface elements were placed in a user control and a wrapper web part was written to load the same. It was, however, in Visual Studio 2010 that a Visual Web Part template was first introduced and the concept was formalized.

Developing Connected Web Parts

All the web parts you developed so far operate in isolation, completely unaware of the existence of other web parts on a page. However, this concept of working in isolation might not work well in real-world scenarios. Consider a scenario in which a business user working on a sales report, which displays all the products with corresponding sales figures in tabular form, wants to view details for a selected product adjacent to the main report, on the same screen. If you were to develop two web parts working in isolation, one to display the sales report and the other to display product details, the details web part would never know what product has been selected by the business user in the sales report web part. This scenario calls for establishing a connection between web parts, so that you can pass the information related to selected product (which can be, say, a selected product ID) from the sales report web part to the product detail web part. Now when the business user selects a product in the sales report, the selected product value would be passed on to the product details web part, which would refresh its content to display the selected product details.

You can connect two or more web parts together by using web part connections. Web parts connected via the web part connections are labeled as connected web parts. A web part connection is established from a web part, which acts as a connection provider to a web part acting as a connection consumer. When a user adds a connection provider and a connection consumer web part on a page, it is the job of the web part manager to discover the compatible web parts and provide the user with an option to establish a connection. Connectable web parts share a common underlying interface definition. The connection provider implements this common interface, and by making use of interface methods and properties, the consumer can access the provider.

The `ConnectedWebParts` project in the accompanying source code for this hour highlights implementation details for the important steps involved in creating connected web parts. The interface `IConfigurationProvider`, defines two properties, the values for which are passed on from the `ConfigurationProdiver` web part to the `ConfigurationConsumer`. Consider the following interface definition:

```
public interface IConfigurationProvider
    {
        string PictureLibraryName { get; set; }
        string ImageFileName { get; set; }
    }
```

The `ConfigurationConsumer` web part uses these two properties to display the configured image from the picture library. The configuration provider implements this interface and provides values of the properties to the consumer. Apart from implementing the interface, the configuration provider also needs to define a function decorated with the `ConnectionProvider` attribute to provide the web part manager an instance of class implementing the `IConfigurationProvider` interface. Since in this case, the configuration provider is itself implementing the `IConfigurationProvider` interface, the function simply returns a reference to the `ConnectionProvider` class's instance, as shown here:

```
[ConnectionProvider("Image Configuration", AllowsMultipleConnections = true)]
public IConfigurationProvider ConfigurationProviderConnectionPoint()
{
return this;
}
```

Setting `AllowMultipleConnections` allows the configuration provider to connect to multiple consumers. This seems a possible scenario, where consumer multiple web parts may want to connect to the provider to get the Image Configuration data.

Similarly the consumer must define a method decorated with the `ConnectionConsumer` attribute and accepting a reference to the interface object as a parameter, as shown in the following code:

```
[ConnectionConsumer("Image Configuration", AllowsMultipleConnections = false)]
public void ConfigurationProviderConnectionPoint
          (IConfigurationProvider configurationProvider)
{
this.configurationProvider = configurationProvider;
}
```

Since it doesn't make sense for the consumer to receive Image Configuration from multiple providers (as it can display only one image at a time in this case), set the `AllowsMultipleConnections` to false.

> **Watch Out!**
> Be aware of the fact that since it is the end user who ultimately creates connections between the web parts there might be scenarios in which the consumer web part is not connected to any source. In such cases, it is important to do a *null check* before accessing any of the provider's properties; otherwise, you might end up with an *object reference not set to an instance of an object* exception.

HOUR 5: Working with Web Parts and Web Pages

With this, your Connection Consumer and Connection Provider web parts are ready to use. Simply add both to a site page and edit the web parts. As shown in Figure 5.12, you should now have an option to connect the web parts by using the Connections menu item.

FIGURE 5.12
Connected web parts

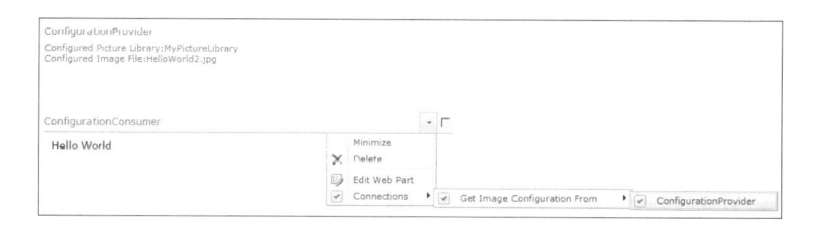

Once a connection is established, the Connection Consumer displays the configured image.

Developing Ajax Web Parts

AJAX, or Asynchronous JavaScript and XML, is a web development technique for creating interactive web applications. AJAX improves "perceived" performance using asynchronous partial page updates, resulting in a better user experience. All the controls and web parts developed so far, cause the entire page to post back and reload to perform an operation on the server. This is fine in scenarios where your web part's contents are mostly static and require less user interaction. However for web parts that take time to load, or are highly interactive, frequent postback and page load delays can degrade the user experience. For example, in the case of a slideshow web part (which you develop next), if the user wants to refresh the contents automatically, say, once every 5 seconds, doing a full page postback and reload results in a lot of flickering and a poor user experience. In scenarios like these ASP.NET AJAX comes to the rescue by enabling partial page updates so that only the contents inside the slideshow web part are refreshed and not the entire container page.

Developing web parts with ASP.NET AJAX in SharePoint 2007, required developers to perform a number of activities, before they could begin with the actual web part development; these included registering a number of libraries in web.config, programmatically adding script manager to their code, and so on. In SharePoint 2010 things have changed considerably and ASP.NET AJAX is now supported out of the box.

Try It Yourself
Create an Ajax Web Part

To better appreciate the built-in AJAX support, let's develop a slideshow web part (similar to the out of box one, but a trimmed down version) with the following features:

- Allows the user to specify picture library to be displayed as slideshow
- Allows the user to configure the time interval between slide transitions
- Allows the user to play and pause the slideshow and manually browse through the images

To develop the slideshow web part, we use the Visual Web Part project template and create the user interface for the web part using the underlying user control. We use the following ASP.NET controls to design the user interface:

- **Update Panel**—(Present under the Ajax Extensions section in the toolbox), to get support from APS.NET AJAX to update only the contents of the update panel in case of a postback initiated by a control contained in the update panel

- **Update Progress**—(Present under the AJAX Extensions section in the toolbox), to indicate to the user that a partial page update is in progress

- **Timer**—(Present under the AJAX Extensions section in the toolbox), to cause postbacks after the configured interval and load the next image in the sequence

- **Image**—To render the image

- **ImageButton**—(Three of these), to allow the user to move to the previous image, move to the next image, and play/pause the slideshow

Follow these steps:

1. Fire up Visual Studio and create a new Empty SharePoint project named SlideShowWebPart.

2. Add a new Visual WebPart item to the project. Name this item SlideShowWebPart.

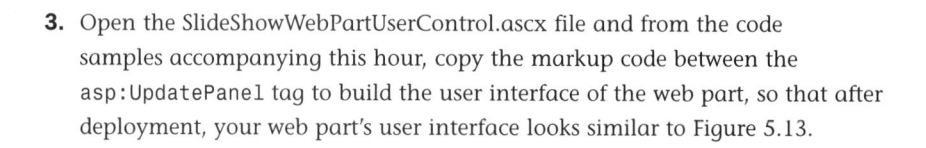

FIGURE 5.13
Slideshow web part—Play, Pause, and Refresh states

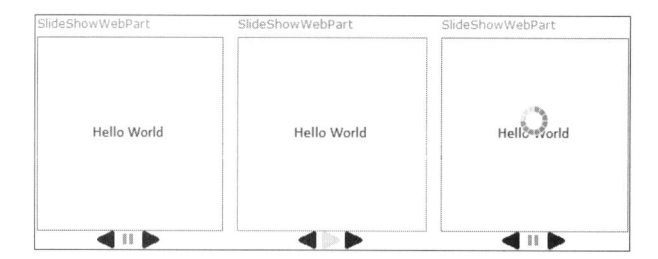

3. Open the SlideShowWebPartUserControl.ascx file and from the code samples accompanying this hour, copy the markup code between the asp:UpdatePanel tag to build the user interface of the web part, so that after deployment, your web part's user interface looks similar to Figure 5.13.

4. Once the preceding user interface elements are in place, most of the work is already done. Now like a regular web part you need to add two properties, namely, picture library name and timer tick interval to allow the end user to configure the web part. These properties should be added to the wrapper web part, which loads the underlying user control and configuration values passed on to the user control. Refer to the following code to achieve the effect:

```
public class SlideShowWebPart : WebPart
{
    // Visual Studio might automatically update this path
➥when you change the Visual Web Part project item.
    private const string _ascxPath =
@"~/_CONTROLTEMPLATES/SlideShowWebPart/
➥SlideShowWebPart/SlideShowWebPartUserControl.ascx";

    [WebBrowsable, Personalizable(PersonalizationScope.Shared),
    Category("SlideShow Settings")]
    public string PictureLibraryName { get; set; }

    [WebBrowsable, Personalizable(PersonalizationScope.Shared),
    Category("SlideShow Settings")]
    public int TimerInterval { get; set; }

    protected override void CreateChildControls()
    {
        if (this.TimerInterval > 0 &&
        !string.IsNullOrEmpty(this.PictureLibraryName))
        {
            SlideShowWebPartUserControl control =
            Page.LoadControl(_ascxPath)
            as SlideShowWebPartUserControl;
            control.PictureLibraryName = this.PictureLibraryName;
            control.TimerInterval = this.TimerInterval;
            Controls.Add(control);
        }
        else
```

```
            {
                if (this.TimerInterval <= 0)
                {
                    this.Controls.Add(new LiteralControl(
                    "Please configure a value greate"+
                    "than 0 for timer<br/>"));
                }
                if (string.IsNullOrEmpty(this.PictureLibraryName))
                {
                    this.Controls.Add(new LiteralControl(
                    "Please configure a picture library<br/>"));
                }
            }
        }
    }
```

5. Finally, add the code for timer tick, Back, Play/Pause, and Next buttons. On clicking the Next button and timer tick event, you simply move on to the next image in the list, and on clicking the Back button, you move to the previous item in the list, as shown in the following code snippet:

```
protected void ImageTransitionTimer_Tick(object sender, EventArgs e)
{
    // Load the next image on timer tick
    currentImageID += 1;
    this.DisplayImage();
}

protected void ImageButtonNext_Click(object sender, ImageClickEventArgs e)
{
    // Load next image
    currentImageID += 1;
    this.DisplayImage();
}

protected void ImageButtonBack_Click(object sender, ImageClickEventArgs e)
{
    // Load previous image
    currentImageID -= 1;
    this.DisplayImage();
}
```

6. Similarly, on clicking the Play/Pause slideshow button, you toggle between playing/pausing the image and enabling/disabling the timer accordingly, as demonstrated in the following code:

```
protected void ImageButtonPlayPause_Click(object sender,
➥ImageClickEventArgs e)
{
    // Toggle play/pause functionality which includes:
    // 1. Toggling between play/pause images
    // 2. Enabling/disabling timer
    if (Path.GetFileName(this.ImageButtonPlayPause.ImageUrl).
➥ToLower().Equals("pause.jpg"))
```

HOUR 5: Working with Web Parts and Web Pages

```
    {
        // Enable timer
        this.ImageTransitionTimer.Enabled = false;

        // Switch to play image
        this.ImageButtonPlayPause.ImageUrl = "~/_layouts/
➥images/SlideShowWebPart/play.jpg";
    }
    else
    {
        // Disable timer
        this.ImageTransitionTimer.Enabled = true;

        // Switch to pause image
        this.ImageButtonPlayPause.ImageUrl = "~/_layouts/
➥images/SlideShowWebPart/pause.jpg";
    }
}
```

7. The most important method in the slideshow web part is the `DisplayImage()` function, which is responsible for loading and displaying images from the picture library configured by the user. The following code sample provides the implementation of this function:

```
private void DisplayImage()
{
if (!string.IsNullOrEmpty(this.PictureLibraryName))
{
try
{
// Load next image
SPWeb rootWeb = SPContext.Current.Site.RootWeb;
SPPictureLibrary pictureLibrary =
rootWeb.GetList(this.PictureLibraryName)
as SPPictureLibrary;

if (pictureLibrary != null)
{
    if (currentImageID == pictureLibrary.ItemCount)
    {
        currentImageID = 0;
    }

    if (currentImageID < 0)
    {
        currentImageID = pictureLibrary.ItemCount - 1;
    }

    if (pictureLibrary != null)
    {
        this.Image1.ImageUrl =
        Path.Combine(
            rootWeb.Url,
            pictureLibrary.Items[currentImageID].Url);
        this.Image1.Visible = true;
        int height, width;
```

```
            int.TryParse(
        pictureLibrary.Items[currentImageID]
                ["Picture Height"].ToString(),
        out height);
        int.TryParse(
        pictureLibrary.Items[currentImageID]
                ["Picture Width"].ToString(),
        out width);

        // Don't let image dimensions exceed
        // 200 by 200 container box
        // In case dimensions exceed the box,
        // reduce the size preserving aspect ratio
        if (width > 200 || height > 200)
        {
            if (width > height)
            {
                this.Image1.Width = 200;
                this.Image1.Height = height * 200 / width;
            }
            else
            {
                this.Image1.Height = 200;
                this.Image1.Width = width * 200 / height;
            }
        }
        else
        {
            this.Image1.Width = width;
            this.Image1.Height = height;
        }

        // Vertically center the image
        this.PanelTopMargin.Height =
        new Unit((200 - Image1.Height.Value) / 2,
        UnitType.Pixel);
    }
}
}
catch
{
    // Eat any errors and restart the image loading on error
    currentImageID = 0;
}
}
}
```

This function fetches a reference to the picture library configured by the user and retrieves the next image in the navigation flow. Next we scale down the images (if required), since we are rendering the images in a fixed area of 200px by 200px dimensions, preserving the image aspect ratio. Finally we adjust the top margin to ensure that image is centered both vertically and horizontally in the display area. Refer to the accompanying code samples for the complete implementation details. To keep the things simple, we will not be

HOUR 5: Working with Web Parts and Web Pages

▼

implementing the editor parts to configure the picture library and the timer interval.

8. Build and deploy the web part using Visual Studio.

9. Once deployed you should see the follow configuration options under the SlideShow Settings section, in the web part editor, as shown in Figure 5.14.

FIGURE 5.14
Configuring the slideshow web part

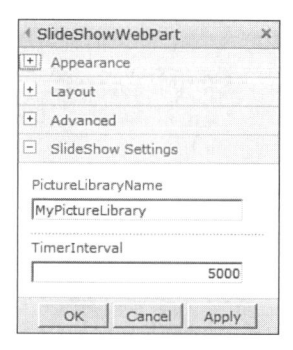

10. Once configured, the web part loads the images from the configured picture library and displays in the form of a slideshow.

By the Way

> An important point to note here is that although on every postback caused by our web part (whether by timer tick, or by user clicks) we see only the contents of the web part being refreshed and not any other item on the page, on the server, the entire page is being generated and sent back to the client on every postback. Thus there are no benefits involved on the server side with this approach, other than an improved user experience on the client side.

▲

As you dirty your hands with AJAX development, you will discover that to achieve performance benefits on the server side, developers often develop an underlying script service (consumed directly by the client) and provide the contents for partial page updates. The slideshow web part created in this hour serves as a really good example to break the ice and get you started with AJAX development.

SharePoint 2010 Safeguard Against XSS

XSS, better known as cross site scripting, is a term given to script injection techniques used by attackers to inject malicious scripts into web pages. The common way to attack is to inject JavaScript into the data entry columns and form fields, to achieve effects such as bypassing user authentication; retrieving, modifying, or deleting important user data; redirecting users to malicious websites; and so on. Without proper safeguards, XSS attacks can be fatal in the case of SharePoint 2010, due to a comprehensive client-side object model introduced in SharePoint 2010.

To equip yourself to better deal with XSS attacks, you must understand the new safeguards provided by SharePoint 2010 against XSS attacks. Unlike SharePoint 2007, in SharePoint 2010 users with Contributor privileges can no longer modify web part properties. To alter this default behavior, SharePoint 2010 introduces a new attribute called `SafeAgainstScript` that you can modify while registering your web part as a safe control in the site's web.config. By default this attribute is set to false; changing it to true, would restore the SharePoint 2007 behavior and every user with appropriate privileges would be able to modify the web part properties. Another attribute, `RequiresDesignerPermissionAttribute` (false by default), allows the users with designer permissions to modify the properties of your web part. You can decorate your web part class with this attribute and once set to true, no matter what the value of `SafeAgainstScript` is, only the user with designer permissions would be able to alter your web part properties. Apart from safeguards against the XSS attacks, correct configuration of the previous attributes is important, since now by default the contributors cannot modify your web part properties as they could in SharePoint 2007.

Web Part Pages and Wiki Pages

Web part pages are special types of content pages that host the web parts in one or more web part zones. Web part pages are created based on specific page templates that define the order, number, and arrangement of web part zones inside a web part page. Users can also create web part pages from scratch or customize the existing pages, using the tools like Microsoft Office SharePoint Designer. Privileged users (site administrators and contributors generally) can add or remove web parts in the various web part zones, on the web part pages, using the web browser. Thus web part pages provide an important dimension in customization and extension of SharePoint.

Web part pages have been in existence since previous releases of SharePoint. SharePoint 2010 introduces new types of pages called wiki pages. Wiki pages allow users to add web parts anywhere on the page, unlike web part pages where adding web parts is restricted to web part zones. Many site templates (for example, team sites) have a wiki page as their home page. Wiki pages make managing page layout easier and more intuitive, as there is no ordering of web parts and web parts can be

HOUR 5: Working with Web Parts and Web Pages

added alongside the text. Behind the scenes, wiki pages have a hidden web part zone inside which the web parts are rendered, and the rendered contents are moved to their respective inline locations.

A privileged user (having Add and Customize Pages permission) can add a new page to a SharePoint site either by using the create content screen and selecting a page template or by using the SharePoint Designer, as shown in Figure 5.15, Figure 5.16, and Figure 5.17.

FIGURE 5.15
Creating a new page

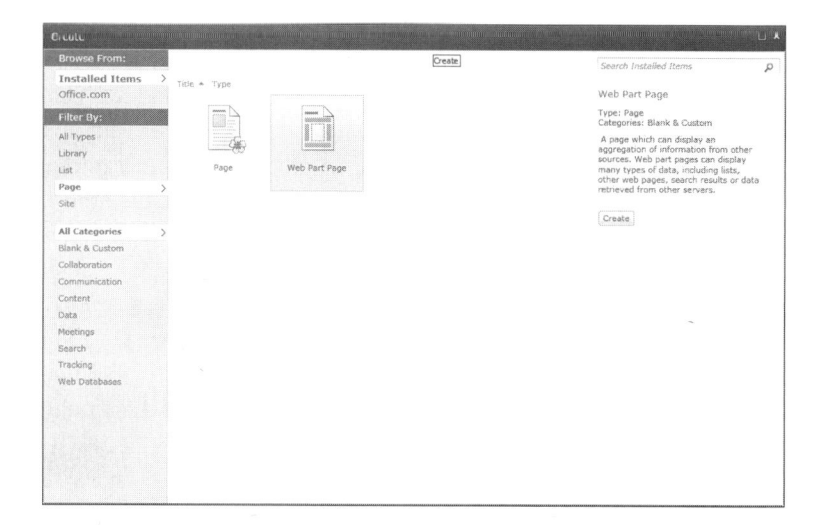

FIGURE 5.16
Selecting a layout template and document library

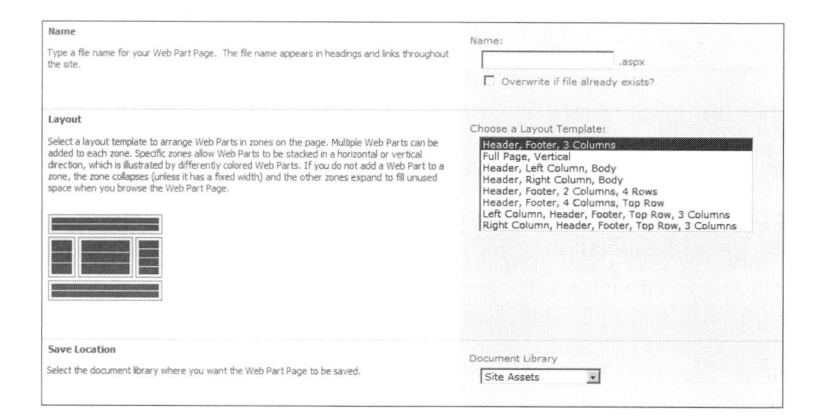

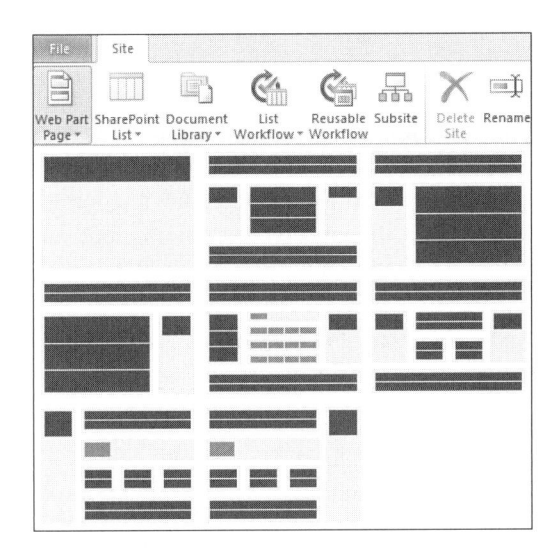

FIGURE 5.17
Creating a web part page using SharePoint Designer

Summary

This hour explored the process of developing various types of controls for SharePoint and explained that web parts are not the only types of controls that you can develop to extend SharePoint. You also learned how visual web parts, introduced in SharePoint 2010, ease the process of web part development, by providing design time support for developing a web part user interface. Along the way you also had a look at new safeguards against XSS attacks in SharePoint 2010. Finally the hour ended with a quick look at web part pages and wiki pages.

Q&A

Q. *My web part is performing poorly and takes too much time to render. Is there any way I can monitor my code for performance bottlenecks?*

A. Yes, you can do this easily using the SPMonitoredScope class, which helps you define your own monitored scope and display performance results on the developer dashboard. This is discussed more in Hour 8, "Understanding Client Object Model in SharePoint 2010."

Q. *Is there any way I can specify default values for my web part properties using an XML file?*

A. Yes, you can specify default values in the .webpart file, which is an XML file that describes your web part and makes it available in the Web Part Gallery. You can add new properties under the properties tag and specify their values, or you can edit the values of any already existing properties. The file is created automatically for you when developing a web part in Visual Studio 2010.

Q. *I want to develop a web part to connect to an already created web part. How do I know which interface I should implement?*

A. In such a scenario, you should refer to the documentation for the existing web part as a first step. Otherwise, for the target web part examine the .webpart file in the Web Part Gallery and look for the assembly defining the underlying type by examining the value of the metadata element. Next you can reflect the assembly thus determined using the Red Gate's reflector and look for the function decorated with the `ConnectionConsumer` or `ConnectionProvider` attribute, depending on the type of web part you are planning to create (that is, connection consumer or provider). By examining the signature of the function thus determined, you can find out the interface that your provider/consumer web part should implement.

HOUR 6

Working with More SharePoint 2010 User Interface Components

What You'll Learn in This Hour:

- ▶ Writing custom actions
- ▶ Programming ribbons
- ▶ Understanding master pages
- ▶ Understanding applications pages
- ▶ Understanding SharePoint 2010 navigation

> **By the Way**
>
> Due to the complexity of the topics discussed, some figures in this book are very detailed and are intended only to provide a high-level view of concepts. Those figures are representational and not intended to be read in detail.

Up to this point you have looked at two important components that form the user interface of a SharePoint application, that is, web parts and web part pages. In addition there are a few other components that you need to understand to build an effective user interface for your SharePoint application. These components are discussed in detail in this hour.

Writing Custom Actions

By now you should be familiar with the various SharePoint components such as the ribbon, the Site Actions menu, and the context menu that appears in a list (more accurately the Edit menu). All these components represent various important tasks within SharePoint and form an indispensible part of the SharePoint user interface. These are also the components that you may need to modify or add to when customizing your SharePoint application.

HOUR 6: Working with More SharePoint 2010 User Interface Components

SharePoint provides a rich, consistent, and simple mechanism to customize these components through custom actions. According to Microsoft a custom action represents a server ribbon, menu, or link customization that a user can see.

> **By the Way**
>
> Custom actions can be bound to a list type, content type, file type, or programmatic identifier (ProgID). (Refer to http://msdn.microsoft.com/en-us/library/ms458635.aspx.)

Try It Yourself
Write a Simple Custom Action

You will now develop your first custom action by adding a link to the Site Actions menu. The link simply takes the user to the ChangeSiteMasterPage.aspx application page from where the user can change the master page for the site.

Follow these steps:

1. Create a new Empty SharePoint project called FirstCustomAction.

2. Right-click the project and add a new item of type Module. Name it CustomActionModule1.

3. Delete the Sample.txt file and edit the Elements.xml as follows:

   ```
   <?xml version="1.0" encoding="utf-8"?>
   <Elements xmlns="http://schemas.microsoft.com/sharepoint/">
     <CustomAction
         Id="MyCustomAction"
         Description="This a shortcut to the change master page screen"
         Title="Change Master Page"
         GroupId="SiteActions"
         Location="Microsoft.SharePoint.StandardMenu"
         ImageUrl="/_layouts/images/icsmrtpg.gif"
         Sequence="10">
       <UrlAction Url="~site/_layouts/ChangeSiteMasterPage.aspx"/>
     </CustomAction>
   </Elements>
   ```

4. Deploy the project through Visual Studio. This should activate the feature associated with the custom action. Browse the site and open the Site Actions menu (see Figure 6.1). You should be able to the see your new custom action as a menu item in the Site Actions menu. Clicking on the menu item takes you to the ChangeSiteMasterPage.aspx.

FIGURE 6.1
Newly created Change Master Page Custom action

Now take a look at XML. The `<CustomAction>` tag defines a new custom action. The `Id` attribute specifies a unique identifier for the custom action. The `Title` and `Description` attributes specify the text and description for the custom action. The `GroupId` is an optional attribute that specifies the group that contains the custom action. In this case the group is `SiteActions`. The `Location` attribute along with the `GroupId` specifies the location where the custom action appears. In this case the location is `Microsoft.SharePoint.StandardMenu`. You can find the list of the default custom action group IDs that are used in Microsoft SharePoint Foundation at http://msdn.microsoft.com/en-us/library/bb802730.aspx.

The other attributes you can see are the `ImageUrl` attribute, which specifies the icon for the custom action, and the `Sequence` attribute, which specifies the ordering priority for the custom action. In addition you can see the `UrlAction` element, which specifies the URL to which the custom action points.

In addition to the ones just mentioned, there are many other attributes and elements that we see later on in this hour.

Programming Ribbons

The ribbon interface was introduced in SharePoint 2010 and is an important element of the user interface. Most of the commands in SharePoint 2010 are available through the ribbons. The ribbons are context sensitive—that is, they change according to the current user interface area. For example, when you edit the page and select an existing web part on the page, the ribbon menu changes to show commands related to the web part as shown in Figure 6.2.

FIGURE 6.2
Options tab in the ribbon for a web part

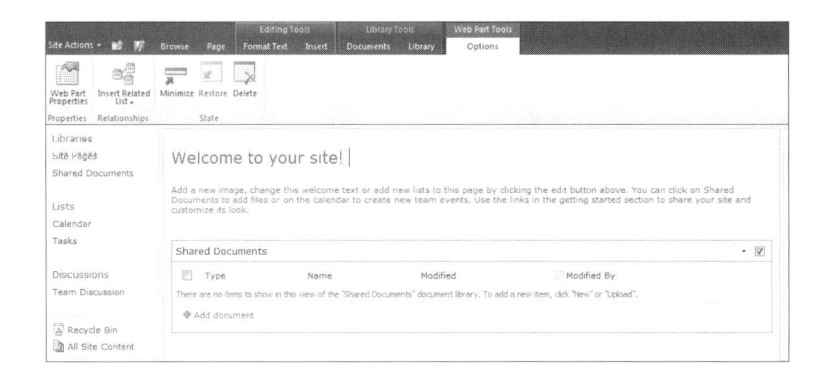

Customizing a ribbon is also done through `CustomActions`. For ribbons the `Location` attribute of the `CustomAction` element has to be one of the following:

- **`Ribbon.DisplayForm`**—Location corresponds to the display form for the list.
- **`CommandUI.Ribbon.ListView`**—Location corresponds to the list view.
- **`CommandUI.Ribbon.NewForm`**—Location corresponds to the new form for the list.
- **`CommandUI.Ribbon.EditForm`**—Location corresponds to the edit form for the list.

You use the `CommandUIExtension` element to extend the ribbon interface. The `CommandUIDefinitions` element, which is a child of the `CommandUIExtension`, contains a collection of the `CommandUIDefinition` element. The `CommandUIDefinition` element defines a new command in the ribbon.

Similarly there is a hierarchy in which the `CommandUIHandlers` element, which is a child of the `CommandUIExtension` element, contains a collection of `CommandUIHandler` elements. The `CommandUIHandler` element defines an event handler for the ribbon commands.

This entire hierarchy is demonstrated in Figure 6.3.

Programming Ribbons 129

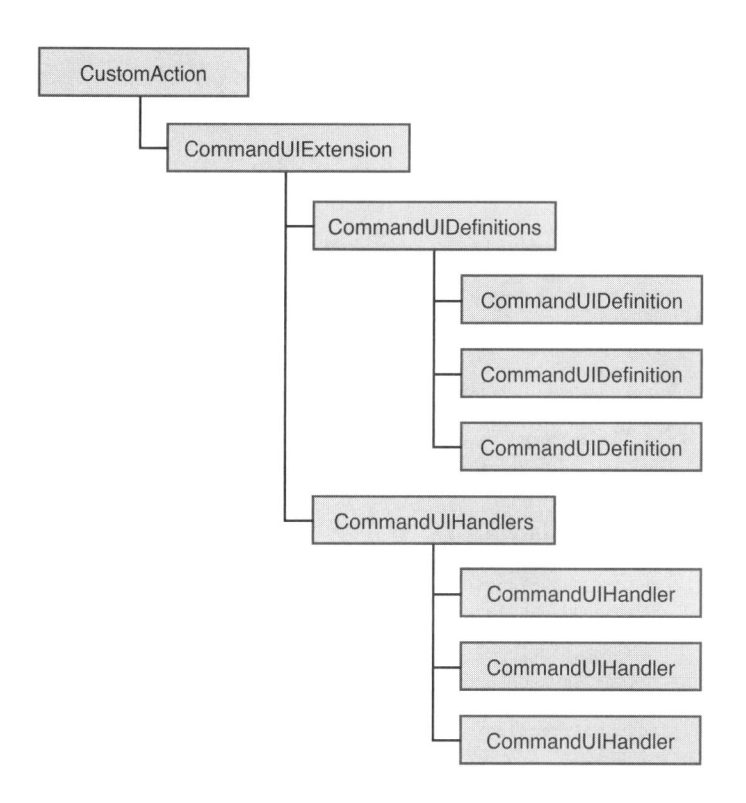

FIGURE 6.3
Custom action XML schema hierarchy

Try It Yourself
Add a Custom Command to a Ribbon

Enough of theory; let's now dive straight into writing some code and write your first custom action. First you write a new command that appears next to the New Folder command in the Items tab on the ribbon for a custom list. Clicking on the command shows a "Hello World" message box.

Follow these steps:

1. Create a new Empty SharePoint project called CustomRibbonDemo.

2. Add a new item of type Module named HelloWorldRibbon. Delete the sample.txt file and add edit the Elements.xml as follows:

   ```
   <?xml version="1.0" encoding="utf-8"?>
   <Elements xmlns="http://schemas.microsoft.com/sharepoint/">
     <CustomAction
       Id="CustomListRibbon"
       Location="CommandUI.Ribbon"
   ```

HOUR 6: Working with More SharePoint 2010 User Interface Components

```xml
          RegistrationId="100"
          RegistrationType="List"
          >
          <CommandUIExtension>
            <CommandUIDefinitions>
              <CommandUIDefinition Location="Ribbon.ListItem.New.Controls._
➥children">
              <Button
           Id="SharePoint.Ribbon.ListItem.New.HelloWorld"
           Sequence="40"
           Command="SharePoint.Ribbon.ListItem.New.HelloWorld.CommandHelloWorld"
           Image16by16="/_layouts/images/webAnalytics.png"
           Image16by16Top="-94"
           Image16by16Left="-16"
           Image32by32="/_layouts/images/webAnalytics.png"
           Image32by32Top="0" Image32by32Left="-96"
           LabelText="Hello World"
           ToolTipTitle="Hello world demo command"
           ToolTipDescription="Click to see hello world message box"
           TemplateAlias="o1"/>
              </CommandUIDefinition>
            </CommandUIDefinitions>
            <CommandUIHandlers>
              <CommandUIHandler
      Command="SharePoint.Ribbon.ListItem.New.
➥HelloWorld.CommandHelloWorld"
      CommandAction="javascript:ShowHelloWorldDialog()" />
            </CommandUIHandlers>
          </CommandUIExtension>
      </CustomAction>

      <CustomAction
      Id="SharePoint.Ribbon.ListItem.New.HelloWorld.Script"
      Location="ScriptLink"

                  ScriptBlock="
                      function ShowHelloWorldDialog()

                      {

                         var _html = document.createElement('div');
                               _html.innerHTML =
                                   '&lt;b&gt;Hello World!
➥SharePoint is amazing!!! &lt;b&gt;';
                               var _options = { html: _html };
                               SP.UI.ModalDialog.showModalDialog(_options);

                      }"

                      />
  </Elements>
```

3. Deploy the solution. Browse to any custom list in your SharePoint site, and you should be able to see a new button next to the New Folder button as shown in Figure 6.4.

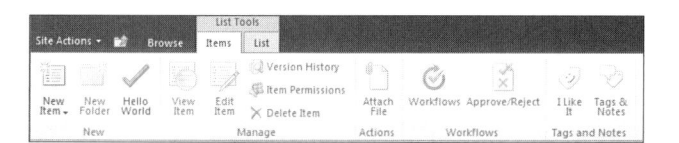

FIGURE 6.4 Custom command in the ribbon

Click the Hello World button and you should see a dialog with the text "HelloWorld! SharePoint is amazing!!!"

Let's see what exactly we defined in the XML. First a new custom action was defined with `Location` as `CommanUI.Ribbon`. The `RegistrationType` and `RegistrationID` attributes indicate that the new custom action will be scoped to a custom list. Then a new command is defined using the `CommandUIDefinition` element with the location of the command as `Ribbon.ListItem.New.Controls._children`. `Ribbon.ListItem.New` is the id of the group in the tab Item of the ribbon. This is defined in <14 Hive>\TEMPLATE\GLOBAL\XML\CMDUI.XML file. You can find a list of all the possible values of the `Location` attribute at http://msdn.microsoft.com/en-us/library/ee537543.aspx. Now that we have got the group name, use the syntax `Controls._children` to specify that we are going to add a child control. Since we want the user interface of our command to be a button, we define the `Button` element and give it some id. The `Command` attribute of the `Button` element refers to the Id of a `CommandUIHandler` defined within the `CommandUIHandlers` tag. The `CommandUIHandler` specifies the JavaScript function to be called when the button is clicked. The JavaScript function itself is defined through another custom action with the `Location` as `ScriptLink`. This JavaScript function calls the client side library of SharePoint to show a modal dialog.

The other things to understand are the attributes starting with `Image`. This is the image rendered for the button that you defined. These define the image for the button. We use the out of the box image /_layouts/images/webAnalytics.png. This is a special image where a collection of images is basically in one image. When you use this image or any other image where a collection of images is in a single file, you have to use the `Image32by32Top` and the `Left` attributes to render properly. These define the top and left coordinates of the image within the larger image. The value is always a negative integer or zero. You can easily find these coordinates by opening the image in Microsoft Paint software and hovering your mouse over the top left of the images. The coordinates are shown in the left-hand side of the status bar. The `TemplateAlias` property is used to specify which template alias to use from the Group Template Layout, which is defined by the CMDUI.XML file. This specifies how the control is positioned. In this case we use "o1" to display a large button. We could have used "o2" for a medium button.

HOUR 6: Working with More SharePoint 2010 User Interface Components

▼ **Try It Yourself**

Create a Custom Tab for a Ribbon

Follow these steps to define a new tab for the ribbon that appears for a SharePoint list:

1. Add a new module named as HelloWorldRibbon. Delete the sample.txt and modify the elements.xml as shown here:

```xml
<?xml version="1.0" encoding="utf-8"?>
<Elements xmlns="http://schemas.microsoft.com/sharepoint/">
  <CustomAction
    Id="SharePoint.Ribbon.DemoTab"
    Location="CommandUI.Ribbon" RegistrationType="List"
RegistrationId="100">
    <CommandUIExtension>
      <CommandUIDefinitions>
        <CommandUIDefinition Location="Ribbon.Tabs._children">
          <Tab Id="SharePoint.Ribbon.DemoTab"
            Title="Demo Tab"
            Description="This is a demo tab with dummy buttons"
            Sequence="1000">
            <Scaling Id="SharePoint.Ribbon.DemoTab.Scaling">
              <MaxSize Id="SharePoint.Ribbon.DemoTab.DemoGroup1.MaxSize"
                    GroupId="SharePoint.Ribbon.DemoTab.DemoGroup1"
                    Size="LargeTemplate"/>
              <MaxSize
    Id="COB.SharePoint.Ribbon.DemoTab.DemoGroup2.MaxSize"
                    GroupId="SharePoint.Ribbon.DemoTab.DemoGroup2"
                    Size="MediumTemplate"/>
              <Scale
                    Id="SharePoint.Ribbon.DemoTab.
➥DemoGroup1.Scaling.DemoTabScaling"
                    GroupId="SharePoint.Ribbon.DemoTab.DemoGroup1"
                    Size="LargeTemplate" />
              <Scale
                    Id="SharePoint.Ribbon.DemoTab.
                       ➥DemoGroup2.Scaling.DemoTabScaling"
                    GroupId="SharePoint.Ribbon.DemoTab.DemoGroup2"
                    Size="MediumTemplate" />
            </Scaling>

            <Groups Id="SharePoint.Ribbon.DemoTab.Groups">
              <Group
                Id="SharePoint.Ribbon.DemoTab.DemoGroup1"
                Description="This is a new Group in a tab"
                Title="Group One"
                Sequence="10"
                Template="Ribbon.Templates.LargeTemplate">
                <Controls
    Id="SharePoint.Ribbon.DemoTab.DemoGroup1.Controls">
                    <Button
                  Id="SharePoint.Ribbon.DemoTab.DemoGroup1.HiMsgBox"
                  Sequence="10"
                  Command="SharePoint.Ribbon.DemoTab.DemoGroup1.
                       ➥HiMsgBox.CommandHiMsgBox"
```

▼

```xml
            Image16by16="/_layouts/images/webAnalytics.png"
            Image16by16Top="-94"
            Image16by16Left="-16"
            Image32by32="/_layouts/images/webAnalytics.png"
            Image32by32Top="0"
            Image32by32Left="-96"
            LabelText="Hi"
            ToolTipTitle="SharePoint Message Box with text as Hi"
            ToolTipDescription="Click to see the Hi message box"
            TemplateAlias="temp1"/>
            </Controls>
          </Group>

          <Group
             Id="SharePoint.Ribbon.DemoTab.DemoGroup2"
             Description="Just another group in the tab"
             Title="Group Two"
             Sequence="20"
             Template="Ribbon.Templates.MediumTemplate">
             <Controls
   Id="SharePoint.Ribbon.DemoTab.DemoGroup2.Controls">
             <Button
           Id="SharePoint.Ribbon.DemoTab.DemoGroup2.StatusNotification0"
            Sequence="20"
            Command="SharePoint.Ribbon.DemoTab.DemoGroup2.
              ➥StatusNotification0.CommandStatusNotification0"
            Image16by16="/_layouts/images/webAnalytics.png"
            Image16by16Top="-94"
            Image16by16Left="-16"
            Image32by32="/_layouts/images/webAnalytics.png"
            Image32by32Top="0"
            Image32by32Left="-96"
            LabelText="Button 1 Status"
            ToolTipTitle="Some text in notification area"
            ToolTipDescription="Click to see some text in notification area"
            TemplateAlias="temp2"/>
             <Button
           Id="SharePoint.Ribbon.DemoTab.DemoGroup2.StatusNotification1"
            Sequence="30"
            Command="SharePoint.Ribbon.DemoTab.DemoGroup2.
              ➥StatusNotification1.CommandStatusNotification1"
            Image16by16="/_layouts/images/webAnalytics.png"
            Image16by16Top="-94"
            Image16by16Left="-16"
            Image32by32="/_layouts/images/webAnalytics.png"
            Image32by32Top="0"
            Image32by32Left="-96"
            LabelText="Button 2 Status"
            ToolTipTitle="Some text in notification area"
            ToolTipDescription="Click to see some text in notification area"
            TemplateAlias="temp3"/>
             </Controls>
           </Group>
         </Groups>
       </Tab>
    </CommandUIDefinition>
    <CommandUIDefinition Location="Ribbon.Templates._children">
      <GroupTemplate Id="Ribbon.Templates.LargeTemplate">
```

HOUR 6: Working with More SharePoint 2010 User Interface Components

```xml
                        <Layout Title="LargeTemplate" >
                          <Section Alignment="Top" Type="OneRow">
                            <Row>
                              <ControlRef DisplayMode="Large" TemplateAlias="temp1" />
                            </Row>
                          </Section>
                        </Layout>
                      </GroupTemplate>
                    </CommandUIDefinition>
                    <CommandUIDefinition Location="Ribbon.Templates._children">
                      <GroupTemplate Id="Ribbon.Templates.MediumTemplate">
                        <Layout Title="MediumTemplate" >
                          <Section Alignment="Top" Type="TwoRow">
                            <Row>
                              <ControlRef DisplayMode="Medium" TemplateAlias="temp2" />
                            </Row>
                            <Row>
                              <ControlRef DisplayMode="Medium" TemplateAlias="temp3" />
                            </Row>
                          </Section>
                        </Layout>
                      </GroupTemplate>
                    </CommandUIDefinition>
                  </CommandUIDefinitions>
                  <CommandUIHandlers>
                    <CommandUIHandler
                  Command="SharePoint.Ribbon.DemoTab.DemoGroup1.
➥HiMsgBox.CommandHiMsgBox"
                  CommandAction="javascript:ShowCustomDialog('Hi from SharePoint');" />
                    <CommandUIHandler
                  Command="SharePoint.Ribbon.DemoTab.DemoGroup2.StatusNotification0.
➥CommandStatusNotification0"
                  CommandAction="javascript:SP.UI.Notify.addNotification
➥('Status 1 from SharePoint');" />
                    <CommandUIHandler
                  Command="SharePoint.Ribbon.DemoTab.DemoGroup2.
➥StatusNotification1.CommandStatusNotification1"
                  CommandAction="javascript:SP.UI.
➥Notify.addNotification('Status 2 from SharePoint');" />
                  </CommandUIHandlers>
                </CommandUIExtension>
              </CustomAction>
              <CustomAction Id="SharePoint.Ribbon.DemoTab.Script" Location="ScriptLink"
                        ScriptBlock="
                            function ShowCustomDialog(message)
                            {
                               var _html = document.createElement('div');
                                      _html.innerHTML = message;
                                      var _options = { html: _html };
                                      SP.UI.ModalDialog.showModalDialog(_options);
                            }"
                            />
</Elements>
```

2. Deploy the Solution and Browse to a custom list. You should see the new tab with the custom commands.

That looks like a lot of code, but it's really simple. The various elements are defined here:

- We define a new tab using the Tab element within the `CommandUIDefinition`.
- Then we define two groups using the Group elements within the Groups element.
- The template for each Group is defined in other `CommandUIDefinition` elements through the `GroupTemplate` element. Here we define the layout using the Row element within the Section element. The `ControlRef` element specifies the size of the `DisplayMode` of the button, that is, Large or Medium. We associate this with our button using the `TemplateAlias` attribute.
- The Scaling section and its child elements define how the user interface should behave when the window is resized and there's not enough room. The `MaxSize` and `Scale` define the size and layout the element(s) should be when at "max" and also what to change to when the window is smaller.
- Finally we have the `CommandUIHandler` elements to handle the click of the buttons. These simply call SharePoint JavaScript APIs to display dialogs and notifications on the UI.

You would by now have realized that SharePoint provides a rich mechanism for customizing ribbons. It's a good idea to go through the MSDN and explore the various options involved in the ribbon customizations.

Understanding Master Pages

SharePoint uses the master page concept to achieve a uniform look and feel across a site, and you will find yourself extensively working with master pages in SharePoint.

> **Did You Know?**
> Master pages were introduced in ASP.NET 2.0 and allow you to create a consistent layout for the pages in your site.

A master page defines user interface elements common across the site. In addition it defines content placeholders that can be overridden by the individual pages to achieve the user interface specific to the pages. This allows you to have a consistent look and feel across the site. You can use a single master page for the entire site or use multiple master pages. You can also have nested master pages. All this gives you a lot of flexibility to achieve the desired look and feel.

HOUR 6: Working with More SharePoint 2010 User Interface Components

SharePoint 2010 comes out of the box with a few master pages. The default master page used by SharePoint 2010 is v4.master. This will be the master page you use most. It provides the ribbon bar and all the other new visual UI changes such as the Site Actions menu on the left side.

Then there is the default.master, which is similar to the default.master in SharePoint 2007. This master page renders the look and feel of SharePoint 2007 and will be used by sites that have upgraded from SharePoint 2007 to SharePoint 2010 and want to use the old user interface.

The search pages and the Office web applications use minimal.master. This is a really slimmed down master page with next to nothing on it.

There are also the mwsdefault.master and the mwsdefaultv4.master, which are used by the meeting workspaces.

You can find these master pages at the <14 Hive>\TEMPLATE\GLOBAL directory.

Let's now look at the structure of the SharePoint master page. If you open the v4.master you find the following:

- Various tag prefixes registered at the start. These are required for the various controls used in the page.
- Various SharePoint controls declared in the head section. These are required to include the CSS and JavaScript files required by the SharePoint site.
- You find the `ScriptManager` tag immediately after the `forms` tag. SharePoint 2010 now supports AJAX.NET out of the box.
- A `SPWebPartManager` is declared after the `ScriptManager` tag.
- Many `ContentPlaceHolders`. Most of the content placeholders are overridden by the individual pages. When creating your own custom master page you might add new `ContentPlaceHolders` or remove some. There are a few required `ContentPlaceHolders` that must always be present in your master page. These are listed in Table 6.1.

TABLE 6.1 Required Content Placeholders in a SharePoint Master Page

Placeholder Control	Description
`<asp:ContentPlaceHolder id="PlaceHolderPageTitle" runat="server"/>`	This is the first ContentPlaceHolder in the master page. This shows the title of the site.

TABLE 6.1 Continued

Placeholder Control	Description
`<asp:ContentPlaceHolder id="PlaceHolderQuickLaunchTop" runat="server">`	This `ContentPlaceHolder` is just above the Quick Launch menu. Override this in the page when you want to display something just above the Quick Launch.
`<asp:ContentPlaceHolder id="PlaceHolderQuickLaunchBottom" runat="server">`	This `ContentPlaceHolder` is just below the Quick Launch menu. Override this in the page when you want to display something just below the Quick Launch.
`<asp:ContentPlaceHolder id="PlaceHolderAdditionalPageHead" runat="server"/>`	Placeholder in the head section of the page used to add extra components such as ECMAScript (JavaScript, JScript) and Cascading Style Sheets (CSS) to the page.
`<asp:ContentPlaceHolder ID="SPNavigation" runat="server">`	Control used for additional page editing controls.
`<asp:ContentPlaceHolder id="PlaceHolderSiteName" runat="server">`	Name of the site where the current page resides.
`<asp:ContentPlaceHolder id="PlaceHolderPageTitleInTitleArea" runat="server" />`	Title of the page, which appears in the title area on the page.
`<asp:ContentPlaceHolder id="PlaceHolderPageDescription" runat="server"/>`	Description of the current page.
`<asp:ContentPlaceHolder id="PlaceHolderSearchArea" runat="server">`	Section of the page for the search controls.
`<asp:ContentPlaceHolder id="PlaceHolderGlobalNavigation" runat="server">`	Breadcrumb control on the page.
`<asp:ContentPlaceHolder id="PlaceHolderTitleBreadcrumb" runat="server">`	Breadcrumb text for the breadcrumb control.
`<asp:ContentPlaceHolder id="PlaceHolderGlobalNavigationSiteMap" runat="server">`	List of subsites and sibling sites in the global navigation on the page.

TABLE 6.1 Continued

Placeholder Control	Description
`<asp:ContentPlaceHolder id="PlaceHolderTopNavBar" runat="server">`	Container used to hold the top navigation bar.
`<asp:ContentPlaceHolder id="PlaceHolderHorizontalNav" runat="server">`	The navigation menu that is inside the top navigation bar.
`<asp:ContentPlaceHolder id="PlaceHolderLeftNavBarDataSource" runat="server" />`	The placement of the data source used to populate the left navigation bar.
`<asp:ContentPlaceHolder id="PlaceHolderCalendarNavigator" runat="server" />`	Date picker used when a calendar is visible on the page.
`<asp:ContentPlaceHolder id="PlaceHolderLeftNavBarTop" runat="server"/>`	Top section of the left navigation bar.
`<asp:ContentPlaceHolder id="PlaceHolderLeftNavBar" runat="server">`	Quick Launch bar.
`<asp:ContentPlaceHolder id="PlaceHolderLeftActions" runat="server">`	Additional objects above the Quick Launch bar.
`<asp:ContentPlaceHolder id="PlaceHolderMain" runat="server">`	Main content of the page.
`<asp:ContentPlaceHolder id="PlaceHolderFormDigest" runat="server">`	Container where the page form digest control is stored.
`<asp:ContentPlaceHolder id="PlaceHolderUtilityContent" runat="server"/>`	Additional content at the bottom of the page. This is outside the form tag.
`<asp:ContentPlaceHolder id="PlaceHolderTitleAreaClass" runat="server"/>`	The class for the title area (now in the head tag). Customizations that add a WebPartZone in a content tag to this placeholder will cause an error.

In addition to those listed in Table 6.1, the following content placeholders are not part of the user interface but are used for backward compatibility:

▶ `<asp:ContentPlaceHolder id="PlaceHolderPageImage" runat="server"/>`

▶ `<asp:ContentPlaceHolder id="PlaceHolderTitleLeftBorder" runat="server">`

▶ `<asp:ContentPlaceHolder id="PlaceHolderMiniConsole" runat="server"/>`

▶ `<asp:ContentPlaceHolder id="PlaceHolderTitleRightMargin" runat="server"/>`

▶ `<asp:ContentPlaceHolder id="PlaceHolderTitleAreaSeparator" runat="server"/>`

▶ `<asp:ContentPlaceHolder id="PlaceHolderNavSpacer" runat="server">`

▶ `<asp:ContentPlaceHolder id="PlaceHolderLeftNavBarBorder" runat="server">`

▶ `<asp:ContentPlaceHolder id="PlaceHolderBodyLeftBorder" runat="server">`

▶ `<asp:ContentPlaceHolder id="PlaceHolderBodyRightMargin" runat="server">`

Try It Yourself
Create a Custom Master Page

The best way to create a new master page is to copy the out of the box master page and customize it as per the requirements. We will now create a custom master page. Although you will not be making too many changes to it now, you will use this master page to demonstrate other concepts later in this and subsequent hours.

1. Create a new empty SharePoint project and name it CustomMasterPage. Right-click the project, select Add a New Item, and add a module name CustomV4MasterPage. Copy the v4.master from the <14 Hive>\TEMPLATE\ GLOBAL directory and include it in the module. Rename the v4.master to v4Custom.master. Delete the sample.txt file. The project structure should look something like Figure 6.5.

FIGURE 6.5
CustomMaster
Page project
hierarchy

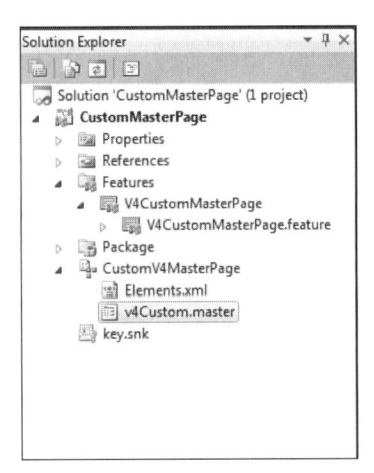

2. Edit the contents of Elements.xml as follows:

```
<?xml version="1.0" encoding="utf-8"?>
<Elements xmlns="http://schemas.microsoft.com/sharepoint/">
  <Module Name="CustomV4MasterPage" Url="_catalogs/masterpage">
    <File \
      Path="CustomV4MasterPage\v4Custom.master"
      Url="v4Custom.master"
      Type="GhostableInLibrary"/>
  </Module>
</Elements>
```

3. Open the v4Custom.master and search for the content placeholder having the id `PlaceHolderPageTitleInTitleArea`. Just before the content placeholder within the H2 tags, add the text `Custom Master Title >>` as shown in the following code:

```
<h2>
Custom Master Title >>
<asp:ContentPlaceHolder
    id="PlaceHolderPageTitleInTitleArea"
    runat="server" />
</h2>
```

4. The preceding module deploys the v4Custom.master to the master page gallery. Right-click and deploy the project from Visual Studio. Browse to the SharePoint site and from the Site Actions menu click Change Master Page. (If you haven't done the steps in the section "Custom Actions" this link won't be present. In this case, go to Site Actions, Site Settings, and click Master Page in the Look and Feel section.

Understanding Master Pages 141

5. You should be able to see your master page in the drop-down lists for Site Master Page and System Master Page as shown in Figure 6.6. The site master page is used by the Publishing pages in the site while the system master page is used for all forms and view pages in the site.

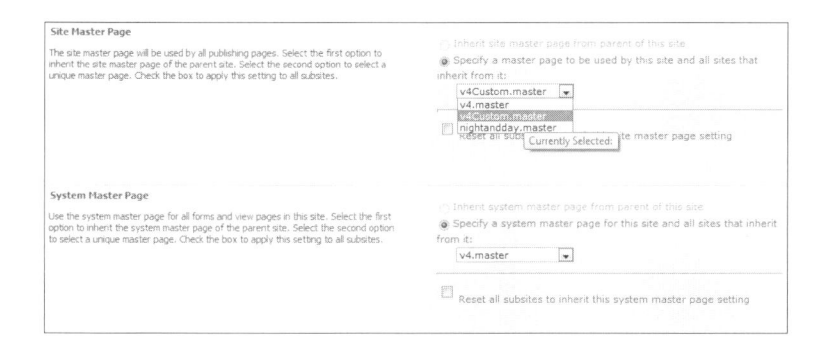

FIGURE 6.6 Change the master page

6. Select v4Custom.master for both the Site Master Page and the System Master Page and click OK. Browse to the home page and you can see the Custom Master Title >> text (see Figure 6.7).

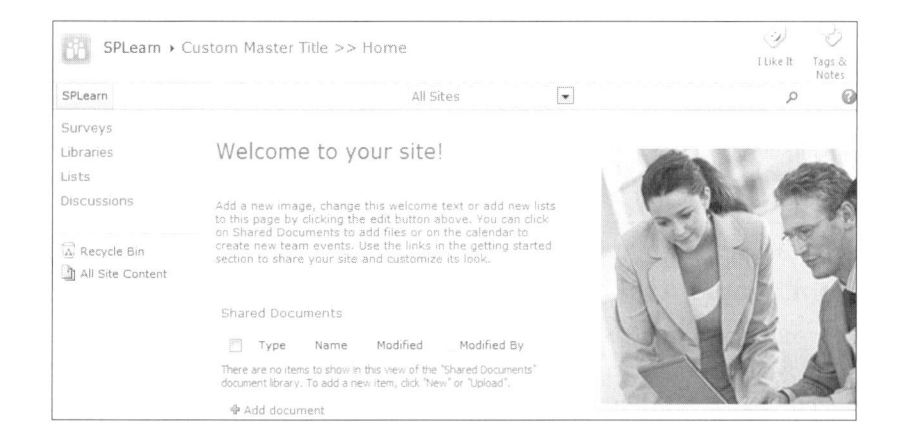

FIGURE 6.7 Site after setting the custom master page

7. You can also apply the master page programmatically. This generally is done through a feature receiver. Right-click the V4CustomMasterPage feature and click Add Event Receiver.

8. Uncomment the `FeatureActivated` event and add the following code:
   ```
   public override void
           FeatureActivated(SPFeatureReceiverProperties properties)
   {
       SPWeb web = properties.Feature.Parent as SPWeb;
       web.CustomMasterUrl = "/_catalogs/masterpage/v4Custom.master";
       web.MasterUrl = "/_catalogs/masterpage/v4Custom.master";
       web.Update();
   }
   ```

9. The `CustomMasterUrl` property gets or sets the site master page, and the `MasterUrl` property sets the system master page. Also note the following statement:
   ```
   SPWeb web = properties.Feature.Parent as SPWeb;
   ```

10. Here we are typecasting the `SPFeatureReceiverProperties.Feature.Parent` to `SPWeb`. This is because our feature is scoped at the web level. If it was at the site level we would have casted it to `SPSite` object.

Understanding Applications Pages

Application pages reside in the file system. These are different from web part pages, which are stored in the database. Unlike web part pages, application pages are not customizable. Application pages reside in the Layouts folder under the <14 Hive>\Template folder. An application page is really like the usual ASP.NET page that inherits from the `Microsoft.SharePoint.WebControls.LayoutsPageBase` class.

Try It Yourself

Write a Simple Application Page

1. Create a new empty SharePoint project and name it DemoApplicationPage. Add a new item of type Application Page named as SiteInfo.aspx. A new ASPX page and code behind file gets added to the project under the Layouts\DemoApplicationPage folder, as shown in Figure 6.8.

Understanding Applications Pages | 143

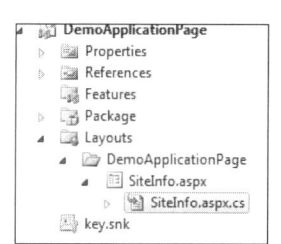

FIGURE 6.8
Demo-
ApplicationPage
project hierarchy

2. Edit the SiteInfo.aspx and update as follows:

```
<%@ Assembly Name="$SharePoint.Project.AssemblyFullName$" %>
<%@ Import Namespace="Microsoft.SharePoint.ApplicationPages" %>
<%@ Register
    Tagprefix="SharePoint"
    Namespace="Microsoft.SharePoint.WebControls"
    Assembly="Microsoft.SharePoint,
    ➥Version=14.0.0.0, Culture=neutral, PublicKeyToken=71e9bce111e9429c" %>
<%@ Register
    Tagprefix="Utilities"
    Namespace="Microsoft.SharePoint.Utilities"
    Assembly="Microsoft.SharePoint, Version=14.0.0.0,
    ➥Culture=neutral, PublicKeyToken=71e9bce111e9429c" %>
<%@ Register
    Tagprefix="asp"
    Namespace="System.Web.UI"
    Assembly="System.Web.Extensions, Version=3.5.0.0, Culture=neutral,
    ➥PublicKeyToken=31bf3856ad364e35" %>
<%@ Import Namespace="Microsoft.SharePoint" %>
<%@ Assembly
    Name="Microsoft.Web.CommandUI, Version=14.0.0.0,
    ➥Culture=neutral, PublicKeyToken=71e9bce111e9429c" %>
<%@ Page
    Language="C#"
    AutoEventWireup="true"
    CodeBehind="SiteInfo.aspx.cs"
    Inherits="DemoApplicationPage.Layouts.DemoApplicationPage.SiteInfo"
    DynamicMasterPageFile="~masterurl/default.master" %>

<asp:Content
    ID="PageHead"
    ContentPlaceHolderID="PlaceHolderAdditionalPageHead"
    runat="server">

</asp:Content>

<asp:Content ID="Main" ContentPlaceHolderID="PlaceHolderMain" runat="server">
<asp:Literal runat="server" ID="LiteralInfo"></asp:Literal>
</asp:Content>

<asp:Content
    ID="PageTitle"
    ContentPlaceHolderID="PlaceHolderPageTitle"
    runat="server">
Site Info
</asp:Content>
```

```
<asp:Content
    ID="PageTitleInTitleArea"
    ContentPlaceHolderID="PlaceHolderPageTitleInTitleArea"
    runat="server" >
Site Info
</asp:Content>
```

3. Edit the code behind as follows:.

```
using System;
using Microsoft.SharePoint;
using Microsoft.SharePoint.WebControls;
using System.Text;

namespace DemoApplicationPage.Layouts.DemoApplicationPage
{
    public partial class SiteInfo : LayoutsPageBase
    {
        protected void Page_Load(object sender, EventArgs e)
        {
            SPWeb web = SPContext.Current.Web;

            StringBuilder html = new StringBuilder();
            html.Append("Some random info. about the current site <BR/>");
            html.Append("<OL>");
            html.AppendFormat("User Name: {0} <BR/>", web.CurrentUser.Name);
            html.AppendFormat("Url : {0} <BR/>", web.Url);
            html.AppendFormat("User Name: {0} <BR/>", web.CurrentUser.Name);
            html.AppendFormat("Site Master Url: {0} <BR/>", web.CustomMasterUrl);
            html.AppendFormat("System Master Url: {0} <BR/>", web.MasterUrl);
            html.Append("</OL>");

            this.LiteralInfo.Text = html.ToString();
        }
    }
}
```

4. Build and deploy the solution. Browse to the application page by going to the URL http://localhost/_layouts/DemoApplicationPage/SiteInfo.aspx. You see the screen shown in Figure 6.9.

Application pages are really simple. They are built mostly for administration tasks and you will find that most links in the Site Settings page point to application pages.

FIGURE 6.9
SiteInfo.aspx

Understanding SharePoint 2010 Navigation

Navigation elements are an essential part of any user interface. SharePoint provides navigation features in the form of a top navigation bar, the Quick Launch menu on the left, and the breadcrumbs. The navigation in SharePoint is based on the ASP.NET Provider model, which encapsulates the user interface from the underlying data source. The following sections look at the various user interface elements of the SharePoint navigation in more detail.

Top Navigation Bar

The top navigation bar displays a tab for each site and pages contained within the root site of the site collection based on the navigation settings. A dynamic drop-down menu displays the subsites and pages for each tab.

By default for a team site the top navigation bar does not display subsites and pages. To display the subsites and pages in the top navigation bar, browse to the Site Settings page and go to Navigation under the Look and Feel section. In the Global Navigation section select the Show Subsites and Show Pages options, as shown in Figure 6.10.

> **Did You Know?**
> If the Show Pages option is disabled, you need to enable the Publishing features at both the site collection scope and site scope.

HOUR 6: Working with More SharePoint 2010 User Interface Components

FIGURE 6.10
Global Navigation settings

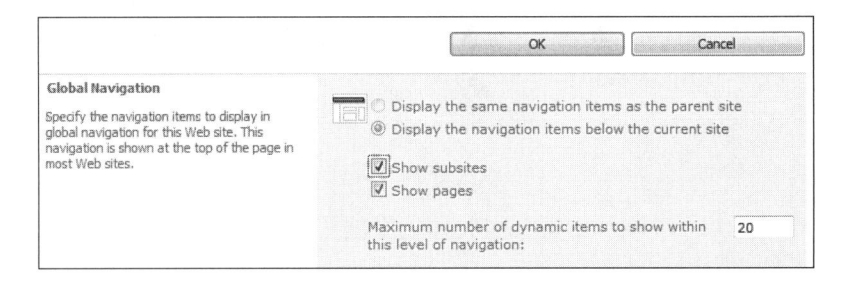

Click OK and you see the subsite and pages in the top navigation bar, as shown in Figure 6.11.

> **By the Way**
>
> The top navigation bar tabs display dynamic drop-down menus for the subsites of a subsite only if the navigation settings of the subsite also have the Show Subsites option set in their global navigation.

FIGURE 6.11
Global Navigation showing subsites

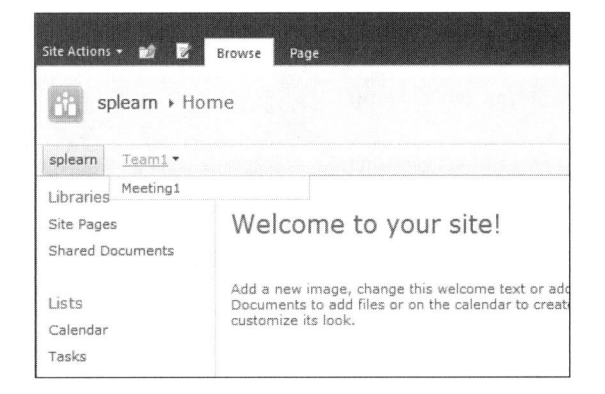

Note that you can set these options programmatically by setting the appropriate properties on the `PublishingWeb` object as shown in the following code:

```
using (SPSite site = new SPSite("http://splearn"))
{
    using (SPWeb web = site.OpenWeb())
    {
        Console.WriteLine(
"Setting the Show subites and Show pages property for global navigation to
➥true");
        PublishingWeb pubWeb = PublishingWeb.GetPublishingWeb(web);
        pubWeb.Navigation.GlobalIncludeSubSites = true;
```

Understanding SharePoint 2010 Navigation

```
            pubWeb.Navigation.GlobalIncludePages = true;
            pubWeb.Update();
        }
    }
```

In addition to the previous settings the items shown in the top navigation menu are also governed by the Global Navigation nodes. Browse to the Site Settings page and open the navigation settings. In the Navigation Editing and Sorting section, add a new node with the title Bing.com and URL http://www.bing.com to the Global Navigation and click OK, as shown in Figure 6.12.

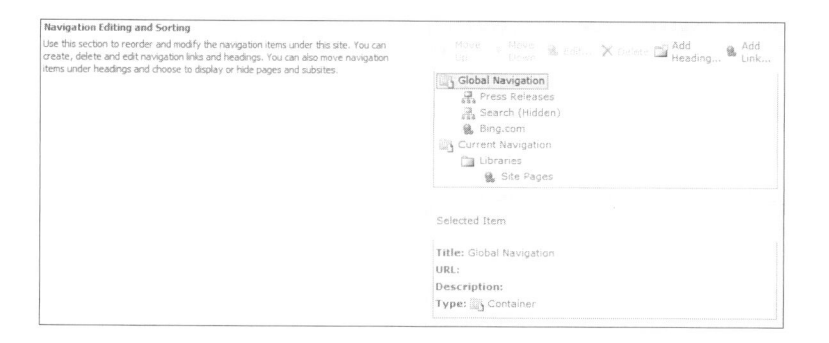

FIGURE 6.12 Navigation and sorting options

You see the new item appear in the top navigation menu (see Figure 6.13).

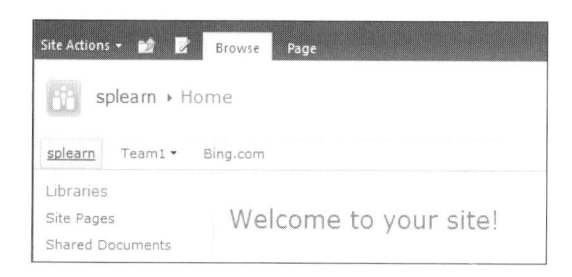

FIGURE 6.13 Custom link in Global Navigation

Quick Launch Menu

Like the top navigation menu the Quick Launch menu displays subsites and pages based on the settings in the Current Navigation section of the Navigation settings for the site (see Figure 6.14). However, this is limited to the subsites and pages within the current site. In addition the Quick Launch displays the nodes present under the Current Navigation of the Navigation settings of the current site.

FIGURE 6.14
Current Navigation options

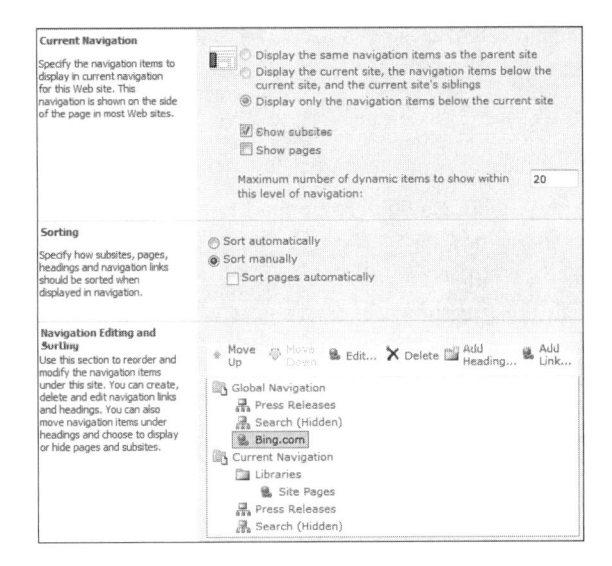

Summary

This hour looked at the building blocks of the SharePoint user interface, including custom actions, ribbons, and various navigation elements of a SharePoint site. Master pages, which are responsible for providing the branding to a SharePoint site, were discussed in addition to application pages, which are ASP.NET pages residing on the file system. This knowledge should give you enough power to configure and customize the SharePoint user interface as per your requirements.

Q&A

Q. *Can a SharePoint master page have a code behind file?*

A. Yes. A SharePoint master is not different from an ASP.NET master page except that it has controls specific to the user interface of SharePoint. You can have a code behind file for a master page.

Q. *Can we have nested master pages?*

A. Yes. You can have nested master pages, and they provide great flexibility in defining a UI that is mostly consistent and at the same time slightly variant across modules within the application.

Q. *Can we embed web parts in an application page?*

A. Web parts can be embedded like any other web control within an application page. However, these will not be editable and cannot be configured through the user interface.

HOUR 7

Understanding SharePoint 2010 Server Side Development

What You'll Learn in This Hour:

- ▶ Jump start programming with the object model
- ▶ Exploring the object model
- ▶ Understanding the object model in relation to server and site architecture
- ▶ Troubleshooting and monitoring performance with the developer dashboard
- ▶ Creating a custom timer job
- ▶ Modifying the web.config with SPWebConfigModifications
- ▶ Understanding the event receivers

> **By the Way**
>
> Due to the complexity of the topics discussed, some figures in this book are very detailed and are intended only to provide a high-level view of concepts. Those figures are representational and not intended to be read in detail.

SharePoint has a well-structured server side object model, with Microsoft.SharePoint.dll assembly containing the core components of the same. Classes such as SPFarm, SPServer, SPContext, SPSite, SPWeb, and SPList defined in this assembly represent various elements of a SharePoint site. SharePoint developers can program against these classes to perform operations such as adding, editing, or deleting data, or manipulate various other aspects of a SharePoint website. This hour looks at various APIs and features offered by the SharePoint server side object model, explores features and facilities provided by Visual Studio 2010 for developers to consume these APIs, and also looks at the process of creating a custom timer job, programmatic modifications to web.config, and programming the event receivers.

Jump Start Programming with the Object Model

To better appreciate the intuitiveness and ease of programming with the object model, let's quickly create a console application that displays all the lists in a top-level SharePoint site under a given site collection.

▼ **Try It Yourself**

Display Lists in a SharePoint Site

To display lists in a SharePoint site, follow these steps:

1. Fire up Visual Studio, create a new console application, and add a reference to Microsoft.SharePoint.dll assembly. As discussed in Hour 3, "Starting Development with SharePoint 2010," make sure that your console application targets .NET Framework 3.5 and has either X64 or Any CPU set under the Platform Target property present in the project's Build configuration tab. By default Visual Studio 2010 sets this value to *X86*.

2. Next create a `DisplayAllLists` function to navigate through all the lists in a site and write their title to the console window, as illustrated in the following code:

   ```
   public static void DisplayAllLists(string url)
   {
   using (SPSite siteCollection = new SPSite(url))
   {
   SPWeb web = siteCollection.RootWeb;
   foreach (SPList list in web.Lists)
   {
   Console.WriteLine(list.Title);
   }
   }
   }
   ```

   The preceding code starts off by instantiating a new `SPSite` object and obtains a reference to its top-level site (or the root web). Then using an `SPList` object the code iterates through all the lists in the root web and writes their titles to the console window.

3. Make a call to the `DisplayAllLists` function from the `Main` function by passing in the URL of a SharePoint site. For complete source code refer to the `ListRetrieverApp` project in the source code for this hour.

▼

4. Run the console application either by pressing F5 or clicking the Start Debugging button. This causes all the lists under the top-level SharePoint site of the current site collection to be displayed in the console window.

Exploring the Object Model

When working with the server side object model, the typical approach involves starting out at a particular level in the object hierarchy and navigating through the hierarchy to reach the object of interest. A number of tools are available that you can use to familiarize yourself with the object hierarchy and examine properties of various objects in the hierarchy. To begin with, Visual Studio's Object Browser is a handy tool that you can use from within Visual Studio to examine the Microsoft.SharePoint.dll assembly.

Next in the list is Visual Studio's Server Explorer. Using Server Explorer, you can Add a SharePoint Connection to your site collection and start exploring the contents of the same using a friendly user interface as illustrated in Figure 7.1.

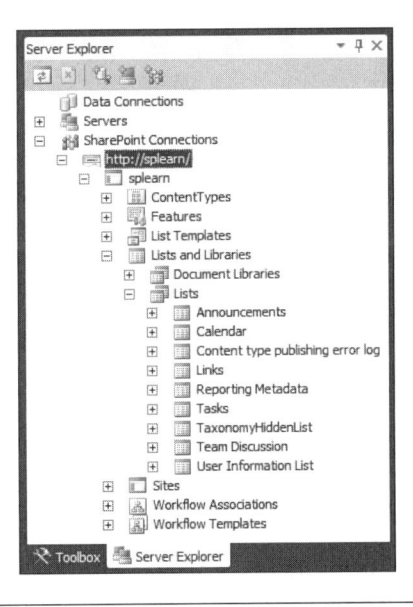

FIGURE 7.1
Visual Studio 2010 Server Explorer

> **By the Way**
>
> Note that Server Explorer actually displays fewer lists than your DisplayAllLists console application displays. This is because Server Explorer does not display hidden lists.

HOUR 7: Understanding SharePoint 2010 Server Side Development

Apart from the Server Explorer and the Object Browser, another tool (not part of Visual Studio) is popular in the SharePoint developer community. It's called SharePoint Manager 2010 and is available for free download on CodePlex at http://spm.codeplex.com/. SharePoint Manager starts off at a much higher level (farm level configuration) and provides more detail compared to Visual Studio's Server Explorer (see Figure 7.2). Further, you get the option of modifying certain properties as well when using SharePoint Manager.

FIGURE 7.2
Exploring the Object Model using SharePoint Manager 2010

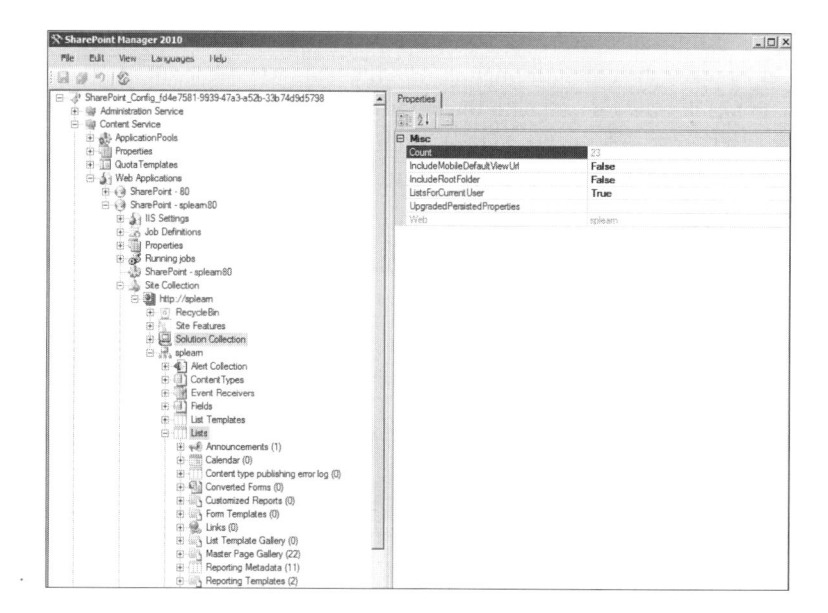

Did You Know?

CodePlex is Microsoft's open source project hosting website. You can also share your solutions with the developer community on codeplex or join other developers and contribute in various open source projects. For more information on codeplex, starting a new project, or joining an existing one, refer to http://www.codeplex.com/site/help.

Understanding the Object Model in Relation to Server and Site Architecture

Every time you intend to program against the SharePoint server side model you need to refer to Microsoft.SharePoint.dll in your code. This assembly contains the object model's core classes inside the Microsoft.SharePoint namespace, as shown in Figure 7.3.

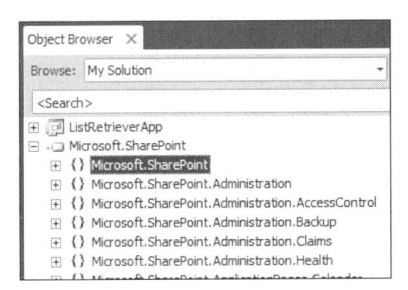

FIGURE 7.3 Exploring Microsoft.SharePoint.dll assembly using Object Browser

You need to understand the role of various core classes in this assembly in the context of SharePoint's server and site architecture, discussed in the following sections.

Understanding the Object Model in Relation to Server Architecture

Let's explore the core classes in the object model corresponding to various nodes in the SharePoint server architecture. At the top of the hierarchy is an object of the SPFarm class, representing a server farm, as shown in Figure 7.4.

SPFarm has two important properties namely, Servers and Services. The Servers property gets a collection of all the servers (SPServer objects) in the farm while the Services property gets a collection of SPService objects, representing logical services on the farm.

SPServer object, representing a server, has an important property called ServiceInstances, which provides references to individual service instances (SPServiceInstance objects) running on the server.

Two important classes, SPWindowsService and SPWebService inheriting from the SPService class, form the base classes for various Windows and web services, respectively. For example, implementation for a timer service (which is actually a Windows service) is provided by the SPTimerService class. As you would expect, this class inherits from the SPWindowsService class.

Further, the WebApplications property of the SPWebService gets the collection of web applications (SPWebApplication objects) that run the service. The Sites property gets the collection of site collections within the web application, and the ContentDatabases property gets the collection of content databases (objects of the SPContentDatabase class) used in the web application.

FIGURE 7.4
Object model in relation to the server architecture

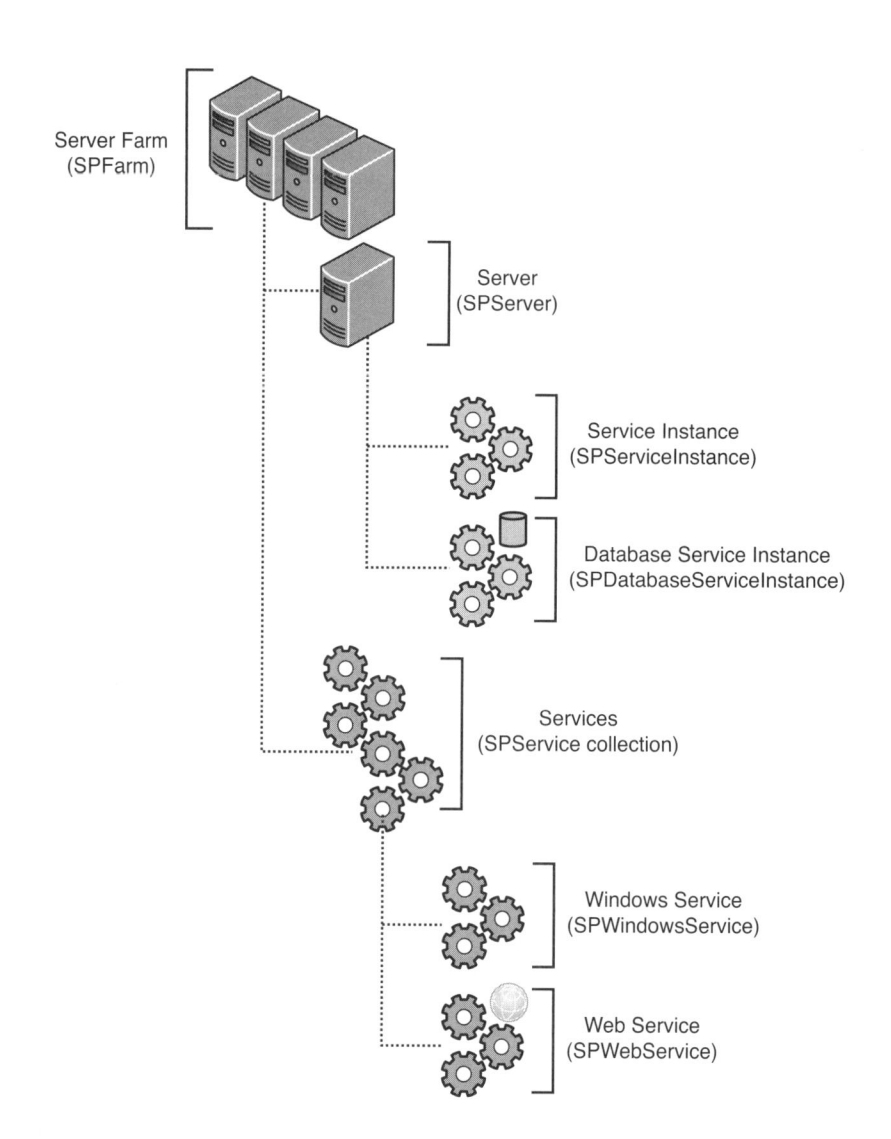

SharePoint 2010 introduces a new concept called Service Application Framework, which is actually a replacement of SharePoint 2007's Shared Services Provider. Services implementing the Service Application Framework inherit from the `SPServiceInstance` class, which represents a single instance of a service that runs on a server and therefore associates services with servers. Services implementing the Service Application Framework can have multiple configured farm-scoped instantiations (CFSI), each having its own configuration settings.

Understanding the Object Model in Relation to Server and Site Architecture

Consider an example of the SPDatabaseServiceInstance class, which extends the SPServiceInstance class and represents a single instance of a database service running on the database server. There can be multiple instances of SPDatabaseServiceInstance running on different servers, each having its own configuration settings. Each service instance can access any farmwide settings that apply to the parent service of this instance (database service in our case) by using the Service property of the SPServiceInstance class.

Try It Yourself
List All the Servers and Services in a Farm

Let's write a small piece of code to list all the servers and services installed on a farm. As discussed, we put to use the Server and the Services properties of an SPFarm object here to get a collection of the servers and services in the farm.

1. Fire up Visual Studio, create a new console application, and add a reference to Microsoft.SharePoint.dll assembly. Make sure your console application targets .NET Framework 3.5 and has either X64 or Any CPU set under the Platform Target property present in the project's Build configuration tab.

2. To obtain a reference to the server farm, invoke the static Open method of the SPFarm class, passing it to the connection string for the configuration database of the server farm. The Open method returns the SPFarm object that represents the server farm, as illustrated in the following code:

   ```
   SPFarm farm = SPFarm.Open(connectionString);
   ```

3. Next create the function ListAllServersAndServices that accepts the SPFarm object, retrieves references to servers, and services collection from it, iterates through the respective collections, and lists out the names of their members on the console window, as shown in the following code:

   ```
   public static void ListAllServersAndServices(SPFarm farm)
   {
   Console.WriteLine("***All Servers***");
   foreach (SPServer server in farm.Servers)
   {
   Console.WriteLine(server.DisplayName);
   }

   Console.WriteLine("***All Services***");
   foreach (SPService service in farm.Services)
   {
   Console.WriteLine("{0} {1}", service.Name, service.TypeName);
   }
   }
   ```

4. Run the console application either by pressing F5 or clicking the Start Debugging button to view all the servers and services in the server farm.

For complete source code of this example, refer to the ServerSideOMDemo project in the source code for this hour.

Understanding the Object Model in Relation to Site Architecture

Next consider the core classes modeling various aspects of a SharePoint website. The SPSite class represents a site collection and can include any number of SPWeb objects representing subsites. Each subsite can further have a number of subsites. The Webs property (of SPWeb) returns a SPWebCollection object that represents all the subsites of a specified site. Further the Lists property of SPWeb returns an SPListCollection object that represents all the lists in the site. The SPList class represents a list containing a collection of list items (the Lists property), represented by SPListItem. Figure 7.5 represents this arrangement visually.

FIGURE 7.5
Object model in relation to the site architecture

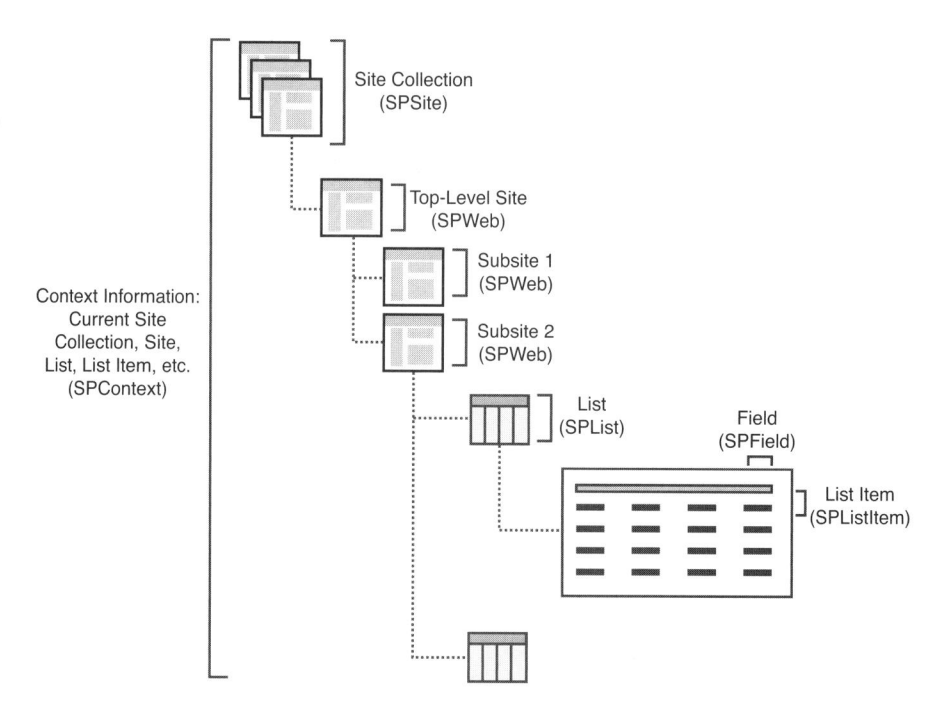

The object hierarchy shown in Figure 7.5 is a much simplified and scaled-down version of the actual SharePoint object model. However, it effectively highlights the

Understanding the Object Model in Relation to Server and Site Architecture

basic thought process behind the SharePoint object model and should get you going in the right direction.

Getting the Context Information

The SPContext class, shown previously in Figure 7.5, has so far not been discussed much. In the SharePoint world, the SPContext class gets the context of the current HTTP request. The static Current property of the SPContext class provides properties that return context information about the current web application, site collection, site, list, list item, and so on.

The following code illustrates how you can use the properties of the SPContext class to return the current list, site, site collection, and web application:

```
SPList currentList = SPContext.Current.List;
SPWeb currentWeb = SPContext.Current.Web;
SPSite currentSite = SPContext.Current.Site;
SPWebApplication currentWebApplication = SPContext.Current.Site.WebApplication;
```

Try It Yourself

Program with the SPContext Class

To better understand the role of the SPContext class, let's convert our ListRetrieverApp to ListRetriever web part. The ListRetrieverWebPart would list all the lists in the list collection of the current site. Earlier while developing ListRetrieverApp we passed site URL as a parameter to the DisplayAllLists function. In place of that we now use the SPContext class to get the information about the current site where the part is hosted and display all the lists in the list collection of that site.

1. Fire up Visual Studio, create a new Empty SharePoint Project, and add a new web part item to the project and name it ListRetrieverWebPart.

2. Add the following code snippet to the ListRetrieverWebPart class:

```
public class ListRetrieverWebPart : WebPart
{
    protected override void CreateChildControls()
    {
        // Get reference to current site
        SPWeb web = SPContext.Current.Web;

        this.DisplayAllLists(web);
    }

    public void DisplayAllLists(SPWeb web)
    {
        // Display Site Title
```

```
                        LiteralControl siteTitle = new LiteralControl(web.Title +
            "<br/>");
                        this.Controls.Add(siteTitle);

                        // Loop through the list collection and display the list title
                        foreach (SPList list in web.Lists)
                        {
                            LiteralControl listTitle =
                            new LiteralControl(list.Title + "<br/>");
                            this.Controls.Add(listTitle);
                        }
                    }
                }
```

In this code snippet, first we get a reference to the current site using the `SPContext.Current.Web` property and pass it on as a parameter to the `DisplayAllLists` function, which creates a `LiteralControl` for each list title and adds it to the controls collection of the web part.

3. Build and deploy the web part using Visual Studio.

Notice that when you add the web part onto the pages in different sites and navigate to the respective pages, the web part produces results (that is, list titles) specific to the particular site. This demonstrates the role of the `SPContext` class in furnishing server side code with the relevant context information.

Security Context and Security Elevation

The ListRetrieverWebPart runs under the security context of the authenticated user. This means that if you try to perform any operation in your server side code that the authenticated user is not authorized to perform, the user receives an Access Denied message. For example, if you create a `DisplayAllWebs` method (similar to `DisplayAllLists`) to list all the subsites under a given site, any user with read privileges (that is, added to your site's visitor group) receives an Access Denied message on navigating to a page hosting your web part. Visitor group users have permissions to enumerate through collection of lists in a site but not thorough collection of subsites, hence the access denied message. Let's discuss the `SPSecurity` class's `RunWithElevatedPrivileges` method to deal with this issue.

The `SPSecurity` class provides methods and properties for security management. By using the `RunWithElevatedPrivileges` method of this class, you can run a block of code in an application pool account context (which is typically the System Account). Because the `SPSecurity` class is not allowed in sandboxed code, sandboxed solutions don't support security elevation.

Understanding the Object Model in Relation to Server and Site Architecture

> **By the Way**
> While employing Security Elevation, the highest level of impersonation you can obtain is "impersonating the application pool account."

An important point to note while using the security elevation is that in the case we take reference of site object from the SPContext as shown in the following code, the associated security context will still be that of the current user.

```
// getting reference to the current site from SPContext won't work
// with elevated permissions
SPWeb site = SPContext.Current.Web;
```

Therefore, while employing security elevation we need to ensure that we create a new SPWeb instance from within the block of code that is to be executed inside the security elevated code block, as shown in the following code:

```
public void DisplayAllWebsElevatedSecurity()
    {
        // Get curent site collection and web ID
        Guid siteCollectionID = SPContext.Current.Site.ID;
        Guid webID = SPContext.Current.Web.ID;

        // Create new site collection and web objects
        using (SPSite newSite = new SPSite(siteCollectionID))
        {
            using (SPWeb newWeb = newSite.OpenWeb(webID))
            {
                // Display Site Title
                LiteralControl siteTitle =
                new LiteralControl(newWeb.Title + "<br/>");
                this.Controls.Add(siteTitle);

                // Loop through the webs collection and display the web title
                foreach (SPWeb web in newWeb.Webs)
                {
                    LiteralControl webTitle =
                    new LiteralControl(web.Title + "<br/>");
                    this.Controls.Add(webTitle);
                }
            }
        }
    }
```

This ensures that a new security context (that is, the application pool account) is loaded when the `DisplayAllWebs` method is called with security elevation. To call the previous method, you need to instantiate the `SPSecurity.CodeToRunElevated` delegate, pointing to the `DisplayAllWebsElevatedSecurity` method, as shown here:

```
SPSecurity.RunWithElevatedPrivileges(newSPSecurity.
➥CodeToRunElevated(DisplayAllWebsElevatedSecurity));
```

Build and deploy your web part again and navigate to the same page where a user with read permissions got an access denied error earlier. This time the code runs under the security context of the application pool account and therefore the user is not presented with an access denied screen.

> **Did You Know?**
>
> No matter how much confidence you have in your programming skills, it is always recommended to unit test your custom code by creating users with different set of privileges (administrator, contributor, visitor, and so on) and making your custom code execute in these different security contexts. This approach is useful for tracking improperly employed security elevation.

Allowing Unsafe Updates

When executing code with `RunWithElevatedPrivileges`, if you try to perform updates to SharePoint objects and the user does not have the privileges to do so, you receive a security exception. Even though your code block is executing with elevated permissions, still to perform updates you need to perform one additional task and that is setting the `AllowUnsafeUpdates` property to true. Setting this property to true allows your code to bypass security validation when making changes to SharePoint objects.

For example, consider a web part to upload images to a picture library. Recall that we developed such a web part (ImageUploaderWebPart) in Hour 5, "Working with Web Parts and Web Pages," when exploring web part development concepts. If a user with read permissions tries to upload an image to a picture library, he receives the following error, even when the block of code to upload file is executed with elevated privileges, as illustrated in Figure 7.6 as well:

The security validation for this page is invalid. Click Back in your Web browser, refresh the page, and try your operation again.

To fix this error, set the `AllowUnsafeUpdates` property of the related `SPWeb` object to true, as shown in the following code:

```
// Get root web reference
Guid rootWebID = SPContext.Current.Site.RootWeb.ID;
Guid siteID = SPContext.Current.Site.ID;
using (SPSite site = new SPSite(siteID))
{
    using (SPWeb rootWeb = site.OpenWeb(rootWebID))
    {
```

Understanding the Object Model in Relation to Server and Site Architecture

```
        // Get reference to MyPictureLibrary
        SPPictureLibrary myPictureLibrary =
rootWeb.GetList(this.PictureLibraryName) as SPPictureLibrary;

        // Get the FileBytes from the File Upload Control
        byte[] fileBytes = this.fileUpload.FileBytes;

        // Prepare destination Url and upload the file
        string fileName = Path.GetFileName(this.fileUpload.PostedFile.FileName);

        // Set Allow unsafe updates to true
        rootWeb.AllowUnsafeUpdates = true;

        SPFile file =
myPictureLibrary.RootFolder.Files.Add(fileName, fileBytes, true);
        file.Update();
        this.labelUploadResult.Text = "Upload Successful!";
    }
}
```

FIGURE 7.6
Security exception even when code is run with elevated permissions

The idea behind `AllowUnsafeUpdates` is to protect you from cross-site scripting attacks. There are basically two scenarios where you would need to fiddle with its value:

▶ In case of an HTTP POST request, when using `RunWithElevatedPrivileges` for a user not having sufficient privileges to make changes to SharePoint objects

▶ In case of an HTTP GET request, when performing any changes to SharePoint objects, **even for a user who has the required privileges** to perform the operation

Although it is generally recommended not to set `AllowUnsafeUpdates` to true, there are always exceptions. While the second scenario just presented should be avoided as much as possible (that is, strictly no updates in HTTP GET), the first scenario can be dealt with more gracefully. To understand how, have a look at the concept of form digest.

Form digest basically contains information about the previous request that has generated the postback. When processing an HTTP POST request always make sure that you call the `SPUtility.ValidateFormDigest` method before performing any operation. This ascertains that the POST request is validated (that is, not a cross-site scripting attack). Thereafter you don't need to worry about the value of

AllowUnsafeUpdates as it automatically is set to true once the form digest is validated.

To understand the second scenario, consider the following code to update the title of the current web when the ImageUploaderWebPart is loaded:

```
protected override void OnLoad(EventArgs e)
{
    SPWeb web = SPContext.Current.Site.RootWeb;
    web.Title = "New Title";
    web.Update();
}
```

While a user with read privileges will definitely receive an Access denied message when trying to perform the preceding operation, even a user having the required level of privileges to update the site title will receive the following error, asking for AllowUnsafeUpdates to be set to true, as shown in Figure 7.7.

FIGURE 7.7
Changes to SharePoint objects in HTTP GET require AllowUnsafeUpdates to be set to true

> Server Error in '/' Application.
>
> <nativehr>0x80004005</nativehr><nativestack></nativestack>Updates are currently disallowed on GET requests. To allow updates on a GET, set the 'AllowUnsafeUpdates' property on SPWeb.

The reason you get an error message on an HTTP GET request, even when having required privileges to perform the operation, is that changes to SharePoint objects in an HTTP GET request are considered unsafe. For example, in the case of a cross-site scripting attack, malicious code can redirect you to the page performing such an operation and you might unintentionally modify the site title or delete a list item. That is why the SharePoint security model prompts you to set the AllowUnsafeUpdates property to true and entrusts you, the developer, with the responsibility of ensuring the correctness of your action. There are scenarios in which you might want to do such a thing—for example, you want to log whenever a user accesses a particular web part. In such cases the AllowUnsafeUpdates allows you to perform such a task.

The ImageUploaderWebPart, in the code samples for this hour, highlights all the scenarios discussed previously. You can uncomment specific sections in the source code to better understand various topics discussed in this section.

Using Disposable Objects

When working with the SharePoint object model, one must be aware of the fact that the object model contains objects that implement the IDisposable interface. The Microsoft .NET Framework requires such objects to be explicitly disposed once you are finished using them.

Understanding the Object Model in Relation to Server and Site Architecture

> **Watch Out!**
> In case you fail to explicitly dispose the disposable objects, such objects might be retained for the long term in memory and might lead to issues like high memory consumption by the IIS worker process, frequent application pool recycling, and poor system performance.

As an example, both `SPWeb` and `SPSite` implement the IDisposable interface. So in your code, if you create a new instance of, say, the `SPSite` class, as shown here:

```
SPSite siteCollection = new SPSite("http://YourSiteCollection");
```

Then you must explicitly call the `Dispose` method on the object once you are done working with it, as follows:

```
// Disposing SPSite object instance after use
siteCollection.Dispose();
```

Another important point to note here is that in case your code throws an exception, the `Dispose` method might not actually get called. To ensure that the `Dispose` method is always called in such scenarios, either use a `try..finally` block or place the instant creation code inside a `using` block, as shown in the following code snippet:

```
try
{
    SPSite siteCollection = null;
    siteCollection = new SPSite("http://YourSiteCollection");
    // Your code to manipulate siteCollection object here
}
finally
{
    if (siteCollection != null)
    {
        // Dispose is always called even when
        // code in try block throws exception
        siteCollection.Dispose();
    }
}

// Compiler automatically generates required code to dispose the object
using (SPSite siteCollection = new SPSite("http://YourSiteCollection"))
{
    // Your code to manipulate siteCollection object here
}
```

As a general rule, you should ensure the proper disposal of objects created in your code. Do not try to dispose the objects obtained from the SharePoint context objects. For example, calling the `Dispose` method on an `SPWeb` object obtained using `SPContext.Current.Web` (as showing in the following code) should be avoided:

```
// Do not try to do this. SharePoint will manage such objects
SPWeb web = SPContext.Current.Web
web.Dispose()

// Do not place such objects in the using block as well
using (SPWeb web = SPContext.Current.Web)
{
}
```

Note that apart from explicitly creating objects using new keyword, calls to certain methods, for example, the SPSite class's OpenWeb method, can cause creation of new objects, which must be disposed as well in your code. For example, SPSite. AllWebs [] index operator creates a new SPWeb instance when accessed, which must be disposed properly in your code. The following code demonstrates this scenario:

```
using (SPSite siteCollection = new SPSite("http://YourSiteCollection"))
{
    // Creates a new SPWeb object, which must also be disposed
    SPWeb web = siteCollection.AllWebs[0];
}
using (SPSite siteCollection = new SPSite("http://YourSiteCollection"))
{
    // SPWeb object correctly disposed
    using (SPWeb web = siteCollection.AllWebs[0])
    {
    }
}
```

> **Did You Know?**
>
> The MSDN article http://msdn.microsoft.com/en-us/library/aa973248 (v=office.12).aspx describes some more best practices for working with disposable objects. Refer to this article to further understand common mistakes and best practices when working with SharePoint objects that implement the IDispose interface.

Working with the SharePoint Dispose Checker Tool

Knowing when to call the Dispose method on a particular object and when not to can be confusing. Fortunately, a tool called SPDisposeCheck comes to the rescue when you're in doubt. SPDisposeCheck analyzes your assemblies and validates them against known Microsoft dispose best practices. For more details on the SPDisposeCheck project, visit the http://code.msdn.microsoft.com/SPDisposeCheck site. You can choose to integrate the tool with Visual Studio by selecting the two options shown in Figure 7.8 at the time of installing the tool.

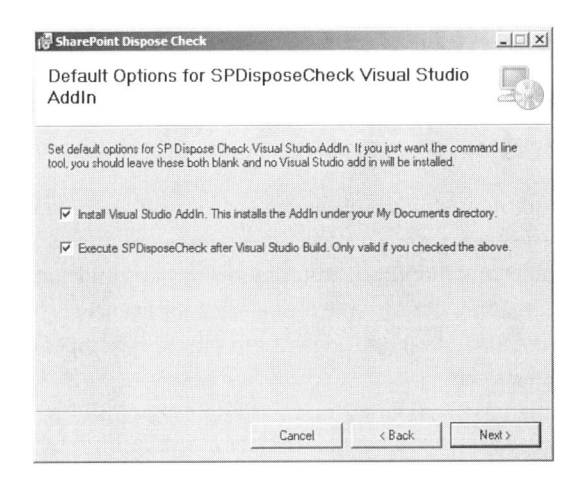

Understanding the Object Model in Relation to Server and Site Architecture 167

FIGURE 7.8 Integrating the SPDispose-Check tool with Visual Studio

You can also choose to run the tool from the command line. By default it is installed at C:\Program Files (x86)\Microsoft\SharePoint Dispose Check. You can fire up SPDisposeCheck.exe present at this location against your assemblies and analyze them for possible memory leaks.

For example, consider the following code. Clearly, we should be disposing the `siteCollection` and web objects, since they are created within our code.

```
// Would be flagged by the SPDisposeCheck tool for a possible memory leak
SPSite siteCollection = new SPSite("http://YourSiteCollection");
SPWeb web = siteCollection.OpenWeb();
```

As expected the `SPDisposeCheck` tool notifies you about the problem with the Disposable type not disposed error as shown in Figure 7.9.

FIGURE 7.9 The SPDispose-Check tool notifying about the "Disposable type not disposed" errors

As indicated in the error message as well, the tool's recommendations may not be correct in all scenarios. In spite of that it's a handy utility to have and you should also analyze your code from the same for possible memory leaks.

Troubleshooting and Monitoring Performance with the Developer Dashboard

Hour 3 talked about the usefulness of the developer dashboard for diagnosis and troubleshooting server side code. The developer dashboard provides a number of performance counters and diagnostic information sections and can be set up in few simple steps. This section looks at some of the advanced concepts related to the developer dashboard, including creating custom monitored scopes and working with performance counters.

Try It Yourself

Troubleshoot with the Developer Dashboard

1. Create a web part called DevDashBoardDemo to demonstrate some of the advanced debugging and monitoring features provided by the developer dashboard.

2. Add the following code to the web part:

   ```
   private void UsingDisposedObject()
   {
       SPList list = null;
       using (SPSite site = new SPSite("http://splearn"))
       {
           using (SPWeb web = site.RootWeb)
           {
               list = site.RootWeb.Lists[0];
           }
       }

       // Attempting to access the list title when
       // SPWeb and SPSite objects have been disposed
       string listTitle = list.Title;
   }
   ```

   Clearly, we are trying to get the list title, after the parent SPWeb and SPSite objects have been disposed.

3. Deploy the web part and enable the developer dashboard on the page.

4. Once the developer dashboard is enabled, we receive an Unexpected General error message in the Asserts and Critical Events section, as shown in Figure 7.10.

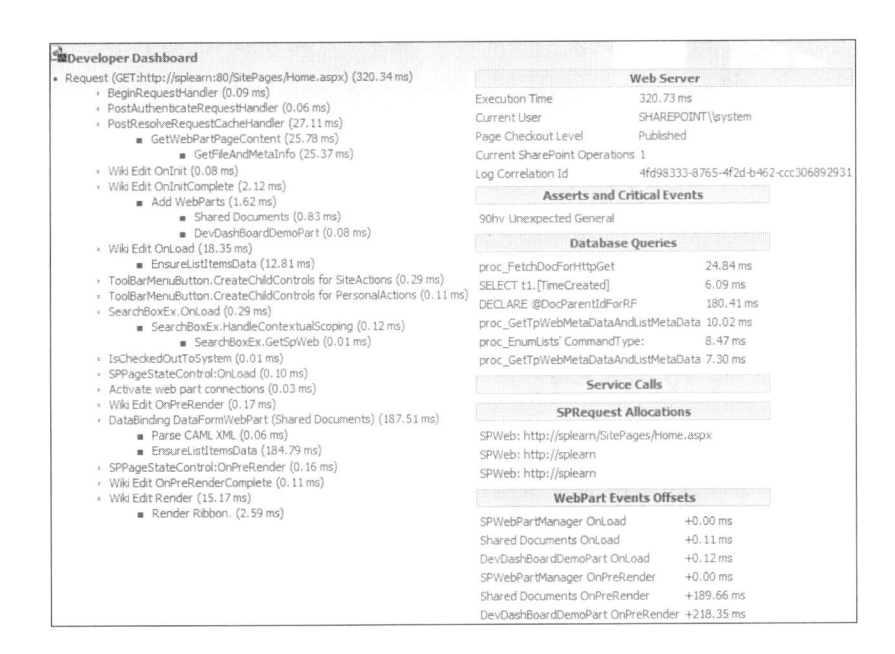

Troubleshooting and Monitoring Performance with the Developer Dashboard

FIGURE 7.10 Developer dashboard warning on accessing a disposed object

5. Click the error message to view more details, as illustrated in Figure 7.11. The detailed message *"Please close SPWeb objects when you are done with all objects obtained from them, but not before"* clearly indicates our attempt to get the list title after the parent SPWeb has been disposed.

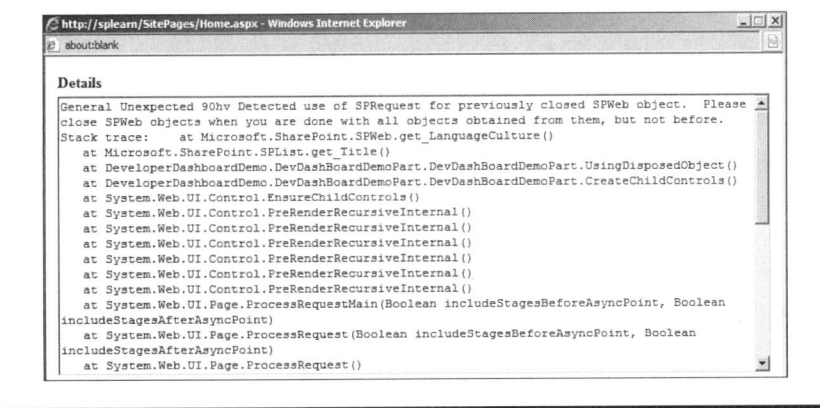

FIGURE 7.11 Detailed error message on accessing a disposed object

Next let's look at a common scenario, where as a developer you want to monitor usage statistics for your code to determine any performance bottlenecks. SharePoint 2010 introduces the SPMonitoredScope class to assist you with this.

HOUR 7: Understanding SharePoint 2010 Server Side Development

Using the SPMonitoredScope class you can create your own monitored scopes to get usage statistics and performance counters for your custom code. All you need to do is wrap the section of code to be monitored in an SPMonitoredScope block, as shown in the following code:

```
// Using SPMonitoredScope to monitor performance
using (SPMonitoredScope monitoredScope =
new SPMonitoredScope("My Monitored Scope"))
{
    TimeConsumingOperation();
}
```

Redeploy the web part and examine the developer dashboard contents. You should now have the My Monitored Scope being displayed on the dashboard, as shown in Figure 7.12.

FIGURE 7.12
Creating a custom monitored scope

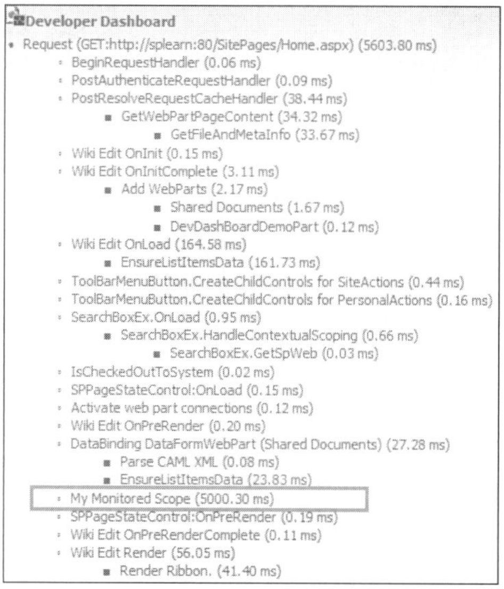

There are a number of performance counters that you can use with the SPMonitoredScope class to measure execution time (via the SPExecutionTimeCounter class), number of SPRequest objects (via the SPRequestUsageCounter class), and the number of SharePoint SQL Server queries (via the SPSqlQueryCounter class).

For example, the following code uses the SPExecutionTimeCounter class to display a critical message to the user if the TimeConsumingOperation takes more than 2 seconds to execute:

Troubleshooting and Monitoring Performance with the Developer Dashboard

```
// Using SPMonitoredScope to monitor performance with performance counters
SPExecutionTimeCounter timeCounter = new SPExecutionTimeCounter(2000);
using (SPMonitoredScope monitoredScope =
       new SPMonitoredScope("My Monitored Scope", 2000, timeCounter))
{
    TimeConsumingOperation();

    if (timeCounter.ValueIsExcessive)
    {
        string message = String.Format(
                    "Operation TimeConsumingOperation"+
                    "expected to take {0}ms time"+
                    "took {1}ms time.",
                        timeCounter.MaximumValue,
                        timeCounter.Value);

        SPCriticalTraceCounter.AddDataToScope(
                        1,
                        "Performance Monitoring",
                        1,
                        message);
    }
}
```

Since the `TimeConsumingOperation` takes around 5 seconds to execute, the developer dashboard displays the Critical Performance Monitoring message in the Asserts and Critical Events section, as shown in Figure 7.13.

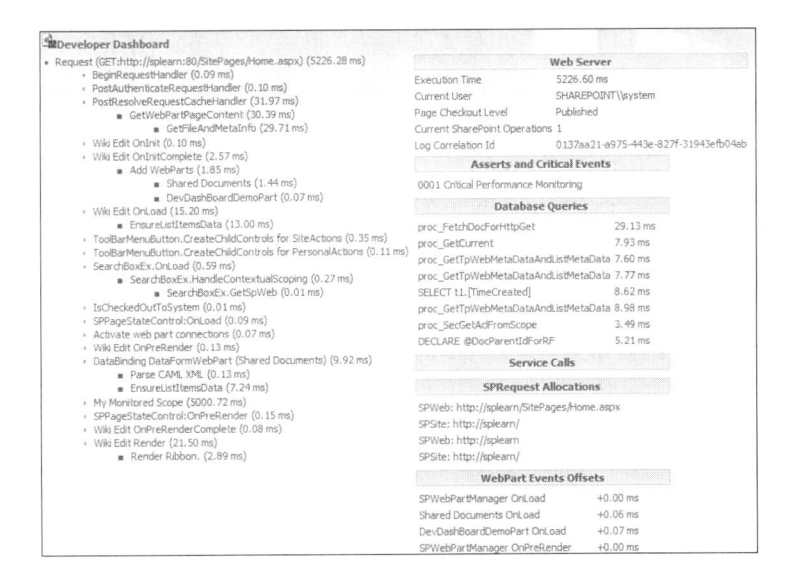

FIGURE 7.13 Using performance counters

On clicking the Critical Performance Monitoring message, you get further details related to the event, as shown in Figure 7.14.

FIGURE 7.14
Logging to the developer dashboard using the `SPCritical TraceCounter. AddDataTo Scope` method

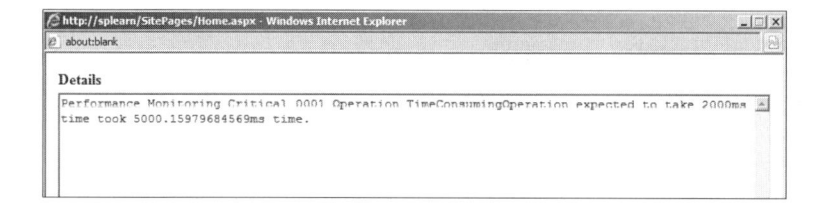

To write the performance monitoring related information to the developer dashboard's Asserts and Critical Events section, we use the `SPCriticalTraceCounter` class's `AddDataToScope` method in the preceding code. The method requires a `TagID`, `Category`, `TraceLevel`, and `Message` as parameters.

> **By the Way**
>
> `SPMonitoredScope` does not work with sandboxed solutions. Even if you try to use the `SPMonitoredScope` in a sandboxed solution, no related information or statistics will appear in the developer dashboard.

Creating a Custom Timer Job

So far you have explored the core classes of the object model either by developing console applications or by developing custom web parts. This section discusses another interesting topic in SharePoint server side development—developing a custom timer job.

Timer jobs are primarily used to run scheduled workloads, for example, performing some custom housekeeping activity in a SharePoint site or sending out daily or weekly email notifications to users based on certain business rules. In such a scenario you can create a timer job and schedule it to run accordingly.

▼ **Try It Yourself**

Create a Custom Timer Job

Let's create a new timer job to add a new announcement to the Announcements list of the top level site in a site collection. We will schedule the job to run every 5 minutes and populate the Announcements list with new announcements in the format shown in Figure 7.15.

Creating a Custom Timer Job 173

FIGURE 7.15
Creating announcements with a custom timer job

1. Fire up Visual Studio and create a new empty SharePoint project.

2. Add a new class called `TimerJobDemo` in the project.

3. To create a timer job definition, you inherit the `TimerJobDemo` class from the `SPJobDefinition` class and override its `Execute` method to specify a set of actions to perform when the job is executed, as demonstrated in the following code:

```
public override void Execute(Guid targetInstanceId)
{
    // Get reference to web application
    SPWebApplication webApp = this.Parent as SPWebApplication;

    if (webApp != null && webApp.Sites.Count != 0)
    {
        // Get reference to root web of the
        // first site collection in the web application
        SPWeb web = webApp.Sites[0].RootWeb;

        // Get reference to the announcements list
        SPList announcements = web.Lists["Announcements"];

        // App new announcement to the list
        SPListItem newAnnouncement = announcements.AddItem();
        newAnnouncement["Title"] =
        "New Announcement, creation time: " +
        DateTime.Now.ToShortTimeString();
        newAnnouncement.Update();
    }
}
```

In the preceding code, we get a reference to the root web of the first site collection in the web application and add a new announcement to the same.

4. Further, the job definition should be associated either with a web application or with a service. In our case, we would associate it with a web application. This requires creating a constructor to accept the `SPWebApplication` object as a parameter, as demonstrated in the following code snippet.

```
public TimerJobDemo(SPWebApplication webApp)
    : base("TimerJobDemo", webApp, null, SPJobLockType.None)
{
}
```

By the Way

> Don't forget to include a default constructor in your timer job class; otherwise, you end up with the error *"TimerJobDemo cannot be deserialized because it does not have a public default constructor."* when activating the feature that installs the job.

5. To deploy this timer job, we create a Web Application scoped feature and add event receivers to handle the FeatureActivated and FeatureDeactivating events. In the FeatureActivated event, we instantiate the TimeJobDemo class and create a schedule to run it after 5 minutes at any time between 0th and 59th second of the minute, as shown in the following code:

```
public override void FeatureActivated(SPFeatureReceiverProperties properties)
{
    SPWebApplication webApp = properties.Feature.Parent as SPWebApplication;

    // Create the timer job
    TimerJobDemo timerJob = new TimerJobDemo(webApp);

    // Schedule it to run after 5 minutes at any time
    // between 0th and 59th second of the minute
    SPMinuteSchedule schedule = new SPMinuteSchedule();
    schedule.BeginSecond = 0;
    schedule.EndSecond = 59;
    schedule.Interval = 5;
    timerJob.Schedule = schedule;
    timerJob.Update();
}
```

6. In the FeatureDeactivating event, we loop through the web application's job definitions and delete the timer job from the same, as shown in the following code:

```
public override void FeatureDeactivating(SPFeatureReceiverProperties properties)
{
    // Delete the timer job
    SPWebApplication webApp = properties.Feature.Parent as SPWebApplication;
    foreach (SPJobDefinition job in webApp.JobDefinitions)
    {
        if (job.Name == "TimerJobDemo")
        {
            job.Delete();
            break;
        }
    }
}
```

Creating a Custom Timer Job   175

> **Did You Know?**
> When deploying the solution through Visual Studio, it is better to set the Activate on Default property to false, as shown in Figure 7.16. Otherwise, the timer job would be activated by default for all the web applications.

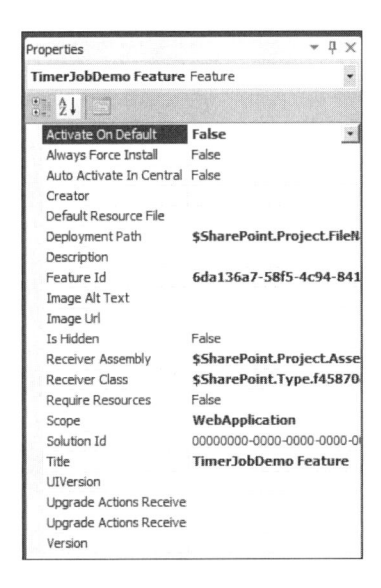

FIGURE 7.16
Setting the Activate on Default property to false

7. Next deploy the feature, navigate to Central Administration, and activate the TimerJobDemo feature for your web application. Once the feature is activated and the timer job starts running, you should see the timer job in the Job Definitions screen for your web application in Central Administration, as shown in Figure 7.17.

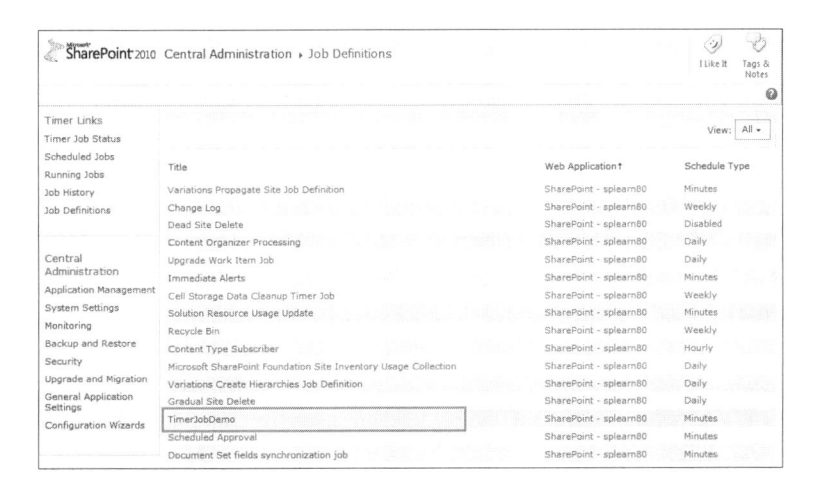

FIGURE 7.17
Examining the TimerJobDemo's job definition in Central Administration

HOUR 7: Understanding SharePoint 2010 Server Side Development

8. Click the timer job and further verify that the job has been scheduled to run after an interval of 5 minutes, as shown in Figure 7.18.

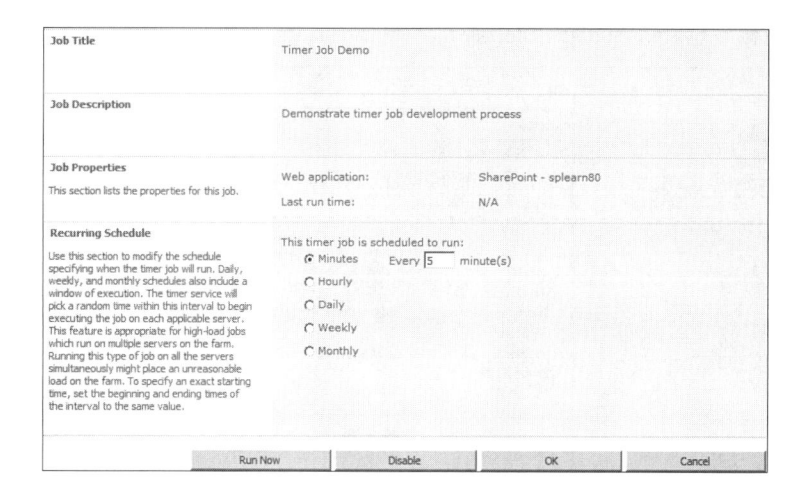

FIGURE 7.18
Verifying the TimerJobDemo's schedule

> **Did You Know?**
>
> At certain times on redeploying your source code for an already existing timer job, you may find that your changes are not getting reflected. To resolve the issue you can restart the Timer Service from the Windows Services Management console (services.msc).

Modifying the web.config with SPWebConfigModifications

Recall that in Hour 5, in the discussion on the delegate controls, you had to register your custom sitemap provider by putting the following entry in the providers section of the web.config:

```
<add name="CustomSiteMapProvider"
siteMapFile="_layouts/DelegateControlDemo/custom.sitemap"
type="Microsoft.SharePoint.Navigation.SPXmlContentMapProvider,
Microsoft.SharePoint, Version=14.0.0.0,
Culture=neutral, PublicKeyToken=71e9bce111e9429c" />
```

At that time you did this manually, and it might just work quite well in a development environment. But imagine in a production environment, where you have more than one WFEs (Web Front Ends), you would end up modifying manually

Modifying the web.config with SPWebConfigModifications

web.config on the web front end. Fortunately the `SPWebConfigModifications` class comes to the rescue.

The `SPWebConfigModification` class helps you to define modifications to web.config that can then be applied by calling the `ApplyWebConfigModifications` method on the current content web service object. To demonstrate the use of the `SPWebConfigModification` class and the `ApplyWebConfigModifications` let's create a web application scoped feature that on activation adds the previous custom sitemap provider into the web application's web.config and on deactivation, removes the previous entry.

The following code segment illustrates this process. As shown, we create the `SPWebConfigModification` class's object, get a reference to the current content web service, and apply the modifications to the same by calling the ApplyWebConfigModifications method:

```
public override void FeatureActivated(SPFeatureReceiverProperties properties)
{
    SPWebApplication webApp = properties.Feature.Parent as SPWebApplication;
    SPWebService webService = webApp.WebService;

    // Create new modification
    SPWebConfigModification myModification = new SPWebConfigModification();
    myModification.Path = "configuration/system.web/siteMap/providers";
    myModification.Name = "add[@name='CustomSiteMapProvider'][@siteMapFile="+
"'_layouts/DelegateControlDemo/custom.sitemap'] "+
" [@type='Microsoft.SharePoint.Navigation.SPXmlContentMapProvider, "+
"Microsoft.SharePoint, Version=14.0.0.0, Culture=neutral, "+
"PublicKeyToken=71e9bce111e9429c']";
    myModification.Sequence = 0;
    myModification.Owner = properties.Feature.DefinitionId.ToString();
    myModification.Type = SPWebConfigModification.SPWebConfigModificationType.
➥EnsureChildNode;
    myModification.Value = "<add name='CustomSiteMapProvider'"+
"siteMapFile='_layouts/DelegateControlDemo/custom.sitemap'"+
"type='Microsoft.SharePoint.Navigation.SPXmlContentMapProvider,"+
"Microsoft.SharePoint, Version=14.0.0.0, Culture=neutral, "+
"PublicKeyToken=71e9bce111e9429c' />";

    // Add the modification and save the changes
    webService.WebConfigModifications.Add(myModification);
    webService.Update();
    webService.ApplyWebConfigModifications();
}
```

We track the modification, by assigning our feature's definition id as the owner of the modification. On feature deactivation, we loop through all the modification objects and get the one modified by our feature. Finally we call the `ApplyWebConfig Modifications` method to save the changes, as demonstrated in the following code sample:

```
public override void FeatureDeactivating(SPFeatureReceiverProperties properties)
{
    SPWebConfigModification modificationFound = null;
    SPWebApplication webApp = properties.Feature.Parent as SPWebApplication;
    SPWebService webService = webApp.WebService;
    Collection<SPWebConfigModification>
    modificationCollection =
    webService.WebConfigModifications;

    // Find the modification by owner
    foreach (SPWebConfigModification modification in modificationCollection)
    {
        if (modification.Owner == properties.Feature.DefinitionId.ToString())
        {
            modificationFound = modification;
            break;
        }
    }

    // Remove the modification and save the changes
    webService.WebConfigModifications.Remove(modificationFound);
    webService.Update();
    webService.ApplyWebConfigModifications();
}
```

> **Watch Out!**
>
> When deploying your web application scoped feature through Visual Studio, it is better to set the Activate on Default property to false to prevent the feature from being activated for all the web applications. Otherwise, the feature would get activated on all the web applications and modify each web application's web.config file.

Further, note that the modifications done using the preceding methodology are persisted in the configuration database, and on call to the `SPWebService.ApplyWeb ConfigModifications` these changes become effective. For example, the owner related information that we are using in the preceding example to track the modifications by owner will not be present in the web.config itself and would be maintained in the configuration database. Due to this reason, manual modifications to the web.config should be avoided as these will not be persisted in the configuration database and application of a Service Pack might actually wipe these out.

Understanding the Event Receivers

Event receivers, as the name suggests, allow you to subscribe and respond to events that occur to SharePoint items such as sites, lists, list items, and so on. For example, you may want to send out a notification when a new site is provisioned or prevent deletion of a list item based on certain conditions. Event receivers help you to achieve just that, by enabling your code to subscribe to various events and then responding accordingly.

Hour 11, "Understanding Advanced Data Management Concepts in SharePoint 2010," looks at event receivers for lists and list items. This section explores event receivers associated with sites in more detail.

Consider a scenario where you want to log information about every newly provisioned site and disallow users to delete a site. To deal with the scenarios, create a new Event Receiver project or create an Empty SharePoint Project and add then an event receiver project item.

Choose to handle the Web Events and select the A Site Is Being Deleted and A Site Was Provisioned events, as shown in Figure 7.19.

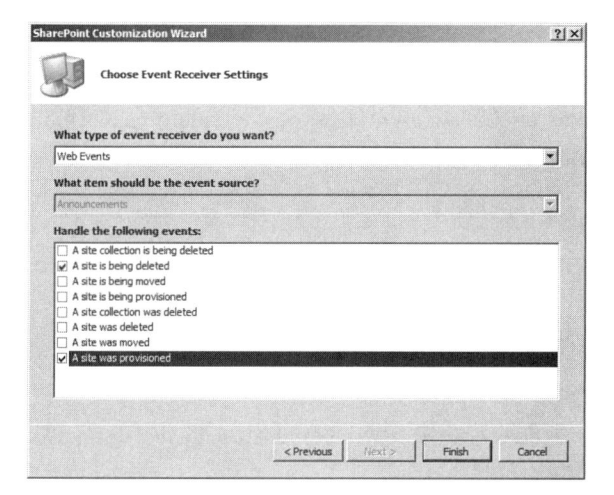

FIGURE 7.19
Creating an Event Receiver project

A Site Is Being Deleted event is called at the time of site deletion but before the actual site deletion, so that you have the option of programmatically cancelling the deletion request. A Site Was Provisioned is called after a new site has been created. In case you have a requirement to cancel the site creation based on some criteria, you should be handling the A Site Is Being Provisioned event instead.

Now look at the code you need to put into the A Site Was Provisioned event receiver:

```
public override void WebProvisioned(SPWebEventProperties properties)
{
    // Get reference to current web and the root web
    SPWeb currentWeb = properties.Web;
    SPWeb rootWeb =currentWeb.Site.RootWeb;
```

HOUR 7: Understanding SharePoint 2010 Server Side Development

```
    // Get reference to the SiteProvisioningTrackerList
    SPList list = rootWeb.GetList("/Lists/SiteProvisioningTracker");

    // Create a new list item and update its titile
    SPListItem listItem = list.AddItem();
    listItem["Title"] = "Web Provisioned: " + properties.Web.Title;
    listItem.Update();

    // Activate our EventReceiverDemoFeature in the newly provisioned site
    currentWeb.Features.Add(new Guid("{c5c61302-6296-4c9c-ad77-130b5af56407}"));
    currentWeb.Update();
}
```

As demonstrated previously, we get a reference to the root web and add a new list item in the SiteProvisioningTracker list indicating the provisioning of a new site. Further, note that we are deploying the event receivers via site scoped feature. Hence we activate the feature in the newly provisioned site as well by calling the Features.Add method and passing the ID of our feature to the same as a parameter.

The preceding code results in the entries shown in Figure 7.20 being made in the SiteProvisioningTracker list:

FIGURE 7.20
Logging site provisioning information to a list

Next examine the code we need to write to disable site deletion and also display the appropriate error message to the user:

```
public override void WebDeleting(SPWebEventProperties properties)
{
    // Prevent site deletion and throw "Site deletion is not Allowed." error
    // message to the user trying to delete the site
    properties.Status = SPEventReceiverStatus.CancelWithError;
    properties.ErrorMessage = "Site deletion is not Allowed.";
    properties.Cancel = true;
}
```

Now whenever an end user tries to delete a site that has our feature activated, she receives the error message as shown in Figure 7.21.

Thus you can see that event receivers make it convenient to plug in our custom code and respond to various events that occur to SharePoint items.

FIGURE 7.21
Preventing site deletion

Summary

This hour explored various features offered by SharePoint's server side object model. You looked at different tools that can be used to explore the object model and also the functionality offered by core classes (`SPFarm`, `SPServer`, `SPSPContext`, `SPSite`, `SPWeb`, `SPList`, and so on) in Microsoft.SharePoint assembly. You learned the importance of explicitly disposing the objects implementing the IDisposable interface and how system administrators and developers can use the developer dashboard for diagnosis and troubleshooting the server side code. Finally, the hour concluded by exploring the development steps involved in creating a custom timer job, modifying web.config, and programming event receivers.

Q&A

Q. Can I use SharePoint Manager to modify object properties?

A. Although SharePoint Manager is a handy tool and allows modification of certain object properties as well, this should generally be avoided. Always go via Central Administration or site settings for any modifications or configuration changes. It is easy to mess up your SharePoint installation via random and unplanned updates done using SharePoint Manager.

Q. Can I keep the AllowUnsafeUpdates always set to true to tackle any access related errors?

A. The idea behind AllowUnsafeUpdates is to protect you from cross-site scripting attacks. While at times it is lucrative to set it to true to escape debugging any access related errors, doing so would expose you to XSS attacks. Therefore, enable unsafe updates very selectively and only under exceptional circumstances.

Q. *Why do I have to worry about disposing objects when Garbage Collector is there to work for me?*

A. Although garbage collection will definitely set in at some stage to destroy the objects no longer in use, this will cause the unused objects to be retained for the long term in memory, leading to poor system performance. Therefore, as a best practice try to explicitly call `Dispose` on disposable objects to free up unmanaged resources as soon as possible after use and also to indicate an object's availability for garbage collection.

Q. *I was able to get the WebProvisioned event receiver working, but the WebDeleting event receiver refuses to trigger. Did I miss something?*

A. When provisioning a new subsite, the web provisioned event receiver for the current site gets triggered as expected. However, now when you try to delete the subsite, it is the subsite's web deleting event receiver that is triggered and not the parent site one. Hence you should reassociate your event receiver with every newly provisioned site for this to work. In our discussion on event receivers we try to achieve this by activating the feature responsible for event receiver registration for every newly provisioned site, which does the trick.

HOUR 8

Understanding Client Object Model in SharePoint 2010

What You'll Learn in This Hour:

▶ Understanding client object model fundamentals
▶ Exploring context in client object model
▶ Exploring the JavaScript client object model

> Due to the complexity of the topics discussed, some figures in this book are very detailed and are intended only to provide a high-level view of concepts. Those figures are representational and not intended to be read in detail.

By the Way

SharePoint has always had a great server side object model. But the server side object model was never adequate to address the needs of the emerging trend of rich Internet applications. Web applications are becoming more and more sophisticated all the time. Each user interaction in Microsoft Office SharePoint Server (MOSS) was followed by a postback, which is really annoying to the end user. Prior to SharePoint 2010, client side functionality was achieved by out of the box web services provided by SharePoint. But these were never complete, and each time a new functionality was needed, developers were required to create custom web services that used server side objects internally. Another concern for SharePoint developers was they had to install SharePoint on a server operating system to start learning or developing applications in SharePoint. Having to get a licensed version of a server operating system such as Win2k3 largely limited the number of people who could play around with SharePoint.

But enough about the limitations of previous versions of SharePoint. This hour delves into what's available as part of SharePoint 2010 to address the issues just mentioned.

Understanding Client Object Model Fundamentals

The client object model introduced as part of SharePoint 2010 enables users to build solutions that can consume SharePoint data and objects from applications that do not run on a SharePoint server. These applications can be anything ranging from simple websites using AJAX/Silverlight to Windows Presentation Foundation (WPF) applications. You can use the client object model for developing the following:

- .NET applications
- ECMAScript client
- Silverlight applications
- WPF applications

There are three different client object models:

- Managed model
- JavaScript model
- Silverlight model

This hour covers the first two models. A separate hour, Hour 9, "Creating Silverlight User Interfaces for SharePoint 2010 Solutions," is dedicated to Silverlight integration with SharePoint 2010.

Figure 8.1 shows the architecture of the client object model.

The architecture for enabling communication between the client object model and the SharePoint content database is provided through a WCF service called Client.svc located in the ISAPI directory. The client object model batches the operations as an XML request and calls the Client.svc. Once the XML request from the client is received, Client.svc uses the server object model to retrieve relevant information from the SharePoint content database, and the results obtained are returned to the client as JavaScript Object Notation (JSON).

The client object model is actually a set of several different assemblies that provide the same functionalities for different types of applications. You refer to the appropriate assemblies in an application based on the application type you are developing. For developing Windows Forms applications or WPF applications, you use Microsoft.SharePoint.Client.dll and Microsoft.SharePoint.ClientRuntime.dll. For Silverlight applications you use Microsoft.SharePoint.Client.Silverlight.dll and

Understanding Client Object Model Fundamentals

Microsoft.SharePoint.Client.Silverlight.Runtime.dll. For invoking the client object model through JavaScript you have to add the SP.js file. Table 8.1 shows where each client object model is located.

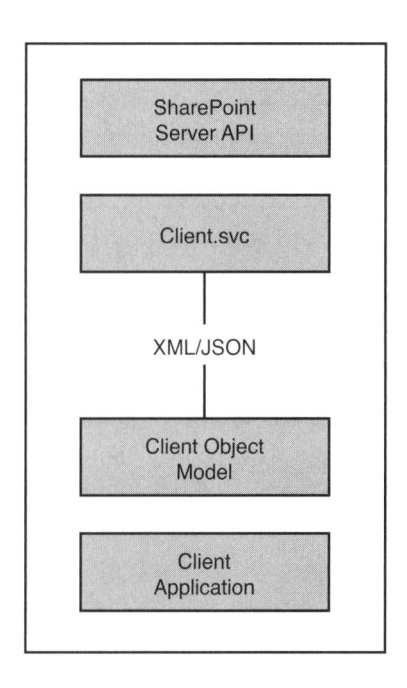

FIGURE 8.1 Client object model architecture

TABLE 8.1 SharePoint DLL Locations for Client Side API

Model	Library	Location (Folder)
Managed	Microsoft.SharePoint.Client.dll Microsoft.SharePoint.ClientRuntime.dll	ISAPI
Silverlight	Microsoft.SharePoint.Client.Silverlight.dll Microsoft.SharePoint.Client.Silverlight.Runtime.dll	Layouts\ClientBin
JavaScript	SP.js	Layouts

The client object model mimics the majority of the functionalities available as part of the server side API. While developing the client object model, Microsoft also had to keep in mind that it should resemble the server side API as closely as possible. This would help developers have an easier learning curve. Table 8.2 makes it clear how the client object model is similar to server APIs.

TABLE 8.2 Mapping of Client Side Classes to Server Side Classes

Server Model	Client Model
SPContext	ClientContext
SPSite	Site
SPWeb	Web
SPList	List
SPListItem	ListItem
SPField	Field

Exploring Context in Client Object Model

The process of communicating with the SharePoint server from the client side starts through the `ClientContext` class, which inherits from `ClientRuntimeContext`. This class provides the capability to control the communication with the SharePoint server. You can specify the following while accessing the SharePoint server:

- URL
- Site
- Web
- Authentication Mode
- Credentials

This hour does not delve into the authentication mode and credentials now as this is outside the scope of this book. For now, just remember that you can use forms authentication as well to access the SharePoint site, and the client object model provides the means to pass the credentials as well.

Try It Yourself

Retrieve Site Title Through Client Side Object Model

To understand things better, let's get started with our first sample application. This example creates a console application to print the title of the SharePoint site. Make sure that you add the references to Microsoft.SharePoint.Client.dll and Microsoft.SharePoint.ClientRuntime.dll in the newly created console application.

```
using System;
using System.Collections.Generic;
using System.Linq;
using System.Text;
using Microsoft.SharePoint.Client;

namespace ClientOMSample
{
    class Program
    {
        static void Main(string[] args)
        {
            using (ClientContext context = new ClientContext(@"http://splearn"))
            {
                Web web = context.Web;
                context.Load(web);
                context.ExecuteQuery();
                Console.WriteLine("Title :" + web.Title);
                Console.Read();
            }
        }
    }
}
```

Now if you run the preceding example, you see the title of your website. But as you have noticed by now, the code is little different from server side code. The main things to notice here are the `Load()` method and the `ExecuteQuery()` method. These two methods of `ClientContext` are responsible for bringing the data from the server to the client side.

Understanding the Role of the `Load()` Method

In this method you specify in which objects you are interested. Suppose if you want to load the `List`, you can just specify the name of the list you want. The main advantage of this is that specifying only the items you are interested in helps reduce network traffic. Generally the `Load()` method returns simple references to types, and not the whole object. If you try to access the child objects right now, you get a `PropertyOrFieldNotInitializedException`. If you need access to those, you have to mention those explicitly in your `Load()` method. Each time you call the `Load()` method, it adds one more query to the batch. Another interesting point is it's not necessary for you to load the parent first to gain access to the child nodes. You take a look into this in the next example.

Now in the previous example comment the `context.ExecuteQuery()` and run the application. You get a `PropertyOrFieldNotInitializedException`. You might be thinking we had mentioned exactly what to load, but why is it throwing an exception? This is where `ExecuteQuery` comes into the picture.

Exploring the `ExecuteQuery()` Method

As mentioned earlier, even though you mentioned the items to load in the `Load()` method, it doesn't load until you explicitly call the `ExecuteQuery()` method. This method is responsible for calling the Client.svc with the current batch mentioned earlier in the `Load()` method. This method can also be used to commit the changes back to the server once you have made changes to the client side as well.

Now that you understand the functionality of both `Load()` and `ExecuteQuery()`, let's take a look into a slightly more complex example. This example uses a list named Books that is available under http://splearn. So before running this example, create a list named Books under splearn. This example tries to load fields in a list from SharePoint without actually loading the web object or the complete list object. This helps you understand how efficient the `Load()` method is.

```
using (ClientContext context = new ClientContext(@"http://splearn"))
{
    Web web = context.Web;
    List books = web.Lists.GetByTitle("Books");
    context.Load(books.Fields);
    context.ExecuteQuery();
    FieldCollection collection = books.Fields;
    Console.WriteLine(collection[0].InternalName);
    //Console.WriteLine(books.ItemCount);
    Console.Read();
}
```

Now as you saw in the previous example, you can access the fields of the list without actually loading the complete web object or the list object. This is achieved by mentioning specifically what to load in the `Load()` method. As we mentioned just the list to load in the `Load()` method, just the list and nothing related to the web object is loaded. To prove this, let's uncomment the code in the preceding example and execute the application.

```
using (ClientContext context = new ClientContext(@"http://splearn"))
{
    Web web = context.Web;
    List books = web.Lists.GetByTitle("Books");
    context.Load(books.Fields);
    context.ExecuteQuery();
    FieldCollection collection = books.Fields;
    Console.WriteLine(collection[0].InternalName);
    Console.WriteLine(books.ItemCount);
    Console.Read();
}
```

We get the `PropertyOrFieldNotInitializedException` because we specifically mentioned the fields to be loaded.

Using Lambda Expressions

If you noticed the signature of the Load() method by now, it should not come as a surprise that you can specify a lambda expression as part of the Load() method. Take a quick look into the following sample application:

```
using (ClientContext context = new ClientContext(@"http://splearn"))
{
    Web web = context.Web;
    List books = web.Lists.GetByTitle("Books");
    context.Load(books, x => x.Title);
    context.ExecuteQuery();
    Console.WriteLine(books.Title);
    //Console.WriteLine(books.Description);
    Console.Read();
}
```

As you can see, the ExecuteQuery() method loads only the items mentioned in the lambda expression. If you uncomment the code and try to access the description of the list, you get a PropertyOrFieldNotInitializedException as you haven't mentioned Description in the lambda expression.

Understanding the LoadQuery() Method

LoadQuery() is an alternative to the Load() method in the SharePoint 2010 client model. Sometimes it may not be easy to mention the items to load in the Load() method. In that case, you can create a query and pass it as a parameter to the LoadQuery() method.

> **By the Way**
>
> A notable difference between Load() and LoadQuery() is that Load() returns a collection of objects, whereas LoadQuery() returns an IEnumerable<T>.

```
using (ClientContext context = new ClientContext(@"http://splearn"))
{
    Web web = context.Web;
    IEnumerable<List> genericLists = context.LoadQuery(web.Lists.Where(
        list => list.BaseType == BaseType.GenericList));

    context.ExecuteQuery();
    foreach (List list in genericLists)
    {
        Console.WriteLine(list.Title);
    }
    Console.Read();
}
```

As seen in the preceding code, the query is much easier to read. Remember, you still have to use the `ExecuteQuery()` method to load the items mentioned in the query.

Creating, Updating, and Deleting Data Using the Client Object Model

You can use the client object model to insert data into SharePoint as well. The following example creates a new item in SharePoint and adds a new `ListItem` to the list:

```
using (ClientContext context = new ClientContext(@"http://splearn"))
{
    //Create a new list
    ListCreationInformation newList = new ListCreationInformation();
    newList.Title = "New List";
    newList.Description += "A new list created with Managed Client OM";
    newList.TemplateType = (int)ListTemplateType.GenericList;
    List list = context.Web.Lists.Add(newList);
    context.ExecuteQuery();

    //Create a new list item
    ListItemCreationInformation newListItem = new
➥ListItemCreationInformation();
    ListItem item = list.AddItem(newListItem);
    item["Title"] = "New List Item";
    item.Update();
    context.ExecuteQuery();
}
```

For creating a new `List` and `ListItem` in SharePoint you have to use the `ListCreationInformation` and `ListItemCreationInformation` classes. As you can see the `Update()` method is used to update the changes made to the website. As in previous cases, you still have to call the `ExecuteQuery()` method to update the changes back to the SharePoint database. You can verify whether the new list got created by going to the SharePoint site.

The following code example illustrates how you can update a website's description and a list's description using the client object model:

```
using (ClientContext context = new ClientContext(@"http://splearn"))
{
    // Update Site Description
    Web web = context.Web;
    web.Description = "Learn SharePoint";
    web.Update();
    context.ExecuteQuery();
    Console.WriteLine(web.Description);
    Console.Read();

    // Update List Description
    List list = web.Lists.GetByTitle("Books");
    list.Description = "Updated Description";
```

```
    list.Update();
    context.ExecuteQuery();
    Console.WriteLine(list.Description);
    Console.Read();
}
```

> **By the Way**
> The most important thing to keep in mind here is you don't have to load the item you are updating into context.

The preceding example sets the Description of web first and then calls the Update(). But still this won't get reflected in the site until you call the ExecuteQuery() method.

For deleting data in SharePoint using the client object model, you use the DeleteObject() method. As in previous examples, call ExecuteQuery() to complete the deletion process:

```
using (ClientContext context = new ClientContext(@"http://splearn"))
{
    Web web = context.Web;
    List list = web.Lists.GetByTitle("ToDelete");
    list.DeleteObject();
    context.ExecuteQuery();
}
```

Understanding Exceptions

Because the client object model works in a disconnected way, error handling becomes all the more important. Table 8.3 depicts the various exceptions that can arise while working with the client object model.

TABLE 8.3 List of Exceptions Thrown by the Client Object Model

Exception	Reason
PropertyOrFieldNotInitializedException	Usually this arises when ExecuteQuery() is not called or you haven't mentioned the specific item in the Load() method.
InvalidQueryExpressionException	Query being passed as part of LoadQuery() is invalid.
ClientRequestException	Thrown when the operation fails at the client side.
ServerException	Thrown when the operation fails at the server side.

Exploring the JavaScript Client Object Model

Until now you have been working with the client object model for the managed applications. This section takes a look into the JavaScript client object model (referred to as ECMAScript from now on), which provides rich script-based programming support. You can greatly improve the user experience in SharePoint by integrating it with AJAX and the JavaScript client object model.

ECMAScript provides a lot more flexibility than the managed object model and Silverlight since it contains a larger set of libraries, which facilitates user interface development. The entirety of ECMAScript allows you to work on user interface elements of SharePoint as well. Using ECMAScript you can control the ribbon, the SharePoint dialogs, and so on, which is not possible with other variants of client object models. Using ECMAScript enables you to create SharePoint solutions that are browser agnostic. While working with ECMAScript, you will see several differences from the managed client model. This is mostly due to the programming conventions used in JavaScript.

> **By the Way**
>
> JavaScript does not support all the data types found in the .NET Framework.

Many files make up the ECMAScript library. They are

- SP.js
- SP.Runtime.js
- SP.Core.js
- SP.Ribbon.js
- SP.UI.js
- CUI.js
- SP.UI.Rte.js

Covering all these files is outside the scope of this book. To provide the functionalities similar to that of the managed object model, you must load the SP.js file.

Using the ECMAScript Library

For using ECMAScript, the hosting page should meet the following requirements:

- Register the `Microsoft.SharePoint.WebControls` namespace on the page. The pages created using the designer will already have the namespace registered:

  ```
  <%@ Register Tagprefix="SharePoint" Namespace="Microsoft.
  ➥SharePoint.WebControls"
  Assembly="Microsoft.SharePoint, Version=14.0.0.0, Culture=neutral,
  PublicKeyToken=71e9bce111e9429c" %>
  ```

- Reference the SP.js file. For pages created using the designer, the reference will be already available in the master page. If you need to add it explicitly, you can use the `ScriptLink` control, which is included in the `Microsoft.SharePoint.WebControls` namespace. Use the following code to add ScriptLink explicitly:

  ```
  <SharePoint:ScriptLink ID="SPScriptLink" runat="server" LoadAfterUI="true"
  Localizable="false" Name="sp.js" />
  ```

- If you plan to make any updates to the SharePoint resources using JavaScript, then make sure that you have a `FormDigest` control in the page. This control is also part of the `Microsoft.SharePoint.WebControls` namespace. This is also added as part of the default master page. To add explicitly, use the following code:

  ```
  <SharePoint:FormDigest runat="server" />
  ```

After all the preceding requirements are met, you are good to start using the ECMAScript library in your application.

Try It Yourself

Use the JavaScript API to Display the Site Title

Now look at a simple example to display the title of the website.

1. First open the site "splearn" in the SharePoint designer, navigate to Site Pages, and add a new page named TestECMAScript.aspx. Once created, add a link to the page.

   ```
   <a href="" onclick="getSiteTitle();return false;">Get Site Title</a>
   ```

2. To display the site title, use the following code:

   ```
   <script type="text/javascript">
       function getSiteTitle() {
   ```

HOUR 8: Understanding Client Object Model in SharePoint 2010

```
            var context = new SP.ClientContext.get_current();
            this.web = context.get_web();
            context.load(this.web);
            context.executeQueryAsync(Function.createDelegate(this,
➥this.onSuccess),
                Function.createDelegate(this, this.onFailure));
        }
        function onSuccess(sender, args) {
            alert('Success');
        }
        function onFailure(sender, args) {
            alert('Failure : ' + args.get_message());
        }
</script>
```

Into the preceding code, as in the managed model, the execution starts by creating a `ClientContext` object. Since the syntax of JavaScript is different from C#, you have to use `get_property()` to gain access to different objects and `set_property()` to update the objects. Here `get_web()` returns the current web. Then the `ClientContexts` load method is used to retrieve the web object. Finally we use the `executeQueryAsync` method by passing the handlers for both success and failure conditions. To display the title of the website, simply call the `getSiteTitle ()` method from anywhere in the page. It might be required that you use the JavaScript function during page loads.

> **Watch Out!**
>
> If the SP.js file is not loaded before the call to the library is made, the JavaScript code will fail. To address this problem, make sure that your JavaScript code runs only after the SP.js file is loaded. To achieve this, use the `ExecuteOrDelayUntilScriptLoaded` JavaScript function.
>
>   ExecuteOrDelayUntilScriptLoaded(getSiteTitle, "sp.js");
>
> Using this statement helps to delay the call to `getSiteTitle()` until the SP.js is completely loaded.

Programming for Add, Delete, and Update Using ECMAScript

To add an item to the list, use the `ListItemCreationInformation` object. After you set the corresponding properties using `set_item`, call the update and ExecureQueryAsync methods:

```
function addItem(title,author){
        var context = new SP.ClientContext.get_current();
        var lstBooks = context.get_web().get_lists().getByTitle('Books');
        var listItemCreationInfo = new SP.ListItemCreationInformation();
```

```
        var newItem = lstBooks.addItem(listItemCreationInfo);
        newItem.set_item('Title', title);
        newItem.set_item('Author', author);
        newItem.update();
    context.executeQueryAsync(Function.createDelegate(this, this.onSuccess),
            Function.createDelegate(this, this.onFailure));
}
```

To delete an item, use the `deleteObject` method:

```
function deleteItem(id) {
var context = new SP.ClientContext.get_current();
var lstBooks = context.get_web().get_lists().getByTitle('Books');
var itemToDelete = lstBooks.getItemById(id);
    itemToDelete.deleteObject();
context.executeQueryAsync(Function.createDelegate(this, this.onSuccess),
            Function.createDelegate(this, this.onFailure));
}
```

To update a resource in SharePoint using ECMAScript, use the `update()` method of the corresponding resource:

```
function updateListDescription(){
var context = new SP.ClientContext.get_current();
var lstBooks = context.get_web().get_lists().getByTitle("Books");
context.load(lstBooks);
lstBooks.set_description("Updated description using ECMAScript");
lstBooks.update();
context.executeQueryAsync(Function.createDelegate(this, this.onSuccess),
            Function.createDelegate(this, this.onFailure));
}
```

Summary

In this hour you learned how to create SharePoint applications using the client object model. By now you should be comfortable using this in various client applications and decide which one suits your needs the best. Client side technologies are more powerful than in earlier versions of SharePoint and should address most of your client requirements. In the next hour you learn how to use Silverlight with SharePoint.

Q&A

Q. *Can you still use web services in SharePoint 2010 in place of the client side API?*

A. Yes. You can still use the web services in SharePoint 2010. These are available in the _vti_bin virtual directory of your SharePoint website.

Q. *Can you use the JavaScript API in custom ASP.NET sites?*

A. The JavaScript API can be used only in SharePoint sites. You cannot use the JavaScript API to provide SharePoint functionalities in an ASP.NET site as this leads to cross-site scripting issues.

Q. *Can you use the JavaScript API to access SharePoint resources in another SharePoint Site?*

A. No. The JavaScript API cannot be used to access SharePoint resources in another SharePoint site. Suppose the script is running in site1.com, you cannot use the JavaScript API to access resources in site2.com.

HOUR 9

Creating Silverlight User Interfaces for SharePoint 2010 Solutions

What You'll Learn in This Hour:

- ▶ Introducing Silverlight
- ▶ Understanding Silverlight architecture
- ▶ Creating the Hello World Silverlight application
- ▶ Hosting the Silverlight application in SharePoint 2010
- ▶ Consuming Silverlight data in SharePoint 2010

> **By the Way**
> Due to the complexity of the topics discussed, some figures in this book are very detailed and are intended only to provide a high-level view of concepts. Those figures are representational and not intended to be read in detail.

Introducing Silverlight

Silverlight is a fast growing and powerful technology used to build rich Internet applications (RIA). For those new to the concept, RIAs are web applications with the features and functionality of traditional desktop applications. While traditional web applications consist of both server side and client side processing, server side processing is more dominant, and a typical website involves a lot of postbacks to the server. Even though there has been an effort to improve this experience through client side scripting and AJAX, the experience cannot be compared to a traditional desktop experience. Rich Internet applications move more of the processing, especially the rendering part, to the client side, thereby drastically reducing postbacks done to the server and vastly improving the user experience. Server side processing still occurs mostly in the form of calls to web/Windows Communication Foundation (WCF) services.

The following are the benefits of RIAs:

- Improved user experience
- Reduced load on server with more processing done on the client side
- Reduced network traffic

However, there are also some disadvantages of the RIAs:

- Need to download entire script/package first before the processing on the client side can start, which may cause a wait time for users
- Loss of ability for search engines to index content of RIAs
- Dependence on client system security to access system resources may cause the application to fail in case users have restricted the permissions on their system

Silverlight can be considered a subset of another Microsoft technology called as the Windows Presentation Framework (WPF). Microsoft created WPF as the next generation of user interface technology for desktop applications. WPF is based on vector graphics and user Extensible Application Markup Language (XAML), which is a form of XML. The earliest version of Silverlight is 1.0 and was first called WPF/E or Windows Presentation Framework/Everywhere.

Understanding Silverlight Architecture

The Silverlight platform consists of the components listed in Table 9.1.

TABLE 9.1 Silverlight Platform Components

Component	Description
Core presentation framework	Components and services for the user interface and user interaction, including user input, lightweight UI controls for use in web applications, media playback, digital rights management, data binding, and presentation features, including vector graphics, text, animation, and images. This also includes the Extensible Application Markup Language (XAML) for specifying layout.
.NET Framework for Silverlight	A set of APIs that is a subset of the .NET Framework. This framework contains components and libraries, including data integration, extensible Windows controls, networking, base class libraries, garbage collection, and the common language runtime (CLR).

Understanding Silverlight Architecture

TABLE 9.1 Continued

Component	Description
Installer and updater	An installation and update control that simplifies the process of installing the application for first-time users and subsequently provides low-impact, automatic updates.

Figure 9.1 represents the architecture of Silverlight as per the MSDN and depicts all the components described in Table 9.1.

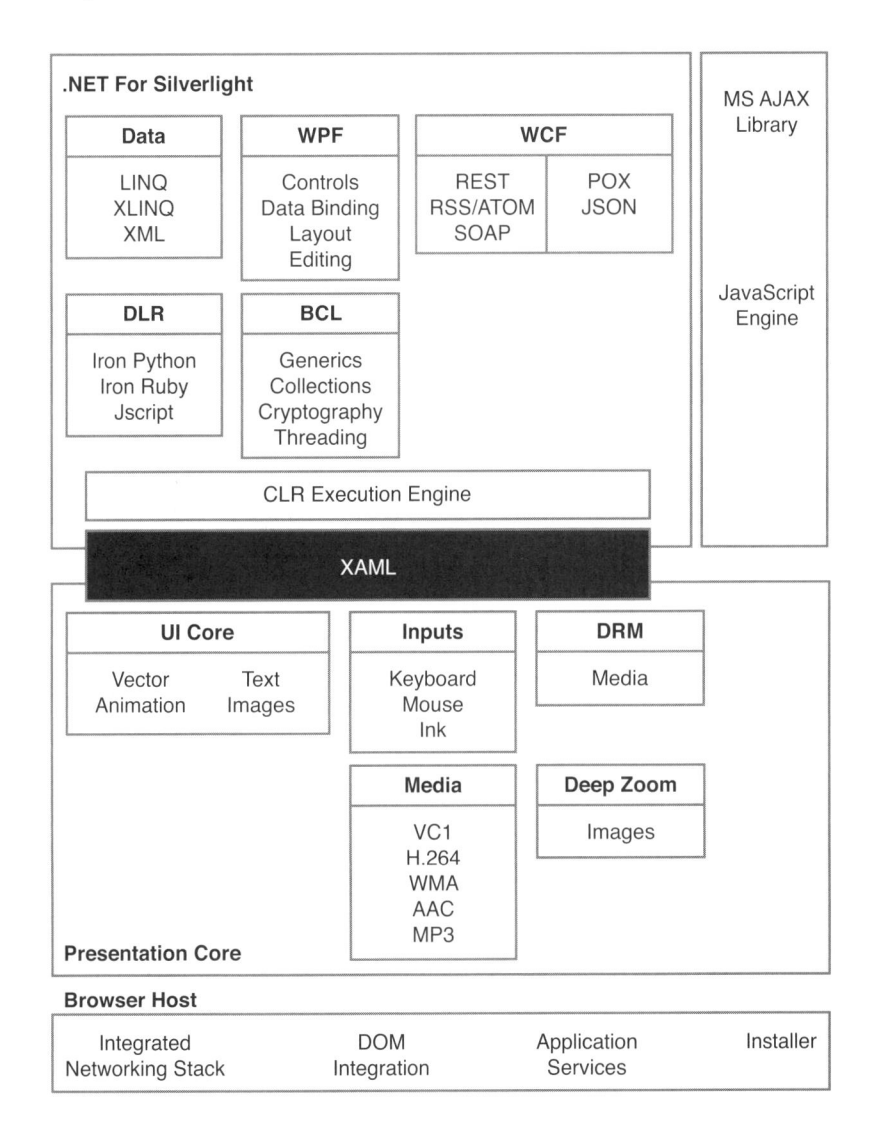

FIGURE 9.1 Silverlight architecture

.NET For Silverlight

Data	WPF	WCF
LINQ XLINQ XML	Controls Data Binding Layout Editing	REST / RSS/ATOM / SOAP POX / JSON

DLR	BCL
Iron Python Iron Ruby Jscript	Generics Collections Cryptography Threading

CLR Execution Engine

MS AJAX Library — JavaScript Engine

XAML

Presentation Core

UI Core	Inputs	DRM
Vector Text Animation Images	Keyboard Mouse Ink	Media

Media	Deep Zoom
VC1 H.264 WMA AAC MP3	Images

Browser Host

Integrated Networking Stack   DOM Integration   Application Services   Installer

Creating the Hello World Silverlight Application

In this section you write a simple Silverlight application that consists of a label, textbox, and a button. On clicking the button a message box displays to the user with a custom message concatenated with the text entered by the user in the textbox.

Open Visual Studio and create a new project of type Silverlight Application. Name it HelloWorldSLApp as shown in Figure 9.2.

FIGURE 9.2
Creating a new Silverlight project

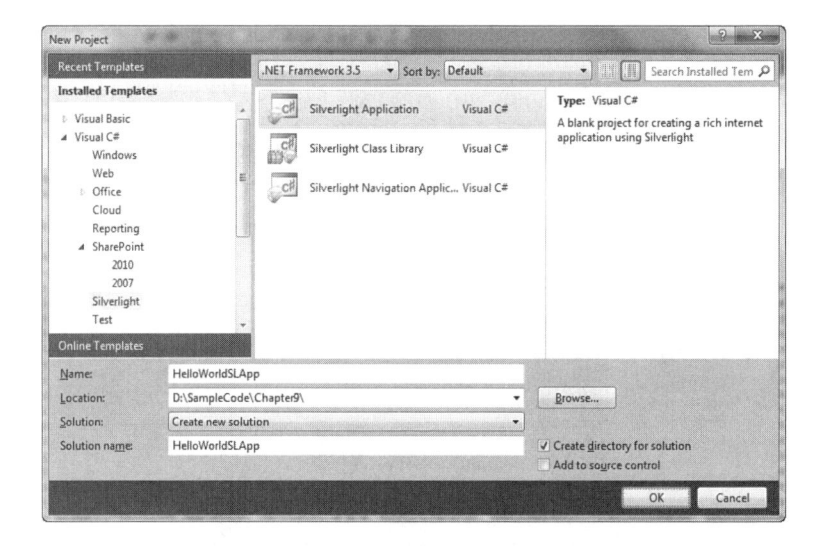

Click OK, and you see the New Silverlight Application screen as shown in Figure 9.3. This screen allows you specify the hosting application for the Silverlight application and select the version of Silverlight to use for the current project. Every Silverlight application needs to be hosted on a web page. Create a new ASP.NET application to host your new Silverlight application. Later on you see how to host this Silverlight application in SharePoint.

Keep the default settings and click OK.

> **Did You Know?**
>
> Even if you are creating a Silverlight application for hosting on SharePoint it is a good idea to create an ASP.NET web application to host the Silverlight application as it makes it easier to debug and test the Silverlight application before finally deploying to the SharePoint site.

Creating the Hello World Silverlight Application

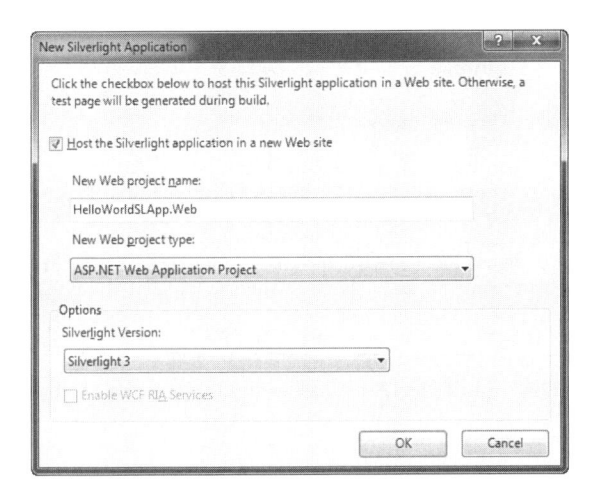

FIGURE 9.3
Options to host the new Silverlight application

You see the Silverlight and the ASP.NET web application projects created in the Visual Studio solution, as shown in Figure 9.4.

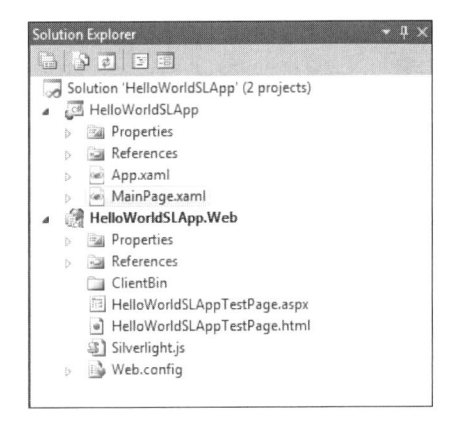

FIGURE 9.4
The HelloWorld-SLApp solution structure

You see two files with the .xaml extension in the Silverlight project. The App.xaml file contains the entry point for the Silverlight application in the form of the function Application_Startup. Also the MainPage.xaml represents your Silverlight form.

> **By the Way**
>
> App.xaml and the MainPage.xaml consist of a codebehind file having the extension .xaml.cs. The .xaml file contains the XAML markup for controls, styles, and resources. The codebehind files contain the class declarations and events. This model is similar to the ASP.NET projects where we have the .aspx and the codebehind .aspx.cs files.

Open the MainPage.xaml file and update the markup as shown in the following code:

```
<UserControl x:Class="HelloWorldSLApp.MainPage"
    xmlns="http://schemas.microsoft.com/winfx/2006/xaml/presentation"
    xmlns:x="http://schemas.microsoft.com/winfx/2006/xaml"
    xmlns:d="http://schemas.microsoft.com/expression/blend/2008"
    xmlns:mc="http://schemas.openxmlformats.org/markup-compatibility/2006"
    mc:Ignorable="d"
    d:DesignHeight="300" d:DesignWidth="400" xmlns:dataInput="clr-namespace:
➥System.Windows.Controls;assembly=System.Windows.Controls.Data.Input">

    <Grid x:Name="LayoutRoot" Background="White">
        <Grid.ColumnDefinitions>
            <ColumnDefinition Width="130" />
            <ColumnDefinition Width="*" />
        </Grid.ColumnDefinitions>
        <Grid.RowDefinitions>
            <RowDefinition Height="100" />
            <RowDefinition Height="*" />
        </Grid.RowDefinitions>
        <dataInput:Label Height="50" HorizontalAlignment="Left" Margin=
➥"20,48,0,0" Name="LabelName" VerticalAlignment="Top" Width="100"
➥Content="Enter Name" />
        <TextBox Grid.Column="1" Height="23" HorizontalAlignment="Left"
➥Margin="6,48,0,0" Name="TextboxName" VerticalAlignment="Top" Width="206" />
        <Button Content="Submit" Grid.Column="1" Grid.Row="1" Height="23"
➥HorizontalAlignment="Left" Margin="22,30,0,0" Name="ButtonSubmit"
➥VerticalAlignment="Top" Width="75" Click="ButtonSubmit_Click" />
    </Grid>
</UserControl>
```

Open the Main.xaml.cs file and update the code as follows:

```
using System;
using System.Collections.Generic;
using System.Linq;
using System.Net;
using System.Windows;
using System.Windows.Controls;
using System.Windows.Documents;
using System.Windows.Input;
using System.Windows.Media;
using System.Windows.Media.Animation;
using System.Windows.Shapes;

namespace HelloWorldSLApp
{
    public partial class MainPage : UserControl
    {
        public MainPage()
        {
            InitializeComponent();
        }

        private void ButtonSubmit_Click(object sender, RoutedEventArgs e)
        {
```

Creating the Hello World Silverlight Application

```
            MessageBox.Show(string.Format("'{0}' - Welcome to the world of
➥Silverlight", TextboxName.Text));
        }
    }
}
```

Rebuild the entire solution. The HelloWorldSLApp.xap file is added to the ASP.NET web application project under the ClientBin folder.

Silverlight applications are packaged as .xap files, which are nothing but zip files. You can view the contents of this file by renaming it to .zip and opening it in Windows Explorer. Right-click HelloWorldSLAppTestPage.aspx and click View in Browser. You can see the Silverlight form in the browser. Enter some text and click Submit. You see the message box shown in Figure 9.5.

FIGURE 9.5
HelloWorld-SLApp Silverlight application

Let's review what exactly you wrote in this first Silverlight application. The XAML defines the user interface. The `Grid` control in the XAML is used to achieve the desired layout. Two rows and two columns are defined using the `Grid.ColumnDefinitions` and `Grid.RowDefinitions` tags. The width of the first column is 130 px, and the other column takes the remaining width by defining `Width="*"`. The desired height for rows is specified in a similar manner:

```
<Grid.ColumnDefinitions>
        <ColumnDefinition Width="130" />
        <ColumnDefinition Width="*" />
    </Grid.ColumnDefinitions>
    <Grid.RowDefinitions>
        <RowDefinition Height="100" />
        <RowDefinition Height="*" />
    </Grid.RowDefinitions>
```

HOUR 9: Creating Silverlight User Interfaces for SharePoint 2010 Solutions

The various controls for the Silverlight application are then defined. The positioning of the controls in the `Grid` is defined through the `Grid.Columns` and `Grid.Rows` attributes. The absence of the attributes indicates the first row or first column.

By the Way

> The `Grid` control is one of the few controls in Silverlight used to achieve the desired layout. The other controls are `StackPanel` and `Canvas`. While the `Grid` control defines the layout through rows and columns the `StackPanel` allows you to lay the control next to each other horizontally or vertically, similar to a stack. The `Canvas` allows you lay controls through absolute positioning in pixels. You can use a combination of these controls nested within each other to achieve complex layouts.

Finally the code behind the `MessageBox.Show` function is called to display the name entered by the user along with some custom text message.

Right-click the HelloWoldSLApp.Web project and click Properties. Go to the Silverlight tab, and you can see your Silverlight project listed there as shown in Figure 9.6. This setting is responsible for copying the HelloWorldSLApp.xap file to the ClientBin folder of the web application.

FIGURE 9.6
Silverlight Applications tab in ASP.NET project properties

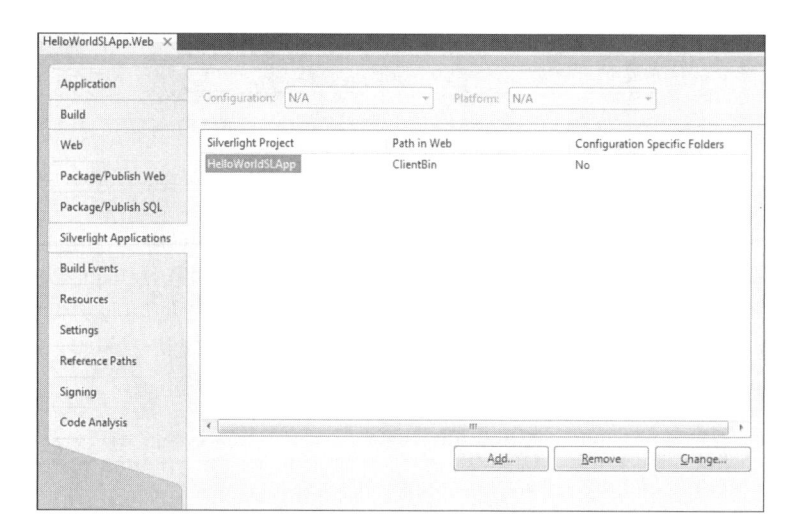

Open the HelloWorldSLAppTestPage.aspx file. You can see the object tag that renders your Silverlight application on the ASP.NET page.

```
<div id="silverlightControlHost">
    <object data="data:application/x-silverlight-2," type="application/
x-silverlight-2" width="100%" height="100%">
        <param name="source" value="ClientBin/HelloWorldSLApp.xap"/>
```

Hosting the Silverlight Application in SharePoint 2010

```
        <param name="onError" value="onSilverlightError" />
        <param name="background" value="white" />
        <param name="minRuntimeVersion" value="3.0.40818.0" />
        <param name="autoUpgrade" value="true" />
        <a href="http://go.microsoft.com/fwlink/?LinkID=149156&v=3.0.40818.0"
➥style="text-decoration:none">
             <img src="http://go.microsoft.com/fwlink/?LinkId=161376"
➥alt="Get Microsoft Silverlight" style="border-style:none"/>
        </a>
      </object><iframe id="_sl_historyFrame" style=
➥"visibility:hidden;height:0px;width:0px;border:0px"></iframe></div>
```

The source parameter specifies the path of the .xap file to be loaded. The onError parameter specifies the JavaScript function to handle errors that might occur while loading the Silverlight application.

> **By the Way**
>
> You can also pass custom data to your Silverlight application from the `object` tag through the `initParams` parameter, which is not mentioned in this code sample. This data is accessible in the Silverlight application in the Application_Startup event of App.xaml through the InitParams property of the `StartupEventArgs` object, which is passed as a parameter to the Application_Startup event.

> **Did You Know?**
>
> If you are hosting your Silverlight application within an ASP.NET site you can use the ASP.NET Silverlight control. This control is available in the System.Web.Silverlight.dll.

Hosting the Silverlight Application in SharePoint 2010

The Silverlight application created in the previous section was hosted on an ASP.NET page, but we now want to host the Silverlight application on a SharePoint site. Hosting a Silverlight application involves two steps:

1. Deploy the XAP file either to some folder in <14 Hive>, ideally the Layouts folder, or to some document library in the SharePoint site.

2. Reference the XAP file in the out of the box Silverlight web part or some custom web part.

Add a new Empty SharePoint project to the HelloWorldSLApp solution and name it HelloWorldSLDeploy. Right-click the SharePoint project and click Add, SharePoint "Layouts" Mapped Folder. The Layouts folder gets added to the Project. A subfolder HelloWorldSLDeploy also gets added under the Layouts folder.

Right-click the HelloWorldSLApp Silverlight project and open the properties. Go to Build Events and add the following in the Post-build event command line section.

```
xcopy /Y $(ProjectDir)$(OutDir)HelloWorldSLApp.XAP
➥$(SolutionDir)HelloWorldSLDeploy\Layouts\HelloWorldSLDeploy
```

Build the HelloWorldSLApp project. If the build is successful the XAP gets copied to the Layouts\HelloWorldSLDeploy folder in the HelloWorldSLDeploy project. Include the XAP file in the project. The final solution structure is shown in Figure 9.7.

FIGURE 9.7
HelloWorldSL-Deploy project structure

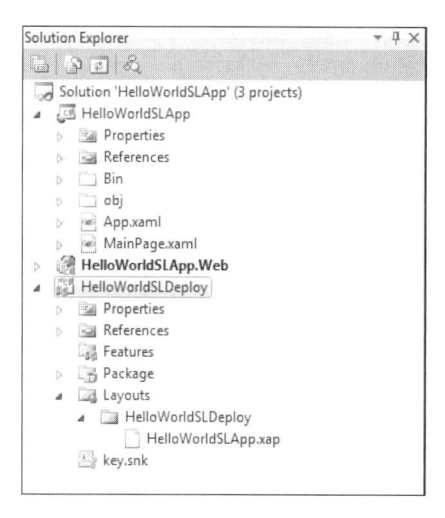

Now any changes in the Silverlight project are reflected in the HelloWorldSLApp.xap file in the HelloWorldSLDeploy project thanks to your Post-build command. This XAP file gets deployed to the <14 Hive>\Layouts\HelloWorldSLDeploy folder. Deploy the HelloWorldSLDeploy solution.

Browse to the SharePoint site and add the Silverlight web part. This web part is available under the Media and Content category.

You are prompted to specify the URL of the Silverlight XAP file after adding the web part. Specify the URL as /_Layouts/HelloWorldSLDeploy/HelloWorldSLApp.xap and click OK. Save the page, and you should see the Silverlight application hosted within the SharePoint site.

Hosting the Silverlight application within a custom web part is a simple exercise. You just need to generate the object tag with the appropriate parameters or use the ASP.NET Silverlight control.

Consuming Silverlight Data in SharePoint 2010

Accessing SharePoint data in Silverlight involves using the SharePoint client side object model. The following DLLs represent the APIs for accessing SharePoint data in Silverlight:

- Microsoft.SharePoint.Client.Silverlight.dll
- Microsoft.SharePoint.Client.Silverlight.Runtime.dll

In this section you create a Silverlight web part that displays data from a list in a grid. It will show data from a custom list called Books. The user can filter the data according to the book category, which he can select from a drop-down list.

Create a new custom list and call it Books. Add the custom columns listed in Table 9.2.

TABLE 9.2 Columns for Books List

Column Name	Type
Author	Single line text field
Publisher	Single line text field
Year	Single line text field
Category	Single line text field

Create a new Silverlight project named ListDataSLApp.

Add a reference to the Microsoft.SharePoint.Client.Silverlight.dll and Microsoft.SharePoint.Client.Silverlight.Runtime.dll from the <14 Hive>\Templates\Layouts\ClientBin folder.

Edit the MainPage.xaml as follows:

```
<UserControl x:Class="ListDataSLApp.MainPage"
    xmlns="http://schemas.microsoft.com/winfx/2006/xaml/presentation"
    xmlns:x="http://schemas.microsoft.com/winfx/2006/xaml"
    xmlns:d="http://schemas.microsoft.com/expression/blend/2008"
    xmlns:mc="http://schemas.openxmlformats.org/markup-compatibility/2006"
```

```
        mc:Ignorable="d"
        d:DesignHeight="350" d:DesignWidth="550" xmlns:dataInput="clr-namespace:
➥System.Windows.Controls;assembly=System.Windows.Controls.Data.Input" xmlns:
➥data="clr-namespace:System.Windows.Controls;assembly=
➥System.Windows.Controls.Data">
    <Grid x:Name="LayoutRoot" Background="White" Height="350" Width="550">
        <Grid.RowDefinitions>
            <RowDefinition Height="40" />
            <RowDefinition Height="40" />
            <RowDefinition Height="*" />
        </Grid.RowDefinitions>

        <dataInput:Label Height="20" HorizontalAlignment="Left" Margin=
➥"10,10,0,0" Name="label1" VerticalAlignment="Top" Width="200" Content=
➥"Select the Category" />
        <ComboBox Grid.Row="1" Height="20" HorizontalAlignment="Left" Margin=
➥"10,10,0,0" Name="ComboCategory" VerticalAlignment="Top" Width="211"
➥SelectionChanged="ComboCategory_SelectionChanged" />
        <data:DataGrid AutoGenerateColumns="False" Grid.Row="2" Height="200"
➥HorizontalAlignment="Left" Margin="10,10,10,10" Name="dataGrid1"
➥VerticalAlignment="Top" Width="525" >
            <data:DataGrid.Columns>
                <data:DataGridTextColumn Header="Title" Binding="{Binding
➥BookTitle}" />
                <data:DataGridTextColumn Header="Author" Binding="{Binding
➥Author}" />
                <data:DataGridTextColumn Header="Publisher" Binding="{Binding
➥Publisher}" />
                <data:DataGridTextColumn Header="Year" Binding="{Binding Year}"
/>
            </data:DataGrid.Columns>
        </data:DataGrid>
    </Grid>
</UserControl>
```

The preceding code defines a drop-down list and a data grid. It also specifies the handler for a drop-down list selection changed event. In addition the example defines the columns and binds to the data grid.

Open the MainPage.xaml.cs and update as shown in the following code:

```
using System;
using System.Collections.Generic;
using System.Linq;
using System.Net;
using System.Windows;
using System.Windows.Controls;
using System.Windows.Documents;
using System.Windows.Input;
using System.Windows.Media;
using System.Windows.Media.Animation;
using System.Windows.Shapes;
using Microsoft.SharePoint.Client;
using System.Collections.ObjectModel;
```

Consuming Silverlight Data in SharePoint 2010

```
namespace ListDataSLApp
{
    public partial class MainPage : UserControl
    {
        ClientContext ctx = null;
        IEnumerable<ListItem> categoryItems = null;
        IEnumerable<ListItem> filteredItems = null;

        public MainPage()
        {
            InitializeComponent();
            using (ctx = ClientContext.Current)
            {
                CamlQuery camlQuery = new CamlQuery();

                var query = from item in
➥ctx.Web.Lists.GetByTitle("Books").GetItems(camlQuery)
                            select item;

                categoryItems = ctx.LoadQuery(query);

                ctx.ExecuteQueryAsync(categorySucceededCallBack,
➥categoryFailedCallback);
            }
        }

        void categorySucceededCallBack(object sender,
➥ClientRequestSucceededEventArgs e)
        {
            this.Dispatcher.BeginInvoke(() =>
            {
                List<string> categories = new List<string>();

                foreach (var item in categoryItems)
                {
                    categories.Add(item["Category"].ToString());
                }

                ComboCategory.ItemsSource = categories.Distinct();
            });
        }

        void categoryFailedCallback(object sender,
➥ClientRequestFailedEventArgs e)
        {
            MessageBox.Show("Failed to retrieve list of categories .. "
➥+ e.Message);
        }

        private void ComboCategory_SelectionChanged(object sender,
➥SelectionChangedEventArgs e)
        {
            string category = ComboCategory.SelectedItem.ToString();
            CamlQuery camlQuery = new CamlQuery()
            {
                ViewXml = string.Format(
                @"<View>
                    <Query>
```

```
                    <Where>
                      <Eq>
                        <FieldRef Name='Category'/>
                        <Value Type='Text'>{0}</Value>
                      </Eq>
                    </Where>
                  </Query>
                </View>", category)
        };

        var query = from item in
ctx.Web.Lists.GetByTitle("Books").GetItems(camlQuery)
                    select item;

        filteredItems = ctx.LoadQuery(query);
        ctx.ExecuteQueryAsync(listItemSucceededCallBack,
listItemFailedCallback);
    }

    void listItemSucceededCallBack(object sender,
ClientRequestSucceededEventArgs e)
    {
        this.Dispatcher.BeginInvoke(() =>
        {
            var data = from item in filteredItems
                       select new BookData { BookTitle = item["Title"].
ToString(), Author = item["Author0"].ToString(), Publisher =
item["Publisher"].ToString(), Year = item["Year"].ToString(), Category =
item["Category"].ToString() };
            dataGrid1.ItemsSource = data.ToList();
        });
    }

    void listItemFailedCallback(object sender,
ClientRequestFailedEventArgs e)
    {
        MessageBox.Show("Failed to retrieve data from Books list.. "
+ e.Message);
    }
  }
}

public class BookData
{
    public string BookTitle { get; set; }
    public string Author { get; set; }
    public string Publisher { get; set; }
    public string Year { get; set; }
    public string Category { get; set; }
}
```

The preceding code first populates the drop-down list for Categories. Then `ClientContext.Current` retrieves the `ClientContext` instance. Next the `LoadQuery` method is called to load the list item collection, and then the query is executed asynchronously. The code then retrieves the distinct categories in categorySucceededCallBack method and populates it in the items collection of the category drop-down list.

The ComboCategory_SelectionChanged method gets called when the user selects a category. The filtered records are retrieved and a collection of the BookData class is populated. Finally this collection is bound to the data grid.

You now need to deploy the Silverlight application to your SharePoint site:

1. Add a new Empty SharePoint project to the solution and name it ListDataSLDeploy.

2. Add the SharePoint Mapped Layouts folder to the Empty SharePoint project.

3. Add the following to the Post Build command of the Silverlight project:

   ```
   xcopy /Y $(ProjectDir)$(OutDir)ListDataSLApp.XAP
   ➥$(SolutionDir)ListDataSLDeploy\Layouts\ListDataSLDeploy
   ```

4. Rebuild the solution and the XAP file gets copied to the Layouts\ListDataSLDeploy folder in the SharePoint project. Include the file in the project.

5. Deploy the ListDataSLDeploy SharePoint project.

6. Open the SharePoint site and add a Silverlight web part to the home page. Set the URL for the Silverlight application as /_Layouts/ListDataSLDeploy/ListDataSLApp.xap.

7. Set the width of the Silverlight web part as 550 pixels and height as 350 pixels.

If you added some data to the Books list you can select a category and see the data in the Grid as shown in Figure 9.8.

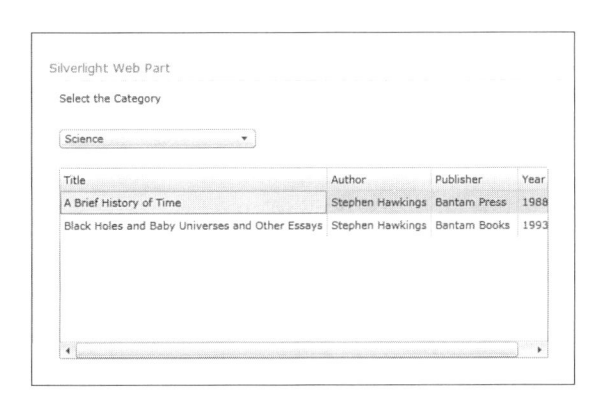

FIGURE 9.8
ListDataSLApp-Silverlight application

Summary

In this hour you were introduced to Silverlight. You created sample applications in Silverlight and hosted the application on the SharePoint 2010 site. Silverlight is a vast program, and an entire discussion of it is outside the scope of this book, but Silverlight is an important technology to learn if you want to build great user interfaces. It is recommended that you go through a good book on Silverlight and gain expertise in it.

Q&A

Q. *Does Silverlight work on all browsers?*

A. Silverlight works on any browser that supports the Silverlight plug-in. As of now Silverlight is supported by all the major browsers.

Q. *Are Silverlight applications as secure as server side applications?*

A. Silverlight is as secure as any web page. You can use SSL to make Silverlight applications even more secure.

HOUR 10

Managing Data in SharePoint 2010

What You'll Learn in This Hour:
- Programming SharePoint lists and libraries
- Understanding site columns
- Understanding content types
- Creating custom list definitions

> **By the Way**
> Due to the complexity of the topics discussed, some figures in this book are very detailed and are intended only to provide a high-level view of concepts. Those figures are representational and not intended to be read in detail.

Data is central to software applications. Every software application ranging from simple text file editors such as Notepad to complex applications such as a big Customer Resource Management system or Enterprise Resource Planning system works on data. Similarly data is central to every SharePoint application. In fact, as you saw in Hour 1, "Introducing SharePoint 2010," from simply acting as a repository for data to performing intelligent operations on data SharePoint can just about do everything in managing data. In this and the next few hours you learn about the features of SharePoint that make it a great application to store and manage all the data of an organization.

Programming SharePoint Lists and Libraries

SharePoint stores all data in lists and libraries. Put simply, lists can be considered data structures that store data in the form of rows and columns. SharePoint libraries are lists that store documents along with information about the document. While internally lists and libraries store data in Microsoft SQL Server, lists and libraries abstract the database. As a SharePoint developer, when working with data you will find yourself working mainly with SharePoint lists and libraries as the back end. Although there is a difference between

HOUR 10: Managing Data in SharePoint 2010

SharePoint lists and libraries, this hour refers to both as SharePoint lists unless specified otherwise.

In Hour 4, "Walking Through the Available Site and List Templates in SharePoint 2010," you created lists and libraries from user interface. In this hour you look at the option of creating lists through code.

▼
Try It Yourself
Create Lists Through a Console Application

Creating a list/library through code is simple. Although you write a console application in this example, you can also do this in a SharePoint feature.

1. Create a new Console Application Project named ListCreateDemo.

2. Add a reference to the Microsoft.SharePoint.dll.

3. If not already done, change the Build Configuration to Any CPU and the Target Framework to .NET Framework 3.5.

4. Update the Program.cs as shown in the following code:

   ```
   using Microsoft.SharePoint;

   namespace ListCreateDemo
   {
       class Program
       {
           static void Main(string[] args)
           {
               using (SPSite site = new SPSite("http://splearn"))
               {
                   using (SPWeb web = site.OpenWeb())
                   {
                       web.Lists.Add("MyCustomList",
   "This list was created programmatically",
   SPListTemplateType.GenericList);
                   }
               }
           }
       }
   }
   ```

5. Build and run the application.

6. Browse to the site and you find the new list has been created at the root site level. Try creating a new record in the list by clicking new item and you can see that the list contains a Title column by default.

▲

Try It Yourself

Create Lists Through a Console Application

To create a new list from the user interface is even easier. To create a new list from the user interface follow these steps:

1. In your SharePoint site, go to Site Actions, More Options.

2. In the Create screen, click List in the left menu.

3. Select Custom List and enter SimpleList as the name. You will be using this list in later sections of this hour.

4. Click Create.

You can also create a document library or any other type of list by specifying the appropriate list template type.

> **By the Way**
>
> To create a list from a custom list template you can pass the feature id through which the custom template is created to one of the overloads of the Add method.

Understanding Site Columns

You saw earlier that SharePoint stores data in the form of rows and columns. Columns define the schema of the data to be stored. You can have two types of columns—site columns and list columns. List columns are scoped to a list and cannot be reused in other lists. Site columns are reusable across multiple lists across multiple SharePoint sites.

SharePoint 2010 comes with a lot of out of the box site columns. In the previous section you saw the Title column in the MyCustomList list. This is an out of the box column that is present in all types of lists and libraries. To view the site columns in your SharePoint site go to Site Actions, Site Settings. Under Galleries click Site Columns link. You see the screen shown in Figure 10.1. Here you see the list of the site columns grouped under various categories. You can also see the type of the column and the source. The source indicates the site at which the column is created. It is important to note that the column is available in the source site and in all sites under the source site. If you create a new subsite and create a site column at the subsite level then the source will be shown as that subsite. In this case the column is available in the subsite and all sites under it, but is not available to the parent site.

HOUR 10: Managing Data in SharePoint 2010

FIGURE 10.1
Site Columns gallery

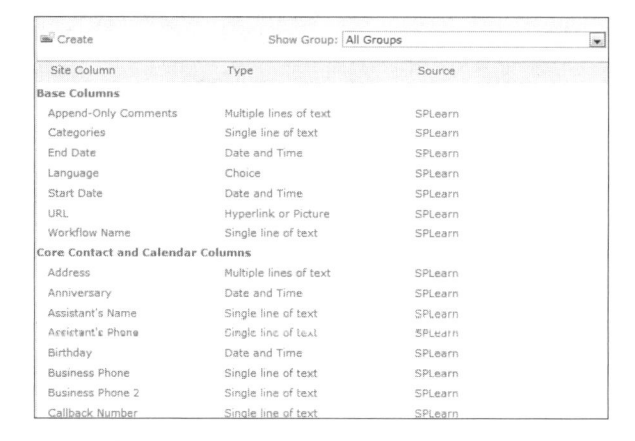

You now create a new site column. To create a new site column follow these steps.

▼ **Try It Yourself**

Create a New Site Column

1. Click the Create button in the Site Column Gallery. You are presented with the screen shown in Figure 10.2 and Figure 10.3.

FIGURE 10.2
Creating a new column

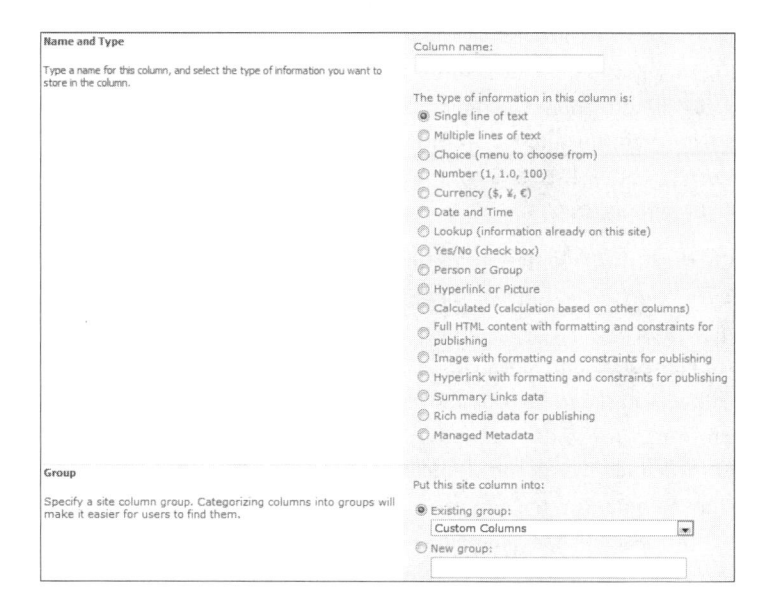

▼

Understanding Site Columns

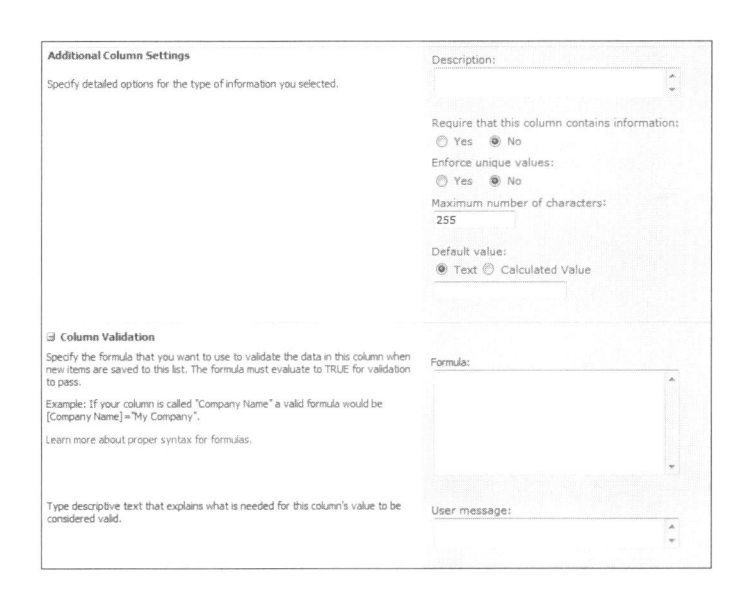

FIGURE 10.3 Setting additional options for a New Column

As you can see in Figure 10.2 and 10.3, the Create New Column screen allows you to specify various properties of the site column, which are listed in Table 10.1.

TABLE 10.1 Create Site Column Configuration Options

Property	Description
Name	This is the title of the site column displayed to the user.
Type of the site column	This specifies the type of information that the site column can store.
Group	This allows you to specify a group for the site column.
Additional Column Settings	Here you can set various properties for the site column based on the type of site column. These properties change based on what type of site column you are creating. For example, for a site column of type "Single Line of Text" you can see the Maximum Number of Characters property while for a site column of type number you can see the Min and Max properties.
Column Validation	This allows you to specify validations through formulae and specify custom error messages when the validation fails.

HOUR 10: Managing Data in SharePoint 2010

2. Enter the column name Additional Comments and select the Multiple Lines of Text type. Click OK. Your new column is created, and you can see it in the Site Columns gallery under the Custom Columns group.

3. Now browse to the list settings of the SimpleList list and click Add from Existing Site Columns. Select Custom Columns in the Select Site Columns From drop-down list and add the Additional Comments column. Figure 10.4 shows the screen to add site columns to the list.

FIGURE 10.4
Adding columns to a list

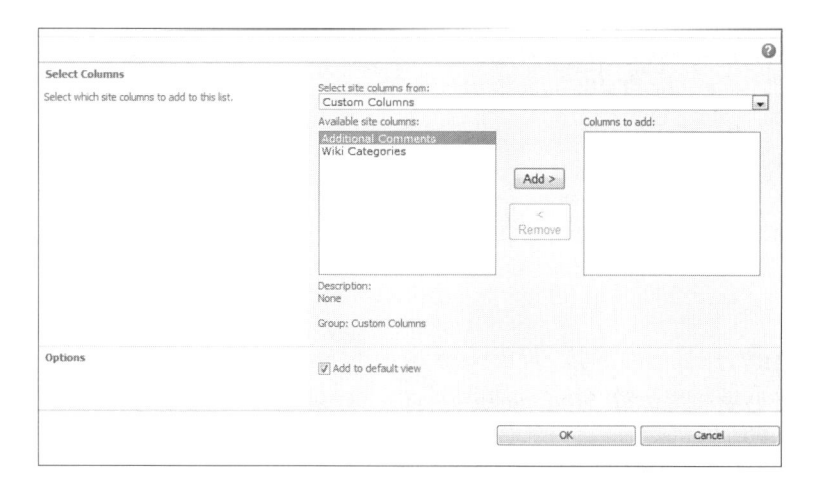

4. Click OK. Add a new item and you can see your new column in the New Item form.

Go back to the list settings for the SimpleList list. Under the columns section, click the Additional Comments column. Change the name to Additional Comments 1. Click OK and try to add a new record to verify the change has reflected. Now go back to the site columns gallery. You can see that the original Additional Comments column is still there. This is an important concept to understand. When you used the Additional Comments column in the list a list column that is a copy of the site column is created. If you make any changes to the column properties from the list settings these will be local to the list column. However, if you make changes to the site column properties these get reflected to the list. The site column you created was of the Multiple Lines of Text type. You can create many other different types of site columns as described in Table 10.2.

TABLE 10.2 Site Column Types in SharePoint

Type of Column	Description
Single Line of Text	Stores a single line of text with a maximum limit of 255 characters.
Multiple Lines of Text	Allows you to create a multiline textbox field. This can be a plain text multiline field or rich text multiline or an enhanced rich text multiline field depending on the configuration selected in the Additional Column Settings.
Choice	Allows you to create a field where users can select a value from a given set of values. The choice can be shown in a drop-down list, radio buttons, or check boxes based on the configuration selected in the Additional Column Settings.
Number	Allows you to create a field for storing numeric values.
Currency	Allows you to store currency data.
Date and Time	Stored date time values.
Lookup (information already on this site)	Allows the user to select a single value or multiple values from the values of an existing column.
Yes/No (check box)	Allows the user to select Yes or No.
Person or Group	Allows the user to select a user or group name.
Hyperlink or Picture	Stores a URL to a link or image.
Calculated (calculation based on other columns)	This column does not allow any user input. It shows data based on the formula entered.
Full HTML Content with Formatting and Constraints for Publishing	Allows you to create a multiline text field.
Image with Formatting and Constraints for Publishing	Allows you to create a field to store and display an image with advanced options.
Hyperlink with Formatting and Constraints for Publishing	Allows you to create a field to store URLs.
Rich Media Data for Publishing	Field to store URLs to digital assets such as audio/video and display them.
Managed Metadata	Allows you to tag terms from the managed metadata service. You learn more about the managed metadata service in Hour 20, "Understanding Service Applications."
Summary Links Data	Stores multiple links and is used for a site page in a publishing site to store summary links.

Creating a Site Column Through Features

You created the site column in the previous section using the user interface provided by SharePoint. This is useful when you are doing minor configurations to your SharePoint application. However in most cases you want to create site columns through features.

Create a new SharePoint empty project named CustomSchema. Add a new module and call it CustomColumns. Delete the sample.txt file. Edit the elements.xml as follows:

```
<?xml version="1.0" encoding="utf-8"?>
<Elements xmlns="http://schemas.microsoft.com/sharepoint/">
  <Field Type="Note"
DisplayName="Additional Comments 2"
Required="FALSE"
EnforceUniqueValues="FALSE"
NumLines="8"
RichText="TRUE"
RichTextMode="FullHtml"
Group="Custom Columns"
ID="{B0980FC7-E50A-4615-BFBD-70EBB71DFE2D}"
StaticName="AdditionalComments2"
Name="AdditionalComments2" />
</Elements>
```

Edit the feature and name it CustomSchema. Change the scope to Site and deploy the solution. Go to the Site columns gallery and you should see your new site column there. The `Field` element is used to define a new site column. Table 10.3 describes some of the important attributes used previously.

TABLE 10.3 Attributes in the `Field` Element for Creating a New Site Column

Attribute	Description
Type	Describes the type of site column to be created. In this case it is a Note for a multiline field.
DisplayName	Title for the column displayed to the user.
Required	Indicates whether the field is a required field.
Group	Group under which the column should appear.
ID	Unique identifier for the site column.
Name	The internal name of a field that will never change for the lifetime of the field definition. It must be unique with respect to the set of fields in a list.
RichText	If true indicates that the multiline field is a richtext field.

You can find the various types of fields you can create and a detailed description of most of these attributes at http://msdn.microsoft.com/en-us/library/ms437580.aspx.

Understanding Content Types

While you have worked with site columns in isolation up to this point, you always find yourself using site columns through content types. A content type is a reusable collection of metadata (columns), workflow, behavior, and many other settings. Content types help to categorize data. Say that you have a list that stores vehicle information. You may be storing information on different types of vehicles like cars, trains, ships, and airplanes. Each of these has some attributes specific to them. You can create separate content types for them. For example, you can have a LandVehicle content type that has attributes such as title, speed, and number of tires. You can have another content type called FlyingVehicles that has attributes such as title, speed, maximum height it can reach, and number of wings. And you can have another content type called SeaVehicles that has its own set of attributes.

A content type can include the following information:

- ▶ The metadata of the content type. These are represented by site columns of the content type.
- ▶ Custom New, Edit, and Display forms to use with this content type.
- ▶ Workflows associated with the content type.
- ▶ For document content types, the document template on which to base documents of this type.
- ▶ Any other custom information that you want to associate with the content type. You can store this information in the content type as one or more XML documents.

You can see the content types available within the site by going to the Site Content Types gallery. To view the Site Content Types gallery, go to Site Actions, Site Settings. Under the Galleries section click Site Content Types. Here you can see the various out of the box and custom content types.

You will now create a new content type named Animal. The content type has title, description and category fields. To create a new content type follow the next steps.

Try It Yourself

Create a New Content Type

1. In the Site Content Types gallery click Create.

2. Enter the Name of the content type as Animal, as shown in Figure 10.5. Your content type needs to inherit from a base content type.

3. In the Select Parent Content Type From drop-down list select List Content Types, and in the Parent Content Type drop-down list select Item.

4. Click OK.

Did You Know?

The out of the box Item content type can be considered as the base content type of all other content types in SharePoint. The Item content type itself inherits from the out of the Box System content type. However, SharePoint does not allow any other content type to inherit from the System content type, and the Item content type is the topmost content type in the hierarchy from which your custom content type can inherit.

FIGURE 10.5
Create new content type screen

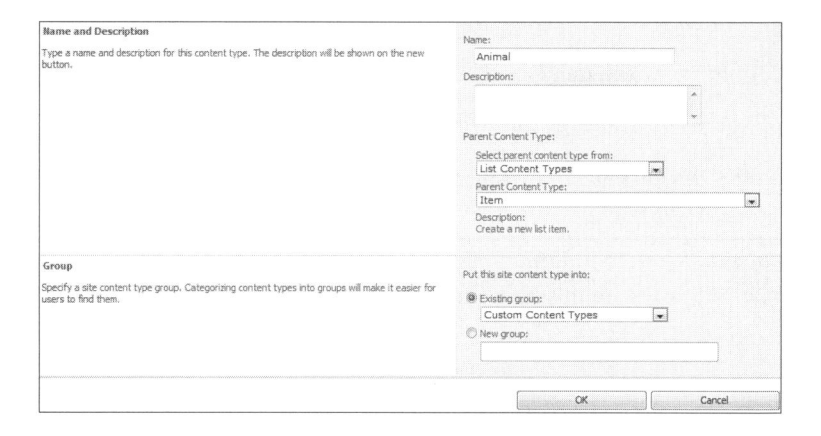

The new content type is created and you are taken to the screen shown in Figure 10.6.

The screen shows many configuration options, most of which are similar to the ones you saw on the list settings page. You can see that the new content type contains the Title site column. This is because you selected the Item content type as the Parent content type when creating the Animal content type.

You can add existing site columns to this content type or create new site columns. To add existing or new site columns to a content type, follow the next steps.

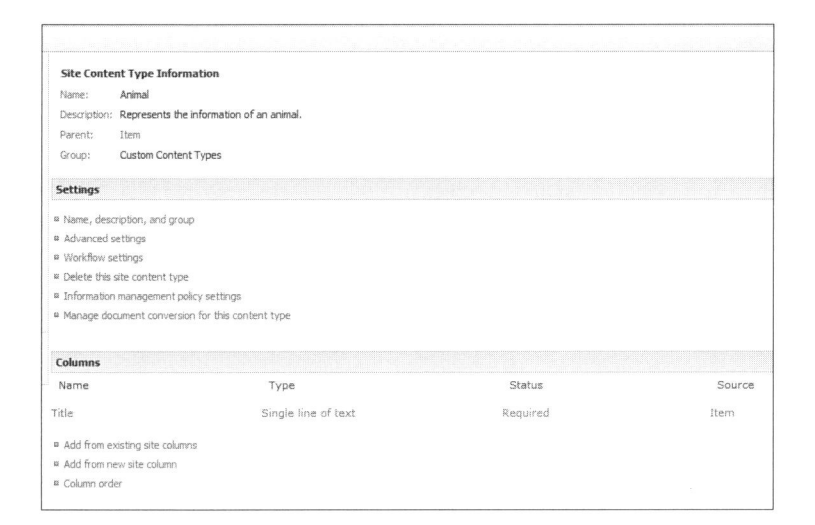

FIGURE 10.6
Site content type information screen

Try It Yourself

Add Site Columns to Content Type

1. In the Site Content Type Information screen, click Add from Existing Site Columns.

2. Add the Description column and click OK.

3. Click Add from New Site Column.

4. Enter the column name as Animal Category. Select the type of column as Choice (Menu to Choose From).

5. In the Additional Column Settings enter the following choice separated by line breaks:

   ▶ Domestic Animal

   ▶ Wild Animal

6. Click OK.

To use the new content type you need to add the content type to a list. To add the content type to the list, follow the next steps.

HOUR 10: Managing Data in SharePoint 2010

▼ **Try It Yourself**

Add Content Type to a List

1. Browse to the list settings page of the SimpleList list.
2. Click Advanced Settings and select Yes for Allow Management of Content Types?
3. Click OK, and you can see a new section for content types.
4. Click Add from Existing Site Content Types and select your newly created Animal content type. Click OK.
5. Browse back to the list and you can see your new content type in the new item menu as shown in Figure 10.7.

FIGURE 10.7
Custom content type in the New Item menu

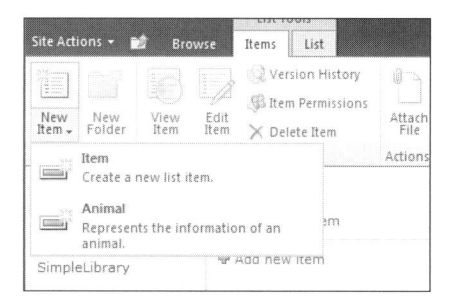

6. Click Animal and you can see the new item form showing fields specific to your new content type as shown in Figure 10.8.

FIGURE 10.8
New Item screen for the Animal content type

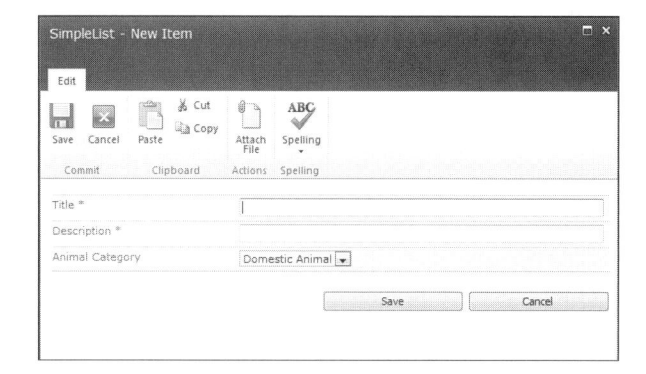

▲

Creating Content Types Through Features

You already saw in the previous section how to create site columns through features. You now create a content type through features. You create a new content type Product based on the item content type. Create the Product Description and Product Category site columns through your feature and add it to the new content type. In addition you use the Title field from the Item content type to store the name of the Product, you also associate the new content type to your SimpleList list.

Open the CustomSchema project created in the previous section. Add a new item of type Content Type and name it Product. Click Add, and you see the screen that appears in Figure 10.9.

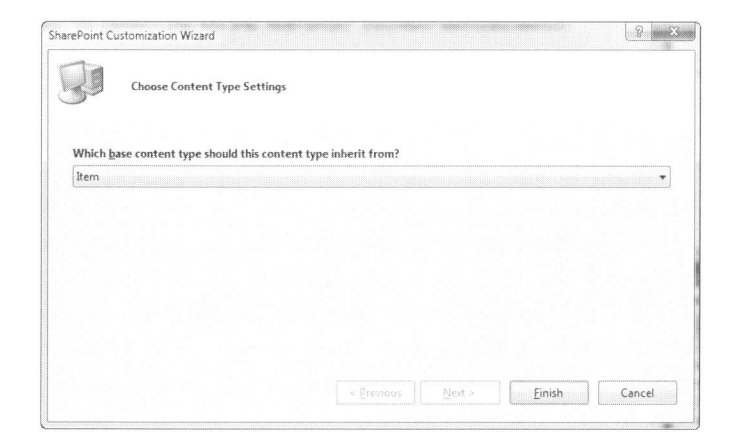

FIGURE 10.9 Selecting a base content type

You can see various content types present in the site collection, including the Animal content type. Select the Item content type. A new elements.xml file is added under the Products folder as shown in Figure 10.10.

Open the elements.xml file, and you can see the following:

```
<?xml version="1.0" encoding="utf-8"?>
<Elements xmlns="http://schemas.microsoft.com/sharepoint/">
  <!-- Parent ContentType: Item (0x01) -->
  <ContentType ID="0x0100acfda71432f84130a72c55b28097ca2b"
               Name="CustomSchema - Product"
               Group="Custom Content Types"
               Description="My Content Type"
               Inherits="TRUE"
               Version="0">
    <FieldRefs>
    </FieldRefs>
  </ContentType>
</Elements>
```

FIGURE 10.10
CustomSchema project structure

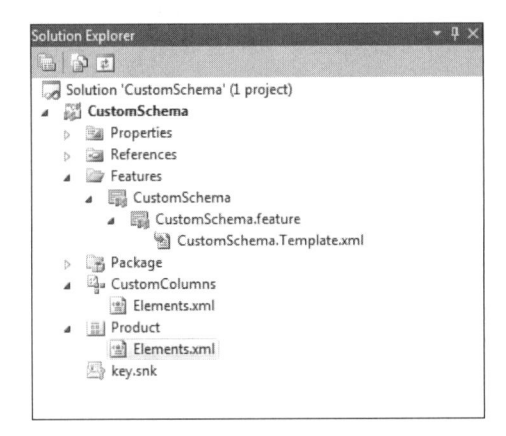

The `ContentType` element defines a new content type. The `ID` attribute uniquely identifies the content type across the site collection. This is represented by the `SPContentTypeId` class in the object model. Content Type IDs are designed to be recursive. The content type ID encapsulates the line of parent content types from which the content type inherits. Each content type ID contains the ID of the parent content type, which in turn contains the ID of that content type's parent, and so on, until System Content Type ID. Hence our new content type starts from 0x01, which is the ID of the Item content type, and the content type ID of the Item content type starts with 0x, which is the content type ID for the System content type. The `Inherits` attribute allows you to specify whether the content type must inherit the fields of the parent content type.

Modify the elements.xml file as shown in the following code:

```
<?xml version="1.0" encoding="utf-8"?>
<Elements xmlns="http://schemas.microsoft.com/sharepoint/">

  <Field Type="Note"
DisplayName="Product Description"
Required="FALSE"
EnforceUniqueValues="FALSE"
NumLines="8"
RichText="TRUE"
RichTextMode="FullHtml"
Group="Custom Columns"
ID="{CA07C01D-B547-4766-A5AD-77D6CA01ABE1}"
StaticName="ProductDescription"
Name="ProductDescription" />

  <Field
Type="Choice"
DisplayName="Product Category"
Required="FALSE"
EnforceUniqueValues="FALSE"
Indexed="FALSE"
```

Understanding Content Types 227

```xml
Format="Dropdown"
FillInChoice="FALSE"
Group="Custom Columns"
ID="{8753041F-629F-48E7-B5C4-B2488A22F5BF}"
StaticName="ProductCategory"
Name="ProductCategory" >
    <Default>Electronics</Default>
    <CHOICES>
      <CHOICE>Electronics</CHOICE>
      <CHOICE>Food and Beverages</CHOICE>
      <CHOICE>Others</CHOICE>
    </CHOICES>
  </Field>

  <!-- Parent ContentType: Item (0x01) -->
  <ContentType ID="0x0100acfda71432f84130a72c55b28097ca2b"
             Name="Product"
             Group="Custom Content Types"
             Description="Represents information about a product"
             Inherits="TRUE"
             Version="0">
    <FieldRefs>
      <FieldRef ID="{CA07C01D-B547-4766-A5AD-77D6CA01ABE1}"
 Name="ProductDescription" />
      <FieldRef ID="{8753041F-629F-48E7-B5C4-B2488A22F5BF}"
Name="ProductCategory" />
    </FieldRefs>
  </ContentType>
  <ContentTypeBinding
    ContentTypeId="0x0100acfda71432f84130a72c55b28097ca2b"
    ListUrl="Lists/SimpleList"/>
</Elements>
```

Deploy the solution. Browse to the SimpleList, and you should be able to see the new content type in the New Item menu, as shown in Figure 10.11.

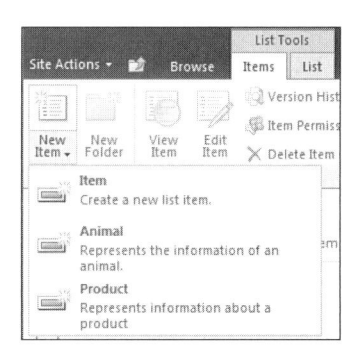

FIGURE 10.11
The Product content type in the New Item menu

Now take a look back at the XML we just wrote. You can see two new site columns, `ProductDescription` and `ProductCategory`, defined. The site columns are associated with the content type using the `FieldRef` element. The `ID` attribute matches the ID of your site column, and the `Name` attribute matches the `StaticName` of the site column. Finally the content type is associated to the lists SimpleList using the `ContentTypeBinding` element. The `ContentTypeId` attribute represents the ID of the content type to be associated with the list at the URL given by the `ListUrl` attribute.

Creating Custom List Definitions

You have created a list and a library using out of the box list templates. At times you will want to define your own list template and create a list using that. It's easy to create a new list template using Visual Studio. This section shows the process of creating a new list definition.

Open the CustomSchema project created earlier. Select List Definition from Content Type and name it Product List. Click the Add button. You are shown the Choose List Definition Settings as shown in Figure 10.12.

FIGURE 10.12
Choose List Definitions Settings screen

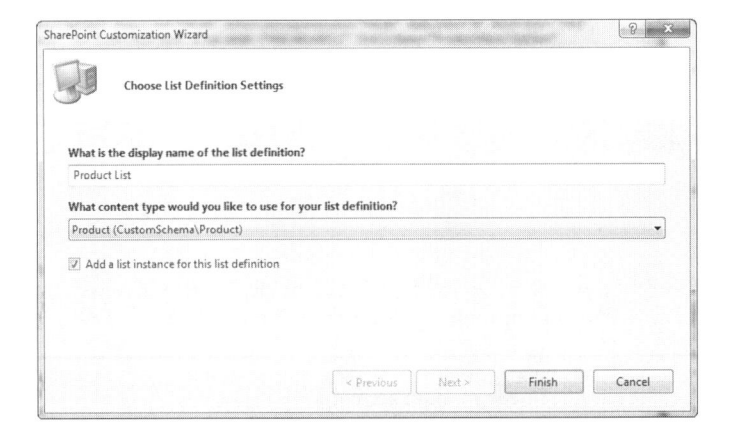

Change the display name to Product List. Select the Product content type and check the Add a List Instance for This List Definition box. Click Finish. You see two elements.xml files created and a schema.xml created as shown in Figure 10.13.

FIGURE 10.13
Visual Studio 2010 project structure for Product List

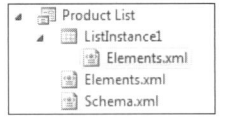

Open the Schema.xml file and the Elements.xml directly under the Product List folder. You can see the list definition XML. The schema.xml specifies the content types used by the list; the views; the new, edit, and display forms; and a lot of other information. The elements.xml file specifies the list template information such as the name, display name, description, template type (this is a unique number that will be used by the list instances), and base type.

Open the elements.xml file under the ListInstance1 folder. You can see that a new list instance is defined using your new list template. Note the `TemplateType` is the same as the type in the `ListTemplate` element.

Deploy the solution. Browse to the SharePoint site and you should see the new list in the Quick Launch menu. Also try to create a new list. You can see the new list template in the list of templates shown in Figure 10.14.

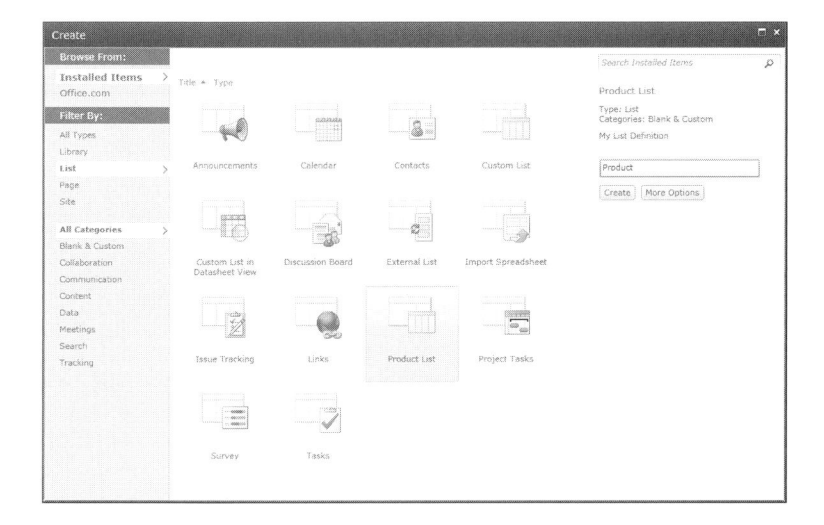

FIGURE 10.14
The Product List template option in the Create New List screen

Summary

In this hour you looked at one of the most important features of SharePoint—lists and libraries. You created site columns and content types through the user interface and through features. In addition you looked at creating custom field controls. Custom field controls provide a lot of flexibility to achieve things that out of the box SharePoint might not offer.

In addition to all this you learned how to create custom list definitions. In the next hour you explore the more advanced topics on managing data in SharePoint.

Q&A

Q. *Can you access list data directly from SQL?*

A. It is not recommended to access data directly from SQL. No documented APIs are available for this. Data manipulation should be done on the lists and libraries only.

Q. *Can you do bulk operations on a SharePoint list?*

A. You can perform batch inserts/updates on a SharePoint list using the `SPWeb.ProcessBatchData` method. This API has been available since SharePoint 2007 and is documented at http://msdn.microsoft.com/en-us/library/cc404818(v=office.12).aspx.

Q. *Can you customize the list forms?*

A. SharePoint 2010 makes it easy to customize list forms. You learn about this in subsequent hours.

HOUR 11

Understanding Advanced Data Management Concepts in SharePoint 2010

What You'll Learn in This Hour:
- ▶ Creating custom field types
- ▶ Understanding lists and list item event receivers
- ▶ Performing list data querying and manipulation

> **By the Way**
>
> Due to the complexity of the topics discussed, some figures in this book are very detailed and are intended only to provide a high-level view of concepts. Those figures are representational and not intended to be read in detail.

In the previous hour you learned about managing data in SharePoint. You looked at site columns, content types, SharePoint lists and libraries, and custom field controls. This hour examines some advanced features provided by SharePoint for managing data such as creating custom field types, event receivers, and querying data using CAML and LINQ to SharePoint.

Creating Custom Field Types

While SharePoint allows you to create many different types of site columns, you will find yourself at times creating custom site column types. For example, you may want to create a new site column type that displays a drop-down list that gets data from the database or some other source. To create a custom site column type you need to create the following:

- ▶ A new field type class. This is a class that must inherit from `Microsoft.SharePoint.SPField` or one of its inherited classes.

- ▶ A new field type definition. This is defined in an XML file that has a naming convention such as fldTypes_*.xml and is deployed to <14 hive>\Template\XML.

The field definition file tells SharePoint information related to the field type such as the name of the field and the underlying parent field type.

- A new custom field control. This is a class that inherits from the `BaseFieldControl` or one of its inherited classes and defines the user interface of the field type.

In this section you create a new field type called Country Drop Down List. This field control simply renders a drop-down list that displays a list of 10 countries. For now, you will hard code this list. You could also get the data from a database or some other source, but for now you should see how to write the new field type.

Try It Yourself

Create a Custom Field Type

1. Create a new Empty SharePoint project called AdvancedDropDownList.
2. Add a user control named CountryDropDownListTemplateControl.
3. Remove the codebehind and designer files.
4. Move the user control directly to the ControlTemplates folder.
5. Edit the user control as shown in the following code:

```
<%@ Assembly Name="$SharePoint.Project.AssemblyFullName$" %>
<%@ Assembly Name= "Microsoft.Web.CommandUI,
Version=14.0.0.0, Culture=neutral,
PublicKeyToken=71e9bce111e9429c" %>
<%@ Register TagPrefix="SharePoint"
Namespace="Microsoft.SharePoint.WebControls"
    Assembly="Microsoft.SharePoint,
Version=14.0.0.0, Culture=neutral,
PublicKeyToken=71e9bce111e9429c" %>
<%@ Register TagPrefix="Utilities"
Namespace="Microsoft.SharePoint.Utilities"
Assembly="Microsoft.SharePoint,
Version=14.0.0.0, Culture=neutral,
PublicKeyToken=71e9bce111e9429c" %>
<%@ Register TagPrefix="asp"
Namespace="System.Web.UI"
Assembly="System.Web.Extensions, Version=3.5.0.0,
Culture=neutral, PublicKeyToken=31bf3856ad364e35" %>
<%@ Import Namespace="Microsoft.SharePoint" %>
<%@ Register TagPrefix="WebPartPages"
Namespace="Microsoft.SharePoint.WebPartPages"
    Assembly="Microsoft.SharePoint,
    Version=14.0.0.0, Culture=neutral,
    PublicKeyToken=71e9bce111e9429c" %>
<%@ Control Language="C#" %>
<SharePoint:RenderingTemplate ID="CountryDropDownListTemplate"
```

Creating Custom Field Types 233

```
runat="server">
    <Template>
        <asp:DropDownList runat="server" ID="countryDropDownList" >
        </asp:DropDownList>
    </Template>
</SharePoint:RenderingTemplate>
```

The preceding code creates a user control for the field control. As you see in the following example this will be the rendering template for your field control. Note that this class must not have any codebehind and must be directly in the ControlTemplates folder and not in its subdirectory.

6. Add two new classes, CountryDropDownListField and CountryDropDownListFieldControl.

7. Update the code for the `CountryDropDownListFieldControl` class as follows:

```
using System;
using System.Collections.Generic;
using System.Linq;
using System.Text;
using Microsoft.SharePoint.WebControls;
using System.Web.UI.WebControls;
using Microsoft.SharePoint;

namespace AdvancedDropDownList
{
    public class CountryDropDownListFieldControl : BaseFieldControl
    {
        protected DropDownList countryDropDownList;

        public override object Value
        {
            get
            {
                EnsureChildControls();
                return countryDropDownList.SelectedValue;
            }
            set
            {
                EnsureChildControls();
                countryDropDownList.SelectedValue = this.ItemFieldValue as String;
            }
        }

        protected override void CreateChildControls()
        {
            if (this.Field == null || this.ControlMode == SPControlMode.Display)
                return;
            base.CreateChildControls();
            countryDropDownList =
            TemplateContainer.FindControl("countryDropDownList")
            as DropDownList;

            string []countries =new string[]{
```

```
                    "Australia",
                    "Brazil",
                    "Canada",
                    "France",
                    "Germany",
                    "India",
                    "Russia",
                    "U.K.",
                    "U.S.A."
                };

                // we could bind data from database or external source here
                countryDropDownList.DataSource = countries;
                countryDropDownList.DataBind();
            }

            protected override string DefaultTemplateName
            {
                get
                {
                    return "CountryDropDownListTemplate";
                }
            }
        }
    }
```

The preceding class represents your field control, which inherits from the `BaseFieldControl`, which is the base for all the other field controls. The interesting thing to note is the `DefaultTemplateName` property. The code overrides this property and returns the id of the rendering template defined in the user control you created.

8. Edit the `CountryDropDownListField` class and update as shown in the following code:

```
using System;
using System.Collections.Generic;
using System.Linq;
using System.Text;
using Microsoft.SharePoint;
using Microsoft.SharePoint.WebControls;

namespace AdvancedDropDownList
{
    public class CountryDropDownListField : SPFieldChoice
    {
        public CountryDropDownListField(
SPFieldCollection fields, string fieldName) :
            base(fields, fieldName) { }

        public CountryDropDownListField(
SPFieldCollection fields,
string typeName, string displayName) :
            base(fields, typeName, displayName) { }
```

```
        public override BaseFieldControl FieldRenderingControl
        {
            get
            {
                BaseFieldControl fieldControl =
                new CountryDropDownListFieldControl();
                fieldControl.FieldName = InternalName;
                return fieldControl;
            }
        }
    }
}
```

This class is simple. The important thing to note is the `FieldRenderingControl` property where the field type is associated with the custom country field control. Finally you need to create your field type definition file.

9. Add a mapped folder for TEMPLATE\XML and inside that folder add a new XML file; name it fldTypes_SearchableDropDownList.xml. Edit the XML as shown here:

```
<?xml version="1.0" encoding="utf-8" ?>
<FieldTypes>
  <FieldType>
    <Field Name="TypeName">CountryDropDownList</Field>
    <Field Name="ParentType">Choice</Field>
    <Field Name="TypeDisplayName">Country Drop Down List</Field>
    <Field Name="TypeShortDescription">Country Drop Down List</Field>
    <Field Name="UserCreatable">TRUE</Field>
    <Field Name="ShowInListCreate">TRUE</Field>
    <Field Name="ShowInSurveyCreate">TRUE</Field>
    <Field Name="ShowInDocumentLibraryCreate">TRUE</Field>
    <Field Name="ShowInColumnTemplateCreate">TRUE</Field>
    <Field Name="FieldTypeClass">
      AdvancedDropDownList.CountryDropDownListField,
      AdvancedDropDownList, Version=1.0.0.0, Culture=neutral,
      PublicKeyToken=d7df0b2df995d128
    </Field>
  </FieldType>
</FieldTypes>
```

This code specifies information like the `TypeName`, which is a unique name for the field type in the entire SharePoint farm. In addition you specify the field type class and assembly used for this field type.

Note that the final project structure should look as shown in Figure 11.1.

FIGURE 11.1
AdvancedDropDownList project structure

10. Deploy the solution.
11. Try to add a new site column to the simple list. You see the option to create a field using your new field type as shown in Figure 11.2.

FIGURE 11.2
Creating a new site column from a custom field type

12. Create the new site column and add it to the SimpleList created earlier.
13. Try to create a new item. You should see the drop-down list with the list of countries as shown in Figure 11.3.

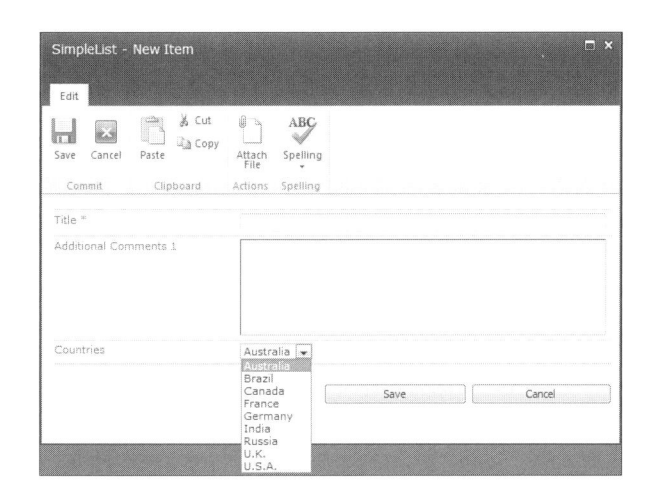

FIGURE 11.3
The Create New Item Screen with a custom field

You can also create the site column using features. Note that the value of the TypeName is used for the type attribute in the field element when creating a site column of this field type using features. The following is an example of the Field element you use to create a new site column:

```xml
<?xml version="1.0" encoding="utf-8"?>
<Elements xmlns="http://schemas.microsoft.com/sharepoint/">
  <Field Type=" CountryDropDownList"
  DisplayName="Countries" Required="FALSE"
  Group="Custom Columns"
  ID="{410BCF29-E156-4256-91E7-CCFED3482DAC}"
  StaticName=" Countries" Name=" Countries" />
</Elements>
```

Understanding Lists and List Item Event Receivers

In Hour 8, "Understanding Client Object Model in SharePoint 2010," you learned how SharePoint enables you to hook the events in the life cycle of a SharePoint site collection and a SharePoint site through various event receivers provided by SharePoint. This section looks at the event receivers for a list and for list items. The event receivers for a list and list items can be categorized in two ways. One is the event receivers that get called when an event is happening and before it is completed. For example, the FieldAdding event is called before a new field is added to the list, and the ItemAdding event gets called before a new list item is created. Similarly some event receivers get called after the event has happened. For example, the `FieldAdded` event receiver gets called after a new field has been added to the list, and the `ItemAdded` event receiver gets called after a new list item has been created. You will find that the name of Before events end with "ing" and the name of the After events end with "ed."

The other way to categorize events is synchronous events and asynchronous events. The `ItemAdding` event occurs synchronously, which allows you to set the `Cancel` property of the event argument to the item creation. The `ItemAdded` event on the other hand is called asynchronously after the item has been added. This means the user might sometimes see the added list item before the `ItemAdded` event receiver has been processed or at times after it is processed.

Table 11.1 lists the various events for a SharePoint list. Notice that the names of most of these events are self-describing.

TABLE 11.1 List Events

Event Name	Description
FieldAdding	Called before a new field has been added to the list
FieldUpdating	Called before the properties of a list field have been updated
FieldDeleting	Called before a field has been deleted
FieldAdded	Called after a new field has been added to the list
FieldUpdated	Called after the properties of a list field have been updated
FieldDeleted	Called after a field has been deleted

Note that these event handlers are defined in the `SPListEventReceiver` class, which is the class that provides methods to trap events that occur for lists. This class is never instantiated, and your event receiver class inherits from this class and overrides the require methods.

Table 11.2 lists the various events for a list item.

TABLE 11.2 List Item Events

Event Name	Description
ItemAdded	An asynchronous event called after an event that occurs after a new item has been added to its containing object.
ItemAdding	A synchronous event called before an event that occurs when a new item is added to its containing object.
ItemAttachmentAdded	An After event that occurs after a user adds an attachment to an item. This is asynchronous.

Event Name	Description
ItemAttachmentAdding	A synchronous Before event that occurs when a user adds an attachment to an item.
ItemAttachmentDeleted	An asynchronous After event that occurs after a user removes an attachment from an item.
ItemAttachmentDeleting	A Before event that occurs when a user removes an attachment from an item. This is synchronous.
ItemCheckedIn	An asynchronous After event that occurs after an item is checked in.
ItemCheckedOut	An asynchronous After event that occurs after an item is checked out.
ItemCheckingIn	A synchronous Before event that occurs as a file is being checked in.
ItemCheckingOut	A synchronous Before event that occurs after an item is checked out.
ItemDeleted	An asynchronous After event that occurs after an existing item is completely deleted.
ItemDeleting	A synchronous Before event that occurs before an existing item is completely deleted.

Try It Yourself
Write a List Item Event Receiver

You now look at an example of list item events. This example handles the
ItemAdded and ItemUpdated events of a custom list called Presentations that has
the following columns:

- **Title**—Out of the box single line title field
- **ViewerComments**—Custom multiline plain text field
- **History**—Custom multiline plain text field

The user first creates a new item and enters a title and comment in the list item. The
ItemAdded event copies the contents of the Title and ViewerComments fields into the
History field in some specific format and clears the ViewerComments field. When
the user edits the list item and adds new ViewerComments to it the ItemUpdating
event appends the existing title and the newly added comment to the History field.
This way the History field shows a history of the list item. Note that the multiline

HOUR 11: Understanding Advanced Data Management Concepts in SharePoint 2010

field has a property that allows you to append the changes to the field, thus effectively storing the history. However, for demonstration purposes this example does it through event receivers.

Follow these steps to create the event receiver:

1. Create a new custom list called Presentations and add two multiline plain text fields called `ViewerComments` and `History` to it. Open Visual Studio 2010 and create a new Empty SharePoint Project called PresentationsListEvents. Add a new item of type Event Receiver named `PresentationsListEventsReceiver`. After clicking on Add you see the Choose Event Receiver Settings screen shown in Figure 11.4. Select List Item Events as the type of event receiver and Custom List for the event source. In the Handle the Following Events section select the An Item Was Added and An Item Was Updated events.

FIGURE 11.4
Event receiver settings

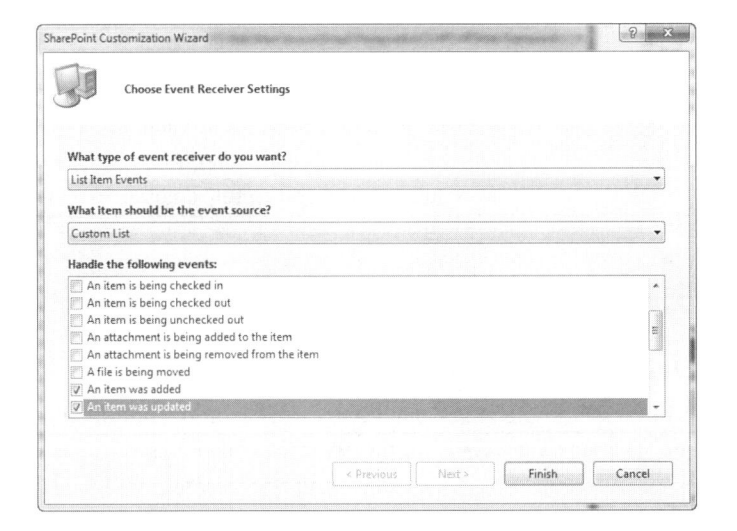

2. Click the Finish button. A new folder is added that has an XML and class file. Rename the newly added feature to some appropriate name. The project structure should look similar to Figure 11.5.

3. Open the PresentationsListEventReceiver.cs. You see a class that inherits from SPItemEventReceiver. This is the base class for handling list item events. Open the elements.xml file. You find the following code:

```
<?xml version="1.0" encoding="utf-8"?>
<Elements xmlns="http://schemas.microsoft.com/sharepoint/">
  <Receivers ListTemplateId="100">
    <Receiver>
      <Name>PresentationsListEventsReceiverItemAdded</Name>
```

```xml
      <Type>ItemAdded</Type>
      <Assembly>$SharePoint.Project.AssemblyFullName$</Assembly>
      <Class>
      PresentationsListEvents.
      PresentationsListEventsReceiver.
      PresentationsListEventsReceiver
      </Class>
      <SequenceNumber>10000</SequenceNumber>
    </Receiver>
    <Receiver>
      <Name>PresentationsListEventsReceiverItemUpdated</Name>
      <Type>ItemUpdated</Type>
      <Assembly>$SharePoint.Project.AssemblyFullName$</Assembly>
      <Class>
      PresentationsListEvents.
      PresentationsListEventsReceiver.
      PresentationsListEventsReceiver
      </Class>
      <SequenceNumber>10000</SequenceNumber>
    </Receiver>
  </Receivers>
</Elements>
```

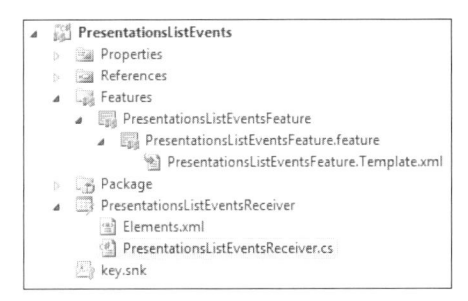

FIGURE 11.5 The PresentationsListEvents project structure

4. This XML is responsible for associating your event handler with the list. The value of the `ListTemplateId` in the `Receivers` tag is set to 100, which represents a custom list template id and hence your event receivers get associated to a custom list. The `Name`, `Type`, and `Assembly` elements specify the name of the event receiver, the type of the event receiver, and the assembly containing the event receiver. The `Class` element specifies the class containing the event handler code. In addition the `Sequence` element specifies the sequence of the event receiver to execute in case multiple event receivers of the same type are associated with the same template id.

5. Note that you could also have programmatically associated your event receivers with the Presentations list in the `FeatureActivated` event of the feature. The following code programmatically associates an event receiver in the feature activated event and removes it in the feature deactivated event:

```
public override void FeatureActivated(SPFeatureReceiverProperties
properties)
    {
        SPWeb web = properties.Feature.Parent as SPWeb;
        SPList list = web.Lists["Presentations"];
        SPEventReceiverDefinition newReceiver =
list.EventReceivers.Add();
        newReceiver.Assembly =
        "PresentationsListEvents, Version=1.0.0.0,
        Culture=neutral; PublicKeyToken=e05ebc5d87c6e48c";
        newReceiver.Class = "PresentationsListEventsReceiver";
        newReceiver.Type = SPEventReceiverType.ItemAdded;
        newReceiver.SequenceNumber = 10000;

    }

public override void FeatureDeactivating(
SPFeatureReceiverProperties properties)
    {
        SPWeb web = properties.Feature.Parent as SPWeb;
        SPList list = web.Lists["Presentations"];
        int count = list.EventReceivers.Count;

        while (count > 0)
        {
            SPEventReceiverDefinition curReceiver =
            list.EventReceivers[count - 1];
            if (curReceiver.Type ==
            SPEventReceiverType.ItemAdded
            && curReceiver.Class ==
            "PresentationsListEventsReceiver"
            && curReceiver.Assembly ==
            "PresentationsListEvents, Version=1.0.0.0,
            Culture=neutral; PublicKeyToken=e05ebc5d87c6e48c")
            {
                curReceiver.Delete();
            }
            count--;
        }
    }
}
```

6. Now look at the event receiver code. Open the PresentationsListEventsReceiver.cs file, and you find the ItemAdded and ItemUpdated methods overridden here. Edit the code in the ItemAdded and ItemUpdated event as shown in the following code:

```
public override void ItemAdded(SPItemEventProperties properties)
    {
        base.ItemAdding(properties);

        if (properties.List.Title != "Presentations")
            return;

        SPListItem curItem = properties.ListItem;

        curItem["History"] =
```

Understanding Lists and List Item Event Receivers 243

```
            string.Format(
            "Time:{0} \n User: {1}\n Title:{2}\n Comments:{3}\n",
            curItem["Modified"],
            curItem["Modified By"].ToString().Split('#')[1],
            curItem["Title"],
            curItem["ViewerComments"]);

            curItem["ViewerComments"] = string.Empty;

            // disable event firing else the item updated event will get
➥called
            this.EventFiringEnabled = false;
            curItem.Update();

            // enable event firing
            this.EventFiringEnabled = true;
        }

        public override void ItemUpdated(SPItemEventProperties properties)
        {
            base.ItemUpdating(properties);

            if (properties.List.Title != "Presentations")
                return;

            SPListItem curItem = properties.ListItem;

            curItem["History"] =
            string.Format(
            "Time:{0} \n User: {1}\n Title:{2}\n Comments:{3}\n\n {4}",
            curItem["Modified"],
            curItem["Modified By"].ToString().Split('#')[1],
            curItem["Title"],
            curItem["ViewerComments"],
            curItem["History"]);

            curItem["ViewerComments"] = string.Empty;

            // disable event firing else the item updated event will get
➥called
            this.EventFiringEnabled = false;
            curItem.Update();

            // enable event firing
            this.EventFiringEnabled = true;
    }
}
```

7. The preceding code updates the current list item represented by properties. ListItem. The History field also is updated with the data from the other fields, and the ViewerComments field is made blank. Also before starting any processing the code checks for the title of the list on which this event was fired. If the list title does not match Presentations we do not do any processing and return from the function. An interesting line of code is where this.EventFiringEnabled is set to false and then to true. Setting the

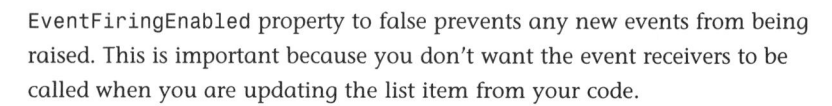

HOUR 11: Understanding Advanced Data Management Concepts in SharePoint 2010

EventFiringEnabled property to false prevents any new events from being raised. This is important because you don't want the event receivers to be called when you are updating the list item from your code.

8. Build the solution and deploy it. Add a new item (see Figure 11.6) and save it.

FIGURE 11.6
The New Item screen for Presentations List

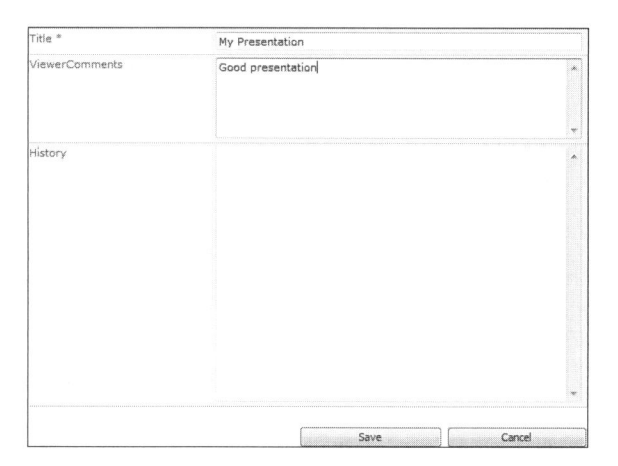

9. You can see that the ViewerComments field got cleared and the History field was updated as shown in Figure 11.7.

FIGURE 11.7
Presentation List item

10. Edit the list item, enter something in ViewerComments, and click Save. You see the History field is updated.

11. At times you may need to refresh the screen to see the changes. This is because the event receivers are running asynchronously. You can make the events run synchronously through the Synchronization element. Update the Elements.xml as shown here:

```
<?xml version="1.0" encoding="utf-8"?>
<Elements xmlns="http://schemas.microsoft.com/sharepoint/">
  <Receivers ListTemplateId="100">
    <Receiver>
      <Name>PresentationsListEventsReceiverItemAdded</Name>
      <Type>ItemAdded</Type>
      <Assembly>$SharePoint.Project.AssemblyFullName$</Assembly>
```

```
      <Class>
        PresentationsListEvents.
        PresentationsListEventsReceiver.
        PresentationsListEventsReceiver
      </Class>
      <SequenceNumber>10000</SequenceNumber>
      <Synchronization>Synchronous</Synchronization>
    </Receiver>
    <Receiver>
      <Name>PresentationsListEventsReceiverItemUpdated</Name>
      <Type>ItemUpdated</Type>
      <Assembly>$SharePoint.Project.AssemblyFullName$</Assembly>
      <Class>
        PresentationsListEvents.
        PresentationsListEventsReceiver.
        PresentationsListEventsReceiver
      </Class>
      <SequenceNumber>10000</SequenceNumber>
      <Synchronization>Synchronous</Synchronization>
    </Receiver>
  </Receivers>
</Elements>
```

Note that the preceding code indicates that our event receivers must run synchronously by setting the `Synchronization` element to `Synchronous`. Deploy the solution and test the changes. You should now be able to see the changes correctly after saving, and a browser refresh will not be needed anymore.

You can also define the event receivers on content types. To bind an event receiver to a content type you can call the `SPContentType.EventReceivers.Add()` method.

> **Watch Out!**
>
> While the event receivers framework seems to provide the developer with a lot of flexibility and power and it does provide it, you must be careful about the code written in event receivers as it can drastically impact performance.

Performing List Data Querying and Manipulation

Hour 7, "Understanding SharePoint 2010 Server Side Development," looked at how to query and manipulate data in lists using the object model—the `SPList` and `SPListItem` class. While this is good for a simple scenario, this is not the best way to query and edit data in lists. This section shows other better and recommended ways to do the same.

Querying List Data Using CAML

CAML (Collaborative Application Markup Language) is an XML-based query language used in conjunction with the `SPQuery` and `SPSiteDataQuery` classes to perform data operations on SharePoint lists. While the `SPQuery` class is used to retrieve data from a specific list, the `SPSiteDataQuery` class is used to retrieve data from multiple lists across different sites in a particular site collection. To query data from a list using the `SPQuery` class, you need to specify the properties of an `SPQuery` object as shown in Table 11.3.

TABLE 11.3 CAML Query Properties

SPQuery Property	Description
Query	CAML query that you want to execute against a SharePoint list
ViewFields	List of columns that you want to retrieve
Joins	Join predicates for the query, to join to a foreign list (similar to concept of joins in relational databases)
ProjectedFields	Fields from the foreign list, which you want to refer to in the `ViewFields` or the `Query` property

Consider a scenario where you have the following two lists in your SharePoint site:

- **Departments**—Having fields like Department ID, Department Name, and Department Location

- **Employees**—Having fields like Employee Number, First Name, Last Name, Designation, and Department ID (a lookup column to the Departments list), Department Name (linked to Department Name in the Departments list via the Department ID lookup column)

Department related information for an employee is present in the Departments *list*, which is linked to the Employees list via the Department ID column. In SharePoint, columns (such as Department ID) defining relationships between lists are of type lookup, and SharePoint provides you the option to select an existing column from the foreign list while defining a column of this type. For example, Figure 11.8 shows how the Department ID column should be defined in the Employees list.

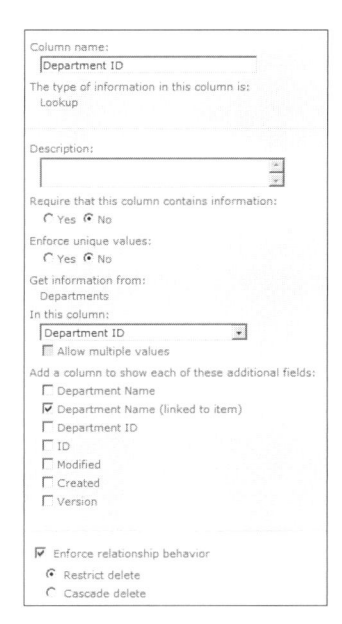

Performing List Data Querying and Manipulation 247

FIGURE 11.8
Defining the Department ID lookup column in the Employees list

Now let's use the SPQuery class and retrieve all employees from the Employees list having the designation of Manager. The following code helps achieve this:

```
// Create SPQuery object
SPQuery allManagersQuery = new SPQuery
{
    Query =
    "<Where>
       <Eq>
         <FieldRef Name='Designation' />
         <Value Type='Text'>Manager</Value>
       </Eq>
     </Where>",
    ViewFields =
    "<FieldRef Name='Last_x0020_Name' />
     <FieldRef Name='LinkTitle' />
     <FieldRef Name='Department_x0020_ID_x003a_Depart' />",
};

// Call GetItems method on Employees list passing SPQuery instance
SPListItemCollection results =
SPContext.Current.Web.Lists
["Employees"].GetItems(allManagersQuery);

if (results != null && results.Count != 0)
{
    // Enumerate through the result set and
    // display Last Name, First Name and
    // Department fields
    foreach (SPListItem listItem in results)
```

```
        {
            writer.Write("{0} {1} {2}<br/>",
              listItem["Last_x0020_Name"],
              listItem["LinkTitle"],
              listItem["Department_x0020_ID_x003a_Depart"]);
        }
}
```

The easiest way to build a CAML query for the preceding scenario is to create a view (on the Employees list) to get all managers with the filter criteria configured as shown in Figure 11.9.

FIGURE 11.9
Specifying filter criteria for the AllManagers view

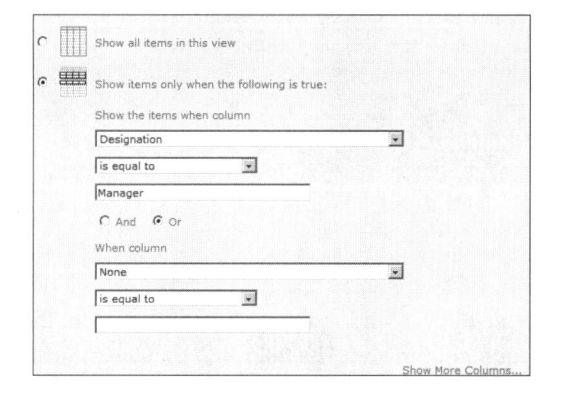

Once the view is ready, use Visual Studio's Server Explorer to connect to the SharePoint site and examine the view's property. Copy the contents of the `SchemaXml` property to Notepad and extract the value of the `Query` and `ViewFields` elements, as shown in Figure 11.10. The value of these elements is used directly in the preceding code while creating a new instance of the `SPQuery` class.

If you examine the contents of the AllManagersWebPart, you will notice that the lookup fields containing an employee's department name, displays a number followed by semicolon and hash characters and finally the department name, as shown in Figure 11.11.

This is because the lookup fields store the Lookup ID along with the actual Lookup value, separated by ";#" characters. The `SPFieldLookupValue` class's `LookupValue` property helps to obtain the actual lookup value. The following code demonstrates how to use this class to get only the department name from the lookup:

```
SPFieldLookupValue DepartmentLookup =
new SPFieldLookupValue(
listItem["Department_x0020_ID_x003a_Depart"].ToString());
string departmentName = DepartmentLookup.LookupValue;
```

FIGURE 11.10 Extracting contents of the Query and ViewFields elements from the AllManagers view's schema definition

FIGURE 11.11 The Lookup field contains the Lookup ID and Lookup Value separated by ";#" characters

Next, try to get all employees located in the north wing. Since the Department Location column is not a linked lookup column (via the Department ID field), you need to include a join predicate here to join the Employees and Department lists and apply the filter on the Department Location column to get the employees located in the North Wing. Make the following modifications to your SPQuery object:

```
SPQuery northWingEmployeesQuery = new SPQuery
{
    Query = @"<Where>
                <Eq>
                    <FieldRef Name='EmployeeDepartmentLocation' />
                    <Value Type='Text'>North Wing</Value>
                </Eq>
            </Where>",
    ViewFields = @"<FieldRef Name='Last_x0020_Name' />
                <FieldRef Name='LinkTitle' />
                <FieldRef Name='EmployeeDepartmentLocation' />",
    Joins = @"<Join Type='INNER' ListAlias='EmployeeDepartmentList'>
                <Eq>
                    <FieldRef Name='Department_x0020_ID' RefType='Id' />
                    <FieldRef List='EmployeeDepartmentList' Name='ID' />
                </Eq>
            </Join>",
```

```
    ProjectedFields = "<Field Name=' EmployeeDepartmentLocation' Type='Lookup'
↪List='EmployeeDepartmentList' ShowField='Department_x0020_Location' />"
};
```

First, understand the `Joins` property in the preceding code. We specify here that we want an Inner Join with the Department ID (internal name `Department_x0020_ID`) being the join field, and we assign the `EmployeeDepartmentList` alias to the join result. The `ProjectedFields` property helps to specify (and assign an alias as well) the columns to retrieve from the foreign list. We retrieve `DepartmentLocation` in this case and call it `EmployeeDepartmentLocation`. Once the `EmployeeDepartmentLocation` field is defined as a projected field, it can be used in the `Query` to filter the list items having the department name of North Wing. Further, because you want to display the department's location in the result, this field is included in the `ViewFields` property as well.

The rest of the procedure of obtaining the results remains the same, as in the case of the all managers query. Refer to the NorthWingEmployeesWebPart in the DataAccessDemo project in the sample code for this hour for a complete listing of the code.

Now look at the usage of the `SPSiteDataQuery` class, which is used to retrieve data from multiple lists across different sites in a particular site collection. Retrieve the value of title field for all the list items across all the generic lists in the current site collection. The following code represents the `SPSiteDataQuery` object for this operation:

```
// Create SPSiteDataQuery object
SPSiteDataQuery siteDataQuery = new SPSiteDataQuery
{
    ViewFields = @"<FieldRef Name='Title'/>",
    Lists = @"<Lists BaseType='0' />",
    Webs = "<Webs Scope='SiteCollection' />",
    RowLimit = 10
};

// Call GetSiteData method on the current web
DataTable results = SPContext.Current.Web.GetSiteData(siteDataQuery);
```

> **By the Way**
>
> In the `Lists` property, a value of zero for the `BaseType` attribute indicates that you are looking for all the Generic lists. Other values that you can specify for this property include 1 to look for a document library, 3 to look for a discussion forum, 4 to look for a vote or survey, and 5 to look for an Issues list.

Further, you can also restrict your results to lists of a particular server template by specifying a value for the `ServerTemplate` attribute.

Using the `Webs` property, you can restrict the scope of your query in the following manner:

- `<Webs Scope='SiteCollection' />` searches the entire site collection.
- `<Webs Scope='Recursive' />` searches the current web and its child webs recursively.

`SPSiteDataQuery` does not support Joins and projected fields. Refer to the AllListTitlesWebPart in the code samples for this hour for complete source code of this example.

Querying List Data Using LINQ

CAML takes some amount of time to gain expertise in. Debugging CAML is not easy, and often you get cryptic error messages that are difficult to interpret. Language-Integrated Query (LINQ) to SharePoint offers an alternative. However, you cannot completely do away with CAML as it is still the most appropriate choice in certain scenarios. Even internally CAML queries are generated corresponding to the LINQ statements, which ultimately perform the specified data operations.

LINQ provides a SQL-like syntax that can be used to query data. It operates against strongly typed entities that represent the items in your lists. These entities can be generated with the help of a command-line tool, shipped with SharePoint, called SPMetal.

Try It Yourself
Write LINQ to Query Data

Let's look at the approach to get employees located in the North Wing, using LINQ to SQL. Earlier you retrieved the related records using CAML in the NorthWingEmployees WebPart.

1. To start using LINQ to SharePoint, add a reference to the Microsoft.SharePoint.Linq.dll located in the 14\ISAPI directory and include the following using statements in your code:

   ```
   using System.Linq;
   using Microsoft.SharePoint.Linq;
   ```

2. Next create entities for the lists you want to manipulate with LINQ. You can use SPMetal.exe, located in the 14\BIN folder, to generate these.

   ```
   SPMetal /web:http://SiteUrl /code:C:\EntityFileName.cs /language:csharp
   ```

3. At this point you are ready to write your LINQ query and query the results. The following code demonstrates exactly how to do this:

   ```
   // Create Data Context object
   using (HumanResourceEntitiesDataContext dataContext =
       new HumanResourceEntitiesDataContext("http://YourSiteUrl"))
   {
   
   // LINQ query to get employees located in North Wing
   var results = from employee in dataContext.Employees.ToList()
                 join department in dataContext.Departments
                 on employee.DepartmentID.DepartmentID
                 equals department.DepartmentID
                 where department.DepartmentLocation == "North Wing"
                 select new
                 {
                     employee.LastName,
                     employee.Title,
                     department.DepartmentLocation
                 };
   
   if (results != null && results.Count() != 0)
   {
       // Enumerate through the result set and
       // display Last Name, First Name and
       // Employee Location
       foreach (var resultItem in results)
       {
           writer.Write("{0} {1} {2}<br/>",
                       resultItem.LastName,
                       resultItem.Title,
                       resultItem.DepartmentLocation);
       }
   }
   }
   ```

The preceding LINQ query joins the Employees and Departments entities on the Department ID field. Next you specify filter criteria in the where statement to get the employees at the North Wing location. Finally, you select the employee's last name, first name (which is the title field internally), and the department location.

Because LINQ to SharePoint operates against strongly typed entities (generated using SPMetal.exe) you get a good amount of IntelliSense support from Visual Studio while writing LINQ queries (see Figure 11.12).

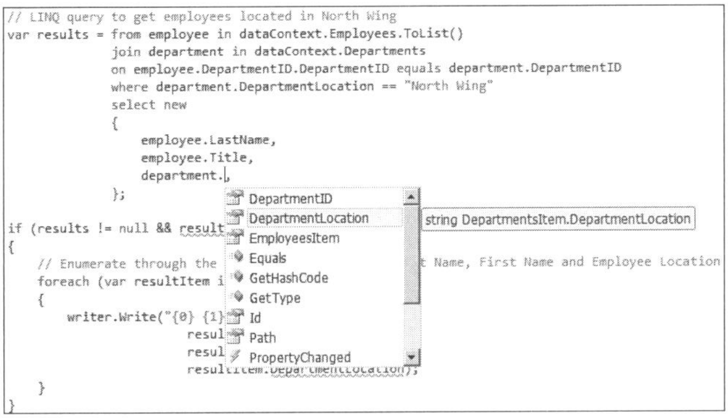

FIGURE 11.12
Visual Studio provides IntelliSense support for LINQ queries.

Querying lists using LINQ is much easier than writing CAML queries directly. However, at certain times, when you have complex LINQ queries, you may want to ensure that your LINQ expressions translate into efficient CAML queries. In such cases it can be useful to review a CAML query generated by the LINQ to SharePoint provider. To do so, you can use the Log property of the DataContext to specify a TextWriter object and log the results to a text file or event log, as illustrated in the following code:

```
// Create Data Context object
using (HumanResourceEntitiesDataContext dataContext =
    new HumanResourceEntitiesDataContext("http://YourSiteUrl"))
{
    // Specify TextWriter object instance to the DataContext class
    StringBuilder sb = new StringBuilder();
    StringWriter stringWriter = new StringWriter(sb);
    dataContext.Log = stringWriter;

    // Your CAML query goes here
    // ............
    // ............

    // Write the generated CAML to event log
    EventLog.WriteEntry("CAML Query", sb.ToString());
}
```

Summary

This hour continued the lesson from the previous hour on managing data better in SharePoint. SharePoint provides so many features that managing data in SharePoint can also be complex. Hopefully by now you have a good hold on the various concepts involved in managing data in SharePoint 2010. This also prepares you for the next two important hours that discuss enterprise content management in SharePoint.

Q&A

Q. *Can you have multiple event receivers of the same type on a list/library?*

A. Yes. You can have multiple event receivers of the same type on a list/library. Their execution sequence depends on the sequence property specified in elements.xml.

Q. *Can you temporarily disable event firing?*

A. To disable the event firing you need to remove the association of the event receiver with the list/list item. This is not temporary unless you associate the event receiver with the list/list item again.

HOUR 12

Enterprise Content Management—Understanding Document Management

What You'll Learn in This Hour:

- ▶ Understanding Enterprise Content Management
- ▶ Managing documents using document IDs
- ▶ Managing document sets
- ▶ Understanding managed metadata
- ▶ Synchronizing content types with the content type publishing hubs

> **By the Way**
>
> Due to the complexity of the topics discussed, some figures in this book are very detailed and are intended only to provide a high-level view of concepts. Those figures are representational and not intended to be read in detail.

Remember the last time you lost a critical e-mail or when you were struggling to free up space on your hard drive deciding what *content* to keep and what to throw away? Managing content has always been a challenge whether at the individual level or an enterprise level, especially in this age of information overload. With the advent of so many new sources of data, for example, unstructured data from social networking sites, audio-visual data from online meetings, and so on, modern-day organizations have to deal with a lot more content today than they had to a decade ago. From the collection of data, to its retention over a period of time, and later to its archival and eventual disposal, the entire life cycle of content management has become even more complex in the present age.

While ECM solutions have been around for many years to aid organizations with the process of content management, their criticality and importance have increased manifold in the recent years. This hour looks at the basics of ECM and the Enterprise Content Management features available in SharePoint. First you must understand exactly what ECM is.

Understanding Enterprise Content Management

The Association for Information and Image Management (AIIM) International, the worldwide association for enterprise content management, defines ECM this way: *"Enterprise Content Management (ECM) is the strategies, methods and tools used to capture, manage, store, preserve, and deliver content and documents related to organizational processes. ECM tools and strategies allow the management of an organization's unstructured information, wherever that information exists."*

ECM encompasses areas such as document management, records management, web content management, electronic forms management, workflow management, search, and collaboration. Primarily, ECM is focused on managing the life cycle of content from its birth to death. Yes, regardless of its type or category, content does have a life cycle, which includes content creation, storage and archival, and eventual disposition based on certain business rules and workflows.

In this age of information overload, ECM becomes even more important with the increasing need to better organize information with improved efficiency, better control, and reduced costs. Although there is no limit to content arriving from various sources, such as documents, emails, audio and video, meeting notes and records, discussion forums, and unstructured data from social networking sites, there is certainly a limit to the amount of data that an organization can store and archive and retain for longer durations. This definitely calls for adequate content disposal and archival policies. Further accurate categorization and classification of content is equally important so that it can be consumed and analyzed using a business intelligence system that can help organizations use the available information to guide business decisions.

Even digitization has impacted the way ECM systems operate. For example, many organizations now store archived expense reports filed by their employees, along with related bills/receipts, within ECM systems instead of the older method of keeping physical documents in storage warehouses. In older systems (when digital storage was expensive and storage capacity was limited) each document was assigned a unique ID, and depending on the content retention policies as the document's ID moved to the archival stage in digital storage of ECM, the associated physical document was handpicked and put in archived storage manually. With the reduced costs of digital storage and document scanning devices, the physical documents are done away with even sooner while the digital records can be retained perhaps forever.

Now that you understand the role of an ECM system in enterprise content management, you can proceed further and explore various content management features available in SharePoint.

Managing Documents Using Document IDs

A basic expectation from any document management system is that it should ease the process of document retrieval. Preferably, documents should be uniquely identifiable with a document key or an ID. The Document ID Service in SharePoint helps you to achieve just that. You can activate this service at site collection level by activating the Document ID Service site collection feature.

Go ahead and enable the Document ID Service feature. After enabling the feature, if you upload a new document, you find that a new field called Document ID is now present in the document properties, as shown in Figure 12.1.

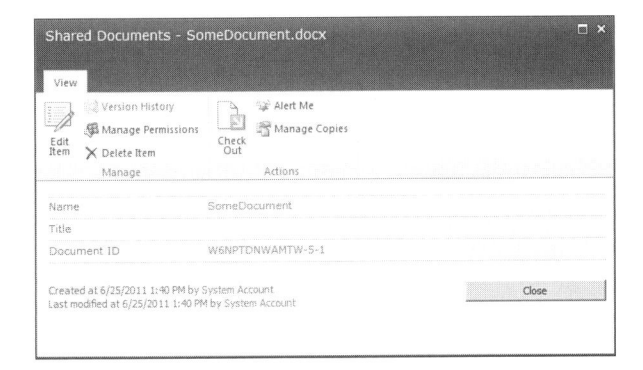

FIGURE 12.1
Document ID assigned to a newly uploaded document by the Document ID Service

> Activating the Document ID Service provisions the timer jobs, Document ID assignment job, and Document ID enable/disable job, to configure the feature. It may take a while at certain times before the timer jobs finish and Document ID Service gets configured. You can find these jobs in Central Administration (_admin/ServiceJobDefinitions.aspx) corresponding to your web application. Further, you can also visit the Document ID Settings under the Site Collection Administration, and until the time the timer jobs don't complete a successful run, you would get the message "Configuration of the Document ID feature is scheduled to be completed by an automated process," as shown in Figure 12.2, and document IDs will not be generated.

By the Way

Once the feature gets configured and the document IDs are generated, inspect the document properties of a recently uploaded document, as shown previously in Figure 12.1. Click the documents ID hyperlink and note the redirection URL, which should be something similar to http://YourSiteCollection/_layouts/DocIdRedir.aspx?ID=W6NPTDNWAMTW-5-1, with a different document ID in your case.

HOUR 12: Enterprise Content Management

Clicking the document ID hyperlink is simply redirecting you to DocIdRedit.aspx page, with the document ID being passed as a query string parameter, and it is worth noting that there is no reference to the document's location in the URL. The Document ID Service evaluates the passed in document ID via the query string and further redirects you to the document's actual location.

FIGURE 12.2
Timer jobs are not yet done with the feature configuration.

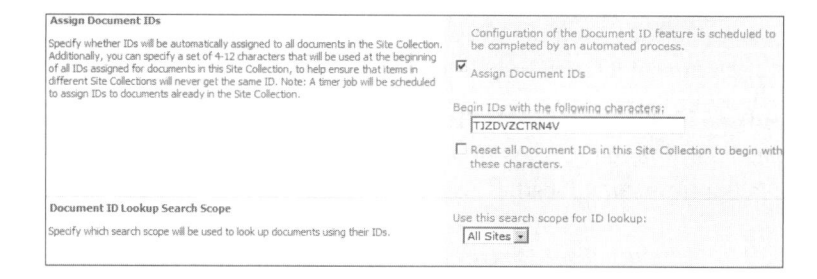

Using the document IDs can be useful to organizations, because as the documents move from one library to the other, corresponding to various business processes of the organization (say from an active to archived documents library), they can still be referred to via the same document ID, which is guaranteed to be unique and independent of the document's location. This also solves the problem of broken links, since a document is guaranteed to be found as long as it is referred to by the location of independent document ID, unless of course it should not have been already disposed by a disposition workflow.

While any new documents you upload get the document IDs assigned as expected, the existing ones are assigned the document IDs once the Document ID assignment job executes, which by default is scheduled to run on a daily basis.

Further, you can also configure the prefix assigned to a document ID by navigating to Document ID Settings under Site Collection Administration. You can even choose to reset the existing document IDs to use the newly configured prefix, as illustrated in Figure 12.3. Again, the existing document IDs would change only once the document ID assignment job executes.

A useful web part while working with the document IDs is the Find by Document ID. The web part is present under the Search folder in the web part gallery. As the name suggests, the web part allows you to find documents based on the *document ID*, as shown in Figure 12.4.

FIGURE 12.3
Configuring the document ID prefix

FIGURE 12.4
Find by Document ID web part

Managing Document Sets

Often, you may want a number of related documents to be treated as one entity, corresponding to a work product in your organization's business process. For example, an expense report submitted by an employee might include a number of bills/receipts, travel tickets or boarding passes, and other supporting documents. Document sets allow all these documents to be grouped together thus facilitating the entire set of documents to participate in the business process as a single entity.

In SharePoint, document sets are implemented as content type. Hence the traditional concepts applicable to a content type (workflows, versioning, and so on) apply to a document set as well.

Try It Yourself
Create a Document Set

Follow these steps to enable and create document sets in SharePoint:

1. Activate the site collection level feature called Document Sets.

2. Set the Allow Management of Content Types option to Yes for a particular library. You can find this option on the Advanced Settings page while configuring document library settings, as illustrated in Figure 12.5.

3. Add the Document Set content type as an allowed content type for the document library by navigating to the Add from Existing Site Content Types link in the document library settings.

4. Click the New Document button, and you see the option to create a document set.

HOUR 12: Enterprise Content Management

FIGURE 12.5
Enabling management of content types

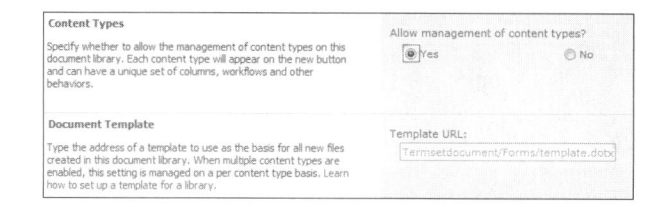

5. Create the new document set and specify a name and description for it. Once the document set is created, you are taken to a welcome page that you can use to manage the content in the document set.

If your library contains both documents and document sets, you can identify the document sets with their unique folder icon as shown in Figure 12.6.

FIGURE 12.6
Identifying the document sets

Now examine the properties of your newly created document set, as illustrated in Figure 12.7.

FIGURE 12.7
Document sets too are assigned document IDs.

By the Way

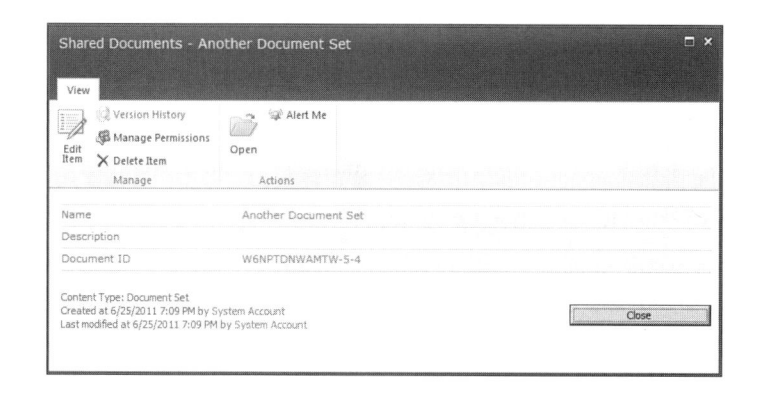

Interestingly, document sets too are assigned document IDs, and clicking on the document ID or navigating to http://YourSiteCollection/_layouts/DocIdRedir. aspx?ID=W6NPTDNWAMTW-5-3 takes you to the document set's welcome page.

Try It Yourself

Configure a Document Set

Because a document set is a content type, it can be configured or customized like any other content type.

You now look at some of the configuration options available for document sets:

1. Navigate to Site Settings, Site Content Types (under Galleries).

2. Select the Document Set content type. This should give you a screen similar to Figure 12.8.

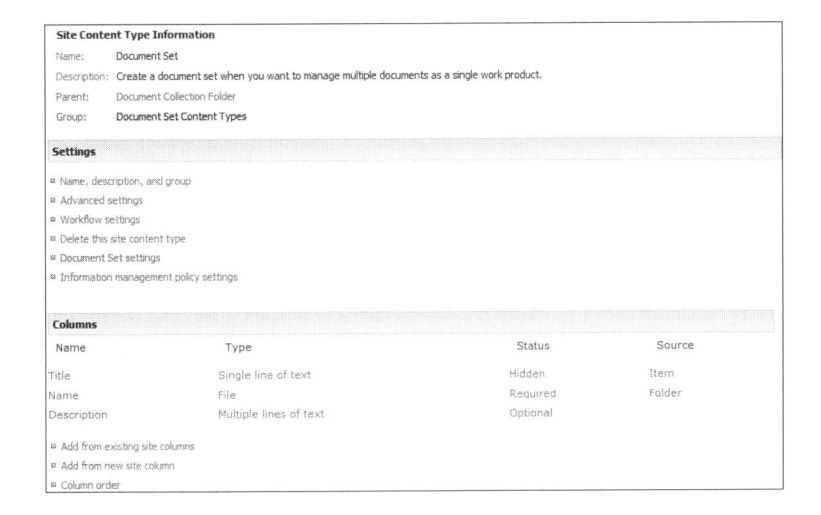

FIGURE 12.8
Configuring the Document Set content type

3. To configure allowed content types under a document set, click Document Set Settings and then choose the content types you want to allow under the document set.

4. You can also choose to prepopulate a newly created document set with default content. For this, on the Document Set Settings screen, in the Default Content section, select a content type for which you want to upload default content and click the Browse button to locate and upload the same.

5. If you want certain columns to be shared among each of the content types in the document set, you can do the required configuration using the Share Columns section on the Document Set Settings screen. Shared columns can be edited only at the document set level and are read-only at the individual document level.

6. You can also customize the welcome page for the document set. You can select the columns to be displayed on the welcome page or customize it using your web-browser and manipulate web parts on the welcome page. You can also use SharePoint Designer to perform more advanced customizations.

Understanding Managed Metadata

This section explores an important concept in content classification and categorization. If you are into blogging and social networking, the concept of tags should not be new to you. Tagging content as a favorite and further categorizing it using relevant category tags is a task that a typical blogger or a social networking site user performs on a daily basis. In fact, the popularity of social networking and various blogging engines has popularized the concept of tags even more than the traditional approach of organizing content in hierarchical folders.

A typical blogging engine allows publishers and readers to apply various tags to blog posts to ease in classification and categorization of content. For example, a technical article on a technology blog can be applicable to both SharePoint and ASP.NET and can be marked with both tags by the author. Later, readers looking for either SharePoint related or ASP.NET related articles would both be able to find the article when searching via related tags. Thus tagging is different from a folder based hierarchical structure in the sense that one piece of content can now come under multiple hierarchies. If you were to use the old school folder based hierarchical navigation, you would end up creating two copies of the same article. Further, blogging engines maintain a dictionary of all these tags so that they can be reused in different blogs.

By drawing parallels to the concept of tagging, as it applies to the blogging engines, let's explore the related concepts in the SharePoint world.

In SharePoint, a tag loosely maps to a *term*. A *term* is a word or a phrase that can be associated with an item in SharePoint. A collection of related terms is called a *term set*. *Managed metadata* refers to the management of the *terms* and *term sets*.

Further, two types of terms are available in SharePoint:

- *Managed terms* (or *taxonomy*) are predefined words or phrases that can only be created by privileged users referred as *Metadata Content Managers*.
- *Enterprise keywords* (or *folksonomy*) are words or phrases that have been added by the end user.

To use terms and managed metadata to tag items in SharePoint, you need to provision an instance of the Managed Metadata Service, which allows you to perform two key tasks:

▶ Use managed metadata.

▶ Share content types across site collections and web applications. (You explore this later in the hour when in the discussion of content type publishing hubs.)

Provisioning the Managed Metadata Service

You can set up and configure an instance of the managed metadata service from the SharePoint central administration. You can find the related options on the Manage Service Applications screen, as illustrated in the following section.

Try It Yourself
Set up the Managed Metadata Service

The following steps are involved in setting up the Managed Metadata Service:

1. Navigate to Central Administration, Application Management, and Manage Service Applications. There might be an instance of the service that is already provisioned out of the box.

2. You are free to use to the existing instance of the service, but to better appreciate the concepts behind metadata management, provision a new service instance from scratch. For this, delete the existing service instance and the data associated with the service as well.

3. Next click the New button and select Managed Metadata Service.

4. Specify the following settings in the pop-up to create and configure a new service instance:

    ▶ **Name**—My Managed Metadata Service.

    ▶ **Database Server and Name**—Choose a database where you want the terms to be stored. Set this to MyManagedMetadataService_DB. Leave the Database Authentication set to Windows Authentication.

    ▶ **Failover Database**—Leave blank.

    ▶ **Application Pool**—You can use an existing one as well, but create a new one called SharePoint - Managed Metadata.

HOUR 12: Enterprise Content Management

Leave the content type hub blank. This is discussed more later in this hour in the section "Synchronizing Content Types with the Content Type Publishing Hubs."

5. Click OK to provision the service.

Creating and Managing Term Sets

When the service is created, click the service hyperlink to access the Term Store Management tool. Using this tool, you can create and manage term sets and also assign managed metadata roles. A user's role determines how the user can work with managed metadata.

By the Way

> If you receive the "The Managed Metadata Service or Connection is currently not available." error message while attempting to use the Term Store Management Tool, make sure that your Managed Metadata Web Service is running by navigating to the Central Admin, Manage Services on Server link (present under System Settings). Click the Start button to start the service in case it is not already started.

Using the Term Store Management tool is intuitive; you can right-click an item in the hierarchy to create a new item under it or perform various other functions such as copy a term, merge terms, deprecate a term, and so on, as shown in Figure 12.9.

FIGURE 12.9
Term Store Management tool

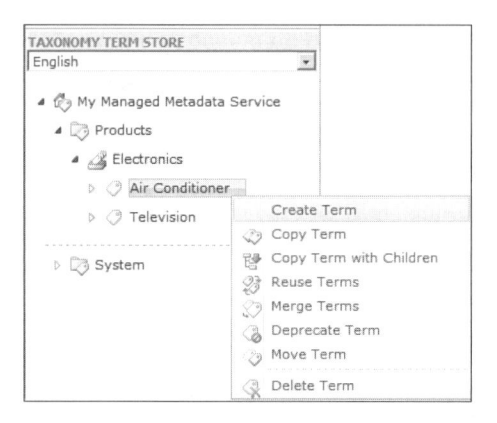

You can configure a number of properties at each level, when creating a new item:

▶ At the group level you can specify a group name, description, group manager (group managers have the same privileges as group contributors and an

Understanding Managed Metadata

additional privilege to add or remove members from the group contributors list), and contributors (contributors can edit the terms and term set hierarchies within the group).

- At the term set level you can specify the term set name, description, term set owner, contact email for receiving term set related suggestions, stakeholders (users who are notified before any major changes are made to the term set), submission policy (a closed submission policy allows only owners of the term set to add terms while an open policy allows term set users as well to add additional terms), and finally whether the term set is available for tagging.
- At the term level you can specify whether the term is available for tagging, language for the label, a default label for the term, and a synonym for the term.

Go ahead and use the Term Store Management tool to create a new group named Products. Create a new term set under this group and call it Electronics. Further create the following set of terms, as shown in Figure 12.10, under the Electronics term set.

FIGURE 12.10 Creating a group, term set, and terms using the Term Store Management tool

Recall that while configuring the Managed Metadata Service, you specified the database name as MyManagedMetadataService_DB. At this point if you happen to connect to the database, using either SQL Server Management Studio or Visual Studio Server explorer and examine the contents of the ECMTermLabel, you find all the terms you just created in this table.

Further, you can also create the Products group and the Electronics term set using the following code:

HOUR 12: Enterprise Content Management

```
using (SPSite site = new SPSite("http://YourSiteCollection/"))
{
    // Instantiate a new TaxonomySession for the root site collection
    TaxonomySession session = new TaxonomySession(site);

    // Instantiate a connection to the My Managed Metadata Service
    TermStore termStore = session.TermStores["My Managed Metadata Service"];

    if (termStore != null)
    {
        // Create Products group
        Group productsGroup = termStore.CreateGroup("Products");

        // Create Electronics term set
        TermSet electronicsTermSet = productsGroup.CreateTermSet("Electronics");

        // Create Air Conditioner term and further Split and Window terms under it
        // 1033 is Locale Identifier for English
        Term airConditionerTerm =
        electronicsTermSet.CreateTerm("Air Conditioner", 1033);
        Term splitTerm = airConditionerTerm.CreateTerm("Split", 1033);
        Term windowTerm = airConditionerTerm.CreateTerm("Window", 1033);

        // Create Television term and further LCD and Plasma terms under it
        Term televisionTerm = electronicsTermSet.CreateTerm("Television", 1033);
        Term lcdTerm = televisionTerm.CreateTerm("LCD", 1033);
        Term plasmaTerm = televisionTerm.CreateTerm("Plasma", 1033);

        // Commit
        termStore.CommitAll();
    }
}
```

All you need to do is add a reference to Microsoft.SharePoint.Taxonomy.dll present under the 14\ISAPI directory, and you can start working with the various classes in the Microsoft.SharePoint.Taxonomy namespace. The preceding code is pretty much self-explanatory. You start by creating a new `TaxonomySession` object and using it to get a reference to a term store provided by the My Managed Metadata Service. Next create a `Products` group with the `Electronics` term set under it and start adding terms to the same. Finally, commit all the changes to the term store. For the complete code listing, see the ManagedMetadataAPIDemo project in the source code for this hour.

Classifying and Tagging Items

Now that the term set is ready, you can utilize this term set to classify and tag items in SharePoint. Create a new custom list called My Products. In this example you add consumer electronics related products data to this list and tag them with the appropriate terms from the Electronics term set. To accomplish this, add a new column of type Managed Metadata to the list. In the Term Set Settings section configure the column to use the Electronics term set, as shown in Figure 12.11.

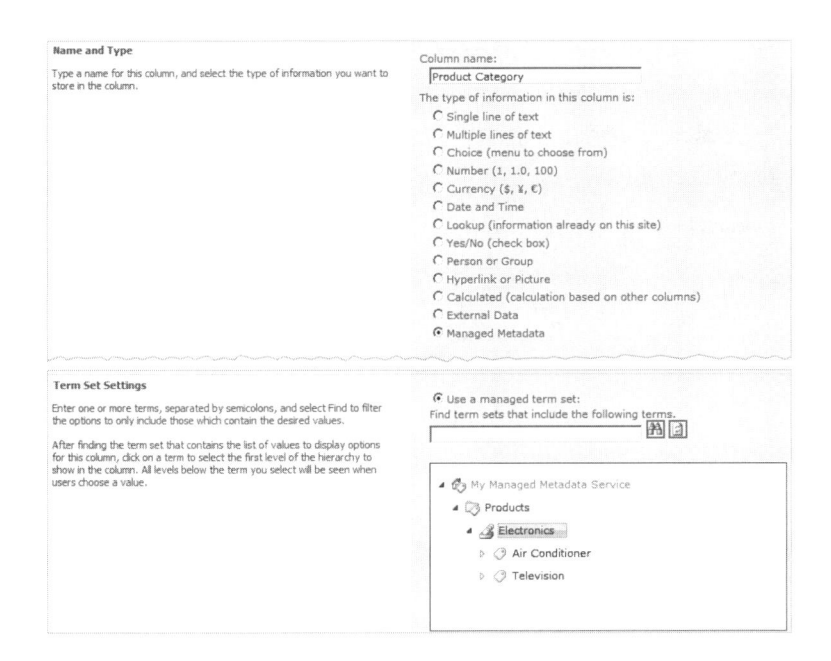

FIGURE 12.11 Adding a Managed Metadata column to a list

With your list set up, add a few items to it. Notice that as you type in a value for the Product Category, SharePoint prompts you with the matching terms from the Electronics term set, as shown in Figure 12.12.

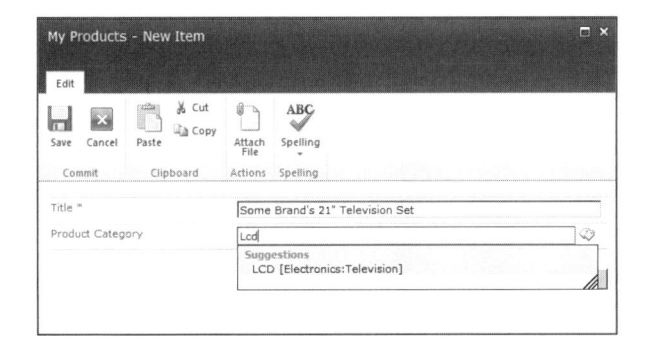

FIGURE 12.12 Tagging products with related terms from the term set

So far so good, but what if a term is better known by another name (or synonyms) as well. For example, what if a user tries to type in "Liquid Crystal Display" instead of "LCD"? Fortunately, the Term Store Management tool allows you to configure

HOUR 12: Enterprise Content Management

synonyms as well for a term. You can do so by typing in the synonyms in the Other Labels section, as shown in Figure 12.13.

FIGURE 12.13
Configuring synonyms

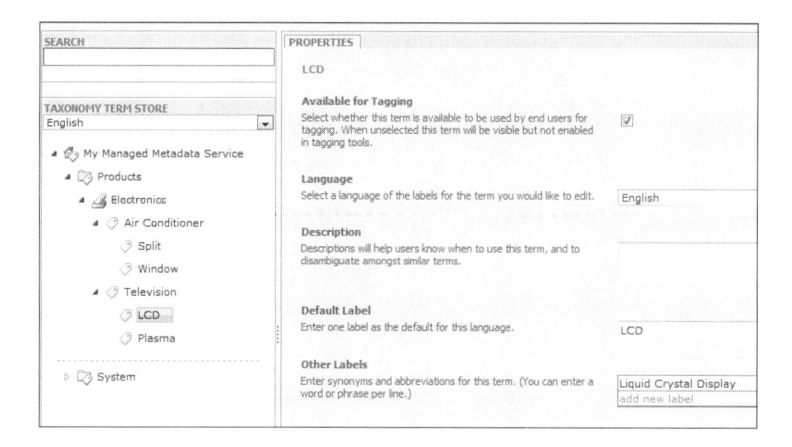

Now because "Liquid Crystal Display" has been configured as a synonym for the term "LCD," as you try to type in the word "Liquid" in the Product Category field, SharePoint identifies it as a synonym for LCD and prompts you. Further, when you select the suggested value, SharePoint intelligently replaces Liquid Crystal Display with LCD.

Content Organization with Managed Metadata

Go ahead and populate the My Products list with a few more products as shown in Figure 12.14.

FIGURE 12.14
Items in the My Products list

Now that your list is populated with a sufficient number of items and appropriate product categories are assigned to each item, you need to understand how managed metadata makes your content better organized and convenient to browse. Go to Metadata Navigation Settings on the List Settings page. Select the Product Category field in the Configure Navigation Hierarchies and Configure Key Filters sections as shown in Figure 12.15.

After you do the configuration specified in Figure 12.15, note that on navigating back to the My Products list you now have the option to select terms from the term set and specify key filters, as shown in Figure 12.16.

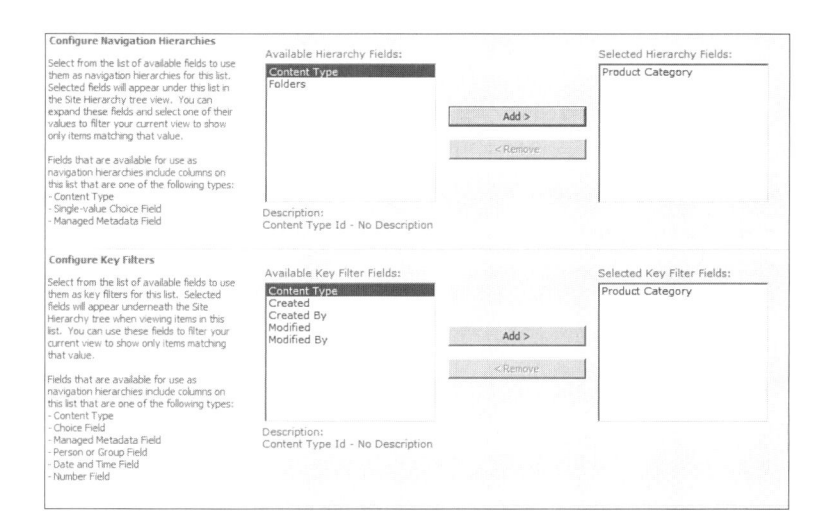

FIGURE 12.15
Configuring the navigation hierarchies and key filters to use in the Product Category field

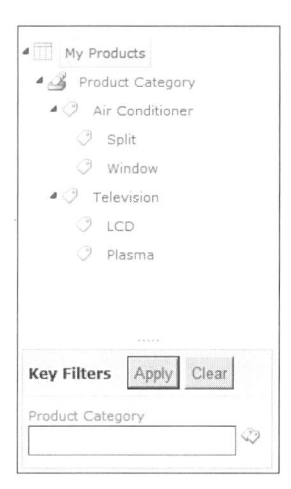

FIGURE 12.16
Using the navigation hierarchy and key filters based on the Product Category field

You can expand the Product Category and select one of the terms in the navigation hierarchy to filter the list to display only the matching items. If you want to filter by multiple terms at a time, you can use key filters. As you can see, list navigation and filtering based on managed metadata is easy to configure and intuitive to use as well.

Understanding the Idea of Enterprise Keywords

So far you have seen how administrators or privileged users can configure the managed terms or taxonomy. Now you see how end users can create and add their own words and phrases, by understanding the idea of enterprise keywords or folksonomy.

HOUR 12: Enterprise Content Management

To understand the concept of enterprise keywords, create a new document library called My Document Library. In the Library Settings for My Document Library, select the Enterprise Metadata and Keywords Settings option. Check the Add an Enterprise Keywords Column to This List and Enable Keyword Synchronization check box.

Now upload a new document to the library and edit its properties. Notice that a new option to specify enterprise keywords appears where you can type in a term, as illustrated in Figure 12.17. If something matches, SharePoint prompts you with the match; otherwise, when you click Save, a new term is created by SharePoint and added to the Keywords term set.

FIGURE 12.17
Using the enterprise keywords

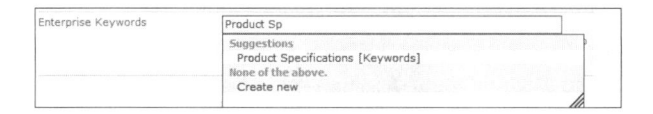

At this stage if you revisit the Term Store Management tool, you would notice that any new keyword that you type in gets added under the Keywords term set in the System group, as shown in Figure 12.18.

FIGURE 12.18
The Keywords term set in the System group

Further, if you were to open any document in this library in a Microsoft Office application, for example, Microsoft Word, you should be able to view Enterprise Keywords in the Document Properties panel, as shown in Figure 12.19. As you would expect, updating the Enterprise Keywords property with a term not already configured as a keyword causes the same to be added as a new enterprise keyword.

At times, you might want to tag content only for your specific needs and don't want the same to appear for all users. To do this, select the desired document in your library and click the Tags and Notes button. A pop-up window similar to one shown in Figure 12.20 appears, allowing you to specify the tags.

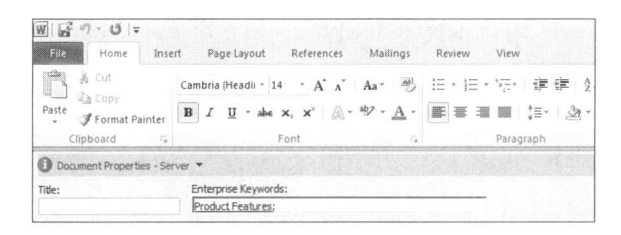

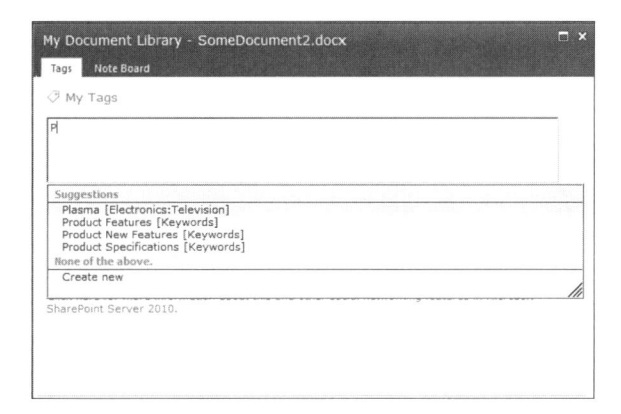

FIGURE 12.19
Configuring a new enterprise keyword from the Document Properties panel in Microsoft Word

FIGURE 12.20
Tagging content for personal use

As you begin typing notice that suggested values are retrieved from both the Keywords and the Products term sets. An interesting implication of this is that as you keep tagging content, this also starts appearing in your activity feed on your My Site.

Synchronizing Content Types with the Content Type Publishing Hubs

While creating a new instance of the Managed Metadata Service, you must have noticed a section to configure the Content Type hub. Another essential function of the Managed Metadata Service is to allow you to share content types across site collections and web applications. Historically, in SharePoint, content types were restricted to use only within a site collection. Using content types consistently across a farm was troublesome and not supported as well. Fortunately, things have changed in SharePoint 2010, and the Managed Metadata Service now makes this possible.

Content type synchronization across site collections is based on a hub and spoke model. A content type publishing hub acts as a central location for content type management and publishing. Spoke site collections subscribe to content type

HOUR 12: Enterprise Content Management

publishing for receiving updates to the published content types and update their local copy accordingly.

Try It Yourself
Configure Content Type Synchronization

In practice various steps are involved in configuring content type synchronization, as presented here:

1. Create two site collections, content type publishing hub (at the root level) and spoke site collection (at the /site/Spoke level).

2. Activate the Content Type Syndication Hub site collection feature in the hub.

3. Next activate the feature with the ID 73EF14B1-13A9-416b-A9B5-ECECA2B0604C on the spoke site collection using the following stsadm command:

```
stsadm -o activatefeature
-url http://splearn/sites/spoke
-id 73EF14B1-13A9-416b-A9B5-ECECA2B0604C
```

4. Visit Central Administration, Managed Service Applications and look for the My Managed Metadata Service created earlier.

5. Select the service and click Properties. If you remember the Content Type Hub section was left blank earlier while you created a new instance of the service. Now populate the content type hub field with your Content Type Publishing Hub's URL.

6. Click OK and view the properties for My Managed Metadata Service Connection, which is located right underneath the My Managed Metadata Service instance.

7. Check the Consumes Content Types from the Content Type Gallery at http://splearn/ Check box on the Properties page as shown in Figure 12.21.

8. Now you need a content type in the Content Type Syndication Hub site collection, which you want to synchronize with the spokes. For this, create a new content type and call it MyDocumentContentType, inheriting from the out-of-the-box Document content type.

Synchronizing Content Types with the Content Type Publishing Hubs 273

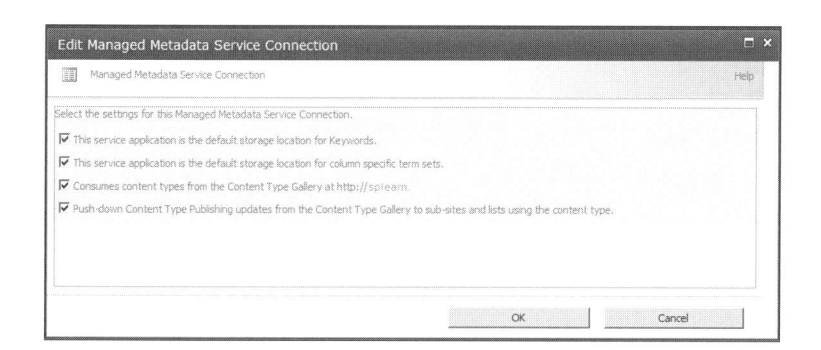

FIGURE 12.21 Configuring Managed Metadata Service Connection

9. Next visit the content type setting page for this content type and select the Manage Publishing for This Content Type option.

   At this point you see the three publishing options as shown in Figure 12.22. Since you have not published this content type before, the options to Unpublish and Republish are disabled at this time. Also, the Last Successful Published Date is empty for the same reason.

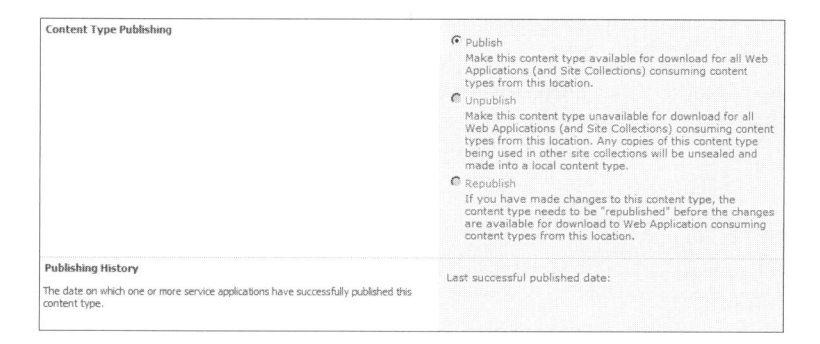

FIGURE 12.22 Publishing the MyDocument-ContentType

10. Go ahead and publish the content type. At this stage you would expect the content type to be published and available for spokes to pull as an update. Not so fast. Two timer jobs should run to do this for us, and by default they run at an interval of 15 minutes. Unless you want to wait for 15 minutes, run these jobs manually and get your work done.

11. Navigate to Central Administration, Monitoring, Review Job Definitions (under Time Jobs), and select the Content Type Hub timer job definition. Click the Run It Now button.

HOUR 12: Enterprise Content Management

12. Once the job executes, the Last Successful Published Date field on the Manage Publishing for This Content Type page gets populated, as shown in Figure 12.23.

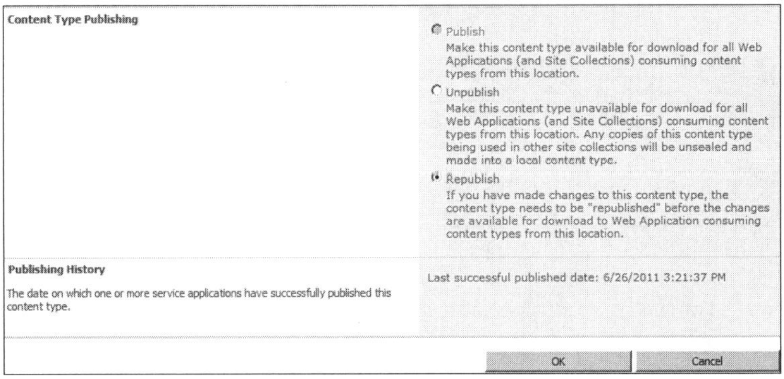

FIGURE 12.23
Last Successful Published Date gets populated after running the Content Type Hub timer job.

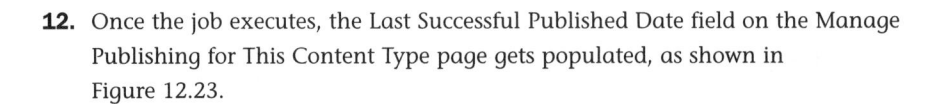

13. Once the Last Successful Published Date is populated, run the Content Type Subscriber job, which is by default scheduled to run hourly. This job would cause the spokes to get the published updates from the hub.

14. Now visit the Content Type Publishing link in the spoke site collection under the Site Collection Administration links. This lists all the subscribed content types. Notice that MyDocumentContentType should now be listed here as well, as shown in Figure 12.24.

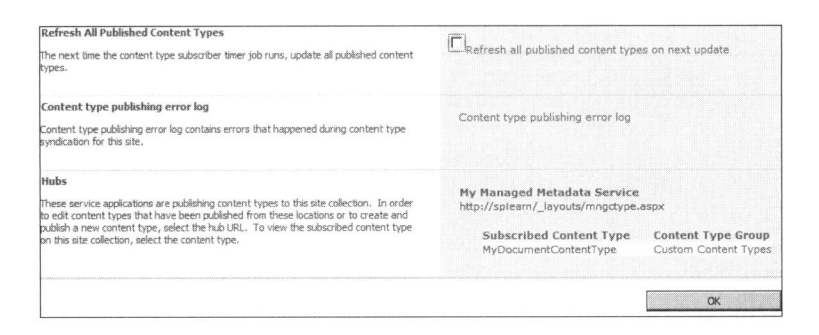

FIGURE 12.24
MyDocument-ContentType appearing in the list of subscribed content types

If you visit the Site Content Types under the galleries, as you would expect, MyDocumentContentType is visible there as well. But if you click the content type, you find that the content type is read-only. This is because any changes to the content type should now be made from the hub site collection and therefore modifications are not allowed at the spoke site collection's level. At this stage if you unpublish the content type by selecting the Unpublish option as shown in Figure 12.23 and rerun the Content Type Hub and Content Type Subscriber jobs, as you would expect, the content type is removed from the list of subscribed content types, as shown in Figure 12.24. However, this does not cause the content type to be deleted from the spoke site collection. In fact the content type would present and would become available for editing.

Summary

This hour explored some of the enterprise content management features offered by SharePoint. The hour started with an introduction to the concept of ECM. Next you learned about the Document ID Service available in SharePoint, which helps you generate document IDs to uniquely identify documents regardless of their location. You also learned about document sets and how they help users to treat a group of related documents as a single entity. Then Managed Metadata Services were discussed, and you learned about the concept of managed terms and enterprise keywords. Finally the hour concluded by exploring the idea of content type publishing hubs, using content types that can now be shared across site collections.

Q&A

Q. *I configured a new prefix to be assigned to all document IDs, but I still don't see this to be working for an existing document. Did I miss something here?*

A. The existing document IDs will be reset only if you selected the Reset All Document IDs in This Site Collection to Begin with These Characters option while configuring the new prefix. Also, the existing document IDs would change only once the Document ID Assignment job executes. You can try to run this job manually from Central Administration as well, or wait for it to run as per the schedule.

Q. *Can I have more than one content type publishing hub?*

A. You can have more than one content type publishing hub as well. All you have to do is create the same number of Managed Metadata Service instances. Even the spoke site collection discussed previously can act as both a spoke and content type hub at the same time, and the content type hub root site collection (which was acting as a publishing hub so far) can as well subscribe for updates from the spoke site collection. Activating the Content Type Syndication Hub feature and provisioning a new instance of the Managed Metadata Service configured to use it as a content type hub would do the trick.

HOUR 13

Enterprise Content Management—Understanding Records and Web Content Management

What You'll Learn in This Hour:
▶ Understanding records management in SharePoint
▶ Exploring the new web content management features

> **By the Way**
> Due to the complexity of the topics discussed, some figures in this book are very detailed and are intended only to provide a high-level view of concepts. Those figures are representational and not intended to be read in detail.

Almost every organization needs to maintain information in the form of records. Records are nothing but documents or other content and data requiring retention over a period of time in a secure and reliable way in conformance with organization practices and regulatory standards. To manage records in an efficient and cost-effective way calls for the need of an intelligent records management system with features such as content discovery, content organization, content disposition, archiving, auditing, and so on.

This hour explores various features provided by SharePoint for records management and also briefly discusses various improvements in SharePoint 2010, as far as records management is concerned, over the earlier versions of SharePoint. The discussion concludes with a brief look at some of the new web content management features in SharePoint 2010 and the steps involved in creating a custom page layout.

Understanding Records Management in SharePoint

Prior to SharePoint 2010 all records management features were restricted to the Records Center site template. The Records Center site served as an archive for records, and

HOUR 13: Enterprise Content Management

documents moved to the archive became records. Although the Records Center site template is still present in SharePoint 2010, a major difference is that in SharePoint 2010 you can activate many of the records management related features on any site, even if it is not based on the Records Center site template. This provides flexibility since users can take advantage of record management related features for documents from within the same document library without the need of moving them to a Records Center site. This is called *in place records management,* or in other words, when you declare a document a record, the document remains in place and SharePoint 2010 manages it as a record.

Now that you've had an introduction to records management, let's begin exploring the Records Center site template and various ideas related to centralized records management.

Exploring the Records Center Site Template

You can create the Records Center as a site or as a site collection. However when creating the Records Center as a separate site collection you get the ability to segregate its content in a separate content database, which gives you the option of moving all the archived content to an alternate storage location when required.

▼ **Try It Yourself**

Provision a Records Library

1. Provision a new Records Center site collection from Central Administration, by selecting the Records Center site template, present under the Enterprise tab.

2. Once the site collection is provisioned navigate to the top-level site's landing page, shown in Figure 13.1. You can customize this landing page to educate the users about your records management policies and organizational compliance. The Submit a Record button lets users upload documents to the Drop Off Library, which are then moved to the correct library/folder according to the configured records management rules.

3. To configure various record management settings, navigate to the Records Center Management page, shown in Figure 13.2, by clicking on the Manage Records Center link under Site Actions.

▼

Understanding Records Management in SharePoint

FIGURE 13.1
Welcome page of the Records Center site

FIGURE 13.2
Records Center Management console

4. The Records Center Management page lists the following steps required to configure the Records Center site:

   a. Create content types.

   b. Create records libraries.

   c. Create content organizer rules.

   d. Customize the Records Center's welcome page.

   Let's go through each of these steps one by one to set up a Records Center site.

HOUR 13: Enterprise Content Management

5. Create a DocumentWithDeptInfo content type, inheriting from the Document content type. Add a new site column called Dept and select the type of information as Choice. Enter the following three departments as values the user can choose for this column:

   ▶ Finance

   ▶ HR

   ▶ Operations

   Keep the other fields as default.

6. Modify the Dept column settings to required; that is, the column must contain information.

7. Next create a new Library with the Records Library template. Name the new library My Records.

8. Modify the library settings and set the document type DocumentWithDeptInfo as the default content type for the library.

Now that you have a content type and a records library ready for use, let's explore various records management related features one by one.

The first topic is the steps involved in configuring and managing document retention policies in a Records Center site. SharePoint allows you to configure a multistage retention policy that you can use to specify the entire life cycle of a document as a single policy. Based on content metadata, you can add multiple retention stages to a policy to perform actions such as kick starting a workflow, moving the content to the recycle bin, or even permanently deleting the content. A retention policy can be configured on a content type, a library, or a folder.

Try It Yourself
Configure a Retention Policy

1. To configure a retention policy, navigate to the library settings page for My Records library.

2. Click the Information Management Policy Settings link. You should now be able to view content types associated with the library and whether any content type has a retention policy defined as shown in Figure 13.3.

Understanding Records Management in SharePoint

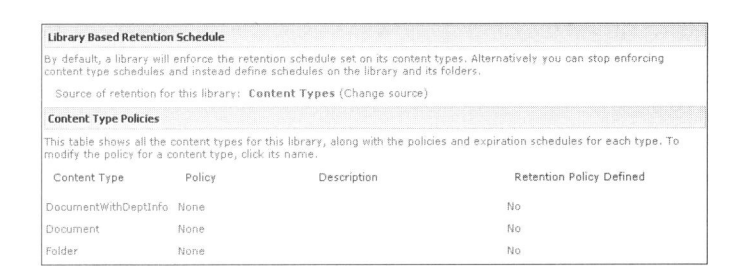

FIGURE 13.3
Configuring the information management policy settings

3. To define a retention policy on DocumentWithDeptInfo content type, select the DocumentWithDeptInfo content type.

4. On the Edit Policy screen, check the Enable Retention check box. Notice that as you do so you get an option to add a retention stage.

5. As discussed earlier, you can add multiple retention stages to a policy, for example, using a custom workflow to send reminders to a user for a particular timeframe, in the case of no action moving to the next retention stage, which may move the content to a different records library or delete the content permanently. Click the Add a Retention Stage link to add a new retention stage.

6. To configure a retention stage, you need to specify an event and an action. Figure 13.4 defines a retention stage to delete all documents not modified for one year.

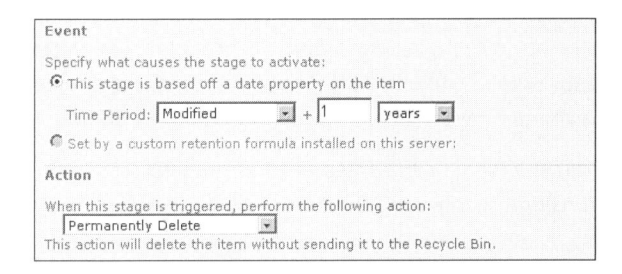

FIGURE 13.4
Configuring a retention stage

7. Click OK to save the changes.

8. The Edit Policy screen provides a number of other options as well, including

    ▶ **Policy Statement**—For the benefit of the end users to explain to them the rules that apply to their content

    ▶ **Auditing**—To log events such as users who opened, downloaded, or viewed the content, modified content properties, and so on

    ▶ **Barcodes and Labels**—For managing nondigital content

As shown in Figure 13.5 enable auditing to track users who opened, downloaded, or viewed the content and also specify a matching policy description.

FIGURE 13.5
Configuring auditing

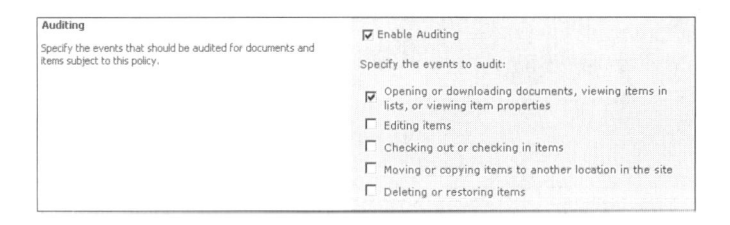

9. You can optionally add an administrative description and a policy statement, which can help other administrators and end users understand the purpose of your policy. Click OK to save the changes and create the policy. The newly created policy should now be visible against the DocumentWithDeptInfo content type.

From now on, any content (associated with the DocumentWithDeptInfo content type) lying unused for more than a year is deleted automatically.

Understanding Hold and eDiscovery

Hold and eDiscovery is a new feature in SharePoint 2010. Using this feature you can discover content and place it on hold—that is, lock it down to prevent editing. Either you can search for content and automatically place it on hold or holds can be set manually as well via the Compliance Details window. Holds and eDiscovery is used especially in scenarios where you need to freeze the content that may be required for a review or inspection in case of litigation, investigation, or audit.

You can configure various options related to Holds and eDiscovery by navigating to Site Settings and using the following three links under the Hold and eDiscovery section:

- **Hold Reports**—Provides information on the items that are on a hold in the site
- **Holds**—Allows you to create a hold and specify a manager for that hold
- **Discover and Hold Content**—Allows you to search content related to a particular litigation, investigation, or audit and add a search result to a hold or send the results to another site.

Try It Yourself

Configure Hold and eDiscovery

1. Upload some documents to My Records library and randomly select the department from Finance/HR/Operations. Assume that you want to place all records related to the Finance department on hold.

2. Select the Discover and Hold Content link (from Site Settings, Hold and eDiscovery section) and configure various attributes as shown in Figure 13.6.

3. Click the Add a New Hold Link as shown in Figure 13.6 to create a Hold Finance Records hold, as illustrated in Figure 13.7, so that it is available for selection in Figure 13.6.

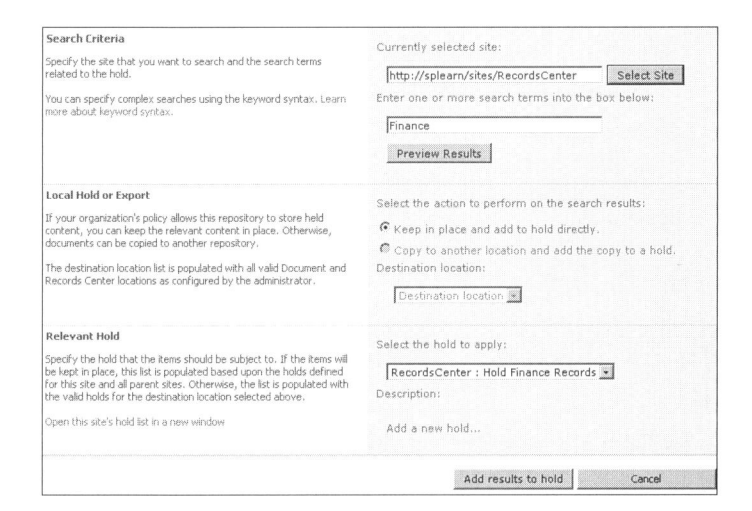

FIGURE 13.6
Creating a hold based on search criteria

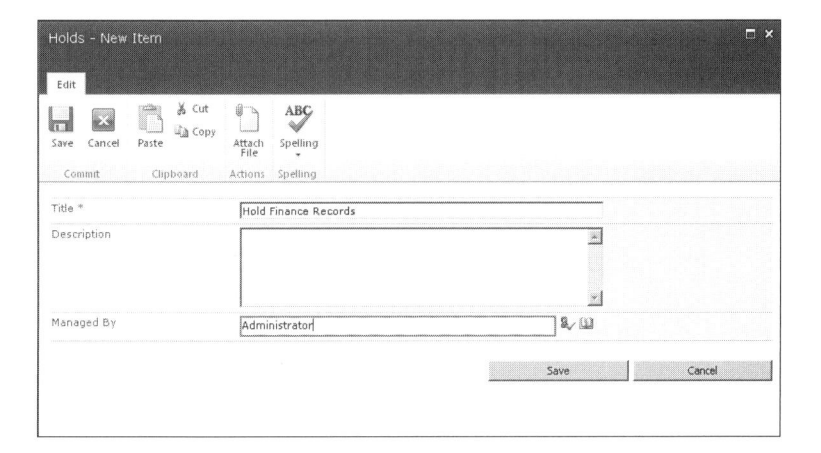

FIGURE 13.7
Creating a new hold

HOUR 13: Enterprise Content Management

4. You can also preview the search result by clicking the Preview Results button. Click the Add Results to Hold button to place the search results on hold.

> **By the Way**
>
> For eDiscovery to work, search should be set up and working. You learn more about search in Hour 18, "Introducing SharePoint Search"; for now, follow these steps to start a crawl so that your eDiscovery search results display the relevant content: Navigate to Manage Service Applications in Central Administration and click Search Service Application. Select the Manage button from the ribbon. Select the Content Sources option under the Crawling section in the left-hand menu. Select the Start Full Crawl option as shown in the Figure 13.8.
>
> Once the crawl is over, your recently uploaded documents start appearing in the search results.

FIGURE 13.8
Starting a full crawl

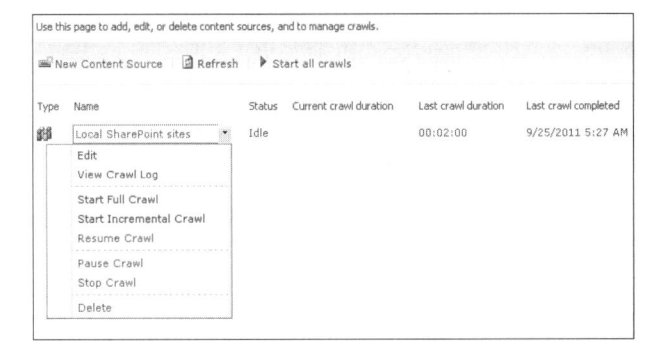

5. Once the items are added to the hold, an email confirmation is sent as indicated in the confirmation message, which you receive by clicking on the Add Results to Hold button.

6. In case you want to select and place individual records on hold, you can do so by selecting the Compliance Details link (as shown in Figure 13.9) and clicking on the Add/Remove from Hold link in the Compliance Details window.

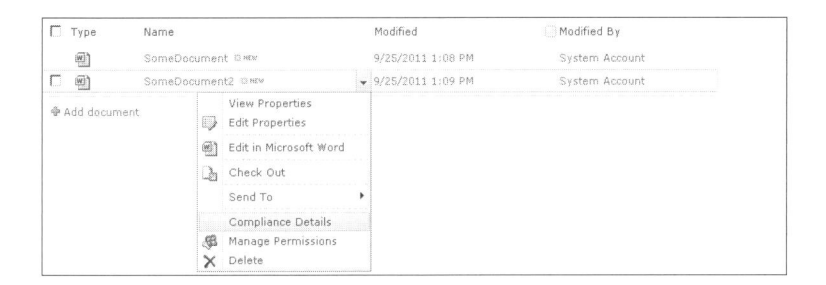

Understanding Records Management in SharePoint | 285

FIGURE 13.9
Viewing compliance details

Once a document or a record is on hold, content disposition rules are not applied to it, and the item is retained until the hold is released. In case the document was editable before, its contents are frozen and it is no longer is available for any further modifications.

Also note that the Compliance Details window provides the option to Generate Audit Log Report. If you remember we discussed auditing and configured the same while setting up an information management policy. Clicking on the link takes you to the View Auditing Reports page with options to view various audit reports from where you can view the configured audit reports.

Content Organizer

Content Organizer is a new routing feature in SharePoint 2010 that allows you to route documents to different libraries and folders within those libraries based on a certain set of routing rules. At the heart of the Content Organizer are the Content Organizer Rules. Rules govern the Content Organizer engine and establish where the content should go.

You can configure the Content Organizer using the following links under the Site Administration section on the Site Settings page:

- Content Organizer Settings
- Content Organizer Rules

As the name suggests you can configure Content Organizer settings from the Content Organizer Settings option and create new routing rules using the Content Organizer Rules option. Any rules that you configure are stored in the Content Organizer Rules list.

HOUR 13: Enterprise Content Management

The Drop Off Library is central to the Content Organizer engine, and any content that users drop off in this library, is routed to various locations according to the configured Content Organizer rules.

To better appreciate the functionality of the Content Organizer, create a routing rule to move documents to subfolders in a document library, depending on their department, whenever a user uploads a new document.

You already have the DocumentWithDeptInfo content type set up that users can use to specify while uploading the content which department the document belongs to.

Now create a new routing rule to move the documents uploaded by the user to the appropriate department folder in the My Records library depending on the value of the Dept field, as selected by the user.

Try It Yourself

Create a Content Routing Rule

1. Navigate to the Content Organizer Rules page (from Site Settings, Site Administration section, Content Organizer Rules link) and click the Add New Item button to create the new rules as per the following attributes (as illustrated in Figure 13.10 as well):

   - **Rule Name**—Document Organizer (by Department).
   - **Rule Status And Priority**—5 (Medium).
   - **Submission's Content Type**—Select DocumentWithDeptInfo content type and leave the other fields as default.
   - **Conditions**—Leave as default.
   - **Target Location**—Select the My Records library by clicking the browse button. Also check the Automatically Create a Folder for Each Unique Value of a Property check box. Select the Dept property for the Select a Property (Must Be a Required, Single Value Property) field and specify the format for folder name as %1.

2. Once the rule is configured, navigate to the Drop Off Library and add a new document to the library or click the Submit a Record button on the site's landing page. Note the message from Content Organizer clearly indicates that documents uploaded to the Drop Off Library are automatically moved to the correct library, as you would expect.

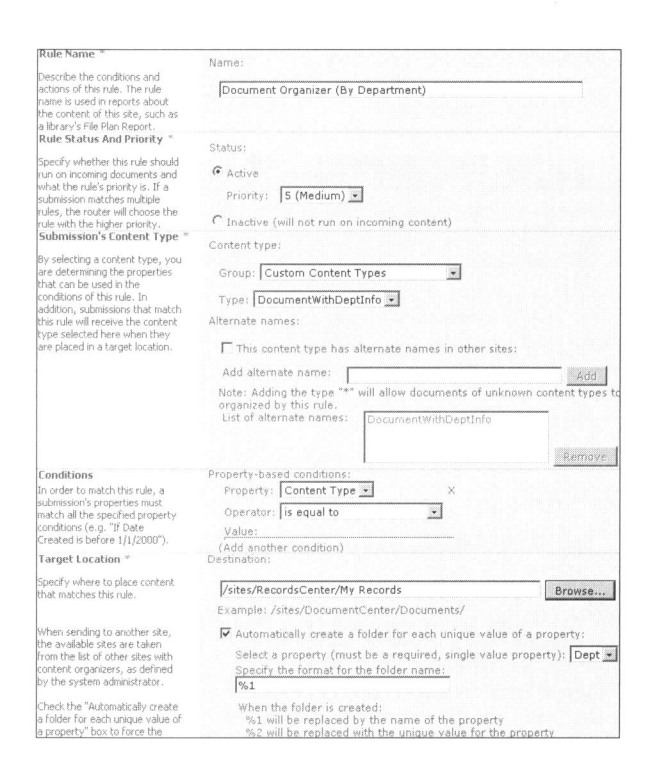

Understanding Records Management in SharePoint

FIGURE 13.10
Configuring the Content Organizer rule

3. Select a department from the drop-down list and click Submit, as shown in Figure 13.11.

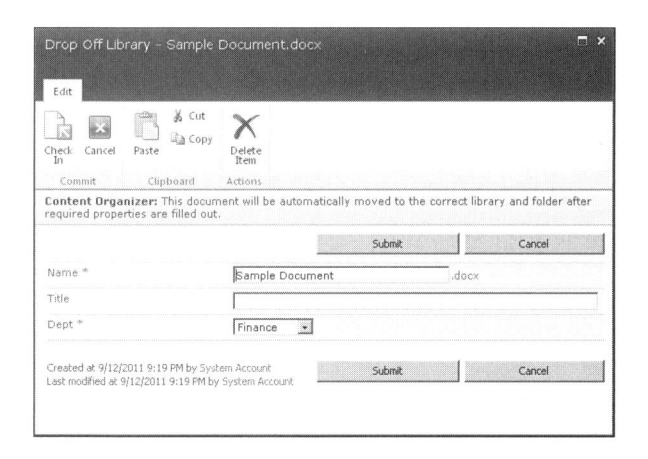

FIGURE 13.11
Selecting a department while uploading a new document

HOUR 13: Enterprise Content Management

Notice that since the Document ID Service feature is active in the Record Center site collection, the uploaded document is assigned a unique document ID as well, as indicated in the URL shown in Figure 13.12.

FIGURE 13.12
Document URL indicates the document has been routed to the correct location.

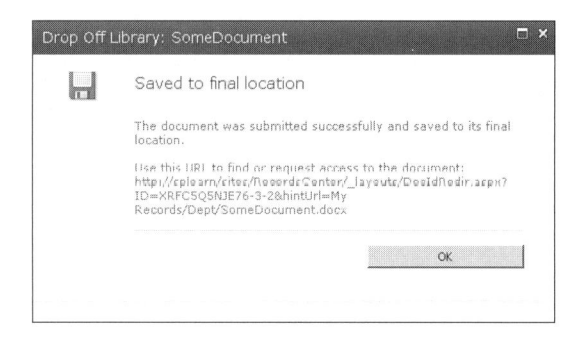

Configuring In-Place Records Management

As discussed earlier, SharePoint 2010 allows you to declare a document as a record "in place," without the need of it being moved to the Records Center site. In a site not created with the Records Center template, you can activate the relevant features and take advantage of the records management related features discussed previously.

For example, first and foremost, to take advantage of in-place records management, enable the In Place Records Management site collection feature from Site Settings, Site Collection Administration, Site Collection Features link.

Activating this feature provides the following new links under Site Administration:

- Record Declaration Settings
- Site Collection Policies

This feature is required if you want to mark incoming documents as records. Further, you are also suggested to activate the Document ID Service to assign document IDs to incoming documents.

Site Collection Policies allows you to define information management policies at the site collection level.

Using the Record Declaration Settings, you can specify at the site collection level users who can declare records and what restrictions to put in place when a document is marked as a record. For example, you can choose to block edit and delete (default) functionality, or you can choose to enforce no additional restrictions, as shown in Figure 13.13.

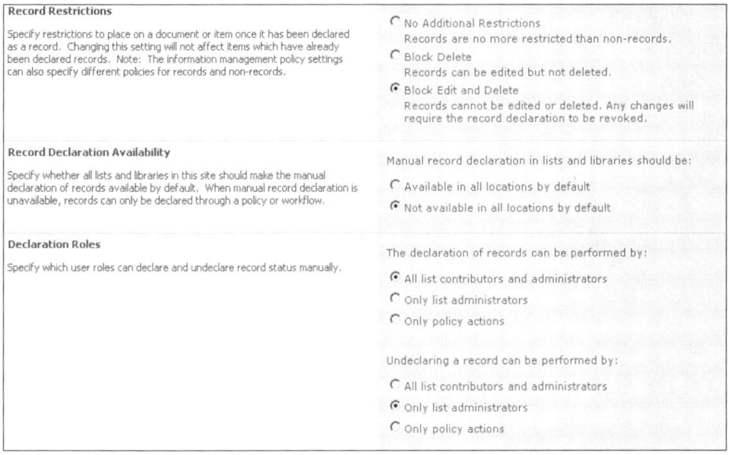

Understanding Records Management in SharePoint

FIGURE 13.13
Configuring record declaration settings

Further, for a document library, you can configure how you want the documents to be converted to records by navigating to the library setting and selecting the Record Declaration Settings option. You can choose to inherit the site collection settings or override them. You can also select the option to automatically declare items as records when added to the library, as shown in Figure 13.14.

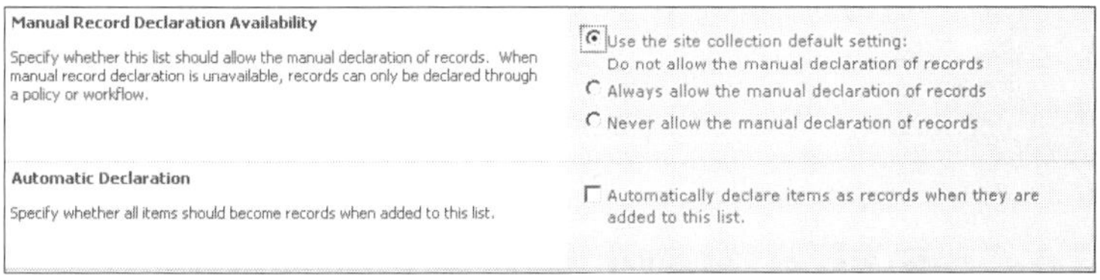

FIGURE 13.14
Configuring record declaration settings for a document library

Further, you can also take advantage of the Hold and eDiscovery feature, by activating the corresponding feature at the site level.

To take advantage of the Content Organizer in place, you need to activate the Content Organizer site feature.

> **By the Way**
>
> The Content Organizer feature has a dependency on the hidden feature DocumentRoutingResources (id: 0c8a9a47-22a9-4798-82f1-00e62a96006e), which must be activated before the Content Organizer feature can be activated. The following `stsadm` statement activates this hidden feature:
>
> ```
> stsadm -o activatefeature
>   -id 0c8a9a47-22a9-4798-82f1-00e62a96006e -url http://splearn
> ```

HOUR 13: Enterprise Content Management

Once the preceding feature is activated, a new content type called Rule is created for you, visible under the site's content type gallery, and a Drop Off Library is created as well, as shown in Figure 13.15. At this stage you can begin configuring Content Organizer rules.

FIGURE 13.15
A content type called Rule is created automatically when the Content Organizer is configured in a site.

Site Content Type	Parent	Source
Content Organizer Content Types		
Rule	Item	Default Site Collection

Site Content Type Information
Name: Rule
Description: Create a rule that moves content submitted to this site to the correct library or folder.
Parent: Item
Group: Content Organizer Content Types

Settings

Columns

Name	Type	Status	Source
Title	Single line of text	Required	Item
Rule Name	Single line of text	Required	
Description	Single line of text	Optional	
Priority	Single line of text	Optional	
Active	Yes/No	Optional	
Submission Content Type	Single line of text	Optional	
Properties used in Conditions	Multiple lines of text	Optional	
Aliases	Single line of text	Optional	
Target Library	Single line of text	Required	
Target Folder	Single line of text	Optional	
Target Path	Single line of text	Optional	
Property for Automatic Folder Creation	Single line of text	Optional	
Custom Router	Single line of text	Optional	
Route To External Location	Yes/No	Optional	

Exploring the New Web Content Management Features

The primary aim of a web content management system is to provide authoring, branding, and publishing tools to enable users to create and manage web content, with little knowledge of web programming techniques. SharePoint 2010 revolutionizes web content management by providing a lot of new, exciting features for different content management requirements. For example, in controlled publishing scenarios, such as Internet facing sites, administrators can exercise greater control over publishing to ensure a consistent look and feel and uniform branding of the site. On the other hand is the need for a loosely controlled process for community-based sites or wiki sites. Apart from publishing features, SharePoint 2010 provides a rich set of new authoring tools and features as well. For example, you can now change the page layout dynamically while creating content. This section briefly explores some of these new enhancements in SharePoint 2010 one by one.

Improved Authoring Tools

With the new set of authoring tools, content creators can now focus only on what rather than how. The new improved user experience and ribbon interface and a rich set of authoring tools enables authors to create content without needing specialized technical skill.

The Ribbon Interface

The ribbon interface was introduced in Office 2007 and has been adapted in SharePoint 2010 for a consistent experience across Office applications. The ribbon makes it easy to discover features and is intuitive to use. In SharePoint 2010 the contents of the ribbon change according to context, that is, the ribbon is context-aware. For example, text formatting options become available when editing a text field, and picture tools are available when editing an image, as demonstrated in Figures 13.16 and 13.17.

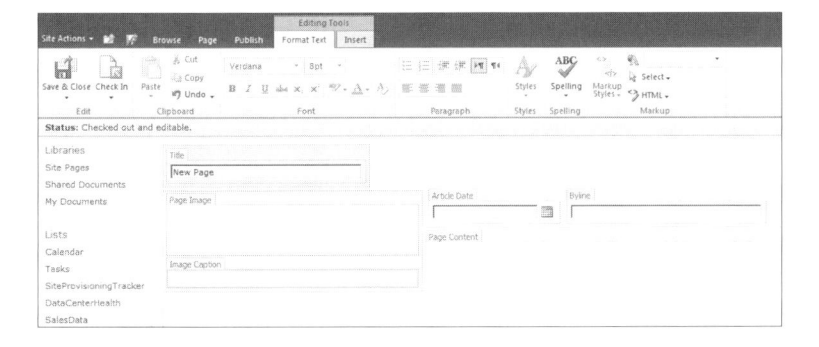

FIGURE 13.16 Text formatting options available when editing a text field

FIGURE 13.17 Picture tools available when working on an image

HOUR 13: Enterprise Content Management

New Page Creation and Page Layout Related Features

SharePoint 2010 allows one-click page creation, where you specify only the page title and the page gets created as shown in Figure 13.18.

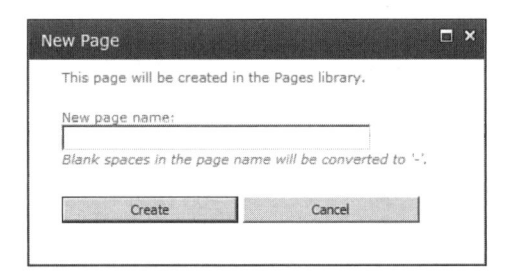

FIGURE 13.18
SharePoint 2010 allows single-click page creation

You can change the page layout later dynamically by picking a page layout from the ribbon as shown in Figure 13.19.

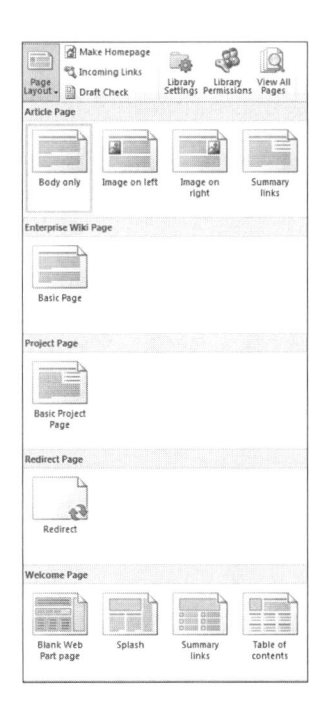

FIGURE 13.19
Dynamically changing page layouts

Other Web Content Management Improvements

Following are some more web content management improvements in SharePoint 2010:

- Improved rich text editor with a rich set of formatting controls and options to embed images and videos directly into rich text.

- Easy to add rich media with options such as preview and play a video before selecting it.

- Specialized Asset Library for rich media, which includes images, audio and video files, and the addition of a new customizable Silverlight media player to deliver the rich media the content.

- New improved content query web part that allows filtering based on metadata of the items being queried or on a value passed as a query string.

- Content administrators can restrict authors to use only fixed styles or approved web parts for maintaining a consistent look and feel of the sites.

- New Web Analytics features for monitoring various aspects of site usage.

- Improved community building tool features allowing users to tag, rate, and comment on site content.

Creating a Custom Page Layout

You can build your own custom page layouts if the out of the box ones don't fit the bill for you. This section shows you how.

Page layouts in SharePoint are tied to content types. You can either choose to use an existing content type or create a new one. In the following Try It Yourself section, you learn to create a new one extending the Page content type (present in Publishing Content Types).

Try It Yourself
Create a New Page Layout

1. Add a new multiline text column to the content type and call it MySectionDescription. Your content type structure should now be something similar to the one shown in Figure 13.20.

FIGURE 13.20
Creating new content type for a custom page layout

2. Next open the SharePoint Designer and connect to your site. Select Page Layouts from Site Objects and click New Page Layout on the ribbon as shown in Figure 13.21.

FIGURE 13.21
Creating a new page layout in SharePoint Designer

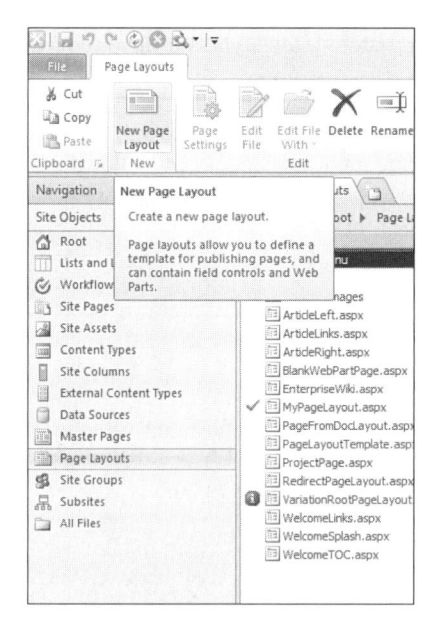

Exploring the New Web Content Management Features   295

3. Select the MyContentType and call the page layout MyPageLayout, as shown in Figure 13.22.

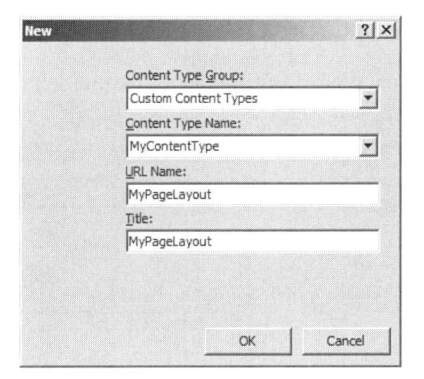

FIGURE 13.22
Selecting content type

4. Next drag and drop fields onto the page from the toolbox. In this case drag and drop the Title and Page Description fields on the page in a table based layout as shown in Figure 13.23.

FIGURE 13.23
Creating a new page layout with SharePoint Designer

HOUR 13: Enterprise Content Management

5. Save the changes and close the SharePoint Designer. Your page layout is ready for use.

6. Now try to create a page using this layout. Navigate to pages library and click Page under the New Document menu.

7. Next select MyPageLayout from the list of available page layouts as shown in Figure 13.24.

FIGURE 13.24
Selecting MyPageLayout from the available page layouts

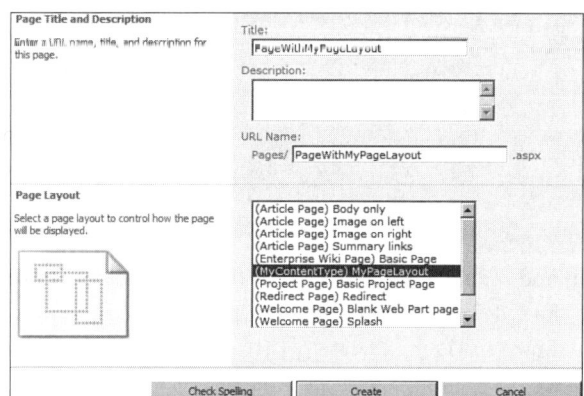

8. Once the page is created, edit the page to verify that your page has title and section description fields as shown in Figure 13.25.

FIGURE 13.25
Editing a page created with MyPageLayout

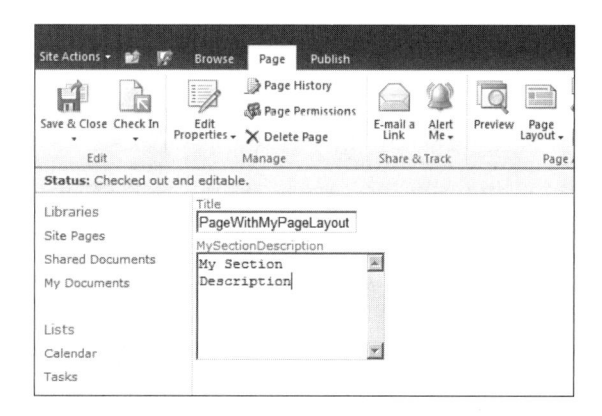

Summary

This hour explored various concepts related to records management and the new web content management features in SharePoint 2010. You explored the Records Center site template, learned about the concept of Holds and eDiscovery, configured the Content Organizer, and learned about in-place records management. You also learned about new web authoring tools, the ribbon interface, the simplified page creation process, and the steps involved in the creation of a custom page layout.

Q&A

Q. *I want to use the Content Organizer to route my documents to different content libraries, but I don't want to create a separate Records Center site for this. Can I use the Content Organizer routing features from within my site?*

A. Yes, you can activate the Content Organizer feature in your site for this to work. This causes a new library called the Drop Off Library to be created where you can upload your documents and configure Content Organizer rules to move them to proper locations.

Q. *Holds and eDiscovery doesn't work for me. None of my documents or records were put on hold. Am I missing something?*

A. The most common reason for this is that search might not be working for you. While configuring Holds and eDiscovery, verify that the preview results button returns the expected search results. Also, any recently uploaded documents may not appear in search results, and you might need to run a crawl from Central Administration for this to work.

Q. *Okay, I understand the new web content management features in SharePoint 2010. But I am still worried about browser compatibility issues. Are there any improvements on that front?*

A. The new fancy web content management features wouldn't be of much use if they were restricted to only one version of Internet Explorer. You'll be glad to know that there is now support for more web browsers, including Internet Explorer 7 and 8 as well and the latest versions of Firefox and Safari. This should resolve most of your concerns on browser compatibility.

HOUR 14

Understanding Business Connectivity Services

What You'll Learn in This Hour

- ▶ Creating external content types and external lists through SharePoint Designer 2010
- ▶ Creating external content types and external lists through Visual Studio

> Due to the complexity of the topics discussed, some figures in this book are very detailed and are intended only to provide a high-level view of concepts. Those figures are representational and not intended to be read in detail.
>
> **By the Way**

As you've seen SharePoint is a great system to store and manage data. However, the capabilities of SharePoint are not limited to data stored within SharePoint. SharePoint connects and works with external data as well. This is possible through Business Connectivity Services, which is a set of features and services that enable SharePoint to connect to external data sources. While SharePoint 2007 had Business Data Connectivity to retrieve external data, it was complex and had limited capability. As you see in this hour the SharePoint team made major improvements in this area, and Business Connectivity Services is a big improvement over its predecessor.

Creating External Content Types and External Lists Through SharePoint Designer 2010

SharePoint 2010 defines the structure of the external data to which it will connect through external content types. External content types are similar to SharePoint content types that define the structure of the data stored in SharePoint. However, external content types define the structure of the data not stored in SharePoint. In addition external content types define the data access capabilities for the external data source.

HOUR 14: Understanding Business Connectivity Services

> **By the Way**
>
> For those who worked on Business Data Connectivity in SharePoint 2007, you can consider an external content type to be equivalent to a BDC entity. However, external content types contain much more information compared to a BDC entity.

External lists are lists based on external content types. They help you interact with the external data in the same way as the normal SharePoint list works.

> **By the Way**
>
> External lists do not physically store data. They are just a medium to interact with the external data.

Follow the next steps to create an external content type and list in SharePoint Designer.

Try It Yourself

Create an External Content Type and List in SharePoint Designer

In this section you define an external content type for the AdventureWorks database provided by Microsoft as a sample database. You can download this database from http://msftdbprodsamples.codeplex.com/releases/view/55926. You use this database for all the code samples in this hour. You can define an external content type from both Visual Studio and SharePoint Designer, but in this example you create your external content type from SharePoint Designer.

> **By the Way**
>
> You were introduced to SharePoint Designer 2010 in Hour 1, "Introducing SharePoint 2010." Although this hour limits the use of SharePoint Designer to creating external content types and external lists, Hour 19, "Working with SharePoint Designer 2010," is dedicated to the topic of SharePoint Designer 2010.

1. Open Microsoft SharePoint Designer 2010. Click Open Site, enter the URL of the SharePoint site where you want to create the external content type, and click Open as shown in Figure 14.1. Enter the appropriate username and password if it prompts for credentials.

Creating External Content Types and External Lists Through SharePoint Designer 2010   301

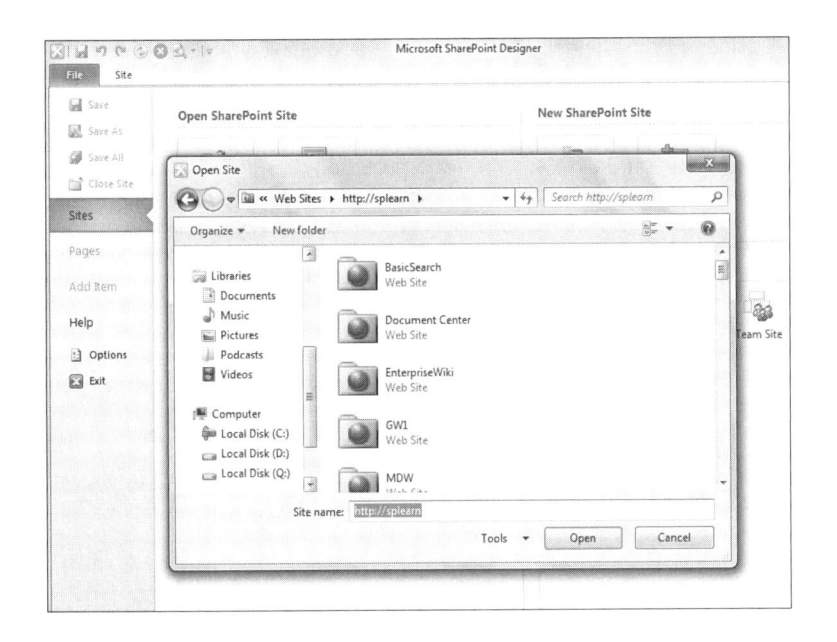

FIGURE 14.1
SharePoint Designer 2010

2. The site opens up in the SharePoint Designer as shown in Figure 14.2.

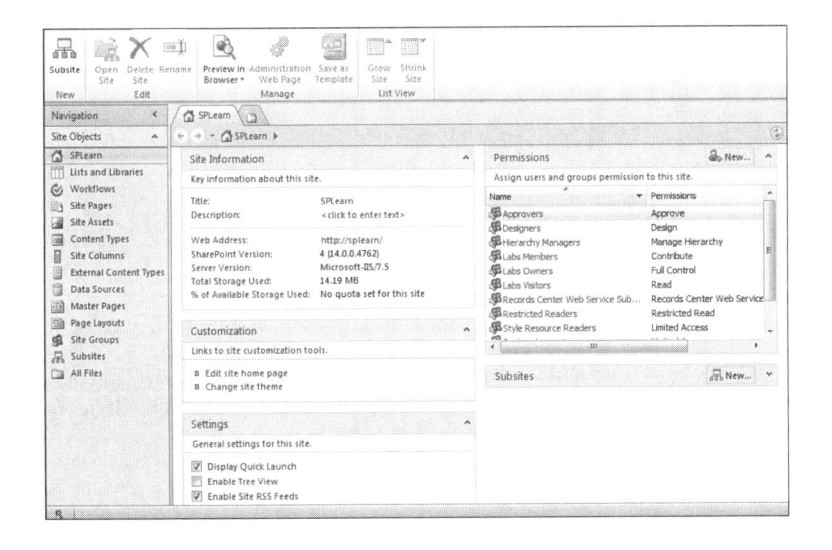

FIGURE 14.2
SharePoint 2010 site in SharePoint Designer 2010

3. Click the External Content Types link in the Site Objects pane on the left. The existing external content types if any are displayed.

> **By the Way**
>
> If the Business Data Connectivity Service is not running, you get the error "The Business Data Connectivity Metadata Store is currently unavailable." To fix this go to SharePoint 2010 Central Administration. Go to Application Management and open Manage Services on Server under the Service Applications section. In the Manage Services on Server screen make sure that the Business Data Connectivity Service has been started. Then go back to the Application Management screen. Click Manage Service Applications and create a new Business Data Connectivity service if none exists. Restart the SharePoint Designer, and you should be able to open the External Content Types screen.

4. Click External Content Type in the New section of the toolbar at the top as shown in Figure 14.3.

FIGURE 14.3
Creating a new external content type

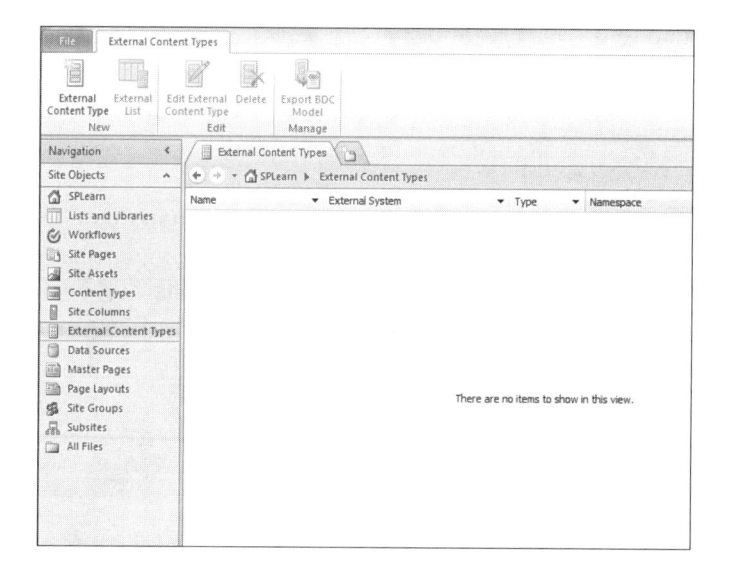

5. The New External Content Type creation screen appears. Specify the Name and Display Name as AdventureWorks_Product. Keep the Office Item Type set to Generic List.

> **By the Way**
>
> The Office Item Type allows you to choose a base type for the external content type. This enables you to use the content type in Office applications. For example, you could have an external contact type based on the Office item type Contact or Appointment, which you could then use in Outlook.

Creating External Content Types and External Lists Through SharePoint Designer 2010

303

6. Click the Click Here to Discover External Data Sources and Define Operations link. This takes you to the screen that allows you to define data sources for the external content type as shown in Figure 14.4.

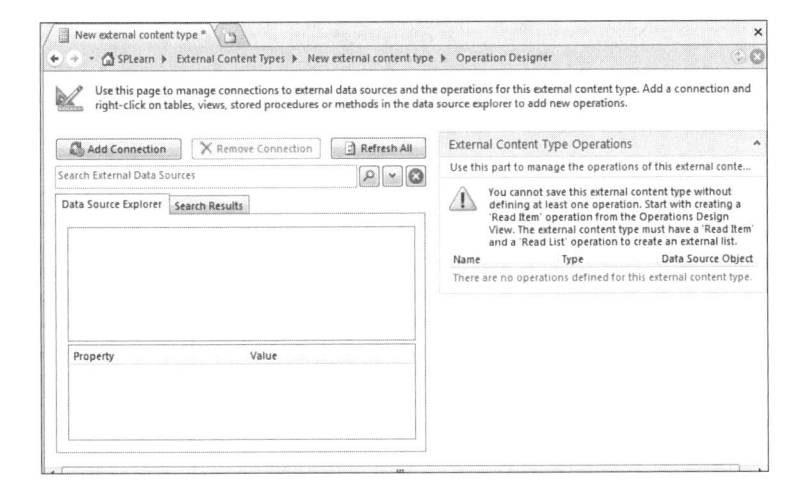

FIGURE 14.4
Creating a new data source in SharePoint Designer 2010

7. Click Add Connection. The External Data Source Type Selection dialog opens as shown in Figure 14.5. Select SQL Server as the Data Source Type and click OK.

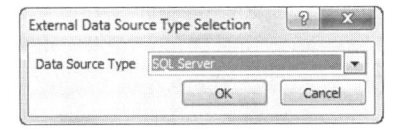

FIGURE 14.5
The External Data Source Type Selection dialog

8. You now are to enter the details for the SQL Server Connection. Enter the details as shown in Figure 14.6. Replace the Database Server Name with the appropriate value.

9. Once the connection is successful, the database tables and views can be visible in the Data Source Explorer window as shown in Figure 14.7. Expand the Tables node and find the Product table. Right-click the Product table and click Create All Operations.

HOUR 14: Understanding Business Connectivity Services

FIGURE 14.6
The SQL Server Connection dialog

FIGURE 14.7
Data Source Explorer

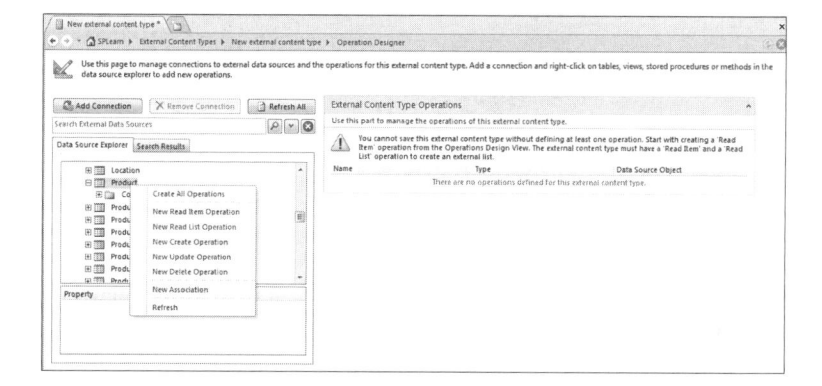

10. The All Operations dialog displays as shown in Figure 14.8. You can click Finish or click Next to change the settings for this data source. You want to go with the default settings, so click Finish.

FIGURE 14.8
The All Operations screen

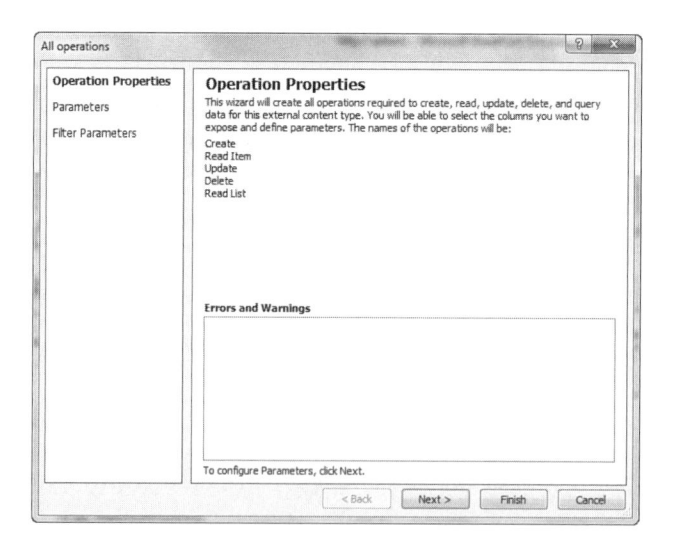

Creating External Content Types and External Lists Through SharePoint Designer 2010

305

11. The various operations for the data source are created. This can be seen in the right section of the SharePoint Designer, as shown in Figure 14.9.

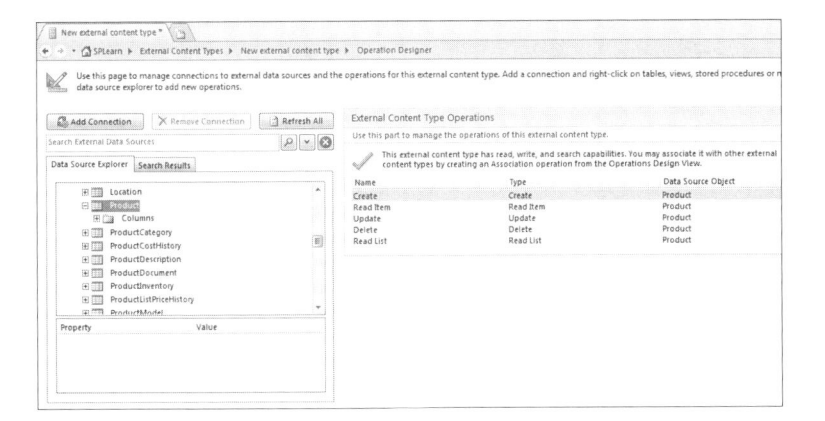

FIGURE 14.9
External content type creation

12. Finally save the content type. Go back to the External Content Types screen, and you can see AdventureWorks.Product. Select it and click create External List in the New section of the toolbar at the top.

13. In the Create External List screen enter AdventureWorks.Products as the name of the list and click OK. The list is created.

14. Before you can view the external list in the browser you need to give the site users permissions on the external content type, or else the call to the various operations for the external content type will fail. For this browse the SharePoint 2010 Central Administration. Go to Application Management and click Manage Service Applications. Click the Business Data Connectivity Service. You should be able to the see your external content type AdventureWorks.Product. Open the pop-up menu for the AdventureWorks.Product and click Set Permissions as shown in Figure 14.10. Add the appropriate users and select Execute permission. This permission needs to be given to all users, regardless of their access level; otherwise, they cannot even read the data. For site administrators, select all the permissions—that is, Edit, Execute, Selectable in Clients, and Set Permissions.

> **By the Way**
>
> You can give permissions to all users by selecting the group NT Authority\Authenticated Users. If you are giving permissions to all users just give the Execute permission. For high-privilege users, add them separately in addition to the NT Authority\Authenticated Users and explicitly give them all permissions.

HOUR 14: Understanding Business Connectivity Services

FIGURE 14.10
Setting permissions on an external content type

15. Browse to the SharePoint site. Go to Site Actions, View All Site Content. You can see the AdventureWorks.Products list. Open the list and you see the data shown in Figure 14.11.

FIGURE 14.11
AdventureWorks. Products external list

16. Add and edit items, and you can see these reflected in the database.

> **Watch Out!**
> When adding or editing the items in the list, make sure you add data that complies with the database constraints. For example, the ProductSubCategoryID and ProductModelID have foreign key constraints and you need to add one of the valid values that you can pick up by looking at the existing records.

> **By the Way**
> You could also create the external list from the browser once the external content type has been defined in SharePoint Designer. To create an external list, create a new list based on the external list template, and it allows you to select the external content type for the list.

Creating External Content Types and External Lists Through Visual Studio

You can also define external content types and external lists through Visual Studio. As you will see Visual Studio provides you complete control over your BCS entities.

Try It Yourself
Create an External Content Type and List in Visual Studio

Now try creating an external content type and list through Visual Studio 2010. Get data from the ContactType table in the AdventureWorks database. Follow these steps to create an external content type and external list in Visual Studio.

1. Create a new empty SharePoint Project named as BCSDemo.

2. In the next screen select the Deploy as a Farm Solution option and enter the appropriate site URL.

3. Add a new Item of type Business Data Connectivity Model and name it BdcContactType as shown in Figure 14.12. Note the name is still Business Data Connectivity Model and not Business Connectivity Services Model. Unfortunately, although the Business Data Connectivity is renamed to Business Connectivity Services, there are still a lot of artifacts for Business Connectivity Services that are using Business Data Connectivity in their names. To avoid confusion any references to Business Data Connectivity in SharePoint 2007 will be explicitly called out.

4. You see a new item named BdcContactType added to the solution. In addition you see a couple of classes added to the solution, and a feature named Feature1 is added. Rename the feature to BdcContactType. The project structure looks as shown in Figure 14.13.

5. The BdcContactType.bdcm is an XML file representing your BCS Model. An entity named Entity1 is automatically created for you by Visual Studio. You can see and design this entity in the SharePoint BDC Designer in the left section of Visual Studio. This is shown in Figure 14.14.

HOUR 14: Understanding Business Connectivity Services

FIGURE 14.12
Business Data Connectivity Model Visual Studio template

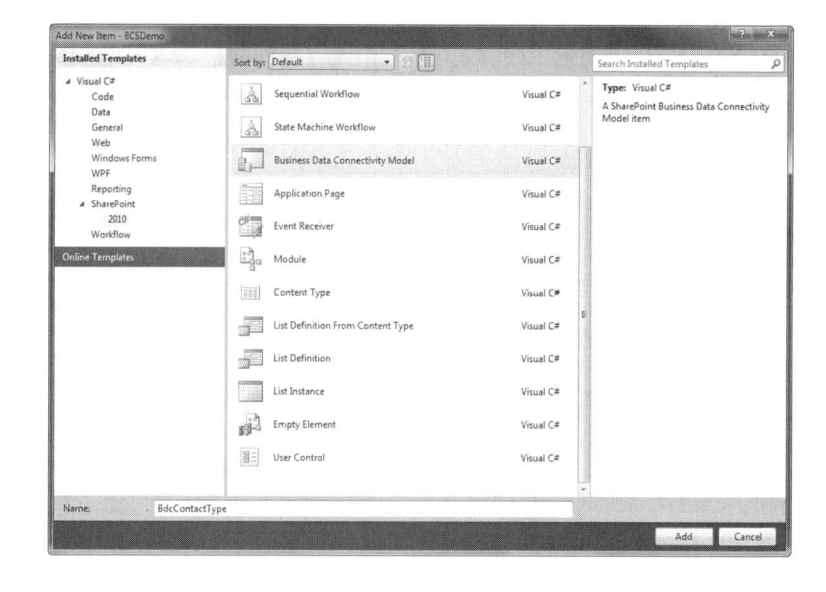

FIGURE 14.13
BCS demo project structure

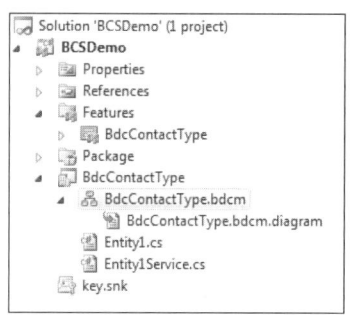

FIGURE 14.14
SharePoint BDC Designer

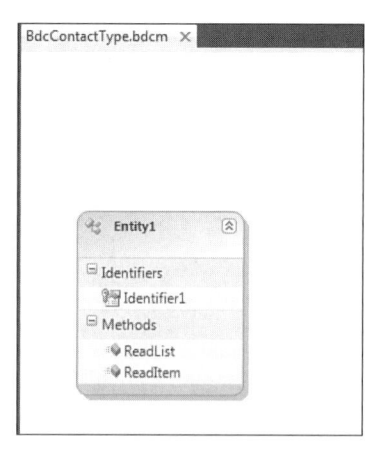

Creating External Content Types and External Lists Through Visual Studio

6. Entity1.cs defines a class that contains the properties for Entity1, which the Entity1Service.cs defines as the various methods such as ReadItem and ReadList. All these are linked together through the BdcContactType.bdcm file. You can verify this by opening the file in a text editor.

> **By the Way**
>
> The ReadItem returns a single instance of the entity and is equivalent to the SpecificFinder method in BDC 2007. As the name indicates, ReadList returns multiple items.

7. In the BDC Designer select the Entity1 entity, and in the properties window change the name from Entity1 to ContactType as shown in Figure 14.15.

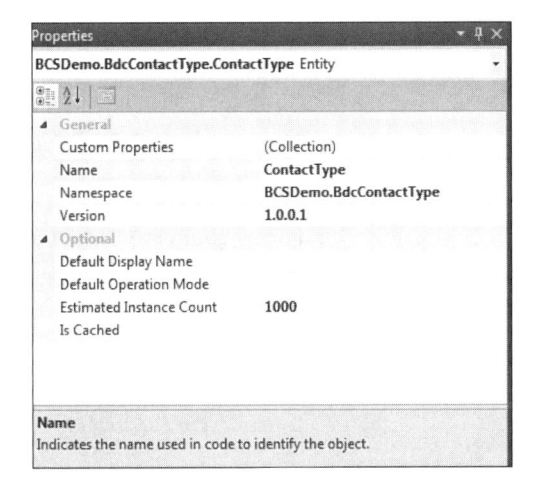

FIGURE 14.15 ContactType entity properties

8. Notice that the Entity1Service class gets automatically renamed to ContactTypeService.

9. Manually rename the Entity1.cs file to ContactType.cs and edit the file as shown here:

```
using System;
namespace BCSDemo.BdcContactType
{
    public partial class ContactType
    {
        public int ContactTypeID { get; set; }
        public string Name { get; set; }
        public DateTime ModifiedDate { get; set; }
    }
}
```

HOUR 14: Understanding Business Connectivity Services

10. Now go back to the BDC Designer and select Identifier1. In the properties window change the Name to ContactTypeID and Type Name to System.Int32 as shown in Figure 14.16.

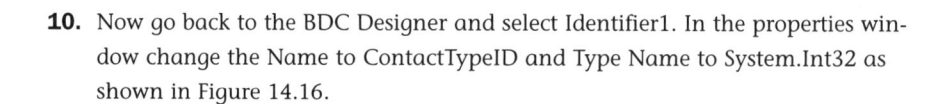

FIGURE 14.16
ContactTypeID identifier properties

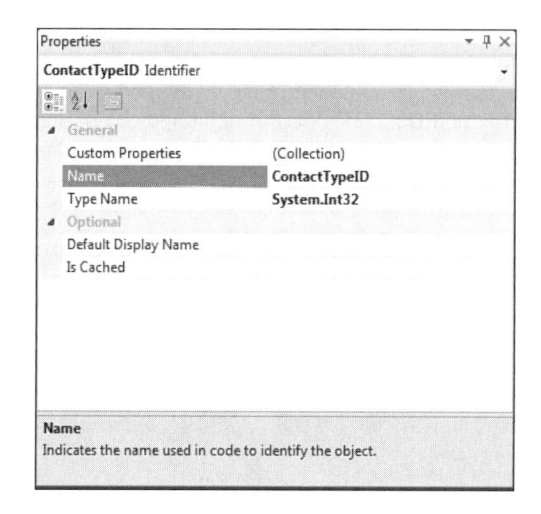

11. Now open the BDC Explorer window by going to View, Other Windows, BDC Explorer. Expand the ReadList node. Select the Entity1list Node under the @returnParameter. Figure 14.17 shows the BDC Explorer.

FIGURE 14.17
BDC Explorer

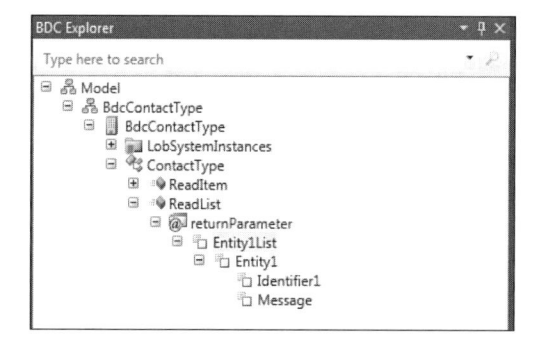

> **By the Way**
>
> The BDC Explorer and the BDC Method Details windows allow you to edit the various configurations for your entity such as the methods and their parameters. You will find yourself using these windows extensively when working with BCS in Visual Studio 2010.

Creating External Content Types and External Lists Through Visual Studio | 311

12. Change the Name to ContactTypeList. Select the drop-down list of Type Name and from the Current Project select ContactType. Keep the Is Enumerable check box selected. This is shown in Figure 14.18.

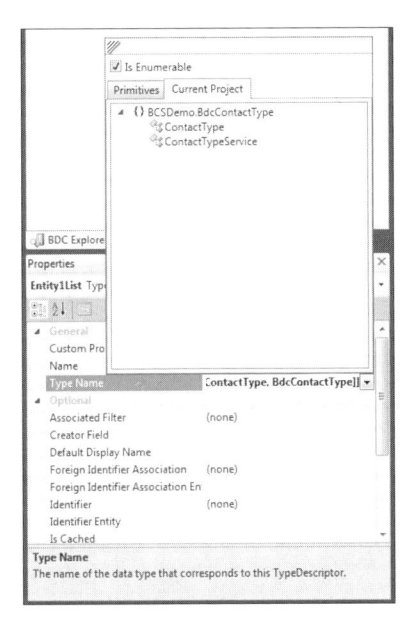

FIGURE 14.18 Setting the Type for ContactTypeList

13. After setting the values the properties window should look similar to Figure 14.19.

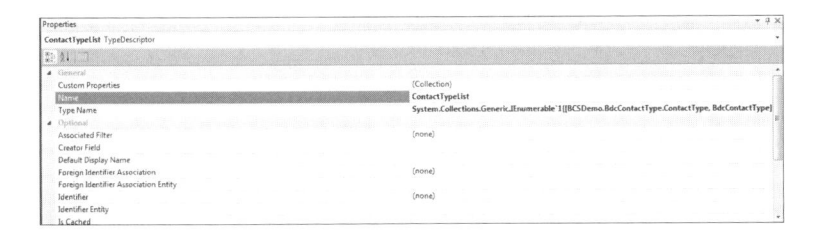

FIGURE 14.19 ContactTypeList properties

14. Right-click and delete the Entity1 node below the ContactTypeList node. Right-click on the ContactTypeList node and click Add Type Descriptor. In the properties window change the Name to ContactType and Type Name to ContactType class.

15. Add the Type descriptors below the ContactType Node as shown in Table 14.1.

HOUR 14: Understanding Business Connectivity Services

TABLE 14.1 Type Descriptors for ContactType

Name	Type Name
ContactTypeID	System.Int32
Name	System.String
ModifiedDate	System.DateTime

Watch Out!

> The ContactType Node below the ContactTypeList node defines the structure for the ContactTypeList collection. If you don't add the ContactType type descriptor you get an error indicating "TypeDescriptor with name 'ContactTypeList' is defined as a collection but does not have a child TypeDescriptor. Collection TypeDescriptors must define a single child TypeDescriptor, representing the structure of each element of the collection."

16. Now Expand the ReadItem node in the BDC Explorer. Select the @Identifier Node under the ID node and change the Name to ContactTypeID and Type Name to System.Int32.

17. Select the Entity1 node under the @returnParameter node and change the Name to ContactType and select the ContactType as the Type Name.

18. Delete the Identifier1 and Message Nodes. Add the Type Descriptors below the ContactType Node as shown in Table 14.2.

TABLE 14.2 Type Descriptors for ContactType

Name	Type Name
ContactTypeID	System.Int32
Name	System.String
ModifiedDate	System.DateTime

19. The final structure should look as shown in Figure 14.20.

20. Modify the ReadItem and ReadList methods so that you can retrieve the data into the entities from the AdventureWorks database.

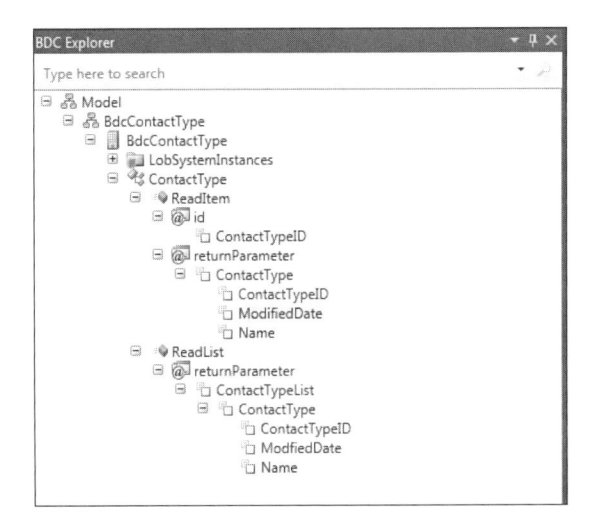

Creating External Content Types and External Lists Through Visual Studio 313

FIGURE 14.20
Final structure in BDC Explorer

21. Edit the code of the ContactTypeService.cs as follows:

```csharp
using System;
using System.Collections.Generic;
using System.Linq;
using System.Text;
using System.Data.SqlClient;

namespace BCSDemo.BdcContactType
{
    /// <summary>
    /// All the methods for retrieving, updating
    ///and deleting data are implemented in this class file.
    /// The samples below show the finder and specific finder method for
➥Entity1.
    /// </summary>
    public class ContactTypeService
    {
        private const string ConnectionString =
"data source=.;initial catalog=AdventureWorks;Integrated Security=SSPI";

        public static ContactType ReadItem(int id)
        {
            SqlConnection conn = new SqlConnection(ConnectionString);

            try
            {
                string query =
" select * from Person.ContactType where ContactTypeID = @ContactTypeId";
                SqlCommand cmd = new SqlCommand(query, conn);
                cmd.Parameters.AddWithValue("@ContactTypeId", id);
                conn.Open();
                SqlDataReader rdr = cmd.ExecuteReader();
```

```csharp
                    if (rdr.Read())
                    {
                        ContactType contactType = new ContactType();
                        contactType.ContactTypeID =
int.Parse(rdr["ContactTypeID"].ToString());
                        contactType.Name = rdr["Name"].ToString();
                        contactType.ModifiedDate =
DateTime.Parse(rdr["ModifiedDate"].ToString());
                        return contactType;
                    }

            }
            finally
            {
                if (conn != null)
                {
                    conn.Close();
                }
            }

            return null;

        }

        public static IEnumerable<ContactType> ReadList()
        {
            List<ContactType> list = new List<ContactType>();

            SqlConnection conn = new SqlConnection(ConnectionString);

            try
            {
                string query = "select * from Person.ContactType";
                SqlCommand cmd = new SqlCommand(query, conn);
                conn.Open();
                SqlDataReader rdr = cmd.ExecuteReader();

                while (rdr.Read())
                {
                    ContactType contactType = new ContactType();
                    contactType.ContactTypeID =
int.Parse(rdr["ContactTypeID"].ToString());
                    contactType.Name = rdr["Name"].ToString();
                    contactType.ModifiedDate =
DateTime.Parse(rdr["ModifiedDate"].ToString());
                    list.Add(contactType);
                }

            }
            finally
            {
                if (conn != null)
                {
                    conn.Close();
                }
            }
```

```
            return list; ;
        }
    }
}
```

22. Build and deploy the solution.

23. Browse to Central Administration and go to Application Management, Manage Service Applications. Go to the administration page of the Business Data Connectivity Service. You should see the ContactType content type listed there. Set the permissions on the ContactType for the appropriate users.

24. Browse to your site and create an external list based on the new content type.

25. You should see the external data in your new external list (Figure 14.21).

ContactTypeID	Name	ModifiedDate
1	Accounting Manager	6/1/1998 5:30 AM
2	Assistant Sales Agent	6/1/1998 5:30 AM
3	Assistant Sales Representative	6/1/1998 5:30 AM
4	Coordinator Foreign Markets	6/1/1998 5:30 AM
5	Export Administrator	6/1/1998 5:30 AM
6	International Marketing Manager	6/1/1998 5:30 AM
7	Marketing Assistant	6/1/1998 5:30 AM
8	Marketing Manager	6/1/1998 5:30 AM
9	Marketing Representative	6/1/1998 5:30 AM
10	Order Administrator	6/1/1998 5:30 AM
11	Owner	6/1/1998 5:30 AM
12	Owner/Marketing Assistant	6/1/1998 5:30 AM
13	Product Manager	6/1/1998 5:30 AM
14	Purchasing Agent	6/1/1998 5:30 AM
15	Purchasing Manager	6/1/1998 5:30 AM

FIGURE 14.21
Contact types external list output

Summary

This hour looked at Business Connectivity Services. On many occasions you need to work with external data in SharePoint. Business Connectivity Services provides you with a structured framework to retrieve external data. In this hour you learned the concepts of external content types and external lists, and you created an external content type and an external list to retrieve data from a SQL database table. In addition you also created an external content type and an external list through Visual Studio 2010. For those who have worked on Business Data Connectivity in SharePoint 2007, what you did in this hour in Business Connectivity Services will appear as a major improvement over BDC. While business connectivity is too vast a topic to cover completely in one hour, you should now have a good understanding of the important aspects of Business Connectivity Services.

Q&A

Q. *Can SharePoint search crawl external data?*

A. One of the capabilities of SharePoint search is that it can crawl external data. For this you need to create a new content source of type Line of Business Data and configure search for your BDC service. You learn more about SharePoint search in Hour 18, "Introducing SharePoint Search."

Q. *Is it possible to upgrade from Business Data Catalog of SharePoint 2007 to Business Connectivity Services?*

A. Yes it is possible to upgrade from Business Data Catalog to Business Connectivity Services. You can find more details at http://technet.microsoft.com/en-us/library/ff607947.aspx.

HOUR 15

Understanding SharePoint 2010 Workflows

What You'll Learn in This Hour

▶ Understanding out of the box SharePoint workflows
▶ Working with workflows in SharePoint Designer
▶ Working with workflows in Visual Studio

> **By the Way**
> Due to the complexity of the topics discussed, some figures in this book are very detailed and are intended only to provide a high-level view of concepts. Those figures are representational and not intended to be read in detail.

Workflows are an important part of the daily business process. Many activities can be represented in the form of workflows. A simple document approval process as well as a more complex human resource process can both be seen as workflows. Automating these processes requires an equivalent representation in the computer world. You see in this hour that SharePoint comes up with a great workflow framework, including out of the box workflows, SharePoint Designer support, and Visual Studio support.

Understanding Out of the Box SharePoint Workflows

SharePoint 2010 provides out of the box many useful workflows. Table 15.1 lists some of the important workflows that you will find yourself using frequently.

TABLE 15.1 Out of the Box Workflows in SharePoint 2010

Workflow Name	Description
Disposition Approval	Used to manage document expiration and retention.
Three-State	Manages the state of a list item and allows the transition between three states.

HOUR 15: Understanding SharePoint 2010 Workflows

TABLE 15.1 Continued

Workflow Name	Description
Approval	Used to route a document for approval. It tracks the approval status and also tracks the approval comments.
Collect Feedback	Used to route a document for review. It tracks the feedback given by the users.
Collect Signature	Used to gather signatures needed to complete a Microsoft Office document.

Using the Out of the Box Three-State Workflow

The Out of the Box Three-State workflow enables you to manage the state of the list item and the transition between the three states. The state of the list item is represented by a field that you can configure when attaching the workflow. The Three-State workflow enables you to create tasks for each state and transition the list item into the appropriate state upon completing the tasks.

Try It Yourself

Use the Three State Workflow

In this example you associate the Three-State workflow to a custom document library. Follow these steps to associate a Three-State workflow to a custom library.

1. Browse to your SharePoint site and create a new document library named ThreeStateDemo.

2. Add a column of type Choice. Name it ItemStatus and add Open, In Progress, and Closed as options, as shown in Figure 15.1.

3. Go to the Library in the ribbon and click the Workflow Settings command in the Settings section.

4. You are shown the Workflow Settings page as shown in Figure 15.2. This page lists all the workflows associated with the list and also provides the option to add a new workflow.

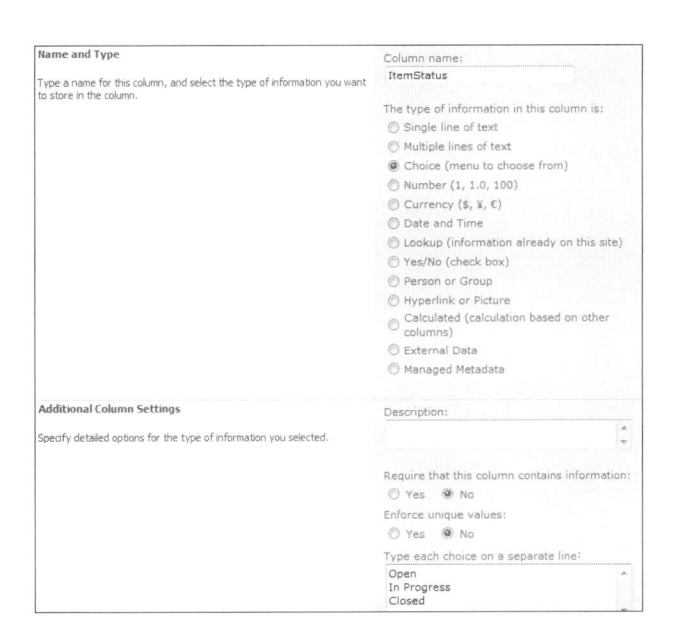

Understanding Out of the Box SharePoint Workflows 319

FIGURE 15.1
Creating a new column—ItemStatus

FIGURE 15.2
Workflow Settings

5. Click the Add a Workflow link to add a new workflow. You see the Add a Workflow page shown in Figure 15.3.

6. Select Three-State from the list of workflow templates. Name the workflow ThreeStateWF.

7. Select an existing task list or a new task list in the Select a Task List dropdown. Any tasks related to the workflow are created in this list.

HOUR 15: Understanding SharePoint 2010 Workflows

8. Select an existing list or a new list in the history list. Select the option Start This Workflow When a New Item Is Created. Click Next.

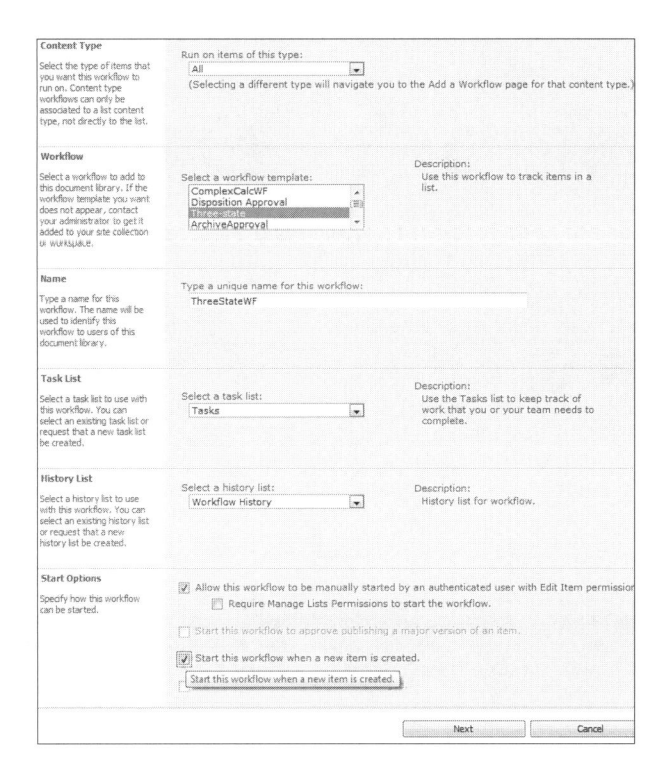

FIGURE 15.3
Adding a workflow

9. You see the Customize the Three-State Workflow screen. This screen allows you to select the field representing the three states of the list item. In addition it allows you to update the details of the tasks created when the item is created and when it is transitioned into its middle state. The ItemStatus field is selected by default, and the values Open, In Progress, and Closed are automatically mapped to the Initial State, Middle State, and Final State, respectively.

10. Modify the Custom Message in the first Task Details to New Request Created. Uncheck the Send E-mail Message check box as you don't need to send any email for now. Figure 15.4 shows the first Task Details.

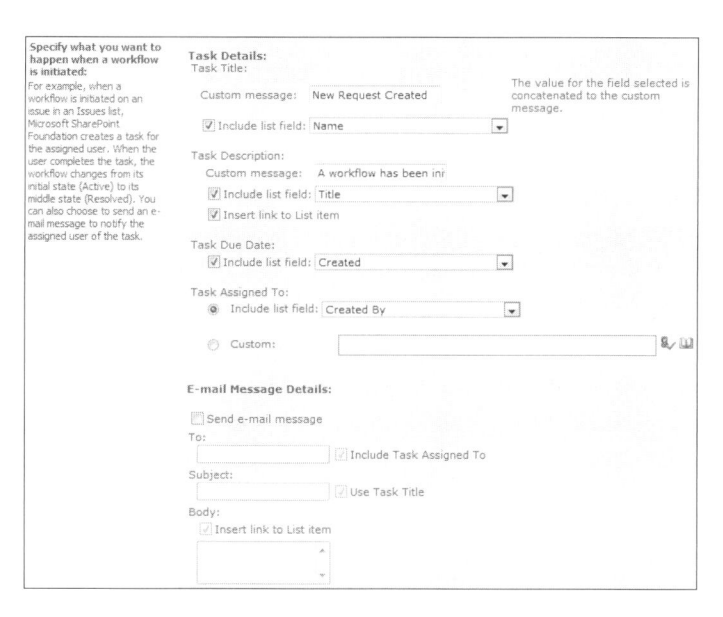

Understanding Out of the Box SharePoint Workflows 321

FIGURE 15.4
Task Details 1

11. Modify the Custom Message in the Second Task Details to Task Started. Uncheck the Send E-mail Message check box. Figure 15.5 shows the second Task Details.

FIGURE 15.5
Task Details 2

12. Click OK. Go back to the Workflow Settings for the ThreeStateDemo library and you can see the new Three-State workflow association listed.

13. Upload a new document to the ThreeStateDemo library. Once you upload the document you see the ThreeStateWF is initiated as shown in Figure 15.6.

FIGURE 15.6
ThreeState Demo Library—three state workflow in progress

14. Click the In Progress link. This takes you to the Workflow Status screen as shown in Figure 15.7. This screen displays the tasks associated with the workflow and the workflow history. You can see that a new task with a title starting with "New Request Created" has been created. This is as per the configuration specified when associating the workflow to the library.

15. Edit the task, set the status to completed, and save the task. You can see that a new task is created with a title starting with "Task Started." Browse to the ThreeStateDemo library and you can see that the ItemStatus for that list item has changed to "In Progress."

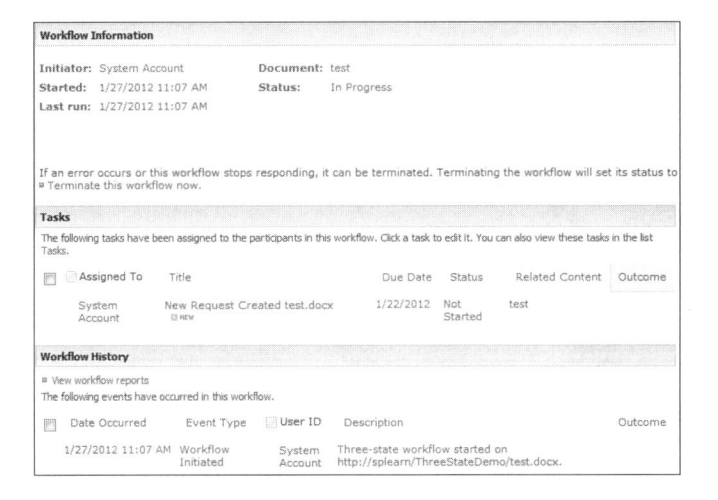

FIGURE 15.7
Workflow status

16. Finally go back to the Workflow Status and update the Task Status to Complete. You can see in the Workflow Status screen that the status of the workflow has changed to completed. If you browse back to the list item you can see that the ItemStatus has also changed to Closed.

> **By the Way**
>
> Sometimes the workflow is queued and you may need to refresh the page to see the changes in the status.

Working with Workflows in SharePoint Designer

Many times you will find that the out of the box workflows are not sufficient to meet your requirements. You may need to modify the out of the box workflows or at times even create workflows from scratch. The easiest way to do this is to create or modify workflows in SharePoint Designer 2010.

> **By the Way**
> You could not modify the out of the box workflows in SharePoint 2007. In SharePoint 2010 you can modify some of the out of the box workflows.

> **By the Way**
> In SharePoint 2007 workflows created in SharePoint Designer could not be exported and reused. This is now possible in SharePoint 2010 in the form of reusable workflows.

Modifying the Out of the Box Approval Workflow

In this example you modify the out of the box approval workflow. The approval workflow routes a document for approval. Approvers can approve or reject the document. You customize the approval workflow to move the approved documents to another list.

Try It Yourself
Modify Out of the Box Workflows

Follow these steps to modify the out of the box approval workflow:

1. Browse to the SharePoint site and create a new document library named ApprovalDemo. This library will use your customized workflow.

2. In addition you need a list where you will move the approved documents. For this create another document library named ApprovedDocuments.

3. Open your SharePoint site in SharePoint Designer 2010. Go to the Workflows section. This shows up as a list of workflows that can be customized. You can see the workflow Approval – SharePoint 2010 listed there. It is a good idea to keep the out of the box workflow unchanged and customize the copy of it.

4. Right-click Approval – SharePoint 2010 and click Copy and Modify.

5. This opens the Create Reusable Workflow dialog as shown in Figure 15.8. Name the workflow ArchiveApproval. Leave the Content Type set to All. Click OK.

HOUR 15: Understanding SharePoint 2010 Workflows

FIGURE 15.8
Creating a reusable workflow

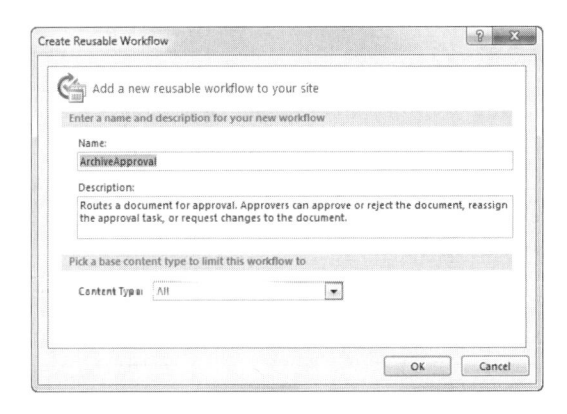

6. You can see the ArchiveApproval workflow screen as shown in Figure 15.9. Save the workflow.

7. Set the focus at the end and add a new condition from the ribbon of type If Any Value Equals Value as shown in Figure 15.10.

FIGURE 15.9
Edit the ArchiveApproval workflow in SharePoint Designer 2010.

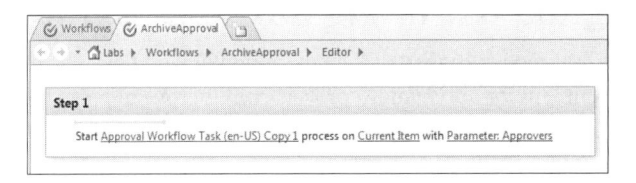

FIGURE 15.10
Adding a condition to the workflow in SharePoint Designer 2010

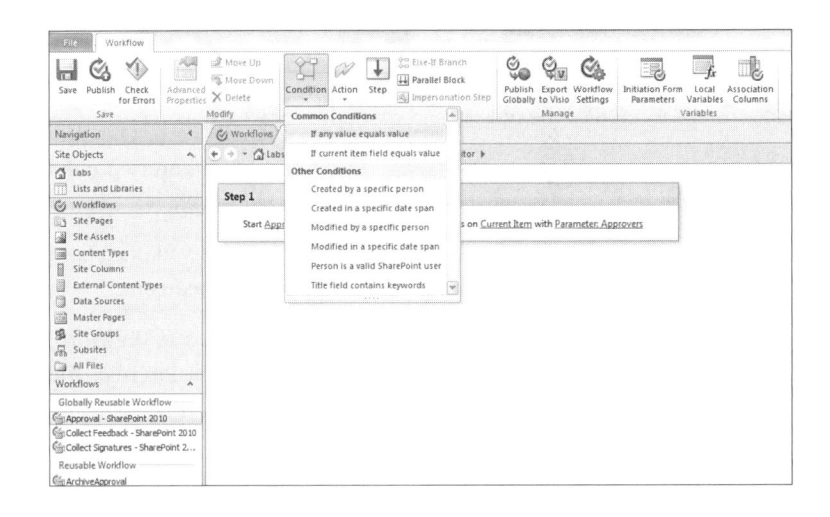

8. The new condition is added to the workflow as shown in Figure 15.11.

Working with Workflows in SharePoint Designer   325

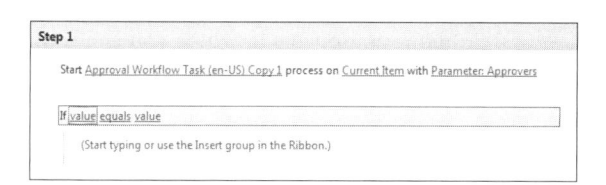

FIGURE 15.11
The new condition added to the ArchiveApproval workflow

9. Click the first Value link. Open the Define Workflow Lookup dialog by clicking on the fx button. In the Define Workflow Lookup dialog select Workflow Variables and Parameters in the Data Source drop-down. Select Variable: IsItemApproved in the Field from Source drop-down. This is shown in Figure 15.12. Click OK.

10. Click the second Value link in the condition. You can see that the options "Yes" and "No" are prepopulated. SharePoint Designer is smart enough to fill this based on the type of variable you are checking for. Select Yes.

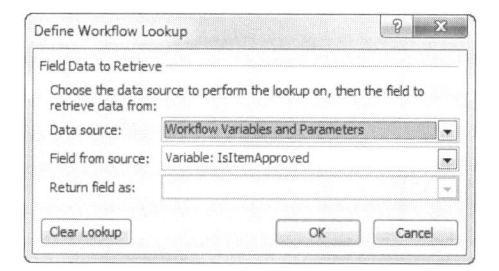

FIGURE 15.12
The Define Workflow Lookup dialog

11. Specify the action you want to do when the condition is satisfied. Add the Copy List Item action. Click the first This List link and select the Current Item in the Choose List Item dialog. Click OK to close the dialog.

12. Click the other This List link and select the ApprovedDocuments library.

13. Add the Delete Item action. Click the This List link and select the Current Item in the Choose List Item dialog.

14. Save the workflow. The designer should look as shown in Figure 15.13.

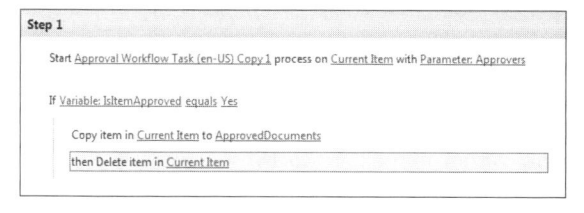

FIGURE 15.13
Final layout of the ArchiveApproval workflow

15. Publish the workflow by clicking on the Publish command in the ribbon.

16. Browse to the ApprovalDemo document library. Browse to the Workflow Settings page and click Add a Workflow. You can see your new workflow along with the other out of the box workflows listed there.

17. Enter the name of the workflow as ArchiveApprovalWF. Click Next.

18. The workflow association form appears in which you can configure the various parameters specific to the workflow as shown in Figure 15.14. Enter some valid user in the list of Approvers and click Save.

19. Add a new document to the ApprovalDemo document library. Open the context menu for the list item and go to the Workflows page. Click the ArchiveApprovalWF link to start the workflow.

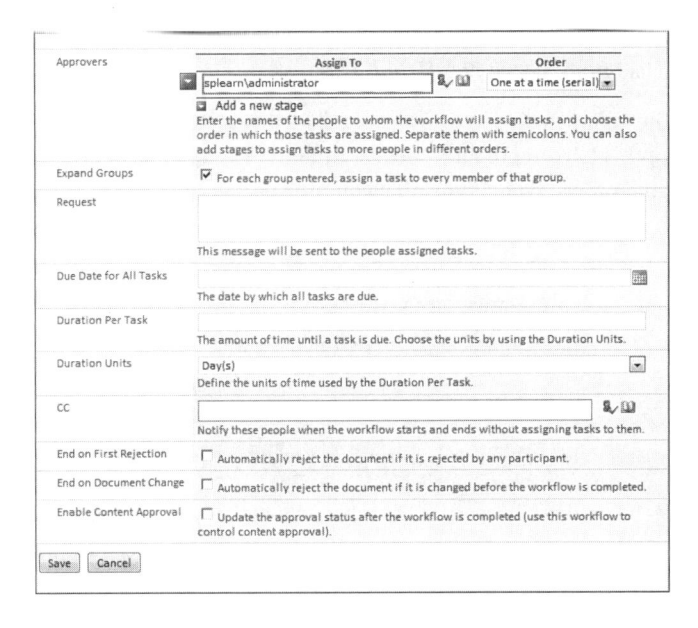

FIGURE 15.14
Associate ArchiveApproval workflow to the ApprovalDemo document library

20. You see the workflow initiation screen. This is similar to the workflow association screen and allows you to configure the individual instance of the workflow. The Approvers field is automatically populated with the name of the user you entered in the workflow association screen. Click Start to start the workflow.

21. You can now see the workflow status as In Progress. Go to the Workflow Status screen by clicking on the In Progress link. You can see a new task has been created for the workflow. Edit the task. This gives you the option to approve or reject the item as shown in Figure 15.15.

22. Approve the item. Browse back to the ApprovalDemo document library. You can see the list item has been deleted from the library. Browse to the ApprovedDocuments library, and you can see the document has been moved there by your workflow.

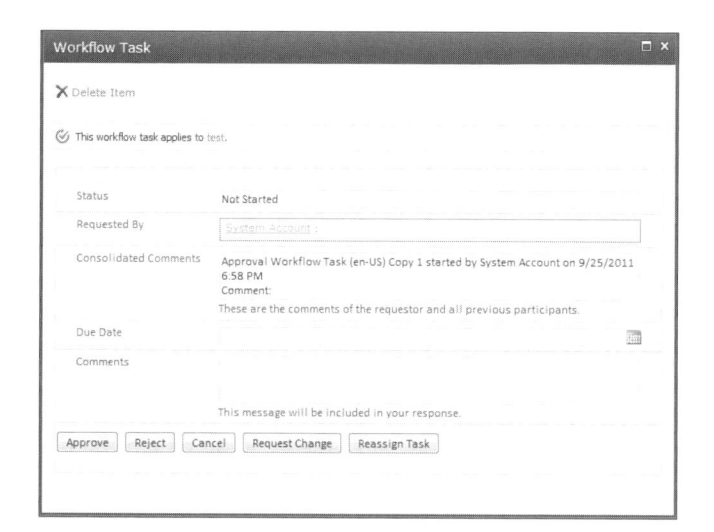

FIGURE 15.15
Starting the ArchiveApproval workflow

Working with Workflows in Visual Studio

At times you will come across scenarios when even SharePoint Designer workflows cannot meet your requirements, and you may need to create workflows in Visual Studio. This may be because you need to call some custom business logic components that do complex processing or access external data sources or external systems that is not possible to do in SharePoint Designer workflows. You might also need to create a Visual Studio workflow because you can use the additional workflow activities not present in the SharePoint Designer workflows.

Creating a SharePoint Workflow in Visual Studio 2010

You now create a new SharePoint workflow in Visual Studio 2010. The workflow is executed when a new item is added to a custom list called Loans. This list stores the LoanAmount, Salary, and LoanStatus. The workflow retrieves the Salary and LoanAmount and calls custom components that, based on some calculations, validate if the user is eligible for the specified LoanAmount. If the user is eligible, the workflow auto-approves the loan by setting the LoanStatus to Approved, or it creates a task for the administrator to manually verify the loan and update the status.

HOUR 15: Understanding SharePoint 2010 Workflows

▼ **Try It Yourself**

Create a SharePoint Workflow in Visual Studio 2010

Follow these steps to create a new SharePoint workflow in Visual Studio 2010:

1. Create a new SharePoint 2010 project of type Sequential Workflow and name it ComplexCalcWF.

2. The SharePoint Customization Wizard appears. Enter the site URL and click Next.

3. In the next screen of the wizard specify the workflow name as ComplexCalcWF and select the type of workflow as List Workflow. Click Next.

4. The next step prompts you to associate the workflow with a list. Uncheck the option as you will manually associate the workflow as shown in Figure 15.16. Click Finish.

FIGURE 15.16
Creating a new workflow in Visual Studio 2010

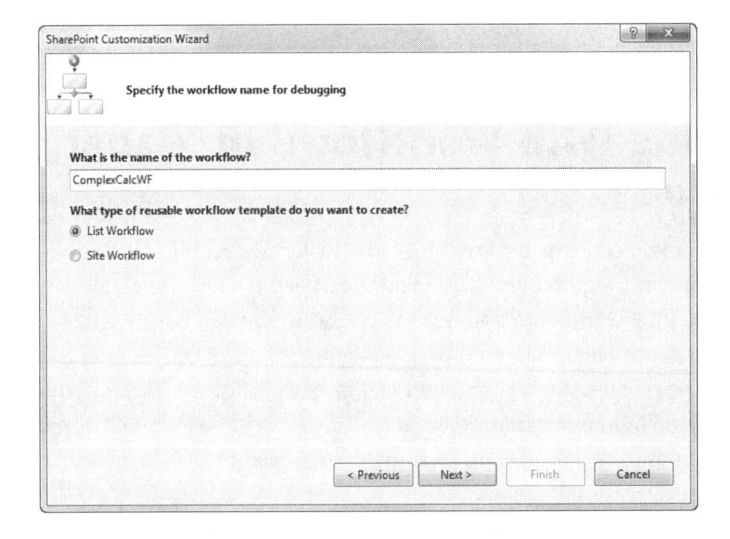

5. The workflow designer appears with OnWorkflowActivity as the first activity as shown in Figure 15.17. The first activity in any SharePoint workflow has to be the onWorkflowActivated activity. The onWorkflowActivity performs various important tasks such as setting the various context variables.

6. Before making any modifications to your workflow create your custom business logic component. Create a new project of type C# class library and name it CalculatorComponent. Ensure that the .Net Framework version for the class library is .Net 3.5.

▼

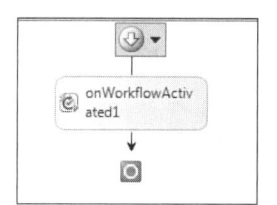

FIGURE 15.17
The OnWorkflow-Activated activity

7. Since the class library needs to be in GAC for the workflow to access it, add a strong name to the assembly.

8. Update the Class1.cs as shown in the following code:

```
namespace CalculatorComponent
{
    public class LoanEligibilityCalculator
    {
        public static bool IsEligible(int salary, int loanAmount)
        {
            if (loanAmount / salary > 10)
            {
                return false;
            }
            else
            {
                return true;
            }
        }
    }
}
```

9. The preceding code checks whether the loan amount is less than 10 times the salary and then passing true or false.

10. Build the CalculatorComponent Project. Add the reference of the CalculatorComponent Project to the workflow project.

11. Go back to the workflow designer and add an IfElse Activity after the onWorkflowActivity1 activity. Go to the code by pressing F7. Add the using for CalculatorComponent. Add the following function in the code:

```
public void Calculate(object sender, ConditionalEventArgs e)
        {
            int salary =
Convert.ToInt32(
workflowProperties.Item["Salary"].ToString());
            int loanAmount =
Convert.ToInt32(
workflowProperties.Item["LoanAmount"].ToString());

            e.Result = LoanEligibilityCalculator.IsEligible(salary,
➥loanAmount);
        }
```

HOUR 15: Understanding SharePoint 2010 Workflows

12. The preceding code retrieves the Salary and LoanAmount and calls the IsEligible method of your custom component. The e.Result indicates whether the condition is true or false.

13. Go back to the workflow designer. Select the first branch of the IfElseActivity and go to the Properties panel. Select the CodeCondition option for Condition property in the Properties panel. As soon as you select the CodeCondition you can expand the Condition property. Expand the condition property and select Calculate as the Condition from the drop-down. This is shown in Figure 15.18.

FIGURE 15.18
Code condition

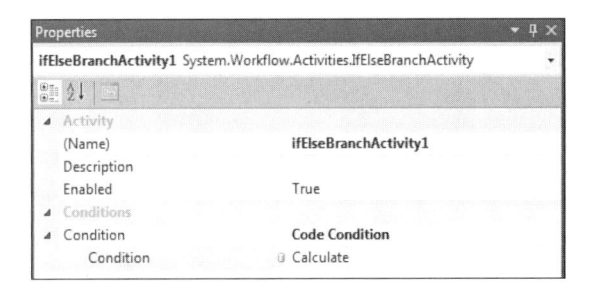

14. Add a code activity to the first branch of the IfElse Activity. This gets executed when the condition evaluates to true. Name the activity automaticApproval. Go to the codebehind file and add the following function. You can see that we are setting the LoanStatus field to Approved in the code.

    ```
    private void ApproveLoan(object sender, EventArgs e)
            {
                workflowProperties.Item["LoanStatus"] = "Approved";
                workflowProperties.Item.Update();
            }
    ```

15. Go back to the designer and select ApproveLoan for the Execute property of the automaticApproval code activity.

16. Create a task when the loan amount exceeds 10 times the salary. Add a CreateTask Activity to the other branch.

> **By the Way**
>
> The create task activity is available under the SharePoint Workflow section in the Toolbox.

17. In the Properties for the CreateTask activity enter the CorrelationToken as correlationToken1.

Working with Workflows in Visual Studio

> **By the Way**
>
> Correlation tokens act as unique identifiers that enable mapping between the objects in a workflow and the environment that is hosting the Windows Workflow Foundation (WF) workflow runtime.

18. Now go to the TaskId property and click the ellipsis button. In the modal dialog that pops up, go to the Bind to a New Member tab and select Create Field as shown in Figure 15.19.

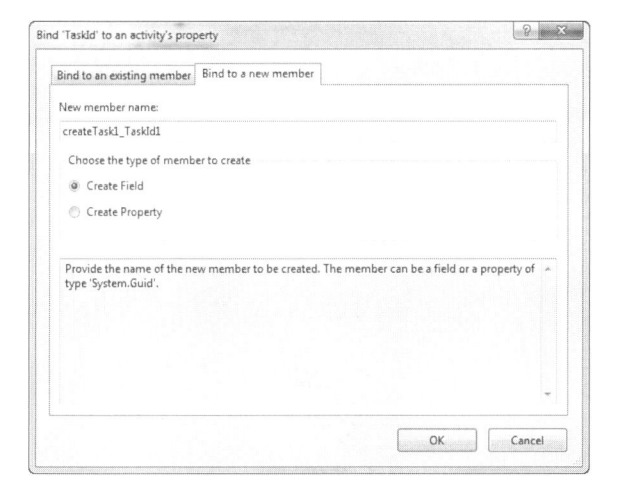

FIGURE 15.19
Bind TaskId

19. Repeat step 18 for TaskProperties in the properties window.

20. Now double-click the createTask1 property. This creates the MethodInvoking event handler in the codebehind. Update the method as in the following code. You can see that we are setting the various properties for the Task in the code.

```
private void createTask1_MethodInvoking(object sender, EventArgs e)
    {
        createTask1_TaskId1 = Guid.NewGuid();

        createTask1_TaskProperties1.Title =
"Loan requires additional Approval";
        createTask1_TaskProperties1.Description =
                    string.Format(@"
Loan amount has exceed 10 times the salary
Loan amount = {0},
Salary = {1}
Cannot perform automated approval.
Requires manual approval from Bank Manager",

workflowProperties.Item["LoanAmount"].ToString(),

workflowProperties.Item["Salary"].ToString());
```

```
                    createTask1_TaskProperties1.SendEmailNotification = true;
                    createTask1_TaskProperties1.AssignedTo =
workflowProperties.Originator;
                }
```

21. The final view of the workflow designer should be as shown in Figure 15.20.

FIGURE 15.20
Final layout of the ComplexCalc-WF workflow

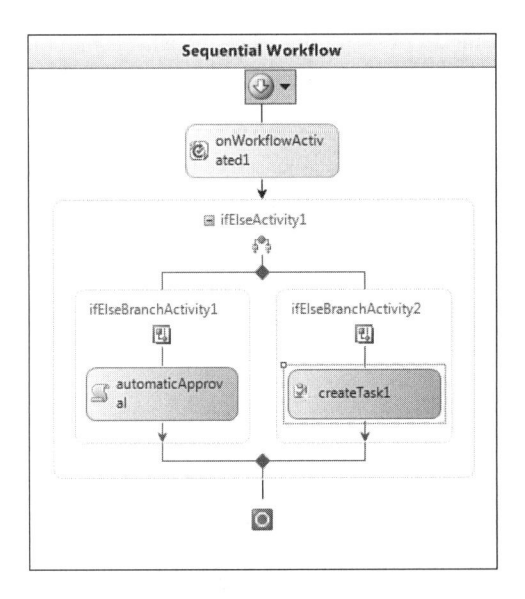

22. Rebuild and deploy the workflow. You also need to add the CalculatorComponent to the GAC. You can do this by simply dragging the CalculatorComponent.dll to the GAC or by running the command gacutil /i CalculatorComponent.dll from the Visual Studio 2010 command prompt.

23. Now create the Loans list. Create a new custom list and add the fields shown in Table 15.2.

TABLE 15.2 Field for the Loans List

Field Name	Type
Salary	Currency
LoanAmount	Currency
LoanStatus	Choice—with options as Pending, Approved, and Rejected

24. Associate your new workflow with the list and set it to start when a new item is created.

25. Create a new list item with Salary as 100, Loan Amount as 900, and Loan Status as Pending. You can see that as soon as you save the list item the loan status is changed to Approved, and you can see that the ComplexCalcWF workflow is completed. This is shown in Figure 15.21.

FIGURE 15.21 ComplexCalcWF status when LoanAmount < (Salary * 10)

26. Create another list item with Salary as 100, Loan Amount as 1100, and Loan Status as Pending. You can see that once you save the list item the workflow shows In Progress, and the Loan Status remains Pending.

27. Click the In Progress link to open the Workflow Status screen. You can see that a new task has been created by the workflow as shown in Figures 15.22 and 15.23.

28. The user can go ahead and manually update the status of the workflow to Approved or Rejected.

FIGURE 15.22 ComplexCalcWF status when LoanAmount > (Salary * 10)

FIGURE 15.23
Task created by the ComplexCalcWF

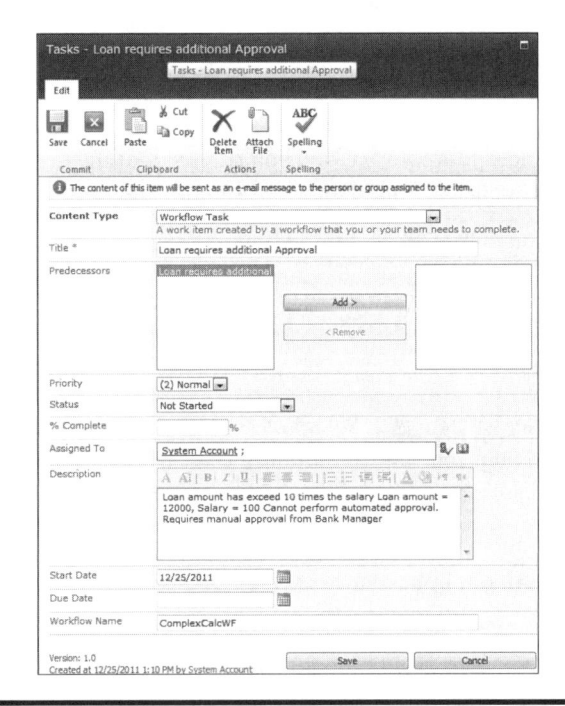

Summary

This hour covered the concept of SharePoint workflows. SharePoint workflows are an important component in automating various business processes. SharePoint 2010 comes with many out of the box workflows. If these workflows fail to meet your requirements you can customize them or create new workflows in SharePoint Designer 2010. In addition you can create custom workflows for advanced scenarios that cannot be handled using SharePoint Designer 2010 workflows.

Q&A

Q. *Can I create custom activities in for SharePoint workflows?*

A. It has been possible to create custom activities for use in Visual Studio since SharePoint 2007. It is now possible to create custom activities for SharePoint Designer 2010 also. Please refer to MSDN to find more details on how to do this.

Q. *What is the difference between sequential workflows and state machine workflows?*

A. Sequential workflows mostly execute in a linear fashion based on branches and are ideal for simple processes such as a linear approval process where the document may be approved or rejected. State machine workflows do not flow in a linear fashion and normally involve transition from one state to another.

HOUR 16

Understanding SharePoint 2010 Central Administration

What You'll Learn in This Hour

- ▶ Starting with SharePoint 2010 Central Administration
- ▶ Understanding Application Management
- ▶ Understanding System Settings in SharePoint Central Administration
- ▶ Understanding Monitoring in SharePoint Central Administration
- ▶ Understanding Backup and Restore in SharePoint Central Administration
- ▶ Understanding Security in SharePoint Central Administration
- ▶ Understanding Upgrade and Migration in SharePoint Central Administration
- ▶ Understanding General Application Settings in SharePoint Central Administration
- ▶ Configuring with PowerShell

> **By the Way**
>
> Due to the complexity of the topics discussed, some figures in this book are very detailed and are intended only to provide a high-level view of concepts. Those figures are representational and not intended to be read in detail.

You will find yourself working frequently with SharePoint 2010 Central Administration, so understanding Central Administration is an important part of your SharePoint know-how even if you are a developer and not an administrator. This hour looks systematically at the various functions performed through SharePoint 2010 Central Administration.

Starting with SharePoint 2010 Central Administration

Those who have worked on SharePoint 2007 will quickly realize that the user interface of SharePoint 2010's Central Administration has changed dramatically. Figure 16.1 shows the SharePoint 2010 Central Administration home page.

HOUR 16: Understanding SharePoint 2010 Central Administration

FIGURE 16.1
SharePoint 2010 Central Administration

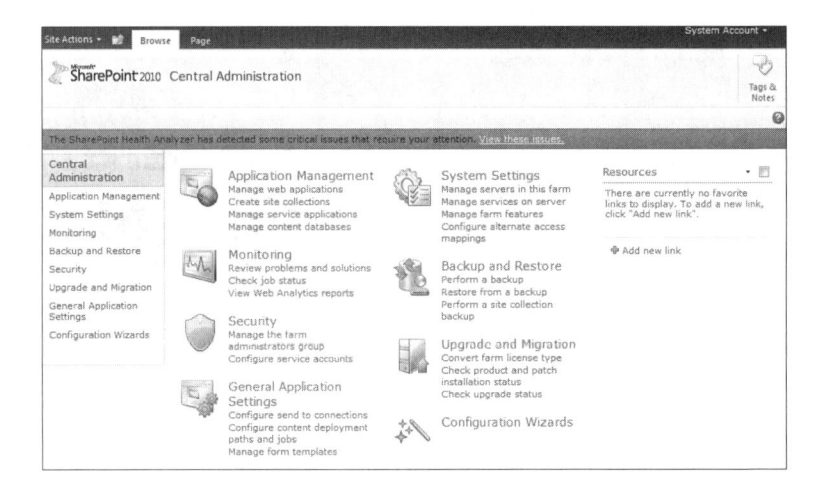

As you can see, the various settings in SharePoint 2010 Central Administration are divided into eight major categories:

- Application Management
- System Settings
- Monitoring
- Backup and Restore
- Security
- Upgrade and Migration
- General Application Settings
- Configuration Wizards

SharePoint 2010 Central Administration is itself a SharePoint site. Being a SharePoint site provides a uniform experience in terms of usability, such as the ribbon interface, site actions, and navigation. The following sections take a look at the various parts of SharePoint 2010 Central Administration.

Understanding Application Management

The Application Management section as the name suggests allows you to perform various functions related to managing your SharePoint Application, such as creating and managing web applications, site collection, service applications, content databases, and managing services on the SharePoint server. Figure 16.2 shows the Application Management screen.

Understanding Application Management | 339

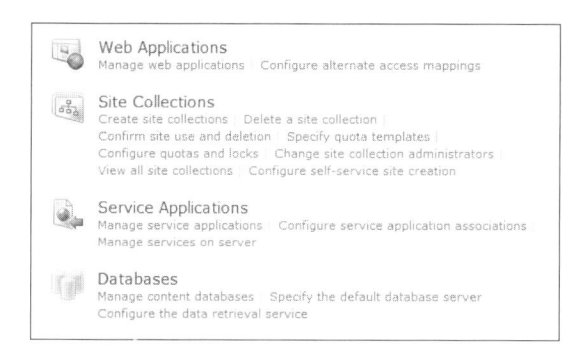

FIGURE 16.2
Application Management

Application Management itself is grouped into four parts, described in the following sections.

Exploring Web Applications

The Web Applications section allows performing various administrative tasks to manage SharePoint web applications. Manage Web Applications takes you to the screen shown in Figure 16.3.

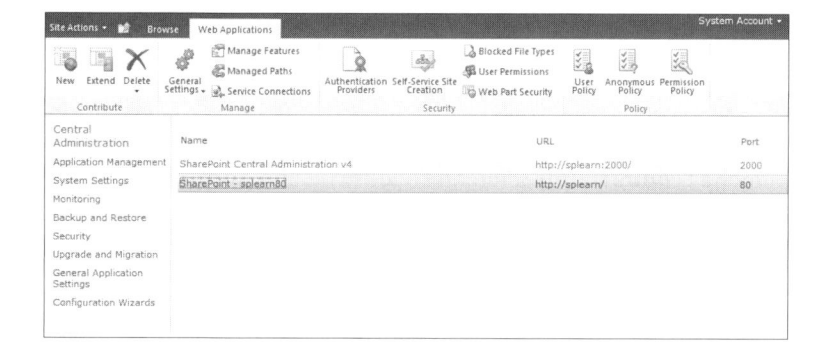

FIGURE 16.3
Manage Web Applications

The Web Applications Management screen allows you to create or delete web applications. Selecting a web application enables additional commands on the ribbon some of which are described here:

- **Extend**—This command allows you to extend an existing web application. Extending a web application means creating a new web application in a different zone that uses the same content database.

Did You Know?

> You may find yourself creating multiple web applications in different zones on multiple occasions. For example, when you have an Internet facing SharePoint site you will create a web application for the Internet zone for end users and a web application in the intranet/default zone for administration purposes. Also the search crawl ideally happens in the default/intranet zone for performance reasons.

- **General Settings**—The General Settings command allows you to manage various settings for web applications, such as the default time zone for the web application, quota information, alerts information, Recycle Bin settings, Resource Throttling settings, general workflow configuration, email configuration, and SharePoint Designer settings.

By the Way

> Resource Throttling settings drive an important configuration that can be critical to the performance of the SharePoint server. This configuration includes the max limit of records that can be retrieved from a list in one query, count of unique permissions on a list (which is also a factor in list performance), and log storage settings.

By the Way

> Quota templates allow you to specify storage limits for users. In addition, in SharePoint 2010 with the introduction of sandboxed solutions, quota templates also enable you to specify the sandboxed solutions resource quota limits.

- **Manage Features**—This command allows you to activate/deactivate web application level features for the selected web application.

- **Managed Paths**—This command allows you to configure managed paths. Managed paths are paths that extend the URL of the web application for creating site collections. An example of the managed path is "/sites".

- **Service Connections**—This allows you to configure service applications associations for the selected web applications.

- **Authentication Providers**—This command allows you to configure the authentication providers for the web application for each extended zone.

- **Self-Service Site Creation**—Self-service site creation allows end users with the Use Self–Service Site Creation permission to create site collections. This command enables you to toggle the Self-Service Site Creation feature on and off.

In addition to the Manage Web Applications function the Configure Alternate Access Mappings function is under the Web Applications group. This option allows you to map alternate URLs to your web application.

Exploring Site Collections

This section allows you to create and manage site collections. The various configuration options are as follows:

- **Create Site Collection**—This screen allows you to create a new site collection within the specified web application. Figure 16.4 shows the Create Site Collection screen.

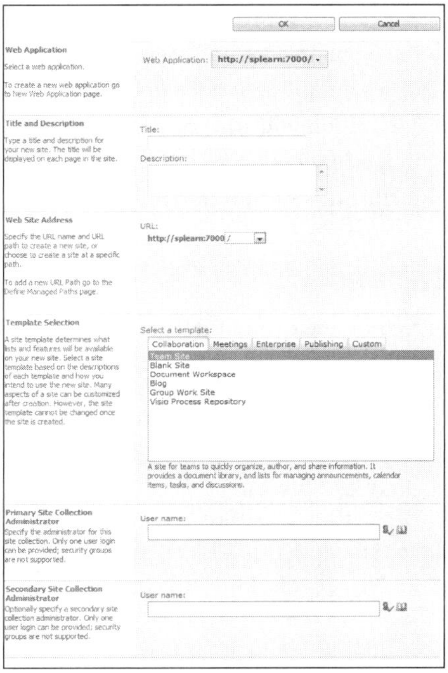

FIGURE 16.4
Create Site Collection

- **Site Usage Confirmation and Deletion**—This is a web application level configuration and allows you to set email notification settings for unused site collections. You can also specify the unused site collections to be deleted automatically after a specific time span.

> **By the Way**
> The options within this screen will be disabled if you have not configured the email settings for the web application. These settings can be configured under the General Settings command of the Web Application Management screen.

- **Specify Quota Templates**—Quota templates specify the storage limits for a SharePoint web application. This screen allows you to create/modify quota templates.

HOUR 16: Understanding SharePoint 2010 Central Administration

- **Site Collection Quota and Locks**—This option allows you to select a quota template for all the site collections within the specified web applications. You also configure Sandbox Solution Resource Quota restrictions in this screen.

- **Change Site Collection Administrators**—This screen allows you to manage the site collection administrators for various site collections centrally.

Exploring Service Applications

This section allows you to create and manage service applications in your SharePoint farm. You can also manage service applications association with your web applications here. In addition you can toggle the state of various services on your server from the Manage Services on Server screen. Hour 20, "Understanding Service Applications," looks at this section in detail.

Exploring Databases

This section allows you to manage content databases. The various configuration options are as follows:

- **Manage Content Databases**—This screen allows you to view and manage the content databases for the specified web applications. Figure 16.5 shows the Manage Content Databases screen.

FIGURE 16.5
Manage Content Databases

Clicking on the database name shows more details of that content database. The Add a Content Database command creates a new content database for the specified web application.

- **Specify the Default Database Server**—This option allows you to specify the default database server to create the new content databases in.

Understanding System Settings in SharePoint Central Administration

The System Settings section contains a lot of configuration options for farmwide settings. Figure 16.6 shows the System Settings section.

Understanding System Settings in SharePoint Central Administration 343

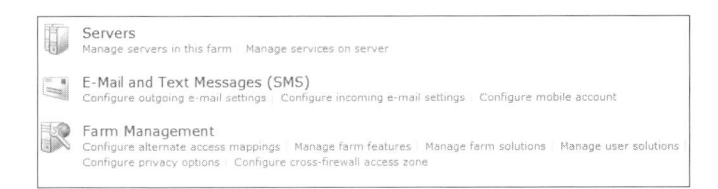

FIGURE 16.6
System Settings

> Servers
> Manage servers in this farm | Manage services on server
>
> E-Mail and Text Messages (SMS)
> Configure outgoing e-mail settings | Configure incoming e-mail settings | Configure mobile account
>
> Farm Management
> Configure alternate access mappings | Manage farm features | Manage farm solutions | Manage user solutions
> Configure privacy options | Configure cross-firewall access zone

As you can see the various configuration options are divided into three major parts, discussed in the following sections.

Servers

The Servers section allows you to configure the servers in the farms. The Manage Servers in This Farm screen lists the servers in the farm and allows you to remove them. The Manage Services on Server screen is the same as the one you saw in the "Understanding Application Management" section earlier in the hour.

> **By the Way**
> To add a new server to the farm you need to run the SharePoint 2010 Products Configuration Wizard in that server.

Email and Text Messages (SMS)

This section allows you to configure the farmwide incoming and outgoing email settings and the SMS settings for sending alerts.

> **By the Way**
> You saw the option to configure outgoing email settings in web application management. That option is specific to that web application and allows you to override the farm level email setting.

> **By the Way**
> The incoming email settings allow SharePoint to receive emails in a list. The SMTP service must be installed as a prerequisite for configuring the incoming email settings.

Farm Management

The Farm Management section contains the following important configuration options:

▶ **Manage Farm Features**—This screen allows you to activate/deactivate the farm scoped features.

▶ **Manage Farm Solutions**—This screen lists the various farm solutions installed in the farm and allows you to deploy, retract, and remove solutions from the farm.

> **By the Way**
>
> You cannot perform the Add solution operation from the user interface of the Manage Farm Solutions screen. This needs to be done through PowerShell or `stsadm` commands.

▶ **Manage User Solutions**—This screen allows you to manage the sandboxed solution restrictions. Figure 16.7 shows the Manage User Solutions screen.

FIGURE 16.7 Manage User Solutions

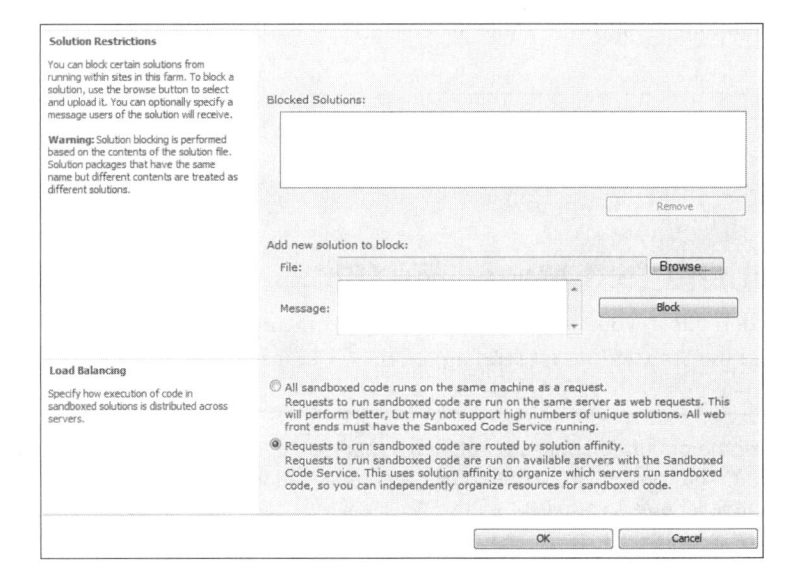

Understanding Monitoring in SharePoint Central Administration

The Monitoring section allows you to configure various options related to timer jobs, logging, and reporting. Figure 16.8 shows the Monitoring section.

The configuration settings in the Monitoring section are discussed in the following sections.

Understanding Monitoring in SharePoint Central Administration   345

FIGURE 16.8
Monitoring

Health Analyzer

The Health Analyzer section lists the health related information about the farm and also provides recommendations. Figure 16.9 shows a sample report. Clicking on one of the items provides more detail and the solution to the issue.

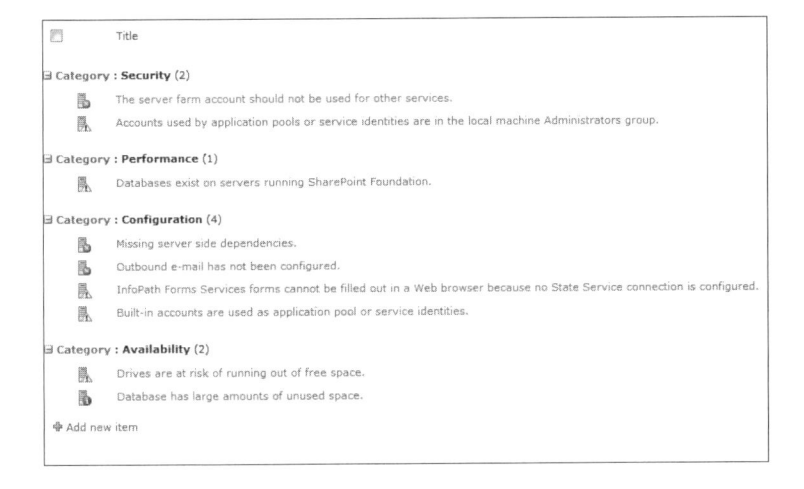

FIGURE 16.9
Sample Health Analyzer report

Timer Jobs

This is an important section that allows you to manage timer jobs. You can see the timer jobs deployed on your farm by clicking Review Timer Job Definitions. Figure 16.10 shows the Job Definitions screen.

In addition you can see the status of the timer jobs by clicking on the Check Job Status screen as shown in Figure 16.11.

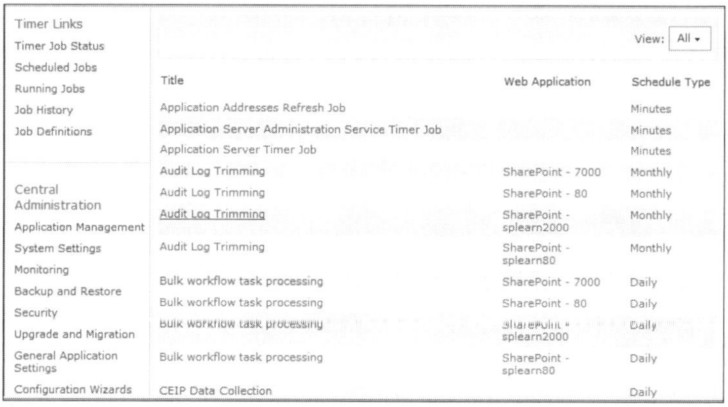

FIGURE 16.10
Timer Job Definitions

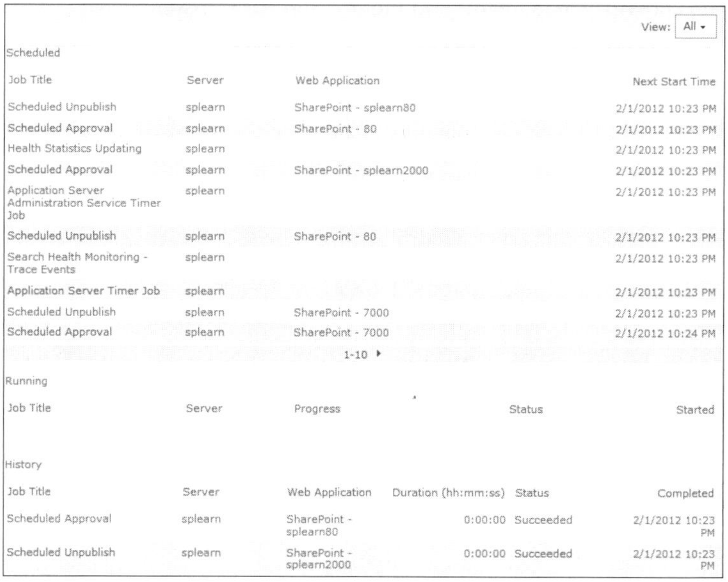

Title	Web Application	Schedule Type
Application Addresses Refresh Job		Minutes
Application Server Administration Service Timer Job		Minutes
Application Server Timer Job		Minutes
Audit Log Trimming	SharePoint - 7000	Monthly
Audit Log Trimming	SharePoint - 80	Monthly
Audit Log Trimming	SharePoint - splearn2000	Monthly
Audit Log Trimming	SharePoint - splearn80	Monthly
Bulk workflow task processing	SharePoint - 7000	Daily
Bulk workflow task processing	SharePoint - 80	Daily
Bulk workflow task processing	SharePoint - splearn2000	Daily
Bulk workflow task processing	SharePoint - splearn80	Daily
CEIP Data Collection		Daily

FIGURE 16.11
Timer Job Status

Scheduled

Job Title	Server	Web Application	Next Start Time
Scheduled Unpublish	splearn	SharePoint - splearn80	2/1/2012 10:23 PM
Scheduled Approval	splearn	SharePoint - 80	2/1/2012 10:23 PM
Health Statistics Updating	splearn		2/1/2012 10:23 PM
Scheduled Approval	splearn	SharePoint - splearn2000	2/1/2012 10:23 PM
Application Server Administration Service Timer Job	splearn		2/1/2012 10:23 PM
Scheduled Unpublish	splearn	SharePoint - 80	2/1/2012 10:23 PM
Search Health Monitoring - Trace Events	splearn		2/1/2012 10:23 PM
Application Server Timer Job	splearn		2/1/2012 10:23 PM
Scheduled Unpublish	splearn	SharePoint - 7000	2/1/2012 10:23 PM
Scheduled Approval	splearn	SharePoint - 7000	2/1/2012 10:24 PM

1-10

Running

Job Title	Server	Progress	Status	Started

History

Job Title	Server	Web Application	Duration (hh:mm:ss)	Status	Completed
Scheduled Approval	splearn	SharePoint - splearn80	0:00:00	Succeeded	2/1/2012 10:23 PM
Scheduled Unpublish	splearn	SharePoint - splearn2000	0:00:00	Succeeded	2/1/2012 10:23 PM

Reporting

The Reporting section allows you to see a variety of reports related to the various aspects of your SharePoint farm. In addition this is the place from where you configure the level of logging you want to perform. Figure 16.12 shows the Diagnostic Logging screen.

Understanding Backup and Restore in SharePoint Central Administration 347

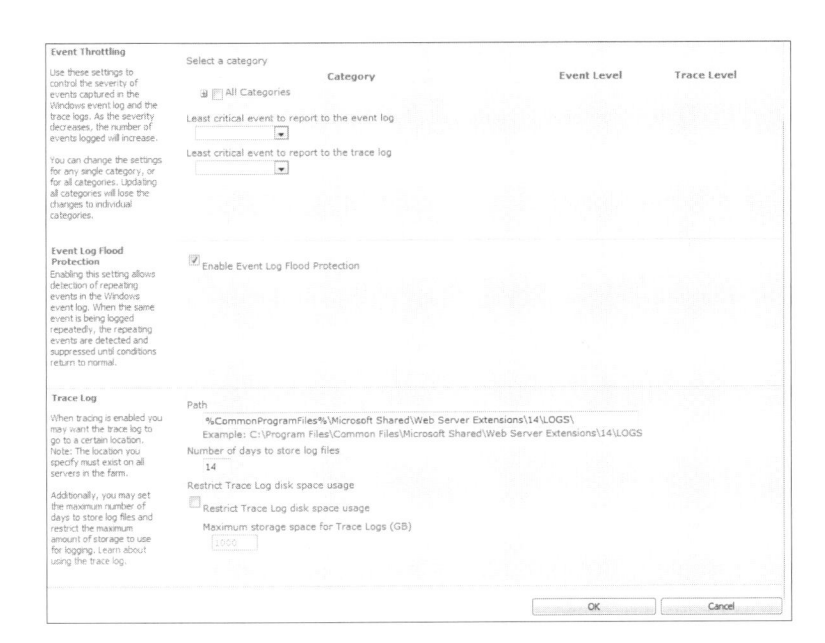

FIGURE 16.12
Diagnostic Logging

Understanding Backup and Restore in SharePoint Central Administration

The Backup and Restore section allows you to perform various operations related to performing and restoring backups on your SharePoint farm. This is divided into mainly two sections—Farm Backup and Restore and Granular Backup.

Farm Backup and Restore

This section allows you to perform backup and restore operations on the entire SharePoint farm. Following are the important screens in this section:

▶ **Perform a Backup**—This screen allows you to back up the entire SharePoint farm. This includes the configuration database, solution store, SharePoint web applications, and shared services. In addition this screen allows you to back up specific components within the farm in case you do not need the entire farm backup.

Try It Yourself ▼

Back Up the SharePoint 2010 Farm

In this example you perform an entire farm backup. Follow these steps:

1. Browse to the Perform Backup screen in Central Administration in the Backup and Restore section.

2. Select all the components of the SharePoint farm as shown in Figure 16.13 and click Next.

▼

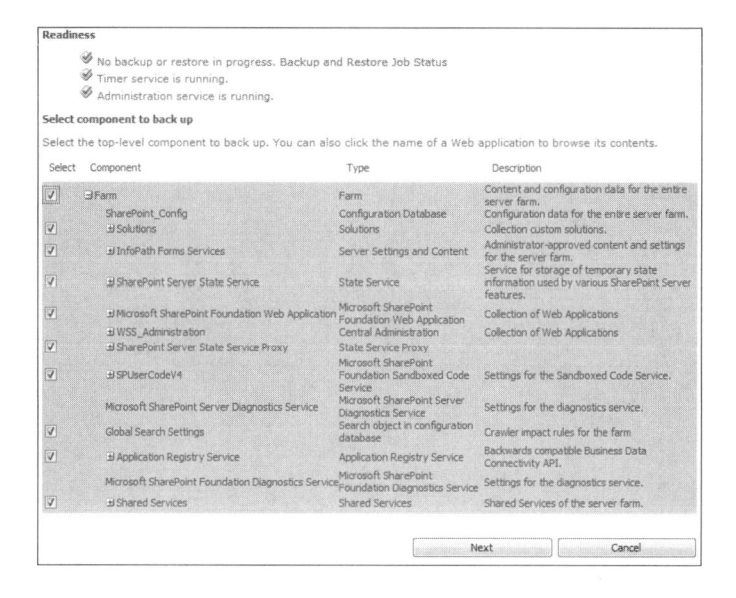

HOUR 16: Understanding SharePoint 2010 Central Administration

FIGURE 16.13
Selecting components to back up

[Figure 16.13: Screenshot showing Select component to back up screen with list of farm components including Farm, SharePoint_Config, Solutions, InfoPath Forms Services, SharePoint Server State Service, Microsoft SharePoint Foundation Web Application, WSS_Administration, SharePoint Server State Service Proxy, SPUserCodeV4, Microsoft SharePoint Server Diagnostics Service, Global Search Settings, Application Registry Service, Microsoft SharePoint Foundation Diagnostics Service, and Shared Services]

3. Select the Full backup type and select an appropriate location to store the backup file, as shown in Figure 16.14. Click Start Backup.

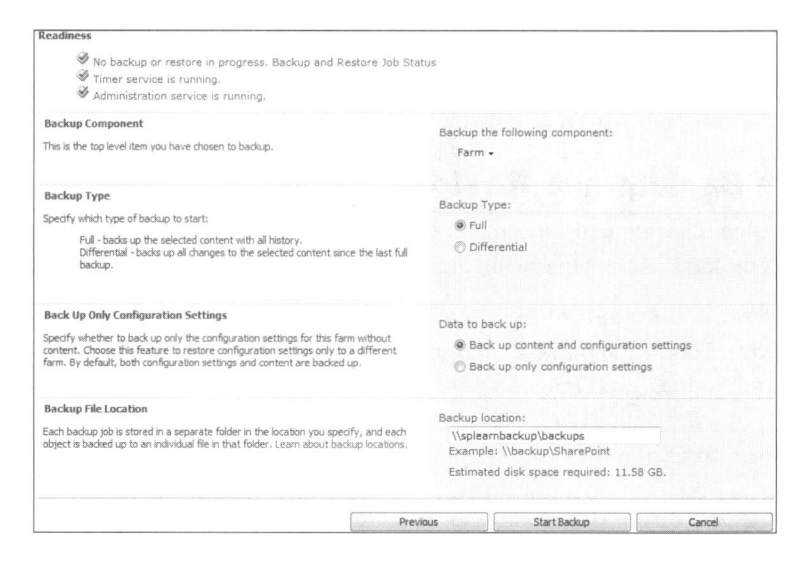

FIGURE 16.14
Backup options

[Figure 16.14: Screenshot of Backup options screen showing Backup Component (Farm), Backup Type (Full or Differential), Back Up Only Configuration Settings options, and Backup File Location with path \\splearnbackup\backups and Estimated disk space required: 11.58 GB]

4. You are taken to the View Backup or Restore Job Status screen. Click Refresh occasionally to see the progress of the backup operation. You see a screen similar to the one shown in Figure 16.15 after the backup job has been completed.

Understanding Backup and Restore in SharePoint Central Administration

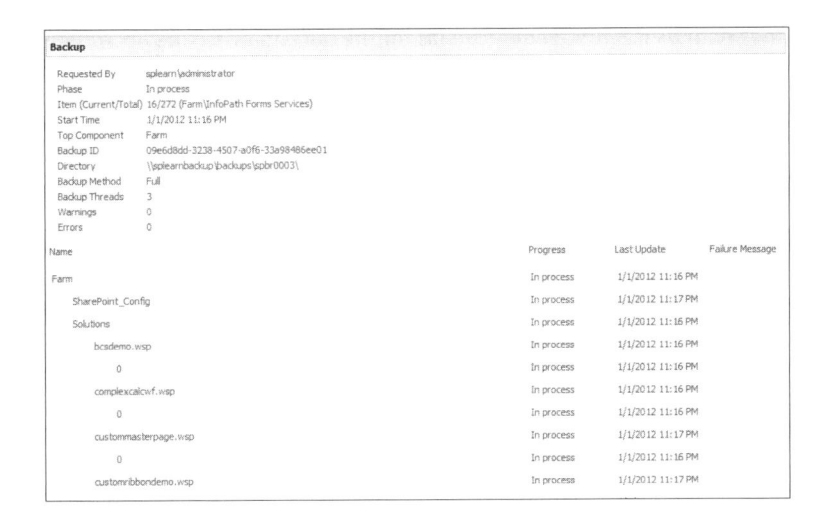

FIGURE 16.15
Backup status

> **By the Way**
> Creating a new backup operation actually schedules the Backup/Restore timer job. You can verify this by going to the Timer Job Status screen; you will find the Backup/Restore job under the list of Running Jobs.

▶ **Restore from a Backup**—This screen allows you to restore a farm backup to the current SharePoint farm. You can see a list of all the backups taken and select and restore one of them. Figure 16.16 shows the Restore Backup screen.

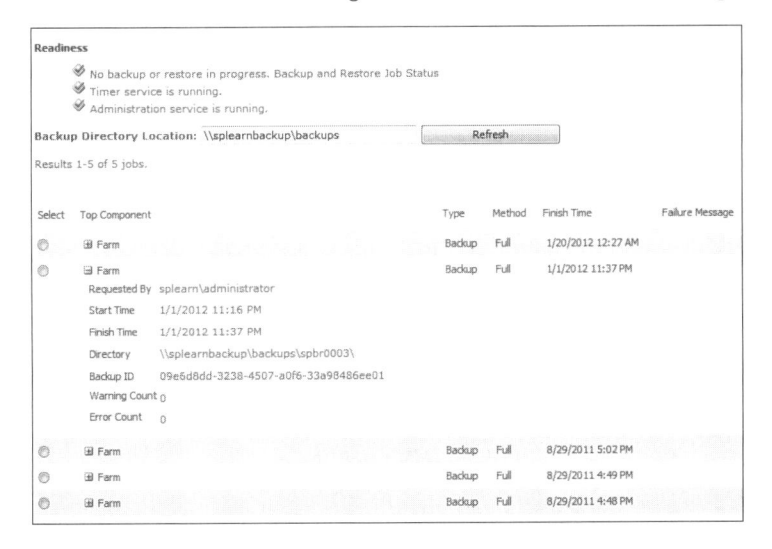

FIGURE 16.16
Restore Backup

▶ **Configure Backup Settings**—This screen allows you to configure various settings such as the number of threads for the backup or restore operations and the default backup location. Figure 16.17 shows the Configure Backup Settings screen.

FIGURE 16.17
Backup and Restore Settings

> By the Way
>
> The number of backup threads and the number of restore threads impact the performance of the backup and restore operations, respectively. The more threads, the faster the respective operations will happen, though the operations will also be more resource intensive.

▶ **View Backup and Restore History**—This screen lists the history about various backup and restore operations performed on the farm.

▶ **View Backup and Restore Job Status**—This screen shows the status of the last backup or restore job operation.

Granular Backup

The Granular Backup section allows you to perform backup and restore operations related to site collections, sites, or lists/libraries. The important screens in this section are as follows:

▶ **Perform a Site Collection Backup**—This section allows you to take the backup of the specified site collection. Figure 16.18 shows the Site Collection Backup screen.

▶ **Export a Site or List**—This screen allows you to back up a single site or a list/library. Figure 16.19 shows the Export a Site or List screen.

Understanding Backup and Restore in SharePoint Central Administration

FIGURE 16.18
Site Collection Backup

FIGURE 16.19
Exporting a site or list

You can see that this screen allows various options such as exporting the security and version information in the backup.

▶ **Recover Data from an Unattached Content Database**—This screen allows you to back up data from a content database. The content database need not be attached. This is particularly useful when you need to back up and restore specific components within a content database.

▶ **Check Granular Backup Job Status**—This screen shows the status of the last backup job. Figure 16.20 shows the Granular Backup Job Status screen.

> **By the Way**
>
> You might have observed there is no screen to restore the site collection backup. In fact you cannot restore the site collection backup from Central Administration. You need to use PowerShell to restore a site collection backup. You learn more about this in the section on PowerShell later in this hour.

FIGURE 16.20
Backup Job Status screen

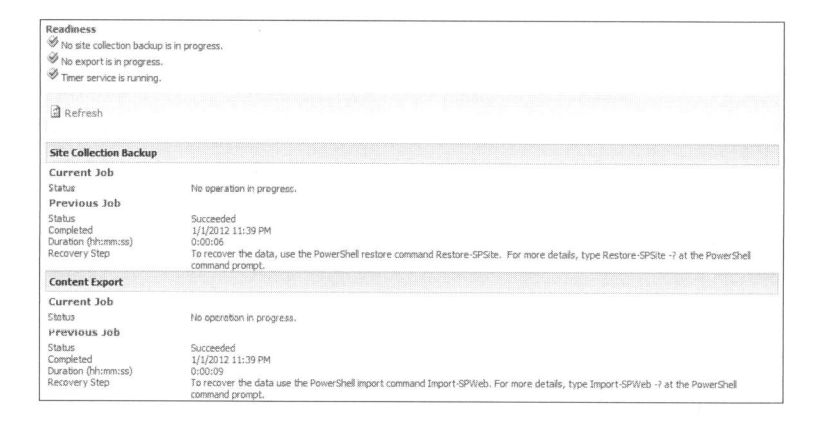

Understanding Security in SharePoint Central Administration

The Security section allows you to configure the security settings for the SharePoint farm. The following sections discuss the important Security screens.

Exploring Users Settings

The Users section contains various settings to manage users in the farm administrators group and to manage users in the Approve or Reject distribution groups. In addition you can provide users access at the web application level through the Specify Web Application User Policy screen.

General Security

This section allows you to configure various security settings as described in the following list:

- ▶ **Configure Managed Accounts**—This screen allows you to add, edit, and delete managed accounts. A managed account is a user account whose credentials are managed by and contained within SharePoint. Figure 16.21 shows the Configure Managed Accounts screen.

- ▶ **Configure Service Accounts**—This allows you to change the accounts under which the service applications run. In addition you can change the user accounts of the application pools used in your SharePoint farm. Figure 16.22 shows the Service Accounts screen.

Understanding Security in SharePoint Central Administration 353

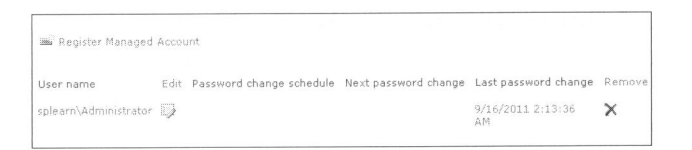

FIGURE 16.21 Configure Managed Accounts

FIGURE 16.22 Service Accounts

- **Configure Password Change Settings**—This screen allows you to configure farm-level settings for automatic password changes and to configure the notification email address that will be used to send all password change notification emails.

- **Specify Authentication Providers**—This screen lists the authentication providers for the selected web applications and allows you to configure those authentication providers. Figure 16.23 shows the Authentication Providers screen.

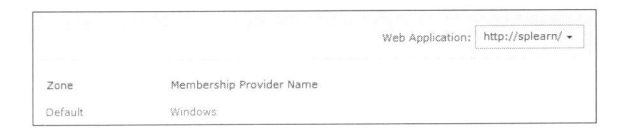

FIGURE 16.23 Authentication Providers

- **Define Blocked File Types**—This allows you to specify file types that are prevented from being uploaded within a document library in a SharePoint site.

- **Manage Web Part Security**—This screen allows you to enable/disable various settings related to web parts such as web part connections, access to the web part gallery, and access to scriptable web parts.

Information Policy

This section allows you to configure the following settings

- **Configure Information Rights Management**—This screen allows you to configure Rights Management Services (RMS) on this server. RMS allows you to use Information Rights Management, which helps you to protect sensitive files from being misused or distributed without permissions once they have been downloaded from the server. Figure 16.24 shows the Information Rights Management screen.

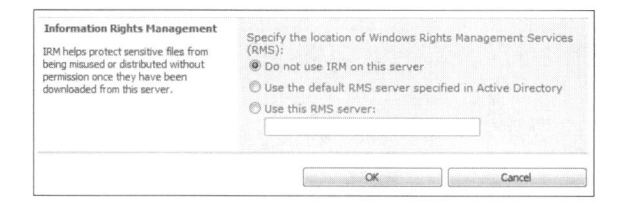

FIGURE 16.24
Information Rights Management

- **Configure Information Management Policy**—This screen allows you to enable/disable the various information management policy features such as Labels, Barcodes, Auditing, and Retention.

Understanding Upgrade and Migration in SharePoint Central Administration

This screen allows you to manage the various settings related to upgrade and patch management. The important screens within this section are the Product and Patch Installation Status, which lists the various components and patches installed in your SharePoint farm as shown in Figure 16.25.

In addition the Review Database Status screen shows the status of the SharePoint databases as shown in Figure 16.26.

FIGURE 16.25
Product and Patch Installation Status

FIGURE 16.26
Review Database Status

Understanding General Application Settings in SharePoint Central Administration

As the name suggests this section allows you to configure many general settings and features, which can be divided as discussed in the following sections.

External Service Connections

This section allows you to configure Send to Connection and Document Conversion settings. Send to Connection allows you to send documents within a document library to a specified location and they appear in a linked menu of a document library item as shown in Figure 16.27.

FIGURE 16.27
Send to options

InfoPath Forms Services

This section enables you to configure various settings related to InfoPath forms, which are as follows:

▶ **Manage Form Templates**—This screen lists the various InfoPath templates available within the farm and also allows you to upload new templates on the server. Figure 16.28 shows the Manage InfoPath form templates screen.

FIGURE 16.28
Manage InfoPath form templates

▶ **Configure InfoPath Forms Services**—This screen enables you to configure a host of settings related to InfoPath forms such as enabling/disabling browse-enabled form templates, data connection timeouts, authentication settings, and so on. Figure 16.29 shows the Configure InfoPath Forms Services screen.

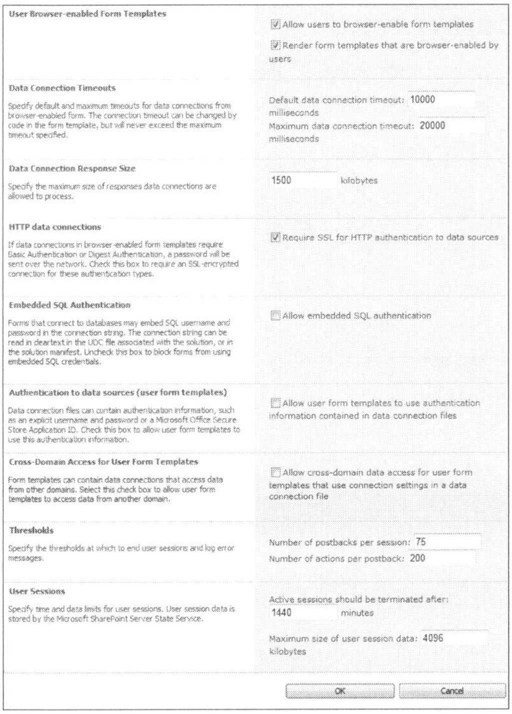

FIGURE 16.29
Configure InfoPath Forms Services

▶ **Upload Form Template**—This screen allows you to upload a new InfoPath template to the server. You can also upgrade an existing form template from here.

▶ **Manage Data Connection Files**—This screen allows you to add new data connection files and manage existing data connection files on the server. Data connection files allow InfoPath forms to connect to data sources to retrieve and work with data.

▶ **Configure InfoPath Forms Services Web Service Proxy**—This screen allows you to enable the InfoPath Forms Services Web Service proxy. The proxy is used for data connections between InfoPath Forms Services forms and web services.

SharePoint Designer

This section allows you to enable/disable use of SharePoint Designer and its features in the farm.

Search

This section enables you to configure search related settings. The Search section is discussed in detail in Hour 18, "Introducing SharePoint Search."

Content Deployment

This section allows you to configure Content Deployment settings. Content Deployment in SharePoint 2010 is basically used to deploy the content from one site to another site.

Configuring with PowerShell

Windows PowerShell is a new command line shell used mainly for administration purposes. Windows PowerShell provides many advantages over other command line scripting mechanisms such as batch files. It is built over the top of the .NET Framework and enables the use of .NET classes within PowerShell, which makes it a powerful scripting language. You can run individual commands in the PowerShell command prompt or execute a batch of commands writing in a file having .ps1 extensions.

Some of the important commands that you use while configuring SharePoint are listed in Table 16.1.

TABLE 16.1 PowerShell Commands

Command	Description
Add-SPSolution	Uploads a SharePoint solution package to the farm
Add-SPUserSolution	Uploads a new sandboxed solution to the solution gallery
Backup-SPConfigurationDatabase	Performs a farm-level configuration-only backup
Install-SPSolution	Deploys an installed SharePoint solution in the farm
Install-SPUserSolution	Activates a sandboxed solution in a site collection
Remove-SPSolution	Removes a SharePoint solution from a farm
Restore-SPFarm	Restores one or more items from a backup
Restore-SPSite	Restores a site collection
Upgrade-SPContentDatabase	Upgrades a content database
Uninstall-SPSolution	Retracts a deployed SharePoint solution
Uninstall-SPUserSolution	Deactivates a sandboxed solution in a site collection

> **By the Way**
>
> You need to load the SharePoint snap-in for PowerShell before executing the commands listed in Table 16.1 or PowerShell will not recognize these commands. To load the snap-in, execute the command Add-PSSnapin "Microsoft.SharePoint.Powershell".

Summary

This hour looked at the various configuration settings available within SharePoint 2010 Central Administration. Although understanding SharePoint administration in detail is a huge topic and could span an entire book, the content covered in this hour gives you a good knowledge of administering SharePoint 2010 and which settings are available where. In addition you also looked briefly at PowerShell, which again is a big topic. It is recommended that you go through MSDN resources for a more detailed understanding of individual topics, but this hour should have provided you a good understanding and ability to administer your SharePoint 2010 farm effectively.

Q&A

Q. *Can we shrink databases directly from the SharePoint2010 Central Administration site?*

A. Yes. It is possible to shrink databases directly from the SharePoint 2010 Central Administration site. To do this, go to Review Problems and Solutions in the Monitoring section. If some databases have too much free space, you should see a warning under the Availability heading indicating "Database has large amounts of unused space." If you click that, you see a Repair Automatically button that will shrink the database.

Q. *The Check Product and Installation Status screen in Upgrade and Migration shows an earlier version even after installing the latest Cumulative Updates.*

A. You need to run the SharePoint 2010 Products Configuration Wizard after installing the cumulative updates or the correct version will not be reflected in the SharePoint 2010 Central Administration site.

HOUR 17

Securing SharePoint 2010

What You'll Learn in This Hour

- ▶ Understanding claims based authentication
- ▶ Configuring claims based authentication for SharePoint 2010
- ▶ Understanding authorization in SharePoint 2010
- ▶ Using the SharePoint security object model

> **By the Way**
> Due to the complexity of the topics discussed, some figures in this book are very detailed and are intended only to provide a high-level view of concepts. Those figures are representational and not intended to be read in detail.

Security is one of the most important requirements of any software application. You don't want to store your data in any application that is not secure enough. SharePoint 2010 has a robust security model that enables you to secure your data at a granular level. This hour discusses how SharePoint manages security. If you have worked on SharePoint 2007 you will see that Claims Based Authentication is a major feature added to SharePoint 2010. In addition this hour looks at authorization in SharePoint 2010 and also the SharePoint Security object model.

Understanding Claims Based Authentication

SharePoint 2010 introduces the concept of claims based authentication, which involves authentication through the use of claims, tokens, and identity providers. On a high level in claims based authentication a user makes a claim about his identity, which is validated by someone.

Consider a real life scenario where someone is trying to prove her identity. She could provide various claims such as a passport, office identity card, or driver's license. These are strong proofs of that person's identity as they have been issued by the government or the person's employer. If you trust the government and the employer you will have no problem accepting that person's identity. On the other hand if that person shows an identity proof certified by a less trustable authority you will not accept the identity of that person.

In more technical terms, in claims based authentication a trusted identity provider performs authentication and validates a claim made by a user. If that claim is successful a security token is issued for that user. This security token enables you to log successfully into the application and access resources within that application.

In SharePoint 2010 a service known as Security Token Service or STS is responsible for issuing tokens that are consumed by the SharePoint 2010 applications. The STS is built over the Windows Identity Foundation formerly known as the Geneva framework. When a client requests access to a SharePoint resource, it is redirected to an identity provider. The identity provider validates the identity and issues a token to the client. This token is then submitted to the STS of SharePoint. SharePoint STS verifies whether the token is from a trusted source and issues a new SAML token to the client. The client can now access the requested resource using the SAML token based on the appropriate authorization.

> **By the Way**
>
> SAML stands for Security Assertions Markup Language (SAML), and SAML tokens are XML representations of claims. SAML tokens carry statements that are sets of claims made by one entity about another entity.

Configuring Claims Based Authentication for SharePoint 2010

You now configure claims based authentication in SharePoint 2010. The new web application will be able to authenticate using a Windows identity or custom identity. It is easy to configure claims based authentication in SharePoint 2010. The following Try It Yourself example enables the web application to use both forms based authentication and active directory authentication by configuring claims based authentication. The forms based authentication uses the `System.Web.Security.SqlMembershipProvider` class. You can easily use any other membership provider class and enable any custom mode of authentication.

To configure claims based authentication for SharePoint 2010, follow the next steps.

Configuring Claims Based Authentication for SharePoint 2010 | 363

Try It Yourself ▼
Configure Claims Based Authentication for a New SharePoint Web Application

1. Create an ASP.NET DB membership provider database. Open a Visual Studio 2010 command prompt and run the following command:
   `aspnet_regsql.exe`.

2. This opens the ASP.NET SQL Server Setup Wizard. Click Next. In the Select a Setup Option screen select the first option as shown in Figure 17.1 and click Next.

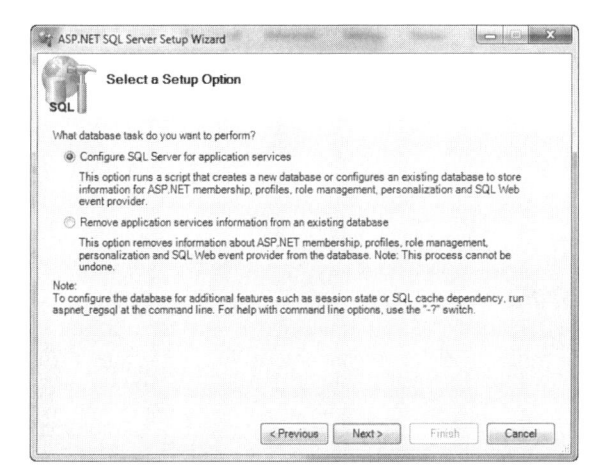

   FIGURE 17.1
   The ASP.NET SQL Server Setup Wizard

3. Select the server and database you want to use as the authentication store as shown in Figure 17.2 and click Next.

   FIGURE 17.2
   ASP.NET SQL Server Setup Wizard—Select Database

▼

HOUR 17: Securing SharePoint 2010

4. Click Next and the various database objects are created. Click Finish to close the wizard.

5. Now you need to create users in your database. The easy way is to create a blank ASP.NET web application (Figure 17.3) that connects to your database through the AspNetSqlMembershipProvider and add users through the Web Site Administration Tool. Create some users and you will be ready for the next steps to configure claims based authentication.

FIGURE 17.3
A new ASP.NET web application

6. Open the web.config and find the connectionStrings section. Add the following at the start of the connectionStrings section. Update the data source name with the correct name of your database server and the password with the correct password for the database server:

```
<add connectionString="Data Source=SPLEARN;
➥Initial Catalog=AuthenticationDB;
➥user id=sa;password=pass@word1"
name=" AuthenticationConnection"/>
```

7. Search for the membership provider by name AspNetSqlMembershipProvider and update the connectionStringName attribute to AuthenticationConnection.

8. Open the ASP.NET Web Site Administration Tool by going to the Project menu and then to ASP.NET configuration. This opens a web page as shown in Figure 17.4.

Configuring Claims Based Authentication for SharePoint 2010

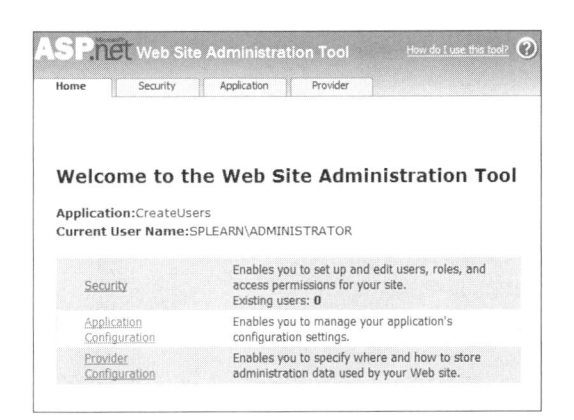

FIGURE 17.4
ASP.NET Web Site Administration Tool

9. Click the Security link. This opens a web page that allows you to create users as shown in Figure 17.5. Create a couple of users by entering the user name, password, email and other details.

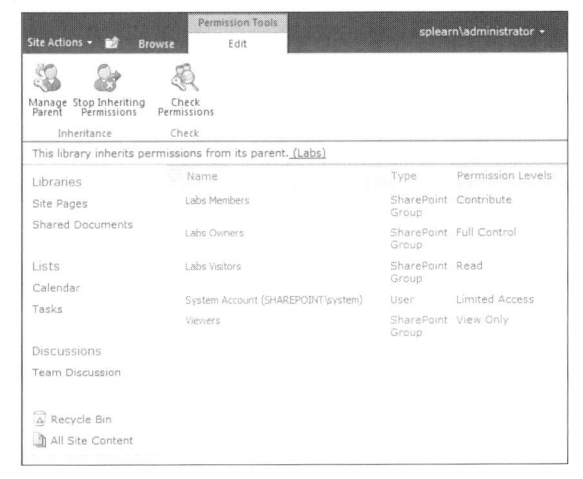

FIGURE 17.5
ASP.NET Web Site Administration Tool—Add Users

10. Now create a new web application that will be configured to use claims based authentication. Browse to SharePoint 2010 Central Administration and go to Manage Web Applications under Application Management. Click the New button under the Web Applications tab in the ribbon.

11. The Create New Web Application dialog is displayed. Select Claims Based Authentication for the authentication type. Enter some appropriate port number. Leave the default settings for the Security Configuration section. These settings are shown in Figure 17.6.

12. In the Claims Authentication Types section select Enable Forms Based Authentication (FBA). Enter FBAMembershipProvider as the ASP.NET Membership Provider Name. The configuration is shown in Figure 17.7.

13. Leave the rest of the settings as the default and click OK to create the new web application. Also create the top level site collection for the new web application.

FIGURE 17.6
New Web Application

FIGURE 17.7
New Web Application—Configure Claims Authentication Type

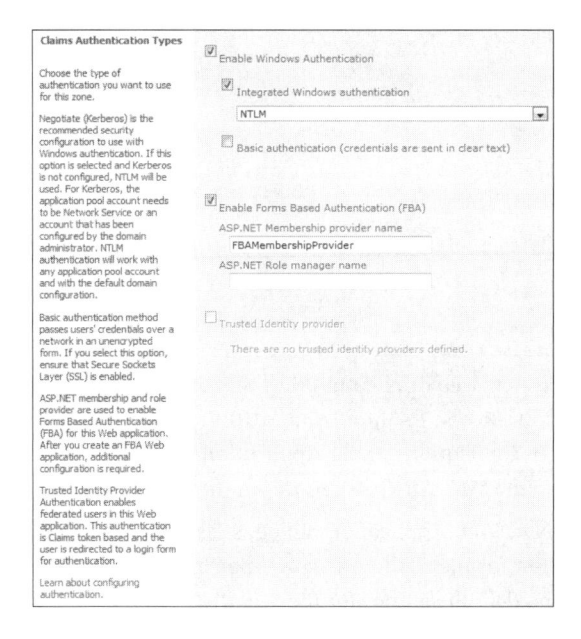

14. You now need to update the web.config files of your web application so that it can connect to your membership provider. In addition you need to update the web.config for the SharePoint 2010 Central Administration and the STS. Open

Configuring Claims Based Authentication for SharePoint 2010 | 367

the web.config for the new web application and add the following tag after the `configSections` tag. Update the database name and the password as appropriate:

```
<connectionStrings>
   <add connectionString="Data Source=splearn;
➥Initial Catalog=AuthenticationDB;
➥user id=sa;password=pass@word1"
name="AuthenticationConnection"/>
  </connectionStrings>
```

15. Add the following tag at the end, inside the `configuration/system.web/membership/providers` tag and save the file:

```
<add name="FBAMembershipProvider"
type="System.Web.Security.SqlMembershipProvider"
connectionStringName="AuthenticationConnection"
enablePasswordRetrieval="false"
enablePasswordReset="true"
requiresQuestionAndAnswer="false"
requiresUniqueEmail="false"
maxInvalidPasswordAttempts="5"
minRequiredPasswordLength="6"
minRequiredNonalphanumericCharacters="0"
passwordAttemptWindow="10"
applicationName="/"/>
```

16. Open the web.config of the SharePoint 2010 Central Administration and add both the connectionStrings and the membership provider entries as you did for the new web application.

17. Finally open the web.config for the STS. This can be found at <14 Hive>\14\WebServices\SecurityToken. Add the following entry after the configuration tag:

```
<connectionStrings>
   <add connectionString="Data Source=splearn;
➥Initial Catalog=AuthenticationDB;
➥user id=sa;password=pass@word1"
name="AuthenticationConnection"/>
  </connectionStrings>
<system.web>
    <membership>
      <providers>
        <add name="FBAMembershipProvider"
type="System.Web.Security.SqlMembershipProvider"
connectionStringName="AuthenticationConnection"
enablePasswordRetrieval="false"
enablePasswordReset="true"
requiresQuestionAndAnswer="false"
requiresUniqueEmail="false"
maxInvalidPasswordAttempts="5"
minRequiredPasswordLength="6"
minRequiredNonalphanumericCharacters="0"
```

```
            passwordAttemptWindow="10"
            applicationName="/"/>
        </providers>
    </membership>
</system.web>
```

18. Go back to SharePoint 2010 Central Administration and proceed to create a new site collection for your web application. Click the book icon next to the username field for the Primary Administrator or the Secondary Administrator. The Select People dialog appears. You can now see the Forms Auth section in it. Select the Forms Auth section and search for the user you created. The user is displayed in the list as shown in Figure 17.8.

FIGURE 17.8
The Select People dialog

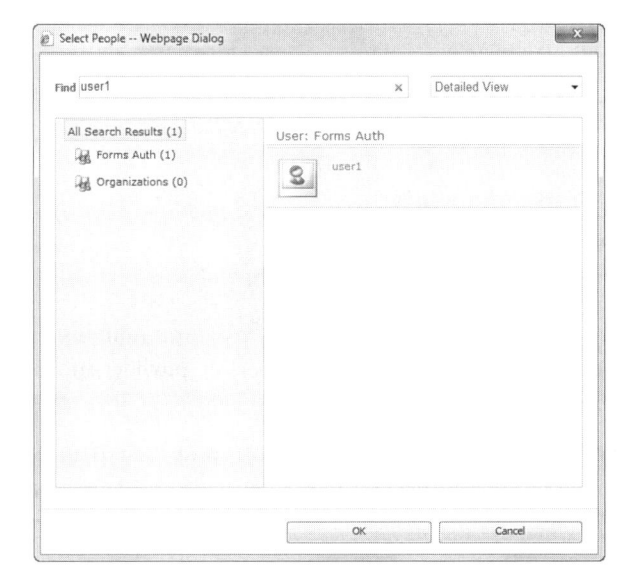

19. Select the user and click OK. Select a Windows user as the other site collection administrator as shown in Figure 17.9. Click OK to create the site collection.

20. Browse to the site collection once created. You see a Sign In page with a drop-down having options to either log in using Windows Authentication or Forms Authentication. This is shown in Figure 17.10.

21. If you select Forms Authentication you are redirected to an out of the box login form. Enter the username and password and click Sign In and you should be able to successfully log in to the site.

22. Sign out of the site and you are redirected to the Sign In page. This time select Windows Authentication and you can log in with the Windows credentials.

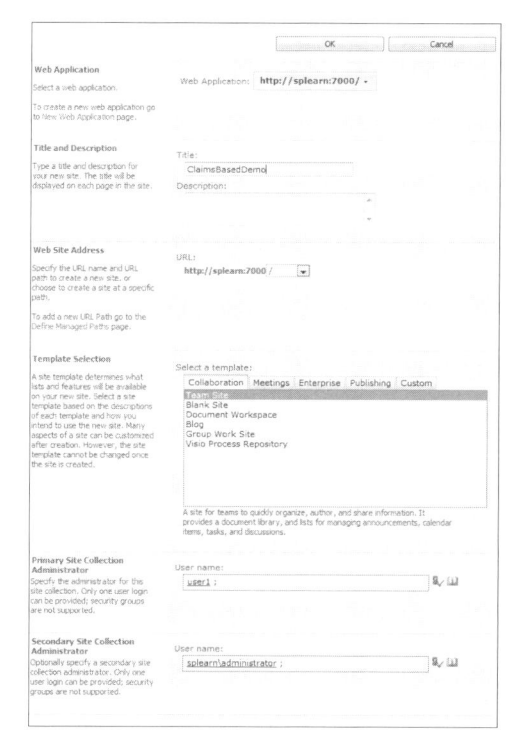

FIGURE 17.9
New site collection

FIGURE 17.10
Sign In page—claim authentication

Understanding Authorization in SharePoint 2010

Authorization is an important aspect of any software application. You don't want someone to access resources that the he is not supposed to even though he might have been successfully authenticated in the system. SharePoint has a robust authorization model, which is discussed in this section.

Authorization in SharePoint starts with the concept of permissions. Permissions represent authorization to perform some action. However, you do not assign permissions directly to a user. Permissions are grouped together to define a permission group. The permission groups are then assigned to a user or a SharePoint group.

HOUR 17: Securing SharePoint 2010

You can see the SharePoint groups by going to People and Groups in the Site Settings. The SharePoint groups are listed on the left-hand side. Click the Groups link to see all the groups as shown in Figure 17.11.

FIGURE 17.11
SharePoint groups

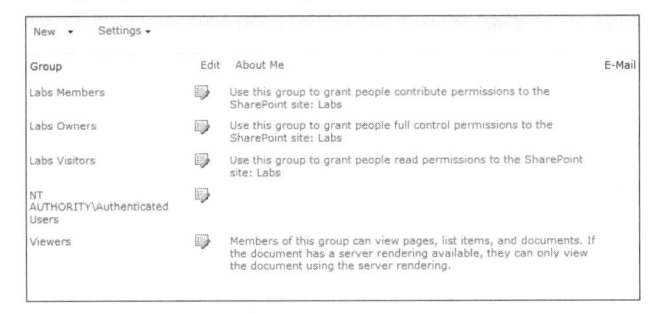

You can see the permission levels assigned to the various groups and users by going to Site Permissions in the Site Settings. This is shown in Figure 17.12.

FIGURE 17.12
Site permissions

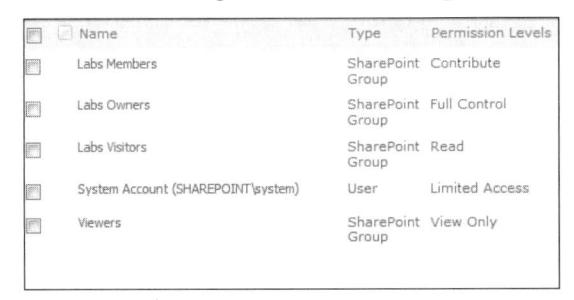

Clicking on Permission Levels in the ribbon shows you the Permission Levels in the site, as shown in Figure 17.13.

FIGURE 17.13
Permission levels

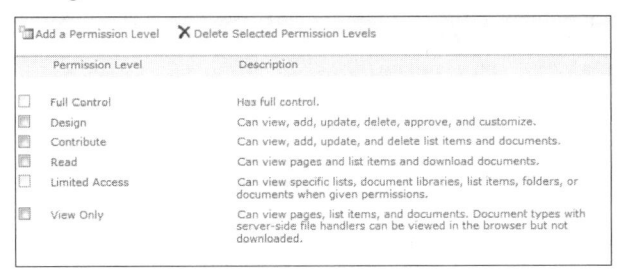

Clicking on the specific permission level displays the permissions assigned to that permission level as shown in Figure 17.14.

The permissions defined for the specific groups or users govern the access to all the objects, including the lists, libraries, and subsites. You can see this by browsing to a list or library and going to library permissions as shown in Figure 17.15.

However, you can give unique permissions to these objects by breaking permission inheritance. To give unique permissions click the Stop Inheriting Permissions button. This copies the parent permissions to the list, and you can modify these permissions at the list level without impacting the site permissions.

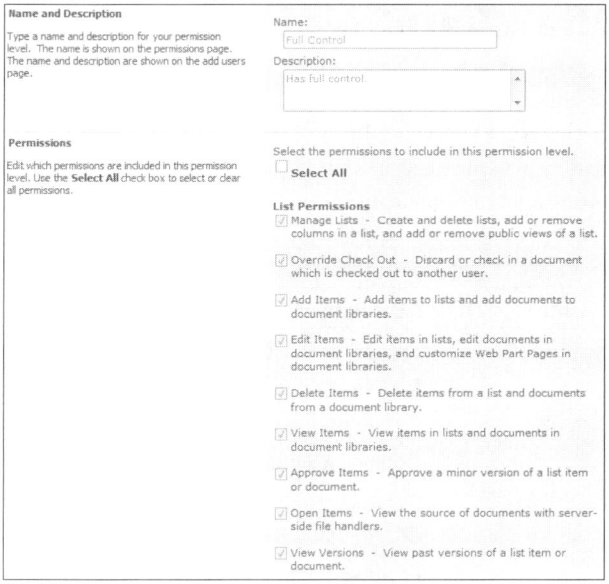

FIGURE 17.14
SharePoint permissions assigned to the Full Control permission level

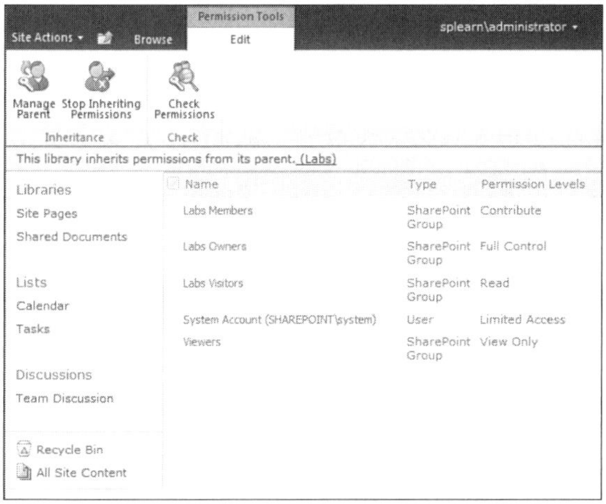

FIGURE 17.15
List permissions

> **By the Way**
>
> The ability to break inheritance gives great flexibility and control in providing permissions. However it can quickly become difficult to manage. It is recommended to avoid breaking inheritance at a very granular level like breaking permissions for every file in a document library. It is more efficient to group these files into a folder based on permissions and then break inheritance at the folder level and not for every file.

Using the SharePoint Security Object Model

SharePoint enables you to do everything that you can do in security through the user interface also through the SharePoint object model. Table 17.1 lists the various classes and objects related to security.

TABLE 17.1 Class and Objects for SharePoint Security Object Model

Class/Object Name	Description
SPBasePermissions	An enumeration that represents the built-in permissions available in SharePoint
SPRoleDefinition	Represents a permission level in SharePoint
SPGroup	Defines a SharePoint group
SPRoleAssignment	Represents the permission levels assigned to a SharePoint group or user
SPUser	Represents a user in SharePoint 2010

The following code illustrates creation of a new permission level:

```
// create a new permission level
SPRoleDefinition roleDefinition = new SPRoleDefinition();

// assign some permissions to the new permission level
roleDefinition.BasePermissions =
SPBasePermissions.AddListItems |
SPBasePermissions.BrowseDirectories |
SPBasePermissions.DeleteListItems |
SPBasePermissions.EditListItems |
SPBasePermissions.ManageLists |
SPBasePermissions.OpenItems |
SPBasePermissions.ViewListItems |
SPBasePermissions.ViewVersions;

roleDefinition.Name = "Test Role";
web.RoleDefinitions.Add(roleDefinition);
```

You can see the newly created permission level in Figure 17.16.

FIGURE 17.16 The Test Role permission level

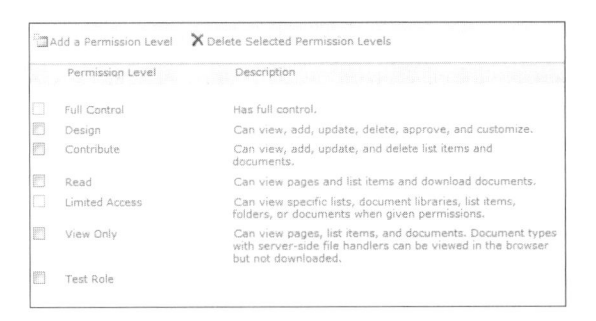

Using the SharePoint Security Object Model

To add a new SharePoint security group you need to use the `SPWeb.SiteGroups.Add` method. The following code adds a new SharePoint group:

```
// create a new SharePoint group
web.SiteGroups.Add("Test Group",
 web.SiteAdministrators[0],
web.SiteAdministrators[0],
"a test group");
```

The new SharePoint group can be seen in your SharePoint site as shown in Figure 17.17.

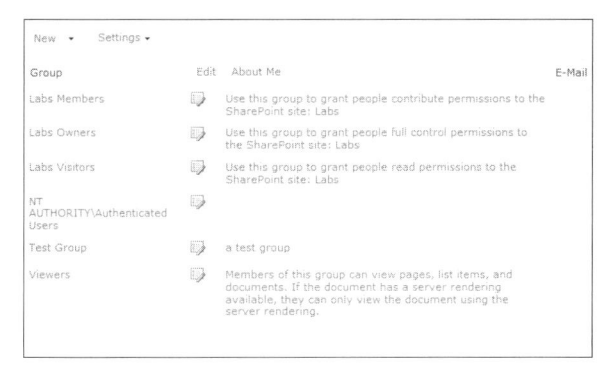

FIGURE 17.17
The Test Group SharePoint group

Finally to assign permission levels to the SharePoint group you can use the following lines of code:

```
// retrieve back the newly created role. We could have used the
SPRoleDefinition testRoleDefinition = web.RoleDefinitions["Test Role"];

//retrieve the sharepoint group
SPGroup group = web.SiteGroups["Test Group"];

SPRoleAssignment roleAssignment = new SPRoleAssignment(group);
roleAssignment.RoleDefinitionBindings.Add(testRoleDefinition);
```

Before ending you should know about the `SPSecurity.RunWithElevatedPrivileges` delegate. Many times your web part performs an action that requires elevated permissions. The code runs fine when the web part is accessed through an account that has sufficient privileges. However, the web part crashes when the page is accessed by a user having limited privileges. In case you want this code to execute successfully regardless of the user access, you need to run that code within `SPSecurity.RunWithElevated Privileges`. The following code shows a sample illustration:

```
SPSecurity.RunWithElevatedPrivileges(delegate()
{
using (SPSite elevatedSite = new SPSite("http://splearn"))
{
using (SPWeb elevatedWeb = site.OpenWeb())
{
// create a new SharePoint group
elevatedWeb.SiteGroups.Add("Test Group",
elevatedWeb.SiteAdministrators[0],
elevatedWeb.SiteAdministrators[0],
```

```
            "a test group");
        }
    }
});
```

The final complete code is as follows:

```
using System;
using System.Collections.Generic;
using System.Linq;
using System.Text;
using Microsoft.SharePoint;

namespace SecurityObjectModelDemo
{
    public class Program
    {
        static void Main(string[] args)
        {
            try
            {
                using (SPSite site =
new SPSite("http://splearn"))
                {
                    using (SPWeb web = site.OpenWeb())
                    {
                        // create a new permission level
                        SPRoleDefinition roleDefinition = new
SPRoleDefinition();

                        // assign some permissions to the new permission level
                        roleDefinition.BasePermissions =
SPBasePermissions.AddListItems |
SPBasePermissions.BrowseDirectories |
SPBasePermissions.DeleteListItems |
SPBasePermissions.EditListItems |
SPBasePermissions.ManageLists |
SPBasePermissions.OpenItems |
SPBasePermissions.ViewListItems |
SPBasePermissions.ViewVersions;

                        roleDefinition.Name = "Test Role";
                        web.RoleDefinitions.Add(roleDefinition);

                        // create a new SharePoint group
                        web.SiteGroups.Add("Test Group",
web.SiteAdministrators[0],
web.SiteAdministrators[0],
"a test group");

                        // retrieve back the newly created role. We could
➥have used the
                        SPRoleDefinition testRoleDefinition =
web.RoleDefinitions["Test Role"];

                        //retrieve the sharepoint group
                        SPGroup group = web.SiteGroups["Test Group"];
```

```
                        SPRoleAssignment roleAssignment = new SPRoleAssignment
➥(group);
                        roleAssignment.RoleDefinitionBindings.Add
➥(testRoleDefinition);

                        SPSecurity.RunWithElevatedPrivileges(delegate()
                        {
                            using (SPSite elevatedSite =
new SPSite("http://splearn"))
                            {
                                using (SPWeb elevatedWeb = site.OpenWeb())
                                {
                                    // create a new SharePoint group
                                    elevatedWeb.SiteGroups.Add(
"Test Group",
elevatedWeb.SiteAdministrators[0],
elevatedWeb.SiteAdministrators[0],
"a test group");
                                }
                            }
                        });

                }
            }
        }
        catch (Exception ex)
        {
            Console.WriteLine("Error in app " + ex.Message);
        }
    }
}
```

> **Watch Out!**
> Objects created outside the `SPSecurity.RunWithElevatedPrivileges` delegate will not run with elevated privileges inside the delegate. This is especially true of objects accessed through the `SPContext`. In such cases even child objects will not run under elevated privileges. So accessing a secured list through the code `SPContext.Current.Web.List["Some List"]` will fail if the list is even within the `SPSecurity.RunWithElevatedPrivileges` delegate. In such cases re-create the objects within the delegate.

Summary

This hour looked at SharePoint security in terms of authentication and authorization. Claims based authentication was introduced, and you also saw how to configure claims based authentication. Claims based authentication enables you to use a variety of authentication mechanisms at the same time, which makes it easier for many enterprises to move to SharePoint and use their traditional authentication. The hour also discussed authorization in SharePoint, including the concepts of permissions, permission levels, SharePoint groups, and inheriting permissions. All this makes the SharePoint security model robust and easy to administer. All the tasks mentioned can be achieved through the SharePoint object model, and the hour briefly looked at the important classes in the SharePoint security object model. Security is an important part of SharePoint, and understanding it well will go a long way toward helping you build robust and secure SharePoint applications.

Q&A

Q. Are there any limitations or performance impact on breaking permissions inheritance in a list?

A. Yes. In addition to making it difficult to manage permissions, breaking inheritance for every granular object like list items can cause a significant impact in performance while accessing the list. Also there are limitations imposed by SharePoint 2010 on breaking permissions inheritance. Refer to the "List and Library limits" at http://technet.microsoft.com/en-us/library/cc262787.aspx#ListLibrary.

Q. Can we disable specific permissions that can be granted to users by the site collection administrator?

A. Yes. It is possible to disable the granting of certain types of permissions to users by the site collection administrator. This is done by going to SharePoint 2010 Central Administration, Application Management, Manage Web Applications. Select the required web application and from the ribbon click User Permissions. Uncheck the permission that you want to disable.

HOUR 18

Introducing SharePoint Search

What You'll Learn in This Hour

- ▶ Understanding search options for SharePoint 2010
- ▶ Understanding the SharePoint 2010 Search components
- ▶ Configuring SharePoint 2010 Search
- ▶ Understanding the search center site
- ▶ Writing custom search queries using the query object model

> **By the Way**
> Due to the complexity of the topics discussed, some figures in this book are very detailed and are intended only to provide a high-level view of concepts. Those figures are representational and not intended to be read in detail.

Searching data in SharePoint is a critical factor in the usability of SharePoint. It is not too helpful to store huge amounts of data in any application if you cannot search it easily and accurately. SharePoint provides rich search capabilities that have been enhanced even further with the integration of FAST Search for SharePoint Server 2010. This hour explores SharePoint 2010's search capabilities.

Understanding Search Options for SharePoint 2010

Before starting with the search configuration for SharePoint 2010 it is good to understand the various flavors in which search is available in SharePoint 2010. You can classify the search capabilities of SharePoint in the following five options:

- ▶ **SharePoint 2010 Foundation**—As indicated in Hour 1, "Introducing SharePoint 2010," SharePoint Foundation 2010 is a basic version of SharePoint that corresponds to Windows SharePoint Services 3.0 in the 2007 version of SharePoint. SharePoint 2010 Foundation provides basic search capabilities limited to searching within the current site. In most cases these capabilities will not be enough unless your requirements around search are truly limited.

- **Search Server 2010 Express**—This is a free, standalone installation for adding better search capabilities to your installation of SharePoint Foundation 2010. You will go with the Search Server 2010 Express when you want to have advanced search capabilities without the complexity of SharePoint Server 2010. The features provided by Search Server 2010 Express include search analytics reporting, user interface–based (UI-based) administration, relevancy tuning by document or site promotions, common connector framework for indexing and federation, search from Windows 7 and Windows Mobile, metadata-based refinement panel, metadata extraction on managed properties, scriptable deployment, and management using Windows PowerShell, relevance improves with social behavior, query suggestions, related searches, and improved "Did you mean?" Search Server 2010 Express has the limitations of processing 300,000 items with SQL Server 2008 Express and 10 million with SQL Server. Also the processing is limited to one server.

- **Search Server 2010**—This provides all the benefits of Search Server 2010 Express. However, it can process 100 million items across multiple servers.

- **SharePoint Server 2010**—This includes a complete search solution with many advanced features. The search of SharePoint Server 2010 includes all the features available in Search Server 2010.

- **FAST Search Server for SharePoint 2010**—This is a separate product and has highly advanced search features. FAST Search for SharePoint Server 2010 provides many features that are missing in SharePoint Server 2010 and also has greater indexing capabilities.

Understanding the SharePoint 2010 Search Components

Before you start configuring search in SharePoint 2010 it is important to understand the various components involved, as described in the following list:

- **Content**—The first thing that you need when you want to perform a search. Some might not consider content a component of search, but it is definitely at the heart of any search application. Content can be of various types such as within the site, from external data sources, and on file shares.

- **Crawler**—Also called the indexing component. This component crawls the content and indexes it for querying purposes.

▶ **Crawl Database**—Stores the indexed data.

▶ **Query Component**—Responsible for performing search against an index.

Figure 18.1 shows a graphical representation of these components.

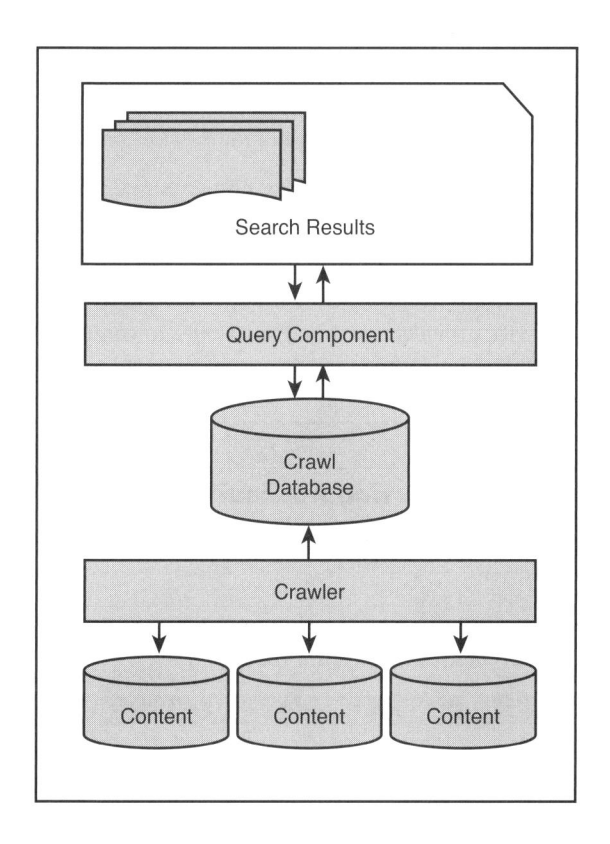

FIGURE 18.1
SharePoint 2010 search components

Configuring SharePoint 2010 Search

You now look at configuring SharePoint 2010 Search. Configuring SharePoint 2010 Search is easy and can be done entirely through the UI of SharePoint 2010 Central Administration. The following sections mention the steps required for simple search requirements and also configuring the search scopes for more advanced requirements such as filtering search data based on content types.

Performing Basic Search Configuration

Perform the following steps for basic search configuration.

HOUR 18: Introducing SharePoint Search

▼ **Try It Yourself**

Configure Search for SharePoint 2010

In this section you go through the basic steps involved in configuring Search for SharePoint 2010.

Start the SharePoint Server Search Service and follow these steps:

1. Browse to Central Administration and go to Application Management.
2. Under Service Applications click the Manage Services on Server link.
3. Start the SharePoint Search Service if not already started.

▲

Now configure the search service application. As you learn in Hour 20, "Understanding Service Applications," service applications have replaced the concept of shared service providers in SharePoint 2007. To configure the search service application, follow the steps in the following Try It Yourself.

▼ **Try It Yourself**

Configure the Search Service Application

1. Browse to Central Administration, Application Management, and Manage Service Application.
2. Create a new search service application from the New menu if it does not already exist. This is shown in Figure 18.2.

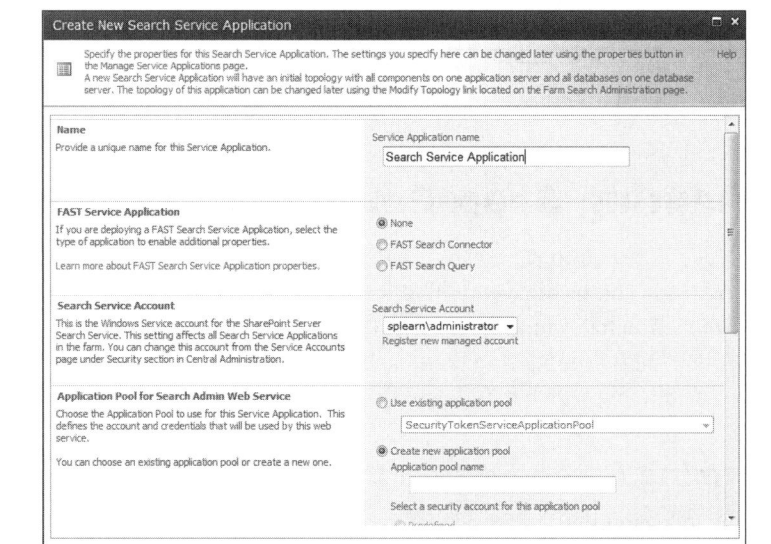

FIGURE 18.2
New search service application screen

▼

3. Browse to the newly created search service application. The home page of the service application with various information related to the status of the search is shown in Figure 18.3.

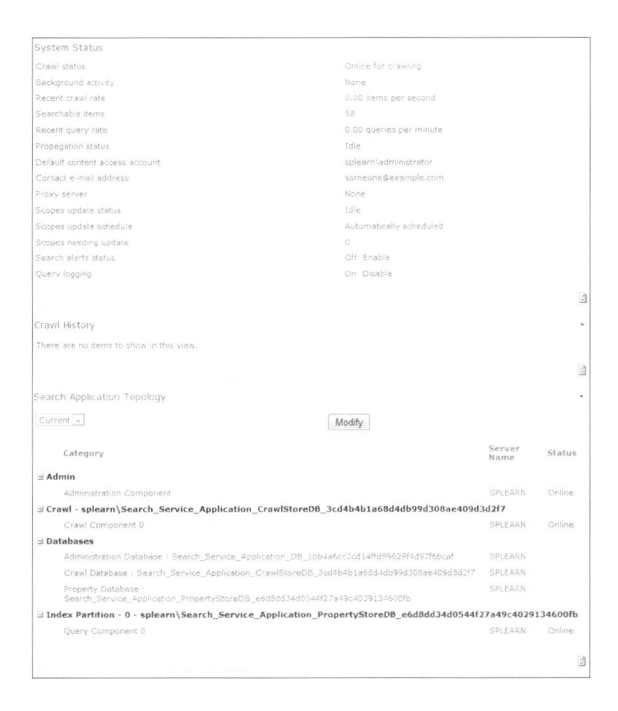

FIGURE 18.3
SharePoint 2010 Search Service Application

4. A content source should have already been configured. To verify click the Content Sources link on the left. You should be able to find the Local SharePoint Sites content source. Edit it to see the sites included in the content source and to modify the crawl schedules for this content source. Figure 18.4 shows the Edit Content Source screen.

FIGURE 18.4
Edit Content Source screen

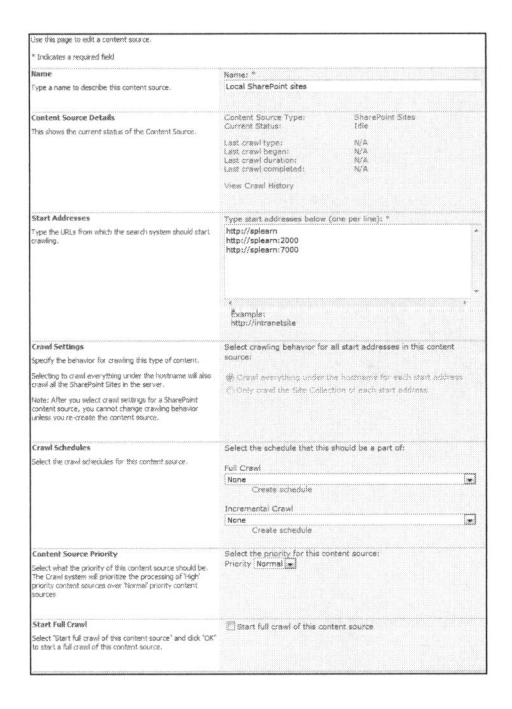

5. You now need to crawl the content source. Browse to the Manage Content Sources page, open the linked menu, and click Start Full Crawl as shown in Figure 18.5. Wait for the crawl to finish.

FIGURE 18.5
Start Full Crawl

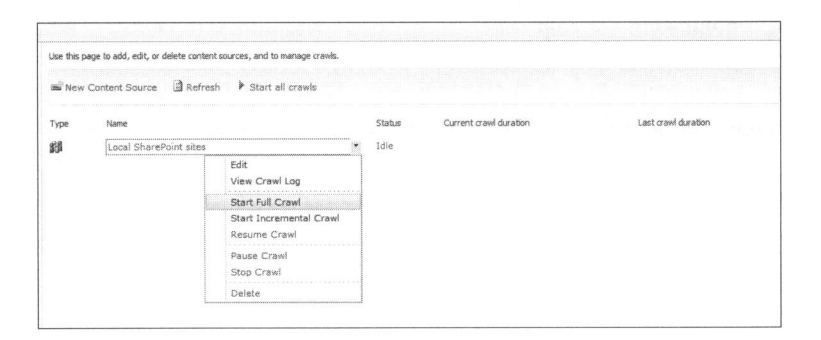

6. You can view the crawl logs by clicking the Crawl Log link on the left. This shows you a summary about the items that were crawled successfully and also errors and warnings that occurred as shown in Figure 18.6. You see more details by clicking on the numbers.

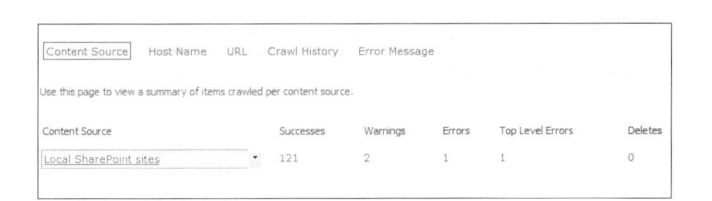

FIGURE 18.6
Search crawl logs

7. Go to your SharePoint site and perform a search for a keyword that you know exists in the site. You should see search results as shown in Figure 18.7.

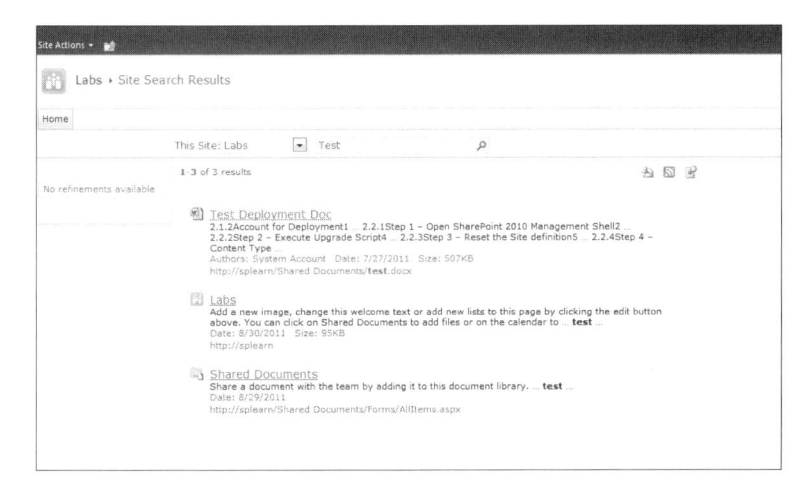

FIGURE 18.7
Search results

> **Watch Out!**
> Search will not show any results even if the crawl logs show data crawled successfully if the scopes show 0 items. You can verify this by clicking on the Scopes link on the left. To resolve this issue edit the permissions of the search services application and give access to the administrator or the appropriate users.

Configuring search is really simple. However, SharePoint Search is rich in its capabilities and you now look at some advanced configuration options.

Understanding Search Scopes

Many times you want to partition search into different categories based on the type of content. For example, you may want to search on technical resources or human resources data. Also at times you might want to filter a search based on specific parameters such as content types. Search scopes help you to achieve such functionality. SharePoint creates two search scopes by default. You can see these search scopes by clicking on the Scopes link on the left in the Search Service Application administration page. You can see the People and All Sites Scopes as shown in Figure 18.8.

HOUR 18: Introducing SharePoint Search

FIGURE 18.8
Search scopes

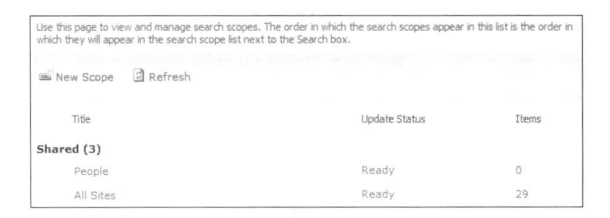

Now try creating a new scope that searches data only for a specific content type.

▼ **Try It Yourself**

Configure Search Scopes

1. Browse to your SharePoint Site and create a new content type named Technical Resources and having Parent Content Type as Document.

2. Add a new site column named TechnicalKeywords of type single line of text.

3. Go ahead and create some document libraries that use the new content type in the current site and subsites. Upload a few documents in these libraries using your new content type. Specify some comma-separated keywords in the TechnicalKeywords field.

4. Go to the Search Services Application and create a new scope called Technical Resource as shown in Figure 18.9 and click OK.

FIGURE 18.9
New search scope

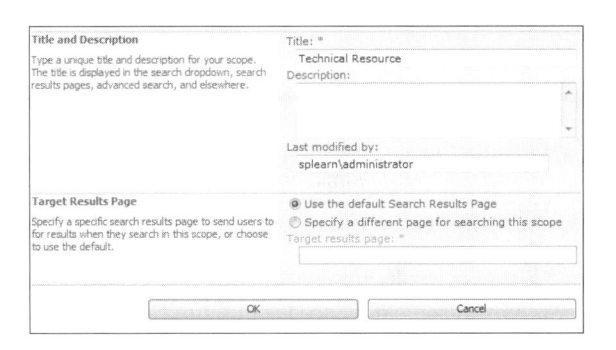

5. Enable the ContentType managed property to be used in search scopes. Click the Metadata Properties link on the left in the home page of the Search Service Application. Search for the Content Type managed property and edit the property as shown in Figure 18.10.

▼

Configuring SharePoint 2010 Search 385

FIGURE 18.10
Managed properties

6. Select Allow This Property to Be Used in Scopes as shown in Figure 18.11 and click OK.

FIGURE 18.11
Edit managed property

> **By the Way**
> Managed properties are used in search queries. You need to map properties extracted from documents during a crawl to managed properties to enable search queries to be executed against these properties.

7. Go back to the View Scopes page and click the Add Rules link beside your new scope.

8. Set Scope Rule Type to Property Query (Author = John Doe).

9. In the Property Query section, select the ContentType property, add the value Technical Resources, and click OK. This is shown in Figure 18.12.

FIGURE 18.12
Edit search scope

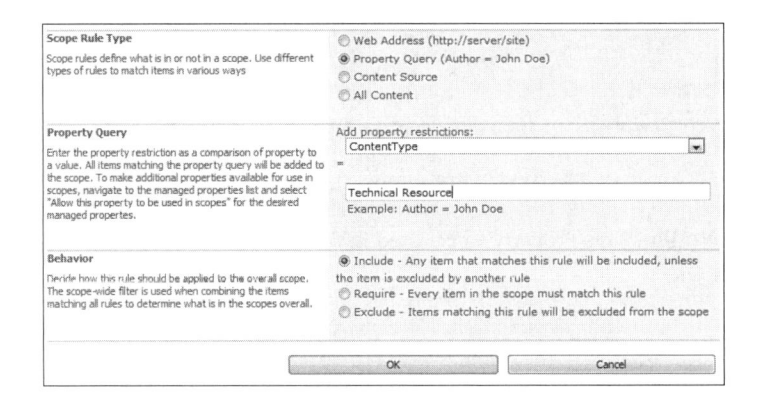

10. Perform an incremental crawl of the Local SharePoint sites content source.

11. Once the crawl is finished browse to the Scopes page. Wait for some time if the scope does not show the status as ready, as shown in Figure 18.13. Once the search scope status is ready proceed to the next step.

FIGURE 18.13
Search scope status

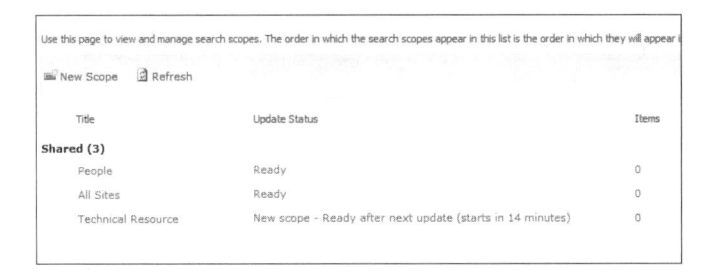

12. To be able to use this scope for searching in your site, first create a search center site. Create a new subsite named BasicSearch of type Basic Search Center in your SharePoint site.

13. Go back to the top level SharePoint site and in Site Settings go to Search Settings.

14. Select the option Enable Custom Scopes (such as "All Sites") by Connecting This Site Collection with the Following Search Center and enter /BasicSearch as the search center URL.

15. Select Show Scopes Dropdown for the Site Collection Search Dropdown Mode. The settings are shown in Figure 18.14.

Configuring SharePoint 2010 Search | 387

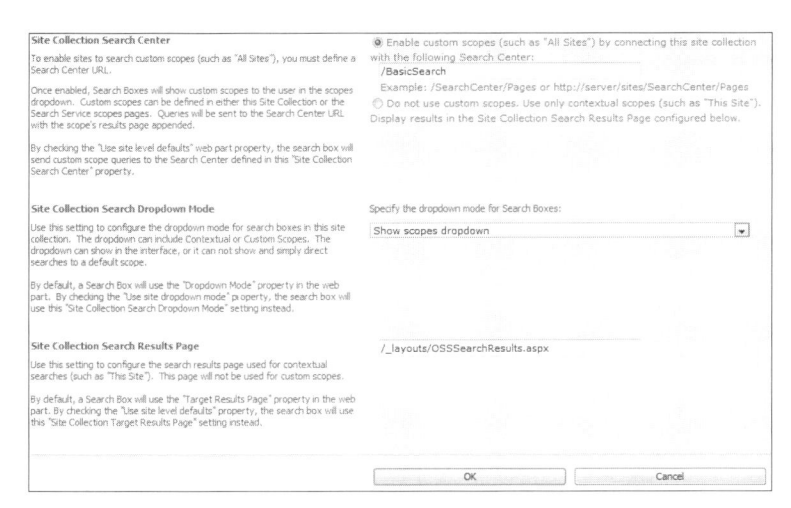

FIGURE 18.14
Site Collection Search Dropdown Mode

16. Now go to Search Scopes in Site Settings. Click Display Groups. Edit the Search Dropdown group and select the Technical Resource scope as shown in Figure 18.15. Click OK.

17. Similarly edit the Advanced Search group and include the Technical Resource scope.

18. Run the `iisreset` command on the server and then browse to the home page of your SharePoint site. You should be able to see the Scopes drop-down list, and your Technical Resource scope will be present there as shown in Figure 18.16.

19. Search within the different scopes and you should see results filtered by the selected scope. Figure 18.17 shows the search results page for a search performed on the Technical Resource scope. Four documents were uploaded in the SharePoint site and its subsite, and the word "Microsoft" was added in the TechnicalKeywords field. Also notice the search redirects you to the BasicSearch site created earlier.

FIGURE 18.15
Edit Search Dropdown group

FIGURE 18.16
Search scopes in search control

FIGURE 18.17
Search results for the Technical Resource scope

Search scopes enable a lot of advanced scenarios in search. As you see in a subsequent section in this hour, you can create custom web parts that perform custom search queries based on the search scopes.

Understanding the Search Center Site

Many times you will find yourself customizing the search center site to suit your requirements. It is important to understand the structure of the search center site and the various search web parts to be able to effectively customize the search center site. This section looks at the BasicSearch site created using the Basic Search template. The various components of a Basic Search Center site are described here:

▶ The home page of a Basic Search Center site contains a single Search Box web part. This simple web part is highly configurable. If you edit this web part you can configure various properties such as the scopes drop-downs, results page, advanced search URL, and many other useful parameters. Figure 18.18 shows the important properties of the Search Box web part.

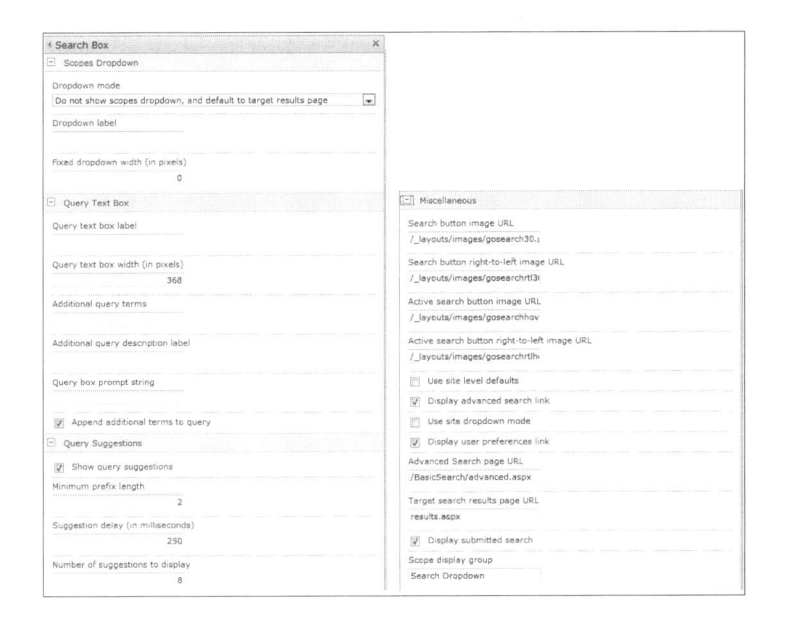

FIGURE 18.18
Search Box web part properties

- The Preferences link allows you to configure user preferences for search. The Advanced link takes you to the configured advanced search page, which by default is the advanced.aspx.

- When you perform a search you are redirected to the results page configured in the Search Box web part along with a query string containing the search keyword you entered. By default this is the results.aspx page.

- The results.aspx contains multiple web parts. At the top is the Search Box web part and Search Summary web part. The Refinement Panel web part on the left allows you to further filter the search results. The Refinement Panel web part is shown in Figure 18.19.

HOUR 18: Introducing SharePoint Search

FIGURE 18.19
Refinement Panel web part

Result Type
Any Result Type
Webpage
Word

Site
Any Site
splearn

Author
Any Author
System Account
User1
User2

Modified Date
Any Modified Date
Past 24 Hours
Past Six Months

▶ In the middle section of results.aspx, you have the following web parts:

▶ **Search Statistics web part**—This web part shows the count of items displayed as shown in Figure 18.20.

FIGURE 18.20
Search Statistics web part

1-10 of 11 results

▶ **Search Action Links web part**—This web part displays various actions related to search such as creating alerts or subscribing to RSS feeds.

▶ **Search Best Bets web part**—This web part shows a single result. This is like the "I am feeling lucky" button on the Google website.

▶ **Top Federated Results web part**—This web parts allows you to see search results from external sources such as Bing and Google. You need to configure the Location Properties as shown in Figure 18.21. Once configured you can see the search results appearing in this web part as shown in Figure 18.22.

Understanding the Search Center Site

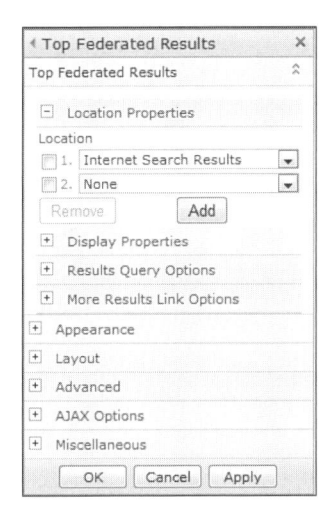

FIGURE 18.21
Top Federated Results web part properties

FIGURE 18.22
Top Federated Results web part

By the Way
The locations for the federated search are configured in the Federated Location screen in the search service application.

- **Search Core Results web part**—This web part displays the search results you saw earlier in Figure 18.19. This web part is also highly configurable.

- **Search Paging web part**—This web part displays the pages to navigate through the search results.

▶ The Advanced.aspx page provides multiple options to customize your search. One interesting option is the ability to filter data directly based on managed properties through the Add Property Restrictions Section. Figure 18.23 shows the Advanced Search page. This is actually the Advanced Search Box web part.

FIGURE 18.23
Advanced Search page

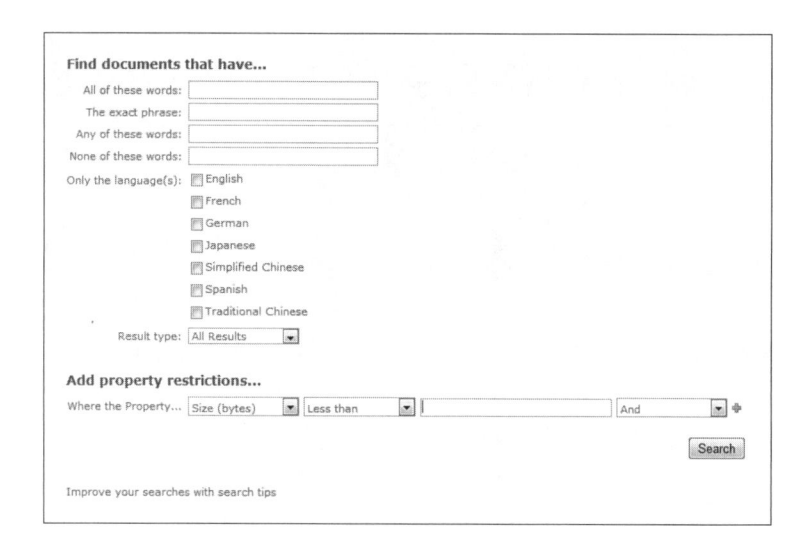

The search center is really a simple SharePoint site preconfigured with the search web parts. You can easily configure these web parts manually on a blank SharePoint site as per your requirements.

Writing Custom Search Queries Using the Query Object Model

You can use the query object model to write custom web parts that consume data from search. At the heart of the query object model are the following two classes.

- `FullTextSqlQuery`—Enables you to execute SQL syntax search queries
- `KeywordQuery`—Enables you to execute Keyword syntax search queries

Try It Yourself

Create a Custom Search Web Part

In this section you create a custom web part that uses the `FullTextSqlQuery` to display data from the Technical Resource scope where the TechnicalKeywords field contains .Net. Follow these steps:

1. Configure the TechnicalKeywords field as a managed property since you will be querying on that field. Browse to the Search Service Application and go to the Metadata Properties screen.

Writing Custom Search Queries Using the Query Object Model | 393

2. Click New Managed Property link on the top menu.

3. In the New Managed Property screen enter the Property name as TechnicalKeyword and click the Add Mapping button. Select the ows_TechnicalKeywords(Text) crawled property and click OK.

4. Leave the rest of the fields set to their default values and click OK.

5. Perform a full crawl.

6. Create a new Empty SharePoint project named SearchDemo in Visual Studio 2010.

7. Add a visual web part named TechnicalResourceDisplayWebPart.

8. Add a reference to Microsoft.Office.Server.dll and Microsoft.Office.Server.Search.dll.

9. Update the code of TechnicalResourceDisplayWebPartUserControl.ascx as shown in the following code:

```
<%@ Assembly Name="$SharePoint.Project.AssemblyFullName$" %>
<%@ Assembly Name="Microsoft.Web.CommandUI,
➥Version=14.0.0.0, Culture=neutral,
➥PublicKeyToken=71e9bce111e9429c" %>
<%@ Register TagPrefix="SharePoint"
Namespace="Microsoft.SharePoint.WebControls"
    Assembly="Microsoft.SharePoint,
➥Version=14.0.0.0,
➥Culture=neutral,
➥PublicKeyToken=71e9bce111e9429c" %>
<%@ Register TagPrefix="Utilities"
Namespace="Microsoft.SharePoint.Utilities"
Assembly="Microsoft.SharePoint,
➥Version=14.0.0.0,
➥Culture=neutral,
➥PublicKeyToken=71e9bce111e9429c" %>
<%@ Register TagPrefix="asp"
Namespace="System.Web.UI"
Assembly="System.Web.Extensions,
➥Version=3.5.0.0, Culture=neutral,
➥PublicKeyToken=31bf3856ad364e35" %>
<%@ Import Namespace="Microsoft.SharePoint" %>
<%@ Register TagPrefix="WebPartPages"
Namespace="Microsoft.SharePoint.WebPartPages"
    Assembly="Microsoft.SharePoint,
➥Version=14.0.0.0, Culture=neutral,
➥PublicKeyToken=71e9bce111e9429c" %>
<%@ Control Language="C#"
AutoEventWireup="true"
CodeBehind="TechnicalResourceDisplayWebPartUserControl.ascx.cs"
    Inherits="SearchDemo.TechnicalResourceDisplayWebPart.
➥TechnicalResourceDisplayWebPartUserControl" %>
<asp:DataList runat="server" ID="dataList1">
    <ItemTemplate>
```

```
            <asp:HyperLink NavigateUrl='<%# Eval("Path") %>'
Text='<%# Eval("Title") %>'
runat="server"></asp:HyperLink>
        </ItemTemplate>
</asp:DataList>
```

10. Update the code of TechnicalResourceDisplayWebPartUserControl.ascx.cs as follows:

```
using System;
using System.Data;
using System.Web.UI;
using Microsoft.Office.Server.Search.Query;
using Microsoft.SharePoint;

namespace SearchDemo.TechnicalResourceDisplayWebPart
{
    public partial class
TechnicalResourceDisplayWebPartUserControl : UserControl
    {
        protected void Page_Load(object sender, EventArgs e)
        {
            GetTechnicalResource();
        }

        protected void GetTechnicalResource()
        {
            using (SPSite site = new SPSite("http://splearn"))
            {
                FullTextSqlQuery myQuery = new FullTextSqlQuery(site);
                myQuery.QueryText = @"
SELECT
    Title,
    Path,
    TechnicalKeywords
FROM SCOPE()
WHERE ""Scope""='Technical Resource'
➥AND Contains(TechnicalKeywords,'.NET')";

                myQuery.ResultTypes = ResultType.RelevantResults;

                // execute the query and load the results into a datatable
                myQuery.RowLimit = 100;
                myQuery.TrimDuplicates = false;
                ResultTableCollection results = myQuery.Execute();
                ResultTable resulttable =
results[ResultType.RelevantResults];
                DataTable data = new DataTable();
                data.Load(resulttable, LoadOption.OverwriteChanges);

                dataList1.DataSource = data;
                dataList1.DataBind();
            }
        }
    }
}
```

11. Deploy the solution and add the TechnicalResourceDisplayWebPart to the home page of your site. You should be able to see data in the web part if the data is crawled, and the word ".NET" is present in the TechnicalKeywords field as shown in Figure 18.24. You can navigate to the individual items by clicking on the links.

FIGURE 18.24
Technical-Resource-DisplayWebPart

```
TechnicalResourceDisplayWebPart
This is a sample document for testing.
This is a sample document for testing.
This is a sample document for testing.
c#
```

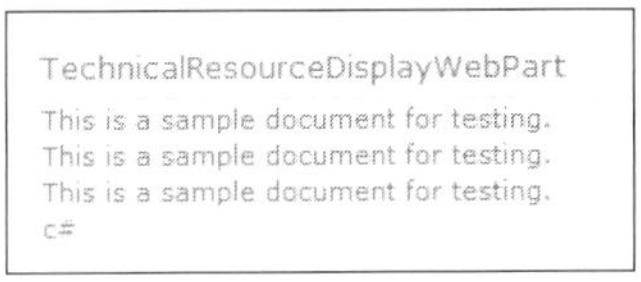

Summary

In this hour you explored the important concepts of SharePoint search. The importance of search in a successful SharePoint implementation cannot be emphasized enough. Although search is an advanced topic and an entire book could be dedicated to it, the concepts explained in this hour should enable you to configure SharePoint search successfully.

Q&A

Q. *Is it possible to modify or further process the information that is returned on the search results?*

Q. Yes. You can modify or do further processing on search results by customizing the XSLT for that particular results page.

Q. *Do we need a search center for advanced search?*

Q. Yes. You need to create a search center site for performing advanced search.

HOUR 19

Working with SharePoint Designer 2010

What You'll Learn in This Hour:

▶ Understanding the SharePoint Designer 2010 interface
▶ Uses of SharePoint Designer 2010

> **By the Way**
>
> Due to the complexity of the topics discussed, some figures in this book are very detailed and are intended only to provide a high-level view of concepts. Those figures are representational and not intended to be read in detail.

In the first hours of this book, you took a quick look at SharePoint Designer (SPD) 2010. You also saw how you can use SPD for Business Connectivity Services (BCS) and for creating workflows. During this hour, you dive into SPD 2010. After this hour you will have a clear understanding of what SPD is and how integral it is for SharePoint development.

SPD is a web and application design program that can be used to create custom no-code solutions for SharePoint 2010. SPD can be used to create sites ranging from small management sites to complex portal solutions. SPD is a single environment through which you can create a SharePoint site, customize individual components, design business processes, and deploy the site, all with zero coding effort. Because you have a single environment for all the tasks, you can spend more time on site customization rather than searching for various components for each task. In the following section you learn about the different user interface sections that make up the SPD 2010.

Understanding the SharePoint Designer 2010 Interface

You can launch SPD from multiple locations, from Windows the Start menu or directly from the site itself, provided you have the necessary permissions. To launch SPD directly from the website, go to Site Actions and click Edit in SharePoint Designer, as shown in Figure 19.1.

FIGURE 19.1
Edit in SharePoint Designer

> **Did You Know?**
>
> You cannot use SPD 2010 to edit sites created using earlier versions of SharePoint.

If you are launching SPD directly to edit a site, click Open Site and select the site you want to open. As you have already created the "splearn" site, open that site.

Once you open the site, the first thing you will notice is the three sections of SharePoint designer. They are

- Navigation pane
- Gallery and Summary pane
- Ribbon pane

Figure 19.2 highlights each section.

The Navigation pane shows the various components that make up your site, such as lists and libraries, workflows, various content types, and so on. Click any of the components and the summary pane for that selection is highlighted. If you click Lists and Libraries, the Summary pane refreshes and highlights all the lists and libraries that are part of the site. Further selection of a particular list shows the various settings for that list in the Gallery pane. As you navigate through various site objects from the Navigation pane, you can see that the ribbon gets updated based on your selection. The ribbon is similar to the ones used in Microsoft Office. The ribbon control highlights the most commonly used commands based on your selection in the Navigation pane.

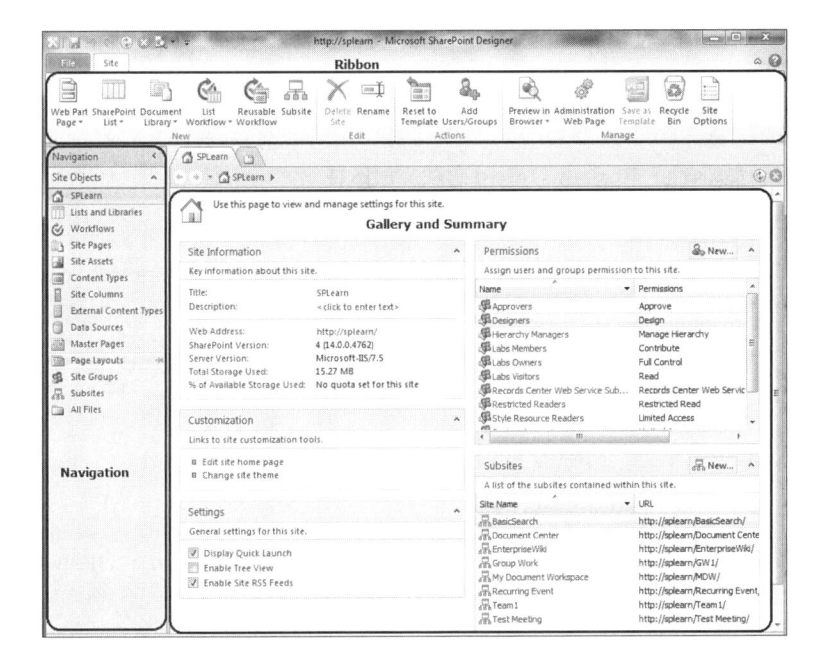

FIGURE 19.2
Sections of SharePoint Designer

Uses of SharePoint Designer 2010

You can use SPD 2010 to achieve the following:

- ▶ Customize the look and feel of the application.
- ▶ Create and manage data sources such as lists.
- ▶ Create views and forms to work with the data sources.
- ▶ Create custom workflows.

You look at the first three items in this hour. Workflows were already covered in Hour 15, "Understanding SharePoint 2010 Workflows."

Customize the Look and Feel of the Application

Often the default master page is not sufficient to address all your needs. Suppose you are creating a SharePoint site for a client, and you have to change the branding based on client requirements. SPD 2010 provides a lot of functionalities to help you address all your UI needs. The following sections look into some of the commonly used UI functionalities in SPD.

Modifying/Creating Master Pages in SPD

You already learned about master pages in Hour 7, "Understanding SharePoint 2010 Server Side Development." You now look at modifying master pages in SharePoint Designer 2010.

Try It Yourself

Modify Master Pages Using SPD 2010

To modify a master page, do the following:

1. Go to Master Pages in the Navigation pane and select the appropriate master page from the Gallery pane.
2. Check Out the master page.
3. Click Edit File.
4. Make the changes in the master page.
5. Check in the master page.
6. Navigate to the home page and verify whether the changes are reflected.

To create a master page, you need to

1. Navigate to Master Pages in the Navigation pane.
2. Make a copy of v4.master.
3. Rename the file to New Master.master.
4. Right-click the new master page and select Set as Default Master. You can now modify this master page to add branding to your site.

> **By the Way**
>
> To understand the various controls in master pages, refer to Hour 7.

Create and Manage Data Sources

SharePoint allows the creation of data sources from the designer itself. The most common sources of data in SharePoint are list and libraries. SharePoint has some generic templates for creating basic lists such as Announcements, Tasks, and so on. You also have the option of creating custom lists.

Try It Yourself

Create Custom Lists Using SPD 2010

In this section you see an example of how to create a custom list through SPD 2010. Follow these steps:

1. Open the website http://splearn in SPD 2010.

2. Select Lists and Libraries in the Navigation pane, as shown in Figure 19.3.

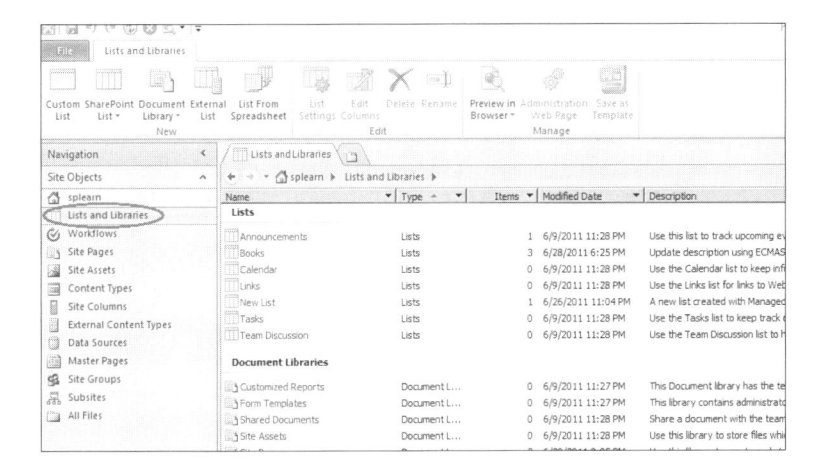

FIGURE 19.3
Selecting Lists and Libraries

3. Select Custom List from the Ribbon pane, as shown in Figure 19.4.

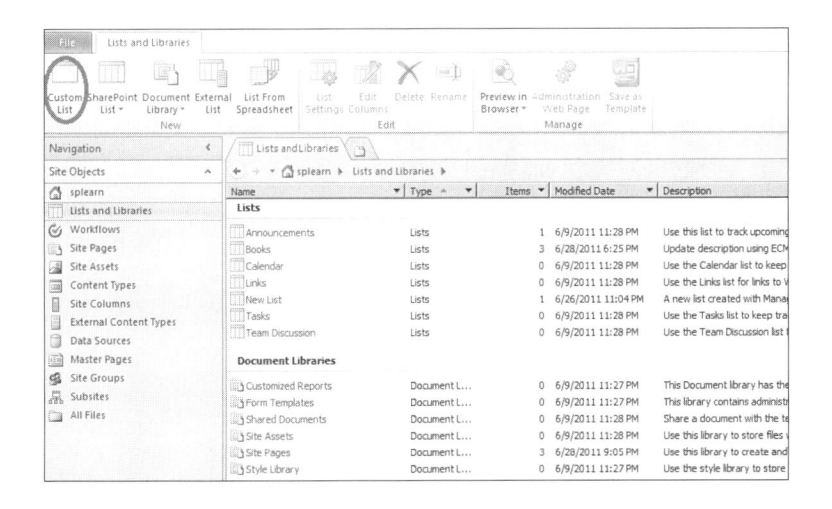

FIGURE 19.4
Selecting Custom List

HOUR 19: Working with SharePoint Designer 2010

4. Name the list Authors and select A Custom List to Store Authors for the Description. Click OK.

You have created a custom list named Authors, and this will appear in the galleries section.

Modifying Site Layouts Using SPD 2010

This section explains how you can edit the site layout using SPD 2010. To edit site layouts, first begin by making a copy of your home page. In this example, change the position of Add Document under the Shared Documents web part, as shown in Figure 19.5.

FIGURE 19.5
Shared Documents web part

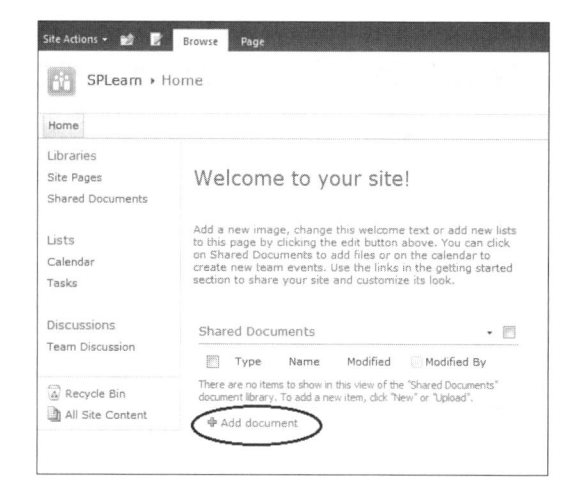

Try It Yourself

Edit Site Layout in SPD 2010

Follow these steps:

1. Navigate to Site Pages under the Navigation section.
2. Make a copy of Home.aspx.
3. Rename the file to New_Home.aspx.
4. Select New_Home.aspx from the Navigation section.
5. Check Out the file.
6. Click Edit File from the Galleries section.
7. Switch the designer to Split mode.

Uses of SharePoint Designer 2010   403

8. Select Add Document from the designer.

9. Add align="right" as a property to the <td> housing the Add Document control, as shown in Figure 19.6.

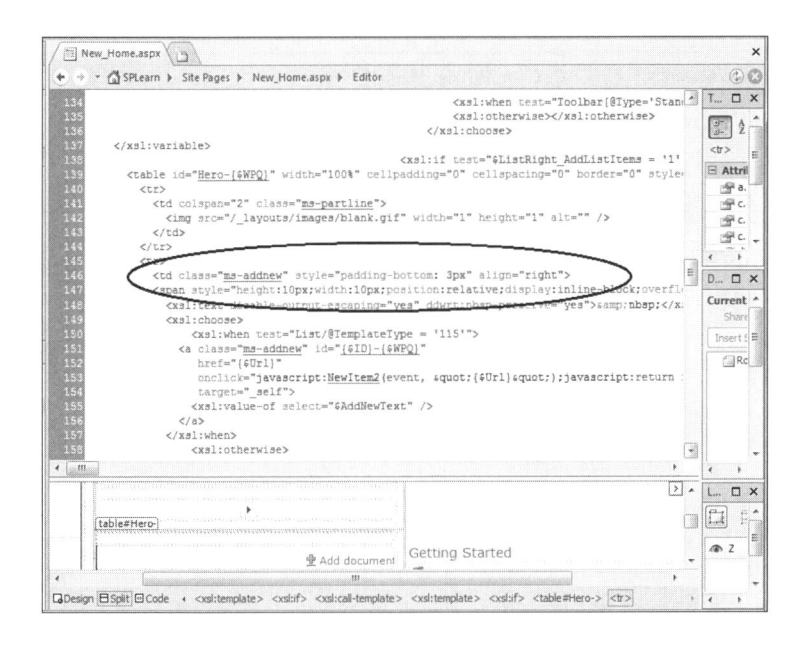

FIGURE 19.6
Modifying site layout in SPD 2010

10. Save the page.

11. Now navigate to New_Home.aspx, and you can see that the changes are reflected in the page, as shown in Figure 19.7.

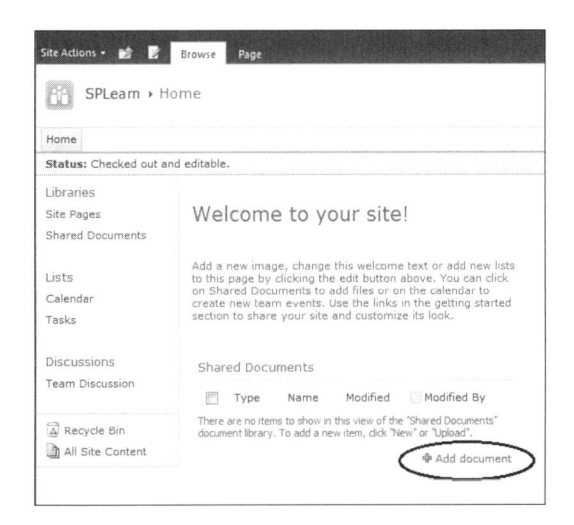

FIGURE 19.7
Modified site layout

Creating Site Columns

Site columns are a fundamental element of SharePoint 2010. These are defined at the site level once and can be reused again and again.

Try It Yourself

Create Site Columns

In this section you learn how to create a site column. Follow these steps:

1. Open http://splearn in SPD 2010.

2. Select Site Columns from the Navigation pane, as shown in Figure 19.8.

FIGURE 19.8
Site Columns in SharePoint Designer

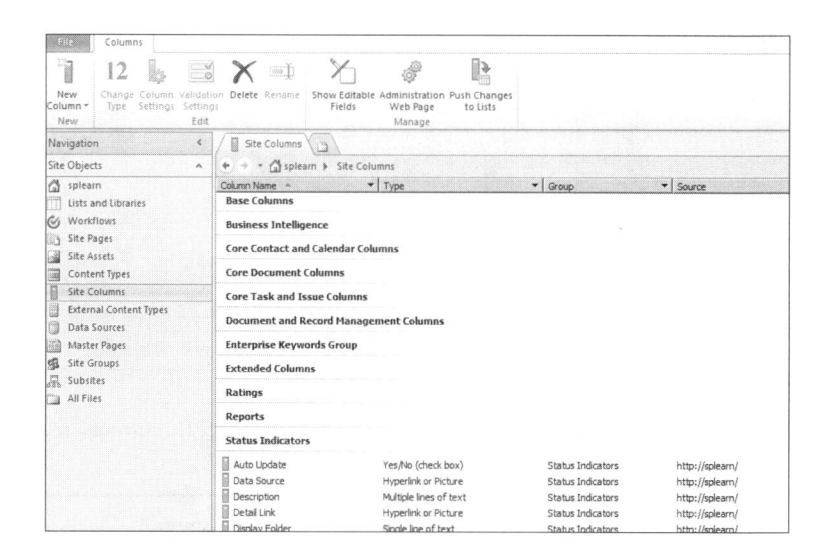

3. Select New Column from the ribbon control, as shown in Figure 19.9, and select Hyperlink or Picture from the drop-down.

4. Name the column Picture and set "Pic of the Author" as the description.

5. Click OK.

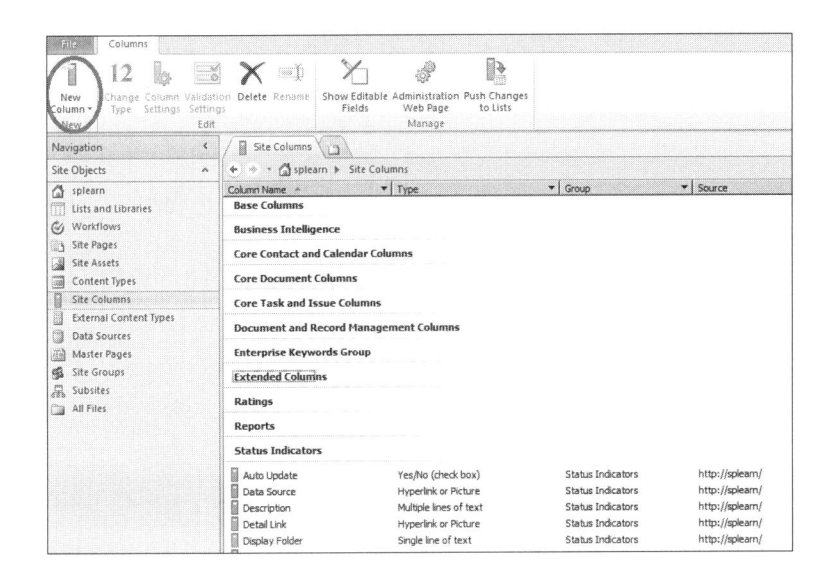

FIGURE 19.9
New Site Column

You just created a new site column named Picture whose scope is the site splearn. You can use this site column throughout the site wherever you need a picture to be embedded in a list.

Creating Content Types Through SPD 2010

You learned about content types in Hour 12, "Enterprise Content Management—Understanding Document Management." SPD 2010 also allows you to create new content types, and these can be added to lists and libraries at the site level. A content type created at a site level is accessible throughout the site/site collections.

Try It Yourself

Create a Content Type in SharePoint Designer 2010

1. Open http://splearn in SPD 2010.
2. Navigate to Content Types in the Navigation pane.
3. Click Content Type from the new section, and the Create a Content Type dialog box appears, as shown in Figure 19.10.
4. Enter the name of the content type in the Name field.
5. Enter a description in the Description field.

FIGURE 19.10
The Create a content type dialog box

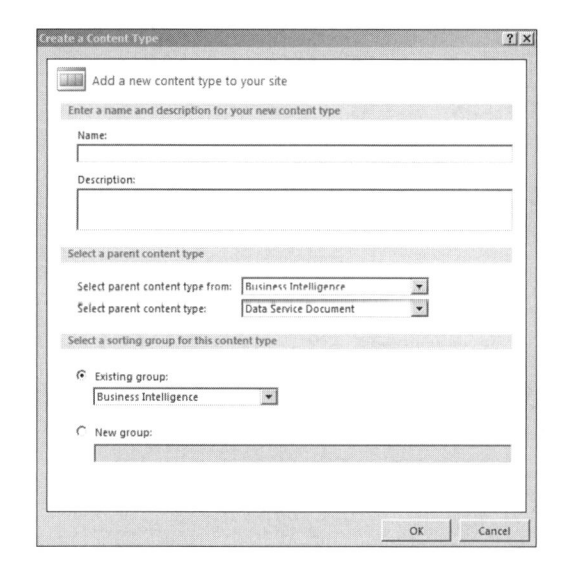

6. From the Select Parent Content Type From list, select the group from which you want to select the parent content type.

7. From the Select Parent Content Type drop-down, select the content type on which you want to base your content type.

8. To create the content type under a new group, select the New Group button and enter the new group name.

9. To create the content type under an existing group, select the Existing Group button and choose the existing group from the drop-down.

10. Click OK to create a new content type.

To edit a content type, follow these steps:

1. Open http://splearn in SPD 2010.

2. Navigate to Content Types in the Navigation pane.

3. Select the content type to be edited.

4. Under Content Type Information in the Galleries section, click Name to edit the name of the content type, click Description to update the description, and select the new group from the Group drop-down to update the group.

5. Click Save to update the changes.

You can select the group as _Hidden to prevent others from using it.

Did You Know?

Adding Data View Through SPD 2010

A data view web part allows you to display data from SharePoint lists with filtering, grouping, and desired formatting. You can add a DataView web part to a page through SPD 2010.

Try It Yourself
Add DataView through SPD 2010

Now add a data view web part to a page and configure it through SharePoint Designer 2010.

1. Open http://splearn in SPD 2010.
2. Navigate to Site Pages in the Navigation pane.
3. Create a new page named DataViewExample.aspx.
4. Select Data View under the Insert tab, as shown in Figure 19.11.

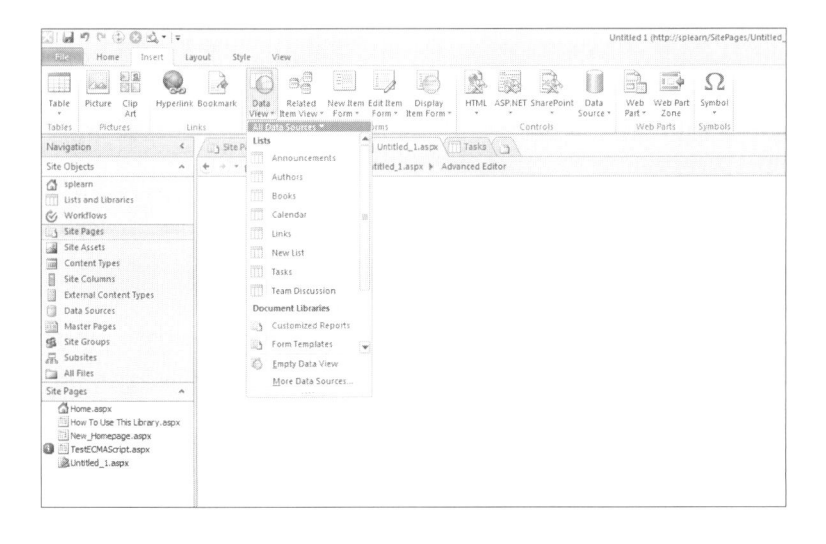

FIGURE 19.11
Adding a data view web part

5. Select the list for which the data view needs to be added.
6. Save the page.
7. Navigate to the DataViewExample.aspx file in the browser.

HOUR 19: Working with SharePoint Designer 2010

You can add and remove columns in the DataView web part. Follow these steps:

1. Open http://splearn in SPD 2010.
2. Navigate to Site Pages in the Navigation pane.
3. Navigate to DataViewExample.aspx.
4. Select the DataView web part and click Add or Remove columns, as shown in Figure 19.12.

FIGURE 19.12
Adding and removing columns in the DataView web part

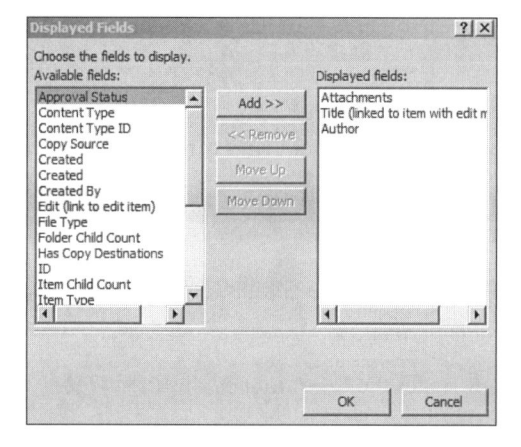

5. To add a new field, select the column under Available Fields and click Add.
6. To remove a particular field, select the column from Displayed Fields and click Remove.
7. To change the order of the columns, select the column under Displayed Columns and select Move Up or Move Down.
8. Click OK.

Filter Data View

The DataView web part comes with built-in filtering capabilities. In this section you see how you can add filtering to your DataView web part:

Try It Yourself

Filter Data View Using SPD 2010

1. Open the view in SPD 2010.

2. Click Filter under the Options tab. The Filter Criteria dialog box appears, as shown in Figure 19.13.

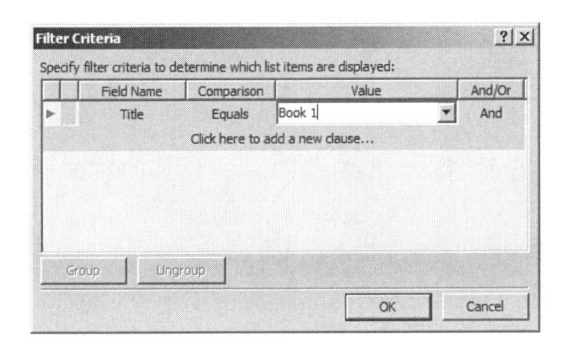

FIGURE 19.13
The Filter Criteria dialog

3. Under the Field Name select the field you want to filter.

4. Select the operator you want to use under the Comparison column.

5. Type the criteria for filtering under the Value box.

6. To add another criteria, click the And/Or box and select the operator.

7. Select the Click Here to Add a New Clause link to add new criteria.

8. Repeat steps 3 through 6.

9. Click OK.

Sorting and Grouping

Try It Yourself

Sort Data View

To sort columns in a data view web part, follow these steps:

1. Click Sort and Group in the Options tab. The Sort and Group dialog box appears, as shown in Figure 19.14.

FIGURE 19.14
The Sort and Group dialog

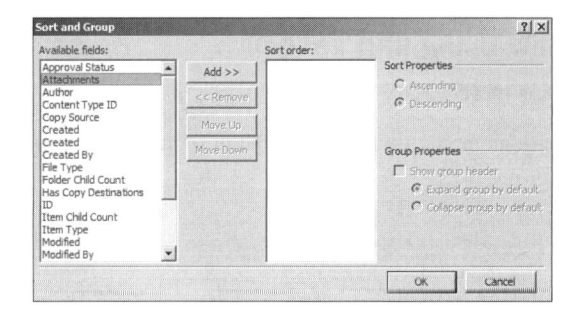

2. From Available Fields, select the fields to be sorted on and click Add.

3. Under Sort Properties, select how the fields are to be sorted (Ascending or Descending).

4. If sorting is to be applied on multiple fields, select the columns from the Available Fields.

5. To change the sort order, click Move Up or Move Down.

6. Click OK.

Try It Yourself

Group Data View

Follow these steps to group columns in a data view web part:

1. Click Sort and Group in the Options tab.

2. From Available Fields, select the fields to be grouped on and click Add.

3. Under Sort Order, select the fields to be grouped on.

4. To show a header for each group, select the Show Group Header check box under Group Properties.

5. To expand and collapse the group by default, select Expand Group By Default or Collapse Group By Default, respectively.

6. Click OK.

Paging in a DataView Web Part

Try It Yourself
Page a Data View
To implement paging in a data view web part, follow these steps:

1. Click Paging under the Options tab as shown in Figure 19.15.

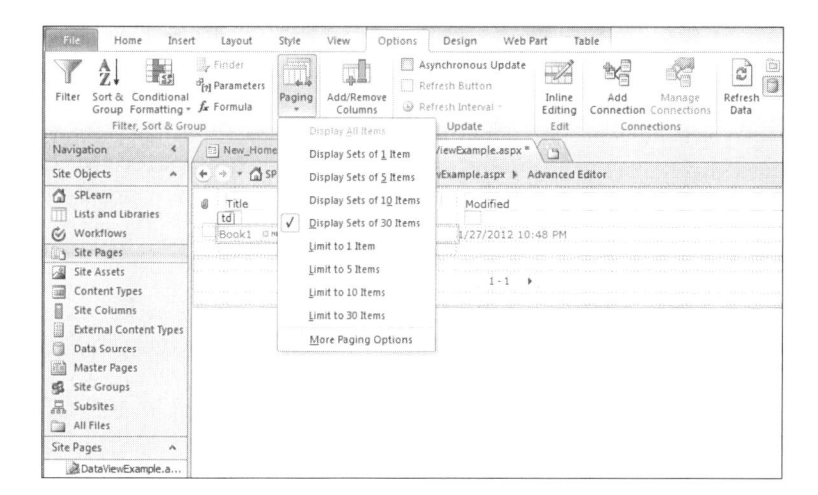

FIGURE 19.15
Paging options

2. Choose the number of records to be displayed per page.

Summary

This hour introduced SharePoint Designer 2010. You used SharePoint Designer 2010 in earlier hours, but this hour gave you a better understanding of SharePoint Designer 2010. You looked at the various user interface elements of SharePoint Designer 2010. You also looked at the various customizations you can do through SharePoint Designer 2010. SharePoint Designer 2010 is a powerful tool that makes SharePoint 2010 an even more compelling product to work with. Any user using SharePoint Designer 2010 does not need to be very technical. In fact SharePoint Designer 2010 is used by semitechnical users and UX developers. You will find yourself working frequently with this tool. SharePoint Designer 2010 has many other capabilities. The important features were covered in this hour, and it is recommended that you read some good books specifically on SharePoint Designer 2010.

HOUR 19: Working with SharePoint Designer 2010

Q&A

Q. *Is it possible to revert changes I have done to a page layout or master page in SharePoint Designer 2010?*

A. Yes. Right-click the page layout or master page and select the Reset to Site Definition option from the context menu to revert the changes done to a page layout or master page.

Q. *The site is giving access denied errors for most users after changing the default master page to a newly created master page in SharePoint Designer 2010.*

A. Make sure that you have published the master page or the master page will not be available to other users and the site will give an access denied error for all users except the one who created the master page.

HOUR 20

Understanding Service Applications

What You'll Learn in This Hour:

- ▶ Understanding the service applications architecture
- ▶ Understanding the existing service applications in SharePoint 2010

> **By the Way**
> Due to the complexity of the topics discussed, some figures in this book are very detailed and are intended only to provide a high-level view of concepts. Those figures are representational and not intended to be read in detail.

Service applications are a new concept in SharePoint that have replaced shared services providers. Understanding service applications is an important part of administering SharePoint 2010. You already worked with some service applications in earlier hours. In this hour you look at service applications in detail.

Understanding the Service Applications Architecture

The concept of shared services was introduced in SharePoint Portal Server 2003 in the form of portals. Portals can be considered site collections that offered services such as federated search, a single user profile store for caching details of the user, audiences, and My Sites. This concept was further enhanced in SharePoint 2007 in the form of shared services providers or SSPs. SSP organized all the services under a single service provider. SSPs were created in their own web applications with the required services configured in them to which other web applications would then subscribe. SSPs had two main disadvantages:

- ▶ Individual services could not vary in their configuration based on the web applications accessing the service. This meant that two web applications requiring the same user profile service configuration but different search configuration would need to have two different SSPs.

- ▶ The services were not extensible.

HOUR 20: Understanding Service Applications

Service applications in SharePoint 2010 represent the next level of enhancement to the concept of shared services. SharePoint service applications consist of multiple components described in Table 20.1.

TABLE 20.1 Service Application Components

Component	Description
Service	The service represents a set of binaries installed on the server farm. This service performs some functionality related to the service applications.
Service application	A service configured for a specific SharePoint farm represents a service application.
Service application proxy	The proxy service is a pointer to a service application within the farm that exists on the web front-end.
Service instance	The instance of the service application running on the application server.
Service consumer	Any component that utilizes the service application to achieve the desired functionality.

Every service application has an associated service running. You can see the services by going to SharePoint 2010 Central Administration. Browse to Application Management and open the link Manage Services on Server. Here you can see the list of services installed on the server as shown in Figure 20.1.

FIGURE 20.1 Manage Services on Server

You can configure the service applications by going to the Manage Service Applications link in the Application Management screen as shown in Figure 20.2. To configure, select a service application and click Manage.

Understanding the Existing Service Applications in SharePoint 2010

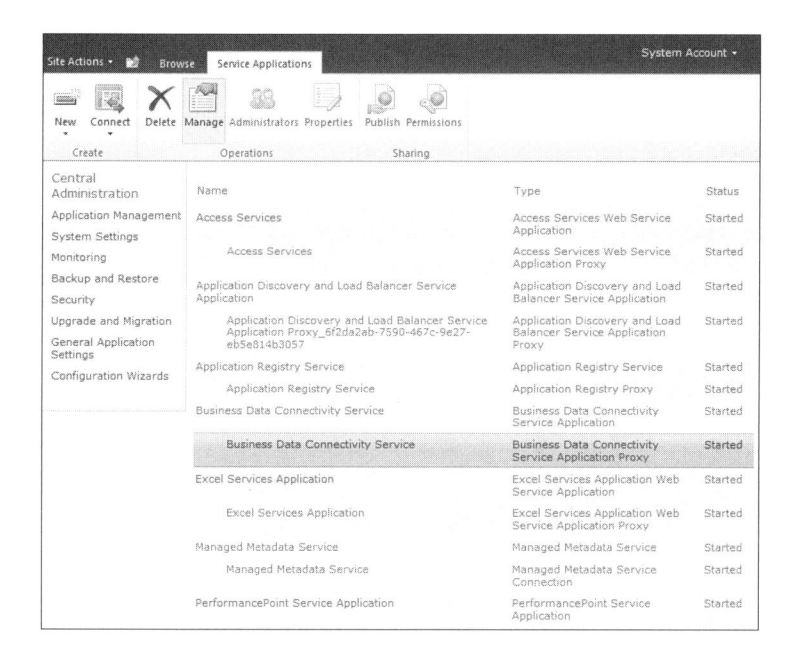

FIGURE 20.2 Manage Service Applications

In addition, service applications have associations with web applications. You can see these associations by going to the Application Management screen and clicking on the Manage Service Application Associations link. You can see the application proxies created for the association with the web application. Figure 20.3 shows the Service Applications Associations screen. Note the Application Proxy Group and Application Proxies columns.

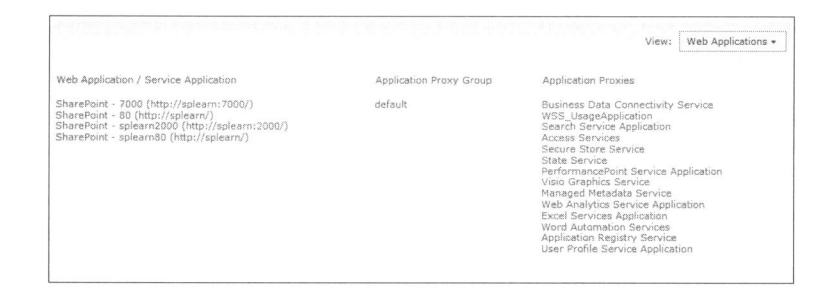

FIGURE 20.3 Service application associations

Understanding the Existing Service Applications in SharePoint 2010

This section looks at some important service applications available in SharePoint 2010. You already indirectly worked with some service applications, including the

Business Data Connectivity service application in Hour 14, "Understanding Business Connectivity Services," and the search service application in Hour 18, "Introducing SharePoint Search." This hour covers three other service applications that you must be aware of.

Understanding Excel Services Application

The Excel Services application enables you to manage the Excel Services. Excel Services supports sharing, securing, managing, and using Excel 2010 workbooks in a SharePoint Server website or document library. Figure 20.4 shows the Manage Excel Services Application screen.

FIGURE 20.4
Manage Excel Services application

> Global Settings
> Define load balancing, memory, and throttling thresholds. Set the unattended service account and data connection timeouts.
>
> Trusted File Locations
> Define places where spreadsheets can be loaded from.
>
> Trusted Data Providers
> Add or remove data providers that can be used when refreshing data connections.
>
> Trusted Data Connection Libraries
> Define a SharePoint Document Library where data connections can be loaded from.
>
> User Defined Function Assemblies
> Register managed code assemblies that can be used by spreadsheets.

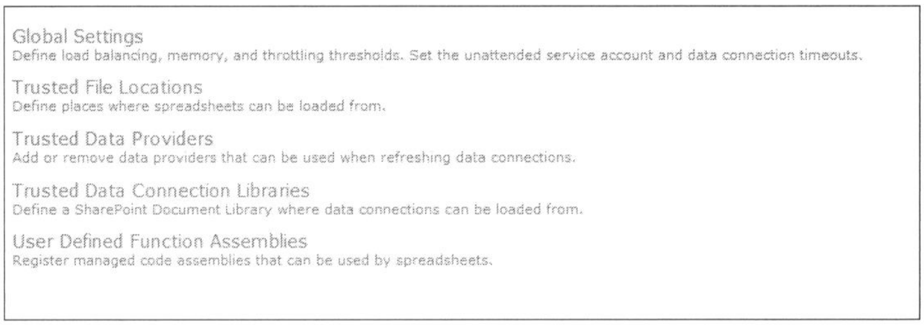

The following are the various screens in the Excel Services application:

- **Global Settings**—This screen allows you to configure various settings such as the authentication method used to access the Excel workbook files from non-SharePoint trusted locations, connection encryption, cross domain access, load balancing scheme, and session and cache settings.

- **Trusted File Locations**—This screen allows you to specify trusted file locations. A trusted file location represents a location such as a SharePoint document library, a UNC path, or an HTTP website from which the Excel workbook can be loaded. Figure 20.5 shows the Trusted File Locations screen. You can see that a trusted location is already added by default.

- **Trusted Data Providers**—Many times you will find yourself accessing external data sources in your Excel workbook. In such cases you need to add the external data sources in the list of Trusted Data Providers.

- **Trusted Data Connection Library**—You can store the data sources used by an Excel workbook in a special type of document library called the Data Connection Library rather than hard coding in the Excel workbook itself. In such cases you need to add the URL of the Data Connection Library in the list of Trusted Data Connection Library.

▶ **User Defined Function Assemblies**—This screen allows you to register .NET assemblies used by the Excel workbook.

FIGURE 20.5
Trusted File Locations

Understanding Managed Metadata Service

The Managed Metadata Service in SharePoint 2010 acts as a central store for keywords and a hierarchically organized metadata. It allows organizations to create a taxonomy store as per the organization needs and enables use of this taxonomy in a consistent manner. Users can tag SharePoint data with the terms defined in the managed metadata term store. This also has major benefits for the search system in the form of better search results.

Try It Yourself
Create and Use Managed Metadata

In this example you use the Managed Metadata Service application to tag content. You create a term store and a custom list and use the terms in the custom list to tag the list items. Follow these steps:

1. Select the Manage Metadata Service Application in Central Administration and click the Manage command in the ribbon. (If the service application is not present create it by clicking on the New command in the ribbon.)

2. You are taken to the Term Store Management Tool screen as shown in Figure 20.6.

3. This screen lists the taxonomy hierarchy. By default there is a single term set group—System. Term set groups are a security boundary. You can assign specific users to manage specific term set groups, though users can normally see all term sets. The System term set group contains two term sets—Keywords and Orphaned Terms—by default. Terms sets group terms.

418 HOUR 20: Understanding Service Applications

FIGURE 20.6
Term Store Management Tool

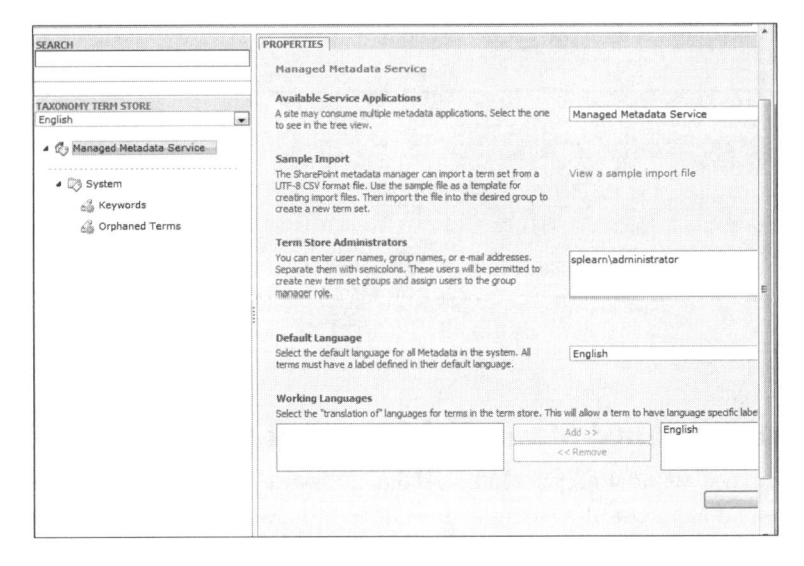

4. Create a new group named DemoGroup. You can create a new group by moving the mouse pointer to the end of the text Managed Metadata Service. This causes a down arrow to appear that enables you to open the context menu. Click the New Group option in the context menu as shown in Figure 20.7.

FIGURE 20.7
Creating a new term group

> **By the Way**
> If the down arrow does not show up, add the current user in the list of Term Store Administrators and click Save. The down arrow and the context menu should appear after that.

5. Add a new TermSet under the DemoGroup named Ticket Priority. To add a new term set move the mouse pointer to the end of the text DemoGroup to open the context menu as shown in Figure 20.8.

6. Similarly add three terms—High, Normal, and Low—under the Ticket Priority term set.

Understanding the Existing Service Applications in SharePoint 2010

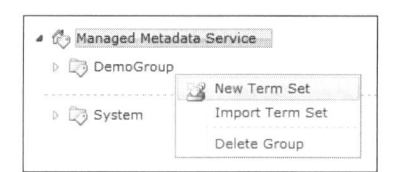

FIGURE 20.8
Creating a new term set

7. Add another term set called Region and add the terms listed here:

   a. Asia

      China

      India

   b. Africa

      South Africa

      Kenya

   c. Australia

   d. Europe

      U.K.

      France

      Germany

   e. North America

      Canada

      U.S.A

   f. South America

> **By the Way**
>
> Creating the term set manually can be a tedious task especially if the term set is big. Also you may not want to keep creating term sets manually when creating multiple environments for the same application (such as QA, Test, and Prod). An easier way is to define a CSV file once and import it in whichever environment you need. The Term Store Tool points a link to a sample CSV file for import.

8. The final hierarchy should look as shown in Figure 20.9.

9. Now browse to your SharePoint site and create a custom list called Tickets. Add a new column called Ticket Description of type Multiple Lines of Text.

HOUR 20: Understanding Service Applications

FIGURE 20.9
DemoGroup term group hierarchy

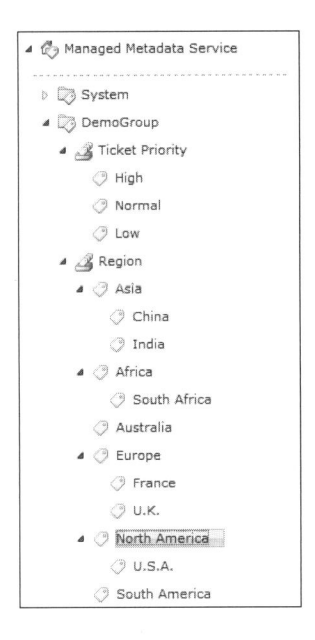

10. Add two columns of type Managed Metadata pointing to the new term sets just created. Create a new column named Ticket Priority of type Managed Metadata. Selecting the type Managed Metadata causes various settings to appear related to the Managed Metadata, including the Term Set settings.

11. Select the Ticket Priority term set as shown in Figure 20.10. Leave the rest of the settings as is and click OK.

FIGURE 20.10
New Managed Metadata column

Understanding the Existing Service Applications in SharePoint 2010

12. Add another column named Region and point it to the Region term set. Select the Allow Multiple Values check box and click OK.

13. Add a new item to the list. You can tag the item with a single ticket priority and multiple regions for the list item as shown in Figure 20.11.

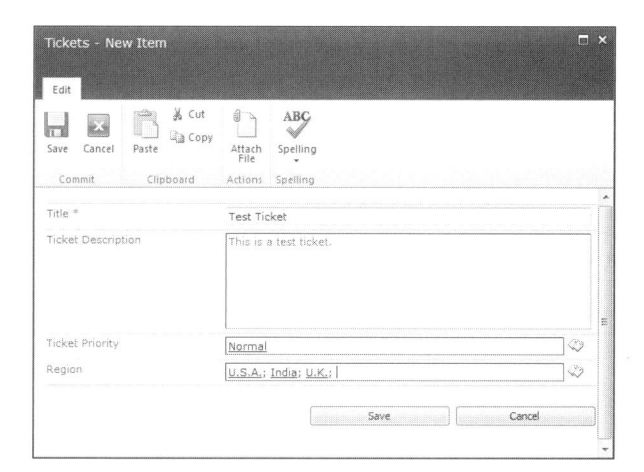

FIGURE 20.11
New list item

You can tag the region with both a parent and a child region. To avoid this you can uncheck the Available for Tagging property for the specific parent terms.

Did You Know?

Understanding User Profile Service Application

The User Profile service application enables you to store information about users in a central location. This information can be accessed by other applications for a variety of purposes. You need to enable the User Profile service application to create My Sites, enable social computing features such as social tagging and newsfeeds, and create and distribute profiles across multiple sites and farms. Figure 20.12 shows the User Profile Service Application page.

As you can see this screen is divided into four sections: People, Synchronization, Organizations, and My Site Settings. In addition the right section displays various statistics related to the User Profile and Audiences. The functions performed by the User Profile Service Application can be classified as follows:

▶ **Managing user profiles**—User profiles store information about a user. You can view a user profile by clicking on the Manage User Profiles link. Search for the specific profile by entering the username in the Find Profiles text box as shown in Figure 20.13.

FIGURE 20.12
User Profile Service Application

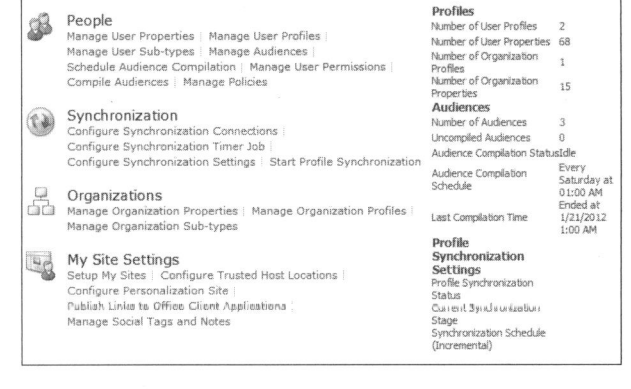

FIGURE 20.13
Managing user profiles

Edit the user profile and you can update the various properties for the user as shown in Figure 20.14.

FIGURE 20.14
Editing a user profile

You can define these properties by going to the Manage User Properties link in the User Profile Service Application page. You can also create a profile manually by clicking on the New Profile link in the Manage User Profile page.

Understanding the Existing Service Applications in SharePoint 2010

▶ **Audiences**—Audiences is a feature of SharePoint that enables targeting of content to a specific group of users. To create a new Audience, go to the Manage Audiences screen and click New Audience. This opens the Create Audience screen as shown in Figure 20.15. Enter the name for the Audience and click OK.

FIGURE 20.15
Creating an audience

The next screen prompts you to specify rules based on which users are included in this audience. Choose the Property option and select the Department property. Keep the Operator as = and enter HR in the Value field as shown in Figure 20.16. Click OK.

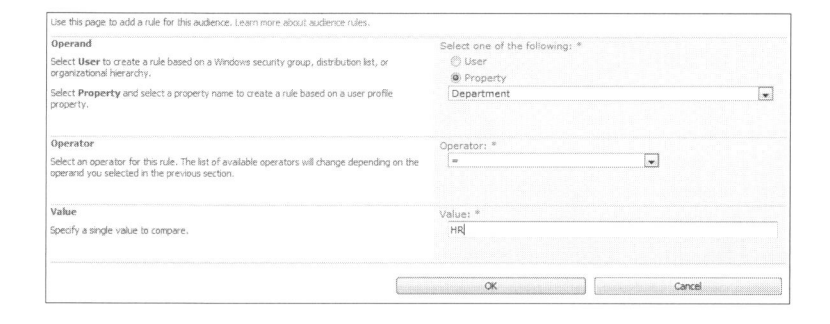

FIGURE 20.16
Create Audience—Add Rule

Though the audience is now created, no users will be part of it until the audience is compiled. You can schedule the compilation of the audience or manually compile by clicking on the Compile Audiences link in the User Profile Service Application page.

▶ **My Sites**—My Sites are personalized sites that can be created for each user and allow the users to share personal information with others much like Facebook or Orkut. The My Site settings are managed through the User Profile service application. The Setup My Sites link enables you to specify various settings for My Sites, which include the URL of the My Site host, Personal Site location, and Permissions as shown in Figure 20.17.

FIGURE 20.17
Setting up My Sites

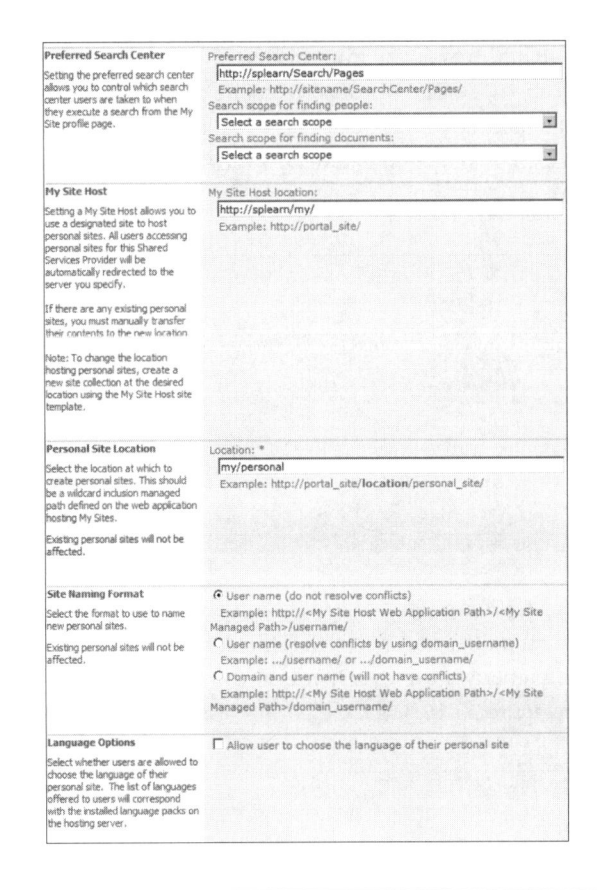

> **By the Way**
>
> The My Site Host site template was covered in Hour 4, "Walking Through the Available Site and List Templates in SharePoint 2010." You need to use this template to create My Sites.

Another important link is the Configure Trusted Host Locations. There will be scenarios when you will have more than one My Site Hosts created. You can target specific users to specific My Site Hosts by creating audiences and mapping these with the My Site Host URLs in the Trusted My Site Host Locations screen. Here you have two audiences—North America Users and Asia Users. These are mapped to two different My Site Hosts. So when a user who falls under the North America Users audience tries to browse his My Site for the first time, the My Site is created at the location http://splearn/sites/MySite. Similarly, for a user falling under the Asia Users audience, the My Site will be created at URL http://splearn_asia/sites/MySite. This is a powerful feature and enables you to distribute the load of My Sites.

> **By the Way**
>
> You can control the permissions indicating what personalization features a user can use by clicking on the Manage User Permissions link under the People section.

Summary

This hour looked at the architecture and components of the SharePoint service application. You saw that the enhanced service application architecture in SharePoint 2010 enables better scalability and flexibility. The hour also covered the three major service applications that you need to be aware of. Many other service applications also are available that you should have a look at.

Q&A

Q. *The Managed Metadata Service is showing an error indicating "The Managed Metadata Service or Connection is currently not available. The Application Pool or Managed Metadata Web Service may not have been started. Please Contact your Administrator."*

A. Make sure that the Managed Metadata Web Service is started by going to Manage Services on Server page in Application Management or you will get that error.

Q. *The User Profile service application is throwing an unexpected error even after starting the User Profile Synchronization Service.*

A. You need to run `iisreset` after starting the User Profile Synchronization Service.

HOUR 21

Understanding the Architecture of Sandboxed Solutions

What You'll Learn in This Hour:

- ▶ Understanding sandboxed solutions
- ▶ A look under the hood
- ▶ Administering sandboxed solutions
- ▶ A brief look at sandboxed solution restrictions
- ▶ Developing a full trust proxy
- ▶ Developing sandboxed solution validators

> **By the Way**
>
> Due to the complexity of the topics discussed, some figures in this book are very detailed and are intended only to provide a high-level view of concepts. Those figures are representational and not intended to be read in detail.

SharePoint 2010 introduces the concept of sandboxed solutions and provides a new technique for deployment and execution of custom code. Sandboxed solutions can be deployed by a site collection administrator, which implies that farm level privileges are no longer required for custom code deployment. Further, since the custom code runs inside a restricted execution environment or the "sandbox," sandboxed solutions offer a great way to protect the rest of the environment from badly written code. However, all these benefits come at a cost; some additional restrictions are imposed on custom code in terms of access to resources and limited access to a subset of the object model. In this hour you explore sandboxed solutions in more depth, understand the architecture of sandboxed solutions, learn the additional restrictions they impose on custom code, and have a look at deployment and monitoring related features and their usefulness in safeguarding the server environment from badly written code.

HOUR 21: Understanding the Architecture of Sandboxed Solutions

Understanding Sandboxed Solutions

A sandboxed solution is packaged as a web solutions package (.wsp) and deployed to the Solution Gallery of a site collection. Since a sandboxed solution is not allowed to access anything outside the site collection, features deployed as a part of sandboxed solutions cannot be scoped beyond the level of a site collection. Further, only a restricted subset of the SharePoint object model is available to sandboxed solutions.

The most important thing to note when developing sandboxed solutions is that you cannot deploy anything to the file system of servers. This implies that you cannot deploy components such as application pages, user controls, and so on, requiring access to the file system using sandboxed solutions.

In spite of the above restrictions and limitations associated with sandboxed solutions when compared to farm solutions, many factors may favor the former over the latter in certain scenarios:

▶ Sandboxed solutions enable the site collection administrator to install custom solutions, which implies that for custom code deployment farm level administration privileges are not required.

▶ Since sandboxed solutions run in a separate process, you can deploy them without worrying about impacting any processes outside the sandbox.

▶ Farm administrators can monitor the health and resource consumption of the sandboxed solutions.

▶ Any solutions causing problems can be blocked by the farm administrator.

Did You Know?

Since there were no sandboxed solutions in SharePoint 2007, all the code developers wrote ran under full trust. Any bad piece of code could easily bring down the entire farm and often created immense headaches for farm administrators. Thanks to sandboxed solutions in SharePoint 2010, farm administrators can now easily monitor custom solutions for resource usage and block any rogue solution from execution.

Since the sandboxed solutions protect the farm from problematic code, they are useful when you want to deploy custom code that has not been rigorously tested for reliability. Also since sandboxed solutions cannot access anything outside the site collection and can be deployed with site collection level administration privileges, they are useful in hosting environments where you may not have farm level privileges and you are guaranteed that anybody else's custom code won't affect your site collection.

A Look Under the Hood

Unlike farm solutions (which run in the IIS worker process), sandboxed solutions run in the sandboxed worker process (SPUCWorkerProcess.exe), which is a restricted execution environment. Each sandboxed solution runs in its own application domain within this process. The sandboxed worker process can run on only those servers in the farm that are configured to run the Sandboxed Code Service (SPUCHostService.exe), also called User Code Host Service. Using Central Administration, farm administrators can configure to run this service either on all servers in the farm or only on a subset. The sandboxed worker process is associated with a special proxy process SPUCWorkerProcessProxy.exe that runs in full trust and is managed by the Sandboxed Code Service. The proxy allows consumers (for example, a web part) to remotely communicate with the service.

> **Did You Know?**
>
> Since the sandboxed solutions run the sandboxed worker process, you must attach your debugger to this process if you ever want to debug your custom code. If you are developing a solution with Visual Studio, it automatically attaches the debugger to this process when you press F5.

Further, you can also configure load balancing for sandboxed solutions. There are two load-balancing schemes to choose from. Depending on the configured scheme, SharePoint determines the server that would be used to run the sandboxed solution. The following are the two available load balancing schemes:

- **Local mode**—Sandboxed code runs on the same server that received the user request.
- **Remote mode**—In this mode, the sandboxed solution is run on a server where it is has already been run. This mode allows the distribution of the execution load on different servers and also reduces the time required for servicing a request.

While local mode configuration works just fine in a development environment, for production environments, where you have multiple servers in a farm, to obtain better performance and scalability remote load balancing mode is the preferred choice.

Further, as stated earlier, only a restricted subset of the SharePoint object model is available to sandboxed solutions. This restriction is imposed via a special version of Microsoft.SharePoint.dll assembly present in the 14\UserCode\assemblies folder. This version of the assembly contains only a subset of the classes available in the standard version.

Administering Sandboxed Solutions

Farm administrators can exercise control over sandboxed solutions in a number of ways. The SharePoint Central Administration portal provides a farm administrator with a number of configuration options, and using those farm administrators can administer sandboxed solutions with ease. This section explains how a farm administrator can do the following:

- Start or stop Sandboxed Code Service on a server
- Configure load balancing for the sandboxed solutions
- Block sandboxed solutions
- Configure resource restrictions for sandboxed solutions

Configuring Sandboxed Code Service

As stated earlier, the sandboxed worker process can run only on those servers in the farm that are configured to run the Sandboxed Code Service. To understand how a farm administrator can start or stop this service on a server, navigate to System Settings from Central Administration and select the Manage Services on Server link. As shown in Figure 21.1, the Microsoft SharePoint Foundation Sandboxed Code Service is already started, since for us everything is set up on a single machine.

Configuring Load Balancing for the Sandboxed Solutions

Further, let's quickly look at how a farm administrator can configure load balancing for the sandboxed solutions. Navigate to the Manage User Solutions link under System Settings and examine the contents of the Load Balancing section as shown in Figure 21.2. The two load balancing techniques discussed earlier in the hour can be configured from here.

Administering Sandboxed Solutions | 431

Service	Status	Action
Access Database Service	Started	Stop
Application Registry Service	Started	Stop
Business Data Connectivity Service	Started	Stop
Central Administration	Started	Stop
Claims to Windows Token Service	Started	Stop
Document Conversions Launcher Service	Started	Stop
Document Conversions Load Balancer Service	Started	Stop
Excel Calculation Services	Started	Stop
Lotus Notes Connector	Stopped	Start
Managed Metadata Web Service	Started	Stop
Microsoft SharePoint Foundation Incoming E-Mail	Started	Stop
Microsoft SharePoint Foundation Sandboxed Code Service	Started	Stop
Microsoft SharePoint Foundation Subscription Settings Service	Started	Stop
Microsoft SharePoint Foundation Web Application	Started	Stop
Microsoft SharePoint Foundation Workflow Timer Service	Started	Stop
PerformancePoint Service	Started	Stop
Search Query and Site Settings Service	Started	Stop
Secure Store Service	Started	Stop
SharePoint Foundation Help Search	Started	Stop
SharePoint Server Search	Started	Stop
User Profile Service	Started	Stop
User Profile Synchronization Service	Stopped	Start
Visio Graphics Service	Started	Stop
Web Analytics Data Processing Service	Started	Stop
Web Analytics Web Service	Started	Stop
Word Automation Services	Started	Stop

FIGURE 21.1
Configuring the Microsoft SharePoint Foundation Sandboxed Code Service

Load Balancing
Specify how execution of code in sandboxed solutions is distributed across servers.

○ All sandboxed code runs on the same machine as a request.
Requests to run sandboxed code are run on the same server as web requests. This will perform better, but may not support high numbers of unique solutions. All web front ends must have the Sandboxed Code Service running.

● Requests to run sandboxed code are routed by solution affinity.
Requests to run sandboxed code are run on available servers with the Sandboxed Code Service. This uses solution affinity to organize which servers run sandboxed code, so you can independently organize resources for sandboxed code.

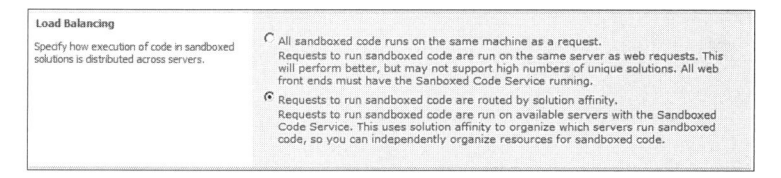

FIGURE 21.2
Configuring load balancing for sandboxed solutions

Blocking Sandboxed Solutions

Apart from providing options to configure load balancing, the Manage User Solutions screen also allows farm administrators to block sandboxed solutions, with the option to specify a message for the users of the solution. This can be seen in Figure 21.3.

Assume that you have an exception thrower web part behaving badly, throwing exceptions now and then. The farm administrator can block the solution by uploading the solution file, providing an error message, and clicking on the Block button, as shown in Figure 21.4.

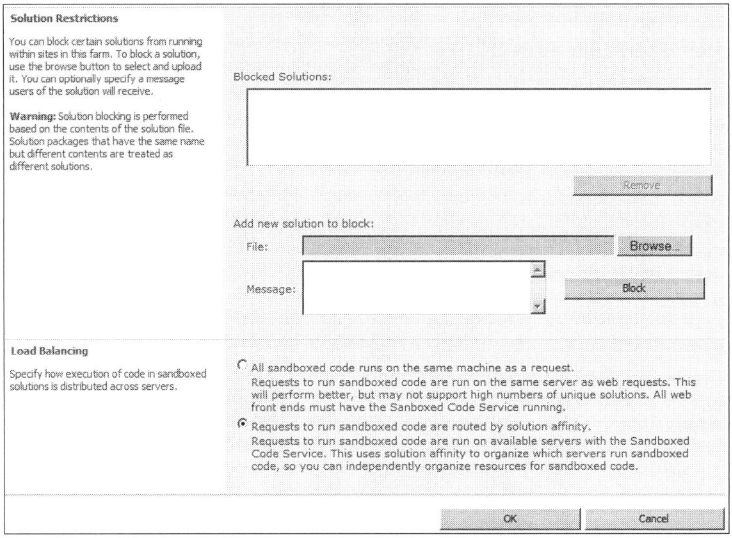

FIGURE 21.3
The Manage User Solutions screen

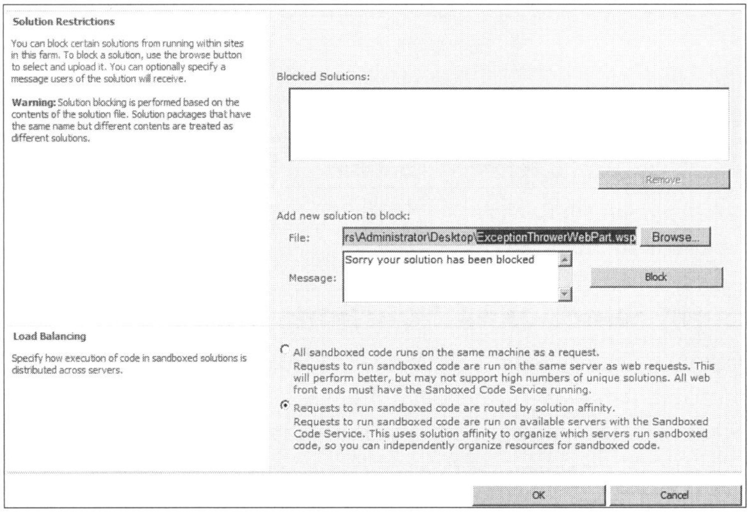

FIGURE 21.4
Blocking a rogue solution

Once the solution is blocked, it appears in the Blocked Solutions list along with the message the administrator keyed in at the time of blocking the solution, as shown in Figure 21.5. The administrator can remove the solution from the blocked list by selecting the solution and clicking on the Remove button.

Now if you navigate to a page where the exception thrower web part was added earlier, you get a message similar to the one shown in Figure 21.6, indicating that the web part has been blocked, along with a message from the administrator.

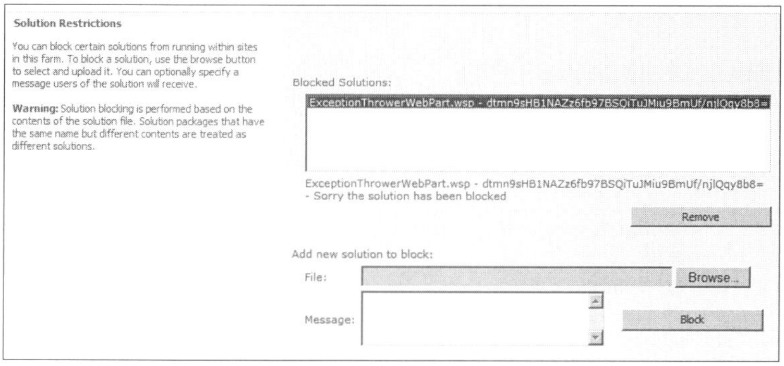

FIGURE 21.5 A blocked solution

FIGURE 21.6 The exception thrower web part showing the message that it has been blocked

Configuring Resource Restrictions for Sandboxed Solutions

Next you see how a farm administrator can configure resource restrictions for sandboxed solutions. To do so navigate to the Application Management, Configure Quotas and Locks page in Central Administration. You should have a view similar to Figure 21.7. By default sandboxed solutions in your site collection are limited to 300 resource points, per day, and you can also choose to send a warning email when the usage per day reaches the configured number of points, which is set to 100 points by default.

The restrictions imply that if combined resource consumption per day for all the sandboxed solutions in your site collection exceeds 300 points, all the sandboxed solutions in your site collection will be blocked for a day. The following 15 resource categories are considered for resource point calculation:

- `AbnormalProcessTerminationCount`
- `CPUExecutionTime`
- `CriticalExceptionCount`
- `IdlePercentProcessorTime`
- `InvocationCount`

HOUR 21: Understanding the Architecture of Sandboxed Solutions

- `PercentProcessorTime`
- `ProcessCPUCycles`
- `ProcessHandleCount`
- `ProcessIOBytes`
- `ProcessThreadCount`
- `ProcessVirtualBytes`
- `SharePointDatabaseQueryCount`
- `SharePointDatabaseQueryTime`
- `UnhandledExceptionCount`
- `UnresponsiveprocessCount`

FIGURE 21.7
Configuring quotas and locks

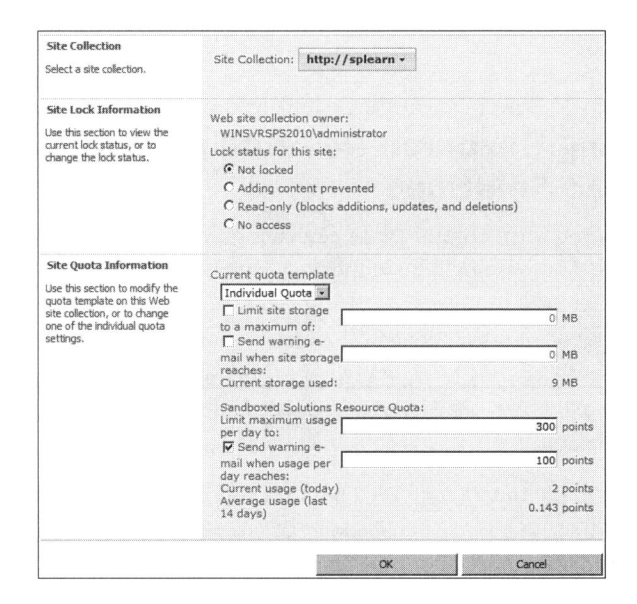

For example, a single abnormal process termination causes consumption of 1 resource point. Refer to the MSDN article at http://msdn.microsoft.com/en-us/library/gg615462.aspx for more details on points associated with each category.

Administering Sandboxed Solutions   435

Try It Yourself
Configure Resource Monitoring

1. To see the resource monitoring in action, set the points for Limit Maximum Usage Per Day To and Send Warning Email to 1 for your site collection, as shown in Figure 21.8 and click OK.

FIGURE 21.8 Setting the Sandboxed Solutions Resource Quota to a low value

2. Now build an exception thrower web part, which does nothing but throw an unhandled exception when the Throw Exception button is clicked, as shown in Figure 21.9.

FIGURE 21.9 Exception thrower web part throws an unhandled exception.

3. Create a new project in Visual Studio and configure the solution to be deployed as a sandboxed solution, as shown in Figure 21.10.

4. Do not provide any implementation for the Throw Exception button Click event and let it throw a not implemented exception as demonstrated in the following code:

```
void buttonThrowException_Click(object sender, EventArgs e)
{
    throw new NotImplementedException();
}
```

5. Build and deploy the solution using Visual Studio and navigate to the Solutions Gallery (click Solutions under the Galleries section on the Site Settings page).

HOUR 21: Understanding the Architecture of Sandboxed Solutions

FIGURE 21.10
Configuring a solution to be deployed as a sandboxed solution

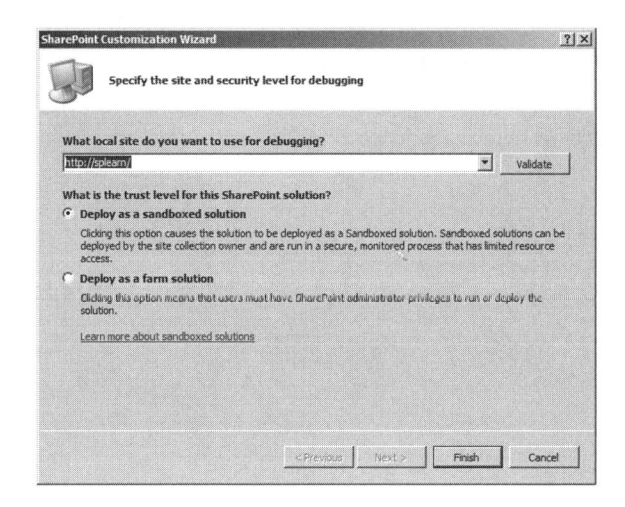

6. On the Solutions Gallery page make note of the message stating that your resource quota is 1 server resources, and on exceeding the quota solutions may be temporarily disabled, which is as per our configuration and illustrated in Figure 21.11.

FIGURE 21.11
Monitoring a sandboxed solution for resource usage

7. Add the exception thrower web part onto a page and click the Throw Exception button a couple of times. The web part should throw the exception as shown in Figure 21.12 each time you click the button.

FIGURE 21.12
Unhandled exception thrown by the exception thrower web part

8. As stated earlier, an unhandled exception causes certain resource points to be consumed. However if you visit the Solutions Gallery at this point and examine the resource usage for the solution, you still see it set to zero. The reason for this is that resource usage and logging are updated via the following two timer jobs:

▶ **Solution Resource Usage Log Processing**—Scheduled to run at 5 minute intervals by default

▶ **Solution Resource Usage Update**—Scheduled to run at 15 minute intervals by default

9. To get the resource usage updated, you can run these two jobs manually from Central Administration for your web application or wait for 15 minutes for the jobs to run and statistics to get updated.

10. Navigate again to the Solutions Gallery once both jobs are executed and examine the resource usage details again. You should now see the updated values, as shown in Figure 21.13.

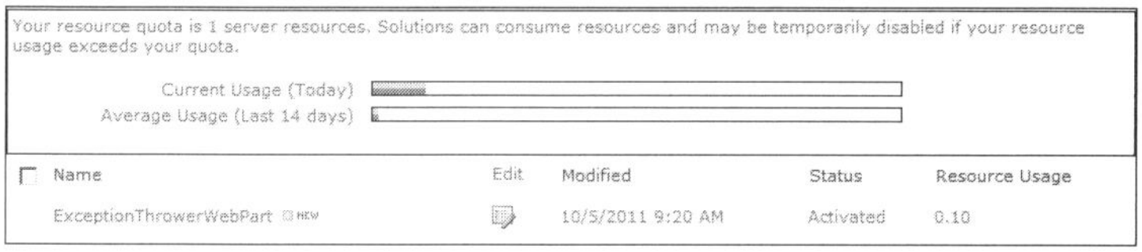

FIGURE 21.13
Resource usage consumptions increases due to unhandled exception

It is possible that at certain times you might exceed your daily quota and all your site collection's sandboxed solutions are blocked from execution. In such a scenario you can request the farm administrator to reset your daily resource consumption so that your solutions start working again. To do so, the farm administrator can run the Solution Daily Resource Usage Update timer job to reset your usage back to zero.

A Brief Look at Sandboxed Solution Restrictions

As stated earlier, only a restricted subset of the SharePoint object model is available to sandboxed solutions. These restrictions reduce the risk of badly written custom code from destabilizing the farm. The allowed subset of the object model includes

▶ `Microsoft.SharePoint` namespace, except `SPSite` constructor, `SPSecurity` object, `SPWorkItem` and `SPWorkItemCollection`, `SPAlertCollection.Add`, `SPAlertTemplateCollection.Add`, `SPUserSolution` and `SPUserSolutionCollection`, and `SPTransformUtilities`

- `Microsoft.SharePoint.Navigation` namespace
- `Microsoft.SharePoint.Utilities` namespace, except `SPUtility.SendEmail` and `SPUtility.GetNTFullNameandEmailFromLogin`
- `Microsoft.SharePoint.Workflow` namespace
- `Microsoft.SharePoint.WebPartPages` namespace, except `SPWebPartManager`, `SPWebPartConnection`, `WebPartZone`, `WebPartPage`, `ToolPane`, and `ToolPart`

To aid you in sandboxed solution development, Visual Studio trims the IntelliSense and does not list the objects and methods not supported in sandboxed solutions.

Apart from the preceding restrictions, code access security (CAS) imposes the following additional restrictions on sandboxed solutions:

- Calls to managed code are not allowed.
- Access to databases is not allowed.
- Read and write operations to file system are not allowed.
- No access to reflection APIs.
- No access to registry.
- Only those assemblies of .NET 3.5 Framework that have the `AllowPartiallyTrustedCallersAttribute` attribute set to true can be called from sandboxed solutions.

The policy is defined in the wss_usercode.config file present at 14\CONFIG location. You should abstain from editing this file, since any modifications to this file are not supported by Microsoft.

Developing a Full Trust Proxy

Not all SharePoint solutions can fit within the boundary of a sandbox. You may have scenarios where you need to write a file to the disk, access databases, or web service. As discussed earlier you are restricted to performing these operations in custom code to be deployed as a sandboxed solution. In such cases, you can overcome these restrictions by developing a full trust proxy. Using a full trust proxy, your sandboxed code can make a call to a trusted assembly that is deployed as a farm solution. This assembly performs the restricted operation on behalf of your sandboxed code and returns the operation execution result.

You may be wondering what the benefit is of such a complicated approach to break the sandbox boundaries. Since in any case we are crossing sandbox limits, why not build a full-fledged farm solution instead? The question is valid; however, the benefit of using a full trust proxy is that your proxy can dictate what restrictions the sandbox is allowed to break. For example, using a full trust proxy, you can expose APIs to allow sandboxed solutions to, say, read or write a file to a particular folder on the file system. However, if you were to build a farm solution instead, the custom code would get full access to the file system and privileges to modify files at other locations of the file system as well or perform any other operation without any restrictions. Thus a full trust proxy lets you decide which part of the boundary you want your sandboxed code to cross.

Following are the essential steps involved in developing a full trust proxy:

1. Create a solution to be deployed at the farm level.
2. Create a class inheriting from the `Microsoft.SharePoint.Usercode.SPProxyOperation` class. This class would provide the implementation of the operation you want to perform via the proxy.
3. Create a serializeable class inheriting from the `Microsoft.SharePoint.Usercode.SPProxyOperationArgs` class. This class is used to pass arguments from the sandboxed solution to the proxy.
4. Override the `Execute` method of the `SPProxyOperation` class and provide implementation of your operation.
5. Create a feature to register the proxy with the Sandboxed Code Service.
6. Add the `AllowPartiallyTrustedCallers` attribute to the assembly since we have to refer to it later in the sandboxed solution.
7. Build and deploy this solution.

Once the proxy is created and deployed, you can create a sandboxed solution and add a reference to the preceding assembly from GAC.

Now let's see the preceding steps in action and create a simple sandboxed solution to deploy a TaskCreatorWebPart that creates new tasks via a call to TaskCreatorProxy. The logic for task creation is implemented in the TaskCreatorProxy's Execute method, and the task creation details are passed to the proxy via the TaskDetails class, as shown in the following code:

```
public class TaskCreationOperation : SPProxyOperation
{
    public override object Execute(SPProxyOperationArgs args)
    {
```

```
            TaskDetails taskDetails = args as TaskDetails;

            if (taskDetails != null)
            {
                SPWeb currentWeb = SPContext.Current.Web;
                SPList taskList = currentWeb.Lists["Tasks"];
                if (taskList != null)
                {
                    // Create new task
                    SPListItem task = taskList.AddItem();
                    task["Title"] = taskDetails.TaskName;
                    task["Description"] = taskDetails.TaskDescription;
                    task.Update();

                    // Task Created
                    return true;
                }

                // Task creation failed
                return false;
            }

            // Task Creation Failed
            return false;
        }
    }

    public class TaskDetails : SPProxyOperationArgs
    {
        public string TaskName { get; set; }
        public string TaskDescription { get; set; }
    }
```

Next you need to register the proxy with the Sandboxed Code Service. You do so via the `FeatureActivated` event receiver. The following code demonstrates exactly how to do that:

```
        public override void FeatureActivated(
        SPFeatureReceiverProperties properties)
        {
            SPProxyOperationType proxyOperationType = new SPProxyOperationType(
                                                    "$SharePoint.
➥Project.AssemblyFullName$",
                                                    "TaskCreatorProxy
➥FeatureEventReceiver.TaskCreationOperation");
            SPUserCodeService userCodeService = SPUserCodeService.Local;
            userCodeService.ProxyOperationTypes.Add(proxyOperationType);
        }
```

Build and deploy the proxy. Now that your proxy is ready, let's see how to make calls to the same through the task creator web part. The web part asks for Task Name and Description from the user and creates a new task via a call to the proxy when the user clicks the Create Task button, as shown in Figure 21.14.

Developing Sandboxed Solution Validators

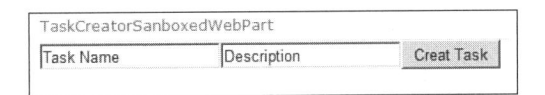

FIGURE 21.14 The task creator web part

Create a new project to be deployed as a sandboxed solution and add a reference to your proxy assembly from GAC, so that you can refer to the `TaskDetails` and `TaskOperation` classes in the code. First construct the `TaskDetails` object using the task name and description entered by the user. Next call the proxy's `Execute` method and pass the task details as a parameter, as demonstrated in the following code:

```
void createTask_Click(object sender, EventArgs e)
{
    TaskDetails taskDetails = new TaskDetails();
    taskDetails.TaskName = taskName.Text;
    taskDetails.TaskDescription = taskDescription.Text;

    TaskCreationOperation proxyOperation = new TaskCreationOperation();
    bool result =
Convert.ToBoolean(proxyOperation.Execute(taskDetails));
    if (result)
    {
        resultLabel.Text = "Task creation successful!";
    }
    else
    {
        resultLabel.Text = "Task creation failed!";
    }
}
```

The web part displays a task creation success or failure message accordingly, as shown in Figure 21.15.

FIGURE 21.15 Task created successfully via a call to a full trust proxy

Developing Sandboxed Solution Validators

While farm administrators can always go and block a rogue solution from the Manage User Solutions screen, there is another proactive way in which solutions can be checked for validations at the time of activation, and any solutions failing validation can be prevented from activation. This can be achieved by developing a sandboxed solution validator.

HOUR 21: Understanding the Architecture of Sandboxed Solutions

The following steps are used to develop a solution validator:

1. Create a class inheriting from `Microsoft.SharePoint.UserCode.SPSolutionValidator` class.

2. Provide a `System.Runtime.InteropServices.Guid` for the validator that will be used as `ProviderID` for the validator.

3. Define a default constructor in the validator that takes no arguments.

4. Define another constructor that takes a `Microsoft.SharePoint.UserCode.SPUserCodeService` object.

5. Set the `Signature` property to a unique value in the second constructor.

6. Override the `ValidateSolution` and `ValidateAssembly` methods. `ValidateSolution` is called once for each solution, and `ValidateAssembly` is called once for each assembly in the solution.

7. Specify an error page to display when a solution fails validation.

8. Register the solution validator with the Sandboxed Code Service.

The following code demonstrates the preceding steps, where we are trying to block any solution having a solution name beginning with the letters `FailValidation`.

```
[Guid("45861A3A-71FB-438C-9B60-DA57DE2F94ED")]
class CustomSolutionValidator : SPSolutionValidator
{
    private const string validatorName = "Custom Solution Validator";

    public CustomSolutionValidator() { }

    public CustomSolutionValidator(SPUserCodeService userCodeService)
        : base(validatorName, userCodeService)
    {
        this.Signature = 2222;
    }

    public override void
    ValidateSolution(
    SPSolutionValidationProperties properties)
    {
        base.ValidateSolution(properties);

        //Check the name of the package
        if (properties.PackageFile.Location.StartsWith("FailValidation",
                             StringComparison.CurrentCultureIgnoreCase))
        {
           properties.ValidationErrorMessage =
          "Sorry, your solution failed Validation.";
           properties.ValidationErrorUrl =
            "/_layouts/CustomSolutionValidator/CustomValidationError.aspx";
```

```
            properties.Valid = false;
        }
        else
        {
            properties.Valid = true;
        }
    }

    public override void ValidateAssembly(
        SPSolutionValidationProperties properties, SPSolutionFile assembly)
    {
        base.ValidateAssembly(properties, assembly);
        properties.Valid = true;
    }
```

Create a new project that can be deployed at farm level. Create the `CustomSolutionValidator` class as per the steps discussed previously. Add a new farm level feature to the solution. To register the validator with the sandboxed user code service, add a feature activated event receiver as demonstrated in the following code:

```
public override void FeatureActivated(SPFeatureReceiverProperties properties)
{
    SPUserCodeService userCodeService = SPUserCodeService.Local;
    CustomSolutionValidator validator =
    new CustomSolutionValidator(userCodeService);
    userCodeService.SolutionValidators.Add(validator);
}
```

Next add a new application page to the solution to be deployed under the layouts folder under the SharePoint root. This application page displays as an error page when a solution fails validation. Build and deploy the solution. Make sure that your farm level custom solution validator feature is active, using Central Administration, as demonstrated in Figure 21.16.

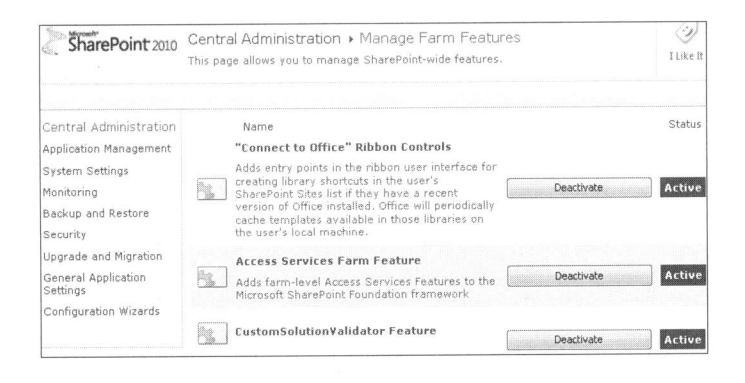

FIGURE 21.16
Make sure that Custom Solution Validator feature has been activated.

HOUR 21: Understanding the Architecture of Sandboxed Solutions

Now test the validator by uploading a solution with a solution name beginning with FailValidation. Upload the solution and click the Activate button, as demonstrated in Figure 21.17.

FIGURE 21.17
Activating a solution that would fail your validation criteria

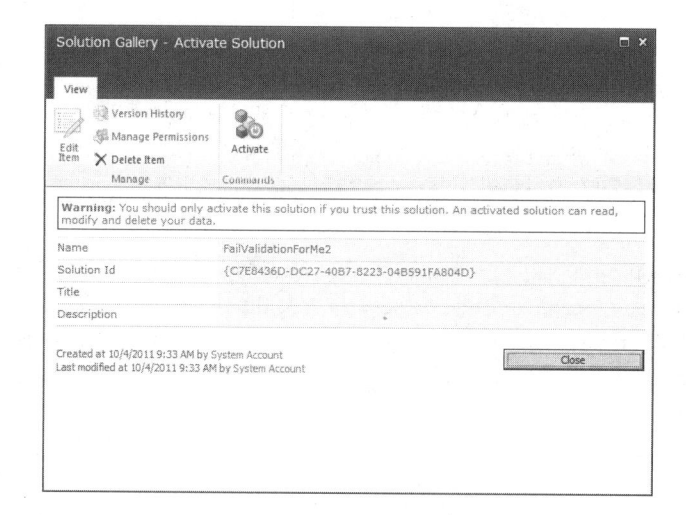

If all goes well, the solution fails validation and is not activated. Instead you are taken to the custom error page as shown in Figure 21.18.

FIGURE 21.18
Custom error page displayed when a solution fails validation

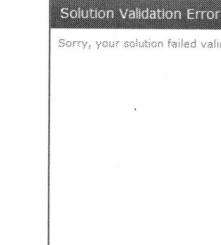

Thus you can see that solution validators offer a proactive way of blocking rogue solutions from activation.

Summary

In this hour you explored the architecture and concept of sandboxed solutions. You also learned how sandboxed solutions can be deployed, monitored, and administered. You learned how to develop a full trust proxy and how to break the boundaries of a sandbox using the same. Finally you learned about solution validators, which enable administrators to prevent activation of any rogue solutions and thus proactively safeguard the farm against bad code.

Q&A

Q. *I want to convert a farm solution to a sandboxed solution. How can I ensure that my solution doesn't use any objects or functions restricted in the sandboxed solution?*

A. Visual Studio IntelliSense does show you a trimmed list of classes and functions when developing a sandboxed solution. However, because in your case the code is already written, although IntelliSense will trim the restricted functions and objects, your solution will still compile successfully even when you set it to be deployed as a sandboxed solution. To ensure that you are not using any restricted functionality of the object model, try compiling your code against the version of the Microsoft.SharePoint.dll assembly present in the 14\UserCode\assemblies folder. In this case you will get compilation errors if you try to use any restricted subset of the object model.

Q. *My sandboxed solution did not exceed the resource usage limit for the site collection. It was another solution that caused the problem. But still my solution is blocked, why is this so?*

A. Even if one sandboxed solution consumes all the resource points for a site collection, all the sandboxed solutions in your site collection will be blocked for a day. Thus even though your sandboxed solution may not have caused any issue, it still gets blocked. In such a scenario, you can request the farm administrator to reset the daily resource usage for your site collection and block the rogue solution from execution.

HOUR 22

Introducing Business Intelligence with SharePoint 2010—Working with Visio and Excel Services

What You'll Learn in This Hour:

- ▶ Exploring the Business Intelligence Center site template
- ▶ Exploring Business Intelligence web parts
- ▶ Consuming Visio diagrams with Visio Services
- ▶ Exploring Excel Services

> **By the Way**
>
> Due to the complexity of the topics discussed, some figures in this book are very detailed and are intended only to provide a high-level view of concepts. Those figures are representational and not intended to be read in detail.

Business Intelligence (BI) tools are used for analysis and presentation of data in a manner that can help business users and executives make informed business decisions. Historically data aggregation, data mining, and reporting were restricted to developers and IT professionals. However using the various Business Intelligence tools available in SharePoint 2010, information workers can now take the control into their own hands and no longer need to depend on developers for their reporting needs. In this hour you explore different Business Intelligence tools available in SharePoint 2010.

Exploring the Business Intelligence Center Site Template

SharePoint 2010 includes a new Business Intelligence Center site template, which is an evolution of the Reporting Center template in SharePoint 2007. The template acts as a starting point for BI and contains links to BI samples to get users accustomed to new BI features in SharePoint 2010. The template also contains predefined lists for Excel and performance point services, as illustrated in Figure 22.1.

FIGURE 22.1
Business Intelligence Center site template

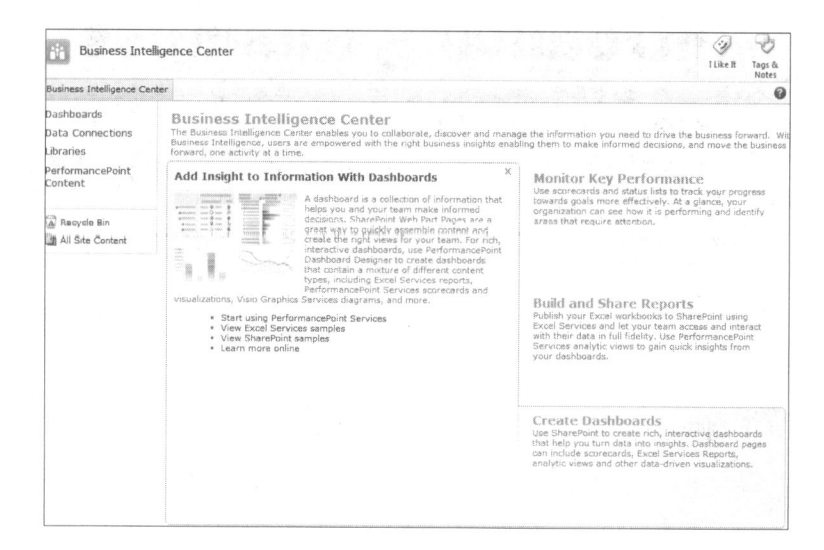

> **Did You Know?**
>
> Although the Business Intelligence Center site is primarily meant for your BI needs, Business Intelligence features are not restricted to the BI Center template and can be used in sites created with other templates as well. You can enable the required features in sites provisioned with other templates, as needed.

Exploring Business Intelligence Web Parts

SharePoint provides chart and status indicator web parts that allow you to create and add charts and KPIs (key performance indicators or the status indicators) to a SharePoint site. Using these web parts you can represent data stored in SharePoint lists, external lists, Business Data Services, Excel Services, and so on, graphically and create visually appealing information dashboards.

This section introduces charting and status indicator web parts and explains with examples how you can use these web parts in your SharePoint site to build interesting dashboards.

Working with the Chart Web Part

Chart web part helps you visualize your data on SharePoint sites and portals. You can connect the chart web part to a variety of data sources. Further, the web part supports a number of chart types, which include bar chart, area chart, line chart, point/bubble chart, pie chart, range chart, and so on.

Try It Yourself

Graphically Represent Tasks with the Chart Web Part

To better appreciate the features of the chart web part, in this section you create a pie chart to display tasks in the task list along with the number of days it would require to complete a task, as shown in Figure 22.2.

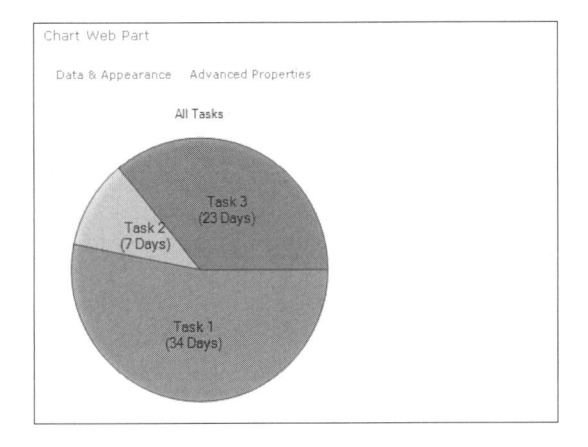

FIGURE 22.2
Pie chart displaying tasks along with days required to complete a task

1. To achieve this, add an integer value calculated column (call it Time Required), to the task list to calculate the number of days required to complete a task. Let the calculation be based on the formula [Due Date]-[Start Date].

2. Populate the task list with some tasks, as shown in Figure 22.3.

FIGURE 22.3
Random tasks added to a task list

3. Next insert a chart web part on a wiki or a web page. The chart web part is present under the Business Data folder, as shown in Figure 22.4.

HOUR 22: Introducing Business Intelligence with SharePoint 2010

FIGURE 22.4
Inserting a chart web part on a page

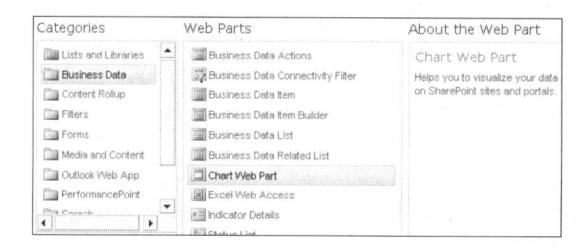

4. When not configured, the chart web part initially displays a dummy bar chart image, as shown in Figure 22.5.

FIGURE 22.5
Chart web part added to a page

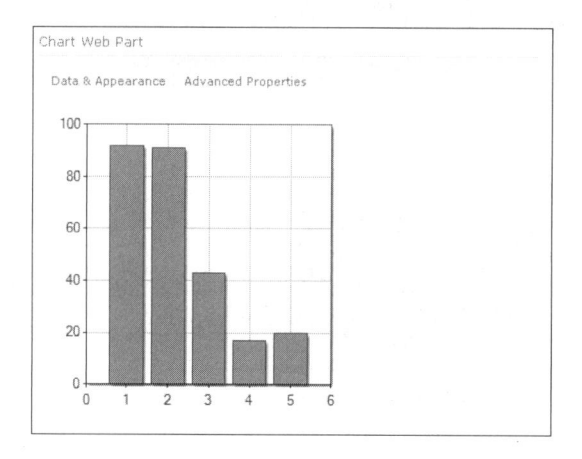

5. Click the Data & Appearance link (refer to Figure 22.5) to either customize your chart or connect the chart to data, as shown in Figure 22.6.

FIGURE 22.6
Configuring data and appearance of a chart web part

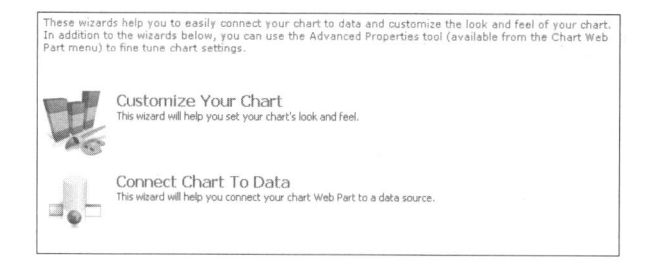

6. Select the Connect Chart To Data option to launch the wizard to connect your chart web part to a data source, which is a SharePoint list in this case.

Exploring Business Intelligence Web Parts 451

7. In step 1 of the wizard, select the Connect To a List option, as shown in Figure 22.7 and click the Next button.

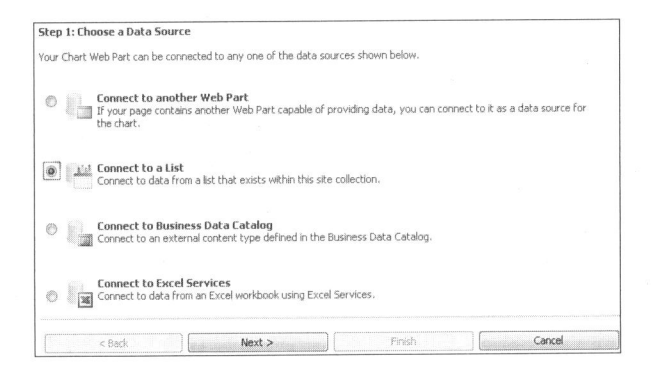

FIGURE 22.7
Choosing a data source

8. In step 2, select the Tasks list, as shown in Figure 22.8 and again click Next.

FIGURE 22.8
Selecting the Tasks list

9. In step 3, you should see the screen shown in Figure 22.9 displaying data retrieved from the selected list. Review the data and click Next.

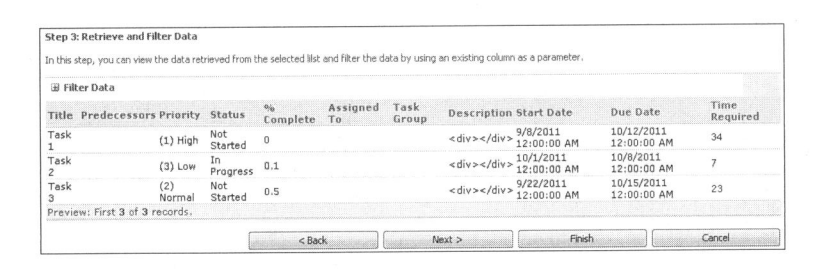

FIGURE 22.9
Data retrieved from the Tasks list

HOUR 22: Introducing Business Intelligence with SharePoint 2010

10. In step 4, select Time Required as the Y axis field and Title as the X axis, as shown in Figure 22.10.

FIGURE 22.10
Binding chart to data

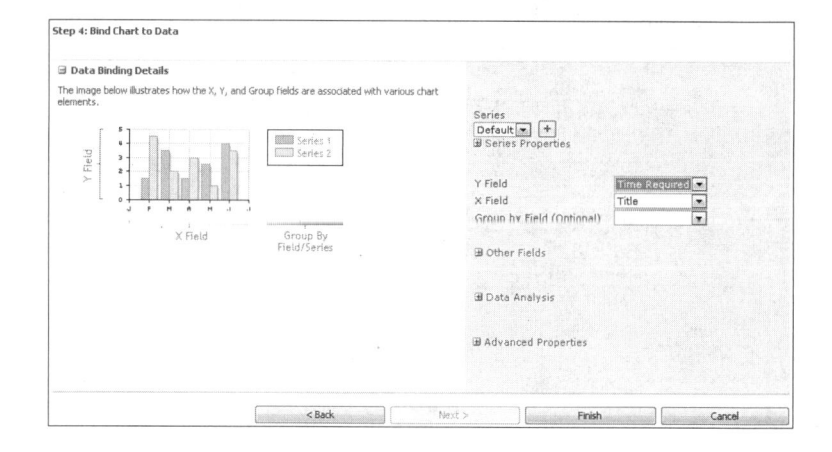

11. That's it. You are done with the initial configuration. Click Finish and your chart should look similar to the one shown in Figure 22.11.

FIGURE 22.11
Tasks versus Time Required plotted as a bar chart

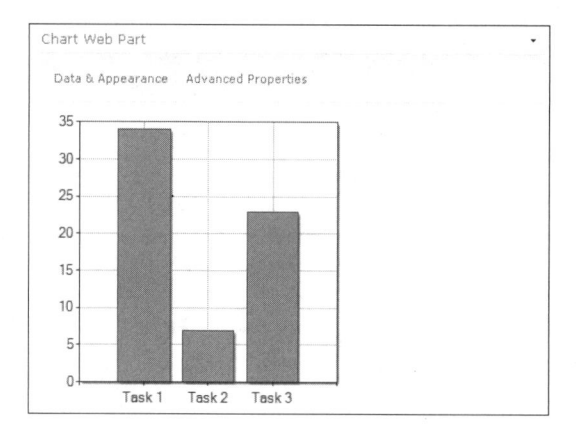

12. Next you see how to convert this bar chart to a pie chart.

13. Again click the Data & Appearance link, and this time select the Customize Your Chart option (refer to Figure 22.6). Select Pie chart from the next screen as shown in Figure 22.12.

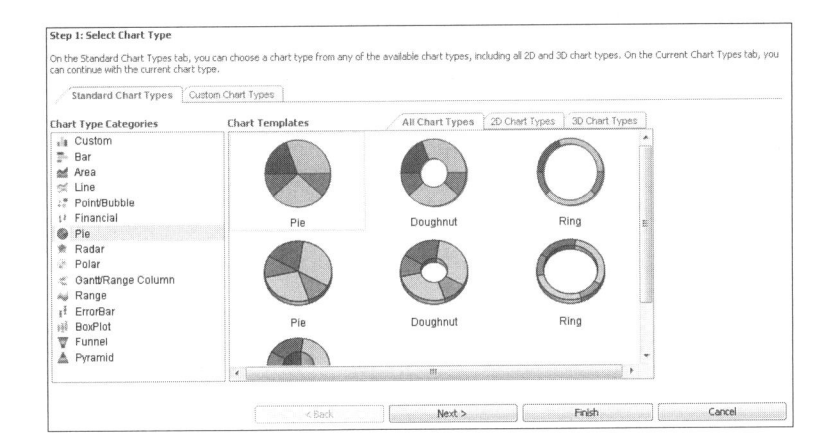

Exploring Business Intelligence Web Parts   453

FIGURE 22.12
Selecting a chart type

14. Click Next and set the chart title as All Tasks, as shown in Figure 22.13.

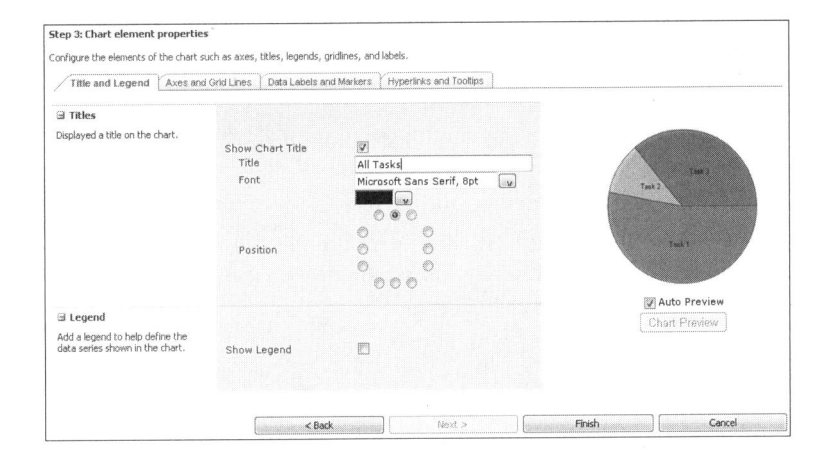

FIGURE 22.13
Configuring the chart title

15. Click the Data Labels and Markers tab and enter the *#VALX\n(#VALY Days)* value in the Custom Value text box, as shown in Figure 22.14. This causes Task Name and Days Required to appear in the format shown in Figure 22.14.

16. That's it. Click Finish to see the effect of your changes. You should now see the pie chart as shown previously in Figure 22.2.

HOUR 22: Introducing Business Intelligence with SharePoint 2010

FIGURE 22.14
Configuring chart labels

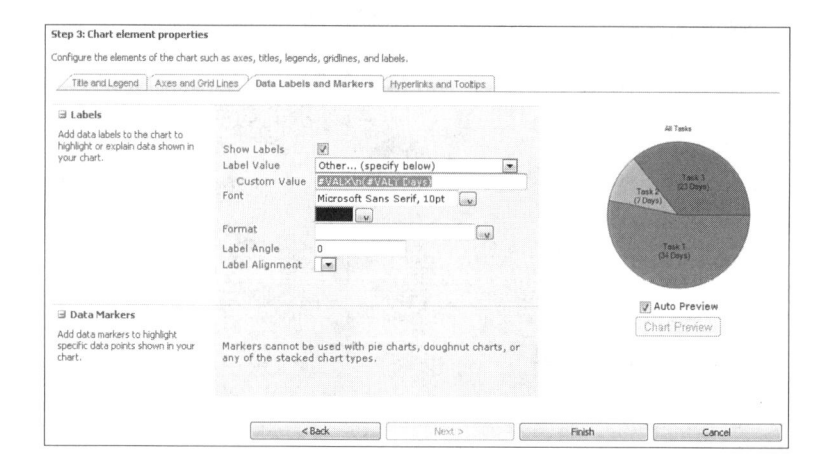

Working with the Status Indicator Web Part

This section looks at the status indicator web part. As the name suggests, the status indicator web part displays a visual indicator, against a chosen measure, indicating the value is good or bad. For example, suppose that for all the tasks in the tasks list, you want to visually know whether you are on track as far as completion of the tasks is concerned—that is, if the average completion % of all tasks is above 80, you are in good shape. If it's between 50% and 80% you are still okay, but anything below 50% is real danger. Let's see how to set up a status indicator to display this information visually, as shown in Figure 22.15.

FIGURE 22.15
Status indicator web part configured to display task completion status

Try It Yourself

Display Task Completion Status Using the Status Indicator Web Part

1. Create a new Status List called Task Status List, as shown in Figure 22.16.

2. Once the list is created, click the New button and select the option to create a SharePoint list based status indicator, as shown in Figure 22.17, since your list is going to be based on a SharePoint task list.

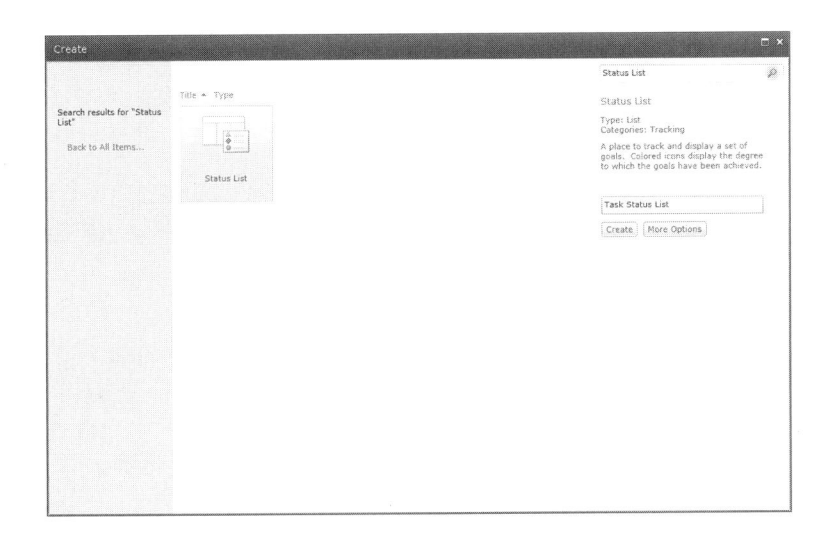

Exploring Business Intelligence Web Parts 455

FIGURE 22.16
Creating a Task Status List

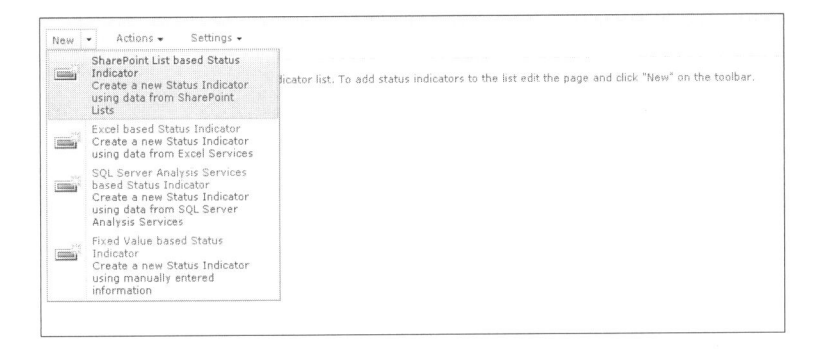

FIGURE 22.17
Creating a SharePoint task list based status indicator

3. Enter All Tasks Status as the name of the indicator and configure the List URL to point to the Tasks list, as shown in Figure 22.18. Since you are going to do this for all tasks in the list, base your indicator on the All Tasks view.

4. Next configure the criteria for the indicator, that is, the value on the basis of which a red, green, or orange indicator would be displayed. Base the criteria on the average of % Complete for all tasks, as shown in Figure 22.19.

5. Finally, complete the configuration by configuring the Status Icon Rules, as shown in Figure 22.20. Anything above 80% is green, between 50% and 80% is orange, and anything else is red.

FIGURE 22.18
Configuring the status indicator name and list URL

FIGURE 22.19
Configuring the indicator value

FIGURE 22.20
Configuring Status Icon Rules

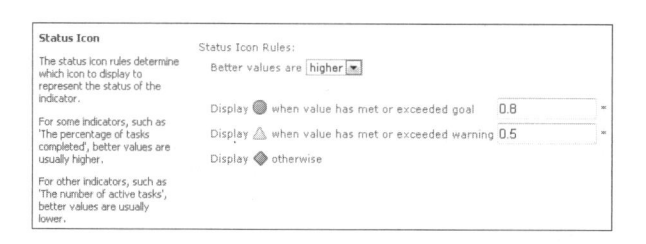

You can also display the status indication data on a web part or wiki page, by adding the Status List web part to the page and configuring it to display data from the Task Status list, as shown in Figure 22.21.

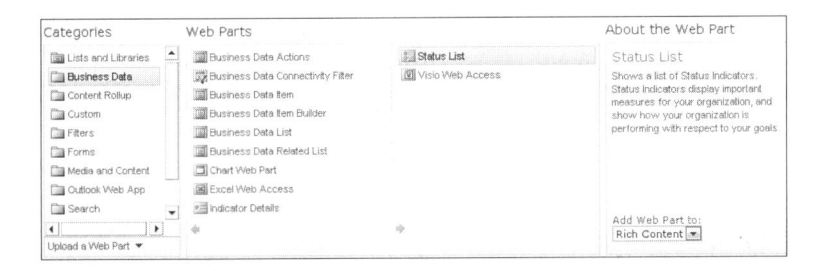

FIGURE 22.21
The Status List web part can be used to display status data on a page.

Consuming Visio Diagrams with Visio Services

Visio Services enables users to bring their Visio diagrams to the web world. Other users can view the Visio documents using a web browser, without needing to install the Visio client on their machine. Moreover Visio diagrams can be connected to various data sources, and Visio Services can be configured to refresh the diagrams with any change in the underlying data.

To better understand the features offered by Visio Services, consider a scenario in which an organization wants to monitor the health of its data centers around the world using visual status indicators. Let's say the health data is fed into a SharePoint list at regular intervals, and using Visio Services you need to design a mechanism to represent that data visually.

Try It Yourself
Represent Data Center Health Indicators Visually Using Visio Services

1. Create a new SharePoint list; call it Data Center Health, with the columns and data shown in Figure 22.22.

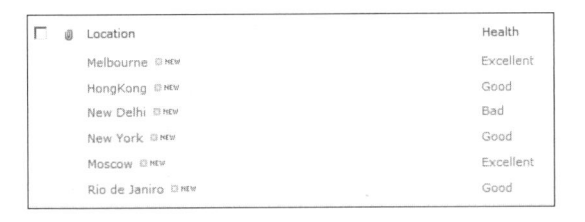

FIGURE 22.22
Data Center Health list

2. Next create a blank Visio drawing (we're using Visio 2010) and insert a world map image from the clipart gallery.

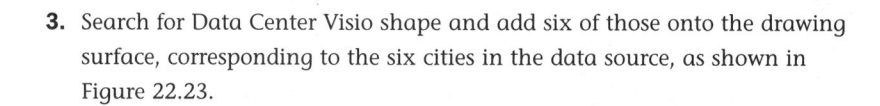

458 HOUR 22: Introducing Business Intelligence with SharePoint 2010

3. Search for Data Center Visio shape and add six of those onto the drawing surface, corresponding to the six cities in the data source, as shown in Figure 22.23.

FIGURE 22.23
Static data center location diagram

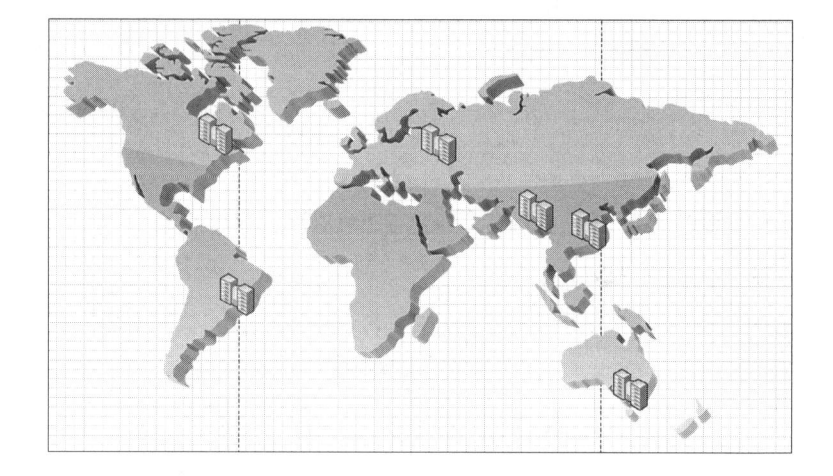

4. With this you have a static data center location diagram ready. Next you bind this diagram to your list and update the health indicators based on changes to the health data. In Visio, select the Data tab from the ribbon and click Link Shapes to Data Symbol to launch the Data Selector Wizard. Select Microsoft SharePoint Foundation List as the source, as shown in Figure 22.24.

FIGURE 22.24
Selecting a data source

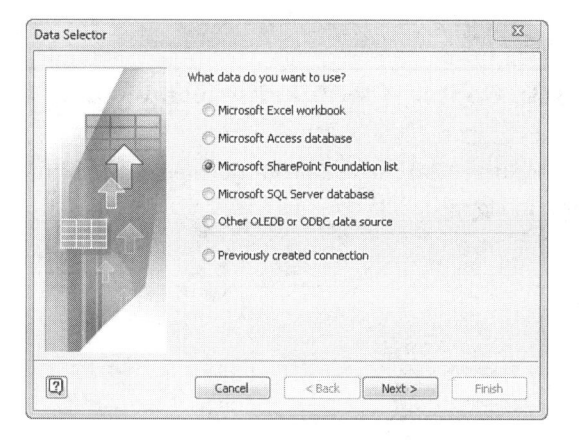

5. Enter the URL of your SharePoint site on the next screen and click Next to view the lists in your site, as shown in Figure 22.25. Select the Data Center Health list and click Next.

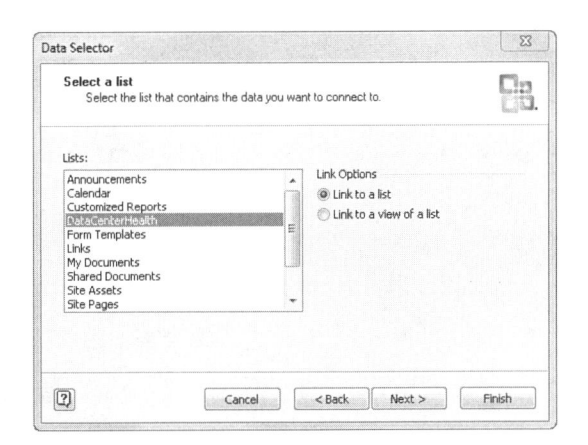

Consuming Visio Diagrams with Visio Services   459

FIGURE 22.25
Configuring a SharePoint list as data source

6. Click Finish to save the changes. The data from the list will be fetched and displayed in Visio, as shown in Figure 22.26.

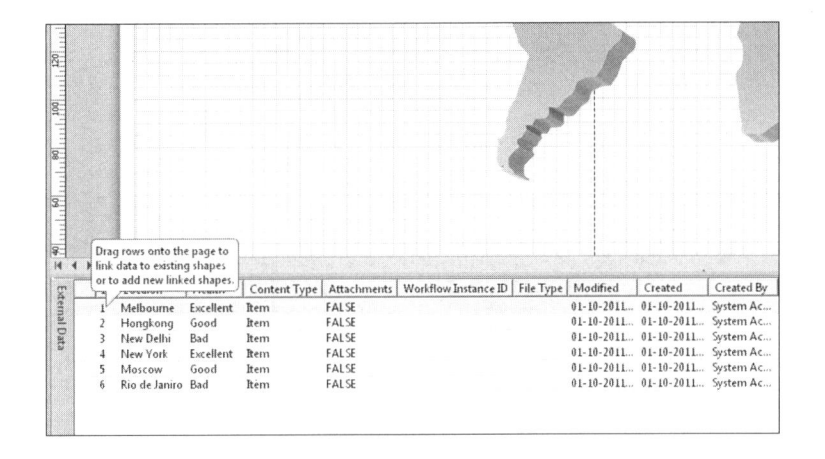

FIGURE 22.26
External data fetched and displayed by Visio

7. Next select the data center symbol located in the vicinity of Melbourne (Australia) on the world map. Right-click the first row (corresponding to Melbourne) displayed in the external data window and select the Link to Selected Shapes option from the context menu. Repeat this for all the other shapes as well, linking them to their respective data items.

8. With this, you are done linking data to shapes; now do some more configurations to format the data in a nicer way. For this, click the Edit Data Graphic menu as shown in Figure 22.27.

HOUR 22: Introducing Business Intelligence with SharePoint 2010

FIGURE 22.27
Editing data graphic

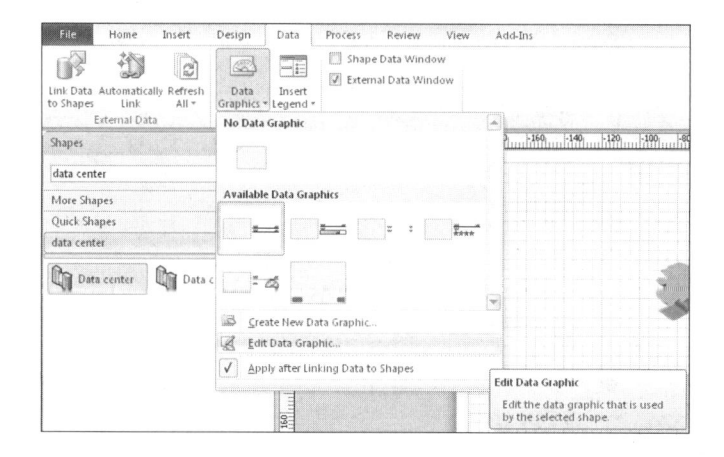

9. You see a window similar to one shown in Figure 22.28. Select the Location field and click the Edit Item button.

FIGURE 22.28
Configuring data fields

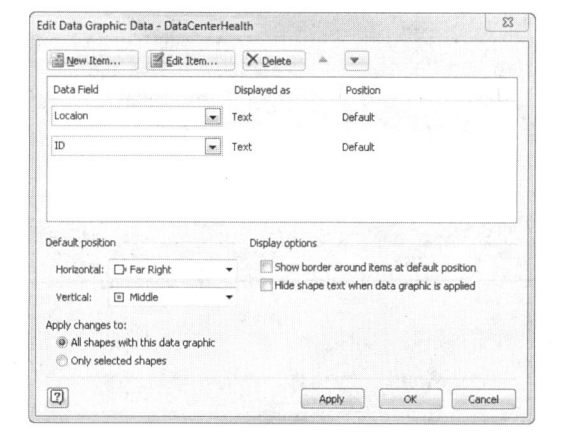

10. Make sure that your font size, positioning, and other properties are set to values as shown in Figure 22.29.

11. The ID field shown previously in Figure 22.28 is not of much use to you; swap it with the Health field instead. Select the ID field and click Edit Item. In the next screen (shown in Figure 22.30) set Data Field to Health and set the Displayed As property to Icon Set. Also configure the rules to display icons as per the values configured in Figure 22.30.

Consuming Visio Diagrams with Visio Services

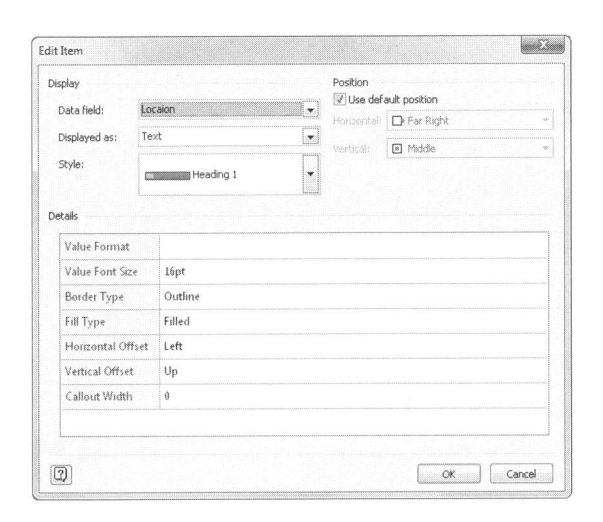

FIGURE 22.29
Configuring the location field

FIGURE 22.30
Configuring the Health field

12. With these configurations you are all set with the Visio diagram. Click OK to save the changes.

13. You can save your file as a Visio web drawing (.vdw) and upload it manually to a SharePoint document library or you can also select the Save and Send (Save to SharePoint) option from the File menu to directly upload your Visio drawing to your site.

14. Once the drawing is uploaded to a document library in the SharePoint site, click the Visio file to open it in the web browser, as shown in Figure 22.31.

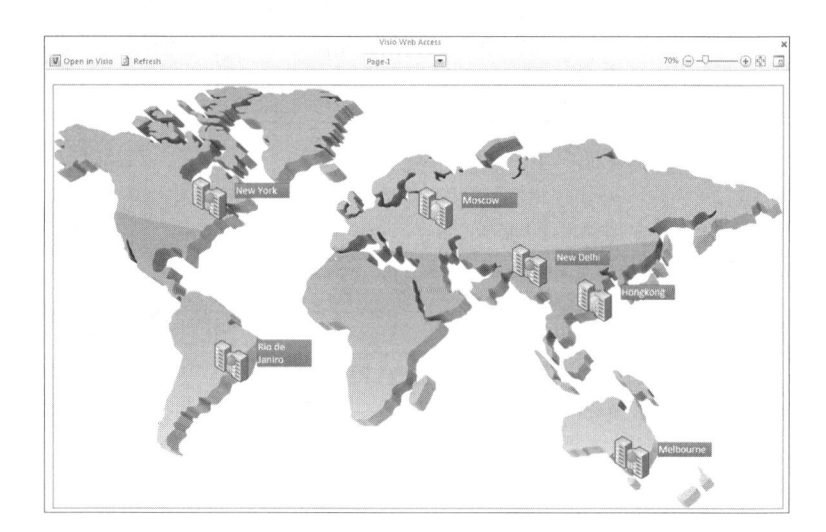

HOUR 22: Introducing Business Intelligence with SharePoint 2010

FIGURE 22.31
Visio diagram opened using a web browser

You can also display this drawing on a web part or wiki page by using the Visio Web Access web part and configuring the path to the Visio drawing file in the web part, as shown in Figure 22.32.

FIGURE 22.32
Visio Web Access web part

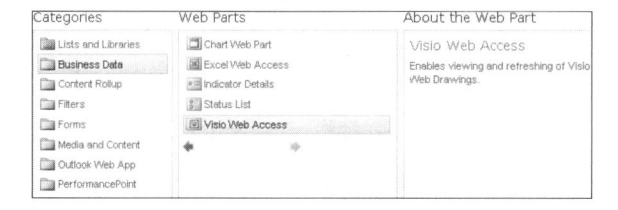

You can also configure other options such as refresh duration from the web part to decide how frequently you want to update the Visio diagram with any changes in data.

Exploring Excel Services

Just like Visio Services, Excel Services allows you to store and selectively publish an Excel workbook on a SharePoint site. Using a web browser, users can view data and interact with the workbook, without needing to install the Excel client. All this is possible using the Excel Web Access web part.

With this basic introduction to Excel Services, let's see it in action.

Try It Yourself
Work with Excel Services

1. Create an Excel workbook, using the Excel client (we are using Excel 2010), having a sales data table and a pie chart representing the total sales graphically, as shown in Figure 22.33.

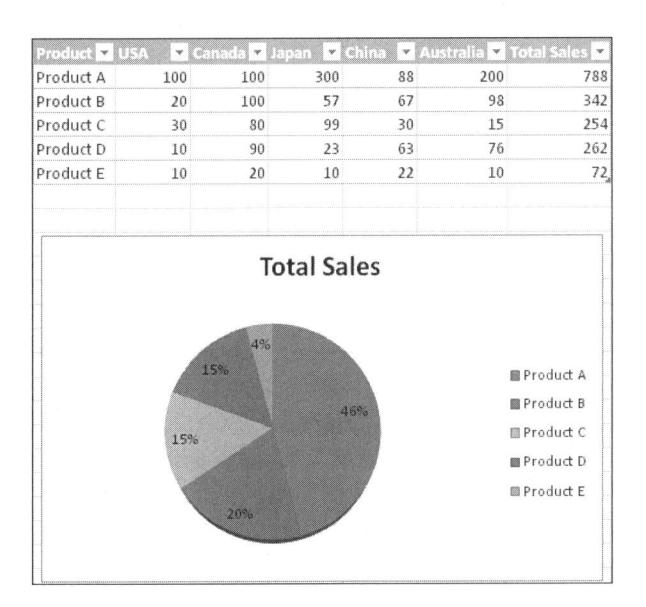

FIGURE 22.33
Excel workbook containing sales data

2. You can publish the workbook to a SharePoint site either by saving the workbook and uploading it to a document library or by selecting the Save and Send (Save to SharePoint) option from the File menu to directly upload your workbook to a SharePoint site.

3. Once the workbook is uploaded to a document library, click the workbook, and SharePoint opens the same for you in the Excel Web Access web part (shown in Figure 22.34). It's as simple as that!

FIGURE 22.34
Excel Web Access web part

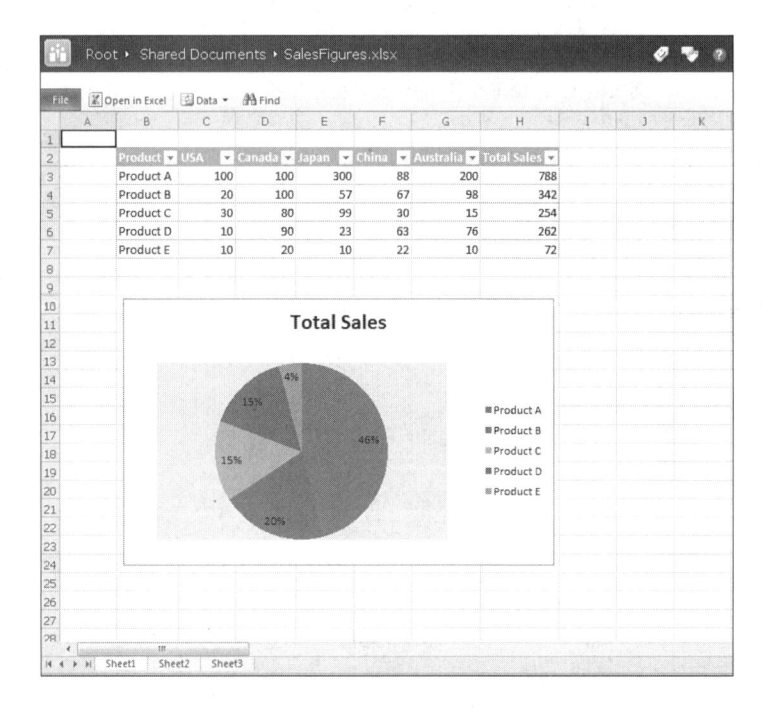

This opens up a whole new world of possibilities. Especially because Excel is popular among business users, Excel Services makes it convenient for them to publish their workbooks to the Web and share with stakeholders, easily and without involving an IT guy.

Another interesting feature of Excel Services is exposing the content of an Excel workbook programmatically using the REST Services. To access the REST services, add _vti_bin/ExcelRest.aspx/ to the URL of your workbook. For example, if your workbook is present in a shared documents library, the modified URL would be http://splearn/**_vti_bin**/**ExcelRest.aspx**/Shared%20Documents/SalesFigures.xlsx.

Further, to discover workbook items using a web browser, add /model at the end of the previous URL. If you copy and paste the URL http://splearn/**_vti_bin**/ **ExcelRest.aspx**/Shared%20Documents/SalesFigures.xlsx/**model** in your browser window, you get an atom feed as shown in Figure 22.35.

Click the Charts link to get all the charts in the workbook, as shown in Figure 22.36.

Click the Chart1 link in Figure 22.36. The web browser renders the pie chart created earlier using the Excel client application, as illustrated in Figure 22.37.

FIGURE 22.35
REST Services atom feed

FIGURE 22.36
All the charts in workbook listed as an atom feed

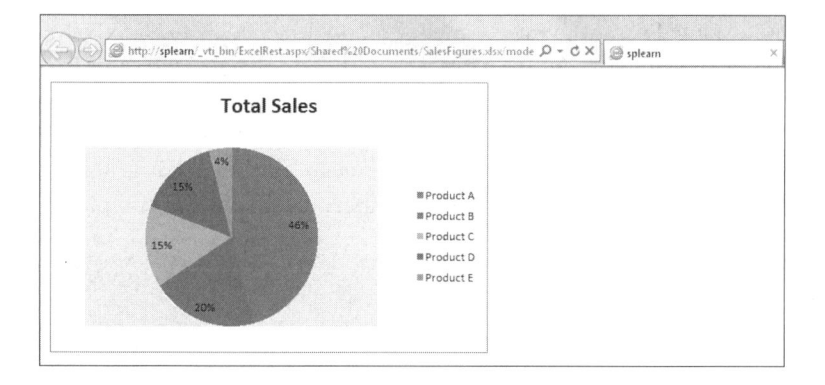

FIGURE 22.37
A pie chart in the workbook exposed using REST Services

Copy the URL from the address bar. You can use this URL to insert the pie chart on any page using the regular image viewer web part.

Similarly, you can access the table containing sales data in the workbook, using the REST Services. So that your web browser can render the table content, replace the

HOUR 22: Introducing Business Intelligence with SharePoint 2010

$format=atom parameter with $format=HTML so that the REST Services returns the table in HTML format, as shown in Figure 22.38.

FIGURE 22.38
Accessing the sales data table as HTML content

Product	USA	Canada	Japan	China	Australia	Total Sales
Product A	100	100	300	88	200	788
Product B	20	100	57	67	98	342
Product C	30	80	99	30	15	254
Product D	10	90	23	63	76	262
Product E	10	20	10	22	10	72

Finally the Excel Web Access web part can also be added to any page and configured to render either the whole workbook or only selected sections of the workbook, as shown in Figure 22.39.

FIGURE 22.39
Configuring the Excel Web Access web part to display only the sales table

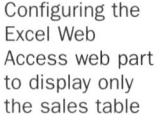

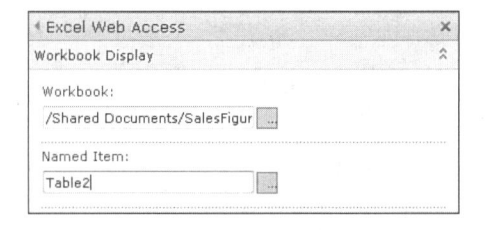

Summary

This hour explored various business intelligence tools available to SharePoint 2010 developers. You learned about the chart web part and the status indicator web part, and the process of adding them to a page on a SharePoint site and connecting them to a data source. You also saw how Visio diagrams can be consumed in SharePoint with the help of Visio Services. The discussion concluded with a look at Excel Services and you learned how easily business users can create and publish Excel workbooks using the Excel Services.

Q&A

Q. *To what other data sources can I connect the charting web part, apart from SharePoint lists?*

A. You can connect the charting web part to the following data sources:

- Connect to another web part capable of providing data
- Connect to external Business Data Catalog (i.e., an external list)
- Connect to Excel Services
- Connect to SharePoint list

Q. *Could you please list the data sources for Visio Services as well?*

A. You can connect Visio diagrams to the following data sources:

- SQL data source
- Excel
- SharePoint lists
- OLEDB data source
- ODBC data Source

Q. *How can I limit the maximum workbook upload size for Excel Services?*

A. Navigate to Manage Service Applications in Central Administration. For the Excel Services Application, click the Manage button. Navigate to the Trusted File Locations page by clicking on the corresponding link. By default Excel Services considers the default web application a trusted site. Click the http:// link (assuming you are using the default web application) to edit the properties for a trusted file location. Look for the Workbook Properties section. You can control the maximum workbook size from here.

HOUR 23

Introducing Business Intelligence with SharePoint 2010—Working with PerformancePoint Services

What You'll Learn in This Hour:

- ▶ Introducing PerformancePoint Services
- ▶ Configuring PerformancePoint Services
- ▶ Downloading and setting up Adventure Works sample databases
- ▶ Exploring the PerformancePoint Services Dashboard Designer
- ▶ Creating your first dashboard

> **By the Way**
>
> Due to the complexity of the topics discussed, some figures in this book are very detailed and are intended only to provide a high-level view of concepts. Those figures are representational and not intended to be read in detail.

Using PerformancePoint Services, you can build dashboards, scorecards, reports, and key performance indicators (KPIs), which are useful for business users to view and analyze performance of their business and help them make well-informed business decisions. In this hour you learn about PerformancePoint Services, including techniques to develop reports, scorecards, and dashboards and how to deploy them to SharePoint.

Introducing PerformancePoint Services

PerformancePoint Services makes the lives of business users easier by allowing them to easily create and publish Business Intelligence dashboards in SharePoint 2010. Using PerformancePoint Services Dashboard Designer, you can build dashboards, scorecards, reports, and key performance indicators (KPIs) and publish them to SharePoint with ease. The Dashboard Designer can be launched directly from the web browser and has been designed especially for business users and information workers so that they can work on it directly without the need of involving an IT guy.

HOUR 23: Introducing Business Intelligence with SharePoint 2010

> **Did You Know?**
>
> Microsoft Office PerformancePoint Server 2007 was earlier available as a stand-alone product, that is, prior to integration with SharePoint Server 2010. The product was discontinued in 2009; however, most features of the product have been preserved apart from various enhancements in the current version of PerformancePoint Services, which are now available as a part of the SharePoint Server Enterprise license.

PerformancePoint Services objects are stored in SharePoint lists and libraries and not in a separate database, as was the case with earlier versions of the product. The integration ensures that the PerformancePoint Services can utilize SharePoint features such as scalability, collaboration, backup and recovery, and disaster recovery capabilities.

Configuring PerformancePoint Services

Configuring PerformancePoint Services in SharePoint 2010 involves the following two main steps:

- Creation and configuration of a PerformancePoint Services service application
- Configuration of the unattended service account for PerformancePoint Services

If you have a single server environment, the PerformancePoint Services application should already be set up and running for you. You can verify this by navigating to the Manage Service Applications screen from Central Administration and looking for the PerformancePoint Services service application.

If the service application is not present, you can create a new one. On the Manage Service Applications screen, click the New button and select PerformancePoint Service Application. Type a name for the service application and select the Add This Service Application's Proxy to the Farm's Default Proxy List option. You can either use an existing application pool or choose to create a new one. Click the Create button, as illustrated in Figure 23.1.

Next configure the unattended service account, which is used to authenticate with the data sources. To specify the credentials for the unattended service account, click the Manage button and make sure that the PerformancePoint Services service application is the active selection. Click the PerformancePoint Service Application Settings link and enter credentials for unattended service account as shown in Figure 23.2.

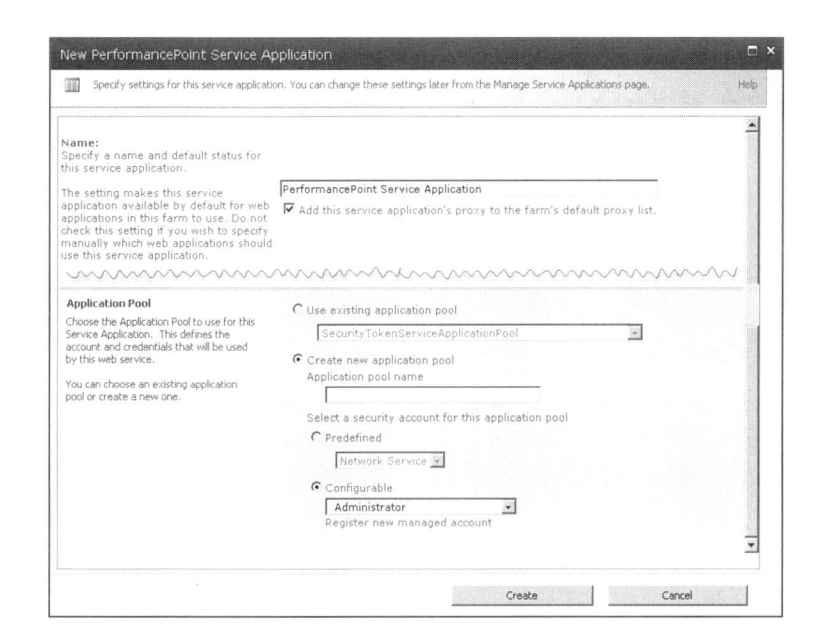

FIGURE 23.1
Creating a new Performance Point service application

FIGURE 23.2
Configuring unattended user account

The Secure Store Service stores the credentials for the service account. You may need to generate a new key for Secure Store Service in case you have not already done that before. In that case you are prompted with an error message asking you to do so before configuring the unattended service account. You can generate a new key for Secure Store Service by clicking on the Manage button on the Manage Service Applications screen and ensuring that Secure Store Service is the current selection. Click the Generate New Key button to begin the process of new key generation.

At this stage you are done with the basic configuration required to start working with the PerformancePoint Services.

Downloading and Setting Up Adventure Works Sample Databases

To create your basic dashboard, you will use the SQL Server Analysis service and Adventure Works cube. Before you can do that, make sure that you have SQL Server Analysis Services up and running.

Download Adventure Works sample databases for Microsoft SQL Server 2008R2 from http://msftdbprodsamples.codeplex.com/releases/view/55926. Run the downloaded .exe, which creates the Adventure Works databases for you.

You need to deploy the Analysis Services project containing the Adventure Works Cube manually. Open the C:\Program Files\Microsoft SQL Server\100\Tools\Samples\AdventureWorks 2008R2 Analysis Services Project\enterprise folder in Windows Explorer. Look for the Adventure Works.sln solution and open it in Visual Studio, as shown in Figure 23.3.

FIGURE 23.3
Adventure Works solution

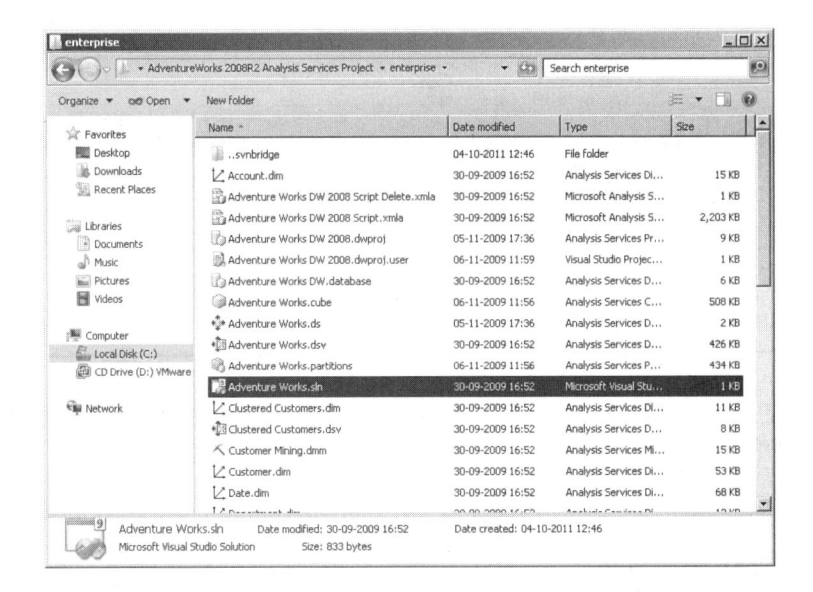

Depending on your environment, you may need to reconfigure the database connection strings. Open the Adventure Works.ds data source, located in the Data Sources folder (in Solution Explorer) and click the Edit button next to the connection string. This brings up the screen shown in Figure 23.4. Specify the SQL Server database engine instance where the Adventure Works sample databases were installed earlier and click the Test Connection button to verify connectivity.

Downloading and Setting Up Adventure Works Sample Databases 473

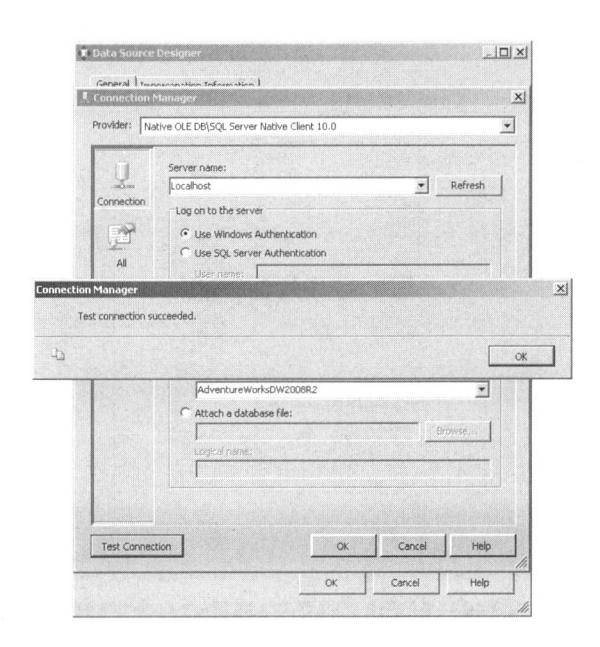

FIGURE 23.4
Configuring the connection string for the Adventure Works.ds data source

Right-click the Adventure Works 2008 DW solution in the Solution Explorer and for the Deployment settings, modify the target server property as per your environment, as illustrated in Figure 23.5.

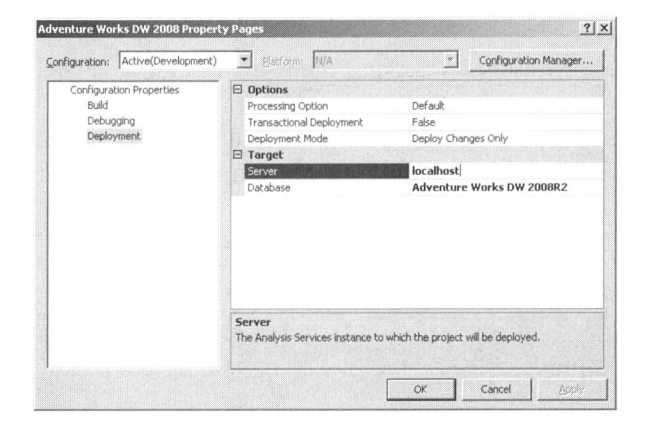

FIGURE 23.5
Specifying the deployment target

Right-click the solution and select the Deploy option to begin the deployment, as shown in Figure 23.6.

Ensure that the deployment completes without any errors.

FIGURE 23.6
Deploying the Adventure Works Analysis Services project

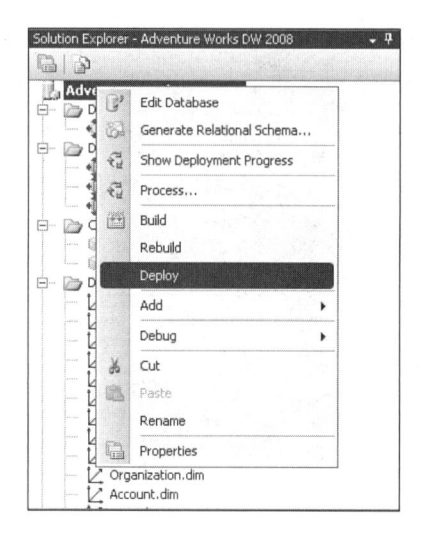

Exploring the PerformancePoint Services Dashboard Designer

The PerformancePoint Services Dashboard Designer is a desktop application for designing and publishing Business Intelligence dashboards. Dashboards represent important business performance related data to enable organizations to measure and monitor business performance more effectively.

You can launch the Dashboard Designer from the web browser itself. Provision a new site collection with Business Intelligence Center template, present under enterprise templates. Once the site collection is provisioned, navigate to the site and select Start Using PerformancePoint Services from the Create Dashboards section. You get a screen similar to Figure 23.7.

Click the Run Dashboard Designer button to launch the PerformancePoint Services Dashboard Designer. Launching the Dashboard Designer for the first time will take some time.

Exploring the PerformancePoint Services Dashboard Designer

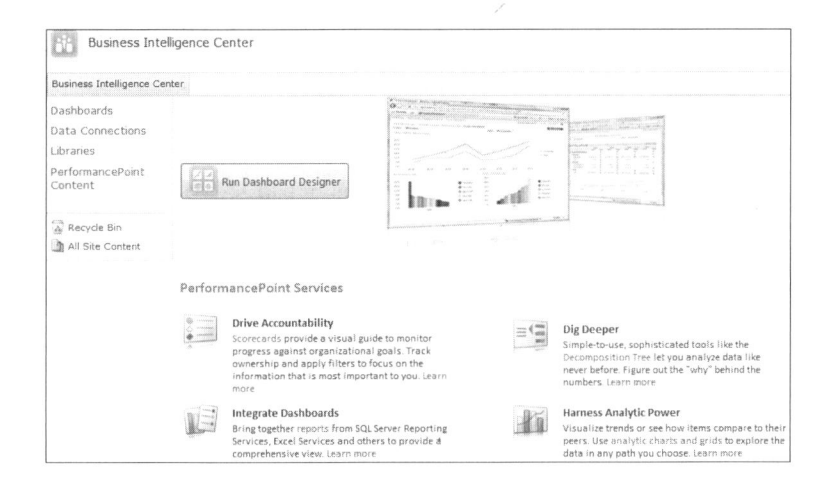

FIGURE 23.7 Launching the PerformancePoint Services Dashboard Designer

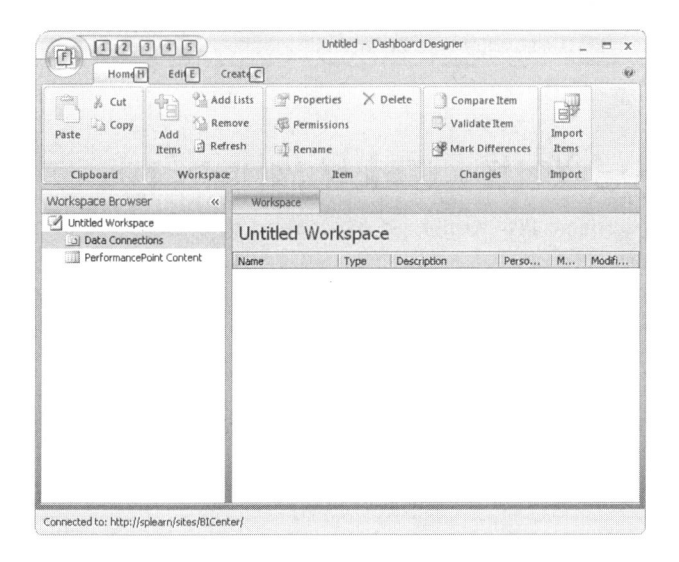

FIGURE 23.8 PerformancePoint Services Dashboard Designer

Table 23.1 summarizes the items you can create with the Dashboard Designer.

TABLE 23.1 Items That Can Be Created with the Dashboard Designer

Item	Description
Data Sources	Contain connection related information for connecting to a back-end data source.
Dashboards	A container for displaying reports and scorecards, organized in a meaningful way that makes sense to business users and decision-makers.
Scorecards	Compare actual results to the target and represents the outcome using visual indicators. Scorecards contain one or more KPIs.
KPIs	Metrics that can be used on scorecards; contain target and actual values and graphical indicators to indicate deviation.
Indicators	Graphical symbols indicating the actual value is on or off track.
Filters	Enable you to filter the dashboard content.
Reports	Contain charts or tables to display information.

Creating Your First Dashboard

As explained earlier, a PPS Dashboard is a container for displaying reports and scorecards, organized in a meaningful way that makes sense to business users and decision-makers. Hence the creation of a dashboard effectively involves planning and creating individual dashboard elements (that is, reports and scorecards) and deploying the dashboard to SharePoint.

At a higher level, to create a PPS dashboard, you need to perform the following tasks, in this sequence:

1. Create a new data source; say, pointing to the Adventure Works cube.
2. Create one or more scorecards and/or reports.
3. Create a dashboard and add the scorecards and reports to it.
4. Deploy the dashboard to SharePoint.

The Try It Yourself section next explores these steps further, by creating a dashboard based on the Adventure Works cube deployed earlier.

Try It Yourself

Create a PerformancePoint Services Dashboard

1. Launch the Dashboard Designer and make sure that you are connected to the BI Center site by examining the URL displayed in the bottom left corner of the Dashboard Designer. You can connect to a different site by clicking the URL and entering the new URL in the Options dialog box, as shown in Figure 23.9.

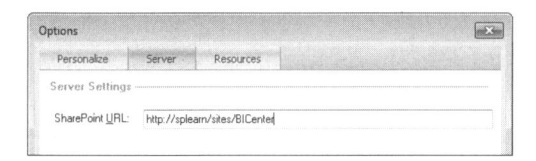

    FIGURE 23.9 Connecting to the Business Intelligence Center site

2. Create a new data source by right-clicking on the Data Connection folder and selecting the New Data Source option, as shown in Figure 23.10.

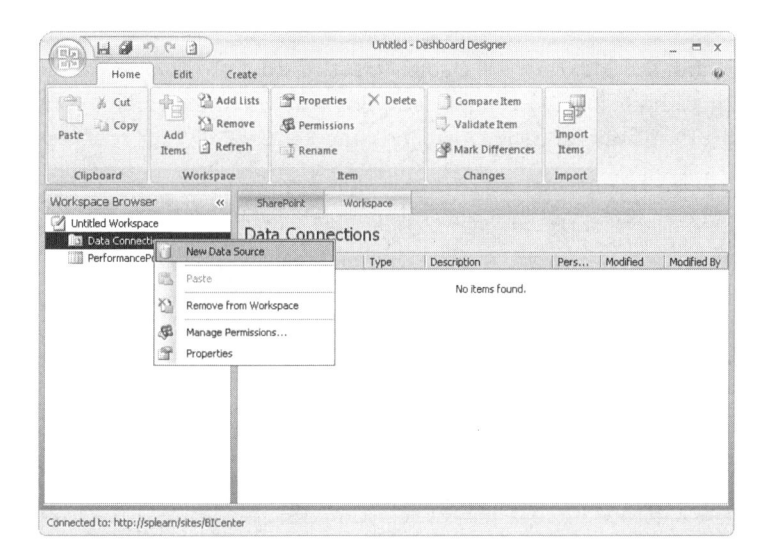

    FIGURE 23.10 Creating a new data source

3. Select Analysis Service from the next screen and configure the values for the Server, Database, and Cube properties, as illustrated in Figure 23.11. This creates a new connection to the Adventure Works cube you downloaded and deployed earlier as a part of the Adventure Works database samples.

4. Click the Test Data Source button to verify the connectivity.

FIGURE 23.11
Configuring the new data source

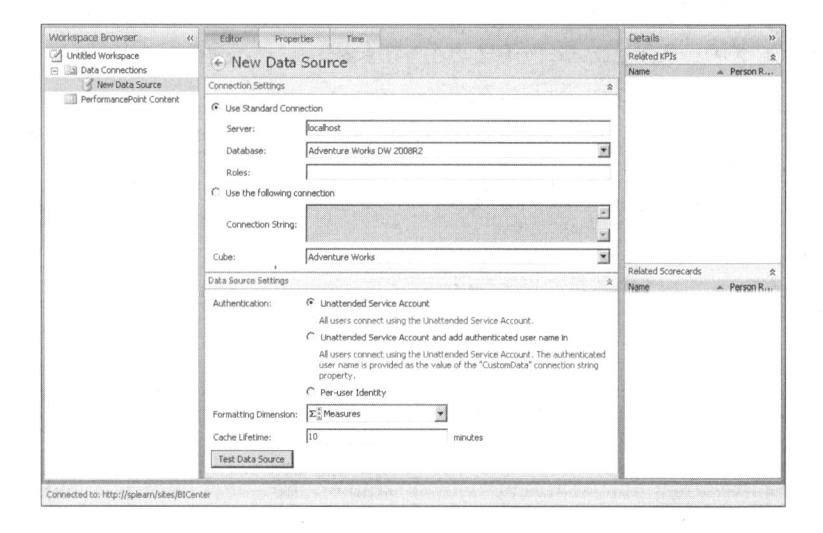

5. Rename the New Data Source to Adventure Works.

6. Now that the data source is created, create a scorecard. Right-click the PerformancePoint Content and select Scorecard from the various options under the New button, as shown in Figure 23.12.

FIGURE 23.12
Creating a new scorecard

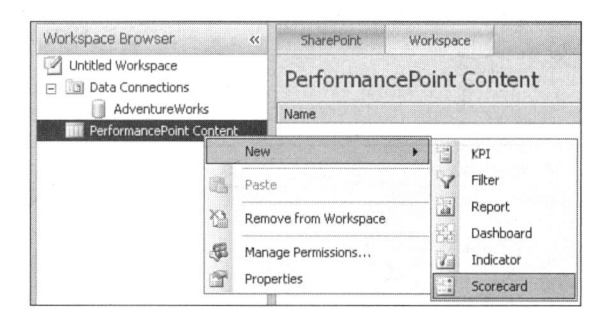

7. Select Analysis Services as the scorecard template and click OK.

8. Select the Adventure Works data connection from the next screen and click Next.

9. Select the Create KPIs from SQL Server Analysis Services Measures from the next screen.

10. Click the Add KPI button a couple of times to add KPIs to your scorecard, as shown in Figure 23.13, and click Next.

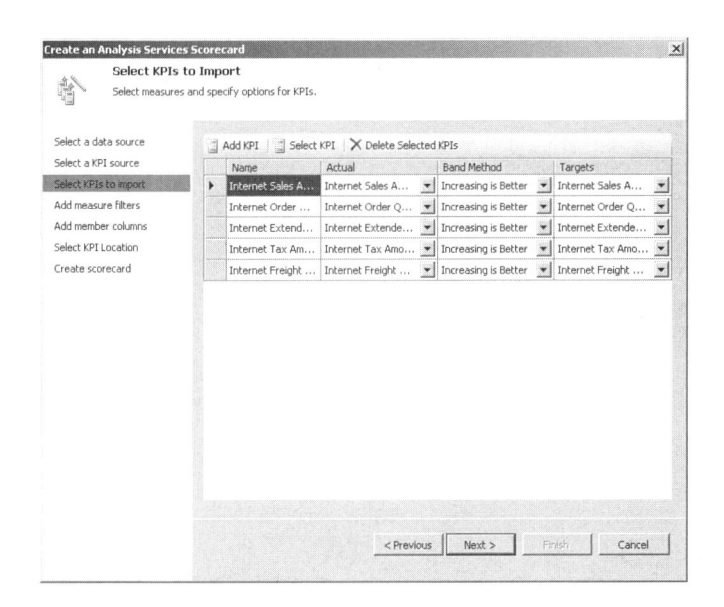

FIGURE 23.13
Adding KPIs to a scorecard

11. Do not check the Add Measure Filters check box and click Next.
12. Do not check the Add Column Members check box and click Next.
13. Leave the location for KPI creation as the default.
14. Click Finish to complete the scorecard creation wizard.
15. Rename your scorecard to AdventureWorksScorecard. Your scorecard should be similar to the one shown in Figure 23.14, depending on the number of KPIs you added to it.

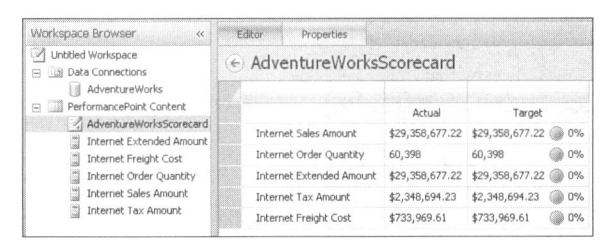

FIGURE 23.14
Adventure Works Scorecard

16. Next create a new Report. Again right-click PerformancePoint content and select Report from various options under the New button.
17. Select Analytic chart as the report template and click OK. Again select the Adventure Works Data Connection and click Finish. Wait for the new report to be created.

HOUR 23: Introducing Business Intelligence with SharePoint 2010

18. Rename the report to Analytic Chart Report, as illustrated in Figure 23.15.

FIGURE 23.15
Creating the Analytic Chart Report

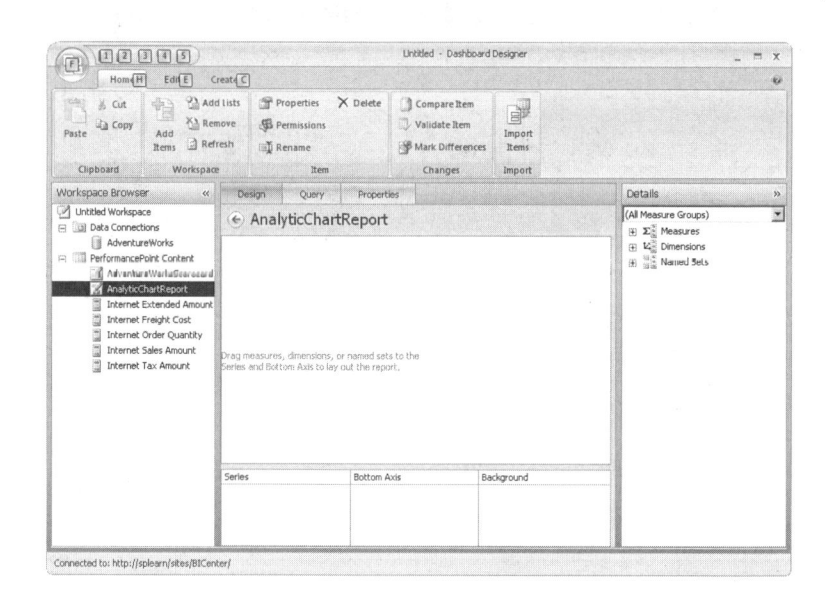

19. As indicated by the message in red, next you need to drag and drop measures, dimensions, or named sets from the Details window on the right to generate the chart. Drag and drop the Customer dimension into the series area, the Geography dimension into the Bottom Axis area, and the Internet Sales measure into the Background area to generate a bar chart, as illustrated in Figure 23.16.

FIGURE 23.16
Adding dimensions and measures to generate the bar chart

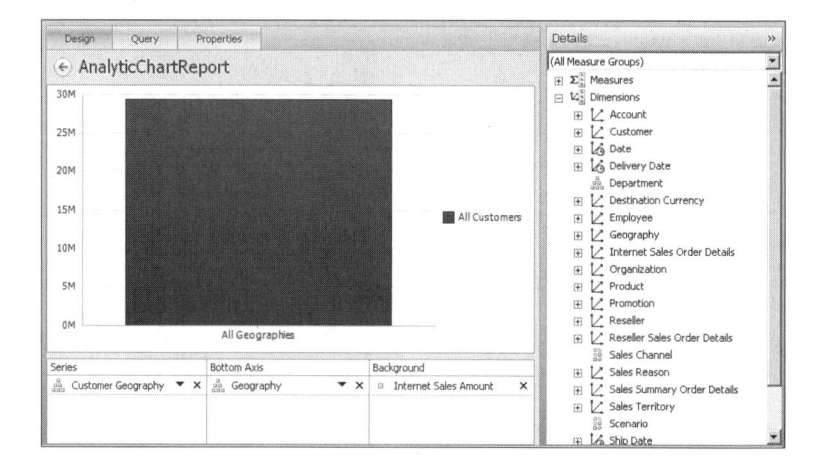

Creating Your First Dashboard   481

20. You can drill down the bar chart by either clicking the blue bar or right-clicking and selecting the drill down option. Drilling down generates a chart for different countries, as shown in Figure 23.17.

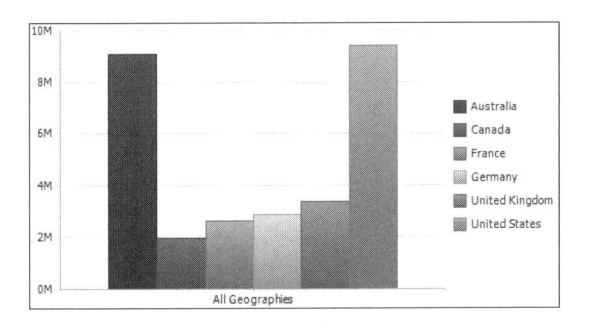

FIGURE 23.17
Drilling down to view the analytic chart for countries

If you are not happy with the bar chart and want a different chart type, right-click an empty area in the chart. You can select a different chart type (say a pie chart) from the Report Type context menu option. Further, you can specify the location of the legend or whether to display the legend under the Format Report context menu option.

Did You Know?

---

21. Finally create a dashboard, add the analytic chart and report to it, and deploy the dashboard to SharePoint.
22. Right-click the PerformancePoint Content and select the New Dashboard option.
23. From the Dashboard Page Template Selection screen, select the 2 Columns template, as shown in Figure 23.18 and click OK.

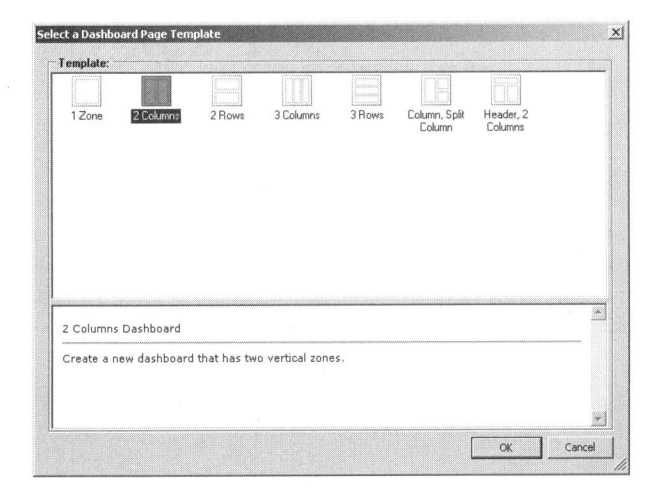

FIGURE 23.18
Selecting a template for the PPS dashboard

HOUR 23: Introducing Business Intelligence with SharePoint 2010

24. Rename the dashboard to Adventure Works Dashboard.
25. Drag and drop the Adventure Works Scorecard and Analytic Chart Report on to the dashboard as shown in Figure 23.19.

FIGURE 23.19
Adding the scorecard and report to the dashboard

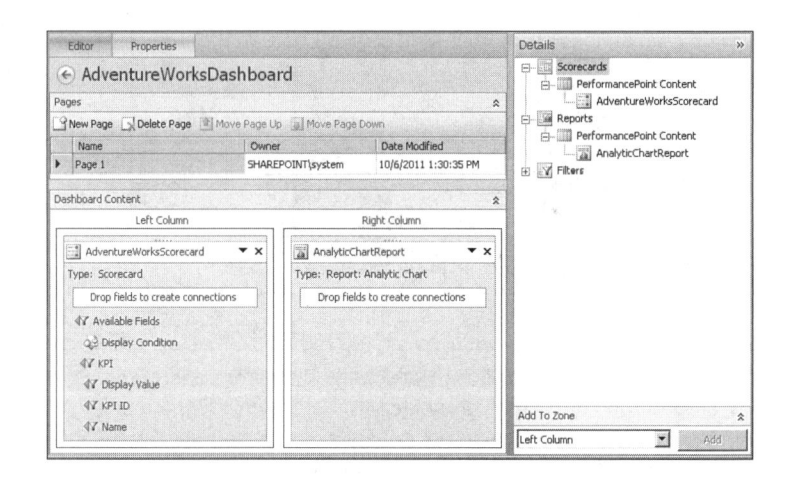

26. Now right-click the dashboard and select the Deploy to SharePoint option, as shown in Figure 23.20.

FIGURE 23.20
Deploying the dashboard to SharePoint

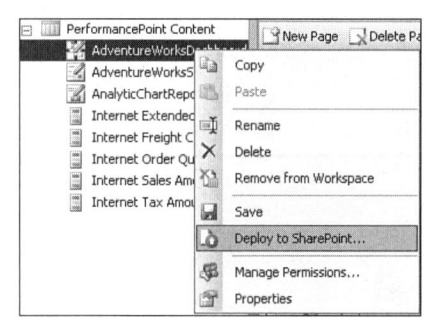

Select the dashboard to be deployed in the Dashboards folder, using the default master page. The PPS Dashboard Designer does the rest of the work for you. Once the dashboard is deployed, you should be able to view it in the web browser, as shown in Figure 23.21.

Creating Your First Dashboard 483

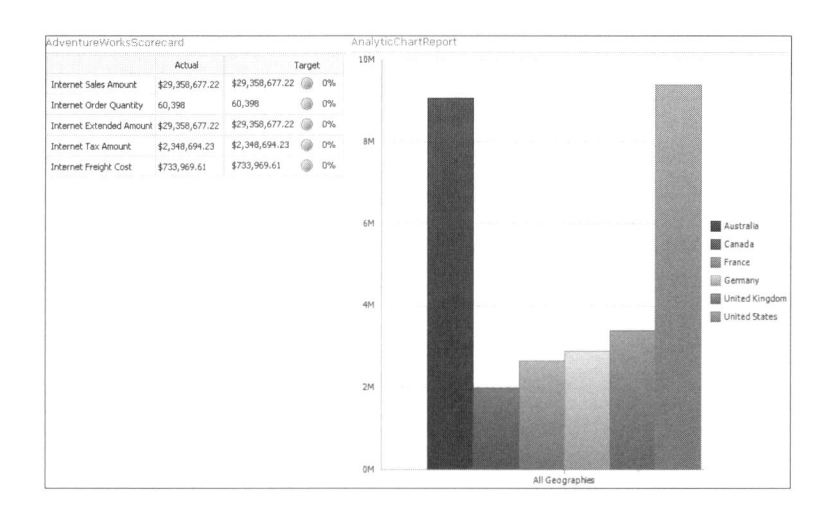

FIGURE 23.21
Dashboard opened in the web browser

Next have a look at a new feature in SharePoint 2010 called decomposition tree. A decomposition tree provides an interactive way to explore hierarchies and contribution relationships. For example, right-click any bar in the analytic chart and select the Decomposition Tree option, as shown in Figure 23.22.

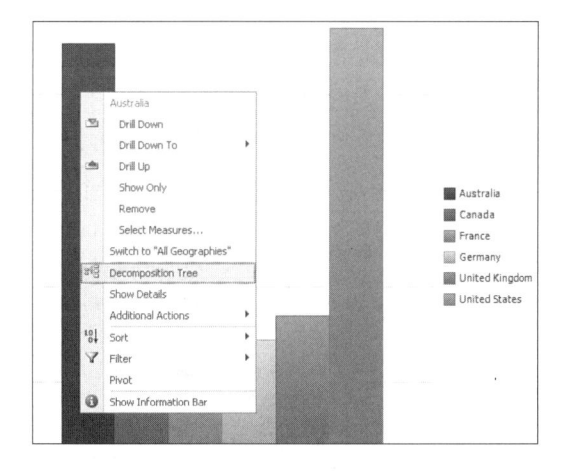

FIGURE 23.22
Viewing the decomposition tree

This brings up a new dialog window with an arrangement of horizontal bar charts, as shown in Figure 23.23. You can click the + symbol next to any of the bars to further drill down to the next level interactively or perform root cause analysis.

FIGURE 23.23
Exploring a decomposition tree

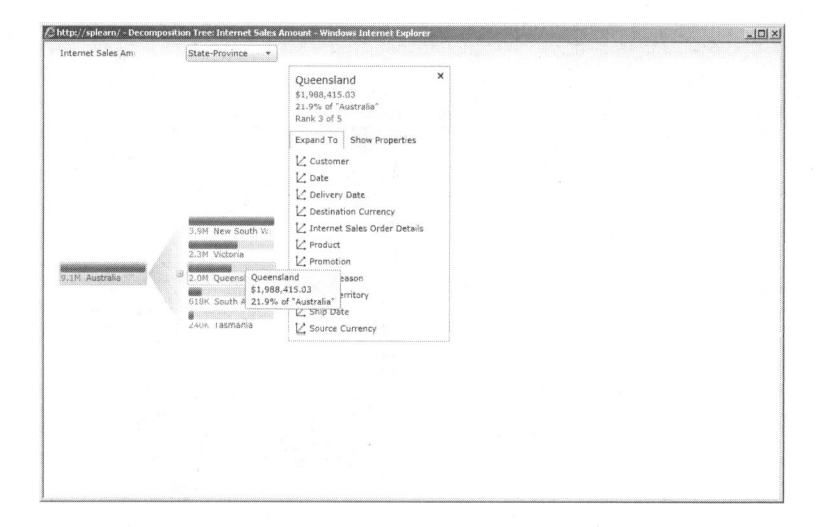

Summary

In this hour you learned about PerformancePoint Services and the steps involved in configuring the PerformancePoint Services service application. You learned how to develop scorecards, analytic chart reports, and dashboards with the Dashboard Designer and publish them to SharePoint. Finally the hour concluded by exploring the concept of decomposition trees.

Q&A

Q. What other data sources can I connect to apart from analysis service?

A. You can connect to a SharePoint list, SQL Server table, import data from an Excel workbook, and connect to Excel Services as well. Some of the data sources supported in the earlier versions of the product such as ODBC data sources and Analysis Services 2000 are not supported anymore.

Q. Can I have multiple pages in a PerformancePoint Services dashboard?

A. Yes, you can have more than one page in a dashboard and also select different templates for different pages. You can add a new page to the dashboard by clicking the New Page button in the Dashboard Designer workspace, while working on a dashboard. You can also rename the existing pages from there.

Q. *The decomposition tree option is not visible (or disabled) for me. Am I missing something here?*

A. The Decomposition Tree feature requires Microsoft Silverlight 3 to be installed. Either you don't have Silverlight installed or it's disabled. In either case the menu command will be either hidden or disabled and you won't be able to use the feature.

HOUR 24

Understanding InfoPath Form Services

What You'll Learn in This Hour:

- ▶ Introducing InfoPath 2010
- ▶ Modifying list forms in InfoPath
- ▶ Creating InfoPath form templates

> **By the Way**
>
> Due to the complexity of the topics discussed, some figures in this book are very detailed and are intended only to provide a high-level view of concepts. Those figures are representational and not intended to be read in detail.

Capturing and storing data from end users is one of the most obvious functions of SharePoint. Considering the variety of scenarios and the fast changing nature of requirements it becomes imperative to have a means of capturing data that is end user friendly and at the same time easy to build. InfoPath plays a major role in satisfying this requirement. You learn about designing and consuming InfoPath forms in this hour.

Introducing InfoPath 2010

InfoPath is a product in the Microsoft Office family that enables you to quickly and easily create electronic forms. InfoPath has become one of the most popular Microsoft products in the last few years due to its ease of use in designing and filling the electronic forms. With every version InfoPath has become more advanced with many features from simple form creation and validation to handling complex business logic. InfoPath Form Services integrates InfoPath with SharePoint and makes it possible to fill the InfoPath forms from the browser, which is a big reason for the increase in InfoPath's popularity in the last few years. InfoPath Form Services enables managing electronic forms in a central location. Also users don't need InfoPath installed on the local machines to fill the form. As long as the form is browser enabled users can fill the form through the browser. As you see in this hour, it is easy for anyone to design InfoPath forms, design a compelling user interface,

HOUR 24: Understanding InfoPath Form Services

and add validations. In addition you can write custom .NET code to do more complex tasks in the InfoPath form. The advantages of using InfoPath are as follows:

- As discussed earlier, filling InfoPath forms does not require InfoPath to be installed locally. A browser-compatible form can be filled from the browser. This is a great cost-saving advantage for enterprises that don't want to buy an InfoPath license for every user.

- Because InfoPath stores data as XML it can communicate between two incompatible data formats.

- Being a part of the Microsoft Office family, InfoPath also integrates better with other Office products such as Excel or Word.

- InfoPath also provides offline support. This means that you don't need to be connected to the network to fill an InfoPath form. Users can save forms locally, work on them offline, and sync back when connected to a network.

- Ease of designing and use makes fast development possible.

Modifying List Forms in InfoPath

Prior to SharePoint 2010 modifying list forms to add custom business logic was difficult. This was because the list forms were simple ASP.NET pages, and you either had to modify these in SharePoint Designer or do some tricks, none of which were very elegant and maintainable. In SharePoint 2010 you can convert your list forms into InfoPath forms, which can be easily modified and are really easy to maintain. You modify the Tasks lists form in InfoPath. To do that, follow the next steps.

Try It Yourself

Modify the Tasks List Form in InfoPath

In this section you modify the Tasks List Add and Edit forms. You add some validations and do some UI style modifications.

1. Browse to the Tasks list in your SharePoint site.

> **By the Way**
>
> If you created the site as indicated in Hour 1, "Introducing SharePoint 2010," you should already have a Tasks list created within your site. If not, create a new list based on the Tasks List template.

2. Go to the List tab and click the Customize Form command in the Customize List section.

3. The InfoPath Designer is launched and you can see the list form in it as shown in Figure 24.1.

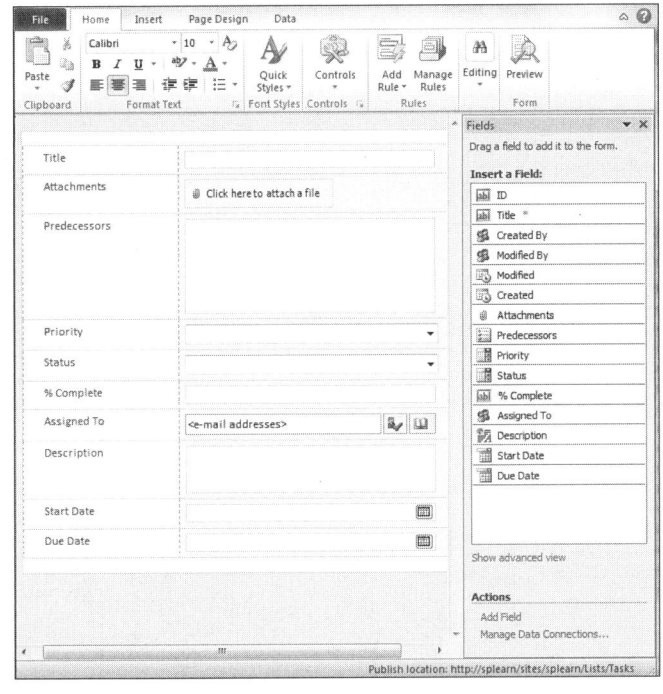

FIGURE 24.1
List form in InfoPath Designer

4. On the right you can see the fields of the Tasks list. You can drag and drop these fields onto the InfoPath form. Add a row at the end of the form by right-clicking the last row and then clicking on Insert, Row Below.

5. Drag the Created By field from the Fields pane into the right column of the new row. Type the Text "Created By" in the left column on the new row.

6. Select the multiline text box for the Description field and delete it.

7. Click the Show Advanced View link in the Fields pane. Select the Description field. An arrow appears next to the Description field. Click it and select Optional Section with Controls from the context menu as shown in Figure 24.2. The Description field is added along with an optional section.

8. Go to the Page Design tab in the ribbon of the InfoPath Designer. Select some theme for the form.

9. Add some validations. Select the Due Date field and click Rules from the context menu.

10. The Rules pane is displayed. Click the New button and select Validation as shown in Figure 24.3.

FIGURE 24.2
Fields pane

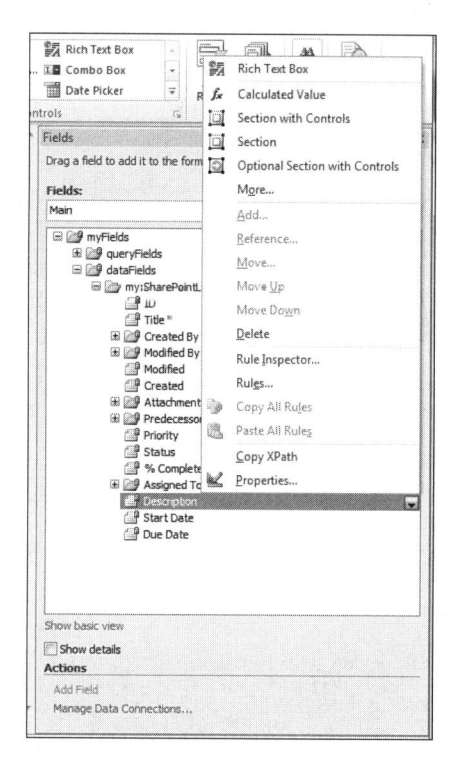

FIGURE 24.3
Rules pane

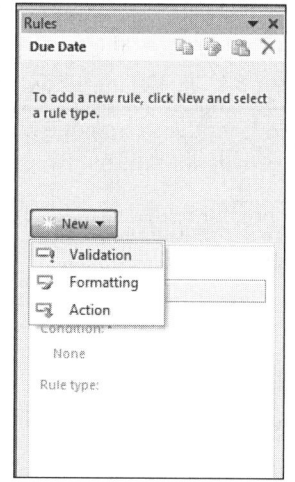

11. Name the rule GreaterThanStartDate.

12. Click the None link in the Condition section. The Condition dialog appears. Select Is Less Than in the second drop-down list.

Modifying List Forms in InfoPath   491

13. In the third drop-down list click Select a Field or Group. Select Start Date in the Select a Field or Group drop-down list and click OK. Figure 24.4 shows the Condition dialog with the appropriate values. Click OK in the Condition dialog.

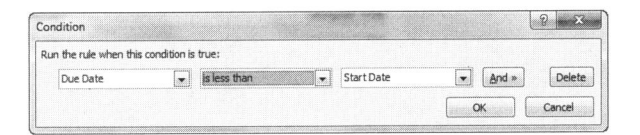

FIGURE 24.4
Condition dialog

14. Enter the text "Due Date must be greater than Start Date" in the ScreenTip. Figure 24.5 shows the Rules pane. The InfoPath form should look similar to Figure 24.6.

15. Publish the updated form by going to the File menu and clicking on the Quick Publish button.

FIGURE 24.5
Due date validation

HOUR 24: Understanding InfoPath Form Services

FIGURE 24.6
Final layout of the list form

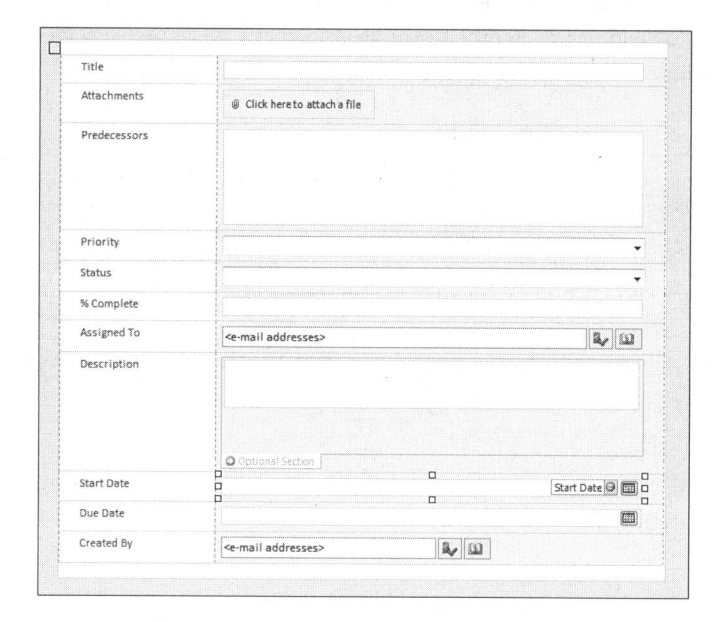

[Form screenshot showing fields: Title, Attachments, Predecessors, Priority, Status, % Complete, Assigned To, Description, Start Date, Due Date, Created By]

16. Now browse to the Tasks list in the SharePoint site and add a new item. You can see the changes in the user interface of the form. The colors are as per the theme selected, and the Description field is unavailable with a link to add it. Also the validation on Due Date will immediately show an error if you enter a value in the Due Date field less than the Start Date.

17. The Created By field also is present on the new form. This is read-only, and a value is shown only for existing items.

18. Correct the errors and save the data. Edit the item and you can see the changes reflected in the Edit form as well. Also you can now see a value in the Created By field.

If you used earlier versions of SharePoint, you will appreciate the ease and power of the InfoPath forms.

> **Did You Know?**
>
> Editing the list forms in InfoPath results in the URL of the display, new, and edit forms of the Tasks list to be changed to displayinfs.aspx, newifs.aspx, and editifs.aspx from the traditional NewForm.aspx and EditForm.aspx. These pages host the InfoPath form in the BrowserFormWebPart.

> **Did You Know?**
>
> You can reset the list settings to use the default list forms in place of the InfoPath forms. For this go to the list's List Settings page and click Form Settings. Select Use the Default SharePoint Form, and click OK.

Creating InfoPath Form Templates

In addition to modifying SharePoint list forms in InfoPath you will find yourself creating custom form templates in InfoPath to capture data from users for a variety of purposes. InfoPath 2010 already comes with many templates by default. In this section you create a new form template that will be used to collect feedback about training from users. This form will have the fields listed in Table 24.1.

TABLE 24.1 Fields for InfoPath Form Template

Field Name	Description
User Name	A read-only field that displays the current logged in username
Training Title	Hard-coded text to SharePoint 2010 training
Department	A drop-down list that displays values from a another list called departments
Rating (1-Highest, 5-Lowest)	A drop-down field showing values from 1-5
Comments	A multiline text field

You now create a custom InfoPath form template. To create a custom InfoPath form template, follow the next steps.

Creating the Form Library and Department Lists

Before creating a custom form template you need to create a form library to store the InfoPath form. A form library is a document library that has an InfoPath form as its template. In addition you need to create the Department lists, which act as the data source for the Department field. Follow the next steps to create a new form library and the Department list.

Try It Yourself

Create a Form Library and Departments List

1. Create a new document library named Training Feedback using the Form Library template.

HOUR 24: Understanding InfoPath Form Services

2. You also need to create a custom list that acts as the data source for the Department field in your InfoPath form. Create a new custom list and name it Department. Add the following values to it:

   ▶ HR
   ▶ Sales
   ▶ R&D

Creating the InfoPath Form Template and Adding Controls

The next step is to create a new InfoPath form template in Microsoft InfoPath Designer 2010 and the required controls for the form template.

▼ **Try It Yourself**

Create a Custom Form Template

To add a new InfoPath Form Template, follow these steps:

1. Open Microsoft InfoPath Designer 2010. You are presented with a screen showing the available form templates to create a new InfoPath form as shown in Figure 24.7.

FIGURE 24.7
New InfoPath form

2. Selecting a template shows the details of the template in the right section. Select the Blank Form template and click the Design Form button in the right section.

3. You are presented with a blank form with two sections. The top section has options to add a title for the form. Enter the Title Business Conduct Training Feedback.

4. Click the bottom section, go to the Insert tab in the ribbon, and click the fourth table (Two Column-4 No Heading), as shown in Figure 24.8.

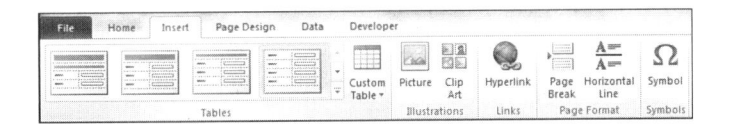

FIGURE 24.8
Insert Table

5. A table with two columns and three rows is inserted. Add two more rows. You can add a new Row by right-clicking on a row and clicking on Insert, Rows Below.

6. You now need to add the controls to the table. To make it easier to add the control, click the arrow at the bottom right of the Controls section in the Home tab of the ribbon. The Controls pane appears on the right side as shown in Figure 24.9.

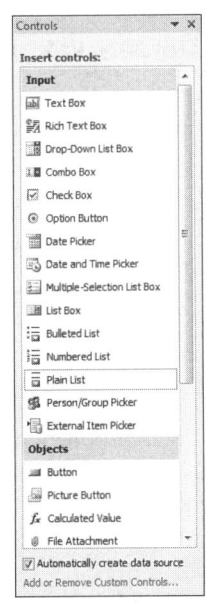

FIGURE 24.9
Controls pane

HOUR 24: Understanding InfoPath Form Services

7. Add the controls as shown in Table 24.2.

TABLE 24.2 Control for Training Feedback InfoPath Form

Label	Control
User Name	Person/Group Picker
Department	Drop-Down List Box
Rating	Drop-Down List Box
Comments	Rich Text Box

8. Add a button in the second column of the last row.

9. Remove the text that was added automatically above the drop-down list and the rich text box controls.

Specifying the Data Source and Default Values for InfoPath Form Template Controls

You now need to specify the data source for the various controls and set the current logged in user name as the default value for the User Name field. To do so, follow the next steps.

Try It Yourself

Set the Data Source and Default Value for Controls

1. Right-click the Person Picker field for User Name and click Person/Group Picker Properties. In the Person/Group Picker Properties dialog change the field name to user_name and click OK.

2. In the Fields pane on the right, click the DisplayName node under the pc:Person node and open the Properties dialog. Click the fx button in the Default value section to open the Formula dialog. Click the Insert Function button, and in the Insert Function dialog select userName function under the User categories as shown in Figure 24.10. Click OK three times to close all the dialogs.

3. Next you need to configure the Department drop-down list to retrieve data from the Departments list. Right-click the Departments drop-down list and open the Drop-Down List Box Properties.

Creating InfoPath Form Templates

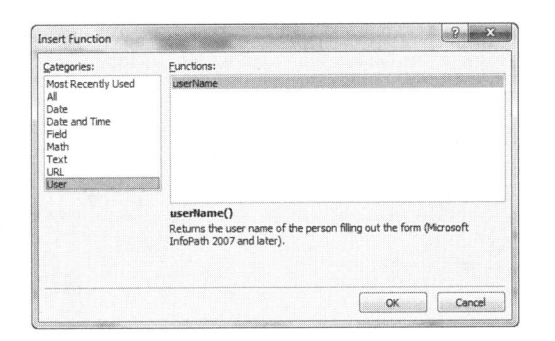

FIGURE 24.10
Insert Function dialog

4. Change the field name to Departments. Under the List Box Choices section select the Get Choices from an External Data Source option as shown in Figure 24.11.

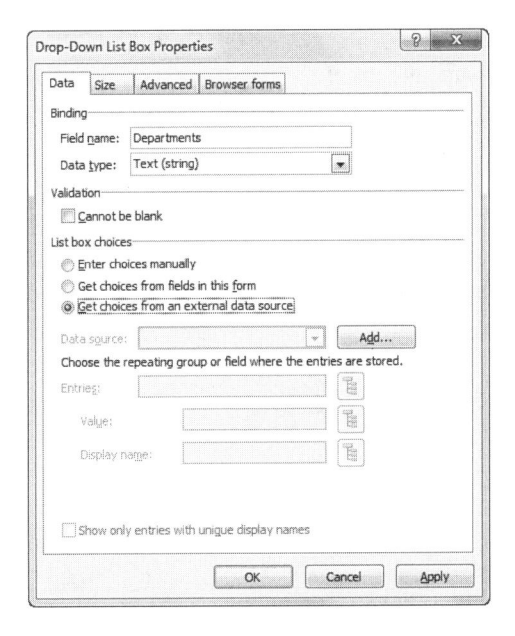

FIGURE 24.11
Drop-Down List Box Properties dialog

5. Click the Add button beside the Data Source drop-down list. This opens the Data Connection Wizard. Select the Create a New Connection To option and select the Receive Data button as shown in Figure 24.12. Click Next.

6. Select the SharePoint Library or List option as the source of the data and click Next.

7. Enter the location of the SharePoint site where you created the Departments list and click Next.

HOUR 24: Understanding InfoPath Form Services

FIGURE 24.12
Data Connection Wizard—Receive Data

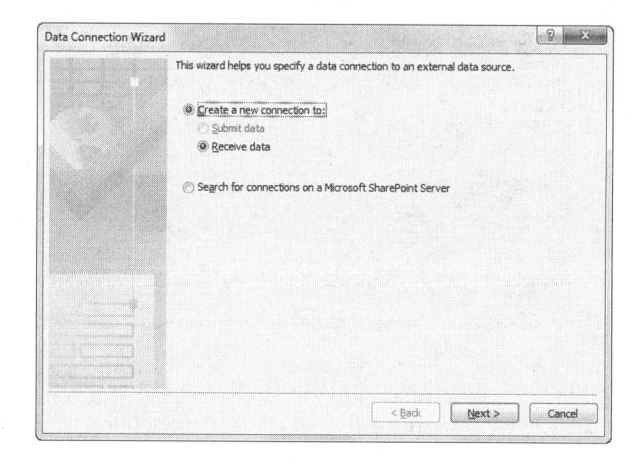

8. The subsequent screen shows a list of the SharePoint lists and libraries in the selected SharePoint site. Select the Departments list as shown in Figure 24.13 and click Next.

FIGURE 24.13
Data Connection Wizard—Select List/Library

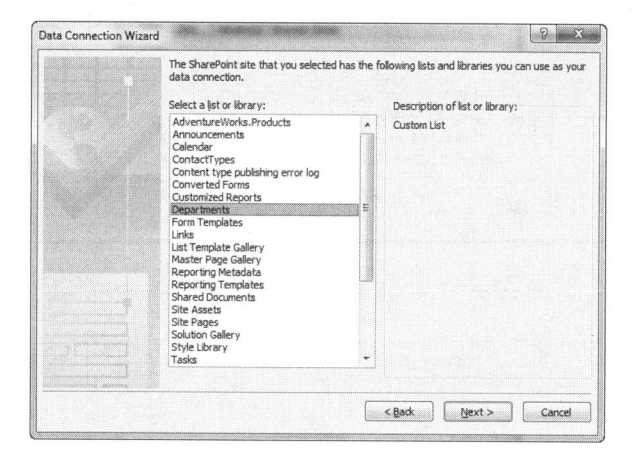

9. In the next screen select the Title field. Set the Sort By field to Title, as shown in Figure 24.14, and click Next.

10. In the next screen select the option Store a Copy of the Data in the Form Template and click Next. This option enables users to work with the InfoPath form offline.

11. Click the button next to Value and select the Title field as shown in Figure 24.15. Do the same for Display Name.

Creating InfoPath Form Templates | 499

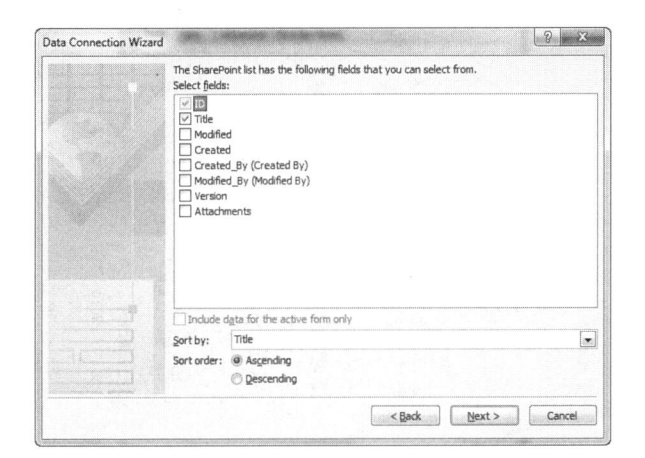

FIGURE 24.14
Data Connection Wizard—Select fields

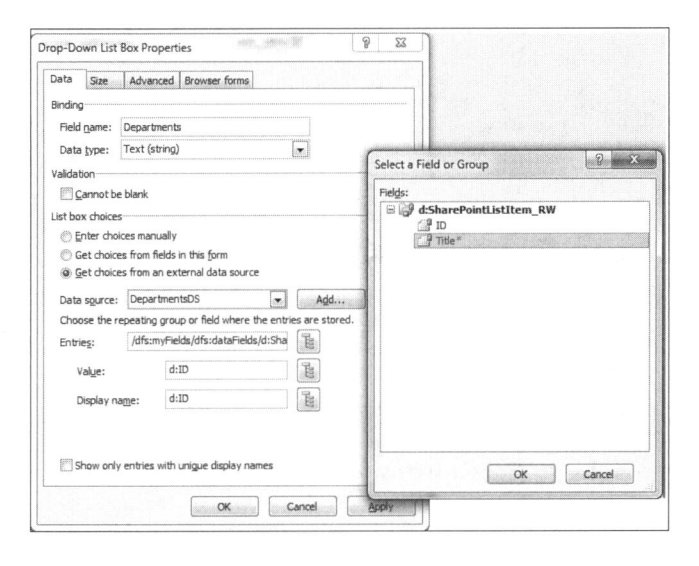

FIGURE 24.15
Drop-Down List Box Properties—Select a field for Value and Display Name

12. Right-click the Rating drop-down list and open the Drop-Down List Box Properties.

13. Change the field name to Rating. Select the Cannot Be Blank check box under the Validation section.

14. Add 1, 2, 3, 4, and 5 as the list box choices as shown in Figure 24.16 and click OK.

15. Right-click the Comments rich text box to open the Rich Text Box properties and change the field name to Comments.

FIGURE 24.16
Drop-Down List Box Properties—Rating drop-down

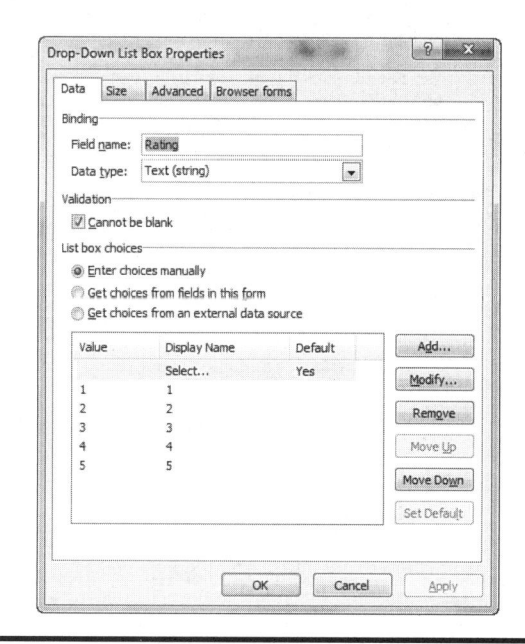

Handling the Submit Button Click

You now need to specify the behavior of the Submit button. The InfoPath template must be saved to the Training Feedback form library that you created earlier.

Try It Yourself

Handle the Submit Button Click

Follow these steps to handle the Submit action:

1. Configure the button to submit the form to the library. Right-click the button and open the Button Properties. Select the Action as Submit. Change the label to Submit Feedback as shown in Figure 24.17.

2. Click the Submit Options button. Select the Allow Users to Submit This Form check box. Select Send Form Data to a Single Destination and select SharePoint Document Library from the drop-down list.

3. Click the Add button, which is next to the Choose a Data Connection for Submit drop-down list as shown in Figure 24.18.

Creating InfoPath Form Templates 501

FIGURE 24.17
Button properties

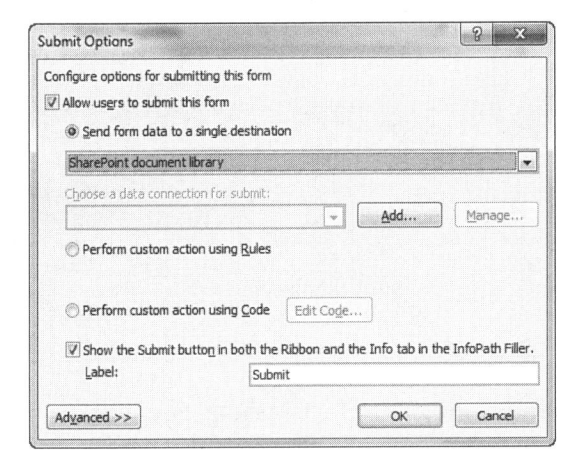

FIGURE 24.18
Submit Options

4. Give the URL of the Training Feedback library. Select the Allow Overwrite if File Exists option. Click the fx button next to File Name field. Enter the text "concat("Feedback_ ", userName())", as shown in Figure 24.19, and click OK. This submits the InfoPath form for each user uniquely.

5. Figure 24.20 shows the Data Connection Wizard. Click Next. The wizard validates the information.

6. Enter the name of the connection as Feedback Submit in the subsequent screen and click Finish.

7. Click OK to close the Button Properties window. The final form should look as shown in Figure 24.21.

HOUR 24: Understanding InfoPath Form Services

FIGURE 24.19
Insert Formula

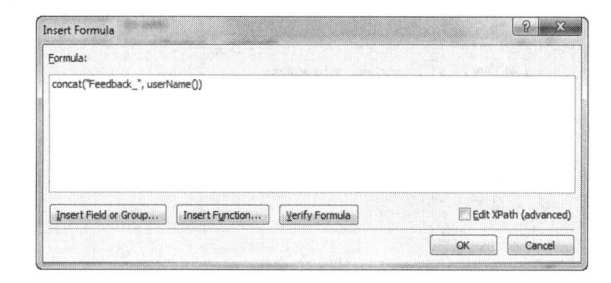

FIGURE 24.20
Data Connection Wizard

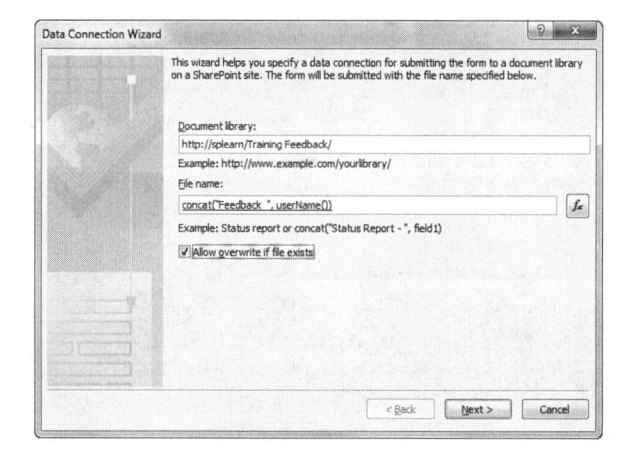

FIGURE 24.21
Business Conduct Training Feedback InfoPath form—final layout

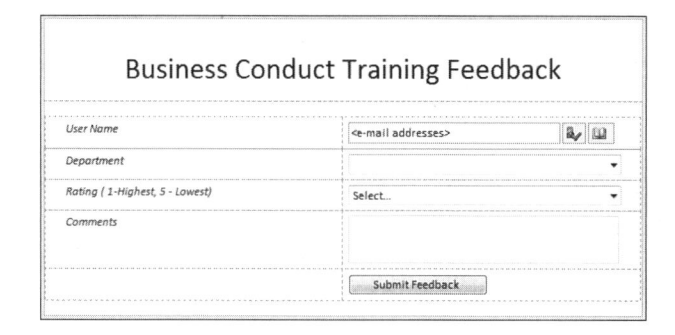

Publishing the Form Template to the Training Feedback Form Library

Finally you need to publish the custom form template so that it is available in the Training Feedback form library.

Try It Yourself

Publish the Custom Form Template

Follow these steps to publish the form template:

1. Save the InfoPath form template. Since you want to enable your form to be edited in the browser you need to validate it for any design errors that can prevent the form from being opened in the browser.

2. Click the File menu and click the Design Checker button as shown in Figure 24.22.

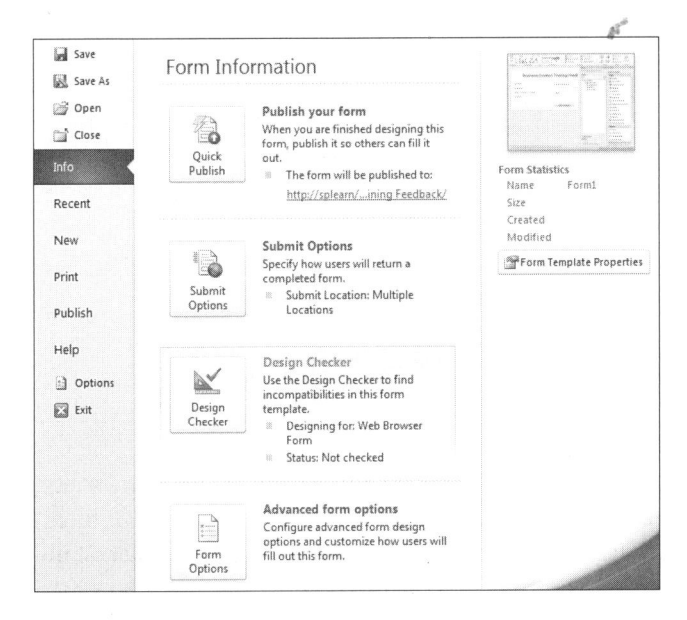

FIGURE 24.22
Design Checker

3. The Design Checker panel is shown with any warning or errors. You can get more information about these by clicking on them. Your form shows one warning that you can safely ignore.

4. Now publish this to the Training Feedback form library.

5. Click the File menu and click the Publish Your Form button.

6. Click the SharePoint Server button on the Publish screen as shown in Figure 24.23.

7. The Publishing Wizard appears. Enter the URL of the SharePoint site and click Next.

8. In the Next screen select the Enable This Form to Be Filled Out By Using a Browser option, select the Form Library option, and click Next.

HOUR 24: Understanding InfoPath Form Services

FIGURE 24.23
Publish InfoPath

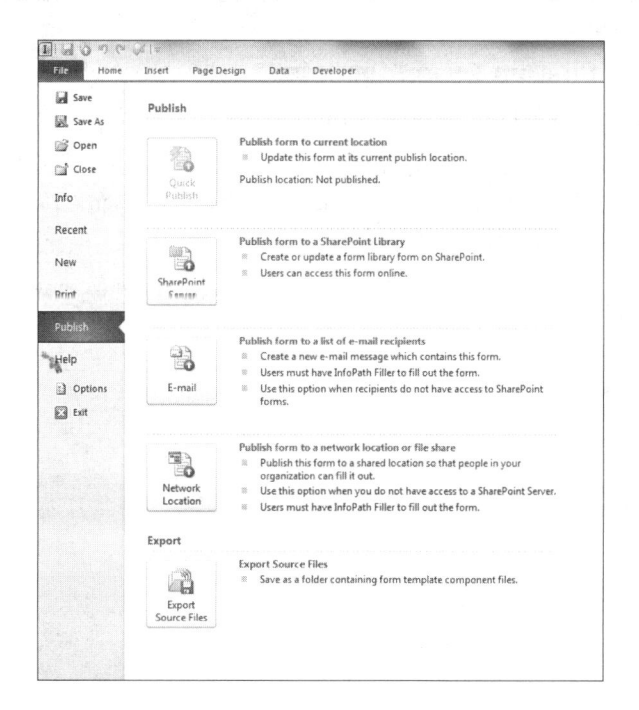

9. Select the Update the Form Template in an Existing Form Library option, select the Training Feedback library, and click Next.

10. The next screen allows you to specify which fields in the InfoPath form can be promoted to the Training Feedback library. This means that these fields will be available as the columns of the Training Feedback list. Add all the fields as shown in Figure 24.24 and click Next.

FIGURE 24.24
Publishing Wizard—Select Fields to Promote

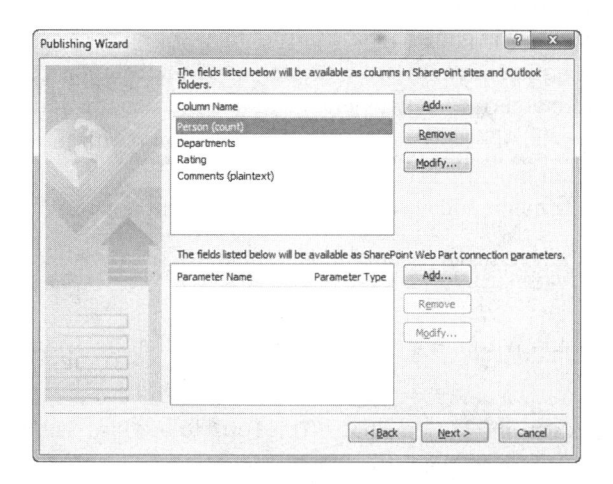

11. Finally click the Publish button.

> **By the Way**
> After publishing the InfoPath form once you can publish any subsequent changes by using the Quick Publish command available in the File menu and in the Title bar at the top of the InfoPath form designer.

12. Once Publishing has been completed successfully, browse to the Training Feedback library. Browse to the Document tab and click the New Document button.

13. The form opens in the browser. You can see the current username populated in the User Name field. Also the Department drop-down list is populated from the Departments list. Fill out the form and submit as shown in Figure 24.25.

FIGURE 24.25
Business Conduct Training Feedback InfoPath form

14. You can see the form is submitted to the Training Feedback library with the name as Feedback_<current user name> as specified in the form template.

Once again the most noticeable thing about the preceding exercise is the ease in designing the form. You can play around with other options in the InfoPath Form Template Designer, especially concerning the look and feel of the form, validations, and data connectivity. It also is a good idea to play around with the existing templates that InfoPath provides out of the box.

Summary

In this hour you were introduced to the concepts of InfoPath forms. You saw how InfoPath makes it easy to modify list forms. You also created a custom InfoPath form template and looked at the various design aspects such as controls, data connection, design checker, and publishing to form libraries. The concepts described here should enable you to easily and quickly create InfoPath forms. InfoPath is a big topic in itself, and it is recommended that you play around with the various features of the InfoPath Form Template Designer.

Q&A

Q. *Can I work in disconnected mode for browser-enabled InfoPath forms?*

A. Browser-enabled InfoPath forms can be filled from the browser, or you can also fill them through the InfoPath Filler. To work in disconnected mode you need InfoPath installed on your machine. You can then download the InfoPath form and fill it later in disconnected mode through the InfoPath Filler. However, you cannot fill the form from the browser when disconnected from the network.

Q. *How can I write custom code for InfoPath?*

A. You need to install Visual Tools for Office to write custom code for InfoPath. This enables you to handle the various events for the InfoPath form and write .NET code in Visual Studio 2010.

Index

Numerics

14 Hive, 29-32

A

AAIM (Association for Information and Image Management), 256

accessing SharePoint data in Silverlight, 207-211

adding
    commands to ribbon, 129-131
    custom tabs to ribbon, 132-135
    data with ECMAScript, 194
    DataView web part with SPD, 407-409
    site columns to content types, 223-224

administration, sandboxed solutions
    blocking, 431-432
    load balancing, configuring, 430
    Sandboxed Service Code, configuring, 430

Adventure Works sample databases, downloading, 472-473

Ajax web parts, developing, 114-120

Announcement lists, 66

Application Management section (Central Administration), 338
    databases, 342
    service applications, 342
    site collections, 341-342
    web applications, 339-340

application pages, writing, 142-144

Approval workflow, modifying with SPD

Approval workflow, modifying
 with SPD, 323-326
architecture
 ASP.NET, 26-27
 of service applications, 413
 of Silverlight, 198
ASP.NET, 26-27
assigning permission levels,
 373-375
associating Three-State workflow
 with custom library, 318-322
authentication, claims based
 authentication, 361
 configuring, 362-369
authoring tools, 291
authorization
 permission levels,
  creating, 372-375
 permissions, 369-370

B

Backup and Restore section
 (Central Administration)
 Farm Backup and Restore
  section, 347-350
 Granular Backup
  section, 350-351
backups
 granular, performing, 350-351
 performing, 343-350
benefits of RIAs, 198
BI (Business Intelligence), 447
 chart web part, 449, 452-453
 status indicator web part,
  454-456

Blank Site template, 77
blocking sandboxed solutions,
 431-432
Blog Site template, 79
Business Intelligence Center site
 template, 447
business solutions provided by
 SharePoint, 3-6
bypassing security
 validation, 162-164

C

Calendar lists, 68
 recurring events, creating,
  69-71
CAML (Collaborative Application
 Markup Language)
 list data, querying,
  246-248, 250-251
CAS (Code Access Security), 438
categorizing events, 238
Central Administration, 337
 Application Management, 338
  site collections
   section, 341-342
  web applications section,
   339-340
 Backup and Restore section
  Farm Backup and Restore
   section, 347-350
  Granular Backup
   section, 350-351

 General Applications section,
  355
  Content Deployment
   section, 358
  InfoPath Forms Services
   section, 356
  Search section, 357
  SharePoint Designer
   section, 357
 Monitoring section, 344
  Health Analyzer
   section, 345
  Reporting section, 346
  Timer Jobs section, 345
 Security section
  General Security
   section, 352-353
  Information Policy
   section, 354
  Users section, 352
 System Settings section
  Email and Text Messages
   section, 343
  Farm Management
   section, 343-344
  Servers section, 343
 Upgrade and Migration
  section, 354
chart web part, 449, 452-453
claims based authentication, 361
 configuring, 362-369
classes
 ClientContext, 186
 mapping client object model
  to server side classes, 185
 security-related, 372

content

SPContext, 159-160
SPFarm, 155
SPQuery, querying list data, 246-248
SPSecurity, 160-162
SPSiteDataQuery, querying list data, 250-251
SPWebConfigModifications, modifying web.config, 177-178
SPWebService, 155
SPWindowService, 155
client object model, 184
   classes, mapping to server side classes, 185
   Client.svc, 184
   context, 186
   creating data, 190
   deleting data, 191
   DLL locations, 185
   ECMAScript, 192
      data, adding, 194
      data, deleting, 195
      data, updating, 195
      hosting page requirements, 193
      site title, displaying, 193-194
   exceptions, 191
   ExecuteQuery() method, 188
   lambda expressions, 189
   Load() method, 187
   LoadQuery() method, 189-190

   site title, retrieving, 186-187
   updating data, 190
Client.svc, 184
ClientContext class, 186
CodePlex, 154
columns, 66
   site columns, 215
      creating, 215, 218-221
      fields, creating, 232-237
command line shells, PowerShell, 358-359
commands
   adding to ribbon, 129-131
   PowerShell, 358-359
communities, 7
comparing
   ASP.NET and SharePoint, 26-27
   user controls and custom controls, 92
components of service applications, 414
composites, 9-10
configuration database, 32
configuring
   claims based authentication, 362-369
   content type synchronization, 271-275
   document sets, 261-262
   Hold and eDiscovery, 283-285
   in-place records management, 288-290
   PerformancePoint Services, 470-471

   retention library, 280-282
   Sandboxed Service Code, 430
   sandboxed solutions
      load balancing, 430
      resource restrictions, 433-436
   search scopes, 383-388
   SharePoint 2010 Search, 379-383
   terms, 266-268
   web parts with editor parts, 106-108
connected web parts, developing, 112-114
console applications
   lists, creating, 214-215
   writing, 41-43
consuming Visio diagrams with Visio Services, 457-462
Contacts lists, 74
content, 8, 378. *See also* **content types**
   ECM, 256
      Document IDs, 258
      document sets, 259-262
      Managed Metadata Service, 263-264
      enterprise keywords, 269-271
   external content types
      creating, 300
      creating with SPD, 299-306
      creating with Visual Studio, 307-315

How can we make this index more useful? Email us at indexes@samspublishing.com

content

    master page placeholders, 136-138
    new types, creating in SPD, 405-406
    organizing with managed metadata, 268-269
    tagging, 266-268, 417-421
    term sets, managing, 264-266

Content Organizer, 285
    content routing rule, creating, 286-288

content types, 221
    creating, 222
        with features, 225-228
    site columns, adding, 223-224
    synchronizing, 271-275

context
    in client object model, 186
    retrieving, 159-160

controls
    custom controls
        developing, 95-97
        web part connections, 112-114
        web parts, 103-105, 109-120
    delegate controls, developing, 100-102
    safe controls, safe mode processing, 98-100
    user controls, developing, 92-94

crawl database, 378-379

creating
    Ajax web parts, 114-120
    content routing rules, 286-288
    content types, 222
        with features, 225-228
        with SPD, 405-406
    custom controls, 95-97
    custom fields, 232-237
    custom lists with SPD, 401-402
    custom timer jobs, 172-176
    data with client object model, 190
    delegate controls, 100-102
    document sets, 259
    event receivers, 179-180
    external content types, 300
        with SPD, 299-306
        with Visual Studio, 307-315
    form templates, 493-496
        data source, specifying, 496-499
        form libraries, 493-494
        publishing to Training Feedback form library, 502-505
        Submit button behavior, specifying, 500-502
    list templates, 228-229
    lists with console application, 214-215
    master pages, 139-142
        with SPD, 400

    page layouts, 293, 296
    PerformancePoint Service applications, 470
    permission levels, 372-375
    PPS dashboards, 476-483
    Silverlight Hello World application, 200-205
    site columns, 215, 218-219
        with features, 220-221
        with SPD, 404-405
    user controls, 93-94
    workflows with Visual Studio, 327-333

custom actions, writing, 125-127

custom controls
    developing, 95-97
    safe mode processing, 98-100
    versus user controls, 92
    web parts, 103
        Ajax web parts, 114-120
        Image Viewer web part, 103-105
        visual web part, 109-112
        web part connections, 112-114

custom errors, disabling, 61
custom fields, creating, 232-237
custom list definitions, creating, 228-229
custom lists, 66-67
    creating in SPD, 401-402
custom page layouts, creating, 293-296

ECMAScript

custom searches, writing with query object model, 392-395
custom tabs, adding to ribbon, 132-135
customization (web parts), 105-106

D

Dashboard Designer (PerformancePoint), 475
   launching, 474
   PPS dashboards, creating, 476-483
data
   adding with ECMAScript, 194-195
   creating with client object model, 190
   deleting with client object model, 191
   Silverlight, consuming in SharePoint, 207-211
   updating with client object model, 190
data source, specifying for form templates, 496-497, 499
databases, 342
   SQL, 32, 35
DataView web parts
   adding with SPD, 407-409
   columns, sorting with SPD, 409-410
   paging, implementing with SPD, 411

debugging
   in Visual Studio, 62
   SharePoint solutions, disabling custom errors, 61
decomposition tree, 483
default values, specifying for form templates, 496-499
delegate controls, developing, 100-102
deleting data
   with client object model, 191
   with ECMAScript, 195
developer dashboard, 62
   monitoring performance, troubleshooting, 168, 171-172
developing
   Ajax web parts, 114-120
   connected web parts, 112-114
   custom controls, 95-97
   delegate controls, 100-102
   full trust proxy, 438-441
   user controls, 92-94
   validators, 441-444
diagrams (Visio), consuming with Visio Services, 457-462
disabling custom errors, 61
disadvantages of RIAs, 198
Discussion Board lists, 71
displaying
   farms, servers and services, 157-158

lists in SharePoint site, 152-153
site title with ECMAScript, 193-194
disposable objects, 164-166
Dispose Checker tool, 166-167
DLL locations for client side API, 185
Document Center template, 85
Document IDs, 257-258
document libraries, 67
document sets
   configuring, 261-262
   creating, 259
document workspaces, 78
downloading Adventure Works sample databases, 472-473

E

ECM (Enterprise Content Management), 256
   Document IDs, 258
   document sets
      configuring, 261-262
      creating, 259
   enterprise keywords, 269-271
   managed metadata, 268-269
   Managed Metadata Service, provisioning, 263-264
   term sets, configuring, 264-266
ECMAScript, 192
   data, adding, 194
   data, deleting, 195

How can we make this index more useful? Email us at indexes@samspublishing.com

ECMAScript

data, updating, 195
hosting page requirements, 193
site title, displaying, 193-194
editing site layouts in SPD, 402-403
editor parts, web parts configuration, 106-108
enterprise keywords, 262, 269-271
Enterprise Wiki template, 88
error handling, exceptions, 191
event receivers, 178, 237
   creating, 179-180
   list item event receivers, writing, 239-245
events
   categorizing, 238
   list events, 238
   of SharePoint features, 60
Excel Services, 462-466
Excel Services application, 416-417
exceptions, 191
ExecuteQuery() method, 188
external content types, creating, 300
   with SPD, 299-306
   with Visual Studio, 307-315

F

farm management, 343-344
Farm scoped features, 58
farm solutions, 44, 47-50
farms, displaying servers and services, 157-158
FAST Search Server for SharePoint 2010, 378
feature receivers, 59
features, 56
   communities, 7
   composites, 9-10
   content, 8
   content types, creating, 225-228
   events, 60
   Farm scoped features, 58
   insights, 8-9
   of web content management system, 293
      authoring tools, 291
      ribbon interface, 291
   search, 8
   site columns, creating, 220-221
   sites, 7
   virtualization, 16-17
fields, creating, 232-237
file system, writing application pages, 142-144
Find by Document ID web part, 258
folders, 14 Hive, 29-32
folksonomy, 262
form libraries, creating, 493-494
forms
   InfoPath, 487
   list forms, modifying, 488-493
templates
   creating, 493-496
   data source, specifying, 496-499
   form libraries, creating, 493-494
   publishing to Training Feedback form library, 502-505
   Submit button behavior, specifying, 500-502
full trust proxy, developing, 438-441

G

General Applications section (Central Administration), 355
   Content Deployment section, 358
   InfoPath Forms Services section, 356
   Search section, 357
   SharePoint Designer section, 357
Geneva Framework, 362
granular backups, performing, 350-351
Group Work Site template, 79, 83

H

hardware requirements for SharePoint 2010 installation, 10-11

load balancing for sandboxed solutions

Hello World Silverlight application, creating, 200-205
history of SharePoint, 6-7
Hold and eDiscovery, configuring, 283-285
home page of search center site, 388
hosting Silverlight applications in SharePoint, 205-207

I

IIS (Internet Information Server), 26
Image Viewer web part, 103-105
implementing DataView web part paging with SPD, 411
improvements to web content management system, 293
in-place records management
  configuring, 288-290
  Content Organizer, 285
    content routing rule, creating, 286-288
  Hold and eDiscovery, configuring, 283-285
  Records Center Site template, 278-280
    retention library, configuring, 280-282
InfoPath, 487
  form templates
    creating, 493-496
    data source, specifying, 496-499

form libraries, 493-494
  publishing to Training Feedback form library, 502-505
  Submit button behavior, specifying, 500-502
  list forms, modifying, 488-493
inheritance, 371
insights, 8-9
installing SharePoint
  hardware requirements, 10-11
  on single Windows Server 2008 R2 machine, 12-16
interface of SPD, 397
  Navigation pane, 398

J-K-L

JavaScript client object model. *See* ECMAScript

lambda expressions, 189
launching
  Dashboard Designer, 474
  SPD, 397
layouts, modifying site layouts in SPD, 402-403
libraries, 65, 213
  custom, associating Three-State workflow, 318-322
  document libraries, 67

LINQ (Language-Integrated Query), querying list data, 251-253
list events, 238
list forms, modifying, 488-493
list item event receivers, writing, 239-245
list templates, creating, 228-229
listing servers and services in farms, 157-158
lists, 65, 213
  Announcement lists, 66
  Calendar lists, 68
    recurring events, creating, 69-71
  columns, 66
  Contacts lists, 74
  custom lists, 66-67
    creating in SPD, 401-402
  Discussion Board lists, 71
  displaying in SharePoint site, 152-153
  document libraries, 67
  external lists, creating, 300
    with SPD, 299-306
    with Visual Studio, 307-315
  in meeting work-spaces, 76
  permissions, 370
  querying with CAML, 246-251
  querying with LINQ, 251-253
  Survey lists, 74-76
  Task lists, 71-73
load balancing for sandboxed solutions, 429

How can we make this index more useful? Email us at indexes@samspublishing.com

Load() method

Load() method, 187
LoadQuery() method, 189-190
local mode load balancing, 429

M

managed metadata, 262, 268-269
Managed Metadata Service, 417-421
    provisioning, 263-264
managed services, service applications, 38
managed terms, 262
managing term sets, 264-266
master pages, 135
    content placeholders, 136-138
    creating, 139-142
    creating in SPD, 400
    structure, 136
meeting workspaces
    lists, 76
    template, 82, 85
Metadata Content Managers, 262
methods
    ExecuteQuery(), 188
    Load(), 187
    LoadQuery(), 189-190
modifying
    Approval workflow with SPD, 323-326

list forms, 488-489, 491-493
master pages in SPD, 400
site layouts with SPD, 402-403
web.config with SPWebConfig-Modifications class, 177-178
monitoring performance, troubleshooting, 168-172
Monitoring section (Central Administration), 344
    Health Analyzer section, 345
    Reporting section, 346
    Timer Jobs section, 345
MOSS (Microsoft Office SharePoint Server), 183
My Site Host template, 87

N

navigation elements
    quick launch menu, 147
    top navigation bar, 145-147
Navigation pane (SPD), 398
new content types
    creating, 222
    creating with SPD, 405-406
    site columns, adding, 223-224
null checks, 113

O

Object Browser (Visual Studio), 153
object model, 152-153
    and server architecture, 155
    and site architecture, 158
    disposable objects, 164-166
objects, security-related, 372
organizing content, managed metadata, 268-269
Out of the Box Three-State workflow, associating with custom library, 318-322

P

page layouts, creating, 293-296
performance, troubleshooting monitoring performance, 168-172
PerformancePoint Services, 469
    Adventure Works sample databases, 472-473
    configuring, 470
    Dashboard Designer, 474-475
        PPS dashboards, creating, 476-483
    unattended user account, configuring, 470-471

sandboxed solutions

performing backups, 347, 349-350
  granular backups, 350-351
permission levels, creating, 372-375
permissions, 369-370
personalization, 105-106
portals, 413
PowerShell commands, 358-359
programming server-side object model, 152-153
project templates (Visual Studio 2010), 18-19
provisioning
  Managed Metadata Service, 263-264
  records library, 278-280
publishing form templates to Training Feedback form library, 502-505
Publishing Portal template, 87

Q

query component (search), 379
query object model, writing custom searches, 392-395
querying lists
  with CAML, 246-251
  with LINQ, 251-253
Quick Launch menu, 147

R

Records Center Site template, 278-280
  retention library, configuring, 280-282
Records Center template, 86
records library, provisioning, 278-280
records management
  Content Organizer, 285
    content routing rule, creating, 286-288
  Hold and eDiscovery, configuring, 283-285
  in-place records management, configuring, 288-290
  Records Center Site template, 278-280
    retention library, configuring, 280-282
recurring events, creating, 69-71
remote mode load balancing, 429
reports, 346
resource monitoring, configuring, 435-436
restrictions for sandboxed solutions, 55, 437-438
results page of search center site, 389
retention library, configuring, 280-282

retrieving
  context information, 159-160
  site title through client side object model, 186-187
RIAs (rich Internet applications), 197
  benefits of, 198
  Silverlight, hosting in SharePoint, 205-207
ribbons, 127 291
  commands, adding, 129, 131
  custom tabs, adding, 132-135
routing, Content Organizer, 285
  content routing rule, creating, 286-288

S

safe mode processing, 98-100
safeguarding against XSS, 120-121
SAML (Security Assertions Markup Language), 362
Sandboxed Service Code, configuring, 430
sandboxed solutions, 51, 428-429
  blocking, 431-432
  full trust proxy, developing, 438-441
  load balancing, 429-430

How can we make this index more useful? Email us at indexes@samspublishing.com

sandboxed solutions

resource restrictions, configuring, 433-436
restrictions, 55, 437-438
Sandbox Service Code, configuring, 430
validators, developing, 441-444
web part, creating, 52-54

scoped features, 58
scopes, SharePoint 2010 Search, 384
search center site, 388
   home page, 388
   results page, 389
   web parts, 390-392
search feature, 8
search queries
   content, 378
   options, 377
   writing with query object model, 392-395
search scopes, configuring, 383-388
Search Server 2010, 378
Search Server 2010 Express, 378
security
   authorization
      permission levels, creating, 372-375
      permissions, 369-370
   CAS, 438
   claims based authentication, 361
      configuring, 362-369
   elevating, 161-162

safe mode processing, 98-100
XSS, protecting against, 120-121
security context, 160-162
security object model, 372
Security section (Central Administration)
   General Security section, 352-353
   Information Policy section, 354
   Users section, 352
security validation, bypassing, 162-164
server architecture and object model, 155
Server Explorer (Visual Studio), 153
server-side object model, 152-153
   and server architecture, 155
   and site architecture, 158
   disposable objects, 164-166
servers in farms, listing, 157-158
Service Application Framework, 156
service applications, 38, 342
   architecture, 413
   components of, 414
   Excel Services application, 416-417
   Managed Metadata Service, 417-421
   PerformancePoint, creating, 470

User Profile service application, 421-425
services in farms, listing, 157-158
shared services, 413
   service applications
      components of, 414
      Excel Services application, 416-417
      Managed Metadata Service, 417, 421
      User Profile service application, 421-425
SharePoint 2010
   farms, 35
   history of, 6-7
   installing
      hardware requirements, 10-11
      on single Windows Server 2008 R2 machine, 12-16
   web applications, 27
SharePoint 2010 Foundation, 377
SharePoint 2010 Search
   configuring, 379-383
   scopes, creating, 384
SharePoint Manager 2010, 154
Silverlight
   applications, hosting in SharePoint, 205-207
   architecture, 198
   Hello World application, creating, 200-205
   SharePoint data, accessing, 207-211

Submit button, specifying form template behavior

site architecture and object model, 158
site collections, 35, 341-342
   sandboxed solutions, 428-429
site columns, 215
   adding to content types, 223-224
   creating, 215, 218-219
      with features, 220-221
   creating in SPD, 404-405
   fields, creating, 232-237
Site Content Types gallery, viewing, 221
site layouts, modifying in SPD, 402-403
site templates
   Blank Site template, 77
   Blog Site template, 79
   Document Center template, 85
   document workspaces, 78
   Enterprise Wiki template, 88
   Group Work Site template, 79, 83
   meeting workspace template, 82, 85
   My Site Host template, 87
   Publishing Portal template, 87
   Records Center template, 86
   Team Site template, 77
site title
   displaying with ECMAScript, 193-194

   retrieving through client side object model, 186-187
sites, 7, 35
   lists, displaying, 152-153
solutions
   custom errors, disabling, 61
   farm solutions, 44, 47-50
   provided by SharePoint, 3-6
   sandboxed solutions, 51
      restrictions, 55
   web part, creating, 52
sorting DataView web part columns with SPD, 409-410
SPContext class, 44, 159-160
SPD
   Approval workflow, modifying, 323-326
   content types, creating, 405-406
   custom lists, creating, 401-402
   DataView web part
      adding, 407, 409
      columns, sorting, 409-410
      paging, 411
   external content types, creating, 299-306
   launching, 397
   master pages, modifying, 400
   site columns, creating, 404-405
   site layouts, modifying, 402-403
   user interface, 397
      Navigation pane, 398

SPD (SharePoint Designer), 22-23
SPDisposeCheck tool, 166-167
SPFarm class, 43, 155
SPQuery class, querying list data, 246-248
spreadsheets, Excel Services, 462-466
SPSecurity class, 160-162
SPSecurity.RunWithElevated-Privileges delegate, 373
SPServer object, 155
SPSiteDataQuery class, querying list data, 250-251
SPUCWorkerProcess.exe, 429
SPWebApplication class, 43
SPWebConfigModifications class, modifying web.config, 177-178
SPWebService class, 155
SPWindowService class, 155
SQL Server, databases, 32, 35
SSPs (shared service providers), 413
status indicator web part, 454-456
structure
   of master pages, 136
   of search center site, 388
      home page, 388
      results page, 389
      web parts, 390-392
STS (Security Token Service), 362
stsadm tool, 48
Submit button, specifying form template behavior, 500-502

How can we make this index more useful? Email us at indexes@samspublishing.com

Survey lists

Survey lists, 74-76
synchronizing content types, 271-275
synonyms, 266-268
Systems Settings section (Central Administration)
    Email and Text Messages section, 343
    Farm Management section, 343-344
    Servers section, 343

T

tabs, adding to ribbon, 132-135
tagging, 262, 266-268
    content, 417-421
Task lists, 71-73
taxonomy, 262
Team Site template, 77
templates
    form templates
        creating, 493-496
        data source, specifying, 496-499
        form libraries, creating, 493-494
        publishing to Training Feedback form library, 502-505
        Submit button behavior, specifying, 500-502
    list templates, creating, 228-229

site templates
    Blank Site template, 77
    Blog Site template, 79
    Document Center template, 85
    document workspaces, 78
    Enterprise Wiki template, 88
    Group Work Site template, 79, 83
    meeting workspace template, 82, 85
    My Site Host template, 87
    Publishing Portal template, 87
    Records Center template, 86
    Team Site template, 77
term sets, 262
    managing, 264-266
Term Store Management tool, 264-266
terms, 262
    enterprise keywords, 269-271
    synonyms, configuring, 266-268
Three-State workflow, associating to custom library, 318-322
timer jobs, 36-37, 345-346
    creating, 172-176
top navigation bar, 145-147
Training Feedback form library, publishing form templates to, 502-505
troubleshooting monitoring performance, 168-172

U

unattended user account (PerformancePoint), configuring, 470-471
unsafe updates, allowing, 162-164
updating
    data
        with client object model, 190
        with ECMAScript, 195
    security, bypassing, 162-164
Upgrade and Migration section (Central Administration), 354
user controls
    developing, 92-94
    versus custom controls, 92
user interface
    Central Administration
        Application Management section, 338-342
        Backup and Restore section, 347-350
        General Applications section, 355-358
        Granular Backup section, 350-351
        Monitoring section, 344-346
        Security section, 352-354
        System Settings section, 343-344
        Upgrade and Migration section, 354

custom actions, writing, 125-127
master pages, 135
   content placeholders, 136-138
   creating, 139-142
   structure, 136
navigation elements
   Quick Launch menu, 147
   top navigation bar, 145-147
of SPD, 397
   Navigation pane, 398
ribbons, 127
   custom commands, adding, 129-131
   custom tabs, adding, 132-135
User Profile service application, 421-425

V

validators, developing, 441-444
viewing
   Site Content Types gallery, 221
   WSP file contents, 49-50
virtual directories, 29-32
virtualization, 16-17
Visio Services, consuming Visio diagrams, 457-462

Visual Studio
   workflows, creating, 327-333
   debugging, 62
   external content types, creating, 307-315
   list templates, creating, 228-229
   Object Browser, 153
   Server Explorer, 153
Visual Studio 2010
   SharePoint 2010 support, 17-21
   SharePoint project templates, 18-19
visual web parts, 109-112

W

web applications, 339-340
   features, 57
web content management system
   features, 293
   authoring tools, 291
   ribbon interface, 291
   page layouts, creating, 293-296
Web Part Manager, 103
web part pages, 121
web parts, 103
   Ajax web parts, 114-120

chart web part, 449, 452-453
configuring with editor parts, 106-108
customization, 105-106
DataView web part
   adding with SPD, 407-409
   columns, sorting with SPD, 409-410
   paging, implementing with SPD, 411
Find by Document ID, 258
Image Viewer web part, 103-105
personalization, 105-106
for sandboxed solution, creating, 52-54
of search center site, 390-392
status indicator web part, 454-456
visual web part, 109-112
web part connections, 112-114
writing, 44, 47-48
web.config, modifying with SPWebConfigModifications class, 177-178
wiki pages, 121-122
Windows PowerShell, 358
   commands, 358-359
Windows Server 2008 R2 machine, installing SharePoint, 12-16

How can we make this index more useful? Email us at indexes@samspublishing.com

workflows

workflows, 317
    creating with Visual Studio, 327-333
    Three-State, associating with custom library, 318-322

WPF (Windows Presentation Framework), 198

writing
    application pages, 142-144
    custom actions, 125-127
    custom search queries with query object model, 392-395
    list item event receivers, 239-245
    web parts, 44, 47-48

WSP files, 428-429
    viewing contents, 49-50

X-Y-Z

XSS, protecting against, 120-121

Sams Teach Yourself

When you only have time for the answers™

Whatever your need and whatever your time frame, there's a Sams **Teach Yourself** book for you. With a Sams **Teach Yourself** book as your guide, you can quickly get up to speed on just about any new product or technology—in the absolute shortest period of time possible. Guaranteed.

Learning how to do new things with your computer shouldn't be tedious or time-consuming. Sams **Teach Yourself** makes learning anything quick, easy, and even a little bit fun.

Visual C# 2010 in 24 Hours
Scott Dorman
ISBN-13: 9780672331015

SharePoint Foundation 2010 in 24 Hours
Mike Walsh
ISBN-13: 9780672333163

ASP.NET 4.0 in 24 Hours
Scott Mitchell
ISBN-13: 9780672333057

Visual Basic 2010 in 24 Hours
James Foxall
ISBN-13: 9780672331138

Windows Phone 7 Game Programming in 24 Hours
Jonathan Harbour
ISBN-13: 9780672335549

Sams Teach Yourself books are available at most retail and online bookstores. For more information or to order direct, visit our online bookstore at **informit.com/sams**.

Online editions of all Sams Teach Yourself titles are available by subscription from Safari Books Online at **safari.informit.com**.

SAMS

REGISTER THIS PRODUCT

informit.com/register

Register the Addison-Wesley, Exam Cram, Prentice Hall, Que, and Sams products you own to unlock great benefits.

To begin the registration process, simply go to **informit.com/register** to sign in or create an account. You will then be prompted to enter the 10- or 13-digit ISBN that appears on the back cover of your product.

Registering your products can unlock the following benefits:
- Access to supplemental content, including bonus chapters, source code, or project files.
- A coupon to be used on your next purchase.

Registration benefits vary by product. Benefits will be listed on your Account page under Registered Products.

About InformIT — THE TRUSTED TECHNOLOGY LEARNING SOURCE

INFORMIT IS HOME TO THE LEADING TECHNOLOGY PUBLISHING IMPRINTS Addison-Wesley Professional, Cisco Press, Exam Cram, IBM Press, Prentice Hall Professional, Que, and Sams. Here you will gain access to quality and trusted content and resources from the authors, creators, innovators, and leaders of technology. Whether you're looking for a book on a new technology, a helpful article, timely newsletters, or access to the Safari Books Online digital library, InformIT has a solution for you.

informIT.com
THE TRUSTED TECHNOLOGY LEARNING SOURCE

Addison-Wesley | Cisco Press | Exam Cram
IBM Press | Que | Prentice Hall | Sams
SAFARI BOOKS ONLINE

informIT.com
THE TRUSTED TECHNOLOGY LEARNING SOURCE

PEARSON

InformIT is a brand of Pearson and the online presence for the world's leading technology publishers. It's your source for reliable and qualified content and knowledge, providing access to the top brands, authors, and contributors from the tech community.

Addison Wesley | Cisco Press | EXAM/CRAM | IBM Press | QUE | PRENTICE HALL | SAMS | Safari

LearnIT at InformIT

Looking for a book, eBook, or training video on a new technology? Seeking timely and relevant information and tutorials? Looking for expert opinions, advice, and tips? **InformIT has the solution.**

- Learn about new releases and special promotions by subscribing to a wide variety of newsletters.
  Visit **informit.com/newsletters**.

- Access FREE podcasts from experts at **informit.com/podcasts**.

- Read the latest author articles and sample chapters at **informit.com/articles**.

- Access thousands of books and videos in the Safari Books Online digital library at **safari.informit.com**.

- Get tips from expert blogs at **informit.com/blogs**.

Visit **informit.com/learn** to discover all the ways you can access the hottest technology content.

Are You Part of the IT Crowd?

Connect with Pearson authors and editors via RSS feeds, Facebook, Twitter, YouTube, and more! Visit **informit.com/socialconnect**.

informIT.com
THE TRUSTED TECHNOLOGY LEARNING SOURCE

PEARSON

Addison-Wesley | Cisco Press | EXAM/CRAM | IBM Press | QUE | PRENTICE HALL | SAMS | Safari

Try Safari Books Online FREE

Get online access to 5,000+ Books and Videos

FREE TRIAL—GET STARTED TODAY!
www.informit.com/safaritrial

Find trusted answers, fast
Only Safari lets you search across thousands of best-selling books from the top technology publishers, including Addison-Wesley Professional, Cisco Press, O'Reilly, Prentice Hall, Que, and Sams.

Master the latest tools and techniques
In addition to gaining access to an incredible inventory of technical books, Safari's extensive collection of video tutorials lets you learn from the leading video training experts.

WAIT, THERE'S MORE!

Keep your competitive edge
With Rough Cuts, get access to the developing manuscript and be among the first to learn the newest technologies.

Stay current with emerging technologies
Short Cuts and Quick Reference Sheets are short, concise, focused content created to get you up-to-speed quickly on new and cutting-edge technologies.

FREE Online Edition

Safari Books Online

Your purchase of **Sams Teach Yourself SharePoint® 2010 Development in 24 Hours** includes access to a free online edition for 45 days through the **Safari Books Online** subscription service. Nearly every Sams book is available online through **Safari Books Online**, along with thousands of books and videos from publishers such as Addison-Wesley Professional, Cisco Press, Exam Cram, IBM Press, O'Reilly Media, Prentice Hall, Que, and VMware Press.

Safari Books Online is a digital library providing searchable, on-demand access to thousands of technology, digital media, and professional development books and videos from leading publishers. With one monthly or yearly subscription price, you get unlimited access to learning tools and information on topics including mobile app and software development, tips and tricks on using your favorite gadgets, networking, project management, graphic design, and much more.

Activate your FREE Online Edition at informit.com/safarifree

STEP 1: Enter the coupon code: FZZQUWA.

STEP 2: New Safari users, complete the brief registration form. Safari subscribers, just log in.

If you have difficulty registering on Safari or accessing the online edition, please e-mail customer-service@safaribooksonline.com